D1126280

# THE AMERICAN MARKETPLACE

# THE AMERICAN MARKETPLACE

Demographics and Spending Patterns

5th EDITION

BY THE EDITORS OF NEW STRATEGIST PUBLICATIONS

New Strategist Publications, Inc.
Ithaca, New York

New Strategist Publications, Inc.
P.O. Box 242, Ithaca, New York 14851
800/848-0841; 607/273-0913
www.newstrategist.com



ISBN 1-885070-33-0

Printed in the United States of America

# Table of Contents

**Introduction** .......... 1

**Chapter 1. Education Trends**

*Highlights* .......... 3
Americans Are Well Educated .......... 4
Asian Americans Are the Best-Educated .......... 7
Educational Attainment Varies Widely by State .......... 10
Some Metros Are Better Educated Than Others .......... 12
School Enrollment Reaches Baby-Boom Peak .......... 15
Most Parents Are Satisfied with the Local Elementary School .......... 18
School Enrollment Is Projected to Stabilize .......... 20
Fewer High School Dropouts .......... 22
More High School Graduates .......... 24
SAT Scores Rise .......... 26
Most Children from Affluent Families Go to College .......... 28
College Enrollment Rate Has Soared .......... 30
Most Older Students Are Part-Timers .......... 33
More Than One in Five College Students Is a Minority .......... 35
Women Earn Most Degrees .......... 39
A Growing Number of College Students Will Be Aged 18 to 21 .......... 46
The Number of Full-Time Students Will Grow the Fastest .......... 48
Most Couples Are Alike in Education .......... 54
More Americans Are Participating in Adult Education .......... 56

**Chapter 2. Health Trends**

*Highlights* .......... 59
Most Americans Feel Good or Excellent .......... 60
American Diet Has Both Improved and Worsened .......... 62
Vitamin Use Rises with Age .......... 66
Births to Rise above 44 Million Again in 2004 .......... 68
More Than One-Third of Newborns Are Black or Hispanic .......... 70
Men Get More Exercise Than Women .......... 75
Fewer People Smoke Cigarettes .......... 78
Millions of Americans Lack Health Insurance .......... 82
Acute Conditions Strike the Young .......... 84
Many People Are Disabled .......... 91
Going to the Doctor Is Common for Everyone .......... 95
Hospital Care Is Much Less Common .......... 97
Millions Use Home Health Services .......... 100

Majority of AIDS Victims Are Black, Hispanic ..... 103
Heart Disease and Cancer Are Biggest Killers ..... 106
Life Expectancy Is at a Record High ..... 108

## Chapter 3. Housing Trends

*Highlights* ..... 111
Homeownership Is at a Record High ..... 112
Non-Hispanic Whites Are Most Likely to Own Their Home ..... 116
Homeownership Is Highest in the Midwest ..... 118
Most Americans Live in Single-Family Homes ..... 126
Piped Gas Is the Most Popular Heating Fuel ..... 129
Amenities Are Many in American Homes ..... 131
Most Are Satisfied with Home and Neighborhood ..... 133
Many People Live near Open Space and Woodlands ..... 138
Housing Costs Are Similar for Owners and Renters ..... 141
Median Value of Owned Homes Is More than $100,000 ..... 143

## Chapter 4. Income Trends

*Highlights* ..... 145
Americans Have Never Been Better Off ..... 146
The Rich Get Richer ..... 148
For Most Age Groups, Incomes Are at Record High ..... 150
Female-Headed Families Make Gains ..... 152
Blacks Post Biggest Gains ..... 154
Median Income of Black Couples Tops $50,000 ..... 156
Householders Aged 45 to 54 Have the Highest Incomes ..... 158
Income Peaks in Middle Age for Blacks, Hispanics, and Whites ..... 160
Median Income of Married Couples Exceeds $56,000 ..... 165
From Young to Old, Incomes Vary by Household Type ..... 167
Couples with Children Have Highest Incomes ..... 174
Single Parents Have Low Incomes ..... 177
Older Women Who Live Alone Have Low Incomes ..... 179
College-Educated Householders Earn Top Dollar ..... 182
Women's Incomes Are Growing Faster Than Men's ..... 184
Among Men, Blacks Post Biggest Income Gains ..... 187
Incomes of Men and Women Peak in the 45-to-54 Age Group ..... 190
Earnings Gap between Men and Women Is Smallest among Young Adults ..... 193
Education Boosts Earnings ..... 195
Women Earn 76 Percent as Much as Men ..... 198
Incomes Are Highest in Suburbia ..... 201
Wages and Salaries Rank Number One ..... 205
Majority of Poor Are Black or Hispanic ..... 207

## Chapter 5. Labor Force Trends

*Highlights* .......... 211
More Women, Fewer Men at Work .......... 212
A Record Proportion of Americans Are at Work .......... 214
Labor Force Participation Varies by Race and Hispanic Origin .......... 216
Working Mothers Are the Norm .......... 220
More Than Half of Couples Are Dual Earners .......... 223
Seventeen Percent of Workers Are Part-Timers .......... 225
Occupations of Men and Women Differ .......... 227
Whites Are Most Likely to Be Managers or Professionals .......... 231
Women's Jobs Are More Concentrated Than Men's .......... 236
Job Tenure Falls among Men .......... 239
Self-Employment Rises with Age .......... 242
Twelve Million Workers Have Alternative Jobs .......... 244
More Than 3 Million Americans Get Paid to Work at Home .......... 246
Most Workers Drive to Work Alone .......... 248
Few Benefits for Part-Time Workers .......... 251
Fiftysomething Workers Will Expand Rapidly .......... 254
Number of Asian and Hispanic Workers Will Grow the Fastest .......... 256
White-Collar Jobs Will Grow Fastest .......... 260
Service Industry Projected to Grow the Most .......... 264
Greatest Demand Will Be for Educated Workers .......... 267

## Chapter 6. Living Arrangement Trends

*Highlights* .......... 269
Married Couples Still Account for the Majority of Households .......... 270
Households Headed by 45-to-54-Year-Olds Have Grown Rapidly .......... 272
Households Vary by Age .......... 274
Big Differences between Black and White Households .......... 277
Hispanic Households Are the Youngest .......... 280
Most Households Are Small .......... 282
Seven Million Elderly Women Live Alone .......... 284
More Than One-Third of Households Reside in the South .......... 286
Half the Nation's Households Are in the Suburbs .......... 288
Most Black Children Live with Mother Only .......... 290
Most Young Adults Live at Home .......... 292
Lifestyles of Men and Women Diverge in Old Age .......... 294
Most Married Couples Have Children at Home .......... 296
Most Single Parents Are Women .......... 299
Many Unmarried Couples Are Older .......... 301
Most Americans Are Married .......... 303
Most Blacks Are Not Married .......... 307

## Chapter 7. Population Trends


*Highlights* ..... 311
More Women Than Men ..... 312
Boomers Will Inflate the 55-to-64 Age Group ..... 314
Asians Are Projected to Grow the Fastest ..... 316
Among Hispanics and Asians, Every Age Group Will Grow ..... 318
The South Is the Most Populous Region ..... 324
California Has Minority Majority ..... 327
Most People Live in Metropolitan Areas ..... 332
Americans Are Moving Less ..... 336
Immigration Adds Millions to Population ..... 340
The Foreign-Born Are Diverse ..... 344
The Majority of Americans Are Protestant ..... 348
More Than 40 Percent of Households Have Internet Access ..... 350
Attendance at Art Events Soars with Education ..... 354
Violent Crime Is Most Likely among the Young ..... 357


## Chapter 8. Spending Trends


*Highlights* ..... 361
Spending rose 2 Percent during 1990s ..... 362
Householders Aged 45 to 54 Spend the Most ..... 368
Spending Rises with Income ..... 388
Couples with Children Spend the Most ..... 408
Spending of Blacks, Hispanics Is above Average on Many Items ..... 425
Spending Is Highest in the West ..... 439
College Graduates Spend More ..... 453


## Chapter 9. Wealth Trends


*Highlights* ..... 467
Net Worth Rises for Most ..... 468
The Majority of Households Own Financial Assets ..... 470
Big Gains in Stock Ownership ..... 473
Nonfinancial Assets Are Most Important ..... 476
Most Households Have Debt ..... 479
Pension Plans Cover 44 Percent of Workers ..... 482

**Appendix 1.** A Note on 2000 Census Data ..... 484
**Appendix 2.** For More Information ..... 485
**Glossary** ..... 495
**Bibliography** ..... 502
**Index** ..... 504

# Tables

## Chapter 1. Education Trends


Educational Attainment of Men by Age, 2000 .......... 5
Educational Attainment of Women by Age, 2000 .......... 6
High School Graduates by Race and Hispanic Origin, 2000 .......... 8
College Graduates by Race and Hispanic Origin, 2000 .......... 9
Educational Attainment by State, 2000 .......... 11
Educational Attainment by Metropolitan Area, 2000 .......... 13
Enrollment in Nursery School through 12th Grade, 1999 .......... 16
School Enrollment by Age, 1999 .......... 17
Satisfaction with Local Elementary School by Homeownership Status, 1999 .......... 19
Projected Enrollment in Kindergarten through 12th Grade, 2000 to 2010 .......... 21
High School Dropouts by Sex, Race, and Hispanic Origin, 1972 and 1999 .......... 23
Projections of High School Graduates, 2000 to 2010 .......... 25
Scholastic Assessment Test Scores by Sex, Race, and
Hispanic Origin, 1986–1987 and 1999–2000 .......... 27
Families with Children in College, 1999 .......... 29
College Enrollment Rate by Sex, 1960 to 1999 .......... 31
College Enrollment Rate by Race and Hispanic Origin, 1977 to 1999 .......... 32
College Students by Age and Attendance Status, 1999 .......... 34
College Students by Race and Hispanic Origin, 1976 and 1998 .......... 36
Degrees Conferred by Race and Hispanic Origin, 1997–98 .......... 37
Associate's Degrees Conferred by Field of Study and Sex, 1997–98 .......... 40
Bachelor's Degrees Conferred by Field of Study and Sex, 1997–98 .......... 42
Master's Degrees Conferred by Field of Study and Sex, 1997-98 .......... 43
Doctoral Degrees Conferred by Field of Study and Sex, 1997-98 .......... 44
First-Professional Degrees Conferred by Field of Study, 1997–98 .......... 45
Projections of College Enrollment by Sex and Age, 2000 and 2010 .......... 47
Projections of College Enrollment by Level of Degree, 2000 to 2010 .......... 49
Projections of College Enrollment by Type of Institution, 2000 to 2010 .......... 51
Projections of Degrees Conferred by Sex, 2000 and 2010 .......... 53
Educational Attainment of Husbands and Wives, 1998 .......... 55
Participation in Adult Education by Age, 1995 and 1999 .......... 57


## Chapter 2. Health Trends


Health Status, 1998 .......... 61
Food and Beverage Consumption, 1970 and 1997 .......... 63
Attitudes toward Diet by Sex, 1994–96 .......... 65
Use of Vitamin and Mineral Supplements by Sex and Age, 1994–96 .......... 67
Number of Births, 2000 to 2050 .......... 69

Births by Age, Race, and Hispanic Origin of Mother, 1999 .... 71
Births to Unmarried Women, 1998 .... 72
Births by Age of Mother and Birth Order, 1999 .... 74
Vigorous Exercise by Sex and Age, 1994–96 .... 76
Most Popular Recreational Activities, 1999 .... 77
Cigarette Smoking by Sex and Age, 1965 and 1998 .... 79
Alcohol Use by Age, 1999 .... 80
Illicit Drug Use by Age, 1999 .... 81
Health Insurance Coverage by Age, 1999 .... 83
Acute Health Conditions by Age, 1996 .... 85
Chronic Health Conditions by Age, 1996 .... 87
People with Disabilities by Age, 1997 .... 92
People Aged 15 or Older with Disabilities by Type of Disability and Age, 1997 .... 93
Physician Office Visits by Age, Sex, and Race, 1998 .... 96
Hospital Care, 1980 and 1998 .... 98
Home Health Care Patients by Age, Sex, and Marital Status, 1996 .... 101
Hospice Care Patients by Age, Sex, and Marital Status, 1996 .... 102
AIDS Cases by Sex and Age, through June 1999 .... 104
AIDS Cases by Race and Hispanic Origin, through June 1999 .... 105
Leading Causes of Death in the U.S., 1998 .... 107
Life Expectancy by Age and Sex, 1900 to 1998 .... 109

## Chapter 3. Housing Trends

Homeownership Rate by Age and Household Type, 1990 and 2000 .... 113
Age of Householder by Homeownership Status, 2000 .... 114
Type of Household by Homeownership Status, 2000 .... 115
Race and Hispanic Origin of Householders by Homeownership Status, 1999 .... 117
Region of Residence by Homeownership Status, 2000 .... 119
Metropolitan Residency by Homeownership Status, 1999 .... 120
Homeownership Rate by State, 1990 and 2000 .... 121
Homeownership Rate by Metropolitan Area, 1990 and 2000 .... 123
Units in Structure by Homeownership Status, 1999 .... 127
Size of Housing Unit by Homeownership Status, 1999 .... 128
House Heating Fuel by Homeownership Status, 1999 .... 130
Amenities of Housing Unit by Homeownership Status, 1999 .... 132
Opinion of Housing Unit by Homeownership Status, 1999 .... 134
Opinion of Neighborhood by Homeownership Status, 1999 .... 136
Neighborhood Characteristics by Homeownership Status, 1999 .... 139
Neighborhood Problems by Homeownership Status, 1999 .... 140
Monthly Housing Costs by Homeownership Status, 1999 .... 142
Housing Value and Purchase Price for Homeowners, 1999 .... 144

**Chapter 4. Income Trends**

Distribution of Households by Income, 1980 to 1999 .......... 147
Distribution of Aggregate Household Income, 1980 to 1999 .......... 149
Median Household Income by Age of Householder, 1980 to 1999 .......... 151
Median Household Income by Type of Household, 1980 to 1999 .......... 153
Median Household Income by Race and Hispanic Origin of Householder, 1980 to 1999 .......... 155
Median Household Income by Household Type and Race and Hispanic Origin, 1999 ... 157
Household Income by Age of Householder, 1999: Total Households .......... 159
Household Income by Age of Householder, 1999: Black Households .......... 161
Household Income by Age of Householder, 1999: Hispanic Households .......... 162
Household Income by Age of Householder, 1999: White Households .......... 163
Household Income by Age of Householder, 1999: Non-Hispanic White Households ..... 164
Household Income by Household Type, 1999: Total Households .......... 166
Household Income by Household Type, 1999: Householders under Age 25 .......... 168
Household Income by Household Type, 1999: Householders Aged 25 to 34 .......... 169
Household Income by Household Type, 1999: Householders Aged 35 to 44 .......... 170
Household Income by Household Type, 1999: Householders Aged 45 to 54 .......... 171
Household Income by Household Type, 1999: Householders Aged 55 to 64 .......... 172
Household Income by Household Type, 1999: Householders Aged 65 or Older .......... 173
Household Income of Married Couples by Presence of Children, 1999 .......... 175
Household Income of Dual-Earner Married Couples by Presence of Children, 1999 ....... 176
Household Income of Female- and Male-Headed Families by Presence of Children, 1999 .......... 178
Household Income of Men Who Live Alone, 1999 .......... 180
Household Income of Women Who Live Alone, 1999 .......... 181
Household Income by Education of Householder, 1999 .......... 183
Median Income of Men by Age, 1980 to 1999 .......... 185
Median Income of Women by Age, 1980 to 1999 .......... 186
Median Income of Men by Race and Hispanic Origin, 1980 to 1999 .......... 188
Median Income of Women by Race and Hispanic Origin, 1980 to 1999 .......... 189
Income of Men by Age, 1999 .......... 191
Income of Women by Age, 1999 .......... 192
Median Income of Full-Time Workers by Sex, 1999 .......... 194
Earnings Distribution of Men Aged 25 or Older by Education, 1999 .......... 196
Earnings Distribution of Women Aged 25 or Older by Education, 1999 .......... 197
Median Weekly Earnings by Sex, 2000 .......... 199
Median Household Income by Metropolitan Status and Region of Residence, 1999 ........ 202
Median Income of Households by State, 1998–99 .......... 203
Sources of Income, 1999 .......... 206
People in Poverty by Age, Race, and Hispanic Origin, 1999 .......... 208
Families in Poverty by Race, Hispanic Origin, and Presence of Children, 1999 .......... 209

## Chapter 5. Labor Force Trends

Labor Force Participation by Sex and Age, 1970 to 2000 .......... 213
Employment Status by Sex and Age, 2000 .......... 215
Employment Status of Blacks by Sex and Age, 2000 .......... 217
Employment Status of Hispanics by Sex and Age, 2000 .......... 218
Employment Status of Whites by Sex and Age, 2000 .......... 219
Labor Force Status of Women by Presence of Children, 1999 .......... 221
Labor Force Status of Parents with Children under Age 18, 1999 .......... 222
Dual-Income Couples by Age, 1998 .......... 224
Full-Time and Part-Time Workers by Sex and Age, 2000 .......... 226
Workers by Occupation and Sex, 2000 .......... 228
Female Workers by Occupation, 1983 and 2000 .......... 229
Workers by Occupation, Race, and Hispanic Origin, 2000 .......... 232
Black and Hispanic Workers by Occupation, 1983 and 2000 .......... 233
Employment of Men by Industry and Occupation, 2000 .......... 237
Employment of Women by Industry and Occupation, 2000 .......... 238
Job Tenure by Sex and Age, 1983 and 2000 .......... 240
Long-Term Employment by Sex and Age, 1983 and 2000 .......... 241
Self-Employed Workers by Age, 2000 .......... 243
Workers in Alternative Work Arrangements by Age, 1999 .......... 245
People Who Work at Home, 1997 .......... 247
Journey to Work, 1999 .......... 249
Employee Benefits for Full- and Part-Time Workers by Size of Firm, 1996–97 .......... 252
Labor Force Projections by Sex and Age, 1998 to 2008 .......... 255
Labor Force Projections by Race and Hispanic Origin, 1998 to 2008 .......... 257
Labor Force Entrants and Leavers, 1998 to 2008 .......... 258
Employment by Major Occupational Group, 1998 and 2008 .......... 261
Fastest Growing Occupations, 1998 to 2008 .......... 262
Occupations with the Largest Job Growth, 1998 to 2008 .......... 263
Employment by Major Industry, 1998 to 2008 .......... 265
Industries with Fastest Job Gains, 1998 to 2008 .......... 266
Projections of Employment by Education, 1998 and 2008 .......... 268

## Chapter 6. Living Arrangement Trends

Households by Type, 1990 and 2000 .......... 271
Households by Age of Householder, 1990 and 2000 .......... 273
Households by Household Type and Age of Householder, 2000 .......... 275
Households by Household Type, Race, and Hispanic Origin of Householder, 2000 .......... 278
Households by Age, Race, and Hispanic Origin of Householder, 2000 .......... 281
Households by Size, 2000 .......... 283
People Living Alone by Sex and Age, 2000 .......... 285

Households by Region, Race, and Hispanic Origin, 2000 .......... 287
Households by Metropolitan Status, 2000 .......... 289
Living Arrangements of Children by Race and Hispanic Origin, 1980 and 1998 .......... 291
Living Arrangements of Young Adults, 1998 .......... 293
Living Arrangements of People Aged 65 or Older, 1998 .......... 295
Married Couples with Children at Home by Age of Householder and Age of Children, 1998 .......... 297
Married Couples by Age of Householder and Number of Children under Age 18 at Home, 1998 .......... 298
Female- and Male-Headed Families with Children under Age 18 at Home by Age of Householder, 1998 .......... 300
Characteristics of Cohabiting Couples, 1998 .......... 302
Median Age at First Marriage by Sex, 1890 to 1998 .......... 304
Marital Status of Men by Age, 1998 .......... 305
Marital Status of Women by Age, 1998 .......... 306
Marital Status by Race, Hispanic Origin, and Age, 1998 .......... 308

**Chapter 7. Population Trends**

Population by Age and Sex, 2001 .......... 313
Population by Age, 2001 to 2010 .......... 315
Population by Race and Hispanic Origin, 2001 to 2010 .......... 317
Non-Hispanic Asians by Age, 2001 to 2010 .......... 319
Non-Hispanic Blacks by Age, 2001 to 2010 .......... 320
Hispanics by Age, 2001 to 2010 .......... 321
Non-Hispanic Native Americans by Age, 2001 to 2010 .......... 322
Non-Hispanic Whites by Age, 2001 to 2010 .......... 323
Population by Region, Race, and Hispanic Origin, 2001 .......... 325
Population by State, Race, and Hispanic Origin, 2001 .......... 328
Distribution of State Populations by Race and Hispanic Origin, 2001 .......... 330
Population by Metropolitan Status, 1950 to 1999 .......... 333
Populations of the Top 50 Metropolitan Areas, 1990 and 2000 .......... 334
Geographical Mobility, 1950 to 1999 .......... 337
Geographical Mobility by Selected Characteristics, 1997–98 .......... 338
Immigration to the U.S., 1901 to 1998 .......... 341
Immigrants by Country of Birth and State of Intended Residence, 1998 .......... 342
Foreign-Born Population by Region of Birth and Year of Entry, 2000 .......... 345
Characteristics of the Foreign-Born Population, 2000 .......... 346
Religious Preference, 1978 and 1998 .......... 349
Households with Computers and Internet Access, 2000 .......... 351
Internet Users by Age, 1998 and 2000 .......... 352
Online Activities of Internet Users, 2000 .......... 353
Attendance at Arts Events, 1997 .......... 355

Participation in the Arts, 1997 ........ 356
Violent Crime, 1999 ........ 358
Household Property Crime, 1999 ........ 360

### Chapter 8. Spending Trends

Spending Trends, 1990 and 1999 ........ 363
Spending by Age of Householder, 1999 ........ 370
Indexed Spending by Age of Householder, 1999 ........ 377
Market Shares by Age of Householder, 1999 ........ 384
Spending by Household Income, 1999 ........ 390
Indexed Spending by Household Income, 1999 ........ 397
Market Shares by Household Income, 1999 ........ 404
Spending by Household Type, 1999 ........ 410
Indexed Spending by Household Type, 1999 ........ 415
Market Shares by Household Type, 1999 ........ 420
Spending by Race and Hispanic Origin, 1999 ........ 427
Indexed Spending by Race and Hispanic Origin, 1999 ........ 431
Market Shares by Race and Hispanic Origin, 1999 ........ 435
Spending by Region, 1999 ........ 441
Indexed Spending by Region, 1999 ........ 445
Market Shares by Region, 1999 ........ 449
Spending by Education of Householder, 1999 ........ 455
Indexed Spending by Education of Householder, 1999 ........ 459
Market Shares by Education of Householder, 1999 ........ 463

### Chapter 9. Wealth Trends

Net Worth of Households, 1989 and 1998 ........ 469
Ownership of Financial Assets, 1998 ........ 471
Stock Ownership by Age of Householder, 1989 and 1998 ........ 474
Stock Ownership by Household Income, 1989 and 1998 ........ 475
Ownership of Nonfinancial Assets, 1998 ........ 477
Households with Debt, 1998 ........ 480
Pension Coverage, 1998 ........ 483

# Illustrations

## Chapter 1. Education Trends


Young women are better educated than young men ........ 4
Hispanics are the least educated ........ 7
Non-Hispanic whites have the lowest dropout rate ........ 22
Verbal down, math up ........ 26
College attendance rises with family income ........ 28
Women are more likely to go to college than men ........ 30
There will be more students of traditional college age ........ 46
The educational background of husbands and wives is usually the same ........ 54
Big gains in adult education are in store for the 55-to-64 age group ........ 56


## Chapter 2. Health Trends


Feeling excellent declines with age ........ 60
Vitamin use peaks among women in their fifties ........ 66
Great diversity among the nation's newborns ........ 70
Many women rarely exercise ........ 75
Health insurance coverage varies greatly by age ........ 82
Disability rises sharply with age ........ 91
Teens and young adults are least likely to see a doctor ........ 95
Hospital stays have fallen the most for the oldest Americans ........ 97
Minorities dominate AIDS cases ........ 103


## Chapter 3. Housing Trends


Homeownership rate is highest among older Americans ........ 112
The majority of non-Hispanic whites and Asians are homeowners ........ 116
Two bathrooms are a must for most homeowners ........ 126
The majority of households are centrally air conditioned ........ 131
Many homeowners pay little per month for housing ........ 141
Housing equity has grown rapidly for some homeowners ........ 143


## Chapter 4. Income Trends


Record-breaking affluence ........ 146
Gains in 1990s vary by age ........ 150
Income varies by household type ........ 152
Asians have the highest incomes ........ 154
Household income peaks in middle age ........ 158
Women's incomes are not far behind men's ........ 179
Incomes rise with education ........ 182
Women's median income grew seven times faster than men's ........ 184
Poverty rates are low for married couples ........ 207

### Chapter 5. Labor Force Trends

Divergent trends for men and women ... 212
Gap is biggest between Hispanic men and women ... 216
Most mothers are in the labor force ... 220
Fewer men have long-term jobs ... 239
For most, the commute is short ... 248
Big gains for workers aged 55 to 64 ... 254

### Chapter 6. Living Arrangement Trends

Little growth for married couples ... 270
Fewer householders are aged 25 to 34 ... 272
Married couples head most households in the 25-to-64 age groups ... 274
Non-Hispanic white households are the oldest ... 280
Two-person households are most common ... 282
Women who live alone are older ... 284
Most white children live with two parents ... 290
Older women are more likely than older men to live alone ... 294
More than one in four cohabiting couples are same-sex partners ... 301

### Chapter 7. Population Trends

Women increasingly outnumber men with age ... 312
Hispanics overtake non-Hispanic blacks ... 316
The Midwest is the least diverse region ... 324
Mobility is down ... 336
California is the top state for immigrants ... 340
Many children are online ... 350

### Chapter 8. Spending Trends

Spending peaks in middle age ... 369
High-income households account for a disproportionately large share of spending ... 389
Spending is below average for single parents ... 409
Non-Hispanic black and Hispanic households spend more than average on children's clothing ... 426
Spending varies by region ... 440
College graduates spend big on many items ... 454

### Chapter 9. Wealth Trends

Median net worth rises with age ... 468
Stock ownership peaks in the 45-to-54 age group ... 473

# Introduction

There are many things Americans have in abundance—fast-food restaurants, big-screen television sets, political pundits, and sound bites, for example. Another item we have in abundance is numbers. Billions of statistics await our perusal only a mouse-click away. In this land of plenty, however, perhaps the hardest thing to find is insight—an understanding of the numbers, the story behind the statistics. After all, it is the story—not the numbers—that is most important to researchers. The story reveals the big picture about how Americans live. By knowing the stories behind the statistics, researchers can identify important trends, discovering what works in our complex, fast-moving society and what's broken and needs to be fixed.

*The American Marketplace* cuts through the statistical clutter and tells the American story. It examines our lifestyles in rich detail, from the proportion of immigrants who settle in California to the proportion of babies born out of wedlock, from the net worth of baby boomers to the amount of money people spend on entertainment. It also looks into the future, with projections of populations, college enrollment, and workers.

Since we published the first edition of *The American Marketplace* in 1992, dramatic technological change has reshaped the reference industry. The government's voluminously detailed demographic data, once widely available to all in printed reports, are now accessible almost exclusively to Internet users or in unpublished tables obtained by calling the appropriate government agency with a specific request. The government's web sites, which house enormous spreadsheets of data, are of great value to researchers with the time and skills to download and extract important nuggets of information. The shift from printed reports to web sites, while convenient for number-crunchers, has made demographic analysis a bigger chore. It has become more time-consuming than ever for researchers to get no-nonsense answers to their questions about the demographics of Americans and how those ever-changing demographics are remaking our society.

*The American Marketplace* has the answers. It has the numbers and the stories behind them. Thumbing through its pages, you can gain more insight into the consumer marketplace than you could by spending all day surfing databases on the Internet. By having it on your bookshelf, you can find answers to your questions faster than you could with the fastest modem.

New to this edition of *The American Marketplace* is the chapter profiling the nation's housing. Based on the 1999 American Housing Survey, the statistics reveal the characteristics of houses as well as people's opinions of their home and neighborhood. With homeownership at a record high, keeping tabs on homeowners and renters is more important than ever.

### How to Use This Book

We designed *The American Marketplace* for easy use. Its nine chapters—Education, Health, Housing, Income, Labor Force, Living Arrangements, Population, Spending, and Wealth—appear in alphabetical order.

Most of the tables rely on data collected and published by the federal government, in particular the Census Bureau, the Bureau of Labor Statistics, the National Center for Education Statistics, the National Center for Health Statistics, and the Federal Reserve Board. The federal government continues to be the best source of up-to-date, reliable information on the changing characteristics of Americans. While most of the data we publish are produced by the government, the tables in *The American Marketplace* are not simply reprints of government spreadsheets—as is the case in many other reference books. Instead, New Strategist's editors compiled and created each of the book's tables individually, the calculations designed to reveal the stories behind the statistics.

Each chapter of *The American Marketplace* includes the demographic and lifestyle data most important to understanding American lifestyles. A page of text accompanies most of the tables, analyzing the data and highlighting trends. If you want even more statistical detail than the tables provide, try plumbing the data source listed at the bottom of each table.

The book contains a comprehensive list of tables to help you locate the information you need. For a more detailed search, use the index at the back of the book. Also at the back of the book is the glossary, which defines the terms commonly used in tables and text. A list of telephone and Internet contacts also appears at the end of the book, allowing researchers to access government specialists and web sites.

*The American Marketplace* will help you cut through the clutter and track the trends.

CHAPTER

# 1

# Education Trends

♦ **Americans are much better educated.**

Just 30 years ago, more than half of Americans had not even graduated from high school. Today, the majority have at least some college experience.

♦ **Asian Americans have the highest level of educational attainment.**

Forty-one percent of Asian-American women and 48 percent of Asian-American men are college graduates.

♦ **Most parents are satisfied with their local elementary school.**

Among households with children under age 13, fully 77 percent are satisfied with the elementary school in their area.

♦ **College campuses are becoming more diverse.**

Non-Hispanic whites accounted for 71 percent of college students in 1997, down from 83 percent in 1976. The non-Hispanic black share rose from 9 to 11 percent during those years, while the Hispanic share climbed from 3 to 8 percent.

♦ **Women earn most degrees.**

Sixty-one percent of associate's degrees went to women in 1997-98, as did 56 percent of bachelor's degrees and 57 percent of master's degrees.

♦ **The number of older college students will decline.**

But the number of students in the traditional college age group, 18 to 21, will increase between 2000 and 2010 as the large millennial generation goes to school.

♦ **More Americans are participating in adult education.**

The percentage of people taking adult education courses grew substantially between 1995 and 1999, rising from 40 to 46 percent of people aged 16 or older.

# Americans Are Well Educated

## More than half the adult population has some college experience.

The educational attainment of Americans has increased dramatically over the past few decades. Just 30 years ago, more than half of Americans had not even graduated from high school. The parents of the baby-boom generation changed that, encouraging their children to finish high school and go to college. The well-educated baby-boom generation has lifted the educational level of the population as a whole.

The proportion of men with a high school diploma ranges from a low of 70 percent among men aged 65 or older to more than 89 percent of those aged 45 to 54. The share of men with a college degree peaks among those aged 45 to 54 at 32 percent.

The proportion of women with a high school diploma ranges from a low of 69 percent among women aged 65 or older to 89 percent of women aged 25 to 54. Women are less likely to be college graduates than men, with only 24 percent having a bachelor's degree. Among 25-to-34-year-olds, however, women are more likely to be college graduates than men.

♦ Because the educational attainment of young women is higher than that of young men, women may succeed in closing the income gap with men in the years ahead.

### Young women are better educated than young men

*(percent distribution of people aged 25 to 34 by educational attainment and sex, 2000)*

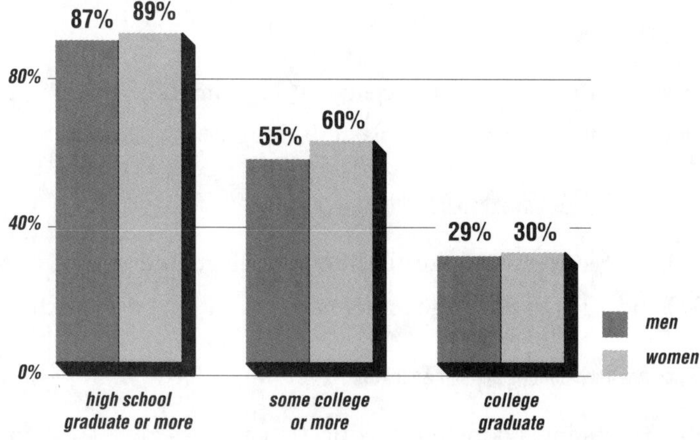

## Educational Attainment of Men by Age, 2000

*(number and percent distribution of men aged 25 or older by highest level of education and age, 2000; numbers in thousands)*

| | *total* | *25 to 34* | *35 to 44* | *45 to 54* | *55 to 64* | *65 or older* |
|---|---|---|---|---|---|---|
| **Total men** | **83,610** | **18,563** | **22,135** | **17,889** | **11,137** | **13,886** |
| Not a high school graduate | 13,217 | 2,385 | 2,622 | 1,990 | 2,025 | 4,223 |
| High school graduate | 26,650 | 5,989 | 7,646 | 5,199 | 3,591 | 4,225 |
| Some college, no degree | 14,540 | 3,483 | 3,934 | 3,416 | 1,760 | 1,947 |
| Associate's degree | 5,952 | 1,387 | 1,864 | 1,502 | 680 | 519 |
| Bachelor's degree | 14,908 | 4,134 | 3,977 | 3,459 | 1,659 | 1,679 |
| Master's degree | 5,166 | 801 | 1,361 | 1,495 | 854 | 655 |
| Professional degree | 1,752 | 241 | 389 | 467 | 331 | 324 |
| Doctoral degree | 1,425 | 142 | 344 | 362 | 264 | 313 |
| High school graduate or more | 70,393 | 16,177 | 19,515 | 15,900 | 9,139 | 9,662 |
| Some college or more | 43,743 | 10,188 | 11,869 | 10,701 | 5,548 | 5,437 |
| Bachelor's degree or more | 23,251 | 5,318 | 6,071 | 5,783 | 3,108 | 2,971 |
| **Total men** | **100.0%** | **100.0%** | **100.0%** | **100.0%** | **100.0%** | **100.0%** |
| Not a high school graduate | 15.8 | 12.8 | 11.8 | 11.1 | 18.2 | 30.4 |
| High school graduate | 31.9 | 32.3 | 34.5 | 29.1 | 32.2 | 30.4 |
| Some college, no degree | 17.4 | 18.8 | 17.8 | 19.1 | 15.8 | 14.0 |
| Associate's degree | 7.1 | 7.5 | 8.4 | 8.4 | 6.1 | 3.7 |
| Bachelor's degree | 17.8 | 22.3 | 17.0 | 19.3 | 14.9 | 12.1 |
| Master's degree | 6.2 | 4.3 | 6.1 | 8.4 | 7.7 | 4.7 |
| Professional degree | 2.1 | 1.3 | 1.8 | 2.6 | 2.0 | 2.3 |
| Doctoral degree | 1.7 | 0.8 | 1.6 | 2.0 | 2.4 | 2.3 |
| High school graduate or more | 84.2 | 87.1 | 88.2 | 88.9 | 82.1 | 69.6 |
| Some college or more | 52.3 | 54.9 | 53.6 | 59.8 | 49.8 | 39.2 |
| Bachelor's degree or more | 27.8 | 28.6 | 27.4 | 32.3 | 27.9 | 21.4 |

*Source: Bureau of the Census,* Educational Attainment in the United States: March 2000, *detailed tables from Current Population Report P20-536, 2000; Internet site <www.census.gov/population/www/socdemo/education/p20-536.html>; calculations by New Strategist*

## Educational Attainment of Women by Age, 2000

*(number and percent distribution of women aged 25 or older by highest level of education and age, 2000; numbers in thousands)*

| | *total* | *25 to 34* | *35 to 44* | *45 to 54* | *55 to 64* | *65 or older* |
|---|---|---|---|---|---|---|
| **Total women** | **91,620** | **19,222** | **22,670** | **18,741** | **12,250** | **18,735** |
| Not a high school graduate | 14,639 | 2,087 | 2,477 | 2,066 | 2,285 | 5,722 |
| High school graduate | 31,435 | 5,557 | 7,466 | 6,169 | 4,767 | 7,476 |
| Some college, no degree | 16,213 | 3,893 | 4,298 | 3,436 | 2,052 | 2,534 |
| Associate's degree | 7,740 | 1,938 | 2,390 | 1,781 | 761 | 871 |
| Bachelor's degree | 14,931 | 4,428 | 4,266 | 3,384 | 1,399 | 1,454 |
| Master's degree | 5,230 | 978 | 1,346 | 1,536 | 812 | 558 |
| Professional degree | 834 | 238 | 250 | 193 | 84 | 69 |
| Doctoral degree | 600 | 106 | 179 | 176 | 88 | 51 |
| High school graduate or more | 76,984 | 17,138 | 20,195 | 16,675 | 9,963 | 13,013 |
| Some college or more | 45,549 | 11,581 | 12,729 | 10,506 | 5,196 | 5,537 |
| Bachelor's degree or more | 21,595 | 5,750 | 6,041 | 5,289 | 2,383 | 2,132 |
| **Total women** | **100.0%** | **100.0%** | **100.0%** | **100.0%** | **100.0%** | **100.0%** |
| Not a high school graduate | 16.0 | 10.9 | 10.9 | 11.0 | 18.7 | 30.5 |
| High school graduate | 34.3 | 28.9 | 32.9 | 32.9 | 38.9 | 39.9 |
| Some college, no degree | 17.7 | 20.3 | 18.0 | 18.3 | 16.8 | 13.5 |
| Associate's degree | 8.4 | 10.1 | 10.5 | 9.5 | 6.2 | 4.6 |
| Bachelor's degree | 16.3 | 23.0 | 18.8 | 18.1 | 11.4 | 7.8 |
| Master's degree | 5.7 | 5.1 | 5.9 | 8.2 | 6.6 | 2.0 |
| Professional degree | 0.9 | 1.2 | 1.1 | 1.0 | 0.7 | 0.4 |
| Doctoral degree | 0.7 | 0.6 | 0.8 | 0.9 | 0.7 | 0.3 |
| High school graduate or more | 84.0 | 89.2 | 89.1 | 88.0 | 81.3 | 69.5 |
| Some college or more | 49.7 | 60.2 | 56.1 | 56.1 | 42.4 | 29.6 |
| Bachelor's degree or more | 23.6 | 29.9 | 26.6 | 28.2 | 19.5 | 11.4 |

*Source: Bureau of the Census,* Educational Attainment in the United States: March 2000, *detailed tables from Current Population Report P20-536, 2000; Internet site <www.census.gov/population/www/socdemo/education/p20-536.html>; calculations by New Strategist*

# Asian Americans Are the Best Educated

## More than 40 percent of Asian Americans are college graduates.

While non-Hispanic Asians are slightly less likely than non-Hispanic whites to be high school graduates, they are much more likely to have a college degree. Behind this disparity are socioeconomic differences within the Asian American population itself, some Asians being immigrants from countries that offer little educational opportunity—such as Vietnam. Forty-one percent of Asian-American women and 48 percent of Asian-American men are college graduates. Among non-Hispanic whites, the corresponding figures are 26 and 31 percent.

The educational attainment of blacks is much lower than that of non-Hispanic whites, but among blacks under age 45 the gap is considerably smaller. Hispanics are the least educated Americans. Only 57 to 58 percent are high school graduates, and just 11 percent have a college diploma.

♦ Millions of Hispanics are immigrants with little schooling. Until immigrants make up a smaller share of the population, the educational attainment of Hispanics is unlikely to rise.

### Hispanics are the least educated

*(percent of people aged 25 or older who have a college degree, by sex, race, and Hispanic origin, 2000)*

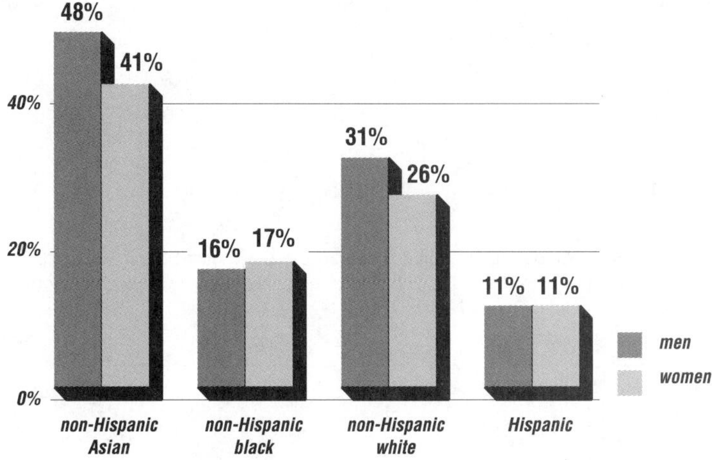

## High School Graduates by Race and Hispanic Origin, 2000

*(percent of people aged 25 or older who are high school graduates by sex, age, race, and Hispanic origin, 2000)*

| | | non-Hispanic | | | |
|---|---|---|---|---|---|
| | *total* | *Asian* | *black* | *white* | *Hispanic* |
| **Total men** | **84.2%** | **88.2%** | **79.1%** | **88.5%** | **56.6%** |
| Aged 25 to 29 | 86.7 | 91.9 | 87.6 | 92.9 | 59.2 |
| Aged 30 to 34 | 87.5 | 93.4 | 89.8 | 93.2 | 58.6 |
| Aged 35 to 39 | 88.2 | 89.7 | 90.4 | 92.8 | 59.8 |
| Aged 40 to 44 | 88.2 | 89.4 | 88.3 | 91.8 | 60.1 |
| Aged 45 to 49 | 89.3 | 89.7 | 84.0 | 93.4 | 59.2 |
| Aged 50 to 54 | 88.4 | 90.8 | 78.3 | 92.7 | 57.5 |
| Aged 55 to 59 | 85.0 | 92.1 | 70.2 | 89.7 | 53.6 |
| Aged 60 to 64 | 78.5 | 84.4 | 55.4 | 84.1 | 42.2 |
| Aged 65 to 69 | 75.4 | 72.6 | 54.4 | 79.9 | 48.1 |
| Aged 70 to 74 | 70.1 | 79.1 | 46.4 | 74.1 | 41.8 |
| Aged 75 or older | 64.9 | 62.6 | 35.5 | 69.3 | 32.6 |
| **Total women** | **84.0** | **83.4** | **78.7** | **88.4** | **57.5** |
| Aged 25 to 29 | 89.4 | 95.0 | 86.2 | 95.2 | 66.4 |
| Aged 30 to 34 | 88.9 | 92.3 | 89.0 | 94.4 | 62.1 |
| Aged 35 to 39 | 88.8 | 89.7 | 87.6 | 92.8 | 66.9 |
| Aged 40 to 44 | 89.4 | 85.7 | 86.4 | 94.1 | 60.8 |
| Aged 45 to 49 | 89.6 | 90.0 | 83.7 | 93.8 | 57.6 |
| Aged 50 to 54 | 88.2 | 81.5 | 84.0 | 93.0 | 55.3 |
| Aged 55 to 59 | 83.1 | 71.8 | 72.0 | 89.0 | 45.1 |
| Aged 60 to 64 | 79.2 | 66.0 | 70.8 | 84.0 | 46.7 |
| Aged 65 to 69 | 75.4 | 66.8 | 54.0 | 82.1 | 38.7 |
| Aged 70 to 74 | 72.8 | 50.7 | 52.1 | 78.8 | 34.3 |
| Aged 75 or older | 64.4 | 50.8 | 40.2 | 68.4 | 31.4 |

*Source: Bureau of the Census,* Educational Attainment in the United States: March 2000, *detailed tables from Current Population Report P20-536, 2000; Internet site <www.census.gov/population/www/socdemo/education/p20-536.html>*

## College Graduates by Race and Hispanic Origin, 2000

*(percent of people aged 25 or older who are college graduates by sex, age, race, and Hispanic origin, 2000)*

| | | non-Hispanic | | | |
|---|---|---|---|---|---|
| | total | Asian | black | white | Hispanic |
| **Total men** | **27.8%** | **47.6%** | **16.4%** | **30.8%** | **10.7%** |
| Aged 25 to 29 | 27.9 | 55.3 | 18.4 | 32.3 | 8.3 |
| Aged 30 to 34 | 29.3 | 45.7 | 17.9 | 34.8 | 8.9 |
| Aged 35 to 39 | 27.3 | 50.2 | 19.7 | 30.4 | 10.3 |
| Aged 40 to 44 | 27.5 | 54.4 | 15.0 | 30.3 | 12.6 |
| Aged 45 to 49 | 30.7 | 45.6 | 18.7 | 33.9 | 12.0 |
| Aged 50 to 54 | 34.2 | 50.2 | 20.8 | 37.0 | 16.8 |
| Aged 55 to 59 | 29.9 | 48.5 | 15.7 | 32.6 | 12.3 |
| Aged 60 to 64 | 25.5 | 39.1 | 11.7 | 28.0 | 9.4 |
| Aged 65 to 69 | 23.4 | 31.5 | 10.1 | 25.5 | 10.6 |
| Aged 70 to 74 | 22.3 | 32.9 | 7.3 | 24.4 | 9.0 |
| Aged 75 or older | 19.3 | 32.4 | 5.3 | 20.7 | 8.2 |
| **Total women** | **23.6** | **40.7** | **16.8** | **25.5** | **10.6** |
| Aged 25 to 29 | 30.1 | 52.7 | 17.4 | 35.8 | 11.0 |
| Aged 30 to 34 | 29.7 | 49.7 | 17.7 | 35.3 | 10.5 |
| Aged 35 to 39 | 27.4 | 45.4 | 20.1 | 29.9 | 14.7 |
| Aged 40 to 44 | 25.9 | 42.4 | 18.7 | 28.2 | 12.1 |
| Aged 45 to 49 | 29.8 | 43.9 | 20.2 | 32.4 | 13.4 |
| Aged 50 to 54 | 26.3 | 37.5 | 21.2 | 28.5 | 10.0 |
| Aged 55 to 59 | 20.7 | 39.1 | 13.7 | 22.4 | 6.7 |
| Aged 60 to 64 | 18.0 | 26.0 | 12.7 | 19.6 | 4.6 |
| Aged 65 to 69 | 14.2 | 20.0 | 11.8 | 15.0 | 6.4 |
| Aged 70 to 74 | 11.8 | 9.6 | 12.5 | 12.4 | 2.4 |
| Aged 75 or older | 9.6 | 14.4 | 3.1 | 10.2 | 6.4 |

*Source: Bureau of the Census,* Educational Attainment in the United States: March 2000, *detailed tables from Current Population Report P20-536, 2000; Internet site <www.census.gov/population/www/socdemo/education/p20-536.html>*

# Educational Attainment Varies Widely by State

## Colorado has the most educated residents, while West Virginia has the least.

The educational attainment of state populations varies widely. Among people aged 25 or older, only 77 percent of those living in West Virginia have a high school diploma—the lowest share among the 50 states. In South Dakota and Washington, 92 percent of residents are high school graduates—15 percentage points higher than in West Virginia.

The figures for college graduates vary as well. In West Virginia, only 15 percent of people aged 25 or older have a college degree, again the smallest share of any state. In contrast, in nine states more than 30 percent of adults are college graduates . The proportion peaks at 35 percent in Colorado (and 38 percent in Washington, D.C.). Since income rises with education, the states with the least-educated populations are also some of the poorest while those with the best-educated populations are some of the richest.

♦ The educational level of the workforce is one factor behind business location decisions. Better-educated populations attract business investment, increasing economic diversity and employment opportunities.

## Educational Attainment by State, 2000

*(percent of people aged 25 or older who are high school or college graduates, by state, 2000)*

| | high school graduate | college graduate | | high school graduate | college graduate |
|---|---|---|---|---|---|
| **United States** | **84.1%** | **25.7%** | Missouri | 86.6% | 26.2% |
| Alabama | 77.5 | 20.4 | Montana | 89.6 | 23.8 |
| Alaska | 90.4 | 28.1 | Nebraska | 90.4 | 24.6 |
| Arizona | 85.1 | 24.6 | Nevada | 82.8 | 19.3 |
| Arkansas | 81.7 | 18.4 | New Hampshire | 88.1 | 30.1 |
| California | 81.2 | 27.5 | New Jersey | 87.3 | 30.1 |
| Colorado | 89.7 | 34.6 | New Mexico | 82.2 | 23.6 |
| Connecticut | 88.2 | 31.6 | New York | 82.5 | 28.7 |
| Delaware | 86.1 | 24.0 | North Carolina | 79.2 | 23.2 |
| District of Columbia | 83.2 | 38.3 | North Dakota | 85.5 | 22.6 |
| Florida | 84.0 | 22.8 | Ohio | 87.0 | 24.6 |
| Georgia | 82.6 | 23.1 | Oklahoma | 86.1 | 22.5 |
| Hawaii | 87.4 | 26.3 | Oregon | 88.1 | 27.2 |
| Idaho | 86.2 | 20.0 | Pennsylvania | 85.7 | 24.3 |
| Illinois | 85.5 | 27.1 | Rhode Island | 81.3 | 26.4 |
| Indiana | 84.6 | 17.1 | South Carolina | 83.0 | 19.0 |
| Iowa | 89.7 | 25.5 | South Dakota | 91.8 | 25.7 |
| Kansas | 88.1 | 27.3 | Tennessee | 79.9 | 22.0 |
| Kentucky | 78.7 | 20.5 | Texas | 79.2 | 23.9 |
| Louisiana | 80.8 | 22.5 | Utah | 90.7 | 26.4 |
| Maine | 89.3 | 24.1 | Vermont | 90.0 | 28.8 |
| Maryland | 85.7 | 32.3 | Virginia | 86.6 | 31.9 |
| Massachusetts | 85.1 | 32.7 | Washington | 91.8 | 28.6 |
| Michigan | 86.2 | 23.0 | West Virginia | 77.1 | 15.3 |
| Minnesota | 90.8 | 31.2 | Wisconsin | 86.7 | 23.8 |
| Mississippi | 80.3 | 18.7 | Wyoming | 90.0 | 20.6 |

*Source: Bureau of the Census,* Educational Attainment in the United States: March 2000, *detailed tables from Current Population Report P20-536, 2000; Internet site <www.census.gov/population/www/socdemo/education/p20-536.html>*

# Some Metros Are Better Educated Than Others

## Educational attainment varies widely by metropolitan area.

Education varies even more widely by metropolitan area than by state. Among the nation's largest metropolitan areas, the proportion of people aged 25 or older who have a high school diploma ranges from a low of 74 percent in Los Angeles to a high of 94 percent in Minneapolis.

The share of college graduates varies by metro as well. More than 40 percent of people aged 25 or older living in Boston, San Jose, and Washington, D.C., are college graduates. In contrast, only 16 percent of the residents of San Antonio, Texas, have a college degree.

Disparities in educational attainment are due to the unique demographics of each metropolitan area. Metros with large Hispanic populations, for example, tend to be less educated because Hispanics are the least-educated Americans. Metros with large Asian populations tend to be more educated because Asians are most likely to be college graduates.

♦ Metropolitan areas with highly educated populations attract different types of businesses than those with less-educated populations. The consequences affect the economy of entire regions.

## Educational Attainment by Metropolitan Area, 2000

*(percent of people aged 25 or older in the nation's largest metropolitan statistical areas who are high school or college graduates, 2000)*

| | high school graduates | college graduates |
|---|---|---|
| **United States** | **84.1%** | **25.7%** |
| Atlanta, GA MSA | 89.0 | 31.4 |
| Boston–Lawrence, MA–NH–ME–CT CMSA | 85.3 | 34.4 |
| Boston, MA–NH PMSA | 87.9 | 41.1 |
| Buffalo–Niagara Falls, NY MSA | 90.2 | 22.6 |
| Charlotte–Gastonia, NC–SC MSA | 81.8 | 23.1 |
| Chicago–Gary–Kenosha, IL–IN–WI CMSA | 85.2 | 30.7 |
| Chicago, IL PMSA | 85.3 | 31.4 |
| Cincinnati–Hamilton, OH–KY–IN CMSA | 86.4 | 27.7 |
| Cincinnati, OH–KY–IN PMSA | 85.8 | 28.8 |
| Cleveland–Akron, OH CMSA | 89.6 | 28.7 |
| Cleveland–Lorain–Elyria, OH PMSA | 88.7 | 28.5 |
| Columbus, OH MSA | 84.9 | 25.0 |
| Dallas–Fort Worth, TX CMSA | 85.6 | 30.7 |
| Dallas–TX PMSA | 84.7 | 33.0 |
| Fort Worth–Arlington, TX PMSA | 87.4 | 25.5 |
| Denver–Boulder–Greeley, CO CMSA | 89.3 | 38.7 |
| Denver, CO PMSA | 91.1 | 38.2 |
| Detroit–Ann Arbor–Flint, MI CMSA | 85.4 | 26.2 |
| Detroit, MI PMSA | 84.8 | 25.7 |
| Hartford, CT MSA | 89.0 | 28.2 |
| Houston–Galveston–Brazoria, TX CMSA | 79.1 | 25.7 |
| Houston, TX PMSA | 78.7 | 26.0 |
| Indianapolis, IN MSA | 83.7 | 25.5 |
| Kansas City, MO–KS MSA | 90.6 | 34.7 |
| Los Angeles–Riverside–Orange, CA CMSA | 77.9 | 25.6 |
| Los Angeles–Long Beach, CA PMSA | 74.4 | 25.0 |
| Orange County, CA PMSA | 86.8 | 31.9 |
| Riverside–San Bernardino, CA PMSA | 78.3 | 19.3 |
| Miami–Fort Lauderdale, FL CMSA | 81.7 | 25.1 |
| Ft. Lauderdale, FL PMSA | 89.7 | 27.1 |
| Miami, FL–PMSA | 75.1 | 23.4 |

*(continued)*

*(continued from previous page)*

| | high school graduates | college graduates |
|---|---|---|
| Milwaukee–Racine, WI CMSA | 87.3% | 26.9% |
| Milwaukee–Waukesha, WI PMSA | 88.0 | 27.6 |
| Minneapolis–St. Paul, MN–WI MSA | 94.0 | 38.4 |
| New Orleans, LA MSA | 87.9 | 26.1 |
| New York–Northern N. J.–Long Island, NY–NJ–CT–PA | 83.4 | 32.6 |
| Bergen–Passaic, NJ PMSA | 86.4 | 30.6 |
| Nassau–Suffolk, NY PMSA | 88.8 | 31.4 |
| New York, NY PMSA | 77.7 | 32.9 |
| Newark, NJ PMSA | 87.9 | 34.7 |
| Norfolk–VA Beach, VA–NC MSA | 89.8 | 29.0 |
| Philadelphia–Atlantic City, PA–NJ–DE–MD CMSA | 86.4 | 27.8 |
| Philadelphia, PA–NJ PMSA | 87.3 | 29.0 |
| Phoenix–Mesa, AZ MSA | 85.1 | 23.9 |
| Pittsburgh, PA MSA | 87.5 | 24.2 |
| Portland–Salem, OR–WA CMSA | 90.0 | 29.4 |
| Portland–Vancouver, OR–WA PMSA | 91.1 | 31.7 |
| Providence–Fall River, RI–MA MSA | 79.3 | 26.2 |
| Sacramento–Yolo, CA CMSA | 90.6 | 31.4 |
| St. Louis, MO–IL MSA | 85.5 | 24.5 |
| Salt Lake City–Odgen, UT MSA | 89.9 | 27.9 |
| San Antonio, TX MSA | 81.1 | 15.9 |
| San Diego, CA MSA | 85.3 | 34.0 |
| San Francisco–Oakland–San Jose, CA CMSA | 88.9 | 37.3 |
| Oakland, CA PMSA | 89.9 | 34.3 |
| San Francisco, CA PMSA | 86.6 | 39.5 |
| San Jose, CA PMSA | 91.4 | 42.2 |
| Seattle–Tacoma–Bremerton, WA CMSA | 93.2 | 33.8 |
| Seattle–Bellevue, WA PMSA | 92.8 | 35.7 |
| Tampa–St. Petersburg–Clearwater, FL MSA | 83.2 | 18.6 |
| Washington, DC–MD–VA–WV CMSA | 87.8 | 37.2 |
| Baltimore, MD PMSA | 85.4 | 30.1 |
| Washington, DC–MD–VA–WV PMSA | 90.0 | 42.0 |

*Note: For definitions of CMSA, MSA, and PMSA, see glossary.*
*Source: Bureau of the Census,* Educational Attainment in the United States: March 2000, *detailed tables from Current Population Report P20–536, 2000; Internet site <www.census.gov/population/www/socdemo/education/p20–536.html>*

# School Enrollment Reaches Baby-Boom Peak

## Forty-nine million Americans were in grades 1 through 12 in 1999, equalling the peak of 1970.

The nation's school districts haven't seen enrollment as high as today since 1970, when the baby-boom generation filled the classrooms. The 49 million children in grades 1 through 12 include 33 million in elementary school and 16 million in high school. Another 8 million students are enrolled in nursery school and kindergarten.

The proportion of 3- and 4- year-olds enrolled in nursery school has grown enormously over the past few decades, from 5 percent in the early 1960s to 54 percent in 1999. Among kindergarteners, 58 percent now attend kindergarten for the full day, up from only 11 percent in 1969.

More than 90 percent of children aged 5 to 17 are in school. Although the share drops with age, a substantial 45 percent of 20- and 21-year-olds are in school, as are 25 percent of 22-to-24-year-olds.

♦ Because working parents need day care, and because education is increasingly important to earnings, the percentage of younger and older Americans enrolled in school will continue to rise in the years ahead.

## Enrollment in Nursery School through 12th Grade, 1999

*(number and percent distribution of people attending nursery school through 12th grade, fall 1999; numbers in thousands)*

| | *number* | *percent* |
|---|---|---|
| **Total students** | **57,193** | **100.0%** |
| Nursery school | 4,578 | 8.0 |
| Kindergarten | 3,825 | 6.7 |
| **Elementary** | **32,874** | **57.5** |
| 1st grade | 4,326 | 7.6 |
| 2nd grade | 3,927 | 6.9 |
| 3rd grade | 4,335 | 7.6 |
| 4th grade | 4,207 | 7.4 |
| 5th grade | 4,148 | 7.3 |
| 6th grade | 4,019 | 7.0 |
| 7th grade | 3,905 | 6.8 |
| 8th grade | 4,007 | 7.0 |
| **High school** | **15,916** | **27.8** |
| 9th grade | 4,172 | 7.3 |
| 10th grade | 3,861 | 6.8 |
| 11th grade | 3,850 | 6.7 |
| 12th grade | 4,033 | 7.1 |

*Source: Bureau of the Census,* School Enrollment—Social and Economic Characteristics of Students: October 1999, *detailed tables for Current Population Report P20-533, 2001; Internet site <www.census.gov/population/www/socdemo/school/p20-533.html>; calculations by New Strategist*

## School Enrollment by Age, 1999

*(number of people aged 3 or older, and number and percent enrolled in school by age, fall 1999; numbers in thousands)*

| | | enrolled | |
|---|---|---|---|
| | *total* | *number* | *percent* |
| **Total people** | **260,936** | **72,395** | **27.7%** |
| Aged 3 to 4 | 7,883 | 4,273 | 54.2 |
| Aged 5 to 6 | 8,097 | 7,774 | 96.0 |
| Aged 7 to 9 | 12,438 | 12,252 | 98.5 |
| Aged 10 to 13 | 16,148 | 15,957 | 98.8 |
| Aged 14 to 15 | 7,886 | 7,741 | 98.2 |
| Aged 16 to 17 | 8,131 | 7,611 | 93.6 |
| Aged 18 to 19 | 7,991 | 4,840 | 60.6 |
| Aged 20 to 21 | 7,196 | 3,256 | 45.3 |
| Aged 22 to 24 | 10,855 | 2,664 | 24.5 |
| Aged 25 to 29 | 18,250 | 2,018 | 11.1 |
| Aged 30 to 34 | 19,501 | 1,215 | 6.2 |
| Aged 35 to 44 | 44,746 | 1,654 | 3.7 |
| Aged 45 to 54 | 35,949 | 871 | 2.4 |
| Aged 55 or older | 55,864 | 269 | 0.5 |

*Source: Bureau of the Census,* School Enrollment—Social and Economic Characteristics of Students: October 1999, *detailed tables for Current Population Report P20-533, 2001; Internet site <www.census.gov/population/www/socdemo/school/p20-533.html>; calculations by New Strategist*

# Most Parents Are Satisfied with the Local Elementary School

## But some are so bothered by their school that they want to move.

Complaints about public schools have become commonplace, but in fact few households with elementary-school-aged children are not satisfied with the local elementary school. Among households with children under age 13, 77 percent are satisfied with the elementary school in their area, and only 7 percent are not satisfied. Three percent of households are so bothered by the local school that they want to move. Renters are slightly more likely than homeowners to be dissatisfied with the local school.

Among households with children aged 5 to 15, 86 percent send at least one child to public school. A substantial 12 percent send a child to private school. Only 1 percent home school their children. Not surprisingly, homeowners are nearly twice as likely as renters to send a child to private school, 14 versus 6 percent.

♦ While the great majority of parents are satisfied with the local elementary school, a significant proportion are not. More than 2 million dissatisfied parents are one of the pressure points for educational reform.

## Satisfaction with Local Elementary School by Homeownership Status, 1999

*(number and percent distribution of households with children aged 5 to 15 by school status and opinion of local elementary school, by homeownership status, 1999; numbers in thousands)*

| | *total* | *owner* | *renter* |
|---|---|---|---|
| **Total households with children aged 5 to 15** | **26,676** | **18,480** | **8,197** |
| Attend public school, K–12 | 22,811 | 15,443 | 7,369 |
| Attend private school, K–12 | 3,094 | 2,562 | 532 |
| Attend ungraded school, preschool | 337 | 187 | 150 |
| Home schooled or no school | 298 | 230 | 68 |
| **Households with children aged 0 to 13** | **30,803** | **20,236** | **10,567** |
| Satisfactory public elementary school | 23,740 | 16,046 | 7,694 |
| Unsatisfactory public elementary school | 2,110 | 1,439 | 671 |
| So bothered by school they want to move | 790 | 438 | 351 |
| **Total households with children aged 5 to 15** | **100.0%** | **100.0%** | **100.0%** |
| Attend public school, K–12 | 85.5 | 83.6 | 89.9 |
| Attend private school, K–12 | 11.6 | 13.9 | 6.5 |
| Attend ungraded school, preschool | 1.3 | 1.0 | 1.8 |
| Home-schooled or no school | 1.1 | 1.2 | 0.8 |
| **Households with children aged 0 to 13** | **100.0** | **100.0** | **100.0** |
| Satisfactory public elementary school | 77.1 | 79.3 | 72.8 |
| Unsatisfactory public elementary school | 6.8 | 7.1 | 6.3 |
| So bothered by school they want to move | 2.6 | 2.2 | 3.3 |

*Note: Numbers will not add to total because "not reported" is not shown.*
*Source: Bureau of the Census,* American Housing Survey for the United States in 1999; *calculations by New Strategist*

# School Enrollment Is Projected to Stabilize

## Now that the millennial generation is in school, enrollment will increase little during the next decade.

The good news is that the nation's already crowded schools will not have to find room for even more students. The bad news is that the overcrowding isn't going away anytime soon. Between 2000 and 2010, enrollment in the nation's elementary and secondary schools is projected to rise just 0.1 percent, remaining at the 53 million level.

Enrollment in kindergarten through eighth grade is projected to decline nearly 2 percent between 2000 and 2010 as millennials age out of the elementary-school years. Enrollment in secondary schools is projected to increase 4 percent between 2000 and 2010 as the youngest millennials enter high school.

Projections are the same for both public and private school. Despite the many complaints about the nation's public schools, the percentage of children who attend private school is projected to remain at 11 percent.

♦ With enrollments stabilizing at high levels, school districts cannot solve overcrowding by simply waiting it out. New schools, more teachers, and higher taxes are required.

## Projected Enrollment in Kindergarten through 12th Grade, 2000 to 2010

*(number of people enrolled in kindergarten through 12th grade by control of institution, fall 2000–10; percent change, 2000–10; numbers in thousands)*

| | total | | | public | | | private | | |
|---|---|---|---|---|---|---|---|---|---|
| | *total* | *K–8th* | *9th–12th* | *total* | *K–8th* | *9th–12th* | *total* | *K–8th* | *9th–12th* |
| 2000 | 52,989 | 38,132 | 14,857 | 47,026 | 33,521 | 13,505 | 5,963 | 4,611 | 1,352 |
| 2001 | 53,155 | 38,172 | 14,982 | 47,176 | 33,557 | 13,619 | 5,979 | 4,616 | 1,363 |
| 2002 | 53,287 | 38,157 | 15,130 | 47,296 | 33,543 | 13,753 | 5,991 | 4,614 | 1,377 |
| 2003 | 53,367 | 38,042 | 15,325 | 47,373 | 33,442 | 13,931 | 5,995 | 4,600 | 1,395 |
| 2004 | 53,429 | 37,809 | 15,620 | 47,436 | 33,237 | 14,199 | 5,993 | 4,572 | 1,422 |
| 2005 | 53,465 | 37,598 | 15,868 | 47,475 | 33,051 | 14,423 | 5,990 | 4,546 | 1,444 |
| 2006 | 53,435 | 37,442 | 15,992 | 47,452 | 32,915 | 14,537 | 5,983 | 4,527 | 1,455 |
| 2007 | 53,336 | 37,352 | 15,985 | 47,365 | 32,835 | 14,530 | 5,971 | 4,517 | 1,455 |
| 2008 | 53,174 | 37,340 | 15,834 | 47,218 | 32,825 | 14,393 | 5,956 | 4,515 | 1,441 |
| 2009 | 53,056 | 37,399 | 15,657 | 47,109 | 32,877 | 14,232 | 5,947 | 4,522 | 1,425 |
| 2010 | 53,016 | 37,538 | 15,478 | 47,068 | 32,999 | 14,069 | 5,948 | 4,539 | 1,409 |
| **Percent change** | | | | | | | | | |
| 2000 to 2010 | 0.1% | –1.6% | 4.2% | 0.1% | –1.6% | 4.2% | –0.3% | –1.6% | 4.2% |

*Source: National Center for Education Statistics,* Projections of Education Statistics to 2010, *NCES 2000071, 2000; calculations by New Strategist*

# Fewer High School Dropouts

## Fewer young adults are gambling with their future.

Among people aged 16 to 24 in 1999, only 11 percent were neither high school graduates nor currently enrolled in school, down from 15 percent in 1972. Dropout rates have fallen for both men and women as well as for every racial and ethnic group.

The dropout rate remains stubbornly high for Hispanics, however. While just 7 percent of non-Hispanic whites and 13 percent of non-Hispanic blacks aged 16 to 24 are dropouts, 29 percent of Hispanics have dropped out of high school. Among Hispanic men, the dropout rate was nearly the same in 1999 as in 1972. Nearly one-third of Hispanic men aged 16 to 24 are high school dropouts.

♦ The arrival of millions of poorly educated Hispanic immigrants to the U.S. during the past few decades explains the high dropout rate. It is likely to remain high as long as recent immigrants make up a large share of the Hispanic population.

**Non-Hispanic whites have the lowest dropout rate**

*(percent of people aged 16 to 24 who were neither enrolled in school nor high school graduates, by race and Hispanic origin, 1999)*

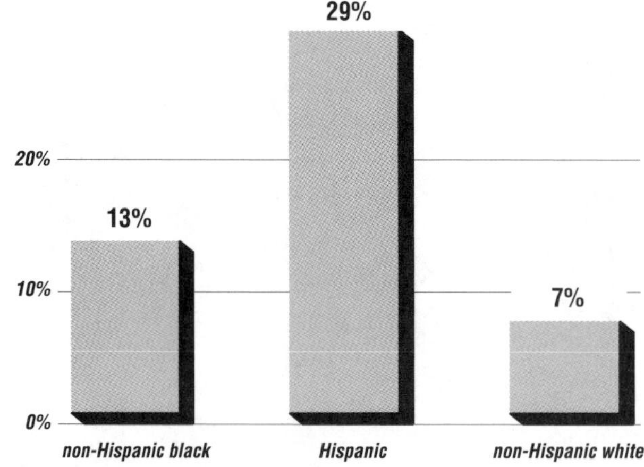

## High School Dropouts by Sex, Race, and Hispanic Origin, 1972 and 1999

*(percent of people aged 16 to 24 who were not enrolled in school and were not high school graduates by sex, race, and Hispanic origin, 1972 and 1999; percentage point change, 1972–99)*

| | *1999* | *1972* | *percentage point change 1972–99* |
|---|---|---|---|
| **Total people** | **11.2%** | **14.6%** | **–3.4** |
| Non-Hispanic black | 12.6 | 21.3 | –8.7 |
| Hispanic | 28.6 | 34.3 | –5.7 |
| Non-Hispanic white | 7.3 | 12.3 | –5.0 |
| **Total men** | **11.9** | **14.1** | **–2.2** |
| Non-Hispanic black | 12.1 | 22.3 | –10.2 |
| Hispanic | 31.0 | 33.7 | –2.7 |
| Non-Hispanic white | 7.7 | 11.6 | –3.9 |
| **Total women** | **10.5** | **15.1** | **–4.6** |
| Non-Hispanic black | 13.0 | 20.5 | –7.5 |
| Hispanic | 26.0 | 34.8 | –8.8 |
| Non-Hispanic white | 6.9 | 12.8 | –5.9 |

*Note: Hispanics may be of any race.*
*Source: National Center for Education Statistics,* Digest of Education Statistics 2001, *NCES 2001034, 2001; calculations by New Strategist*

## More High School Graduates

### The number of people graduating from high school will climb 10 percent between 2000 and 2010.

As the millennial generation moves through high school, the number of high school graduates will climb from 2.8 million in 2000 to 3.1 million in 2010. The annual crop of graduates, which had been shrinking for years, began a steady rise in 1993.

The number of high school graduates will peak in about 2008. Thereafter, the number of graduates should stabilize—unless the nation's school systems can further lower the high school dropout rate.

♦ Colleges are welcoming the growing number of high school graduates because it means applications will increase without a greater investment in recruitment.

## Projections of High School Graduates, 2000 to 2010

*(number of people graduating from high school by control of institution, 2000 to 2010; percent change 2000–10; numbers in thousands)*

| | *total* | *public* | *private* |
|---|---|---|---|
| 2000 | 2,820 | 2,526 | 294 |
| 2001 | 2,837 | 2,542 | 296 |
| 2002 | 2,886 | 2,585 | 301 |
| 2003 | 2,929 | 2,624 | 305 |
| 2004 | 2,935 | 2,630 | 306 |
| 2005 | 2,944 | 2,637 | 307 |
| 2006 | 2,998 | 2,685 | 312 |
| 2007 | 3,069 | 2,750 | 320 |
| 2008 | 3,153 | 2,825 | 328 |
| 2009 | 3,146 | 2,818 | 328 |
| 2010 | 3,115 | 2,791 | 324 |
| **Percent change** | | | |
| 2000 to 2010 | 10.5% | 10.5% | 10.2% |

*Source: National Center for Education Statistics,* Projections of Education Statistics to 2010, *NCES 2000071, 2000; calculations by New Strategist*

# SAT Scores Rise

## Most demographic segments have made gains.

The number of high school students who take the Scholastic Assessment Test expanded enormously over the past few decades. Once limited to the elite, the SAT has been embraced by the masses—as have the nation's college campuses. With larger numbers of "average" students taking the test, overall SAT scores have suffered setbacks, falling in some years.

Most demographic segments have boosted their test scores during the past 13 years, however. While the average verbal score fell 2 points overall between 1986–1987 and 1999–2000, by racial and ethnic group verbal scores rose for all but Mexican Americans. Math scores rose 13 points between 1986–1987 and 1999–2000, including double-digit gains for all but Mexican Americans.

♦ Overall, SAT scores are likely to show slow improvement in the years ahead as minority scores continue to rise.

**Verbal down, math up**

*(average verbal and math SAT scores, 1986–1987 and 1999–2000)*

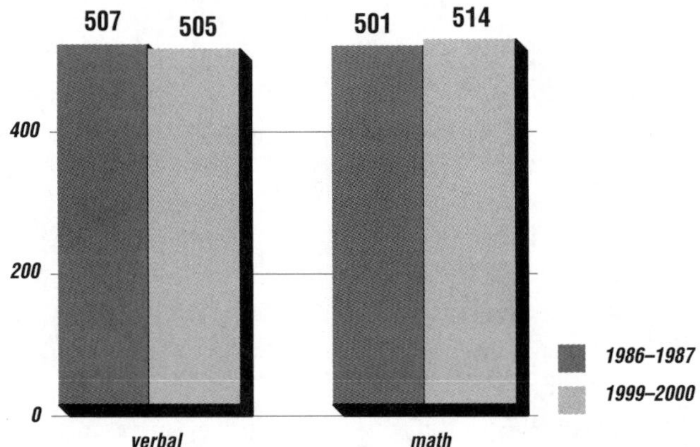

## Scholastic Assessment Test Scores by Sex, Race, and Hispanic Origin, 1986–1987 and 1999–2000

*(average SAT scores and change in scores by sex, race, and Hispanic origin of student, 1986–1987 and 1999–2000)*

| | *1999–00* | *1986–87* | *change* |
|---|---|---|---|
| **VERBAL SAT** | | | |
| **Total students** | **505** | **507** | **–2** |
| Male | 507 | 512 | –5 |
| Female | 504 | 502 | 2 |
| White | 528 | 524 | 4 |
| Black | 434 | 428 | 6 |
| Hispanic or Latino | 461 | 464 | –3 |
| Mexican American | 453 | 457 | –4 |
| Puerto Rican | 456 | 436 | 20 |
| Asian American | 499 | 479 | 20 |
| American Indian | 482 | 471 | 11 |
| Other | 508 | 480 | 28 |
| **MATH SAT** | | | |
| **Total students** | **514** | **501** | **13** |
| Male | 533 | 523 | 10 |
| Female | 498 | 481 | 17 |
| White | 530 | 514 | 16 |
| Black | 426 | 411 | 15 |
| Hispanic or Latino | 467 | 462 | 5 |
| Mexican American | 460 | 455 | 5 |
| Puerto Rican | 451 | 432 | 19 |
| Asian American | 565 | 541 | 24 |
| American Indian | 481 | 463 | 18 |
| Other | 514 | 482 | 32 |

*Source: National Center for Education Statistics,* Digest of Education Statistics 2000*; NCES 2001034, 2001; calculations by New Strategist*

# Most Children from Affluent Families Go to College

## The majority of families with children aged 18 to 24 and incomes of $50,000 or more have at least one child in college.

Family income is one of the best predictors of whether children have the opportunity to go to college. Among the nation's 11 million families with children aged 18 to 24, 47 percent have at least one child in college full-time. The proportion rises with income to a high of 67 percent for families with incomes of $75,000 or more.

Among families with children aged 18 to 24 whose income is below $20,000, only 24 percent have a child in college full-time.

♦ Children of the affluent can devote full attention to their studies because their parents are paying the bills. Many children from less affluent families attend school part-time because they must work to support themselves.

**College attendance rises with family income**

*(percentage of families with children aged 18 to 24 that have at least one child attending college full-time, by household income, 1999)*

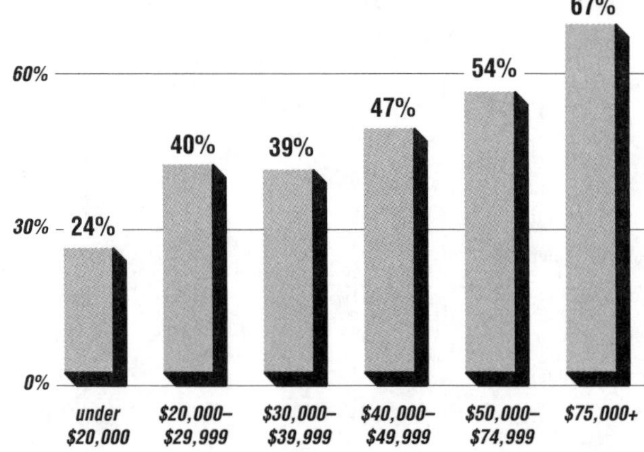

## Families with Children in College, 1999

*(total number of families, number with children aged 18 to 24, and number and percent with children aged 18 to 24 attending college full-time by household income, 1999; numbers in thousands)*

| | | | with one or more children attending college full-time | | |
|---|---|---|---|---|---|
| | total | with children aged 18–24 | number | percent of total families | percent of families with children 18–24 |
| **Total families** | **72,921** | **10,608** | **5,017** | **6.9%** | **47.3%** |
| Under $20,000 | 11,570 | 1,447 | 354 | 3.1 | 24.5 |
| $20,000 to $29,999 | 9,286 | 1,117 | 444 | 4.8 | 39.7 |
| $30,000 to $39,999 | 8,282 | 1,063 | 416 | 5.0 | 39.1 |
| $40,000 to $49,999 | 6,834 | 971 | 455 | 6.7 | 46.9 |
| $50,000 to $74,999 | 12,932 | 2,022 | 1,087 | 8.4 | 53.8 |
| $75,000 or more | 13,765 | 2,497 | 1,671 | 12.1 | 66.9 |

*Note: Numbers will not add to total because "not reported" is not shown.*
*Source: Bureau of the Census,* School Enrollment—Social and Economic Characteristics of Students: October 1999, *detailed tables for Current Population Report P20-533, 2001; Internet site <www.census.gov/population/www/socdemo/school/p20-533.html>; calculations by New Strategist*

# College Enrollment Rate Has Soared

## Rates rose because a college degree has become a necessity for a middle-class lifestyle.

The rate at which high school graduates enroll in college has soared over the past few decades—despite the rising cost of attending college. Once a privilege reserved for the nation's elite, the college experience now belongs to the majority of young adults.

Among women aged 16 to 24 who graduated from high school in 1999, fully 64 percent were enrolled in college within 12 months. The share is sharply higher than the 38 percent of 1960. Women's college enrollment rate now exceeds that of men.

The college enrollment rate has increased for whites, blacks, and Hispanics in the past two decades. For whites, the rate has grown from 51 percent in 1977 to 63 percent in 1999; for blacks, from 50 to 59 percent. The Hispanic rate has also grown slightly, from 49 percent in 1977 to 52 percent in 1999.

♦ Many who start college never finish—which is why fewer than half the nation's young adults have a college degree although the majority enroll in college. Because even a few years of college can boost earnings, however, the rise in enrollment rates is good news.

### Women are more likely to go to college than men

*(percent of people aged 16 to 24 graduating from high school in the previous 12 months who were enrolled in college as of October of each year, by sex, 1960 and 1999)*

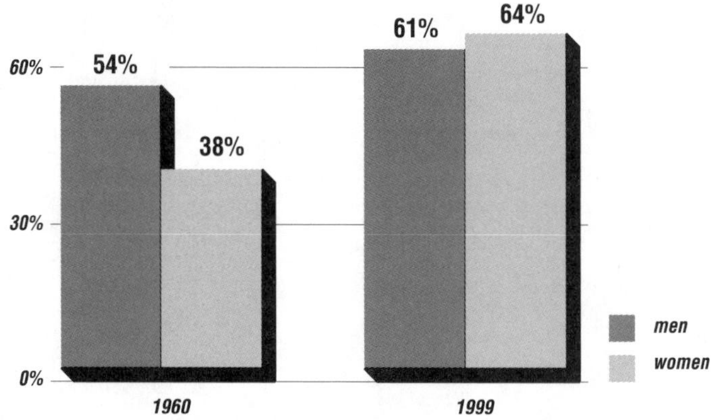

## College Enrollment Rate by Sex, 1960 to 1999

*(percent of people aged 16 to 24 graduating from high school in the previous 12 months who were enrolled in college as of October of each year, by sex; percentage point difference in enrollment rates of men and women, 1960–99)*

| | men | women | percentage point difference |
|---|---|---|---|
| 1999 | 61.4% | 64.4% | –3.0 |
| 1998 | 62.4 | 69.1 | –6.7 |
| 1997 | 63.5 | 70.3 | –6.8 |
| 1996 | 60.1 | 69.7 | –9.6 |
| 1995 | 62.6 | 61.4 | 1.2 |
| 1994 | 60.6 | 63.2 | –2.6 |
| 1993 | 59.7 | 65.4 | –5.7 |
| 1992 | 59.6 | 63.8 | –4.2 |
| 1991 | 57.6 | 67.1 | –9.5 |
| 1990 | 57.8 | 62.0 | –4.2 |
| 1989 | 57.6 | 61.6 | –4.0 |
| 1988 | 57.0 | 60.8 | –3.8 |
| 1987 | 58.4 | 55.3 | 3.1 |
| 1986 | 55.9 | 51.9 | 4.0 |
| 1985 | 58.6 | 56.9 | 1.7 |
| 1980 | 46.7 | 51.8 | –5.1 |
| 1975 | 52.6 | 49.0 | 3.6 |
| 1970 | 55.2 | 48.5 | 6.7 |
| 1965 | 57.3 | 45.3 | 12.0 |
| 1960 | 54.0 | 37.9 | 16.1 |

*Source: National Center for Education Statistics,* Digest of Education Statistics 2000, *NCES 2001034, 2001; calculations by New Strategist*

## College Enrollment Rate by Race and Hispanic Origin, 1977 to 1999

*(percent of people aged 16 to 24 graduating from high school in the previous 12 months who were enrolled in college as of October of each year, by race and Hispanic origin, 1977–99)*

| | white | black | Hispanic |
|---|---|---|---|
| 1999 | 62.8% | 59.2% | – |
| 1998 | 65.8 | 62.1 | 51.7% |
| 1997 | 67.5 | 59.6 | 54.6 |
| 1996 | 65.8 | 55.3 | 55.0 |
| 1995 | 62.6 | 51.4 | 51.1 |
| 1994 | 63.6 | 50.9 | 55.1 |
| 1993 | 62.8 | 55.6 | 55.4 |
| 1992 | 63.4 | 47.9 | 58.1 |
| 1991 | 64.6 | 45.6 | 53.1 |
| 1990 | 61.5 | 46.3 | 53.3 |
| 1989 | 60.4 | 52.8 | 53.2 |
| 1988 | 60.7 | 45.0 | 48.6 |
| 1987 | 56.6 | 51.9 | 45.0 |
| 1986 | 56.0 | 36.5 | 43.0 |
| 1985 | 59.4 | 42.3 | 46.6 |
| 1980 | 49.9 | 41.8 | 49.9 |
| 1977 | 50.7 | 49.6 | 48.9 |

*Note: Hispanic enrollment rates are a three-year moving average.*
*Source: National Center for Education Statistics,* Digest of Education Statistics 2000, *NCES 2001034, 2001; calculations by New Strategist*

# Most Older Students Are Part-Timers

## With families to support, older students cannot afford to go to school full-time.

As the number of older college students has grown, so has the number of students attending college part-time. Many older students have families to support and cannot afford the luxury of full-time study. Instead, they juggle jobs and classes by attending school part-time. In 1999, 33 percent of college students were part-timers.

Most students under age 25 attend school full-time. Ninety percent of college students aged 18 or 19 are full-time students, as are 86 percent of those aged 20 to 21. The figure stands at 75 percent among 22-to-24-year-olds, and drops to 53 percent among students aged 25 to 29.

Among full-time students, 79 percent are under age 25. Among part-time students, 72 percent are aged 25 or older.

♦ The lifestyles of college students differ sharply by age. While younger students have time to party, older students have little free time thanks to jobs, families, and classes.

## College Students by Age and Attendance Status, 1999

*(number of people aged 15 or older enrolled in institutions of higher education by age and attendance status, 1999; numbers in thousands)*

| | | full-time | | part-time | |
|---|---|---|---|---|---|
| | total | number | percent | number | percent |
| **Total people** | **15,202** | **10,111** | **66.5%** | **5,091** | **33.5%** |
| Aged 15 to 17 | 151 | 144 | 95.4 | 6 | 4.0 |
| Aged 18 to 19 | 3,520 | 3,173 | 90.1 | 347 | 9.9 |
| Aged 20 to 21 | 3,119 | 2,696 | 86.4 | 425 | 13.6 |
| Aged 22 to 24 | 2,620 | 1,972 | 75.3 | 647 | 24.7 |
| Aged 25 to 29 | 1,940 | 1,024 | 52.8 | 915 | 47.2 |
| Aged 30 to 34 | 1,156 | 403 | 34.9 | 753 | 65.1 |
| Aged 35 to 39 | 856 | 261 | 30.5 | 595 | 69.5 |
| Aged 40 to 44 | 741 | 212 | 28.6 | 529 | 71.4 |
| Aged 45 to 49 | 502 | 121 | 24.1 | 381 | 75.9 |
| Aged 50 to 54 | 337 | 63 | 18.7 | 274 | 81.3 |
| Aged 55 to 59 | 151 | 30 | 19.9 | 121 | 80.1 |
| Aged 60 to 64 | 39 | 6 | 15.4 | 33 | 84.6 |
| Aged 65 or older | 76 | 6 | 7.9 | 70 | 92.1 |

*Source: Bureau of the Census,* School Enrollment—Social and Economic Characteristics of Students: October 1999, *detailed tables for Current Population Report P20-533, 2001; Internet site <www.census.gov/population/www/socdemo/school/p20-533.html>; calculations by New Strategist*

# More Than One in Five College Students Is a Minority

## Among the nation's 14 million college students, nearly 4 million are black, Hispanic, Asian, or American Indian.

College campuses are becoming more diverse. Non-Hispanic whites accounted for 71 percent of college students in 1997, down from 83 percent in 1976. The non-Hispanic black share rose from 9 to 11 percent during those years, while the Hispanic share climbed from 3 to 8 percent. The Asian share of college students tripled, from 2 to 6 percent. Foreign students (called nonresident aliens) account for only 3 percent of all college students but for a larger 11 percent of graduate students.

Non-Hispanic whites received 76 percent of the bachelor's degrees awarded in 1997–98. Blacks earned 8 percent, Hispanics 6 percent, and Asians 6 percent. Non-Hispanic whites earn a much smaller proportion of degrees at the doctoral level—not because minorities are better represented, but because foreign students make up a large share of those earning degrees. Twenty-five percent of doctoral degrees awarded in 1997-98 went to nonresident aliens.

♦ The educational attainment of blacks and Hispanics is inching upward at a painfully slow rate. More financial aid would hasten the rise.

## College Students by Race and Hispanic Origin, 1976 and 1997

*(number and percent distribution of people enrolled in institutions of higher education by race, Hispanic origin, and level of enrollment, fall 1976 and fall 1997; percent change in number and percentage point change in distribution, 1976–97; numbers in thousands)*

| | number | | percent change | percent distribution | | percentage point change |
|---|---|---|---|---|---|---|
| | 1997 | 1976 | 1976–97 | 1997 | 1976 | 1976–97 |
| **Total enrollment** | **14,345** | **10,986** | **30.6%** | **100.0%** | **100.0%** | – |
| White, non-Hispanic | 10,161 | 9,076 | 11.0 | 70.8 | 82.6 | –11.8 |
| Minority | 3,723 | 1,691 | 120.2 | 25.0 | 15.4 | 10.6 |
| Black, non-Hispanic | 1,533 | 1,033 | 48.4 | 10.7 | 9.4 | 1.3 |
| Hispanic | 1,200 | 384 | 212.7 | 8.4 | 3.5 | 4.9 |
| Asian | 852 | 198 | 330.5 | 5.9 | 1.8 | 4.1 |
| Native American | 139 | 76 | 82.7 | 0.0 | 0.7 | 0.3 |
| Nonresident alien | 461 | 219 | 110.8 | 3.2 | 1.0 | 1.2 |
| **Undergraduate enrollment** | **12,298** | **9,419** | **30.6** | **100.0** | **100.0** | – |
| White | 8,682 | 7,741 | 12.2 | 70.6 | 82.2 | –11.6 |
| Minority | 3,352 | 1,535 | 118.3 | 27.3 | 16.3 | 10.0 |
| Black, non-Hispanic | 1,380 | 943 | 46.3 | 11.2 | 10.0 | 1.2 |
| Hispanic | 1,108 | 353 | 213.0 | 9.0 | 3.7 | 5.3 |
| Asian | 737 | 169 | 335.3 | 5.0 | 1.8 | 4.2 |
| Native American | 127 | 70 | 82.2 | 1.0 | 0.7 | 0.3 |
| Nonresident alien | 265 | 143 | 85.1 | 2.2 | 1.5 | 0.6 |
| **Graduate enrollment** | **1,751** | **1,323** | **32.3** | **100.0** | **100.0** | – |
| White | 1,260 | 1,116 | 12.9 | 72.0 | 84.4 | –12.4 |
| Minority | 302 | 135 | 123.4 | 17.2 | 10.2 | 7.0 |
| Black, non-Hispanic | 132 | 79 | 66.7 | 7.5 | 5.9 | 1.6 |
| Hispanic | 78 | 26 | 201.5 | 4.5 | 1.0 | 2.5 |
| Asian | 82 | 25 | 228.4 | 4.7 | 1.9 | 2.8 |
| Native American | 9 | 5 | 88.0 | 0.5 | 0.4 | 0.1 |
| Nonresident alien | 189 | 72 | 162.2 | 10.8 | 5.5 | 5.3 |
| **First-professional enrollment** | **297** | **244** | **21.5** | **100.0** | **100.0** | – |
| White | 219 | 220 | –0.5 | 73.8 | 90.1 | –16.3 |
| Minority | 70 | 21 | 233.8 | 23.6 | 8.6 | 15.0 |
| Black, non-Hispanic | 21 | 11 | 92.7 | 7.2 | 4.6 | 2.6 |
| Hispanic | 14 | 5 | 178.0 | 4.7 | 1.8 | 2.9 |
| Asian | 33 | 4 | 720.0 | 11.1 | 1.7 | 9.4 |
| Native American | 2 | 1 | 130.0 | 0.8 | 0.5 | 0.3 |
| Nonresident alien | 8 | 3 | 150.0 | 2.5 | 1.3 | 1.2 |

*Source: National Center for Education Statistics,* Digest of Education Statistics 2000, *NCES 2001034, 2001; calculations by New Strategist*

## Degrees Conferred by Race and Hispanic Origin, 1997–98

*(number and percent distribution of degrees conferred by institutions of higher education by level of degree, race, and Hispanic origin of degree holder, 1997–98)*

| | *number* | *percent* |
|---|---|---|
| **Total associate's degrees** | **555,538** | **100.0%** |
| White, non-Hispanic | 411,336 | 74.0 |
| Black, non-Hispanic | 55,008 | 9.9 |
| Hispanic | 45,627 | 8.2 |
| Asian | 25,047 | 4.5 |
| Native American | 6,220 | 1.1 |
| Nonresident alien | 12,300 | 2.2 |
| **Total bachelor's degrees** | **1,183,033** | **100.0** |
| White, non-Hispanic | 900,317 | 76.1 |
| Black, non-Hispanic | 98,132 | 8.3 |
| Hispanic | 65,937 | 5.6 |
| Asian | 71,592 | 6.1 |
| Native American | 7,894 | 0.7 |
| Nonresident alien | 39,161 | 3.3 |
| **Total master's degrees** | **429,296** | **100.0** |
| White, non-Hispanic | 307,587 | 71.6 |
| Black, non-Hispanic | 30,097 | 7.0 |
| Hispanic | 16,215 | 3.8 |
| Asian | 21,088 | 4.9 |
| Native American | 2,049 | 0.5 |
| Nonresident alien | 52,260 | 12.2 |
| **Total doctoral degrees** | **45,925** | **100.0** |
| White, non-Hispanic | 28,747 | 62.6 |
| Black, non-Hispanic | 2,066 | 4.5 |
| Hispanic | 1,270 | 2.8 |
| Asian | 2,664 | 5.8 |
| Native American | 187 | 0.4 |
| Nonresident alien | 11,321 | 24.7 |

*(continued)*

*(continued from previous page)*

| | *number* | *percent* |
|---|---|---|
| **Total first-professional degrees** | **78,353** | **100.0%** |
| White, non-Hispanic | 59,273 | 75.6 |
| Black, non-Hispanic | 5,483 | 6.0 |
| Hispanic | 3,547 | 4.5 |
| Asian | 7,712 | 9.8 |
| Native American | 561 | 0.7 |
| Nonresident alien | 1,777 | 2.3 |

*Source: National Center for Education Statistics,* Digest of Education Statistics 2000, *NCES 2001034, 2001; calculations by New Strategist*

# Women Earn Most Degrees

## Women earned more than half the bachelor's and master's degrees awarded in 1997-98.

As women pursue careers, they are eager for credentials that command a premium wage. Women are now a significant presence in most degree programs and fields of study. Sixty-one percent of associate's degrees went to women in 1997-98, as did 56 percent of bachelor's degrees and 57 percent of master's degrees. Women earned 18 percent of the bachelor's degrees awarded in engineering in 1997-98 and 48 percent of those awarded in business.

Women earned 42 percent of all doctorates in 1997-98 and 43 percent of first-professional degrees. They accounted for 42 percent of newly minted physicians, 44 percent of lawyers, and 67 percent of pharmacists.

♦ Women's share of the nation's doctors, lawyers, and other professionals will expand rapidly in the next few decades as the young women now earning degrees replace older men retiring from the professions.

## Associate's Degrees Conferred by Field of Study and Sex, 1997–98

*(number of associate's degrees conferred by field of study and sex, and percent awarded to women, 1997–98)*

| | | | women | |
|---|---|---|---|---|
| | total | men | number | percent |
| **Total degrees** | **558,555** | **217,613** | **340,942** | **61.0%** |
| Agriculture and natural resources | 6,673 | 4,459 | 2,214 | 33.2 |
| Architecture and related programs | 265 | 90 | 175 | 66.0 |
| Area, ethnic, and cultural studies | 104 | 25 | 79 | 76.0 |
| Biological sciences, life sciences | 2,113 | 782 | 1,331 | 63.0 |
| Business management and administrative services | 91,399 | 24,637 | 66,762 | 73.0 |
| Communications | 2,368 | 1,144 | 1,224 | 51.7 |
| Communications technologies | 1,602 | 1,008 | 594 | 37.1 |
| Computer and information sciences | 13,870 | 7,627 | 6,243 | 45.0 |
| Construction trades | 2,172 | 2,055 | 117 | 5.4 |
| Consumer and personal services | 7,744 | 4,642 | 3,102 | 40.1 |
| Education | 9,278 | 2,174 | 7,104 | 76.6 |
| Engineering | 2,149 | 1,823 | 326 | 15.2 |
| Engineering-related technologies | 32,748 | 28,533 | 4,215 | 12.9 |
| English language and literature, letters | 1,609 | 543 | 1,066 | 66.3 |
| Foreign languages and literatures | 543 | 217 | 326 | 60.0 |
| Health professions and related sciences | 92,031 | 14,260 | 77,771 | 84.5 |
| Home economics | 8,292 | 697 | 7,595 | 91.6 |
| Law and legal studies | 7,797 | 943 | 6,854 | 87.9 |
| Liberal arts and sciences | 186,248 | 70,612 | 115,636 | 62.1 |
| Library science | 96 | 14 | 82 | 85.4 |
| Marketing operations/marketing and distribution | 5,516 | 1,368 | 4,148 | 75.2 |
| Mathematics | 844 | 491 | 353 | 41.8 |
| Mechanics and repairers | 10,616 | 9,901 | 715 | 6.7 |
| Multi/interdisciplinary studies | 9,401 | 4,541 | 4,860 | 51.7 |
| Parks, recreation, leisure, and fitness | 895 | 512 | 383 | 42.8 |
| Philosophy and religion | 94 | 43 | 51 | 54.3 |
| Physical sciences | 2,286 | 1,099 | 1,187 | 51.9 |
| Precision production trades | 11,085 | 8,551 | 2,534 | 22.9 |
| Protective services | 19,002 | 12,820 | 6,182 | 32.5 |

*(continued)*

*(continued from previous page)*

| | total | men | women number | women percent |
|---|---|---|---|---|
| Psychology | 1,765 | 604 | 1,161 | 65.8% |
| Public administration and services | 4,156 | 692 | 3,464 | 83.3 |
| ROTC and military technologies | 22 | 21 | 1 | 4.5 |
| Social sciences and history | 4,196 | 1,564 | 2,632 | 62.7 |
| Theological studies, religious vocations | 570 | 323 | 247 | 43.3 |
| Transportation and material moving | 1,009 | 852 | 157 | 15.6 |
| Visual and performing arts | 14,980 | 6,773 | 8,207 | 54.8 |
| Not classified | 3,017 | 1,173 | 1,844 | 61.1 |

*Source: National Center for Education Statistics,* Digest of Education Statistics 2000, *NCES 2001034, 2001; calculations by New Strategist*

## Bachelor's Degrees Conferred by Field of Study and Sex, 1997–98

*(number of bachelor's degrees conferred by field of study and sex, and percent awarded to women, 1997–98)*

| | total | men | women number | women percent |
|---|---|---|---|---|
| **Total degrees** | **1,184,406** | **519,956** | **664,450** | **56.1%** |
| Agriculture and natural resources | 23,284 | 13,809 | 9,475 | 40.7 |
| Architecture and related programs | 7,652 | 4,966 | 2,686 | 35.1 |
| Area, ethnic, and cultural studies | 6,153 | 2,045 | 4,108 | 66.8 |
| Biological sciences, life sciences | 65,868 | 29,589 | 36,279 | 55.1 |
| Business management and administrative services | 233,119 | 120,069 | 113,050 | 48.5 |
| Communications | 49,385 | 19,631 | 29,754 | 60.2 |
| Communications technologies | 729 | 383 | 346 | 47.5 |
| Computer and information sciences | 26,852 | 19,686 | 7,166 | 26.7 |
| Education | 105,968 | 26,302 | 79,666 | 75.2 |
| Engineering | 59,910 | 48,852 | 11,058 | 18.5 |
| Engineering-related technologies | 14,000 | 12,588 | 1,412 | 10.1 |
| English language and literature | 49,708 | 16,477 | 33,231 | 66.9 |
| Foreign languages and literatures | 14,451 | 4,342 | 10,109 | 70.0 |
| Health professions and related sciences | 84,379 | 15,082 | 69,297 | 82.1 |
| Home economics | 17,296 | 1,980 | 15,316 | 88.6 |
| Law and legal studies | 2,017 | 569 | 1,448 | 71.8 |
| Liberal arts and sciences | 33,202 | 11,866 | 21,336 | 64.3 |
| Library science | 73 | 17 | 56 | 76.7 |
| Mathematics | 12,328 | 6,596 | 5,732 | 46.5 |
| Multi/interdisciplinary studies | 26,163 | 8,866 | 17,297 | 66.1 |
| Parks, recreation, leisure, and fitness | 16,781 | 8,350 | 8,431 | 50.2 |
| Philosophy and religion | 8,207 | 5,178 | 3,029 | 36.9 |
| Physical sciences | 19,416 | 11,955 | 7,461 | 38.4 |
| Precision production trades | 407 | 296 | 111 | 27.3 |
| Protective services | 25,076 | 14,934 | 10,142 | 40.4 |
| Psychology | 73,972 | 18,959 | 55,013 | 74.4 |
| Public administration and services | 20,408 | 3,881 | 16,527 | 81.0 |
| ROTC and military technologies | 3 | 3 | 0 | 0.0 |
| Social sciences and history | 125,040 | 63,537 | 61,503 | 49.2 |
| Theological studies, religious vocations | 5,903 | 4,260 | 1,643 | 27.8 |
| Transportation and material moving | 3,206 | 2,809 | 397 | 12.4 |
| Visual and performing arts | 52,077 | 21,483 | 30,594 | 58.7 |
| Not classified | 1,373 | 596 | 777 | 56.6 |

*Source: National Center for Education Statistics,* Digest of Education Statistics 2000, *NCES 2001034, 2001; calculations by New Strategist*

## Master's Degrees Conferred by Field of Study and Sex, 1997–98

*(number of master's degrees conferred by field of study and sex, and percent awarded to women, 1997–98)*

| | total | men | women number | women percent |
|---|---|---|---|---|
| **Total degrees** | **430,164** | **184,375** | **245,789** | **57.1%** |
| Agriculture and natural resources | 4,475 | 2,552 | 1,923 | 43.0 |
| Architecture and related programs | 4,347 | 2,537 | 1,810 | 41.6 |
| Area, ethnic, and cultural studies | 1,617 | 709 | 908 | 56.2 |
| Biological sciences, life sciences | 6,261 | 2,981 | 3,280 | 52.4 |
| Business management and administrative services | 102,171 | 62,713 | 39,458 | 38.6 |
| Communications | 5,611 | 2,110 | 3,501 | 62.4 |
| Communications technologies | 564 | 282 | 282 | 50.0 |
| Computer and information sciences | 11,246 | 7,987 | 3,259 | 29.0 |
| Education | 114,691 | 27,070 | 87,621 | 76.4 |
| Engineering | 25,936 | 20,813 | 5,123 | 19.8 |
| Engineering-related technologies | 1,152 | 885 | 267 | 23.2 |
| English language and literature | 7,795 | 2,643 | 5,152 | 66.1 |
| Foreign languages and literatures | 2,927 | 932 | 1,995 | 68.2 |
| Health professions and related sciences | 39,260 | 8,751 | 30,509 | 77.7 |
| Home economics | 2,914 | 494 | 2,420 | 83.0 |
| Law and legal studies | 3,228 | 2,070 | 1,158 | 35.9 |
| Liberal arts and sciences | 2,801 | 1,023 | 1,778 | 63.5 |
| Library science | 4,871 | 1,015 | 3,856 | 79.2 |
| Mathematics | 3,643 | 2,151 | 1,492 | 41.0 |
| Multi/interdisciplinary studies | 2,677 | 1,076 | 1,601 | 59.8 |
| Parks, recreation, leisure, and fitness | 2,024 | 1,053 | 971 | 48.0 |
| Philosophy and religion | 1,307 | 848 | 459 | 35.1 |
| Physical sciences | 5,361 | 3,435 | 1,926 | 35.9 |
| Precision production trades | 15 | 10 | 5 | 33.3 |
| Protective services | 2,000 | 1,172 | 828 | 41.4 |
| Psychology | 13,747 | 3,699 | 10,048 | 73.1 |
| Public administration and services | 25,144 | 7,025 | 18,119 | 72.1 |
| ROTC and military technologies | 0 | 0 | 0 | 0.0 |
| Social sciences and history | 14,938 | 7,960 | 6,978 | 46.7 |
| Theological studies/religious vocations | 4,692 | 2,726 | 1,966 | 41.9 |
| Transportation and material moving | 736 | 664 | 72 | 9.8 |
| Visual and performing arts | 11,145 | 4,596 | 6,549 | 58.8 |
| Not classified | 868 | 393 | 475 | 54.7 |

*Source: National Center for Education Statistics,* Digest of Education Statistics 2000, *NCES 2001034, 2001; calculations by New Strategist*

## Doctoral Degrees Conferred by Field of Study and Sex, 1997–98

*(number of doctoral degrees conferred by field of study and sex, and percent awarded to women, 1997–98)*

| | total | men | women number | women percent |
|---|---|---|---|---|
| **Total degrees** | **46,010** | **26,664** | **19,346** | **42.1%** |
| Agriculture and natural resources | 1,302 | 931 | 371 | 28.5 |
| Architecture and related programs | 131 | 80 | 51 | 38.9 |
| Area, ethnic, and cultural studies | 181 | 95 | 86 | 47.5 |
| Biological sciences, life sciences | 4,961 | 2,852 | 2,109 | 42.5 |
| Business management and administrative services | 1,290 | 885 | 405 | 31.4 |
| Communications | 354 | 168 | 186 | 52.5 |
| Communications technologies | 5 | 3 | 2 | 40.0 |
| Computer and information sciences | 858 | 718 | 140 | 16.3 |
| Education | 6,729 | 2,479 | 4,250 | 63.2 |
| Engineering | 5,980 | 5,247 | 733 | 12.3 |
| Engineering-related technologies | 14 | 14 | 0 | 0.0 |
| English language and literature | 1,639 | 670 | 969 | 59.1 |
| Foreign languages and literatures | 959 | 406 | 553 | 57.7 |
| Health professions and related sciences | 2,484 | 931 | 1,553 | 62.5 |
| Home economics | 424 | 108 | 316 | 74.5 |
| Law and legal studies | 66 | 37 | 29 | 43.9 |
| Liberal arts and sciences | 87 | 43 | 44 | 50.6 |
| Library science | 48 | 17 | 31 | 64.6 |
| Mathematics | 1,259 | 936 | 323 | 25.7 |
| Multi/interdisciplinary studies | 508 | 283 | 225 | 44.3 |
| Parks, recreation, leisure, and fitness | 129 | 75 | 54 | 41.9 |
| Philosophy and religion | 585 | 411 | 174 | 29.7 |
| Physical sciences | 4,571 | 3,417 | 1,154 | 25.2 |
| Precision production trades | 0 | 0 | 0 | 0.0 |
| Protective services | 39 | 25 | 14 | 35.9 |
| Psychology | 4,073 | 1,325 | 2,748 | 67.5 |
| Public administration and services | 499 | 223 | 276 | 55.3 |
| ROTC and military technologies | 0 | 0 | 0 | 0.0 |
| Social sciences and history | 4,127 | 2,445 | 1,682 | 40.8 |
| Theological studies, religious vocations | 1,460 | 1,224 | 236 | 16.2 |
| Transportation and material moving | 0 | 0 | 0 | 0.0 |
| Visual and performing arts | 1,163 | 566 | 597 | 51.3 |
| Not classified | 85 | 50 | 35 | 41.2 |

*Source: National Center for Education Statistics,* Digest of Education Statistics 2000, *NCES 2001034, 2001; calculations by New Strategist*

## First-Professional Degrees Conferred by Field of Study, 1997–98

*(number of first-professional degrees conferred by field of study and sex, and percent awarded to women, 1997–98)*

| | | | women | |
|---|---|---|---|---|
| | *total* | *men* | *number* | *percent* |
| **Total degrees** | **78,598** | **44,911** | **33,687** | **42.9%** |
| Chiropractic (D.C. or D.C.M.) | 3,735 | 2,712 | 1,023 | 27.4 |
| Dentistry (D.D.S. or D.M.D.) | 4,032 | 2,490 | 1,542 | 38.2 |
| Medicine (M.D.) | 15,424 | 9,006 | 6,418 | 41.6 |
| Optometry (O.D.) | 1,274 | 594 | 680 | 53.4 |
| Osteopathic medicine (D.O.) | 2,110 | 1,337 | 773 | 36.6 |
| Pharmacy (Pharm.D.) | 3,660 | 1,197 | 2,463 | 67.3 |
| Podiatry (Pod.D., D.P., or D.P.M.) | 594 | 418 | 176 | 29.6 |
| Veterinary medicine (D.V.M.) | 2,193 | 754 | 1,439 | 65.6 |
| Law (LL.B. or J.D.) | 39,331 | 21,876 | 17,455 | 44.4 |
| Theology (M. Div., M.H.L., B.D., or Ord. and M.H.L./Rav.) | 5,873 | 4,343 | 1,530 | 26.1 |
| Other | 372 | 184 | 188 | 50.5 |

*Source: National Center for Education Statistics,* Digest of Education Statistics 2000, *NCES 2001034, 2001; calculations by New Strategist*

# A Growing Number of College Students Will Be Aged 18 to 21

## The number of older students should decline.

After years of rapid growth, the number of older students attending college will decline between 2000 and 2010 as small generation X enters its late thirties. In contrast, the number of students of traditional college age, 18 to 21, will increase as the larger millennial generation goes to school.

On college campuses, the percentage of students aged 25 or older will fall from 41 to 39 percent between 2000 and 2010. The percentage of those aged 18 to 21 will climb from 42 to 44 percent. Because most students today spend more than four years getting their degree, the traditional college ages are expanding into the 22-to-24 age group. Between 2000 and 2010, the share of students aged 22 to 24 will climb slightly from 15 to 16 percent.

♦ With more 18-to-24-year-olds in the population, colleges will find it easier to fill their freshmen classes. For young adults, this abundance means stiffer competition to get into the school of their choice and higher college costs.

**There will be more students of traditional college age**

*(number of students aged 18 to 21 enrolled in college by age, in millions, 2000 and 2010)*

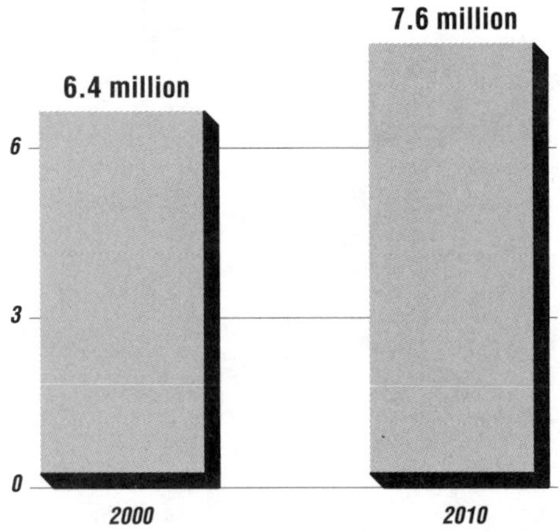

## Projections of College Enrollment by Sex and Age, 2000 and 2010

*(number and percent distribution of people enrolled in institutions of higher education by sex and age, 2000 and 2010; percent change in number, 2000–10; numbers in thousands)*

| | 2000 | | 2010 | | percent change |
|---|---|---|---|---|---|
| | number | percent | number | percent | 2000–10 |
| **Total people** | **15,136** | **100.0%** | **17,491** | **100.0%** | **15.6%** |
| Aged 14 to 17 | 204 | 1.3 | 258 | 1.5 | 26.5 |
| Aged 18 to 19 | 3,409 | 22.5 | 4,077 | 23.3 | 19.6 |
| Aged 20 to 21 | 2,954 | 19.5 | 3,569 | 20.4 | 20.8 |
| Aged 22 to 24 | 2,341 | 15.5 | 2,831 | 16.2 | 20.9 |
| Aged 25 to 29 | 1,956 | 12.9 | 2,383 | 13.6 | 21.8 |
| Aged 30 to 34 | 1,117 | 7.4 | 1,258 | 7.2 | 12.6 |
| Aged 35 or older | 3,155 | 20.8 | 3,115 | 17.8 | -1.3 |
| **Total men** | **6,482** | **100.0** | **7,320** | **100.0** | **12.9** |
| Aged 14 to 17 | 98 | 1.5 | 113 | 1.5 | 15.3 |
| Aged 18 to 19 | 1,519 | 23.4 | 1,761 | 24.1 | 15.9 |
| Aged 20 to 21 | 1,373 | 21.2 | 1,607 | 21.0 | 17.0 |
| Aged 22 to 24 | 1,132 | 17.5 | 1,342 | 18.3 | 18.6 |
| Aged 25 to 29 | 915 | 14.1 | 1,089 | 14.9 | 19.0 |
| Aged 30 to 34 | 428 | 6.6 | 443 | 6.1 | 3.5 |
| Aged 35 or older | 1,017 | 15.7 | 965 | 13.2 | –5.1 |
| **Total women** | **8,654** | **100.0** | **10,170** | **100.0** | **17.5** |
| Aged 14 to 17 | 106 | 1.2 | 145 | 1.4 | 36.8 |
| Aged 18 to 19 | 1,890 | 21.8 | 2,316 | 22.8 | 22.5 |
| Aged 20 to 21 | 1,581 | 18.3 | 1,962 | 19.3 | 24.1 |
| Aged 22 to 24 | 1,209 | 13.0 | 1,488 | 14.6 | 23.1 |
| Aged 25 to 29 | 1,041 | 12.0 | 1,294 | 12.7 | 24.3 |
| Aged 30 to 34 | 689 | 7.0 | 815 | 8.0 | 18.3 |
| Aged 35 or older | 2,138 | 24.7 | 2,150 | 21.1 | 0.6 |

*Source: National Center for Education Statistics,* Projections of Education Statistics to 2010, *NCES 2000071, 2000; calculations by New Strategist*

# The Number of Full-Time Students Will Grow the Fastest

## Four-year schools will see a bigger gain than two-year institutions.

Between 2000 and 2010, the number of college students is projected to increase 16 percent, rising from 15 million to 17 million. As the millennial generation reaches college age, four-year colleges will see enrollment climb more than two-year institutions, the number of students attending school full-time will increase more rapidly than that of part-timers, and the ranks of undergraduates will swell more than those of graduates.

Enrollment at four-year institutions is projected to increase 16 percent between 2000 and 2010 compared with a 14 percent gain for two-year schools. Undergraduate enrollment will increase 16 percent versus an 11 percent gain for graduate schools. The number of full-time students will climb 19 percent versus an 11 percent gain in part-timers. The biggest increase—23 percent—is projected for undergraduate women attending school full-time.

The number of degrees awarded by the nation's colleges will rise 10 percent between 2000 and 2010. The biggest gain is projected for bachelor's and master's degrees with double-digit increases for women. While the number of first-professional degrees granted to men will decline 3 percent between 2000 and 2010, the number of women earning one should increase 14 percent.

♦ Baby-boom parents will be hard-pressed to keep up with college expenses, but anxiety over their children's future will make college mandatory for most.

## Projections of College Enrollment by Level of Degree, 2000 to 2010

*(number of people enrolled in institutions of higher education by level of degree, sex, and attendance status; 2000–10; percent change, 2000–10; numbers in thousands)*

| | | men | | women | |
|---|---|---|---|---|---|
| | total | full-time | part-time | full-time | part-time |
| **Undergraduate enrollment** | | | | | |
| 2000 | 13,080 | 3,457 | 2,131 | 4,277 | 3,215 |
| 2001 | 13,294 | 3,514 | 2,157 | 4,365 | 3,258 |
| 2002 | 13,419 | 3,539 | 2,178 | 4,411 | 3,291 |
| 2003 | 13,584 | 3,578 | 2,201 | 4,483 | 3,323 |
| 2004 | 13,752 | 3,613 | 2,225 | 4,556 | 3,358 |
| 2005 | 13,927 | 3,644 | 2,251 | 4,635 | 3,396 |
| 2006 | 14,162 | 3,694 | 2,279 | 4,751 | 3,438 |
| 2007 | 14,435 | 3,757 | 2,309 | 4,888 | 3,481 |
| 2008 | 14,738 | 3,839 | 2,338 | 5,042 | 3,519 |
| 2009 | 15,002 | 3,916 | 2,362 | 5,175 | 3,549 |
| 2010 | 15,209 | 3,972 | 2,383 | 5,277 | 3,578 |
| **Percent change** | | | | | |
| 2000 to 2010 | 16.3% | 14.9% | 11.8% | 23.4% | 11.3% |
| **Graduate enrollment** | | | | | |
| 2000 | 1,775 | 322 | 413 | 362 | 678 |
| 2001 | 1,786 | 321 | 416 | 364 | 685 |
| 2002 | 1,799 | 321 | 419 | 367 | 691 |
| 2003 | 1,813 | 323 | 422 | 372 | 696 |
| 2004 | 1,832 | 326 | 425 | 379 | 702 |
| 2005 | 1,853 | 329 | 429 | 386 | 710 |
| 2006 | 1,877 | 331 | 433 | 394 | 718 |
| 2007 | 1,905 | 337 | 437 | 406 | 726 |
| 2008 | 1,929 | 342 | 440 | 416 | 731 |
| 2009 | 1,946 | 347 | 442 | 424 | 733 |
| 2010 | 1,963 | 351 | 443 | 432 | 737 |
| **Percent change** | | | | | |
| 2000 to 2010 | 10.6% | 9.0% | 7.3% | 19.3% | 8.7% |

*(continued)*

(continued from previous page)

| | total | men full-time | men part-time | women full-time | women part-time |
|---|---|---|---|---|---|
| **First-professional enrollment** | | | | | |
| 2000 | 281 | 138 | 19 | 110 | 14 |
| 2001 | 281 | 138 | 19 | 110 | 14 |
| 2002 | 283 | 138 | 19 | 111 | 14 |
| 2003 | 285 | 139 | 19 | 113 | 14 |
| 2004 | 289 | 140 | 19 | 115 | 15 |
| 2005 | 292 | 141 | 19 | 117 | 15 |
| 2006 | 297 | 142 | 20 | 120 | 15 |
| 2007 | 303 | 145 | 20 | 123 | 15 |
| 2008 | 308 | 147 | 20 | 126 | 15 |
| 2009 | 313 | 149 | 20 | 129 | 15 |
| 2010 | 317 | 151 | 20 | 131 | 15 |
| **Percent change** | | | | | |
| 2000 to 2010 | 12.8% | 9.4% | 5.3% | 19.1% | 7.1% |

*Source: National Center for Education Statistics,* Projections of Education Statistics to 2010, *NCES 2000071, 2000; calculations by New Strategist*

# Projections of College Enrollment by Type of Institution, 2000 to 2010

*(number of people enrolled in institutions of higher education by type of institution, sex, attendance status, and control of institution; 2000–10; percent change, 2000–10; numbers in thousands)*

| | | *sex* | | *attendance status* | | *control* | |
|---|---|---|---|---|---|---|---|
| | *total* | *men* | *women* | *full-time* | *part-time* | *public* | *private* |
| **Total institutions** | | | | | | | |
| 2000 | 15,135 | 6,481 | 8,655 | 8,666 | 6,470 | 11,795 | 3,340 |
| 2001 | 15,361 | 6,565 | 8,796 | 8,811 | 6,550 | 11,971 | 3,390 |
| 2002 | 15,500 | 6,614 | 8,886 | 8,888 | 6,612 | 12,080 | 3,420 |
| 2003 | 15,683 | 6,681 | 9,001 | 9,007 | 6,675 | 12,221 | 3,462 |
| 2004 | 15,875 | 6,750 | 9,125 | 9,129 | 6,744 | 12,370 | 3,505 |
| 2005 | 16,072 | 6,814 | 9,259 | 9,252 | 6,822 | 12,524 | 3,550 |
| 2006 | 16,336 | 6,899 | 9,437 | 9,433 | 6,903 | 12,727 | 3,610 |
| 2007 | 16,643 | 7,005 | 9,638 | 9,655 | 6,989 | 12,962 | 3,681 |
| 2008 | 16,975 | 7,126 | 9,849 | 9,912 | 7,063 | 13,216 | 3,760 |
| 2009 | 17,261 | 7,235 | 10,025 | 10,139 | 7,121 | 13,434 | 3,827 |
| 2010 | 17,489 | 7,320 | 10,169 | 10,313 | 7,176 | 13,607 | 3,882 |
| **Percent change** | | | | | | | |
| 2000 to 2010 | 15.6% | 12.9% | 17.5% | 19.0% | 10.9% | 15.4% | 16.2% |
| **Two-year institutions** | | | | | | | |
| 2000 | 5,847 | 2,412 | 3,435 | 2,145 | 3,702 | 5,638 | 209 |
| 2001 | 5,931 | 2,444 | 3,487 | 2,181 | 3,750 | 5,718 | 213 |
| 2002 | 5,981 | 2,461 | 3,520 | 2,196 | 3,785 | 5,767 | 214 |
| 2003 | 6,046 | 2,486 | 3,560 | 2,223 | 3,822 | 5,829 | 217 |
| 2004 | 6,119 | 2,514 | 3,605 | 2,256 | 3,862 | 5,899 | 220 |
| 2005 | 6,192 | 2,539 | 3,653 | 2,286 | 3,907 | 5,970 | 223 |
| 2006 | 6,286 | 2,571 | 3,715 | 2,331 | 3,955 | 6,060 | 226 |
| 2007 | 6,394 | 2,611 | 3,783 | 2,389 | 4,006 | 6,163 | 231 |
| 2008 | 6,509 | 2,665 | 3,854 | 2,457 | 4,052 | 6,272 | 237 |
| 2009 | 6,604 | 2,693 | 3,911 | 2,514 | 4,090 | 6,363 | 241 |
| 2010 | 6,675 | 2,719 | 3,956 | 2,551 | 4,124 | 6,431 | 244 |
| **Percent change** | | | | | | | |
| 2000 to 2010 | 14.2% | 12.7% | 15.2% | 18.9% | 11.4% | 14.1% | 16.7% |

*(continued)*

*(continued from previous page)*

| | | sex | | attendance status | | control | |
|---|---|---|---|---|---|---|---|
| | total | men | women | full-time | part-time | public | private |
| **Four-year institutions** | | | | | | | |
| 2000 | 9,288 | 4,069 | 5,220 | 6,521 | 2,768 | 6,157 | 3,131 |
| 2001 | 9,430 | 4,121 | 5,309 | 6,630 | 2,800 | 6,253 | 3,177 |
| 2002 | 9,519 | 4,153 | 5,366 | 6,692 | 2,827 | 6,313 | 3,206 |
| 2003 | 9,637 | 4,195 | 5,441 | 6,784 | 2,853 | 6,392 | 3,245 |
| 2004 | 9,756 | 4,236 | 5,520 | 6,873 | 2,882 | 6,471 | 3,285 |
| 2005 | 9,880 | 4,275 | 5,606 | 6,966 | 2,915 | 6,554 | 3,327 |
| 2006 | 10,050 | 4,328 | 5,722 | 7,102 | 2,948 | 6,667 | 3,384 |
| 2007 | 10,249 | 4,394 | 5,855 | 7,266 | 2,983 | 6,799 | 3,450 |
| 2008 | 10,466 | 4,471 | 5,995 | 7,455 | 3,011 | 6,944 | 3,523 |
| 2009 | 10,657 | 4,542 | 6,114 | 7,625 | 3,031 | 7,071 | 3,586 |
| 2010 | 10,814 | 4,601 | 6,213 | 7,762 | 3,052 | 7,176 | 3,638 |
| **Percent change** | | | | | | | |
| 2000 to 2010 | 16.4% | 13.1% | 19.0% | 19.0% | 10.3% | 16.6% | 16.2% |

*Source: National Center for Education Statistics,* Projections of Education Statistics to 2010, *NCES 2000071, 2000; calculations by New Strategist*

## Projections of Degrees Conferred by Sex, 2000 and 2010

*(number of degrees conferred by sex and level of degree, 2000 and 2010; percent change in number, 2000–10)*

| | *2000* | *2010* | *percent change 2000–10* |
|---|---|---|---|
| **Total degrees** | **2,264,500** | **2,501,700** | **10.5%** |
| Associate's degree | 558,000 | 611,000 | 9.5 |
| Bachelor's degree | 1,185,000 | 1,323,000 | 11.6 |
| Master's degree | 398,000 | 439,000 | 10.3 |
| Doctoral degree | 45,200 | 47,100 | 4.2 |
| First-professional degree | 78,300 | 81,600 | 4.2 |
| **Men, total degrees** | **972,400** | **1,016,300** | **4.5** |
| Associate's degree | 216,000 | 224,000 | 3.7 |
| Bachelor's degree | 517,000 | 547,000 | 5.8 |
| Master's degree | 168,000 | 175,000 | 4.2 |
| Doctoral degree | 26,700 | 27,100 | 1.5 |
| First-professional degree | 44,700 | 43,200 | –3.4 |
| **Women, total degrees** | **1,292,100** | **1,485,400** | **14.0** |
| Associate's degree | 342,000 | 387,000 | 13.2 |
| Bachelor's degree | 668,000 | 776,000 | 16.2 |
| Master's degree | 230,000 | 264,000 | 14.8 |
| Doctoral degree | 18,500 | 20,000 | 8.1 |
| First-professional degree | 33,600 | 38,400 | 14.3 |

*Source: National Center for Education Statistics,* Projections of Education Statistics to 2010, *NCES 2000071, 2000; calculations by New Strategist*

# Most Couples Are Alike in Education

## More than half the nation's married couples have the same level of educational attainment.

Husbands and wives often have comparable levels of education. In 19 percent of couples, both husband and wife earned a high school diploma but went no further in their schooling. The second largest group is couples in which both husband and wife have at least a bachelor's degree, accounting for 17 percent of couples. Both husband and wife are high school dropouts in just 8 percent of couples. In about 10 percent of all couples, both husband and wife have attended college but neither has a degree.

Husbands are likely to be better educated than wives. Overall, 29 percent of husbands have a bachelor's degree compared with 24 percent of wives.

♦ As younger generations replace less-educated older ones, the proportion of couples in which both husband and wife have at least a bachelor's degree will rise. So will the share of couples in which the wife is better educated than the husband.

### The educational background of husbands and wives is usually the same

*(percent of husbands and wives with the same educational attainment, by education, 1998)*

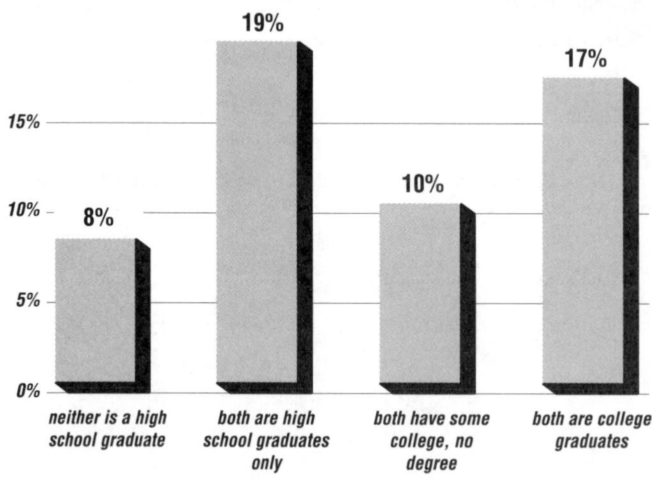

## Educational Attainment of Husbands and Wives, 1998

*(percent distribution of married couples aged 18 or older by educational attainment of husband and wife, 1998)*

| | | education of wife | | | |
|---|---|---|---|---|---|
| | *total wives* | *less than high school* | *high school graduate only* | *some college or associate's degree* | *bachelor's degree or more* |
| **Education of husband** | | | | | |
| **Total husbands** | **100.0%** | **13.6%** | **36.7%** | **25.7%** | **24.1%** |
| Less than high school | 15.9 | 8.4 | 5.5 | 1.6 | 0.4 |
| High school graduate only | 31.7 | 3.6 | 18.7 | 6.7 | 2.6 |
| Some college or associate's degree | 23.9 | 1.2 | 8.2 | 10.1 | 4.5 |
| Bachelor's degree or more | 28.5 | 0.4 | 4.3 | 7.2 | 16.7 |

*Source: Bureau of the Census,* Educational Attainment in the United States: March 1998 (Update), *detailed tables for Current Population Report P20-513, 1998; calculations by New Strategist*

# More Americans Are Participating in Adult Education

## Millions have eagerly embraced lifelong learning.

Educated Americans are more likely to go back to school than those with less education. This is apparent in statistics on participation in adult education. Those most likely to take educational courses outside of postsecondary institutions are people under age 55—who are also the most educated. More than half of people from age 16 to 55 took part in adult education in 1999, not including full-time college students.

The percentage of people involved in adult education grew substantially between 1995 and 1999, rising from 40 to 46 percent of people aged 16 or older. People aged 55 to 64 made the biggest gains. Their participation rose 9 percentage points during those years, from 28 to 37 percent.

♦ The percentage of 55-to-64-year-olds who participate in adult education is likely to soar in the years ahead as the well-educated baby-boom generation enters the age group.

**Big gains in adult education are in store for the 55-to-64 age group**

*(percent of people aged 16 or older participating in adult education, by age, 1999)*

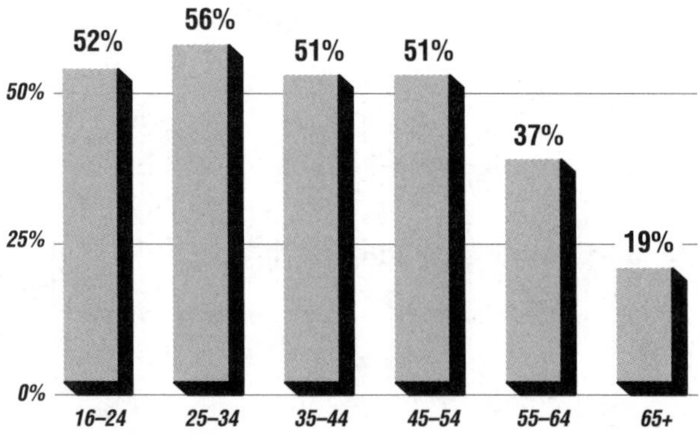

## Participation in Adult Education by Age, 1995 and 1999

*(percent of people aged 16 or older participating in adult education activities, by age, 1995 and 1999; percentage point change, 1995–99)*

| | 1999 | 1995 | percentage point change |
|---|---|---|---|
| **Total people** | **46%** | **40%** | **6** |
| Aged 16 to 24 | 52 | 47 | 5 |
| Aged 25 to 34 | 56 | 48 | 8 |
| Aged 35 to 44 | 51 | 49 | 2 |
| Aged 45 to 54 | 51 | 46 | 5 |
| Aged 55 to 64 | 37 | 28 | 9 |
| Aged 65 or older | 19 | 15 | 4 |

*Note: Adult education activities include apprenticeships, courses for basic skills, personal development, English as a second language, work-related courses, and credential programs in organizations other than postsecondary institutions. Excludes full-time participation in postsecondary institutions leading to a college degree, diploma, or certificate.*

*Source: National Center for Education Statistics, unpublished data from the National Household Education Survey, 1999; and* Statistical Abstract of the United States, *1999; calculations by New Strategist*

CHAPTER

# 2

## Health Trends

♦ **Even among the oldest Americans, most rate their health as excellent or good.**

While the proportion of people who rate their health as excellent falls with age, only 13 percent of the oldest Americans say their health is poor.

♦ **Thanks to a deluge of nutritional advice, eating habits have changed.**

Fully 40 percent of Americans strongly agree that the many recommendations about healthy eating make it difficult to know what to believe.

♦ **Babies born today promise great diversity tomorrow.**

Of the nearly 4 million babies born in 1999, 35 percent were born to black or Hispanic mothers. Only 59 percent were born to non-Hispanic whites.

♦ **Heavy drinking is widespread among young adults.**

Binge drinking is most common among people in their early twenties, more than 40 percent of whom have done so in the past month.

♦ **Hospital stays continue to shorten.**

As insurance companies try to cut costs, the health care industry has been thrown into turmoil while health care providers and patients cope with change.

♦ **Chronic diseases are the biggest killers of Americans.**

Heart disease and cancer each kill more than 500,000 Americans a year, but life expectancy has never been higher.

# Most Americans Feel Good or Excellent

## Only 5 percent say their health is poor.

Overall, 31 percent of adults say their health is excellent, ranging from 39 percent of 18-to-29-year-olds to 15 percent of people aged 70 or older. While the proportion of Americans who rate their health as excellent falls with age, even in the oldest age group only 13 percent say their health is poor. Sixty-one percent of the oldest Americans say their health is good or excellent.

The higher their education, the better people feel. Fully 45 to 46 percent of college graduates say their health is excellent compared with just 13 percent of people who did not graduate from high school. One reason for the poorer health of the less-educated is that older Americans are overrepresented among those with the least education.

Men and women are equally likely to report good or excellent health. In contrast, whites are much more likely than blacks to say their health is excellent, 33 versus 24 percent.

♦ As the population ages, the proportion of Americans who feel excellent is likely to decline while the share of those who feel only fair or poor could grow.

### Feeling excellent declines with age

*(percent of people aged 18 or older who say their health is "excellent," by age, 1998)*

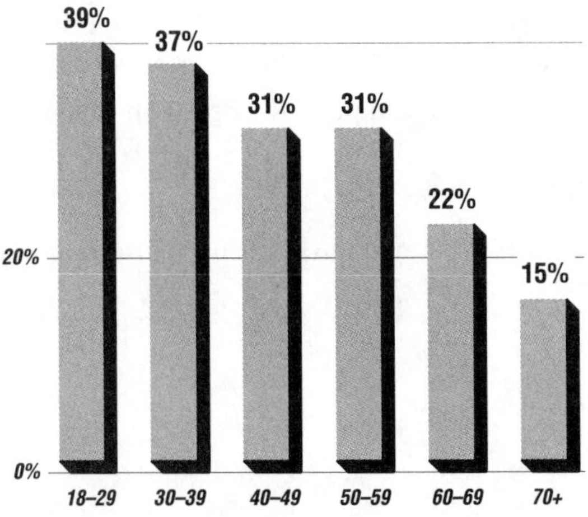

## Health Status, 1998

"Would you say your own health, in general, is excellent, good, fair, or poor?"

*(percent of people aged 18 or older responding by sex, race, age, and education, 1998)*

| | excellent | good | fair | poor |
|---|---|---|---|---|
| **Total people** | **31%** | **48%** | **17%** | **5%** |
| Men | 31 | 48 | 17 | 4 |
| Women | 31 | 48 | 16 | 5 |
| Black | 24 | 48 | 21 | 7 |
| White | 33 | 47 | 16 | 4 |
| Other | 26 | 51 | 16 | 6 |
| Aged 18 to 29 | 39 | 47 | 13 | 1 |
| Aged 30 to 39 | 37 | 51 | 12 | 1 |
| Aged 40 to 49 | 31 | 49 | 16 | 3 |
| Aged 50 to 59 | 31 | 44 | 17 | 8 |
| Aged 60 to 69 | 22 | 46 | 23 | 9 |
| Aged 70 or older | 15 | 46 | 26 | 13 |
| Not a high school graduate | 13 | 43 | 30 | 13 |
| High school graduate | 28 | 51 | 18 | 4 |
| Bachelor's degree | 46 | 45 | 6 | 2 |
| Graduate degree | 45 | 41 | 11 | 2 |

*Note: Numbers may not add to 100 because "don't know" and no answer are not shown.*
*Source: General Social Survey, National Opinion Research Center, University of Chicago; calculations by New Strategist*

# American Diet Has Both Improved and Worsened

## Fruit and vegetable consumption is up, but so is consumption of candy and soft drinks.

Americans ate more bananas, cantaloupe, broccoli, and tomatoes in 1997 than in 1970. They ate less beef and fewer eggs. Some eating trends reflect changing tastes. A growing preference for spicy food, for example, boosted consumption of onions by 77 percent. Consumption of tomatoes and mozzarella cheese has grown along with the popularity of take-out pizza.

Changes in eating habits are also due to the deluge of nutritional advice directed at the public. The majority of Americans "strongly agree" that what they eat affects their health. But a substantial 40 percent also strongly agree that the many recommendations about healthy eating make it difficult to know what to believe. Few think their current diet is optimum, and this belief is confirmed by food consumption trends. Consumption of soft drinks rose 118 percent between 1970 and 1997, corn sweetener consumption was up more than 300 percent, while fat and oil consumption rose 25 percent as people filled up on fast foods.

♦ As the variety of the American diet increases, the biggest nutritional problem facing many people is simply eating too much.

## Food and Beverage Consumption, 1970 and 1997

*(number of pounds of selected foods and gallons of selected beverages consumed per person, 1970 and 1997; percent change in consumption, 1970–97)*

| | 1997 | 1970 | percent change 1970–97 |
|---|---|---|---|
| **Red meat** | **111.0** | **131.7** | **–15.7%** |
| Beef | 63.8 | 79.6 | –19.8 |
| Pork | 45.6 | 48.0 | –5.0 |
| **Poultry** | **64.8** | **33.8** | **91.7** |
| Chicken | 50.9 | 27.4 | 85.8 |
| Turkey | 13.9 | 6.4 | 117.2 |
| **Fish and shellfish** | **14.5** | **11.7** | **23.9** |
| Canned tuna | 3.1 | 2.5 | 24.0 |
| Fresh and frozen fish | 6.1 | 4.5 | 35.6 |
| Fresh and frozen shellfish | 3.8 | 2.4 | 58.3 |
| **Eggs (number)** | **238.7** | **308.9** | **–22.7** |
| Processed | 65.5 | 33.0 | 98.5 |
| Shell | 173.1 | 275.9 | –37.3 |
| **Cheese** | **28.0** | **11.4** | **145.6** |
| Cheddar | 9.6 | 5.8 | 65.5 |
| Mozzarella | 8.4 | 1.2 | 600.0 |
| Swiss | 1.0 | 0.9 | 11.1 |
| **Beverage milk** | **206.9** | **269.1** | **–23.1** |
| Plain whole milk | 70.2 | 213.5 | –67.1 |
| 2% milk | 66.7 | 28.0 | 138.2 |
| Skim milk | 34.4 | 11.6 | 196.6 |
| **Yogurt** | **5.1** | **0.8** | **537.5** |
| **Frozen dairy products** | **28.7** | **28.5** | **0.7** |
| Ice cream | 16.2 | 17.8 | –9.0 |
| **Fats and oils** | **65.6** | **52.6** | **24.7** |
| Butter | 4.2 | 5.4 | –22.2 |
| Margarine | 8.6 | 10.8 | –20.4 |
| Salad and cooking oils | 28.7 | 15.4 | 86.4 |
| **Fresh fruits** | **133.2** | **101.2** | **31.6** |
| Apples | 18.5 | 17.0 | 8.8 |
| Bananas | 27.7 | 17.4 | 59.2 |
| Cantaloupe | 11.7 | 7.2 | 62.5 |
| Grapefruit | 6.3 | 8.2 | –23.2 |
| Grapes | 8.0 | 2.9 | 175.9 |
| Oranges | 14.1 | 16.2 | –13.0 |
| Peaches and nectarines | 5.7 | 5.8 | –1.7 |
| Pears | 3.5 | 1.9 | 84.2 |

*(continued)*

*(continued from previous page)*

| | 1997 | 1970 | percent change 1970–97 |
|---|---|---|---|
| Strawberries | 4.2 | 1.7 | 147.1% |
| Watermelon | 16.1 | 13.5 | 19.3 |
| **Canned fruits** | **18.0** | **23.3** | **–22.7** |
| **Frozen fruits** | **3.3** | **3.3** | **0.0** |
| **Fruit juices** | **9.2** | **5.7** | **61.4** |
| Apple juice | 1.6 | 0.5 | 220.0 |
| Orange juice | 5.9 | 3.8 | 55.3 |
| **Fresh vegetables** | **185.6** | **152.9** | **21.4** |
| Bell peppers | 7.2 | 2.2 | 227.3 |
| Broccoli | 5.2 | 0.5 | 940.0 |
| Cabbage | 10.2 | 8.8 | 15.9 |
| Carrots | 12.5 | 6.0 | 108.3 |
| Celery | 6.0 | 7.3 | –17.8 |
| Corn | 8.1 | 7.8 | 3.8 |
| Cucumbers | 6.3 | 2.8 | 125.0 |
| Garlic | 2.1 | 0.4 | 425.0 |
| Head lettuce | 24.3 | 22.4 | 8.5 |
| Onions | 17.9 | 10.1 | 77.2 |
| Potatoes | 47.9 | 61.8 | –22.5 |
| Tomatoes | 18.9 | 12.1 | 56.2 |
| **Peanuts** | **5.8** | **5.5** | **5.5** |
| Peanut butter | 2.8 | 2.7 | 3.7 |
| **Flour and cereal products** | **200.1** | **135.6** | **47.6** |
| Ready-to-eat cereals | 14.3 | 8.6 | 66.3 |
| Ready-to-cook cereals | 2.6 | 1.7 | 52.9 |
| **Caloric sweeteners** | **154.1** | **122.3** | **26.0** |
| Sugar | 66.5 | 101.8 | –34.7 |
| Corn sweeteners | 86.2 | 19.1 | 351.3 |
| **Candy** | **24.8** | **19.9** | **24.6** |
| **Bottled water** | **13.1** | **1.2*** | **383.3** |
| **Coffee** | **23.5** | **33.4** | **–29.6** |
| **Tea** | **7.4** | **6.8** | **8.8** |
| **Soft drinks** | **53.0** | **24.3** | **118.1** |
| Diet | 11.6 | 2.1 | 452.4 |
| Regular | 41.4 | 22.2 | 86.5 |
| **Alcoholic beverages**** | **38.9** | **35.7** | **9.0** |
| Beer | 33.9 | 30.6 | 10.8 |
| Wine | 3.0 | 2.2 | 36.4 |
| Distilled spirits | 1.9 | 3.0 | –36.7 |

** Data for 1976.*
*** Per person aged 21 or older.*
*Source: USDA, Economic Research Service,* Food Consumption, Prices, and Expenditures, *1970–97; calculations by New Strategist*

## Attitudes toward Diet by Sex, 1994–96

*(percent of people aged 20 or older who "strongly agree" with statements about diet, by sex, 1994–96)*

| | men | women |
|---|---|---|
| What you eat can make a big difference in your chance of getting a disease, like heart disease or cancer | 57.8% | 63.5% |
| There are so many recommendations about healthy ways to eat, it's hard to know what to believe | 39.5 | 40.1 |
| Choosing a healthy diet is just a matter of knowing what foods are good and what foods are bad | 37.3 | 40.3 |
| Eating a variety of foods each day probably gives you all the vitamins and minerals you need | 33.1 | 34.2 |
| The things I eat and drink now are healthy so there is no reason for me to make changes | 16.3 | 15.3 |
| Some people are born to be fat and some thin; there is not much you can do to change this | 13.7 | 12.2 |
| Starchy foods, like bread, potatoes, and rice, make people fat | 11.8 | 12.7 |

*Source: USDA, ARS Food Surveys Research Group,* 1994–96 Diet and Health Knowledge Survey, *1999; Internet site <www.barc.usda.gov/bhnrc/foodsurvey/home.htm>*

# Vitamin Use Rises with Age

## People aged 40 or older are most likely to take vitamin and mineral supplements.

Health concerns increase with age, so it is no surprise that the use of vitamin and mineral supplements is most common among middle-aged and older Americans. Among women, supplement use peaks in the 50-to-59 age group at 63 percent. For men, it peaks among those in their sixties at 48 percent.

In the 6-to-11 age group, boys are more likely than girls to take vitamin supplements (46 versus 42 percent). In all other age groups, females are much more likely than males to take supplements.

Among those who take supplements, males under age 60 and women under age 40 are more likely to take a multivitamin than a single vitamin or mineral supplement. Among men aged 60 or older and women aged 40 or older, single vitamin and mineral supplements are more widely used than multivitamins.

♦ Older Americans seeking to treat or prevent specific health problems are responsible for a substantial portion of supplement sales in the U.S.

### Vitamin use peaks among women in their fifties

*(percent of women aged 20 or older who take vitamin/mineral supplements, by age, 1994–96)*

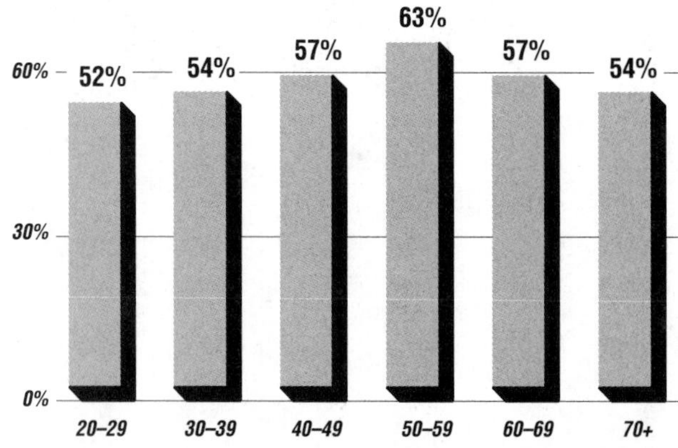

## Use of Vitamin and Mineral Supplements by Sex and Age, 1994–96

*(percent of people taking vitamin/mineral supplements by sex, age, and type of supplement, 1994–96)*

| | | type of supplement | | | |
|---|---|---|---|---|---|
| | *total* | *multivitamin* | *multivitamin with iron or other minerals* | *combination of vitamin C and iron* | *single vitamins or minerals* |
| **Total, both sexes** | **46.8%** | **20.7%** | **16.8%** | **2.9%** | **15.3%** |
| Under age 1 | 15.3 | 5.6 | 5.6 | 0.2 | 4.3 |
| Aged 1 to 2 | 44.9 | 21.3 | 19.0 | 1.6 | 4.3 |
| Aged 3 to 5 | 56.1 | 27.6 | 24.3 | 2.7 | 4.9 |
| **Males** | | | | | |
| Aged 6 to 11 | 46.1 | 23.9 | 17.1 | 2.4 | 5.6 |
| Aged 12 to 19 | 29.2 | 14.6 | 7.6 | 3.0 | 8.8 |
| Aged 20 to 29 | 36.4 | 18.8 | 9.7 | 3.2 | 9.6 |
| Aged 30 to 39 | 39.7 | 20.6 | 14.1 | 3.1 | 10.2 |
| Aged 40 to 49 | 43.8 | 20.6 | 14.1 | 1.5 | 15.6 |
| Aged 50 to 59 | 43.8 | 21.6 | 12.0 | 2.3 | 19.2 |
| Aged 60 to 69 | 47.6 | 20.5 | 15.4 | 1.5 | 22.7 |
| Aged 70 or older | 47.1 | 19.2 | 15.7 | 2.4 | 20.1 |
| **Females** | | | | | |
| Aged 6 to 11 | 41.7 | 20.1 | 15.7 | 2.2 | 6.3 |
| Aged 12 to 19 | 39.3 | 15.7 | 12.5 | 4.0 | 11.8 |
| Aged 20 to 29 | 52.0 | 22.7 | 21.9 | 3.9 | 13.7 |
| Aged 30 to 39 | 54.4 | 19.8 | 25.6 | 3.5 | 17.5 |
| Aged 40 to 49 | 56.7 | 21.9 | 21.8 | 3.7 | 23.8 |
| Aged 50 to 59 | 62.6 | 24.5 | 20.7 | 4.7 | 32.7 |
| Aged 60 to 69 | 57.3 | 21.5 | 19.4 | 2.6 | 30.9 |
| Aged 70 or older | 53.6 | 23.1 | 15.7 | 2.7 | 23.2 |

*Source: USDA, ARS Food Surveys Research Group,* Supplementary Data Tables: USDA's 1994-96 Continuing Survey of Food Intakes by Individuals, *Internet site <www.barc.usda.gov/bhnrc/foodsurvey/home.htm>*

## Births to Rise above 4 Million Again in 2004

### Births will not surpass the 1990 peak until 2008, however.

The 4,158,000 babies born in 1990 were the most since the end of the baby boom in the early 1960s. Those children turn 11 in 2001, marking the high point of the millennial generation.

After peaking in 1990, the annual number of births stabilized right around 4 million for the remainder of the decade. The Census Bureau projects that the annual number of births will remain under 4 million until 2004, then rise steadily. In 2040, the annual number of births will top 5 million.

♦ For the nation's already crowded schools and the taxpayers who support them, there's no relief in sight.

## Number of Births, 2000 to 2050

*(annual number of births, 2000 to 2050; numbers in thousands)*

| | births |
|---|---|
| 1990 | 4,158 |
| 1991 | 4,111 |
| 1992 | 4,065 |
| 1993 | 4,000 |
| 1994 | 3,953 |
| 1995 | 3,900 |
| 1996 | 3,891 |
| 1997 | 3,881 |
| 1998 | 3,941 |
| 1999 | 3,958 |
| 2000 | 3,914 |
| 2001 | 3,932 |
| 2002 | 3,953 |
| 2003 | 3,978 |
| 2004 | 4,009 |
| 2005 | 4,045 |
| 2006 | 4,086 |
| 2007 | 4,133 |
| 2008 | 4,183 |
| 2009 | 4,234 |
| 2010 | 4,283 |
| 2020 | 4,613 |
| 2030 | 4,878 |
| 2040 | 5,286 |
| 2050 | 5,661 |

*Source: Bureau of the Census, Projections of the Resident Population by Age, Sex, Race, and Hispanic Origin: 1999 to 2100, Internet site <www.census.gov/population/www/projections/natproj.html>; National Center for Health Statistics,* Births: Preliminary Data for 1999, *National Vital Statistics Report, Vol. 48, No. 14, 2000; and* Births: Final Data for 1998, *National Vital Statistics Report, Vol. 48, No. 3, 2000*

# More Than One-Third of Newborns Are Black or Hispanic

## Babies born today promise great diversity tomorrow.

Of the nearly 4 million babies born in 1999, 35 percent were born to black or Hispanic mothers. Only 59 percent were born to non-Hispanic whites. As today's children grow up, they will be part of an increasingly multicultural society in which no single racial or ethnic group can lay claim to being the majority of the U.S. population.

In the future, fewer adults will have lived in a two-parent family. Fully 33 percent of births in 1998 were to unwed mothers, up from just 11 percent in 1970. Among blacks, 69 percent of births are out of wedlock versus 22 percent among non-Hispanic whites.

Despite an increase in the number of older women giving birth, most babies are born to women in their twenties. Only among women having their fourth or higher-order birth is the majority aged 30 or older.

♦ Considering that a middle-class lifestyle now requires two incomes, but that so many babies are born to unmarried mothers, reducing poverty among children is an uphill task.

**Great diversity among the nation's newborns**

*(percent distribution of births by race and Hispanic origin of mother, 1999)*

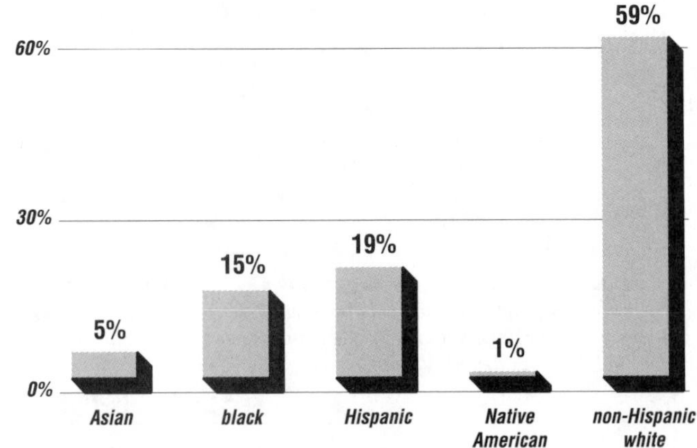

## Births by Age, Race, and Hispanic Origin of Mother, 1999

*(number and percent distribution of births by age, race, and Hispanic origin of mother, 1999)*

| | | race | | | | Hispanic origin | |
|---|---|---|---|---|---|---|---|
| | total | white | black | Asian | Native American | Hispanic | non-Hispanic white |
| **Total births** | **3,957,829** | **3,130,100** | **606,720** | **180,993** | **40,015** | **762,364** | **2,349,536** |
| Under age 15 | 9,049 | 4,723 | 3,981 | 142 | 203 | 2,721 | 2,046 |
| Aged 15 to 19 | 475,745 | 337,323 | 121,262 | 9,255 | 7,905 | 124,352 | 213,223 |
| Aged 20 to 24 | 981,207 | 747,217 | 193,483 | 27,304 | 13,203 | 230,881 | 515,026 |
| Aged 25 to 29 | 1,078,350 | 873,586 | 139,175 | 56,040 | 9,549 | 203,399 | 665,018 |
| Aged 30 to 34 | 892,478 | 739,967 | 91,596 | 55,220 | 5,695 | 131,134 | 601,676 |
| Aged 35 to 39 | 433,793 | 356,546 | 47,244 | 27,182 | 2,822 | 57,926 | 294,585 |
| Aged 40 to 44 | 82,875 | 67,228 | 9,562 | 5,472 | 613 | 11,430 | 55,037 |
| Aged 45 to 49 | 4,330 | 3,509 | 417 | 379 | 26 | 519 | 2,924 |
| **Percent distribution by race and Hispanic origin** | | | | | | | |
| **Total births** | **100.0%** | **79.1%** | **15.3%** | **4.6%** | **1.0%** | **19.3%** | **59.4%** |
| Under age 15 | 100.0 | 52.2 | 44.0 | 1.6 | 2.2 | 30.1 | 22.6 |
| Aged 15 to 19 | 100.0 | 70.9 | 25.5 | 1.9 | 1.7 | 26.1 | 44.8 |
| Aged 20 to 24 | 100.0 | 76.2 | 19.7 | 2.8 | 1.3 | 23.5 | 52.5 |
| Aged 25 to 29 | 100.0 | 81.0 | 12.9 | 5.2 | 0.9 | 18.9 | 61.7 |
| Aged 30 to 34 | 100.0 | 82.9 | 10.3 | 6.2 | 0.6 | 14.7 | 67.4 |
| Aged 35 to 39 | 100.0 | 82.2 | 10.9 | 6.3 | 0.7 | 13.4 | 67.9 |
| Aged 40 to 44 | 100.0 | 81.1 | 11.5 | 6.6 | 0.7 | 13.8 | 66.4 |
| Aged 45 to 49 | 100.0 | 81.0 | 9.6 | 8.8 | 0.6 | 12.0 | 67.5 |
| **Percent distribution by age** | | | | | | | |
| **Total births** | **100.0%** | **100.0%** | **100.0%** | **100.0%** | **100.0%** | **100.0%** | **100.0%** |
| Under age 15 | 0.2 | 0.2 | 0.7 | 0.1 | 0.5 | 0.4 | 0.1 |
| Aged 15 to 19 | 12.0 | 10.8 | 20.0 | 5.1 | 19.8 | 16.3 | 9.1 |
| Aged 20 to 24 | 24.8 | 23.9 | 31.9 | 15.1 | 33.0 | 30.3 | 21.9 |
| Aged 25 to 29 | 27.2 | 27.9 | 22.9 | 31.0 | 23.9 | 26.7 | 28.3 |
| Aged 30 to 34 | 22.5 | 23.6 | 15.1 | 30.5 | 14.2 | 17.2 | 25.6 |
| Aged 35 to 39 | 11.0 | 11.4 | 7.8 | 15.0 | 7.1 | 7.6 | 12.5 |
| Aged 40 to 44 | 2.1 | 2.1 | 1.6 | 3.0 | 1.5 | 1.5 | 2.3 |
| Aged 45 to 49 | 0.1 | 0.1 | 0.1 | 0.2 | 0.1 | 0.1 | 0.1 |

*Note: Numbers will not add to total because Hispanics may be of any race.*
*Source: National Center for Health Statistics,* Births: Preliminary Data for 1999, *National Vital Statistics Reports, Vol. 48, No. 14, 2000; calculations by New Strategist*

## Births to Unmarried Women, 1998

*(total number of births and number and percent to unmarried women, by race, Hispanic origin, and age of mother, 1998)*

| | | to unmarried women | |
|---|---|---|---|
| | total | number | percent |
| **Total births** | **3,941,553** | **1,293,567** | **32.8%** |
| Under age 20 | 494,357 | 390,005 | 78.9 |
| Aged 20 to 24 | 965,122 | 460,367 | 47.7 |
| Aged 25 to 29 | 1,083,010 | 243,280 | 22.5 |
| Aged 30 to 34 | 889,365 | 124,624 | 14.0 |
| Aged 35 to 39 | 424,890 | 61,087 | 14.4 |
| Aged 40 or older | 84,809 | 14,204 | 16.7 |
| **Births to whites** | **3,118,727** | **821,441** | **26.3** |
| Under age 20 | 345,495 | 250,346 | 72.5 |
| Aged 20 to 24 | 736,664 | 291,677 | 39.6 |
| Aged 25 to 29 | 880,688 | 153,310 | 17.4 |
| Aged 30 to 34 | 737,532 | 77,883 | 10.6 |
| Aged 35 to 39 | 349,799 | 38,905 | 11.1 |
| Aged 40 or older | 68,549 | 9,320 | 13.6 |
| **Births to blacks** | **609,902** | **421,383** | **69.1** |
| Under age 20 | 131,226 | 125,728 | 95.8 |
| Aged 20 to 24 | 189,088 | 151,903 | 80.3 |
| Aged 25 to 29 | 139,302 | 79,344 | 57.0 |
| Aged 30 to 34 | 93,785 | 40,927 | 43.6 |
| Aged 35 to 39 | 46,657 | 19,367 | 41.5 |
| Aged 40 or older | 9,844 | 4,114 | 41.8 |
| **Births to Hispanics** | **734,661** | **305,442** | **41.6** |
| Under age 20 | 124,104 | 91,045 | 73.4 |
| Aged 20 to 24 | 223,113 | 106,020 | 47.5 |
| Aged 25 to 29 | 196,012 | 61,079 | 31.2 |
| Aged 30 to 34 | 125,702 | 30,725 | 24.4 |
| Aged 35 to 39 | 54,195 | 13,403 | 24.7 |
| Aged 40 or older | 11,535 | 3,170 | 27.5 |

*(continued)*

*(continued from previous page)*

| | total | to unmarried women number | percent |
|---|---|---|---|
| **Births to non-Hispanic whites** | **2,361,462** | **517,153** | **21.9%** |
| Under age 20 | 221,301 | 159,561 | 72.1 |
| Aged 20 to 24 | 511,101 | 185,985 | 36.4 |
| Aged 25 to 29 | 678,227 | 92,542 | 13.6 |
| Aged 30 to 34 | 603,639 | 47,449 | 7.9 |
| Aged 35 to 39 | 291,202 | 25,491 | 8.8 |
| Aged 40 or older | 55,992 | 6,125 | 10.9 |

*Note: Births by race and Hispanic origin will not add to total because Hispanics may be of any race and because "not stated" is not shown.*
*Source: National Center for Health Statistics,* Births: Final Data for 1998, *National Vital Statistics Report, Vol. 48, No. 3, 2000; calculations by New Strategist*

## Births by Age of Mother and Birth Order, 1999

*(number and percent distribution of births by age of mother and birth order, 1999)*

| | *total births* | *first birth* | *second birth* | *third birth* | *fourth birth or more* |
|---|---|---|---|---|---|
| **Total births** | **3,957,829** | **1,587,971** | **1,285,974** | **652,380** | **413,012** |
| Under age 20 | 484,794 | 379,567 | 85,615 | 14,651 | 2,149 |
| Aged 20 to 24 | 981,207 | 448,102 | 338,720 | 137,232 | 52,762 |
| Aged 25 to 29 | 1,078,350 | 392,762 | 373,887 | 194,879 | 112,263 |
| Aged 30 to 34 | 892,478 | 253,327 | 322,390 | 186,292 | 126,464 |
| Aged 35 to 39 | 433,793 | 95,585 | 141,258 | 101,369 | 93,376 |
| Aged 40 to 44 | 82,875 | 17,577 | 23,118 | 17,200 | 24,499 |
| Aged 45 to 54 | 4,330 | 1,051 | 987 | 757 | 1,499 |
| **Percent distribution by birth order** | | | | | |
| **Total births** | **100.0%** | **40.1%** | **32.5%** | **16.5%** | **10.4%** |
| Under age 20 | 100.0 | 78.3 | 17.7 | 3.0 | 0.4 |
| Aged 20 to 24 | 100.0 | 45.7 | 34.5 | 14.0 | 5.4 |
| Aged 25 to 29 | 100.0 | 36.4 | 34.7 | 18.1 | 10.4 |
| Aged 30 to 34 | 100.0 | 28.4 | 36.1 | 20.9 | 14.2 |
| Aged 35 to 39 | 100.0 | 22.0 | 32.6 | 23.4 | 21.5 |
| Aged 40 to 44 | 100.0 | 21.2 | 27.9 | 20.8 | 29.6 |
| Aged 45 to 54 | 100.0 | 24.3 | 22.8 | 17.5 | 34.6 |
| **Percent distribution by age** | | | | | |
| **Total births** | **100.0%** | **100.0%** | **100.0%** | **100.0%** | **100.0%** |
| Under age 20 | 12.2 | 23.9 | 6.7 | 2.2 | 0.5 |
| Aged 20 to 24 | 24.8 | 28.2 | 26.3 | 21.0 | 12.8 |
| Aged 25 to 29 | 27.2 | 24.7 | 29.1 | 29.9 | 27.2 |
| Aged 30 to 34 | 22.5 | 16.0 | 25.1 | 28.6 | 30.6 |
| Aged 35 to 39 | 11.0 | 6.0 | 11.0 | 15.5 | 22.6 |
| Aged 40 to 44 | 2.1 | 1.1 | 1.8 | 2.6 | 5.9 |
| Aged 45 to 54 | 0.1 | 0.1 | 0.1 | 0.1 | 0.4 |

*Note: Numbers will not add to total because "not stated" is not shown.*
*Source: National Center for Health Statistics,* Births: Preliminary Data for 1999, *National Vital Statistics Reports, Vol. 48, No. 14, 2000; calculations by New Strategist*

# Men Get More Exercise Than Women

## Nearly half of women rarely exercise.

One in four men aged 20 or older exercises vigorously at least five times a week, the figure ranging from 40 percent of men aged 18-to-29 to 24 percent of men aged 70 or older. Among women, the proportions are much smaller: only 14 to 23 percent exercise vigorously at least five times a week.

While 28 percent of men say they rarely exercise, the proportion is a much larger 44 percent among women. The majority of men aged 70 or older and women aged 60 or older rarely take part in vigorous physical exercise.

The most popular recreational activity among Americans is exercise-walking. More than 80 million people aged 7 or older participated in exercise-walking more than once in 1999, 21 percent greater than in 1989. The number of people participating in the fourth ranked activity, exercising with equipment, rose 43 percent between 1989 and 1999—the fastest growth among the top-ten recreational activities.

♦ Women are so busy juggling jobs and home life that many have little time to devote to themselves, which limits their participation in physical exercise.

**Many women rarely exercise**

*(percent of women who rarely participate in vigorous physical exercise, by age, 1994–96)*

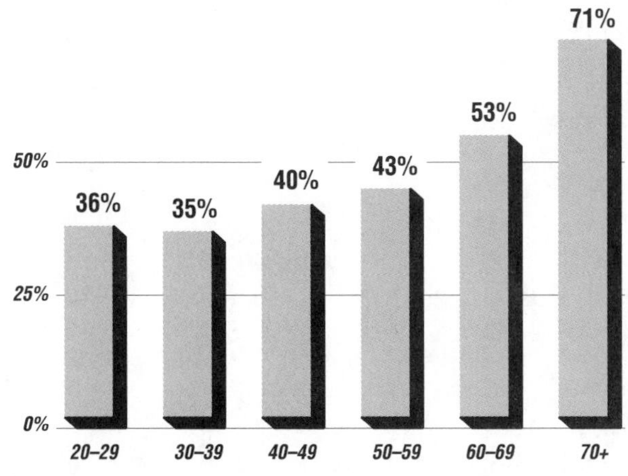

## Vigorous Exercise by Sex and Age, 1994–96

*(percent of people aged 20 or older who exercise vigorously by sex, age, and frequency of vigorous exercise, 1994–96)*

| | total | 5 to 7 times per week | 2 to 4 times per week | 1 to 4 times per month | rarely |
|---|---|---|---|---|---|
| **Total people** | **100.0%** | **25.4%** | **23.8%** | **14.0%** | **36.5%** |
| **Total men** | **100.0** | **32.4** | **25.4** | **13.4** | **28.4** |
| Aged 20 to 29 | 100.0 | 39.6 | 29.0 | 14.5 | 16.6 |
| Aged 30 to 39 | 100.0 | 32.5 | 29.7 | 16.0 | 21.8 |
| Aged 40 to 49 | 100.0 | 30.2 | 26.6 | 15.2 | 27.4 |
| Aged 50 to 59 | 100.0 | 29.6 | 23.4 | 13.0 | 33.4 |
| Aged 60 to 69 | 100.0 | 33.4 | 18.1 | 8.5 | 39.4 |
| Aged 70 or older | 100.0 | 24.2 | 14.3 | 6.1 | 54.6 |
| **Total women** | **100.0** | **18.8** | **22.3** | **14.6** | **43.9** |
| Aged 20 to 29 | 100.0 | 18.3 | 27.1 | 18.4 | 35.8 |
| Aged 30 to 39 | 100.0 | 19.6 | 26.5 | 19.3 | 34.6 |
| Aged 40 to 49 | 100.0 | 17.8 | 25.3 | 16.7 | 39.5 |
| Aged 50 to 59 | 100.0 | 23.3 | 21.2 | 11.7 | 43.2 |
| Aged 60 to 69 | 100.0 | 20.4 | 16.7 | 9.6 | 53.2 |
| Aged 70 or older | 100.0 | 13.5 | 9.8 | 4.9 | 71.1 |

*Note: Numbers will not add to total because "don't know" and no answer are not shown.*
*Source: USDA, ARS Food Surveys Research Group,* Data Tables: Results from USDA's 1994–96 Continuing Survey of Food Intakes by Individuals *and* 1994–96 Diet and Health Knowledge Survey, *1999; Internet site <www.barc.usda.gov/bhnrc/foodsurvey/home.htm>*

## Most Popular Recreational Activities, 1999

*(the 10 recreational activities with the largest number of people aged 7 or older participating more than once, 1989 and 1999; percent change, 1989–99; ranked by number participating in 1999; numbers in millions)*

| | 1999 | 1989 | percent change 1989–99 |
|---|---|---|---|
| Exercise walking | 80.8 | 66.6 | 21.3% |
| Swimming | 57.9 | 70.5 | –17.9 |
| Camping | 50.1 | 46.5 | 7.7 |
| Exercising with equipment | 45.2 | 31.5 | 43.5 |
| Fishing | 46.7 | 46.5 | 0.4 |
| Bicycle riding | 42.4 | 56.9 | –25.5 |
| Bowling | 41.6 | 40.8 | 2.0 |
| Billiards/pool | 32.1 | 29.6 | 8.4 |
| Basketball | 29.6 | 26.2 | 13.0 |
| Golf | 27.0 | 23.2 | 16.4 |
| Hiking | 28.1 | 23.5 | 19.6 |

*Source: National Sporting Goods Association, Internet site <www.nsga.org>; calculations by New Strategist*

# Fewer People Smoke Cigarettes

## More people drink than smoke, with heavy drinking widespread among the young.

The proportion of Americans who smoke cigarettes fell 18 percentage points between 1965 and 1998, from 42 to 24 percent. In 1998, only 26 percent of men smoked cigarettes, down from 52 percent in 1965. Among women, 22 percent smoked in 1998, down from 34 percent in 1965.

Drinking is far more common than smoking among adults. The majority of people between the ages of 19 and 49 had an alcoholic drink in the past month. The figure peaks at 67 percent among 21-year-olds. A large proportion of people binge drink—meaning they had five or more drinks on at least one occasion during the past month. Binge drinking is most common among people in their early twenties, more than 40 percent of whom have done so in the past month. At least 10 percent of people aged 18 to 24 are heavy drinkers, which means they binged on alcohol at least five times in the past month.

While 40 percent of people aged 12 or older have used an illicit drug at some point in their lives, only 7 percent have done so in the past month and 12 percent in the past year. Past-month drug use peaks among people aged 18 to 20, one in five of whom used an illicit drug. Lifetime drug use peaks among people aged 35 to 44, however—the younger members of the baby-boom generation. Nearly 60 percent have used illicit drugs at some point in their lives.

♦ The decline in cigarette smoking over the past few decades is a public health success story with far-reaching consequences for the health of our aging population.

## Cigarette Smoking by Sex and Age, 1965 and 1998

*(percent of people aged 18 or older who currently smoke cigarettes by sex and age, 1965 to 1998; percentage point change, 1965–98)*

| | *1998* | *1965* | *percentage point change* |
|---|---|---|---|
| **Total, both sexes** | **24.1%** | **42.4%** | **–18.3** |
| **Total men** | **26.4** | **51.9** | **–25.5** |
| Aged 18 to 24 | 31.3 | 54.1 | –22.8 |
| Aged 25 to 34 | 28.6 | 60.7 | –32.1 |
| Aged 35 to 44 | 30.2 | 58.2 | –28.0 |
| Aged 45 to 64 | 27.7 | 51.9 | –24.2 |
| Aged 65 or older | 10.4 | 28.5 | –18.1 |
| **Total women** | **21.9** | **33.9** | **–12.0** |
| Aged 18 to 24 | 24.5 | 38.1 | –13.6 |
| Aged 25 to 34 | 24.6 | 43.7 | –19.1 |
| Aged 35 to 44 | 26.4 | 43.7 | –17.3 |
| Aged 45 to 64 | 22.5 | 32.0 | –9.5 |
| Aged 65 or older | 11.2 | 9.6 | 1.6 |

*Source: National Center for Health Statistics,* Health, United States, *2000; Internet site <www.cdc.gov/nchs/products/pubs/pubd/hus/hus.htm>; calculations by New Strategist*

## Alcohol Use by Age, 1999

*(percent of people aged 12 or older who drank alcoholic beverages during the past month, by age and level of alcohol use, 1998)*

| | any time | binge | heavy |
|---|---|---|---|
| **Total people** | **47.3%** | **20.2%** | **5.6%** |
| Aged 12 | 3.9 | 1.7 | 0.1 |
| Aged 13 | 8.5 | 3.7 | 0.4 |
| Aged 14 | 14.6 | 7.3 | 1.2 |
| Aged 15 | 21.2 | 12.1 | 2.2 |
| Aged 16 | 28.8 | 18.1 | 4.4 |
| Aged 17 | 34.5 | 22.4 | 6.5 |
| Aged 18 | 43.7 | 30.5 | 10.0 |
| Aged 19 | 53.0 | 36.6 | 13.5 |
| Aged 20 | 54.7 | 38.7 | 15.8 |
| Aged 21 | 66.6 | 45.6 | 17.4 |
| Aged 22 | 65.1 | 42.5 | 14.6 |
| Aged 23 | 64.2 | 40.0 | 13.5 |
| Aged 24 | 61.5 | 38.3 | 12.4 |
| Aged 25 | 60.6 | 35.6 | 9.2 |
| Aged 26 to 29 | 59.5 | 31.3 | 8.2 |
| Aged 30 to 34 | 56.6 | 28.0 | 6.8 |
| Aged 35 to 39 | 56.5 | 24.0 | 6.5 |
| Aged 40 to 44 | 55.1 | 21.1 | 6.0 |
| Aged 45 to 49 | 52.8 | 20.7 | 6.0 |
| Aged 50 to 64 | 47.2 | 13.8 | 2.9 |
| Aged 65 or older | 32.7 | 5.6 | 1.6 |

*Note: Binge drinking is defined as having five or more drinks on the same occasion on at least one day in the 30 days prior to the survey. Heavy drinking is having five or more drinks on the same occasion on each of five or more days in 30 days prior to the survey. Heavy drinkers include binge drinkers.*
*Source: U.S. Substance Abuse and Mental Health Services Administrations,* National Household Survey on Drug Abuse, *1999; Internet site <www.samhsa.gov/NHSDA.htm>*

## Illicit Drug Use by Age, 1999

*(percent of people aged 12 or older who have used illicit drugs in their lifetime, in the past year, and in the past month, by age, 1999)*

| | *past month* | *past year* | *lifetime* |
|---|---|---|---|
| **Total people** | **6.7%** | **11.9%** | **39.7%** |
| Aged 12 | 4.1 | 7.4 | 10.3 |
| Aged 13 | 5.9 | 11.0 | 15.9 |
| Aged 14 | 9.2 | 17.2 | 25.0 |
| Aged 15 | 12.4 | 24.1 | 31.6 |
| Aged 16 | 16.1 | 29.4 | 38.8 |
| Aged 17 | 17.5 | 32.8 | 43.7 |
| Aged 18 | 20.2 | 34.0 | 48.7 |
| Aged 19 | 20.7 | 34.3 | 53.0 |
| Aged 20 | 20.8 | 34.2 | 54.5 |
| Aged 21 | 17.8 | 30.6 | 54.9 |
| Aged 22 | 16.8 | 28.9 | 53.3 |
| Aged 23 | 15.0 | 28.0 | 54.9 |
| Aged 24 | 12.3 | 22.7 | 53.4 |
| Aged 25 | 10.6 | 19.9 | 48.6 |
| Aged 26 to 29 | 8.5 | 15.7 | 50.8 |
| Aged 30 to 34 | 6.3 | 12.8 | 55.0 |
| Aged 35 to 39 | 6.6 | 12.5 | 59.5 |
| Aged 40 to 44 | 8.6 | 12.7 | 58.0 |
| Aged 45 to 49 | 4.1 | 7.6 | 51.1 |
| Aged 50 to 64 | 1.7 | 2.5 | 25.9 |
| Aged 65 or older | 0.6 | 1.0 | 7.1 |

*Source: U.S. Substance Abuse and Mental Health Services Administrations,* National Household Survey on Drug Abuse, *1999; Internet site <www.samhsa.gov/household99.htm>*

# Millions of Americans Lack Health Insurance

## The proportion is highest among young adults.

While 16 percent of all Americans lack health insurance, the figure is a much higher 29 percent among those aged 18 to 24. Among 25-to-34-year-olds, a substantial 23 percent are without insurance.

Because the federal government's Medicare program covers the elderly, Americans aged 65 or older are most likely to have health insurance. Only 1 percent of the oldest Americans are without health care coverage. In contrast, 14 percent of children under age 18 do not have health insurance—accounting for 24 percent of the nation's uninsured.

♦ The proportion of Americans who lack health insurance could rise substantially if the economy experiences another recession and businesses cut back on benefits.

**Health insurance coverage varies greatly by age**

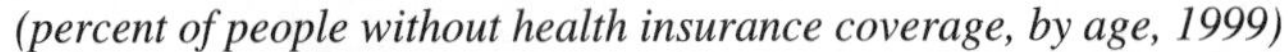

*(percent of people without health insurance coverage, by age, 1999)*

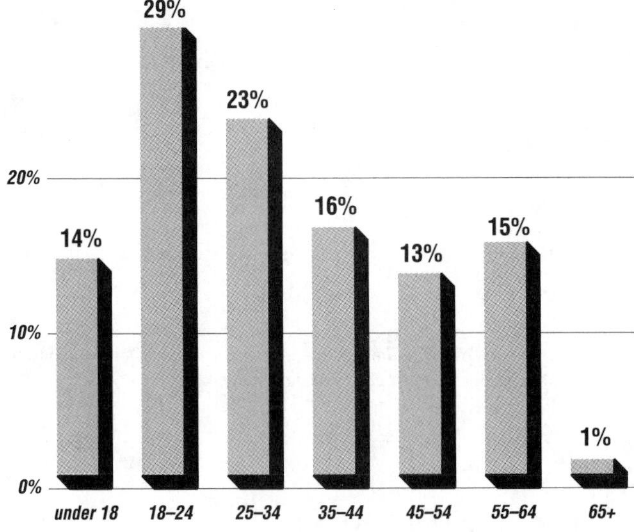

## Health Insurance Coverage by Age, 1999

*(number and percent distribution of people by age and health insurance coverage status, 1999; numbers in thousands)*

| | | covered by private or government health insurance | | | | | | | |
|---|---|---|---|---|---|---|---|---|---|
| | | | private health insurance | | government health insurance | | | | |
| | total | total | total | employment based | total | Medicaid | Medicare | military | not covered |
| **Total** | **274,087** | **231,533** | **194,599** | **172,023** | **66,176** | **27,890** | **36,066** | **8,530** | **42,554** |
| Under 18 | 72,325 | 62,302 | 49,822 | 46,594 | 16,579 | 14,479 | 355 | 2,080 | 10,023 |
| 18 to 24 | 26,532 | 18,844 | 16,438 | 13,535 | 3,450 | 2,643 | 152 | 798 | 7,688 |
| 25 to 34 | 37,786 | 29,031 | 26,567 | 25,150 | 3,429 | 2,344 | 323 | 940 | 8,755 |
| 35 to 44 | 44,805 | 37,428 | 34,624 | 32,423 | 3,988 | 2,340 | 856 | 1,256 | 7,377 |
| 45 to 54 | 36,631 | 31,737 | 29,440 | 27,489 | 3,544 | 1,693 | 1,124 | 1,209 | 4,893 |
| 55 to 64 | 23,387 | 19,992 | 17,654 | 15,662 | 3,874 | 1,474 | 2,024 | 1,014 | 3,395 |
| 65 or older | 32,621 | 32,199 | 20,054 | 11,169 | 31,312 | 2,917 | 31,231 | 1,232 | 422 |
| **Percent distribution by type of coverage** | | | | | | | | | |
| **Total** | **100.0%** | **84.5%** | **71.0%** | **62.8%** | **24.1%** | **10.2%** | **13.2%** | **3.1%** | **15.5%** |
| Under 18 | 100.0 | 86.1 | 68.9 | 64.4 | 22.9 | 20.0 | 0.5 | 2.9 | 13.9 |
| 18 to 24 | 100.0 | 71.0 | 62.0 | 51.0 | 13.0 | 10.0 | 0.6 | 3.0 | 29.0 |
| 25 to 34 | 100.0 | 76.8 | 70.3 | 66.6 | 8.9 | 6.1 | 0.8 | 2.4 | 22.8 |
| 35 to 44 | 100.0 | 83.5 | 77.3 | 72.4 | 8.9 | 5.2 | 1.9 | 2.8 | 16.5 |
| 45 to 54 | 100.0 | 86.6 | 80.4 | 75.0 | 9.7 | 4.6 | 3.1 | 3.3 | 13.4 |
| 55 to 64 | 100.0 | 85.5 | 75.5 | 67.0 | 16.6 | 6.3 | 8.7 | 4.3 | 14.5 |
| 65 or older | 100.0 | 98.7 | 61.5 | 34.2 | 96.0 | 8.9 | 95.7 | 3.8 | 1.3 |
| **Percent distribution by age** | | | | | | | | | |
| **Total** | **100.0%** | **100.0%** | **100.0%** | **100.0%** | **100.0%** | **100.0%** | **100.0%** | **100.0%** | **100.0%** |
| Under 18 | 26.4 | 26.9 | 25.6 | 27.1 | 25.1 | 51.9 | 1.0 | 24.4 | 23.6 |
| 18 to 24 | 9.7 | 8.1 | 8.4 | 7.9 | 5.2 | 9.5 | 0.4 | 9.4 | 18.1 |
| 25 to 34 | 13.8 | 12.5 | 13.6 | 14.6 | 5.2 | 8.4 | 0.9 | 11.0 | 20.6 |
| 35 to 44 | 16.3 | 16.2 | 17.8 | 18.8 | 6.0 | 8.4 | 2.4 | 14.7 | 17.3 |
| 45 to 54 | 13.4 | 13.7 | 15.1 | 16.0 | 5.4 | 6.1 | 3.1 | 14.2 | 11.5 |
| 55 to 64 | 8.5 | 8.6 | 9.1 | 9.1 | 5.9 | 5.3 | 5.6 | 11.9 | 8.0 |
| 65 or older | 11.9 | 13.9 | 10.3 | 6.5 | 47.3 | 10.5 | 86.6 | 14.4 | 1.0 |

*Note: Numbers may not add to total because people may have more than one type of health insurance coverage.*
*Source: Bureau of the Census, unpublished tables from the 2000 Current Population Survey, Internet site <www.census.gov/hhes/hlthins/historic/hihistt2.html>; calculations by New Strategist*

# Acute Conditions Strike the Young

## As acute conditions diminish with age, chronic conditions take their place.

Acute conditions are most common among the young. One-half of all acute conditions that led to a doctor visit or at least half-a-day of bed rest in 1996 occurred to people under age 25 and fully 78 percent to people under age 45. Not only do older people have better immunity than children and young adults, but they are less likely to be around the sick. Fifty-three percent of colds bad enough to keep people in bed for at least half a day or send them to a doctor befell people under age 25, as did 79 percent of influenza cases.

In contrast to acute conditions, the prevalence of most chronic conditions rises with age. The most common chronic conditions among Americans of all ages are arthritis, chronic sinusitis, orthopedic impairments, high blood pressure, hay fever, hearing impairments, and heart disease. People aged 65 or older account for 46 percent of Americans with arthritis, 44 percent of those with hearing impairments, and 41 percent of those with high blood pressure or heart disease. Contrary to this pattern, hay fever and chronic sinusitis are found mostly among the young.

♦ As the baby-boom generation ages into its sixties during the next decades, the number of people with chronic conditions will surge.

## Acute Health Conditions by Age, 1996

*(total number of acute conditions by type, and percent distribution of conditions by age, 1996; numbers in thousands)*

| | total | | | | | | | |
|---|---|---|---|---|---|---|---|---|
| | number | percent | under 5 | 5 to 17 | 18 to 24 | 25 to 44 | 45 to 64 | 65 or older |
| **Total acute conditions** | **432,001** | **100.0%** | **14.8%** | **24.3%** | **10.5%** | **27.9%** | **14.0%** | **8.6%** |
| Infective and parasitic diseases | 54,192 | 100.0 | 21.1 | 35.1 | 10.5 | 18.7 | 10.8 | 3.8 |
| Common childhood diseases | 3,118 | 100.0 | 43.9 | 38.6 | 7.1 | 10.4 | – | – |
| Intestinal virus | 15,980 | 100.0 | 17.9 | 33.2 | 9.6 | 24.6 | 9.4 | 5.3 |
| Viral infections | 15,067 | 100.0 | 30.1 | 32.7 | 4.6 | 14.5 | 15.9 | 2.2 |
| Other | 20,027 | 100.0 | 13.4 | 37.8 | 16.3 | 18.5 | 9.7 | 4.3 |
| **Respiratory conditions** | **208,623** | **100.0** | **12.5** | **25.0** | **10.1** | **30.7** | **14.2** | **7.5** |
| Common cold | 62,251 | 100.0 | 15.7 | 27.8 | 9.4 | 25.1 | 14.0 | 8.0 |
| Other acute upper respiratory infections | 29,866 | 100.0 | 8.8 | 25.7 | 13.3 | 32.3 | 13.4 | 6.4 |
| Influenza | 95,049 | 100.0 | 11.3 | 23.9 | 10.5 | 33.5 | 14.6 | 6.2 |
| Acute bronchitis | 12,116 | 100.0 | 11.9 | 18.3 | 7.8 | 35.2 | 15.2 | 11.5 |
| Pneumonia | 4,791 | 100.0 | 16.3 | 18.4 | 7.2 | 22.6 | 10.2 | 25.1 |
| Other respiratory conditions | 4,550 | 100.0 | 13.0 | 27.2 | 2.4 | 37.0 | 17.1 | 3.2 |
| **Digestive system conditions** | **17,646** | **100.0** | **10.9** | **28.5** | **9.0** | **23.9** | **15.9** | **11.8** |
| Dental conditions | 2,970 | 100.0 | 24.2 | 18.1 | 9.2 | 24.0 | 15.5 | 8.9 |
| Indigestion, nausea, and vomiting | 7,963 | 100.0 | 5.7 | 47.5 | 7.7 | 22.6 | 11.6 | 4.8 |
| Other digestive conditions | 6,713 | 100.0 | 11.2 | 10.5 | 10.3 | 25.4 | 21.1 | 21.5 |

*(continued)*

*(continued from previous page)*

| | total | | | | | | | |
|---|---|---|---|---|---|---|---|---|
| | number | percent | under 5 | 5 to 17 | 18 to 24 | 25 to 44 | 45 to 64 | 65 or older |
| **Injuries** | **57,279** | **100.0%** | **8.0%** | **19.1%** | **13.5%** | **36.2%** | **13.6%** | **9.6%** |
| Fractures and dislocations | 8,465 | 100.0 | 2.9 | 35.7 | 8.7 | 17.8 | 21.7 | 13.3 |
| Sprains and strains | 12,977 | 100.0 | 0.8 | 13.8 | 13.8 | 53.2 | 15.6 | 2.8 |
| Open wounds and lacerations | 9,027 | 100.0 | 15.2 | 11.2 | 18.1 | 40.3 | 9.8 | 5.4 |
| Contusions and superficial injuries | 9,979 | 100.0 | 7.2 | 20.1 | 14.4 | 37.0 | 14.4 | 7.0 |
| Other current injuries | 16,832 | 100.0 | 12.8 | 18.6 | 12.7 | 29.7 | 9.5 | 16.6 |
| **Selected other acute conditions** | **63,090** | **100.0** | **25.4** | **19.8** | **9.9** | **22.2** | **12.9** | **9.7** |
| Eye conditions | 3,478 | 100.0 | 21.9 | 9.7 | 11.0 | 9.6 | 26.7 | 21.0 |
| Acute ear infections | 21,766 | 100.0 | 50.7 | 29.3 | 4.3 | 11.0 | 2.8 | 1.9 |
| Other ear conditions | 3,833 | 100.0 | 15.5 | 30.0 | 4.8 | 25.7 | 17.9 | 6.0 |
| Acute urinary conditions | 8,405 | 100.0 | 5.7 | 12.1 | 8.4 | 30.0 | 20.7 | 23.2 |
| Disorders of menstruation | 839 | 100.0 | – | 15.9 | 20.1 | 64.0 | – | – |
| Other disorders of female genital tract | 1,597 | 100.0 | – | 2.4 | 27.9 | 38.4 | 22.4 | 9.0 |
| Delivery and other conditions of pregnancy | 3,279 | 100.0 | – | 9.5 | 33.4 | 57.1 | – | – |
| Skin conditions | 4,986 | 100.0 | 11.5 | 14.8 | 9.9 | 23.7 | 24.2 | 15.9 |
| Acute musculoskeletal conditions | 8,461 | 100.0 | 7.1 | 5.0 | 15.6 | 29.7 | 21.9 | 20.7 |
| Headache, excluding migraine | 1,738 | 100.0 | – | 22.7 | 16.2 | 33.7 | 21.4 | 5.9 |
| Fever, unspecified | 4,708 | 100.0 | 42.7 | 33.9 | 4.8 | 9.6 | 9.1 | – |
| **Other acute conditions** | **31,170** | **100.0** | **12.3** | **16.8** | **9.2** | **22.9** | **19.7** | **19.1** |

*Note: The acute conditions shown here are those that caused people to seek medical attention or to restrict their activity for at least half a day. (–) means not applicable or sample is too small to make a reliable estimate.*

*Source: National Center for Health Statistics,* Current Estimates from the National Health Interview Survey, 1996, *Series 10, No. 200, 1999; calculations by New Strategist*

## Chronic Health Conditions by Age, 1996

*(total number of chronic conditions by type, and percent distribution of conditions by age, 1996; numbers in thousands)*

| | total | | | | | aged 65 or older | | |
|---|---|---|---|---|---|---|---|---|
| | number | percent | under 18 | 18 to 44 | 45 to 64 | total | 65 to 74 | 75 or older |
| **Skin and musculoskeletal conditions** | | | | | | | | |
| Arthritis | 33,638 | 100.0% | 0.4% | 16.1% | 37.9% | 45.6% | 24.8% | 20.8% |
| Gout, including gouty arthritis | 2,487 | 100.0 | – | 12.9 | 47.8 | 39.3 | 23.5 | 15.8 |
| Intervertebral disc disorders | 6,700 | 100.0 | 1.0 | 34.0 | 49.8 | 15.3 | 10.5 | 4.8 |
| Bonespur or tendinitis | 2,934 | 100.0 | – | 40.3 | 42.0 | 17.7 | 9.2 | 8.6 |
| Disorders of bone or cartilage | 1,730 | 100.0 | 2.0 | 19.3 | 30.8 | 48.0 | 16.6 | 31.4 |
| Bunions | 2,360 | 100.0 | 4.1 | 29.8 | 36.5 | 29.6 | 16.5 | 13.0 |
| Bursitis | 5,006 | 100.0 | 1.1 | 28.2 | 46.6 | 24.1 | 15.8 | 8.3 |
| Sebaceous skin cyst | 1,190 | 100.0 | 2.7 | 51.8 | 40.4 | 5.2 | 5.2 | – |
| Acne | 4,952 | 100.0 | 35.2 | 59.9 | 4.9 | – | – | – |
| Psoriasis | 2,940 | 100.0 | 7.8 | 38.6 | 37.5 | 16.2 | 10.2 | 6.0 |
| Dermatitis | 8,249 | 100.0 | 26.4 | 39.4 | 24.5 | 9.7 | 5.9 | 3.7 |
| Dry, itching skin | 6,627 | 100.0 | 13.6 | 39.8 | 23.2 | 23.4 | 10.4 | 13.0 |
| Ingrown nails | 5,807 | 100.0 | 6.4 | 48.4 | 24.6 | 20.6 | 10.8 | 9.8 |
| Corns and calluses | 3,778 | 100.0 | 2.1 | 37.2 | 35.8 | 24.9 | 13.2 | 11.7 |

*(continued)*

(continued from previous page)

| | total | | | | | aged 65 or older | | |
|---|---|---|---|---|---|---|---|---|
| | number | percent | under 18 | 18 to 44 | 45 to 64 | total | 65 to 74 | 75 or older |
| **Impairments** | | | | | | | | |
| Visual impairment | 8,280 | 100.0% | 5.4% | 31.3% | 31.0% | 32.3% | 15.5% | 16.8% |
| Color blindness | 2,811 | 100.0 | 10.1 | 38.2 | 30.4 | 21.3 | 13.5 | 7.8 |
| Cataracts | 7,022 | 100.0 | 0.5 | 4.3 | 17.7 | 77.6 | 39.8 | 37.8 |
| Glaucoma | 2,595 | 100.0 | – | 8.2 | 21.0 | 70.7 | 33.1 | 37.6 |
| Hearing impairment | 22,044 | 100.0 | 4.1 | 20.5 | 31.7 | 43.7 | 21.3 | 22.4 |
| Tinnitus | 7,866 | 100.0 | 2.4 | 22.0 | 40.3 | 35.4 | 22.5 | 12.9 |
| Speech impairment | 2,720 | 100.0 | 42.6 | 30.8 | 12.8 | 13.7 | 6.8 | 6.9 |
| Absence of extremities | 1,285 | 100.0 | 5.4 | 22.8 | 23.7 | 48.0 | 30.7 | 17.4 |
| Paralysis of extremities | 2,138 | 100.0 | 12.8 | 25.7 | 33.4 | 28.0 | 10.7 | 17.4 |
| Deformity or orthopedic impairment | 29,499 | 100.0 | 6.2 | 44.8 | 32.0 | 17.0 | 10.9 | 6.0 |
| Back | 16,905 | 100.0 | 3.3 | 51.5 | 32.3 | 12.9 | 8.7 | 4.2 |
| Upper extremities | 4,170 | 100.0 | 4.5 | 34.5 | 37.5 | 23.5 | 17.2 | 6.3 |
| Lower extremities | 12,696 | 100.0 | 10.5 | 36.8 | 34.5 | 18.2 | 11.3 | 6.9 |
| **Digestive conditions** | | | | | | | | |
| Ulcer | 3,709 | 100.0 | 2.6 | 34.2 | 37.4 | 25.8 | 18.3 | 7.5 |
| Hernia of abdominal cavity | 4,470 | 100.0 | 2.7 | 26.1 | 36.8 | 34.4 | 15.8 | 18.7 |
| Gastritis or duodenitis | 3,729 | 100.0 | 5.8 | 39.2 | 31.5 | 23.5 | 16.8 | 6.7 |
| Frequent indigestion | 6,420 | 100.0 | 3.7 | 44.9 | 34.9 | 16.6 | 11.1 | 5.5 |
| Enteritis or colitis | 1,686 | 100.0 | 7.1 | 44.2 | 31.4 | 17.4 | 9.1 | 8.3 |
| Spastic colon | 2,083 | 100.0 | 2.3 | 40.8 | 35.0 | 21.8 | 14.9 | 7.0 |
| Diverticula of intestines | 2,529 | 100.0 | – | 10.4 | 37.0 | 52.6 | 26.2 | 26.4 |
| Frequent constipation | 3,149 | 100.0 | 12.1 | 29.0 | 24.9 | 34.1 | 13.9 | 20.1 |

(continued)

*(continued from previous page)*

| | total | | | | | aged 65 or older | | |
|---|---|---|---|---|---|---|---|---|
| | number | percent | under 18 | 18 to 44 | 45 to 64 | total | 65 to 74 | 75 or older |
| **Genitourinary, nervous, endocrine, metabolic, and blood conditions** | | | | | | | | |
| Goiter or other thyroid disorders | 4,598 | 100.0% | 1.5% | 30.6% | 34.7% | 33.2% | 20.1% | 13.1% |
| Diabetes | 7,627 | 100.0 | 1.2 | 16.7 | 40.5 | 41.7 | 23.7 | 17.9 |
| Anemias | 3,457 | 100.0 | 10.4 | 52.0 | 16.5 | 21.1 | 7.3 | 13.9 |
| Epilepsy | 1,335 | 100.0 | 26.3 | 35.8 | 23.1 | 14.8 | 7.4 | 7.4 |
| Migraine headache | 11,546 | 100.0 | 9.4 | 56.1 | 26.7 | 7.8 | 4.6 | 3.3 |
| Neuralgia or neuritis, unspecified | 353 | 100.0 | 4.2 | 8.5 | 36.5 | 50.4 | 13.3 | 37.1 |
| Kidney trouble | 2,553 | 100.0 | 6.6 | 49.8 | 26.6 | 17.0 | 9.9 | 7.1 |
| Bladder disorders | 3,139 | 100.0 | 7.6 | 38.7 | 26.5 | 27.2 | 11.7 | 15.5 |
| Diseases of prostate | 2,803 | 100.0 | – | 8.6 | 27.8 | 63.5 | 32.1 | 31.5 |
| Diseases of female genital organs | 4,420 | 100.0 | 5.5 | 59.2 | 24.9 | 10.5 | 6.9 | 3.6 |
| **Circulatory conditions** | | | | | | | | |
| Rheumatic fever | 1,759 | 100.0 | 4.7 | 42.4 | 31.4 | 21.5 | 8.2 | 13.3 |
| Heart disease | 20,653 | 100.0 | 8.2 | 20.6 | 29.9 | 41.3 | 21.2 | 20.1 |
| Ischemic heart disease | 7,672 | 100.0 | – | 5.9 | 35.8 | 58.3 | 31.4 | 26.9 |
| Heart rhythm disorders | 8,716 | 100.0 | 14.0 | 36.0 | 24.8 | 25.2 | 14.0 | 11.2 |
| Tachycardia or rapid heart | 2,310 | 100.0 | – | 29.7 | 27.8 | 42.4 | 24.7 | 17.7 |
| Heart murmurs | 4,783 | 100.0 | 24.8 | 42.5 | 19.6 | 13.0 | 8.2 | 4.8 |
| Other heart rhythm disorders | 1,624 | 100.0 | 1.8 | 25.9 | 36.0 | 36.4 | 15.7 | 20.7 |
| Other selected diseases of heart | 4,265 | 100.0 | 11.0 | 15.3 | 30.0 | 43.7 | 17.7 | 26.0 |

*(continued)*

*(continued from previous page)*

| | total | | | | | aged 65 or older | | |
|---|---|---|---|---|---|---|---|---|
| | number | percent | under 18 | 18 to 44 | 45 to 64 | total | 65 to 74 | 75 or older |
| High blood pressure (hypertension) | 28,314 | 100.0% | 0.1% | 18.9% | 40.2% | 40.8% | 23.1% | 17.6% |
| Cerebrovascular disease | 2,999 | 100.0 | 1.0 | 7.4 | 22.7 | 68.9 | 24.6 | 44.3 |
| Hardening of the arteries | 1,556 | 100.0 | – | – | 22.8 | 77.2 | 33.5 | 43.7 |
| Varicose veins of lower extremities | 7,399 | 100.0 | – | 32.4 | 33.6 | 34.0 | 18.4 | 2.1 |
| Hemorrhoids | 8,231 | 100.0 | 0.2 | 45.1 | 34.6 | 23.6 | 16.3 | 7.4 |
| **Respiratory conditions** | | | | | | | | |
| Chronic bronchitis | 14,150 | 100.0 | 28.9 | 34.7 | 22.2 | 14.3 | 7.9 | 6.4 |
| Asthma | 14,598 | 100.0 | 30.3 | 42.1 | 17.7 | 9.9 | 5.5 | 4.4 |
| Hay fever or allergic rhinitis | 23,721 | 100.0 | 17.7 | 49.8 | 23.5 | 9.1 | 4.8 | 4.3 |
| Chronic sinusitis | 33,161 | 100.0 | 13.7 | 47.1 | 27.9 | 11.2 | 7.0 | 4.2 |
| Deviated nasal septum | 1,985 | 100.0 | 6.1 | 43.7 | 40.1 | 10.0 | 3.0 | 7.0 |
| Chronic disease of tonsils and adenoids | 2,513 | 100.0 | 57.5 | 35.2 | 6.3 | 1.0 | 1.0 | – |
| Emphysema | 1,821 | 100.0 | – | 4.9 | 38.5 | 56.6 | 32.7 | 23.9 |

*Note: Chronic conditions are those that last at least three months or belong to a group of conditions that are considered to be chronic regardless of when they begin. (–) means sample is too small to make a reliable estimate.*
*Source: National Center for Health Statistics,* Current Estimates from the National Health Interview Survey, 1996, *Series 10, No. 200, 1999; Internet site <www.cdc.gov/nchs/data/nvs48_3.pdf>; calculations by New Strategist*

# Many People Are Disabled

## One in five Americans has a disability.

Fifty-three million Americans were disabled in 1997, 33 million severely so. Not surprisingly, those most likely to be disabled are the oldest Americans. Among people aged 65 or older, more than half are disabled. Thirty-eight percent are severely disabled, although only 17 percent need help in managing their daily life.

The most common disability among people aged 15 or older is difficulty walking and/or using stairs. One in eight experiences these problems. Among people aged 65 or older, 40 percent have difficulty walking or using stairs. Twenty-two percent of the oldest Americans have difficulty seeing, hearing, or speaking. Twelve percent have a mental disability.

♦ As the enormous baby-boom generation ages, the number of Americans with disabilities will grow rapidly.

**Disability rises sharply with age**

*(percent of people with a disability, by age, 1997)*

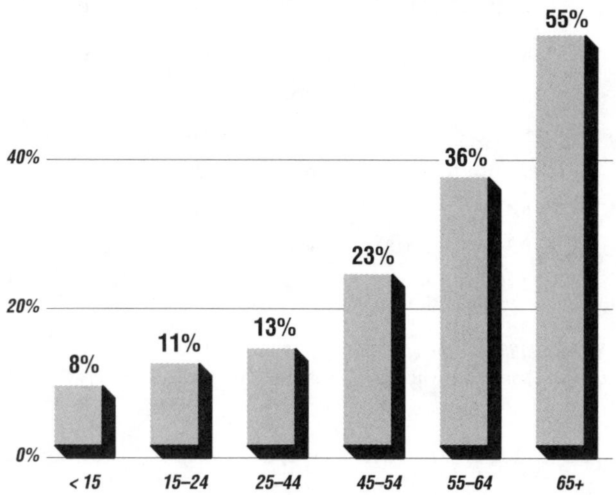

## People with Disabilities by Age, 1997

*(total number of people and number and percent with disabilities, by age and severity of disability, 1997; numbers in thousands)*

| | | with a disability | | | | | |
|---|---|---|---|---|---|---|---|
| | | total | | severe | | needs assistance | |
| | total | number | percent | number | percent | number | percent |
| **Total people** | **267,665** | **52,596** | **19.7%** | **32,970** | **12.3%** | **10,076** | **3.8%** |
| Under age 15 | 59,606 | 4,661 | 7.8 | 2,256 | 3.8 | 224 | 0.4 |
| Aged 15 to 24 | 36,897 | 3,961 | 10.7 | 1,942 | 5.3 | 372 | 1.0 |
| Aged 25 to 44 | 83,887 | 11,200 | 13.4 | 6,793 | 8.1 | 1,635 | 1.9 |
| Aged 45 to 54 | 33,620 | 7,585 | 22.6 | 4,674 | 13.9 | 1,225 | 3.6 |
| Aged 55 to 64 | 21,591 | 7,708 | 35.7 | 5,233 | 24.2 | 1,280 | 5.9 |
| Aged 65 or older | 32,064 | 17,480 | 54.5 | 12,073 | 37.7 | 5,339 | 16.7 |
| **Total females** | **136,680** | **28,265** | **20.7** | **18,216** | **13.3** | **5,927** | **4.3** |
| Under age 15 | 29,112 | 1,646 | 5.7 | 754 | 2.6 | 95 | 0.3 |
| Aged 15 to 24 | 18,235 | 1,795 | 9.8 | 935 | 5.1 | 156 | 0.9 |
| Aged 25 to 44 | 42,316 | 5,797 | 13.7 | 3,470 | 8.2 | 789 | 1.9 |
| Aged 45 to 54 | 17,202 | 4,158 | 24.2 | 2,536 | 14.7 | 690 | 4.0 |
| Aged 55 to 64 | 11,250 | 4,190 | 37.2 | 2,869 | 25.5 | 695 | 6.2 |
| Aged 65 or older | 18,565 | 10,679 | 57.5 | 7,652 | 41.2 | 3,502 | 18.9 |
| **Total males** | **130,985** | **24,331** | **18.6** | **14,754** | **11.3** | **4,149** | **3.2** |
| Under age 15 | 30,494 | 3,015 | 9.9 | 1,502 | 4.9 | 130 | 0.4 |
| Aged 15 to 24 | 18,663 | 2,166 | 11.6 | 1,007 | 5.4 | 216 | 1.2 |
| Aged 25 to 44 | 41,571 | 5,403 | 13.0 | 3,323 | 8.0 | 846 | 2.0 |
| Aged 45 to 54 | 16,418 | 3,427 | 20.9 | 2,138 | 13.0 | 535 | 3.3 |
| Aged 55 to 64 | 10,342 | 3,518 | 34.0 | 2,364 | 22.9 | 584 | 5.7 |
| Aged 65 or older | 13,498 | 6,801 | 50.4 | 4,421 | 32.8 | 1,838 | 13.6 |

*Note: For the definition of disability, see the glossary.*
*Source: Bureau of the Census,* Americans with Disabilities: 1997, *detailed tables from Current Population Reports P70–73, 2001*

## People Aged 15 or Older with Disabilities by Type of Disability and Age, 1997

*(total number of people aged 15 or older and percent with a disability, by type of disability and age, 1997; numbers in thousands)*

| | 15 or older | | 15 to 24 | | 25 to 64 | | 65 or older | |
|---|---|---|---|---|---|---|---|---|
| | number | percent | number | percent | number | percent | number | percent |
| **Total people** | **208,059** | **100.0%** | **36,897** | **100.0%** | **139,098** | **100.0%** | **32,064** | **100.0%** |
| **Disability status** | | | | | | | | |
| No disability | 160,124 | 77.0 | 32,936 | 89.3 | 112,604 | 81.0 | 14,583 | 45.5 |
| With a disability | 47,935 | 23.0 | 3,961 | 10.7 | 26,493 | 19.0 | 17,480 | 54.5 |
| Severe | 30,714 | 14.8 | 1,942 | 5.3 | 16,700 | 12.0 | 12,073 | 37.7 |
| Not severe | 17,221 | 8.3 | 2,019 | 5.5 | 9,794 | 7.0 | 5,408 | 16.9 |
| **Mental** | | | | | | | | |
| With a disability | 14,267 | 6.9 | 2,021 | 5.5 | 8,334 | 6.0 | 3,912 | 12.2 |
| Learning disability | 3,451 | 1.7 | 1,048 | 2.8 | 2,193 | 1.6 | 210 | 0.7 |
| Mental retardation | 1,366 | 0.7 | 264 | 0.7 | 988 | 0.7 | 114 | 0.4 |
| Alzheimers, senility, or dementia | 1,873 | 0.9 | 58 | 0.2 | 595 | 0.4 | 1,219 | 3.8 |
| Frequently depressed or anxious | 5,615 | 2.7 | 511 | 1.4 | 3,848 | 2.8 | 1,256 | 3.9 |
| Trouble getting along with others | 1,816 | 0.9 | 346 | 0.9 | 1,145 | 0.8 | 325 | 1.0 |
| Trouble concentrating | 3,753 | 1.8 | 480 | 1.3 | 2,307 | 1.7 | 967 | 3.0 |
| Trouble coping with stress | 4,659 | 2.2 | 508 | 1.4 | 3,180 | 2.3 | 971 | 3.0 |
| **Seeing/hearing/speaking** | | | | | | | | |
| With a disability | 14,613 | 7.0 | 608 | 1.6 | 6,963 | 5.0 | 7,042 | 22.0 |
| Has difficulty seeing words/letters | 7,673 | 3.7 | 202 | 0.5 | 3,594 | 2.6 | 3,877 | 12.1 |

*(continued)*

*(continued from previous page)*

| | 15 or older | | 15 to 24 | | 25 to 64 | | 65 or older | |
|---|---|---|---|---|---|---|---|---|
| | *number* | *percent* | *number* | *percent* | *number* | *percent* | *number* | *percent* |
| Has difficulty hearing conversation | 7,966 | 3.8% | 262 | 0.7% | 3,400 | 2.4% | 4,304 | 13.4% |
| Has difficulty with speech | 2,270 | 1.1 | 277 | 0.8 | 1,176 | 0.8 | 818 | 2.6 |
| **Walking/using stairs** | | | | | | | | |
| With a disability | 25,138 | 12.1 | 619 | 1.7 | 11,717 | 8.4 | 12,803 | 39.9 |
| Has difficulty walking | 19,465 | 9.4 | 443 | 1.2 | 8,938 | 6.4 | 10,084 | 31.4 |
| Has difficulty using stairs | 19,757 | 9.5 | 461 | 1.2 | 9,223 | 6.6 | 10,073 | 31.4 |
| **Selected physical tasks** | | | | | | | | |
| With a disability | 18,071 | 8.7 | 419 | 1.1 | 8,803 | 6.3 | 8,849 | 27.6 |
| Has difficulty lifting/carrying 10 lbs. | 15,198 | 7.3 | 336 | 0.9 | 7,098 | 5.1 | 7,764 | 24.2 |
| Has difficulty grasping objects | 6,758 | 3.2 | 187 | 0.5 | 3,560 | 2.6 | 3,012 | 9.4 |
| **Special aids** | | | | | | | | |
| Uses a wheelchair | 2,155 | 1.0 | 95 | 0.3 | 843 | 0.6 | 1,216 | 3.8 |
| Uses a cane/crutches/walker | 6,372 | 3.1 | 54 | 0.1 | 2,141 | 1.5 | 4,176 | 13.0 |
| Uses a hearing aid | 3,972 | 1.9 | 95 | 0.3 | 880 | 0.6 | 2,997 | 9.3 |
| Has difficulty hearing | 1,684 | 0.8 | 45 | 0.1 | 340 | 0.2 | 1,300 | 4.1 |
| Does not have difficulty hearing | 2,288 | 1.1 | 50 | 0.1 | 540 | 0.4 | 1,698 | 5.3 |
| **Needs personal assistance** | **9,851** | **4.7** | **372** | **1.0** | **4,140** | **3.0** | **5,339** | **16.7** |

*Note: Use of hearing aid is not part of the disability definition. For the definition of disability, see the glossary.*
*Source: Bureau of the Census,* Americans with Disabilities: 1997, *detailed tables from Current Population Reports P70-73, 2001*

# Going to the Doctor Is Common for Everyone

## Americans visited the doctor more than 800 million times in 1998.

The average American visits a doctor 3.1 times a year. Women visit doctors more often than men, whites more often than blacks, and older people more often than children and young adults.

Among the 829 million doctor visits in 1998, 50 percent were by people aged 25 to 64. Not only is the enormous baby-boom generation between those ages, but most pregnant women are too. Pregnancies account for a large share of women's visits to the doctor. People aged 65 or older account for nearly one in four doctor visits. While the average person visits a doctor 3.1 times a year, those aged 65 or older visit doctors 5.7 to 6.6 times a year.

♦ As the population ages, doctor visits will increase. The cost of medical care will rise significantly unless less-costly practitioners such as nurses or physician assistants provide more care.

### Teens and young adults are least likely to see a doctor

*(average annual number of physician visits per person, by age, 1998)*

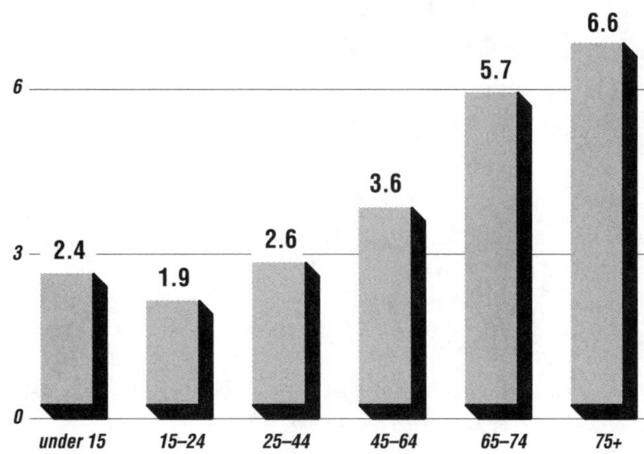

## Physician Office Visits by Age, Sex, and Race, 1998

*(total number, percent distribution, and number of physician office visits per person per year, by age, sex, and race, 1998)*

| | *total* | *female* | *male* | *black* | *white* |
|---|---|---|---|---|---|
| **Number of visits (in 000s)** | | | | | |
| **Total visits** | **829,280** | **500,365** | **328,916** | **89,832** | **702,190** |
| Under age 15 | 145,842 | 68,018 | 77,825 | 22,327 | 113,358 |
| Aged 15 to 24 | 71,283 | 48,750 | 22,532 | 8,417 | 59,927 |
| Aged 25 to 44 | 211,775 | 144,827 | 66,948 | 24,238 | 177,947 |
| Aged 45 to 64 | 203,296 | 120,822 | 82,474 | 20,742 | 173,822 |
| Aged 65 to 74 | 102,306 | 58,808 | 43,498 | 8,271 | 90,379 |
| Aged 75 or older | 94,779 | 59,141 | 35,638 | 5,837 | 86,757 |
| **Percent distribution of visits by age** | | | | | |
| **Total visits** | **100.0%** | **100.0%** | **100.0%** | **100.0%** | **100.0%** |
| Under age 15 | 17.6 | 13.6 | 23.7 | 24.9 | 16.1 |
| Aged 15 to 24 | 8.6 | 9.7 | 6.9 | 9.4 | 8.5 |
| Aged 25 to 44 | 25.5 | 28.9 | 20.4 | 27.0 | 25.3 |
| Aged 45 to 64 | 24.5 | 24.1 | 25.1 | 23.1 | 24.8 |
| Aged 65 to 74 | 12.3 | 11.8 | 13.2 | 9.2 | 12.9 |
| Aged 75 or older | 11.4 | 11.8 | 10.8 | 6.5 | 12.4 |
| **Visits per person per year** | | | | | |
| **Total people** | **3.1** | **3.6** | **2.5** | **2.6** | **3.2** |
| Under age 15 | 2.4 | 2.3 | 2.5 | 2.3 | 2.4 |
| Aged 15 to 24 | 1.9 | 2.6 | 1.2 | 1.5 | 2.0 |
| Aged 25 to 44 | 2.6 | 3.4 | 1.6 | 2.3 | 2.6 |
| Aged 45 to 64 | 3.6 | 4.1 | 3.0 | 3.5 | 3.6 |
| Aged 65 to 74 | 5.7 | 6.0 | 5.4 | 5.1 | 5.7 |
| Aged 75 or older | 6.6 | 6.7 | 6.4 | 5.4 | 6.7 |

*Source: National Center for Health Statistics,* National Ambulatory Medical Care Survey: 1998 Summary, *Advance Data No. 315, 2000; calculations by New Strategist*

# Hospital Care Is Much Less Common

## The average hospital stay was 4.9 days in 1998, down from 7.1 days in 1980.

As insurance companies try to contain costs, hospital stays have shortened and hospital discharges have fallen sharply. The consequence has been turmoil in the health care industry as both hospitals and patients cope with change.

The hospital discharge rate per 1,000 people fell 35 percent between 1980 and 1998, while the number of days of hospital care dropped an even larger 55 percent. Behind the decline is the growing use of outpatient surgery and home health care. The declines in discharges and days of care have occurred for both males and females, in every age group, and in every region of the country.

Not surprisingly, people aged 75 or older have the longest stays in hospitals. But their length of stay has dropped the most, falling more than five days between 1980 and 1998, from 11.4 to 6.3 days.

♦ Public protest against shortening hospital stays has slowed the decline somewhat, but the relentless need to cut costs will continue to push convalescent care into the home.

**Hospital stays have fallen the most for the oldest Americans**

*(average length of a hospital stay in days, by age, 1980 and 1998)*

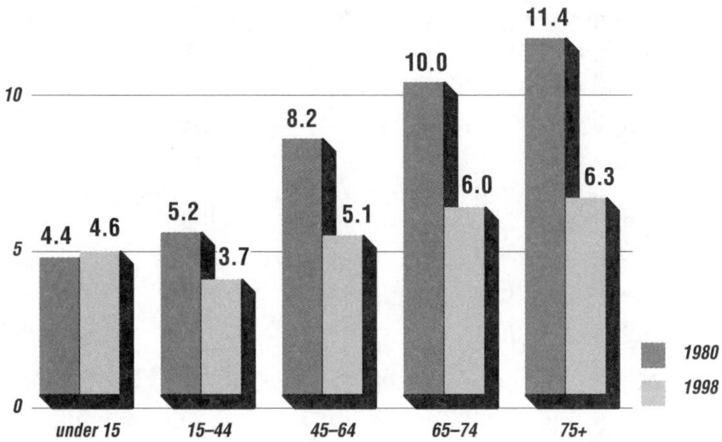

## Hospital Care, 1980 and 1998

*(hospital discharges and days of care per 1,000 persons, and average length of stay in days, for nonfederal short-stay hospitals by sex, age, and region, 1980 and 1998; percent change in rate and change in length of stay, 1980–98)*

| | *1998* | *1980* | *percent change 1980–98* |
|---|---|---|---|
| **Hospital discharges** | **103.0** | **158.5** | **–35.0%** |
| Females | 117.1 | 177.0 | –33.8 |
| Males | 89.0 | 140.3 | –36.6 |
| Under age 15 | 38.3 | 71.6 | –46.5 |
| Aged 15 to 44 | 85.1 | 150.1 | –43.3 |
| Aged 45 to 64 | 117.3 | 194.8 | –39.8 |
| Aged 65 to 74 | 267.6 | 315.8 | –15.3 |
| Aged 75 or older | 477.4 | 489.3 | –2.4 |
| Northeast | 112.9 | 147.6 | –23.5 |
| Midwest | 100.6 | 175.4 | –42.6 |
| South | 110.2 | 165.1 | –33.3 |
| West | 85.0 | 136.9 | –37.9 |
| **Days of hospital care** | **508.1** | **1,129.0** | **–55.0** |
| Females | 530.3 | 1,187.1 | –55.3 |
| Males | 487.2 | 1,076.0 | –54.7 |
| Under age 15 | 178.0 | 315.7 | –43.6 |
| Aged 15 to 44 | 316.1 | 786.8 | –59.8 |
| Aged 45 to 64 | 603.9 | 1,596.9 | –62.2 |
| Aged 65 to 74 | 1,596.1 | 3,147.0 | –49.3 |
| Aged 75 or older | 3,030.8 | 5,578.7 | –45.7 |
| Northeast | 627.2 | 1,204.7 | –47.9 |
| Midwest | 466.6 | 1,296.2 | –64.0 |
| South | 544.2 | 1,105.5 | –50.8 |
| West | 385.1 | 836.2 | –53.9 |

*(continued)*

*(continued from previous page)*

| | *1998* | *1980* | *change 1980–98* |
|---|---|---|---|
| **Average length of stay** | **4.9** | **7.1** | **–2.2** |
| Females | 4.5 | 6.7 | –2.2 |
| Males | 5.5 | 7.7 | –2.2 |
| Under age 15 | 4.6 | 4.4 | 0.2 |
| Aged 15 to 44 | 3.7 | 5.2 | –1.5 |
| Aged 45 to 64 | 5.1 | 8.2 | –3.1 |
| Aged 65 to 74 | 6.0 | 10.0 | –4.0 |
| Aged 75 or older | 6.3 | 11.4 | –5.1 |
| Northeast | 5.6 | 8.2 | –2.6 |
| Midwest | 4.6 | 7.4 | –2.8 |
| South | 4.9 | 6.7 | –1.8 |
| West | 4.5 | 6.1 | –1.6 |

*Source: National Center for Health Statistics,* Health, United States, *2000; calculations by New Strategist*

# Millions Use Home Health Services

## More than 2 million Americans received home health care services in 1996.

As hospital stays have shortened, the need for home health care services has grown. Among the 2.4 million Americans receiving home health care in 1996, 72 percent were aged 65 or older, two-thirds were women, and more than half had never married or were widowed. Home health care services are particularly important to people living alone, such as widows and the never married, because there's no one at home to help them manage after an illness.

The number of Americans being cared for through hospice programs stood at 59,400 in 1996. Hospice programs help the terminally ill spend their final days in comfort. As with home health care, most patients in hospice care are aged 65 or older—fully 78 percent in 1996.

♦ If the cost of home care can be controlled, this alternative to hospital stays is likely to surge in popularity over the next few decades.

## Home Health Care Patients by Age, Sex, and Marital Status, 1996

*(number and percent distribution of current home health care patients by age at admission, sex, and marital status, 1996)*

| | *number* | *percent distribution* |
|---|---|---|
| **Total patients** | **2,427,500** | **100.0%** |
| **Age** | | |
| Under age 45 | 347,400 | 14.3 |
| Aged 45 to 54 | 130,200 | 5.4 |
| Aged 55 to 64 | 187,600 | 7.7 |
| Aged 65 or older | 1,753,400 | 72.2 |
| Aged 65 to 69 | 213,600 | 8.8 |
| Aged 70 to 74 | 314,300 | 12.9 |
| Aged 75 to 79 | 416,200 | 17.1 |
| Aged 80 to 84 | 404,300 | 16.7 |
| Aged 85 or older | 404,900 | 16.7 |
| **Sex** | | |
| Female | 1,628,500 | 67.1 |
| Male | 798,700 | 32.9 |
| **Marital status** | | |
| Never married | 455,100 | 18.7 |
| Married | 703,000 | 29.0 |
| Divorced or separated | 100,100 | 4.1 |
| Widowed | 857,600 | 35.3 |
| Unknown | 311,600 | 12.8 |

*Source: National Center for Health Statistics,* An Overview of Home Health and Hospice Care Patients: 1996 National Home and Hospice Care Survey, *Advance Data, No. 297, 1998*

## Hospice Care Patients by Age, Sex, and Marital Status, 1996

*(number and percent distribution of current hospice care patients by age, sex, and marital status, 1996)*

| | number | percent distribution |
|---|---|---|
| **Total patients** | **59,400** | **100.0%** |
| **Age** | | |
| Under age 45 | 4,300 | 7.3 |
| Aged 45 to 54 | 2,700 | 4.5 |
| Aged 55 to 64 | 6,100 | 10.3 |
| Aged 65 or older | 46,100 | 77.7 |
| Aged 65 to 69 | 5,000 | 8.4 |
| Aged 70 to 74 | 9,600 | 16.2 |
| Aged 75 to 79 | 9,800 | 16.6 |
| Aged 80 to 84 | 9,100 | 15.2 |
| Aged 85 or older | 12,700 | 21.3 |
| **Sex** | | |
| Female | 32,700 | 55.1 |
| Male | 26,600 | 44.9 |
| **Marital status** | | |
| Never married | 5,000 | 8.5 |
| Married | 25,900 | 43.7 |
| Divorced or separated | 5,500 | 9.3 |
| Widowed | 19,100 | 32.2 |
| Unknown | 3,800 | 6.3 |

*Source: National Center for Health Statistics,* An Overview of Home Health and Hospice Care Patients: 1996 National Home and Hospice Care Survey, *Advance Data, No. 297, 1998*

# Majority of AIDS Victims Are Black, Hispanic

## Males account for 83 percent of people diagnosed with AIDS.

As of June 1999, 687,000 people had been diagnosed with AIDS. While new drug therapies have been successful in reducing the AIDS mortality rate, the number of AIDS cases continues to climb.

Men aged 30 to 39 account for the largest share of AIDS victims—38 percent of the total through June 1999. Those aged 40 to 49 account for another 22 percent. Overall, 6 out of 10 AIDS victims are men aged 30 to 49.

Blacks and Hispanics accounted for the 54 percent majority of people diagnosed with AIDS through June 1999. Among males aged 13 or older who have been diagnosed with AIDS, 49 percent are black or Hispanic. Among females, the figure is a much higher 76 percent. Among children under age 13, the proportion is an even larger 81 percent.

♦ Blacks and Hispanics are less likely than non-Hispanic whites to receive expensive new drug therapies for AIDS. Since blacks and Hispanics account for the majority of AIDS cases, the death rate may rise.

**Minorities dominate AIDS cases**

*(percent of people diagnosed with AIDS who are black or Hispanic, by sex and age, through June 1999)*

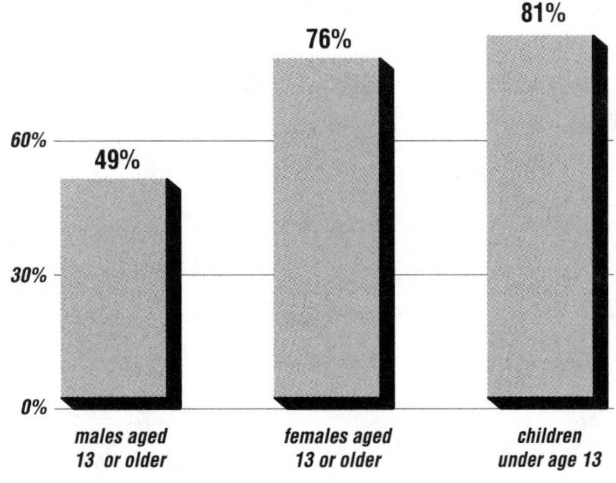

## AIDS Cases by Sex and Age, through June 1999

*(cumulative number and percent distribution of AIDS cases by age at diagnosis and sex for those aged 13 or older, through June 1999)*

| | *number* | *percent of total cases* |
|---|---:|---:|
| **Total cases** | **687,863** | **100.0%** |
| Under age 1 | 3,224 | 0.5 |
| Aged 1 to 12 | 4,969 | 0.7 |
| Aged 13 to 19 | 3,404 | 0.5 |
| Aged 20 to 29 | 116,390 | 16.9 |
| Aged 30 to 39 | 309,456 | 45.0 |
| Aged 40 to 49 | 177,641 | 25.8 |
| Aged 50 to 59 | 53,076 | 7.7 |
| Aged 60 or older | 19,703 | 2.9 |
| **Males** | | |
| Aged 13 or older | 570,211 | 82.9 |
| Aged 13 to 19 | 2,036 | 0.3 |
| Aged 20 to 29 | 92,540 | 13.5 |
| Aged 30 to 39 | 259,917 | 37.8 |
| Aged 40 to 49 | 153,154 | 22.3 |
| Aged 50 to 59 | 46,314 | 6.7 |
| Aged 60 or older | 16,250 | 2.4 |
| **Females** | | |
| Aged 13 or older | 109,459 | 15.9 |
| Aged 13 to 19 | 1,368 | 0.2 |
| Aged 20 to 29 | 23,850 | 3.5 |
| Aged 30 to 39 | 49,539 | 7.2 |
| Aged 40 to 49 | 24,487 | 3.6 |
| Aged 50 to 59 | 6,762 | 1.0 |
| Aged 60 or older | 3,453 | 0.5 |

*Source: National Center for Health Statistics,* Health, United States, *2000; calculations by New Strategist*

## AIDS Cases by Race and Hispanic Origin, through June 1999

*(cumulative number and percent distribution of AIDS cases among people aged 13 or older by sex, and among children under age 13, by race, and Hispanic origin; through June 1999)*

| | *total* | *male* | *female* | *children* |
|---|---|---|---|---|
| **Total cases** | **687,863** | **570,211** | **109,459** | **8,193** |
| White, non-Hispanic | 311,292 | 284,410 | 25,383 | 1499 |
| Black, non-Hispanic | 262,057 | 191,919 | 65,131 | 5007 |
| Hispanic | 106,454 | 86,988 | 17,868 | 1598 |
| American Indian | 2,034 | 1,670 | 335 | 29 |
| Asian or Pacific Islander | 5,104 | 4,475 | 583 | 46 |
| **Percent distribution by race** | | | | |
| **Total cases** | **100.0%** | **100.0%** | **100.0%** | **100.0%** |
| White, non-Hispanic | 45.3 | 49.9 | 23.2 | 18.3 |
| Black, non-Hispanic | 38.1 | 33.7 | 59.5 | 61.1 |
| Hispanic | 15.5 | 15.3 | 16.3 | 19.5 |
| American Indian | 0.3 | 0.3 | 0.3 | 0.4 |
| Asian or Pacific Islander | 0.7 | 0.8 | 0.5 | 0.6 |
| **Percent distribution by sex** | | | | |
| **Total cases** | **100.0%** | **82.9%** | **15.9%** | **1.2%** |
| White, non-Hispanic | 100.0 | 91.4 | 8.2 | 0.5 |
| Black, non-Hispanic | 100.0 | 73.2 | 24.9 | 1.9 |
| Hispanic | 100.0 | 81.7 | 16.8 | 1.5 |
| American Indian | 100.0 | 82.1 | 16.5 | 1.4 |
| Asian or Pacific Islander | 100.0 | 87.7 | 11.4 | 0.9 |

*Source: National Center for Health Statistics,* Health, United States, *2000; calculations by New Strategist*

# Heart Disease and Cancer Are Biggest Killers

## In 1999, more than half the deaths in the U.S. were caused by heart disease or cancer.

Heart disease and cancer each kill more than 500,000 Americans a year. Chronic diseases such as these are by far the leading causes of death in the United States. Other chronic diseases that make the top-ten list are cerebrovascular diseases, chronic obstructive pulmonary disease, diabetes, and chronic liver disease.

Only three causes of death in the top-ten list are not chronic conditions: accidents, pneumonia and influenza, and suicide. Accidental deaths have declined greatly over the past few years thanks to greater use of seat belts and stricter drunk driving laws. Pneumonia is a leading cause of death because it commonly strikes those with weakened immune systems—such as the frail elderly.

♦ Although medical science has made considerable progress in combating heart disease, it will remain the leading cause of death for years to come.

## Leading Causes of Death in the U.S., 1998

*(number and percent distribution of deaths for the 10 leading causes of death, 1998)*

| | | *number* | *percent* |
|---|---|---|---|
| | **All causes** | **2,337,256** | **100.0%** |
| 1. | Diseases of heart | 724,859 | 31.0 |
| 2. | Malignant neoplasms | 541,532 | 23.2 |
| 3. | Cerebrovascular diseases | 158,448 | 6.8 |
| 4. | Chronic obstructive pulmonary diseases and allied conditions | 112,584 | 4.8 |
| 5. | Accidents and adverse effects | 97,835 | 4.2 |
| 6. | Pneumonia and influenza | 91,871 | 3.9 |
| 7. | Diabetes mellitus | 64,751 | 2.8 |
| 8. | Suicide | 30,575 | 1.3 |
| 9. | Nephritis, nephrotic syndrome, and nephrosis | 26,182 | 1.1 |
| 10. | Chronic liver disease and cirrhosis | 25,192 | 1.1 |
| | All other causes | 463,427 | 19.8 |

*Source: National Center for Health Statistics,* Deaths: Final Data for 1998, *National Vital Statistics Reports, Vol. 48, No. 11, 2000; calculations by New Strategist*

# Life Expectancy Is at a Record High

## Americans born in 1998 can expect to live 76.7 years.

Since 1900, life expectancy at birth has climbed almost 30 years, from 47.3 to nearly 77 years. Life expectancy for males has increased 27.5 years while the gain for females has been a larger 31.2 years. At the beginning of the 20th century, newborn girls could expect to outlive newborn boys by just two years. Today, female life expectancy exceeds that of males by 5.7 years.

Many of the gains in life expectancy during the 20th century have been a consequence of declining death rates among infants and children. But life expectancy has grown even at older ages as medical science combats heart disease and other chronic ailments. Life expectancy at age 65 has increased from 11.9 to 17.8 years. Again, the gain for women has been greater than that for men. In 1900, women aged 65 or older could expect to outlive their male counterparts by just half a year. Today's 65-year-old woman can expect to live 19.2 more years, 3.2 years longer than a 65-year-old man.

♦ The costs of extending life at very old age are enormous, raising ethical questions about the equitable distribution of society's medical resources. Those questions will have to be addressed as the baby-boom generation ages.

## Life Expectancy by Age and Sex, 1900 to 1998

*(years of life remaining at birth and age 65 by sex, 1900 to 1998; change in years of life remaining, 1900–98)*

| | *total* | *males* | *females* |
|---|---|---|---|
| **At birth** | | | |
| 1998 | 76.7 | 73.8 | 79.5 |
| 1990 | 75.4 | 71.8 | 78.8 |
| 1980 | 73.7 | 70.0 | 77.4 |
| 1970 | 70.8 | 67.1 | 74.7 |
| 1960 | 69.7 | 66.6 | 73.1 |
| 1950 | 68.2 | 65.6 | 71.1 |
| 1900 | 47.3 | 46.3 | 48.3 |
| Change, 1900–98 | 29.4 | 27.5 | 31.2 |
| **At age 65** | | | |
| 1998 | 17.8 | 16.0 | 19.2 |
| 1990 | 17.2 | 15.1 | 18.9 |
| 1980 | 16.4 | 14.1 | 18.3 |
| 1970 | 15.2 | 13.1 | 17.0 |
| 1960 | 14.3 | 12.8 | 15.8 |
| 1950 | 13.9 | 12.8 | 15.0 |
| 1900 | 11.9 | 11.5 | 12.2 |
| Change, 1900–98 | 5.9 | 4.5 | 7.0 |

*Source: National Center for Health Statistics,* Health, United States, *2000; calculations by New Strategist*

CHAPTER

# 3

# Housing Trends

♦ **Homeownership is at a record high.**

Between 1990 and 2000, householders aged 65 or older made the biggest gain in homeownership.

♦ **Non-Hispanic whites are most likely to own a home.**

Among the nation's 69 million homeowners in 1999, 82 percent were non-Hispanic white.

♦ **The Midwest has the highest homeownership rate.**

Seventy-three percent of households in the Midwest own their home. In the West, only 62 percent do.

♦ **American homes have a median of 1,730 square feet of living space.**

Homes are growing larger as our record level of affluence boosts demand for space.

♦ **Most householders are happy with their home.**

When asked to rate their housing unit on a scale of 1 (worst) to 10 (best), 68 percent of householders rate their home an 8 or higher.

♦ **The median value of owned homes stood at $108,300 in 1999.**

Only 19 percent of homes are worth $200,000 or more, and just 8 percent are valued at $300,000 or more.

# Homeownership Is at a Record High

## Between 1990 and 2000, homeownership rates rose in every age group.

The percentage of householders who own their home is at a record high, thanks to the middle-aging of the population and the booming economy. By 2000, more than two out of three householders owned their home.

Between 1990 and 2000, householders aged 65 or older made the biggest gain in homeownership. Behind the increase was the entry of a more affluent generation into the 65-or-older age group. Homeownership levels off at 80 percent among householders aged 55 or older.

Married couples account for 64 percent of the nation's homeowners. Eighty-two percent of couples owned their home in 2000, the highest rate of homeownership among all household types. Every type of household experienced an increase in homeownership between 1990 and 2000.

♦ Since older Americans are most likely to own their home, the homeownership rate will continue to climb along with the aging of the population.

**Homeownership rate is highest among older Americans**

*(percent of householders who own their home, by age, 2000)*

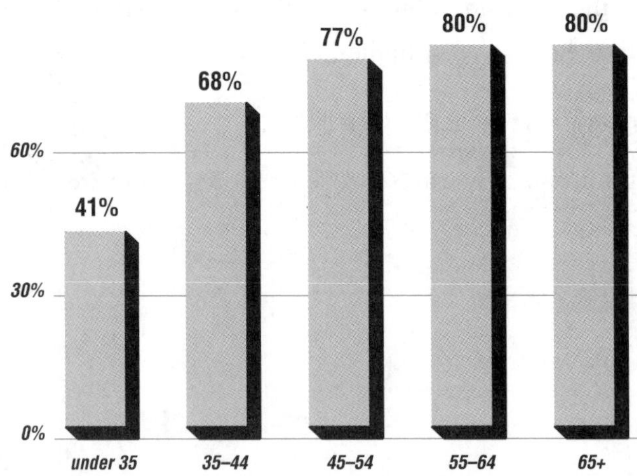

## Homeownership Rate by Age and Household Type, 1990 and 2000

*(percent of householders who own their home by age and household type, 1990 and 2000; percentage point change, 1990–2000)*

| | *2000* | *1990* | *percentage point change 1990–2000* |
|---|---|---|---|
| **Total households** | **67.4%** | **63.9%** | **3.5** |
| **Age of householder** | | | |
| Under age 35 | 40.8 | 38.5 | 2.3 |
| Aged 35 to 44 | 67.9 | 66.3 | 1.6 |
| Aged 45 to 54 | 76.5 | 75.2 | 1.3 |
| Aged 55 to 64 | 80.3 | 79.3 | 1.0 |
| Aged 65 or older | 80.4 | 76.3 | 4.1 |
| **Type of household** | | | |
| Married couples | 82.4 | 78.1 | 4.3 |
| Female householder, no spouse present | 49.1 | 44.0 | 5.1 |
| Male householder, no spouse present | 57.5 | 55.2 | 2.3 |
| Women living alone | 58.1 | 53.6 | 4.5 |
| Men living alone | 47.4 | 42.4 | 5.0 |

*Source: Bureau of the Census, data from the Housing Vacancy Surveys; Internet site <www.census.gov/hhes/www/housing/hvs/annual00/ann00t15.html>; calculations by New Strategist*

## Age of Householder by Homeownership Status, 2000

*(number and percent distribution of householders by age and homeownership status, 2000; numbers in thousands)*

| | total | owner | renter |
|---|---|---|---|
| **Total households** | **105,719** | **71,249** | **34,470** |
| Under age 35 | 24,922 | 10,161 | 14,761 |
| Aged 35 to 44 | 24,211 | 16,429 | 7,782 |
| Aged 45 to 54 | 20,998 | 16,058 | 4,940 |
| Aged 55 to 64 | 13,817 | 11,100 | 2,717 |
| Aged 65 or older | 21,771 | 17,501 | 4,270 |
| **Percent distribution by homeownership status** | | | |
| **Total households** | **100.0%** | **67.4%** | **32.6%** |
| Under age 35 | 100.0 | 40.8 | 59.2 |
| Aged 35 to 44 | 100.0 | 67.9 | 32.1 |
| Aged 45 to 54 | 100.0 | 76.5 | 23.5 |
| Aged 55 to 64 | 100.0 | 80.3 | 19.7 |
| Aged 65 or older | 100.0 | 80.4 | 19.6 |
| **Percent distribution by age** | | | |
| **Total households** | **100.0%** | **100.0%** | **100.0%** |
| Under age 35 | 23.6 | 14.3 | 42.8 |
| Aged 35 to 44 | 22.9 | 23.1 | 22.6 |
| Aged 45 to 54 | 19.9 | 22.5 | 14.3 |
| Aged 55 to 64 | 13.1 | 15.6 | 7.9 |
| Aged 65 or older | 20.6 | 24.6 | 12.4 |

*Source: Bureau of the Census, data from the Housing Vacancy Surveys, <www.census.gov/hhes/www/housing/hvs/historic/histt15.html>; calculations by New Strategist*

## Type of Household by Homeownership Status, 2000

*(number and percent distribution of households by type of household and homeownership status, 2000; numbers in thousands)*

| | *total* | *owner* | *renter* |
|---|---|---|---|
| **Total households** | **105,719** | **71,249** | **34,470** |
| Married couples | 55,294 | 45,535 | 9,759 |
| Female householder, no spouse present | 12,798 | 6,283 | 6,515 |
| Male householder, no spouse present | 4,224 | 2,427 | 1,797 |
| Women living alone | 15,715 | 9,135 | 6,580 |
| Men living alone | 11,573 | 5,480 | 6,093 |
| **Percent distribution by homeownership status** | | | |
| **Total households** | **100.0%** | **67.4%** | **32.6%** |
| Married couples | 100.0 | 82.4 | 17.6 |
| Female householder, no spouse present | 100.0 | 49.1 | 50.9 |
| Male householder, no spouse present | 100.0 | 57.5 | 42.5 |
| Women living alone | 100.0 | 58.1 | 41.9 |
| Men living alone | 100.0 | 47.4 | 52.6 |
| **Percent distribution by household type** | | | |
| **Total households** | **100.0%** | **100.0%** | **100.0%** |
| Married couples | 52.3 | 63.9 | 28.3 |
| Female householder, no spouse present | 12.1 | 8.8 | 18.9 |
| Male householder, no spouse present | 4.0 | 3.4 | 5.2 |
| Women living alone | 14.9 | 12.8 | 19.1 |
| Men living alone | 10.9 | 7.7 | 17.7 |

*Note: Numbers will not add to total because not all household types are shown.*
*Source: Bureau of the Census, data from the Housing Vacancy Surveys, <www.census.gov/hhes/www/housing/hvs/historic/histt15.html>; calculations by New Strategist*

# Non-Hispanic Whites Are Most Likely to Own Their Home

## Hispanics are least likely to be homeowners.

Among the nation's 69 million homeowners in 1999, 82 percent were non-Hispanic white. Only 9 percent of homeowners were black, and 6 percent were Hispanic.

Homeownership is much more common for non-Hispanic whites than for other racial and ethnic groups because white incomes are higher. Three out of four non-Hispanic white householders own their home compared with 51 percent of Asians, 46 percent of blacks and Native Americans, and 45 percent of Hispanics.

Among the nation's 34 million renters, only 59 percent are non-Hispanic white. Twenty percent are black and 15 percent are Hispanic.

♦ Black incomes are growing rapidly, making homeownership more affordable. The black homeownership rate may surpass 50 percent within the decade.

**The majority of non-Hispanic whites and Asians are homeowners**

*(percent of householders who own their home, by race and Hispanic origin, 1999)*

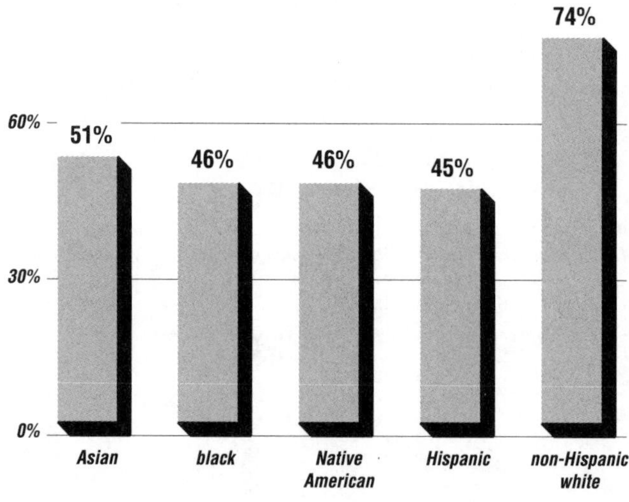

## Race and Hispanic Origin of Householders by Homeownership Status, 1999

*(number and percent distribution of households by race and Hispanic origin of householder, by homeownership status, 1999; numbers in thousands)*

| | *total* | *owner* | *renter* |
|---|---|---|---|
| **Total households** | **102,803** | **68,796** | **34,007** |
| Asian | 3,049 | 1,566 | 1,483 |
| Black | 12,936 | 6,013 | 6,923 |
| Native American | 666 | 306 | 360 |
| Hispanic | 9,041 | 4,087 | 4,955 |
| Non-Hispanic white | 76,891 | 56,716 | 20,175 |
| **Percent distribution by homeownership status** | | | |
| **Total households** | **100.0%** | **66.9%** | **33.1%** |
| Asian | 100.0 | 51.4 | 48.6 |
| Black | 100.0 | 46.5 | 53.5 |
| Native American | 100.0 | 45.9 | 54.1 |
| Hispanic | 100.0 | 45.2 | 54.8 |
| Non-Hispanic white | 100.0 | 73.8 | 26.2 |
| **Percent distribution by race and Hispanic origin** | | | |
| **Total households** | **100.0%** | **100.0%** | **100.0%** |
| Asian | 3.0 | 2.3 | 4.4 |
| Black | 12.6 | 8.7 | 20.4 |
| Native American | 0.6 | 0.4 | 1.1 |
| Hispanic | 8.8 | 5.9 | 14.6 |
| Non-Hispanic white | 74.8 | 82.4 | 59.3 |

*Note: Numbers will not add to total because Hispanics may be of any race.*
*Source: Bureau of the Census,* American Housing Survey for the United States in 1999*; calculations by New Strategist*

# Homeownership Is Highest in the Midwest

## Householders in suburbs and nonmetro areas are most likely to own their home.

The Midwest has the highest homeownership rate in the nation as 73 percent of householders in the region own their home. Housing prices are often much higher than average in the West, and the region has the lowest homeownership rate, at 62 percent.

More than half the nation's homeowners live in the suburbs. Three out of four suburban householders are homeowners, as are an equal share of householders in nonmetropolitan areas. In the central cities, only 50 percent of householders own their home.

By state, the highest homeownership rate is found in Michigan, at 77 percent. The lowest rate (except for the District of Columbia) is in New York, where only 53 percent of households own their home. Most states made gains in homeownership between 1990 and 2000. The biggest gain occurred in Missouri where the homeownership rate rose 10 percentage points during those years.

Among the largest metropolitan areas, homeownership is highest in Grand Rapids-Muskegon-Holland, Michigan, where 80 percent of households own their home. Only 34 percent of households own their home in the New York metropolitan area. Homeownership rates rose more than 10 percentage points in several metropolitan areas between 1990 and 2000, including Buffalo, Charlotte, Cincinnati, Denver, Indianapolis, Kansas City, Minneapolis, Nashville, and St. Louis.

♦ As the population is aging, the homeownership rate should continue to rise in most states and metropolitan areas during the next few decades.

## Region of Residence by Homeownership Status, 2000

*(number and percent distribution of households by region of residence and homeownership status, 2000; numbers in thousands)*

| | *total* | *owner* | *renter* |
|---|---|---|---|
| **Total households** | **105,719** | **71,249** | **34,470** |
| Northeast | 20,149 | 12,780 | 7,369 |
| Midwest | 24,604 | 17,864 | 6,740 |
| South | 37,959 | 26,402 | 11,557 |
| West | 23,008 | 14,204 | 8,804 |
| **Percent distribution by homeownership status** | | | |
| **Total households** | **100.0%** | **67.4%** | **32.6%** |
| Northeast | 100.0 | 63.4 | 36.6 |
| Midwest | 100.0 | 72.6 | 27.4 |
| South | 100.0 | 69.6 | 30.4 |
| West | 100.0 | 61.7 | 38.3 |
| **Percent distribution by region** | | | |
| **Total households** | **100.0%** | **100.0%** | **100.0%** |
| Northeast | 19.1 | 17.9 | 21.4 |
| Midwest | 23.3 | 25.1 | 19.6 |
| South | 35.9 | 37.1 | 33.5 |
| West | 21.8 | 19.9 | 25.5 |

*Source: Bureau of the Census, data from the Housing Vacancy Survey; Internet site <www.census.gov/hhes/www/housing/hvs/historic/histtab9.html>; calculations by New Strategist*

## Metropolitan Residence by Homeownership Status, 1999

*(number and percent distribution of households by metropolitan residence and homeownership status, 1999; numbers in thousands)*

| | *total* | *owner* | *renter* |
|---|---|---|---|
| **Total households** | **102,803** | **68,796** | **34,007** |
| In metropolitan areas | 79,911 | 52,527 | 28,385 |
| In central cities | 31,131 | 15,512 | 15,619 |
| In suburbs | 48,780 | 36,015 | 12,766 |
| Outside metropolitan areas | 22,891 | 17,269 | 5,622 |
| **Percent distribution by homeownership status** | | | |
| **Total households** | **100.0%** | **66.9%** | **33.1%** |
| In metropolitan areas | 100.0 | 65.7 | 35.5 |
| In central cities | 100.0 | 49.8 | 50.2 |
| In suburbs | 100.0 | 73.8 | 26.2 |
| Outside metropolitan areas | 100.0 | 75.4 | 24.6 |
| **Percent distribution by metropolitan residence** | | | |
| **Total households** | **100.0%** | **100.0%** | **100.0%** |
| In metropolitan areas | 77.7 | 76.4 | 83.5 |
| In central cities | 30.3 | 22.5 | 45.9 |
| In suburbs | 47.4 | 52.4 | 37.5 |
| Outside metropolitan areas | 22.3 | 25.1 | 16.5 |

*Source: Bureau of the Census,* American Housing Survey for the United States in 1999*; calculations by New Strategist*

## Homeownership Rate by State, 1990 and 2000

*(percent of householders who own their home by state, 1990 and 2000; percentage point change, 1990–2000)*

| | *2000* | *1990* | *percentage point change 1990–2000* |
|---|---|---|---|
| **United States** | **67.4%** | **63.9%** | **3.5%** |
| Alabama | 73.2 | 68.4 | 4.8 |
| Alaska | 66.4 | 58.4 | 8.0 |
| Arizona | 68.0 | 64.5 | 3.5 |
| Arkansas | 68.9 | 67.8 | 1.1 |
| California | 57.1 | 53.8 | 3.3 |
| Colorado | 68.3 | 59.0 | 9.3 |
| Connecticut | 70.0 | 67.9 | 2.1 |
| Delaware | 72.0 | 67.7 | 4.3 |
| District of Columbia | 41.9 | 36.4 | 5.5 |
| Florida | 68.4 | 65.1 | 3.3 |
| Georgia | 69.8 | 64.3 | 5.5 |
| Hawaii | 55.2 | 55.5 | –0.3 |
| Idaho | 70.5 | 69.4 | 1.1 |
| Illinois | 67.9 | 63.0 | 4.9 |
| Indiana | 74.9 | 67.0 | 7.9 |
| Iowa | 75.2 | 70.7 | 4.5 |
| Kansas | 69.3 | 69.0 | 0.3 |
| Kentucky | 73.4 | 65.8 | 7.6 |
| Louisiana | 68.1 | 67.8 | 0.3 |
| Maine | 76.5 | 74.2 | 2.3 |
| Maryland | 69.9 | 64.9 | 5.0 |
| Massachusetts | 59.9 | 58.6 | 1.3 |
| Michigan | 77.2 | 72.3 | 4.9 |
| Minnesota | 76.1 | 68.0 | 8.1 |
| Mississippi | 75.2 | 69.4 | 5.8 |
| Missouri | 74.2 | 64.0 | 10.2 |
| Montana | 70.2 | 69.1 | 1.1 |
| Nebraska | 70.2 | 67.3 | 2.9 |
| Nevada | 64.0 | 55.8 | 8.2 |
| New Hampshire | 69.2 | 65.0 | 4.2 |
| New Jersey | 66.2 | 65.0 | 1.2 |

*(continued)*

*(continued from previous page)*

| | 2000 | 1990 | percentage point change 1990–2000 |
|---|---|---|---|
| New Mexico | 73.7% | 68.6% | 5.1% |
| New York | 53.4 | 53.3 | 0.1 |
| North Carolina | 71.1 | 69.0 | 2.1 |
| North Dakota | 70.7 | 67.2 | 3.5 |
| Ohio | 71.3 | 68.7 | 2.6 |
| Oklahoma | 72.7 | 70.3 | 2.4 |
| Oregon | 65.3 | 64.4 | 0.9 |
| Pennsylvania | 74.7 | 73.8 | 0.9 |
| Rhode Island | 61.5 | 58.5 | 3.0 |
| South Carolina | 76.5 | 71.4 | 5.1 |
| South Dakota | 71.2 | 66.2 | 5.0 |
| Tennessee | 70.9 | 68.3 | 2.6 |
| Texas | 63.8 | 59.7 | 4.1 |
| Utah | 72.7 | 70.1 | 2.6 |
| Vermont | 68.7 | 72.6 | –3.9 |
| Virginia | 73.9 | 69.8 | 4.1 |
| Washington | 63.6 | 61.8 | 1.8 |
| West Virginia | 75.9 | 72.0 | 3.9 |
| Wisconsin | 71.8 | 68.3 | 3.5 |
| Wyoming | 71.0 | 68.9 | 2.1 |

*Source: Bureau of the Census, data from the Housing Vacancy Surveys, Internet site <www.census.gov/hhes/www/housing/hvs/annual00/ann00t13.html>; calculations by New Strategist*

# Homeownership Rate by Metropolitan Area, 1990 and 2000

*(percent of householders who own their home in the 75 largest metropolitan areas, 1990 and 2000; percentage point change 1990–2000)*

| | *2000* | *1990* | *percentage point change 1990–2000* |
|---|---|---|---|
| **Total metropolitan areas** | **65.5%** | **61.3%** | **4.2%** |
| Akron, OH | 63.6 | – | – |
| Albany–Schenectady–Troy, NY | 71.1 | 69.9 | 1.2 |
| Atlanta, GA | 67.7 | 61.0 | 6.7 |
| Austin–San Marcos, TX | 54.7 | – | – |
| Baltimore, MD | 68.2 | 63.0 | 5.2 |
| Bergen–Passaic, NJ | 63.2 | 61.4 | 1.8 |
| Birmingham, AL | 69.9 | 65.7 | 4.2 |
| Boston, MA–NH | 58.7 | 55.0 | 3.7 |
| Buffalo, NY | 72.5 | 61.4 | 11.1 |
| Charlotte–Gastonia–Rock Hill, NC–SC | 75.8 | 64.8 | 11.0 |
| Chicago, IL | 66.4 | 56.9 | 9.5 |
| Cincinnati, OH–KY–IN | 72.5 | 57.9 | 14.6 |
| Cleveland–Lorain–Elyria, OH | 72.0 | 64.5 | 7.5 |
| Columbus, OH | 61.6 | 61.8 | –0.2 |
| Dallas, TX | 62.4 | 54.0 | 8.4 |
| Dayton–Springfield, OH | 62.8 | 67.6 | –4.8 |
| Denver, CO | 68.2 | 55.7 | 12.5 |
| Detroit, MI | 75.3 | 71.4 | 3.9 |
| Fresno, CA | 56.2 | – | – |
| Ft. Lauderdale, FL | 76.3 | 68.2 | 8.1 |
| Ft. Worth–Arlington, TX | 62.4 | 61.4 | 1.0 |
| Grand Rapids–Muskegon–Holland, MI | 80.1 | – | – |
| Greensboro–Winston-Salem–High Point, NC | 68.9 | 68.2 | 0.7 |
| Greenville–Spartanburg–Anderson, SC | 76.5 | – | – |
| Hartford, CT | 69.7 | 65.5 | 4.2 |
| Honolulu, HI | 56.8 | 52.9 | 3.9 |
| Houston, TX | 53.6 | 53.9 | –0.3 |
| Indianapolis, IN | 67.5 | 55.3 | 12.2 |
| Jacksonville, FL | 70.4 | 61.0 | 9.4 |
| Kansas City, MO–KS | 73.6 | 61.7 | 11.9 |
| Las Vegas, NV–AZ | 61.9 | – | – |

*(continued)*

*(continued from previous page)*

| | 2000 | 1990 | percentage point change 1990–2000 |
|---|---|---|---|
| Los Angeles–Long Beach, CA | 49.0% | 47.9% | 1.1% |
| Louisville, KY–IN | 70.2 | 69.3 | 0.9 |
| Memphis, TN–AR–MS | 61.1 | 60.8 | 0.3 |
| Miami, FL | 56.2 | 47.9 | 8.3 |
| Middlesex–Somerset–Hunterton, NJ | 69.7 | 72.4 | –2.7 |
| Milwaukee–Waukesha, WI | 67.5 | 72.2 | –4.7 |
| Minneapolis–St. Paul, MN–WI | 73.1 | 62.5 | 10.6 |
| Monmouth–Ocean, NJ | 83.5 | 76.1 | 7.4 |
| Nashville, TN | 67.9 | 57.3 | 10.6 |
| Nassau–Suffolk, NY | 79.7 | 81.8 | –2.1 |
| New Orleans, LA | 64.6 | 59.9 | 4.7 |
| New York, NY | 34.1 | 34.0 | 0.1 |
| Newark, NJ | 60.3 | 60.7 | –0.4 |
| Norfolk–Virginia Beach–Newport News, VA | 70.1 | 62.6 | 7.5 |
| Oakland, CA | 60.3 | 54.2 | 6.1 |
| Oklahoma City, OK | 70.5 | 65.1 | 5.4 |
| Omaha, NE–IA | 69.6 | – | – |
| Orange County, CA | 62.3 | 55.1 | 7.2 |
| Orlando, FL | 60.5 | 66.8 | –6.3 |
| Philadelphia, PA–NJ | 74.7 | 73.6 | 1.1 |
| Phoenix–Mesa, AZ | 70.7 | 64.3 | 6.4 |
| Pittsburgh, PA | 71.8 | 71.9 | –0.1 |
| Portland–Vancouver, OR–WA | 62.1 | 66.5 | –4.4 |
| Providence–Fall River–Pawtucket, RI | 61.2 | 59.5 | 1.7 |
| Raleigh–Durham–Chapel Hill, NC | 65.6 | – | – |
| Richmond–Petersburg, VA | 74.1 | 69.4 | 1.3 |
| Rochester, NY | 65.2 | 65.9 | 5.9 |
| Sacramento, CA | 61.6 | 53.5 | 8.6 |
| Salt Lake City–Ogden, UT | 72.1 | 73.6 | –12.4 |
| San Antonio, TX | 66.6 | 57.9 | 7.7 |
| San Bernardino–Riverside, CA | 62.6 | 60.0 | 14.1 |
| San Diego, CA | 59.1 | 51.2 | 14.0 |
| San Francisco, CA | 48.9 | 48.8 | 12.8 |
| San Jose, CA | 60.9 | 63.2 | 8.9 |
| Scranton–Wilkes-Barre–Hazelton, PA | 71.8 | – | – |

*(continued)*

*(continued from previous page)*

| | 2000 | 1990 | percentage point change 1990–2000 |
|---|---|---|---|
| Seattle–Bellevue–Everett, WA | 63.4% | 64.8% | –2.2% |
| St. Louis, MO–IL | 70.6 | 59.4 | –0.3 |
| Syracuse, NY | 59.2 | – | – |
| Tampa–St. Petersburg–Clearwater, FL | 70.0 | 67.0 | –6.1 |
| Tucson, AZ | 60.5 | – | – |
| Tulsa, OK | 65.2 | – | – |
| Ventura, CA | 66.2 | – | – |
| Washington, DC–MD–VA–WV | 67.1 | 63.2 | –4.0 |
| West Palm Beach–Boca Raton, FL | 71.3 | – | – |

*Note: Because many metropolitan area boundaries were different in 2000 and 1990, some of the changes in homeownership rate are due to geographic shifts; (–) means data not available.*
*Source: Bureau of the Censu+s, data from the Housing Vacancy Surveys, Internet site <www.census.gov/hhes/www/housing/hvs/annual00/ann00t14.html>; calculations by New Strategist*

# Most Americans Live in Single-Family Homes

## More than half of homeowners have two or more bathrooms.

America's housing statistics reveal the nation's affluence. The great majority of householders live in single-family detached homes—63 percent in 1999. Only 24 percent dwell in apartments, while 7 percent live in duplexes and another 7 percent in mobile homes. Not surprisingly, renters are far more likely than homeowners to live in apartments.

American homes have a median of 1,730 square feet of living space. The majority of homeowners have six or more rooms to spread out in, while most renters have four or fewer rooms. Fully 76 percent of homeowners have three or more bedrooms, and 54 percent have two or more bathrooms.

Many homes include a room devoted to business. In 1999, 22 percent of homeowners and 13 percent of renters had a room they used for business.

♦ The homes of Americans are growing larger as our record level of affluence boosts demand for space.

### Two bathrooms are a must for most homeowners

*(percent distribution of occupied housing units by number of bathrooms and homeownership status, 1999)*

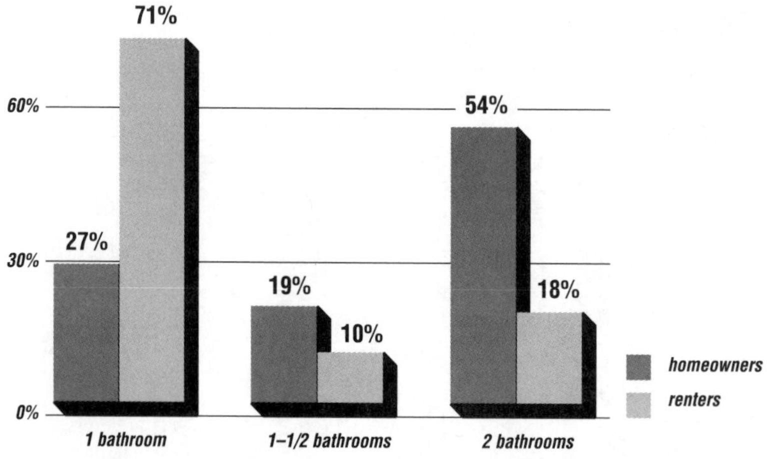

## Units in Structure by Homeownership Status, 1999

*(number and percent distribution of occupied housing units by number of units in structure and homeownership status, 1999; numbers in thousands)*

| | *total* | *owner* | *renter* |
|---|---|---|---|
| **Total occupied housing units** | **102,803** | **68,796** | **34,007** |
| 1, detached | 64,536 | 56,471 | 8,065 |
| 1, attached | 6,963 | 3,499 | 3,465 |
| 2 to 4 units | 8,572 | 1,466 | 7,015 |
| 5 to 9 units | 4,847 | 469 | 4,378 |
| 10 to 19 units | 4,416 | 357 | 4,059 |
| 20 to 49 units | 3,343 | 341 | 3,002 |
| 50 or more units | 3,341 | 544 | 2,797 |
| Mobile home | 6,785 | 5,649 | 1,136 |
| **Percent distribution by number of units in structure** | | | |
| **Total occupied housing units** | **100.0%** | **100.0%** | **100.0%** |
| 1, detached | 62.8 | 82.1 | 23.7 |
| 1, attached | 6.8 | 5.1 | 10.2 |
| 2 to 4 units | 8.3 | 2.1 | 20.6 |
| 5 to 9 units | 4.7 | 0.7 | 12.9 |
| 10 to 19 units | 4.3 | 0.5 | 11.9 |
| 20 to 49 units | 3.3 | 0.5 | 8.8 |
| 50 or more units | 3.2 | 0.8 | 8.2 |
| Mobile home | 6.6 | 8.2 | 3.3 |

*Source: Bureau of the Census,* American Housing Survey for the United States in 1999*; calculations by New Strategist*

## Size of Housing Unit by Homeownership Status, 1999

*(number and percent distribution of occupied housing units by size of unit and homeownership status, 1999; numbers in thousands)*

| | number | | | percent distribution | | |
|---|---|---|---|---|---|---|
| | *total* | *owner* | *renter* | *total* | *owner* | *renter* |
| **Total occupied housing units** | **102,803** | **68,796** | **34,007** | **100.0%** | **100.0%** | **100.0%** |
| **Number of rooms** | | | | | | |
| 1 room | 407 | 6 | 401 | 0.4 | 0.0 | 1.2 |
| 2 rooms | 1,014 | 70 | 943 | 1.0 | 0.1 | 2.8 |
| 3 rooms | 8,973 | 996 | 7,977 | 8.7 | 1.4 | 23.5 |
| 4 rooms | 19,390 | 7,322 | 12,068 | 18.9 | 10.6 | 35.5 |
| 5 rooms | 23,733 | 16,395 | 7,338 | 23.1 | 23.8 | 21.6 |
| 6 rooms | 21,662 | 18,174 | 3,488 | 21.1 | 26.4 | 10.3 |
| 7 rooms | 13,457 | 12,314 | 1,143 | 13.1 | 17.9 | 3.4 |
| 8 rooms | 7,985 | 7,583 | 401 | 7.8 | 11.0 | 1.2 |
| 9 rooms | 3,565 | 3,427 | 137 | 3.5 | 5.0 | 0.4 |
| 10 or more rooms | 2,618 | 2,508 | 110 | 2.5 | 3.6 | 0.3 |
| **Number of bedrooms** | | | | | | |
| None | 858 | 45 | 814 | 0.8 | 0.1 | 2.4 |
| 1 bedroom | 11,986 | 1,731 | 10,255 | 11.7 | 2.5 | 30.2 |
| 2 bedrooms | 29,166 | 14,422 | 14,744 | 28.4 | 21.0 | 43.4 |
| 3 bedrooms | 43,103 | 36,370 | 6,733 | 41.9 | 52.9 | 19.8 |
| 4 or more bedrooms | 17,689 | 16,228 | 1,461 | 17.2 | 23.6 | 4.3 |
| **Complete bathrooms** | | | | | | |
| None | 676 | 263 | 413 | 0.7 | 0.4 | 1.2 |
| 1 bathroom | 42,838 | 18,650 | 24,188 | 41.7 | 27.1 | 71.1 |
| 1 and 1/2 bathrooms | 16,189 | 12,743 | 3,446 | 15.7 | 18.5 | 10.1 |
| 2 or more bathrooms | 43,100 | 37,140 | 5,960 | 41.9 | 54.0 | 17.5 |
| **With rooms used for business** | **19,663** | **15,282** | **4,382** | **19.1** | **22.2** | **12.9** |
| Median square footage of unit | 1,730 | 1,795 | 1,293 | – | – | – |
| Median size of lot (acres) | 0.34 | 0.38 | 0.22 | – | – | – |

*Note: Size of lot does not include multiunit properties; (–) means not applicable.*
*Source: Bureau of the Census,* American Housing Survey for the United States in 1999*; calculations by New Strategist*

# Piped Gas Is the Most Popular Heating Fuel

## Few households depend on alternative sources of energy for heat.

In 1999, the 51 percent majority of households used piped gas as their primary heating fuel. Piped gas is the most popular heating fuel among both homeowners and renters. Fifty-four percent of homeowners depend on piped gas, as do 46 percent of renters.

Electricity is the second most popular heating fuel, used by 26 percent of homeowners and 40 percent of renters. Together, electricity and piped gas are the primary sources of heat for 82 percent of the nation's homes.

Fewer than 2 percent of homes use wood as their primary heating fuel, homeowners being more likely to do so than renters. Just 19,000 homes use solar energy as their primary heating fuel—fewer than 0.5 percent of households.

♦ While many people believe alternative sources of energy hold great promise, cost and convenience of traditional heating fuels have convinced most householders to opt for the status quo.

## House Heating Fuel by Homeownership Status, 1999

*(number and percent distribution of occupied housing units by main house heating fuel and homeownership status, 1999; numbers in thousands)*

| | *total* | *owner* | *renter* |
|---|---|---|---|
| **Total housing units with heating fuel** | **102,259** | **68,590** | **33,669** |
| Electricity | 31,142 | 17,770 | 13,372 |
| Piped gas | 52,366 | 37,031 | 15,335 |
| Bottled gas | 5,905 | 4,954 | 951 |
| Fuel oil | 10,026 | 6,665 | 3,361 |
| Kerosene or other liquid fuel | 724 | 509 | 216 |
| Coal or coke | 168 | 147 | 21 |
| Wood | 1,703 | 1,433 | 270 |
| Solar energy | 19 | 11 | 8 |
| Other | 205 | 68 | 136 |
| **Percent distribution by type of heating fuel** | | | |
| **Total housing units with heating fuel** | **100.0%** | **100.0%** | **100.0%** |
| Electricity | 30.5 | 25.9 | 39.7 |
| Piped gas | 51.2 | 54.0 | 45.5 |
| Bottled gas | 5.8 | 7.2 | 2.8 |
| Fuel oil | 9.8 | 9.7 | 10.0 |
| Kerosene or other liquid fuel | 0.7 | 0.7 | 0.6 |
| Coal or coke | 0.2 | 0.2 | 0.1 |
| Wood | 1.7 | 2.1 | 0.8 |
| Solar energy | 0.0 | 0.0 | 0.0 |
| Other | 0.2 | 0.1 | 0.4 |

*Source: Bureau of the Census,* American Housing Survey for the United States in 1999; *calculations by New Strategist*

# Amenities Are Many in American Homes

## Conveniences once limited to the wealthy are now commonly available.

To find evidence of the affluence of the United States, look no further than inside the American household. The average household is equipped with an array of amenities and conveniences that at one time only the rich could afford.

More than 90 percent of households have a telephone, which is no surprise. More interesting is that 81 percent of households have a porch, deck, balcony, or patio. Washing machines and clothes dryers are in three-quarters of all homes and almost universally present in owned homes. The majority of households also have a garage or carport, a dishwasher, and central air conditioning.

Among homeowners, the majority have a separate dining room. Forty-one percent have two or more living or recreation rooms, and 43 percent have a usable fireplace.

♦ As household incomes have grown, Americans have spent their money on bigger and better homes outfitted with appliances and electronics.

**The majority of households are centrally air conditioned**

*(percent of households with selected amenities, 1999)*

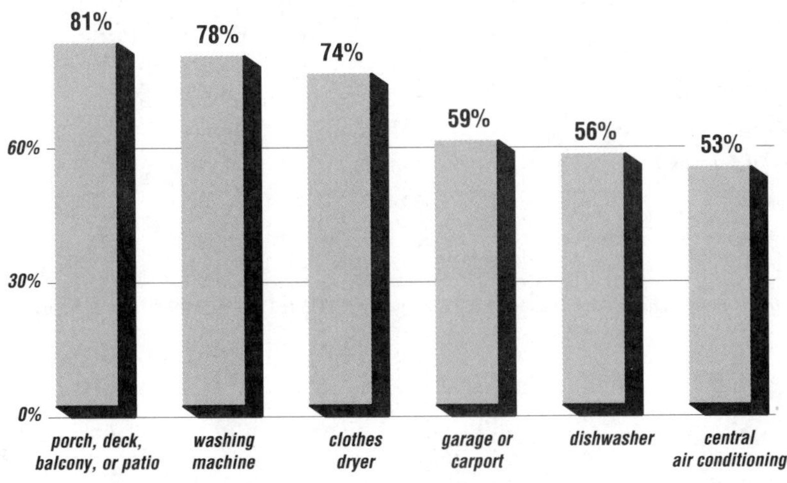

## Amenities of Housing Unit by Homeownership Status, 1999

*(number and percent distribution of occupied housing units by amenities in unit and homeownership status, 1999; numbers in thousands)*

| | total | owner | renter |
|---|---|---|---|
| **Total occupied housing units** | **102,803** | **68,796** | **34,007** |
| Telephone | 98,449 | 66,658 | 31,791 |
| Porch, deck, balcony, or patio | 83,498 | 61,556 | 21,942 |
| Washing machine | 80,543 | 65,140 | 15,403 |
| Clothes dryer | 76,454 | 62,738 | 13,716 |
| Garage or carport | 60,553 | 49,941 | 10,612 |
| Dishwasher | 57,703 | 44,904 | 12,799 |
| Central air conditioning | 54,878 | 41,167 | 13,711 |
| Separate dining room | 45,844 | 36,968 | 8,875 |
| Disposal in kitchen sink | 45,345 | 31,659 | 13,685 |
| Usable fireplace | 33,269 | 29,243 | 4,026 |
| Two or more living/recreation rooms | 30,360 | 28,203 | 2,157 |
| **Percent with amenity** | | | |
| **Total occupied housing units** | **100.0%** | **100.0%** | **100.0%** |
| Telephone | 95.8 | 96.9 | 93.5 |
| Porch, deck, balcony, or patio | 81.2 | 89.5 | 64.5 |
| Washing machine | 78.3 | 94.7 | 45.3 |
| Clothes dryer | 74.4 | 91.2 | 40.3 |
| Garage or carport | 58.9 | 72.6 | 31.2 |
| Dishwasher | 56.1 | 65.3 | 37.6 |
| Central air conditioning | 53.4 | 59.8 | 40.3 |
| Separate dining room | 44.6 | 53.7 | 26.1 |
| Disposal in kitchen sink | 44.1 | 46.0 | 40.2 |
| Usable fireplace | 32.4 | 42.5 | 11.8 |
| Two or more living/recreation rooms | 29.5 | 41.0 | 6.3 |

*Source: Bureau of the Census,* American Housing Survey for the United States in 1999*; calculations by New Strategist*

# Most Are Satisfied with Home and Neighborhood

## Homeowners are happier than renters, but few renters are dissatisfied.

When asked how they rate their housing unit on a scale of 1 (worst) to 10 (best), 68 percent of householders rated their home an 8 or higher. More than one in four gave it a perfect 10. Homeowners rated their homes more highly than renters. While 75 percent of homeowners rated their home an 8 or higher, only 54 percent of renters were that positive. Thirty percent of homeowners, but only 17 percent of renters, gave their home a 10. Although few rated their home below 5, those who did were mostly renters.

The patterns were the same when householders were asked to rate their neighborhood. Sixty-six percent of all householders rated their neighborhood an 8 or higher, including 71 percent of homeowners and 55 percent of renters. Among the few householders who rated their neighborhood at 4 or below, the 60 percent majority were renters.

♦ Householders are likely to rate their homes and neighborhoods highly because most of those who are unhappy find new places to live.

## Opinion of Housing Unit by Homeownership Status, 1999

*(number and percent distribution of occupied housing units by householder's opinion of housing unit and homeownership status, 1999; numbers in thousands)*

| | *total* | *owner* | *renter* |
|---|---|---|---|
| **Total occupied housing units** | **102,803** | **68,796** | **34,007** |
| 1 (worst) | 561 | 168 | 392 |
| 2 | 363 | 121 | 241 |
| 3 | 737 | 228 | 509 |
| 4 | 1,302 | 395 | 907 |
| 5 | 6,376 | 2,743 | 3,633 |
| 6 | 5,564 | 2,746 | 2,817 |
| 7 | 13,902 | 8,044 | 5,858 |
| 8 | 28,184 | 19,376 | 8,807 |
| 9 | 14,516 | 10,978 | 3,539 |
| 10 (best) | 27,147 | 21,207 | 5,940 |
| **Percent distribution by homeownership status** | | | |
| **Total occupied housing units** | **100.0%** | **66.9%** | **33.1%** |
| 1 (worst) | 100.0 | 29.9 | 69.9 |
| 2 | 100.0 | 33.3 | 66.4 |
| 3 | 100.0 | 30.9 | 69.1 |
| 4 | 100.0 | 30.3 | 69.7 |
| 5 | 100.0 | 43.0 | 57.0 |
| 6 | 100.0 | 49.4 | 50.6 |
| 7 | 100.0 | 57.9 | 42.1 |
| 8 | 100.0 | 68.7 | 31.2 |
| 9 | 100.0 | 75.6 | 24.4 |
| 10 (best) | 100.0 | 78.1 | 21.9 |

*(continued)*

*(continued from previous page)*

| | *total* | *owner* | *renter* |
|---|---|---|---|
| **Percent distribution by opinion of housing unit** | | | |
| **Total occupied housing units** | **100.0%** | **100.0%** | **100.0%** |
| 1 (worst) | 0.5 | 0.2 | 1.2 |
| 2 | 0.4 | 0.2 | 0.7 |
| 3 | 0.7 | 0.3 | 1.5 |
| 4 | 1.3 | 0.6 | 2.7 |
| 5 | 6.2 | 4.0 | 10.7 |
| 6 | 5.4 | 4.0 | 8.3 |
| 7 | 13.5 | 11.7 | 17.2 |
| 8 | 27.4 | 28.2 | 25.9 |
| 9 | 14.1 | 16.0 | 10.4 |
| 10 (best) | 26.4 | 30.8 | 17.5 |

*Note: Numbers will not add to total because not reported is not shown.*
*Source: Bureau of the Census,* American Housing Survey for the United States in 1999*; calculations by New Strategist*

## Opinion of Neighborhood by Homeownership Status, 1999

*(number and percent distribution of occupied housing units by householder's opinion of neighborhood and homeownership status, 1999; numbers in thousands)*

| | *total* | *owner* | *renter* |
|---|---|---|---|
| **Total occupied housing units** | **102,803** | **68,796** | **34,007** |
| 1 (worst) | 885 | 354 | 531 |
| 2 | 657 | 248 | 409 |
| 3 | 1,151 | 459 | 692 |
| 4 | 1,621 | 650 | 971 |
| 5 | 7,051 | 3,617 | 3,434 |
| 6 | 5,974 | 3,172 | 2,802 |
| 7 | 13,313 | 8,266 | 5,047 |
| 8 | 26,599 | 18,421 | 8,179 |
| 9 | 15,707 | 11,655 | 4,062 |
| 10 (best) | 25,215 | 18,838 | 6,377 |
| **Percent distribution by homeownership status** | | | |
| **Total occupied housing units** | **100.0%** | **66.9%** | **33.1%** |
| 1 (worst) | 100.0 | 40.0 | 60.0 |
| 2 | 100.0 | 37.7 | 62.3 |
| 3 | 100.0 | 39.9 | 60.1 |
| 4 | 100.0 | 40.1 | 59.9 |
| 5 | 100.0 | 51.3 | 48.7 |
| 6 | 100.0 | 53.1 | 46.9 |
| 7 | 100.0 | 62.1 | 37.9 |
| 8 | 100.0 | 69.3 | 30.7 |
| 9 | 100.0 | 74.2 | 25.9 |
| 10 (best) | 100.0 | 74.7 | 25.3 |

*(continued)*

*(continued from previous page)*

| | total | owner | renter |
|---|---|---|---|
| **Percent distribution by opinion of neighborhood** | | | |
| **Total occupied housing units** | **100.0%** | **100.0%** | **100.0%** |
| 1 (worst) | 0.9 | 0.5 | 1.6 |
| 2 | 0.6 | 0.4 | 1.2 |
| 3 | 1.1 | 0.7 | 2.0 |
| 4 | 1.6 | 0.9 | 2.9 |
| 5 | 6.9 | 5.3 | 10.1 |
| 6 | 5.8 | 4.6 | 8.2 |
| 7 | 13.0 | 12.0 | 14.8 |
| 8 | 25.9 | 26.8 | 24.1 |
| 9 | 15.3 | 16.9 | 11.9 |
| 10 (best) | 24.5 | 27.4 | 18.8 |

*Note: Numbers will not add to total because not reported is not shown.*
*Source: Bureau of the Census,* American Housing Survey for the United States in 1999*; calculations by New Strategist*

# Many People Live near Open Space and Woodlands

## Few are bothered by crime, street noise, or other problems.

Of the 103 million householders in the United States, 79 percent report there are single-family detached houses within 300 feet of their home—84 percent of homeowners and 67 percent of renters. More than two out of three renters report apartment buildings within 300 feet. Forty-one percent of homeowners and 34 percent of renters report having open space, parks, woods, farm, or ranchland close by.

Many householders have commercial or institutional buildings within 300 feet of their home—16 percent of homeowners and 45 percent of renters. Just 4 percent report industries or factories nearby, while a larger 13 percent say a four-lane highway, railroad, or airport is within 300 feet of their home.

Few householders report bothersome neighborhood problems. The biggest problem is street noise or traffic, reported by 10 percent of homeowners and 15 percent of renters. Crime ranks second but is bothersome to only 6 percent of homeowners and 12 percent of renters. People are the third biggest neighborhood problem, bothering 4 percent of householders nationwide.

♦ Despite media reports of rampant crime in urban neighborhoods, few householders say crime is bothersome where they live.

## Neighborhood Characteristics by Homeownership Status, 1999

*(number and percent distribution of occupied housing units by description of area within 300 feet, by homeownership status, 1999; numbers in thousands)*

| | *total* | *owner* | *renter* |
|---|---|---|---|
| **Total occupied housing units** | **102,803** | **68,796** | **34,007** |
| Single-family detached houses | 80,921 | 58,082 | 22,840 |
| Single-family attached | 12,933 | 6,279 | 6,654 |
| 1- to 3-story multiunit | 23,824 | 6,934 | 16,889 |
| 4- to 6-story multiunit | 5,349 | 1,256 | 4,093 |
| 7-or-more-story multiunit | 2,812 | 622 | 2,190 |
| Mobile homes | 11,530 | 9,011 | 2,518 |
| Commerical/institutional | 26,614 | 11,329 | 15,285 |
| Industrial or factories | 3,996 | 1,775 | 2,222 |
| Open space, park, woods, farm, or ranch | 39,742 | 28,217 | 11,525 |
| Four-or-more-lane highway, railroad, or airport | 13,859 | 6,712 | 7,147 |
| Waterfront property | 2,631 | 2,082 | 549 |
| **Percent with characteristic** | | | |
| **Total occupied housing units** | **100.0%** | **100.0%** | **100.0%** |
| Single-family detached houses | 78.7 | 84.4 | 67.2 |
| Single-family attached | 12.6 | 9.1 | 19.6 |
| 1- to 3-story multiunit | 23.2 | 10.1 | 49.7 |
| 4- to 6-story multiunit | 5.2 | 1.8 | 12.0 |
| 7-or-more-story multiunit | 2.7 | 0.9 | 6.4 |
| Mobile homes | 11.2 | 13.1 | 7.4 |
| Commerical/institutional | 25.9 | 16.5 | 44.9 |
| Industrial or factories | 3.9 | 2.6 | 6.5 |
| Open space, park, woods, farm, or ranch | 38.7 | 41.0 | 33.9 |
| Four-or-more-lane highway, railroad, or airport | 13.5 | 9.8 | 21.0 |
| Waterfront property | 2.6 | 3.0 | 1.6 |

*Note: Numbers will not add to total because more than one category may apply to unit.*
*Source: Bureau of the Census,* American Housing Survey for the United States in 1999*; calculations by New Strategist*

## Neighborhood Problems by Homeownership Status, 1999

*(number and percent distribution of occupied housing units by neighborhood conditions considered bothersome by householder, by homeownership status, 1999; numbers in thousands)*

| | *total* | *owner* | *renter* |
|---|---|---|---|
| **Total occupied housing units** | **102,803** | **68,796** | **34,007** |
| Street noise or traffic | 11,624 | 6,632 | 4,992 |
| Crime | 8,384 | 4,435 | 3,949 |
| People | 4,494 | 2,736 | 1,758 |
| Odors | 3,983 | 2,250 | 1,733 |
| Noise | 2,659 | 1,502 | 1,157 |
| Litter or housing deterioration | 1,821 | 1,159 | 662 |
| Poor city or county services | 847 | 532 | 316 |
| Undesirable commercial/institutional/industrial | 759 | 485 | 275 |
| **Percent with problem** | | | |
| **Total occupied housing units** | **100.0%** | **100.0%** | **100.0%** |
| Street noise or traffic | 11.3 | 9.6 | 14.7 |
| Crime | 8.2 | 6.4 | 11.6 |
| People | 4.4 | 4.0 | 5.2 |
| Odors | 3.9 | 3.3 | 5.1 |
| Noise | 2.6 | 2.2 | 3.4 |
| Litter or housing deterioration | 1.8 | 1.7 | 1.9 |
| Poor city or county services | 0.8 | 0.8 | 0.9 |
| Undesirable commercial/institutional/industrial | 0.7 | 0.7 | 0.8 |

*Note: Numbers will not add to total because not reported is not shown and more than one category may apply to unit.*
*Source: Bureau of the Census,* American Housing Survey for the United States in 1999*; calculations by New Strategist*

# Housing Costs Are Similar for Owners and Renters

## But renters pay a much larger share of their income for housing.

Median monthly housing costs for owners and renters are remarkably similar—$581 for homeowners and $580 for renters in 1999. But because homeowners have higher incomes than renters, housing absorbs only 17 percent of homeowners' income versus 28 percent of renters'.

Homeowners pay more than renters for utilities, in part because their homes tend to be larger. Homeowners pay a median of $67 per month for electricity versus $45 paid by renters. Owners pay $29 a month for water while renters pay $21.

Among homeowners with a mortgage, the average monthly payment for principal and interest is $611. Homeowners also pay a median of $93 a month for real estate taxes.

♦ On average, the housing costs of homeowners are low because many have paid off their mortgage and own their home free and clear.

**Many homeowners pay little per month for housing**

*(percent distribution of homeowners by total monthly housing costs, 1999)*

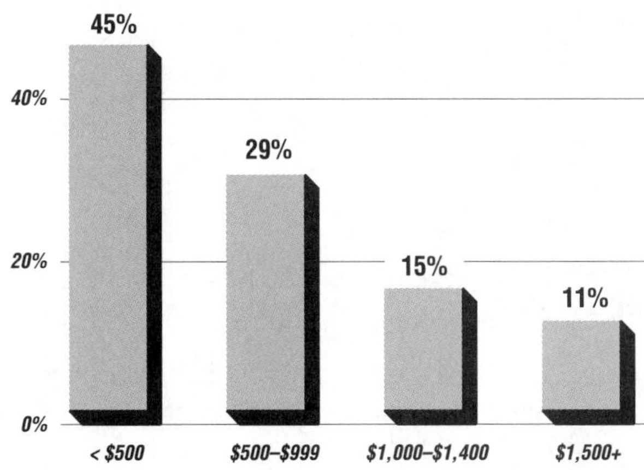

## Monthly Housing Costs by Homeownership Status, 1999

*(total and median monthly housing costs, monthly housing costs as a percent of current income, and median monthly amount paid for selected services and utilities, by homeownership status, 1999)*

| | *total* | *owner* | *renter* |
|---|---|---|---|
| **Total occupied housing units** | **102,803** | **68,796** | **34,007** |
| **Total monthly housing cost** | | | |
| Less than $250 | 16,831 | 14,135 | 2,696 |
| $250 to $499 | 25,557 | 16,529 | 9,028 |
| $500 to $799 | 26,137 | 12,879 | 13,257 |
| $800 to $999 | 10,886 | 7,205 | 3,681 |
| $1,000 to $1,249 | 7,945 | 6,166 | 1,779 |
| $1,250 to $1,499 | 4,892 | 4,240 | 652 |
| $1,500 or more | 8,455 | 7,642 | 813 |
| No cash rent | 2,100 | – | 2,100 |
| Median (excludes no cash rent) | $581 | $581 | $580 |
| Monthly housing cost as a percent of current income | 20% | 17% | 28% |
| **Median monthly cost paid** | | | |
| For electricity | $60 | $67 | $45 |
| For piped gas | 40 | 43 | 28 |
| For fuel oil | 56 | 58 | 44 |
| For property insurance | 35 | 37 | 18 |
| For water | 28 | 29 | 21 |
| For trash removal | 16 | 17 | 15 |
| For principal and interest | – | 611 | – |
| For real estate taxes | – | 93 | – |

*Note: Median costs are for householders with that expense; (–) means not applicable.*
*Source: Bureau of the Census,* American Housing Survey for the United States: 1999, *Current Housing Reports, H150/99, 2000; calculations by New Strategist*

# Median Value of Owned Homes Is More Than $100,000

## Current value greatly exceeds purchase price.

The median value of the homes owned by Americans stood at $108,300 in 1999. Only 19 percent of homes are worth $200,000 or more, and just 8 percent are valued at $300,000 or more by their owners.

The current value of owned homes is much greater than their $61,244 median purchase price. Only 7 percent of homeowners paid $200,000 or more for their house, and fewer than 3 percent paid more than $300,000. Four percent of homeowners received their home as an inheritance or gift.

The largest share of homeowners (48 percent) used savings for the down payment on their current home. Thirty-two percent came up with the down payment by selling their previous home. Only 2 percent received the down payment as a gift, while 7 percent did not have to make a down payment.

♦ Many people have seen the value of their home rise rapidly as the large baby-boom generation entered the housing market. Housing values may not rise as fast in the next few decades as the smaller generation X buys homes.

**Housing equity has grown rapidly for some homeowners**

*(median current value and purchase price of owned homes, 1999)*

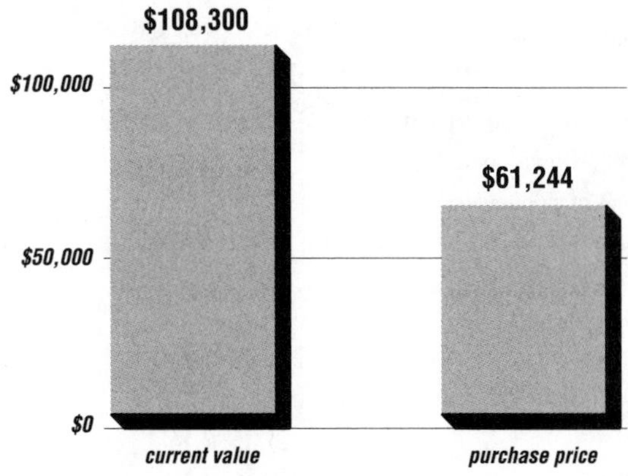

## Housing Value and Purchase Price for Homeowners, 1999

*(number and percent distribution of homeowners by value of home, purchase price, and major source of down payment, 1999; numbers in thousands)*

| | *number* | *percent* |
|---|---|---|
| **Total homeowners** | **68,796** | **100.0%** |
| **Value of home** | | |
| Under $50,000 | 10,665 | 15.5 |
| $50,000 to $99,999 | 20,994 | 30.5 |
| $100,000 to $149,999 | 15,217 | 22.1 |
| $150,000 to $199,999 | 9,129 | 13.3 |
| $200,000 to $249,999 | 4,642 | 6.7 |
| $250,000 to $299,999 | 2,749 | 4.0 |
| $300,000 or more | 5399 | 7.8 |
| Median value | $108,300 | – |
| **Purchase price** | | |
| Home purchased or built | 65,334 | 95.0 |
| Under $50,000 | 25,748 | 37.4 |
| $50,000 to $99,999 | 16,903 | 24.6 |
| $100,000 to $149,999 | 8,150 | 11.8 |
| $150,000 to $199,999 | 4,471 | 6.5 |
| $200,000 to $249,999 | 2,002 | 2.9 |
| $250,000 to $299,999 | 1,080 | 1.6 |
| $300,000 or more | 1,836 | 2.7 |
| Received as inheritance or gift | 2,414 | 3.5 |
| Median purchase price | 61,244 | – |
| **Major source of down payment** | | |
| Sale of previous home | 20,622 | 31.6 |
| Savings of cash on hand | 31,552 | 48.3 |
| Sale of other investment | 603 | 0.9 |
| Borrowing, other than mortgage on this property | 2,279 | 3.5 |
| Inheritance or gift | 1,508 | 2.3 |
| Land where built used for financing | 523 | 0.8 |
| Other | 2,361 | 3.6 |
| No down payment | 4,318 | 6.6 |

*Note: Numbers may not add to total because not reported is not shown; (–) means not applicable.*
*Source: Bureau of the Census,* American Housing Survey for the United States in 1999, *Current Housing Reports, H150/99, 2000; calculations by New Strategist*

CHAPTER

# 4

# Income Trends

♦ **One in eight households had an income of $100,000 or more in 1999.**

The proportion of households with incomes of $100,000 or more stands at 12 percent—the highest level of affluence ever seen in the United States.

♦ **For most householders, incomes are at a record high.**

But householders under age 25 and aged 35 to 44 still lag the income peaks they reached years ago.

♦ **The median income of black married couples now exceeds $50,000.**

The median income of black couples is 89 percent as high as the median for all married couples.

♦ **College-educated householders had a median income of $69,804 in 1999.**

The median income of households headed by college graduates is 66 percent higher than the national average.

♦ **Women have a long way to go before they catch up to men.**

Among full-time workers, women earn 73 percent as much as men—a median of $27,370 for women versus $37,574 for men in 1999.

♦ **Among the nation's 32 million poor, only 46 percent are non-Hispanic white.**

Eight percent of non-Hispanic whites are poor versus 24 percent of blacks and 23 percent of Hispanics.

# Americans Have Never Been Better Off

## One in eight households has an income of $100,000 or more.

The proportion of households with incomes of $100,000 or more reached 12 percent in 1999—the highest level of affluence ever seen in the United States. Only 5.5 percent of households had incomes of $100,000 or more in 1980, after adjusting for inflation. Fully 41 percent of households had incomes of $50,000 or more in 1999—again, the highest proportion ever recorded.

At the other end of the income scale, the share of households with incomes below $25,000 stood at 31 percent in 1999, down from 33 percent in 1990 and 35 percent in 1980.

Behind the rising affluence of American households is the baby-boom generation, now in its peak earning years. Highly educated, dual-income couples in their forties and fifties are benefiting from their investment in higher education and their commitment to the two-earner lifestyle.

♦ The proportion of households with incomes of $100,000 or more should climb for another decade as the entire baby-boom generation fills the peak-earning age groups.

**Record-breaking affluence**

*(percent of households with incomes of $100,000 or more, 1980–99; in 1999 dollars)*

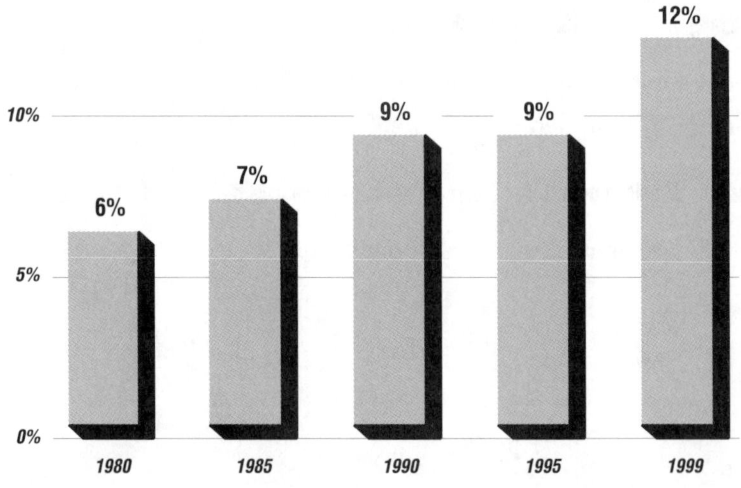

## Distribution of Households by Income, 1980 to 1999

*(number and percent distribution of households by income, 1980–99, in 1999 dollars; households in thousands as of the following year)*

| | total households | total | under $15,000 | $15,000–$24,999 | $25,000–$34,999 | $35,000–$49,999 | $50,000–$74,999 | $75,000–$99,999 | $100,000 or more |
|---|---|---|---|---|---|---|---|---|---|
| 1999 | 104,705 | 100.0% | 16.5% | 14.1% | 12.7% | 15.8% | 18.4% | 10.3% | 12.3% |
| 1998 | 103,874 | 100.0 | 17.7 | 13.8 | 13.1 | 15.8 | 18.7 | 9.8 | 11.1 |
| 1997 | 102,528 | 100.0 | 18.4 | 14.6 | 12.9 | 16.3 | 18.3 | 9.4 | 10.3 |
| 1996 | 101,018 | 100.0 | 19.1 | 14.6 | 13.4 | 16.1 | 18.3 | 9.0 | 9.5 |
| 1995 | 99,627 | 100.0 | 18.8 | 15.0 | 13.6 | 16.6 | 18.0 | 8.9 | 9.0 |
| 1994 | 98,990 | 100.0 | 19.8 | 15.3 | 13.4 | 16.3 | 17.6 | 8.6 | 9.0 |
| 1993 | 97,107 | 100.0 | 20.2 | 14.9 | 13.9 | 16.2 | 17.7 | 8.6 | 8.5 |
| 1992 | 96,426 | 100.0 | 20.1 | 15.1 | 13.2 | 16.9 | 18.2 | 8.4 | 8.1 |
| 1991 | 95,669 | 100.0 | 19.5 | 14.8 | 13.7 | 16.9 | 18.3 | 8.8 | 8.1 |
| 1990 | 94,312 | 100.0 | 18.4 | 14.3 | 13.7 | 17.5 | 18.5 | 9.1 | 8.5 |
| 1989 | 93,347 | 100.0 | 18.1 | 14.2 | 13.3 | 16.9 | 19.1 | 9.2 | 9.2 |
| 1988 | 92,830 | 100.0 | 18.5 | 14.3 | 12.8 | 17.3 | 19.2 | 9.3 | 8.5 |
| 1987 | 91,124 | 100.0 | 18.9 | 14.4 | 13.0 | 16.9 | 19.2 | 9.3 | 8.3 |
| 1986 | 89,479 | 100.0 | 18.9 | 14.6 | 13.3 | 17.1 | 19.0 | 9.1 | 8.0 |
| 1985 | 88,458 | 100.0 | 19.6 | 15.1 | 13.6 | 17.6 | 18.4 | 8.8 | 7.0 |
| 1984 | 86,789 | 100.0 | 19.6 | 15.2 | 13.8 | 17.8 | 18.4 | 8.4 | 6.6 |
| 1983 | 85,290 | 100.0 | 20.0 | 15.5 | 14.4 | 17.5 | 18.5 | 7.9 | 6.1 |
| 1982 | 83,918 | 100.0 | 20.5 | 15.4 | 14.3 | 18.2 | 18.1 | 7.7 | 5.7 |
| 1981 | 83,527 | 100.0 | 20.3 | 15.9 | 13.6 | 18.3 | 18.8 | 7.8 | 5.4 |
| 1980 | 82,368 | 100.0 | 19.8 | 15.3 | 13.9 | 18.4 | 19.4 | 7.6 | 5.5 |

*Source: Bureau of the Census,* Money Income in the United States: 1999, *Current Population Reports, P60-209, 2000*

# The Rich Get Richer

## The poorest households receive a smaller share of income today than in 1980.

If you add up all the money going to American households, including earnings, interest, dividends, Social Security benefits, and so on, the result is called "aggregate household income." Year-to-year changes in how this aggregate is divided among the nation's households can reveal trends in income inequality. The numbers on the next page show how much aggregate income each fifth of households receives, from poorest to richest. It also shows how much accrues to the 5 percent of households with the highest incomes.

Since 1980, incomes have become more unequal, but this trend appears to have halted in the mid-1990s. The percentage of aggregate income the richest 5 percent of households receive rose from 15.8 percent in 1980 to a peak of 21.7 percent in 1997, then fell slightly to 21.5 percent in 1999. The percentage the bottom fifth of households receives fell from 4.3 to 3.6 percent between 1980 and 1999.

♦ A rise or fall in the amount of income accruing to each fifth of households reveals trends in the distribution of income among households, not the economic well-being of individual households. Households headed by young adults, for example, typically start out at the bottom, then rise through the income distribution as the young gain job experience and earn bigger paychecks.

## Distribution of Aggregate Household Income, 1980 to 1999

*(total number of households and percent of income received by each fifth and top 5 percent of households, 1980-99; households in thousands as of the following year)*

| | total households | total | bottom fifth | second fifth | third fifth | fourth fifth | top fifth | top 5 percent |
|---|---|---|---|---|---|---|---|---|
| 1999 | 104,705 | 100.0% | 3.6% | 8.9% | 14.9% | 23.2% | 49.4% | 21.5% |
| 1998 | 103,874 | 100.0 | 3.6 | 9.0 | 15.0 | 23.2 | 49.2 | 21.4 |
| 1997 | 102,528 | 100.0 | 3.6 | 8.9 | 15.0 | 23.2 | 49.4 | 21.7 |
| 1996 | 101,018 | 100.0 | 3.7 | 9.0 | 15.1 | 23.3 | 49.0 | 21.4 |
| 1995 | 99,627 | 100.0 | 3.7 | 9.1 | 15.2 | 23.3 | 48.7 | 21.0 |
| 1994 | 98,990 | 100.0 | 3.6 | 8.9 | 15.0 | 23.4 | 49.1 | 21.2 |
| 1993 | 97,107 | 100.0 | 3.6 | 9.0 | 15.1 | 23.5 | 48.9 | 21.0 |
| 1992 | 96,426 | 100.0 | 3.8 | 9.4 | 15.8 | 24.2 | 46.9 | 18.6 |
| 1991 | 95,669 | 100.0 | 3.8 | 9.6 | 15.9 | 24.2 | 46.5 | 18.1 |
| 1990 | 94,312 | 100.0 | 3.9 | 9.6 | 15.9 | 24.0 | 46.6 | 18.6 |
| 1989 | 93,347 | 100.0 | 3.8 | 9.5 | 15.8 | 24.0 | 46.8 | 18.9 |
| 1988 | 92,830 | 100.0 | 3.8 | 9.6 | 16.0 | 24.3 | 46.3 | 18.3 |
| 1987 | 91,124 | 100.0 | 3.8 | 9.6 | 16.1 | 24.3 | 46.2 | 18.2 |
| 1986 | 89,479 | 100.0 | 3.9 | 9.7 | 16.2 | 24.5 | 45.7 | 17.5 |
| 1985 | 88,458 | 100.0 | 4.0 | 9.7 | 16.3 | 24.6 | 45.3 | 17.0 |
| 1984 | 86,789 | 100.0 | 4.1 | 9.9 | 16.4 | 24.7 | 44.9 | 16.5 |
| 1983 | 85,290 | 100.0 | 4.1 | 10.0 | 16.5 | 24.7 | 44.7 | 16.4 |
| 1982 | 83,918 | 100.0 | 4.1 | 10.1 | 16.6 | 24.7 | 44.5 | 16.2 |
| 1981 | 83,527 | 100.0 | 4.2 | 10.2 | 16.8 | 25.0 | 43.8 | 15.6 |
| 1980 | 82,368 | 100.0 | 4.3 | 10.3 | 16.9 | 24.9 | 43.7 | 15.8 |

*Source: Bureau of the Census, Internet site <www.census.gov/hhes/income/histinc/h02.html>*

# For Most Age Groups, Incomes Are at Record High

## Householders under age 25 and aged 35 to 44 are still below the peak, however.

Household income growth has varied significantly by age over the past two decades. Between 1980 and 1999, the youngest householders have seen their incomes fall 2 percent, after adjusting for inflation. In contrast, householders aged 65 or older have experienced the fastest income growth—up 28 percent. In 1980, the median income of the oldest householders was just 69 percent of the median of the youngest householders. By 1999, the figure had climbed to 91 percent.

While most households now enjoy record-breaking incomes, those under age 25 and those aged 35 to 44 are struggling to match the income peaks they reached years ago. For householders aged 35 to 44, median income grew only 3.5 percent during the 1990s, just half the 6.9 percent gain made by the average household. Their median income in 1999 was still below the peak reached in the late 1980s. Householders under age 25 saw their incomes grow a substantial 9.7 percent during the 1990s, but they have yet to exceed the income peak they reached in 1980.

♦ The incomes of the elderly have grown rapidly because a more affluent generation has replaced the less-affluent in the older age groups.

### Gains in 1990s vary by age

*(percent change in median household income by age, 1990–99)*

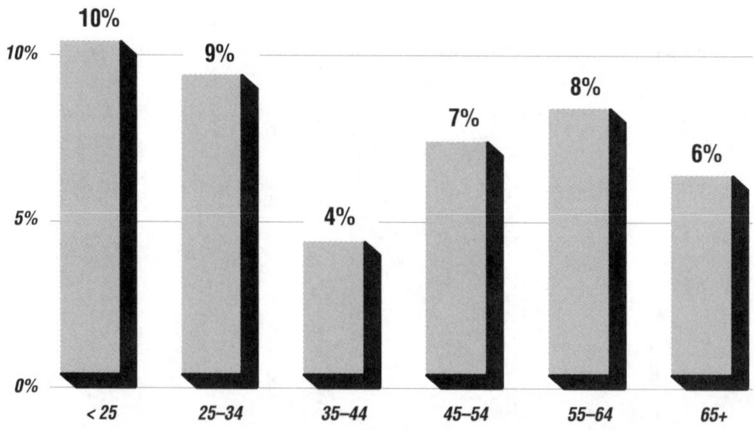

## Median Household Income by Age of Householder, 1980 to 1999

*(median household income by age of householder, 1980–99; percent change for selected years; in 1999 dollars)*

| | total households | under 25 | 25 to 34 | 35 to 44 | 45 to 54 | 55 to 64 | 65 or older |
|---|---|---|---|---|---|---|---|
| 1999 | $40,816 | $25,171 | $42,174 | $50,873 | $56,917 | $44,597 | $22,812 |
| 1998 | 39,744 | 24,084 | 40,954 | 49,521 | 55,344 | 44,120 | 22,209 |
| 1997 | 38,411 | 23,441 | 39,625 | 48,121 | 53,847 | 42,928 | 21,550 |
| 1996 | 37,686 | 22,763 | 38,107 | 47,166 | 53,592 | 42,276 | 20,650 |
| 1995 | 37,251 | 22,934 | 37,934 | 47,515 | 52,536 | 41,625 | 20,875 |
| 1994 | 36,270 | 21,741 | 37,267 | 46,840 | 53,129 | 39,606 | 20,342 |
| 1993 | 36,019 | 22,290 | 36,065 | 47,111 | 53,274 | 38,594 | 20,466 |
| 1992 | 36,379 | 20,974 | 37,095 | 47,324 | 52,766 | 40,365 | 20,347 |
| 1991 | 36,850 | 22,400 | 37,726 | 48,132 | 53,516 | 40,737 | 20,764 |
| 1990 | 38,168 | 22,947 | 38,698 | 49,153 | 53,437 | 41,255 | 21,485 |
| 1989 | 38,837 | 25,075 | 40,069 | 50,564 | 55,788 | 41,407 | 21,189 |
| 1988 | 38,341 | 23,997 | 40,007 | 51,478 | 53,815 | 40,704 | 21,016 |
| 1987 | 38,220 | 24,120 | 39,547 | 51,601 | 54,563 | 40,418 | 21,181 |
| 1986 | 37,845 | 23,272 | 39,367 | 49,839 | 54,206 | 40,701 | 21,045 |
| 1985 | 36,568 | 23,301 | 38,840 | 48,100 | 51,440 | 39,571 | 20,522 |
| 1984 | 35,942 | 22,493 | 38,058 | 47,758 | 50,535 | 38,634 | 20,523 |
| 1983 | 34,934 | 22,417 | 36,374 | 46,298 | 50,770 | 38,101 | 19,601 |
| 1982 | 35,152 | 24,077 | 37,086 | 45,954 | 48,769 | 38,470 | 19,241 |
| 1981 | 35,269 | 24,485 | 37,930 | 46,936 | 50,006 | 38,906 | 18,311 |
| 1980 | 35,850 | 25,731 | 39,144 | 47,828 | 50,852 | 39,569 | 17,775 |
| **Percent change** | | | | | | | |
| 1990–1999 | 6.9% | 9.7% | 9.0% | 3.5% | 6.5% | 8.1% | 6.2% |
| 1980–1999 | 13.9 | –2.2 | 7.7 | 6.4 | 11.9 | 12.7 | 28.3 |

*Source: Bureau of the Census, Internet site <www.census.gov/hhes/income/histinc/h10.html>; calculations by New Strategist*

# Female-Headed Families Make Gains

## During the 1990s, female-headed families experienced the fastest income growth.

Female-headed families may be one of the poorer household types, but they're not as poor as they used to be. During the 1990s, the incomes of female-headed families rose 14 percent, after adjusting for inflation—faster than any other household type. The $26,164 median income of female-headed families was still far below the $56,827 median of married couples, however. It also lagged the $41,838 median of male-headed families. But it surpassed the $24,566 median of nonfamily households.

Regardless of household type, incomes have never been higher. Married couples have the highest incomes, and their median has grown rapidly for two decades—up 21 percent between 1980 and 1999, after adjusting for inflation. Women who live alone were the only householders with faster income growth during those years. Most of them are elderly and benefit from the growing affluence of the older population. The median income of women who live alone rose 28 percent between 1980 and 1999, to $17,347.

♦ Married couples will always have above-average incomes because the majority are dual-earners. Most other household types have only one or even no earners.

**Income varies by household type**

*(median household income by household type, 1999)*

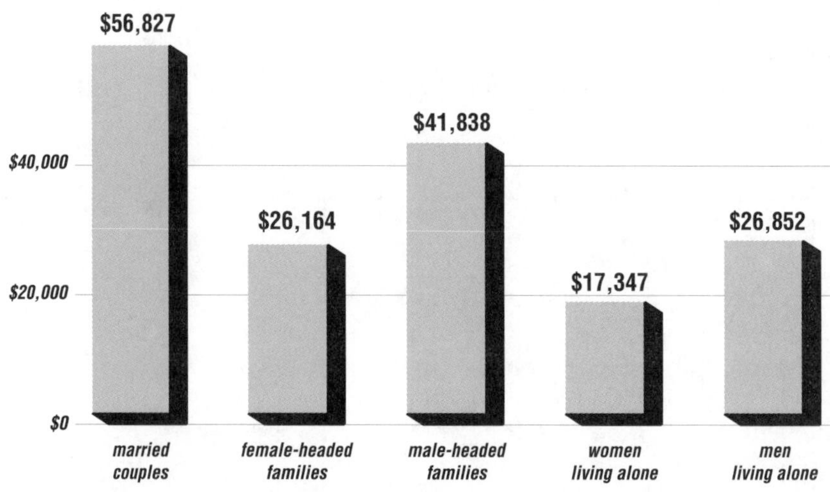

## Median Household Income by Type of Household, 1980 to 1999

*(median household income by type of household, 1980–99; percent change for selected years; income in 1999 dollars)*

| | | family households | | | | nonfamily households | | |
|---|---|---|---|---|---|---|---|---|
| | total households | total | married couples | female hh, no spouse present | male hh, no spouse present | total | women living alone | men living alone |
| 1999 | $40,816 | $49,940 | $56,827 | $26,164 | $41,838 | $24,566 | $17,347 | $26,852 |
| 1998 | 39,744 | 48,517 | 55,475 | 24,932 | 40,284 | 23,959 | 16,768 | 26,596 |
| 1997 | 38,411 | 47,070 | 53,645 | 23,916 | 38,026 | 22,530 | 16,120 | 24,778 |
| 1996 | 37,686 | 45,745 | 52,940 | 22,897 | 37,862 | 22,270 | 15,530 | 25,537 |
| 1995 | 37,251 | 45,065 | 51,520 | 23,337 | 36,659 | 21,786 | 15,666 | 24,690 |
| 1994 | 36,270 | 44,281 | 50,633 | 22,339 | 34,255 | 21,299 | 15,099 | 23,850 |
| 1993 | 36,019 | 43,217 | 49,725 | 21,381 | 34,414 | 21,768 | 14,982 | 24,641 |
| 1992 | 36,379 | 43,925 | 49,833 | 21,809 | 35,992 | 21,054 | 15,357 | 23,724 |
| 1991 | 36,851 | 44,528 | 50,243 | 21,975 | 37,931 | 21,746 | 15,699 | 24,781 |
| 1990 | 38,168 | 45,515 | 50,982 | 23,032 | 40,219 | 22,549 | 15,995 | 25,448 |
| 1989 | 38,837 | 46,531 | 51,947 | 23,355 | 40,758 | 22,995 | 16,378 | 26,356 |
| 1988 | 38,341 | 45,757 | 51,312 | 22,604 | 40,336 | 22,741 | 16,367 | 25,749 |
| 1987 | 38,220 | 45,825 | 51,260 | 22,702 | 39,164 | 21,777 | 15,718 | 24,923 |
| 1986 | 37,845 | 45,212 | 49,974 | 21,793 | 39,981 | 21,508 | 15,164 | 25,033 |
| 1985 | 36,568 | 43,387 | 48,247 | 22,166 | 37,708 | 21,364 | 15,133 | 25,256 |
| 1984 | 35,942 | 42,734 | 47,600 | 21,603 | 39,367 | 20,824 | 15,456 | 24,376 |
| 1983 | 34,934 | 41,454 | 45,713 | 20,472 | 38,275 | 20,089 | 15,290 | 23,618 |
| 1982 | 35,152 | 41,152 | 45,426 | 20,708 | 36,973 | 19,901 | 14,215 | 24,079 |
| 1981 | 35,269 | 41,700 | 46,422 | 21,155 | 37,983 | 19,202 | 13,692 | 23,736 |
| 1980 | 35,850 | 42,838 | 46,923 | 21,923 | 38,006 | 19,142 | 13,543 | 23,334 |
| **Percent change** | | | | | | | | |
| 1990–1999 | 6.9% | 9.7% | 11.5% | 13.6% | 4.0% | 8.9% | 8.5% | 5.5% |
| 1980–1999 | 13.9 | 16.6 | 21.1 | 19.3 | 10.1 | 28.3 | 28.1 | 15.1 |

*Source: Bureau of the Census, Internet site <www.census.gov/hhes/income/histinc/h09.html>; calculations by New Strategist*

## Blacks Post Biggest Gains

### The median income of black households rose 17 percent during the 1990s, after adjusting for inflation.

The median income of black households rose more than twice as fast as the national median during the 1990s, continuing a pattern established in the 1980s. By 1999, the median income of black households was 68 percent as high as the national median, up from 61 percent in 1980.

Overall, Asians have the highest median household income, $51,205 in 1999. This compares with a median of $44,366 for households headed by non-Hispanic whites. Despite rapid gains in household income, blacks continue to have the lowest median, $27,910 in 1999. The median income of Hispanic households was slightly greater, at $30,735. Regardless of race or Hispanic origin, household incomes have never been higher.

♦ The income gap between blacks and whites is due largely to the difference in the composition of black and white households. Black households are much less likely than white households to be headed by married couples—the most affluent household type.

**Asians have the highest incomes**

*(median household income by race and Hispanic origin, 1999)*

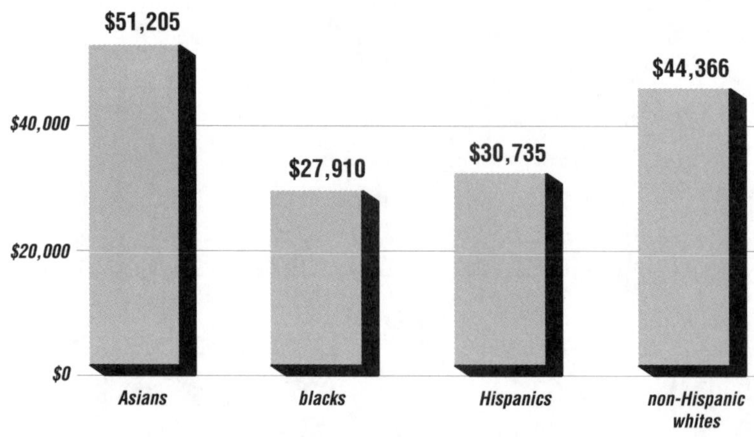

## Median Household Income by Race and Hispanic Origin of Householder, 1980 to 1999

*(median household income by race and Hispanic origin of householder, 1980–99; percent change in median for selected years; in 1999 dollars)*

| | total households | Asian | black | Hispanic | white | non-Hispanic white |
|---|---|---|---|---|---|---|
| 1999 | $40,816 | $51,205 | $27,910 | $30,735 | $42,504 | $44,366 |
| 1998 | 39,744 | 47,667 | 25,911 | 28,956 | 41,816 | 43,376 |
| 1997 | 38,411 | 46,969 | 26,002 | 27,640 | 40,453 | 42,119 |
| 1996 | 37,686 | 45,951 | 24,934 | 26,446 | 39,458 | 41,185 |
| 1995 | 37,251 | 44,398 | 24,479 | 24,990 | 39,099 | 40,642 |
| 1994 | 36,270 | 45,508 | 23,638 | 26,329 | 38,253 | 39,487 |
| 1993 | 36,019 | 44,212 | 22,520 | 26,386 | 38,001 | 39,399 |
| 1992 | 36,379 | 44,887 | 22,271 | 26,833 | 38,247 | 39,530 |
| 1991 | 36,850 | 44,584 | 23,005 | 27,756 | 38,615 | 39,538 |
| 1990 | 38,168 | 49,011 | 23,806 | 28,463 | 39,809 | 40,719 |
| 1989 | 38,837 | 48,505 | 24,295 | 29,452 | 40,852 | 41,731 |
| 1988 | 38,341 | 45,441 | 23,106 | 28,671 | 40,532 | 41,649 |
| 1987 | 38,220 | – | 22,984 | 28,357 | 40,269 | 41,376 |
| 1986 | 37,845 | – | 22,923 | 27,896 | 39,788 | 40,692 |
| 1985 | 36,568 | – | 22,945 | 27,042 | 38,566 | 39,433 |
| 1984 | 35,942 | – | 21,600 | 27,246 | 37,917 | 38,704 |
| 1983 | 34,934 | – | 20,790 | 26,606 | 36,635 | – |
| 1982 | 35,152 | – | 20,856 | 26,450 | 36,800 | 37,417 |
| 1981 | 35,269 | – | 20,911 | 28,291 | 37,264 | 37,802 |
| 1980 | 35,850 | – | 21,790 | 27,634 | 37,822 | 38,492 |
| **Percent change** | | | | | | |
| 1990–1999 | 6.9% | 4.5% | 17.2% | 8.0% | 6.8% | 9.0% |
| 1980–1999 | 13.9 | – | 28.1 | 11.2 | 12.4 | 15.3 |

*Note: (–) means data not available.*
*Source: Bureau of the Census, Internet site <www.census.gov/hhes/income/histinc/h05.html>; calculations by New Strategist*

# Median Income of Black Couples Tops $50,000

## Black married couples have a median income nearly twice that of the average black household.

The median income of all black households is only 68 percent that of the average household, but the median income of black couples is 89 percent as high as the median for all married couples. In 1999, black couples had a median household income of $50,758 versus $56,827 for all couples. The median income of the average black household is a much lower $27,910 because so many black households are female-headed families—one of the poorer household types.

Interestingly, while the median income of the average Hispanic household is slightly higher than that of the average black household ($30,735 versus $27,910), the median income of Hispanic couples is far below that of their black counterparts ($37,583 versus $50,758). Behind this pattern are differences in the lifestyles of Hispanics and blacks. The average Hispanic household has a higher income than the average black household because Hispanic households are more likely to be headed by married couples. But black couples have higher incomes than Hispanic couples because black couples are more likely to be dual-earners.

♦ Hispanic incomes are low regardless of household type because many Hispanics are recent immigrants with little education or earning power.

## Median Household Income by Household Type and Race and Hispanic Origin, 1999

*(median household income by type of household and race and Hispanic origin of householder; index of race/Hispanic origin median to national median by household type, 1999)*

| | total | black | Hispanic | white | non-Hispanic white |
|---|---|---|---|---|---|
| **Total households** | **$40,816** | **$27,910** | **$30,735** | **$42,504** | **$44,366** |
| **Family households** | **49,940** | **33,805** | **33,077** | **51,912** | **54,906** |
| Married couples | 56,827 | 50,758 | 37,583 | 57,242 | 59,853 |
| Female householder, no spouse present | 26,164 | 19,133 | 20,765 | 29,629 | 31,684 |
| Male householder, no spouse present | 41,838 | 37,825 | 34,320 | 42,401 | 44,988 |
| **Nonfamily households** | **24,566** | **19,860** | **20,462** | **25,161** | **25,496** |
| Female householder | 19,917 | 15,886 | 14,682 | 20,311 | 20,571 |
| Living alone | 17,347 | 14,036 | 10,787 | 17,720 | 18,095 |
| Male householder | 30,753 | 24,235 | 24,387 | 31,619 | 32,194 |
| Living alone | 26,852 | 22,022 | 19,637 | 27,375 | 28,177 |
| **INDEX** | | | | | |
| **Total households** | **100** | **68** | **75** | **104** | **109** |
| **Family households** | **100** | **68** | **66** | **104** | **110** |
| Married couples | 100 | 89 | 66 | 101 | 105 |
| Female householder, no spouse present | 100 | 73 | 79 | 113 | 121 |
| Male householder, no spouse present | 100 | 90 | 82 | 101 | 108 |
| **Nonfamily households** | **100** | **81** | **83** | **102** | **104** |
| Female householder | 100 | 78 | 74 | 102 | 103 |
| Living alone | 100 | 81 | 62 | 102 | 104 |
| Male householder | 100 | 79 | 79 | 103 | 105 |
| Living alone | 100 | 82 | 73 | 102 | 105 |

*Note: The index is calculated by dividing median income by race/Hispanic origin by the national median and multiplying by 100.*

*Source: Bureau of the Census,* Money Income in the United States: 1999, *Current Population Reports, P60-209, 2000; calculations by New Strategist*

# Householders Aged 45 to 54 Have the Highest Incomes

## Median household income peaks at $56,917 in the 45-to-54 age group.

One in five householders aged 45 to 54 had an income of $100,000 or more in 1999. The age group accounts for one-third of the 12.8 million households with incomes in the highest category. Householders aged 45 to 54 have the highest incomes because, at that age, workers typically are at the height of their career.

Households headed by people aged 65 or older have the lowest incomes, a median of just $22,812. They are not far behind householders under age 25, however, who had a median income of $25,171 in 1999.

♦ With boomers entering their late fifties and sixties during the next decade, the household incomes of 55-to-64-year-olds should soar as early retirement becomes less common.

### Household income peaks in middle age

*(median income of households by age of householder, 1999)*

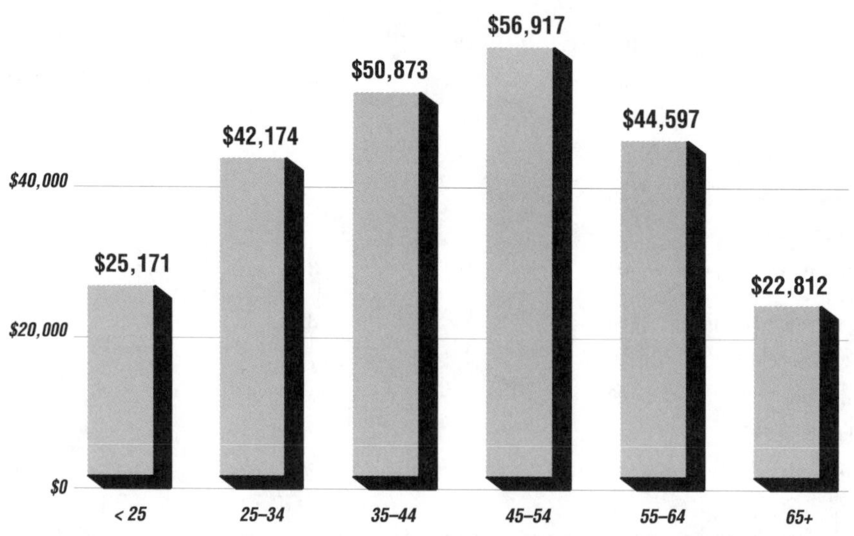

## Household Income by Age of Householder, 1999: Total Households

*(number and percent distribution of households by household income and age of householder, 1999; households in thousands as of 2000)*

| | *total* | *under 25* | *25 to 34* | *35 to 44* | *45 to 54* | *55 to 64* | *65 or older* |
|---|---|---|---|---|---|---|---|
| **Total households** | **104,705** | **5,860** | **18,627** | **23,955** | **20,927** | **13,592** | **21,745** |
| Under $25,000 | 32,036 | 2,903 | 4,688 | 4,827 | 3,853 | 3,838 | 11,929 |
| $25,000 to $49,999 | 29,812 | 1,979 | 6,241 | 6,897 | 5,199 | 3,638 | 5,855 |
| $50,000 to $74,999 | 19,272 | 640 | 4,158 | 5,503 | 4,494 | 2,490 | 1,988 |
| $75,000 to $99,999 | 10,755 | 183 | 1,829 | 3,211 | 3,148 | 1,494 | 890 |
| $100,000 or more | 12,831 | 154 | 1,711 | 3,520 | 4,233 | 2,130 | 1,084 |
| Median income | $40,816 | $25,171 | $42,174 | $50,873 | $56,917 | $44,597 | $22,812 |
| **Total households** | **100.0%** | **100.0%** | **100.0%** | **100.0%** | **100.0%** | **100.0%** | **100.0%** |
| Under $25,000 | 30.6 | 49.5 | 25.2 | 20.2 | 18.4 | 28.2 | 54.9 |
| $25,000 to $49,999 | 28.5 | 33.8 | 33.5 | 28.8 | 24.8 | 26.8 | 26.9 |
| $50,000 to $74,999 | 18.4 | 10.9 | 22.3 | 22.0 | 21.5 | 18.3 | 9.1 |
| $75,000 to $99,999 | 10.3 | 3.1 | 9.8 | 13.4 | 15.0 | 10.0 | 4.1 |
| $100,000 or more | 12.3 | 2.6 | 9.2 | 14.7 | 20.2 | 15.7 | 4.0 |

*Source: Bureau of the Census, data from the 2000 Current Population Survey, Internet site <http://ferret.bls .census.gov/macro/032000/hhinc/new02_001.htm>; calculations by New Strategist*

# Income Peaks in Middle Age for Blacks, Hispanics, and Whites

## Median household income peaks at ages 45 to 54 for all racial and ethnic groups.

Among non-Hispanic whites, the median income of householders aged 45 to 54 stood at a lofty $61,754 in 1999. Fully 23 percent of non-Hispanic white householders in the age group had an income of $100,000 or more. Among blacks and Hispanics, incomes peak in the same age group but at a much lower level. Median household income peaks at $39,638 for blacks, while among Hispanics the income peak is a slightly higher $39,711. Ten percent of black householders aged 45 to 54 have an income of $100,000 or more, as do 8 percent of their Hispanic counterparts.

Among both Hispanics and non-Hispanic whites, the poorest householders are those aged 65 or older. Among blacks, the youngest are the poorest, those under age 25 having a median income of just $15,576 in 1999.

♦ The incomes of black households are far below those of whites because black households are much less likely to be headed by married couples—the most affluent household type. Hispanic household incomes are low because many Hispanics are recent immigrants with little earning power.

## Household Income by Age of Householder, 1999: Black Households

*(number and percent distribution of black households by household income and age of householder, 1999; households in thousands as of 2000)*

| | *total* | *under 25* | *25 to 34* | *35 to 44* | *45 to 54* | *55 to 64* | *65 or older* |
|---|---|---|---|---|---|---|---|
| **Total households** | **12,849** | **1,002** | **2,724** | **3,149** | **2,566** | **1,522** | **1,886** |
| Under $25,000 | 5,775 | 675 | 1,132 | 1,127 | 882 | 667 | 1,289 |
| $25,000 to $49,999 | 3,642 | 241 | 938 | 978 | 730 | 387 | 365 |
| $50,000 to $74,999 | 1,804 | 63 | 375 | 542 | 436 | 249 | 140 |
| $75,000 to $99,999 | 841 | 19 | 152 | 290 | 252 | 95 | 30 |
| $100,000 or more | 788 | 3 | 126 | 211 | 264 | 124 | 60 |
| Median income | $27,910 | $15,576 | $28,766 | $35,061 | $39,638 | $28,631 | $16,312 |
| **Total households** | **100.0%** | **100.0%** | **100.0%** | **100.0%** | **100.0%** | **100.0%** | **100.0%** |
| Under $25,000 | 44.9 | 67.4 | 41.6 | 35.8 | 34.4 | 43.8 | 68.3 |
| $25,000 to $49,999 | 28.3 | 24.1 | 34.4 | 31.1 | 28.4 | 25.4 | 19.4 |
| $50,000 to $74,999 | 14.0 | 6.3 | 13.8 | 17.2 | 16.0 | 16.4 | 7.4 |
| $75,000 to $99,999 | 6.5 | 1.9 | 5.6 | 9.2 | 9.8 | 6.2 | 1.6 |
| $100,000 or more | 6.1 | 0.3 | 4.6 | 6.7 | 10.3 | 8.1 | 3.2 |

*Source: Bureau of the Census, data from the 2000 Current Population Survey, Internet site <http://ferret.bls.census.gov/macro/032000/hhinc/new02_003.htm>; calculations by New Strategist*

## Household Income by Age of Householder, 1999: Hispanic Households

*(number and percent distribution of Hispanic households by household income and age of householder, 1999; households in thousands as of 2000)*

| | total | under 25 | 25 to 34 | 35 to 44 | 45 to 54 | 55 to 64 | 65 or older |
|---|---|---|---|---|---|---|---|
| **Total households** | **9,319** | **871** | **2,477** | **2,494** | **1,546** | **929** | **1,002** |
| Under $25,000 | 3,767 | 451 | 952 | 801 | 510 | 385 | 668 |
| $25,000 to $49,999 | 3,025 | 287 | 910 | 906 | 453 | 256 | 207 |
| $50,000 to $74,999 | 1,414 | 81 | 369 | 453 | 276 | 152 | 80 |
| $75,000 to $99,999 | 627 | 31 | 155 | 179 | 167 | 75 | 18 |
| $100,000 or more | 488 | 17 | 90 | 156 | 139 | 59 | 26 |
| Median income | $30,735 | $24,268 | $31,377 | $34,699 | $39,711 | $30,718 | $16,858 |
| **Total households** | **100.0%** | **100.0%** | **100.0%** | **100.0%** | **100.0%** | **100.0%** | **100.0%** |
| Under $25,000 | 40.4 | 51.8 | 38.4 | 32.1 | 32.0 | 41.4 | 66.7 |
| $25,000 to $49,999 | 32.5 | 32.0 | 36.7 | 36.3 | 29.3 | 27.6 | 20.7 |
| $50,000 to $74,999 | 15.2 | 9.3 | 14.9 | 18.2 | 17.9 | 16.4 | 7.0 |
| $75,000 to $99,999 | 6.7 | 3.6 | 6.3 | 7.2 | 10.8 | 8.1 | 1.8 |
| $100,000 or more | 5.2 | 1.0 | 3.6 | 6.3 | 8.0 | 6.4 | 2.6 |

*Source: Bureau of the Census, data from the 2000 Current Population Survey, Internet site <http://ferret.bls.census.gov/macro/032000/hhinc/new02_004.htm>; calculations by New Strategist*

## Household Income by Age of Householder, 1999: White Households

*(number and percent distribution of white households by household income and age of householder, 1999; households in thousands as of 2000)*

| | total | under 25 | 25 to 34 | 35 to 44 | 45 to 54 | 55 to 64 | 65 or older |
|---|---|---|---|---|---|---|---|
| **Total households** | **87,671** | **4,541** | **14,871** | **19,808** | **17,475** | **11,599** | **19,376** |
| Under $25,000 | 25,109 | 2,046 | 3,312 | 3,501 | 2,793 | 3,051 | 10,410 |
| $25,000 to $49,999 | 25,069 | 1,656 | 4,977 | 5,659 | 4,267 | 3,142 | 5,370 |
| $50,000 to $74,999 | 16,731 | 547 | 3,557 | 4,787 | 3,885 | 2,169 | 1,784 |
| $75,000 to $99,999 | 9,461 | 159 | 1,584 | 2,805 | 2,759 | 1,341 | 816 |
| $100,000 or more | 11,298 | 135 | 1,444 | 3,055 | 3,772 | 1,898 | 995 |
| Median income | $42,504 | $26,787 | $45,230 | $53,034 | $60,370 | $46,483 | $23,344 |
| **Total households** | **100.0%** | **100.0%** | **100.0%** | **100.0%** | **100.0%** | **100.0%** | **100.0%** |
| Under $25,000 | 28.6 | 45.1 | 22.3 | 17.7 | 15.0 | 26.3 | 53.7 |
| $25,000 to $49,999 | 28.6 | 36.5 | 33.5 | 28.6 | 24.4 | 27.1 | 27.7 |
| $50,000 to $74,999 | 19.1 | 12.1 | 23.9 | 24.2 | 22.2 | 18.7 | 9.2 |
| $75,000 to $99,999 | 10.8 | 3.5 | 10.7 | 14.2 | 15.8 | 11.6 | 4.2 |
| $100,000 or more | 12.9 | 2.0 | 9.7 | 15.4 | 21.6 | 16.4 | 5.1 |

*Source: Bureau of the Census, data from the 2000 Current Population Survey, Internet site <http://ferret.bls.census.gov/macro/032000/hhinc/new02_002.htm>; calculations by New Strategist*

## Household Income by Age of Householder, 1999: Non-Hispanic White Households

*(number and percent distribution of non-Hispanic white households by household income and age of householder, 1999; households in thousands as of 2000)*

| | total | under 25 | 25 to 34 | 35 to 44 | 45 to 54 | 55 to 64 | 65 or older |
|---|---|---|---|---|---|---|---|
| **Total households** | **78,819** | **3,721** | **12,533** | **17,440** | **16,008** | **10,704** | **18,412** |
| Under $25,000 | 21,533 | 1,626 | 2,410 | 2,739 | 2,317 | 2,675 | 9,763 |
| $25,000 to $49,999 | 22,174 | 1,380 | 4,113 | 4,785 | 3,829 | 2,893 | 5,174 |
| $50,000 to $74,999 | 15,397 | 470 | 3,216 | 4,363 | 3,619 | 2,020 | 1,708 |
| $75,000 to $99,999 | 8,876 | 127 | 1,439 | 2,640 | 2,597 | 1,273 | 796 |
| $100,000 or more | 10,841 | 118 | 1,355 | 2,912 | 3,643 | 1,844 | 969 |
| Median income | $44,366 | $27,237 | $47,899 | $55,853 | $61,754 | $47,885 | $23,669 |
| **Total households** | **100.0%** | **100.0%** | **100.0%** | **100.0%** | **100.0%** | **100.0%** | **100.0%** |
| Under $25,000 | 27.3 | 43.7 | 19.2 | 15.7 | 14.5 | 24.0 | 53.0 |
| $25,000 to $49,999 | 28.1 | 37.1 | 32.8 | 27.4 | 23.9 | 27.0 | 28.1 |
| $50,000 to $74,999 | 19.5 | 12.6 | 25.7 | 25.0 | 22.6 | 18.9 | 9.3 |
| $75,000 to $99,999 | 11.3 | 3.4 | 11.5 | 15.1 | 16.2 | 11.9 | 4.3 |
| $100,000 or more | 13.8 | 3.2 | 10.8 | 16.7 | 22.8 | 17.2 | 5.3 |

*Source: Bureau of the Census, data from the 2000 Current Population Survey, Internet site <http://ferret.bls.census.gov/macro/032000/hhinc/new02_005.htm>; calculations by New Strategist*

# Median Income of Married Couples Exceeds $56,000

## Married couples are by far the most affluent household type.

Most married couples are dual earners, which accounts for their high incomes. Nearly one in five couples had an income of $100,000 or more in 1999, accounting for fully 81 percent of all households with incomes that high.

Married couples and male-headed families are the only household types whose median incomes are above the all-household median of $40,816. Female-headed families had a median income of just $26,164. While 10 percent of male-headed families had an income of $100,000 or more, only 3 percent of female-headed families had an income that high.

Women who live alone have the lowest incomes, a median of $17,347 in 1999, in part because most women who live alone are older widows. Men who live alone have much higher incomes than their female counterparts—a median of $26,852—because most are under age 55 and in the labor force.

♦ The incomes of women who live alone are likely to rise in the decades ahead as baby-boom women with pensions of their own become widows.

## Household Income by Household Type, 1999: Total Households

*(number and percent distribution of households by household income and type of household, 1999; households in thousands as of 2000)*

| | | family households | | | | nonfamily households | | | | |
|---|---|---|---|---|---|---|---|---|---|---|
| | | | | | | | female householders | | male householders | |
| | total | total | married couples | female hh, no spouse present | male hh, no spouse present | total | total | living alone | total | living alone |
| **Total households** | **104,705** | **72,025** | **55,311** | **12,687** | **4,028** | **32,680** | **18,039** | **15,543** | **14,641** | **11,181** |
| Under $25,000 | 32,036 | 15,480 | 8,425 | 6,072 | 983 | 16,559 | 10,679 | 10,122 | 5,880 | 5,155 |
| $25,000 to $49,999 | 29,812 | 20,574 | 15,153 | 3,992 | 1,429 | 9,237 | 4,538 | 3,737 | 4,699 | 3,677 |
| $50,000 to $74,999 | 19,272 | 15,462 | 13,033 | 1,622 | 807 | 3,810 | 1,646 | 1,058 | 2,164 | 1,343 |
| $75,000 to $99,999 | 10,755 | 9,321 | 8,298 | 621 | 402 | 1,433 | 571 | 317 | 862 | 431 |
| $100,000 or more | 12,831 | 11,187 | 10,399 | 381 | 407 | 1,644 | 607 | 309 | 1,038 | 570 |
| Median income | $40,816 | $49,940 | $56,827 | $26,164 | $41,838 | $24,566 | $19,917 | $17,347 | $30,753 | $26,852 |
| **Total households** | **100.0%** | **100.0%** | **100.0%** | **100.0%** | **100.0%** | **100.0%** | **100.0%** | **100.0%** | **100.0%** | **100.0%** |
| Under $25,000 | 30.6 | 21.5 | 15.2 | 47.9 | 24.4 | 50.7 | 59.2 | 65.1 | 40.2 | 46.1 |
| $25,000 to $49,999 | 28.5 | 28.6 | 27.4 | 31.5 | 35.5 | 28.3 | 25.2 | 24.0 | 32.1 | 32.9 |
| $50,000 to $74,999 | 18.4 | 21.5 | 23.6 | 12.8 | 20.0 | 11.7 | 9.1 | 6.8 | 14.8 | 12.0 |
| $75,000 to $99,999 | 10.3 | 12.9 | 15.0 | 4.9 | 9.0 | 4.4 | 3.2 | 2.0 | 5.9 | 3.9 |
| $100,000 or more | 12.3 | 15.5 | 18.8 | 3.0 | 10.1 | 5.0 | 3.4 | 1.0 | 7.1 | 5.1 |

*Source: Bureau of the Census, data from the 2000 Current Population Survey, Internet site <http://ferret.bls.census.gov/macro/032000/hhinc/new02_000.htm>; calculations by New Strategist*

# From Young to Old, Incomes Vary by Household Type

## In most age groups, married couples have the highest incomes.

Married couples are the most affluent household type, while the middle-aged are the most affluent age group. Combine those characteristics and you've located the most affluent households in the country. Married couples in the 45-to-54 age group had a median income of $74,012 in 1999, with an impressive 29 percent having incomes of $100,000 or more.

Fewer than one-fourth of householders under age 25 are married couples, which is one reason for the low incomes of the age group. Among householders under age 25, male-headed families have the highest incomes, a median of $35,692 in 1999. The same is true among householders aged 65 or older, with the median income of male-headed families standing at $40,257 compared with $33,719 for married couples. One reason for the higher incomes of male-headed families in the oldest and youngest age groups is that they have more earners than their married counterparts. Most older couples are retired, while many of the youngest wives are homemakers caring for young children.

♦ The number of earners in a household is the major determinant of income. Because most married couples are dual earners, their incomes are usually far higher than those of other household types.

## Household Income by Household Type, 1999: Householders under Age 25

*(number and percent distribution of households headed by householders under age 25, by household income and type of household, 1999; households in thousands as of 2000)*

| | | family households | | | | nonfamily households | | | | |
|---|---|---|---|---|---|---|---|---|---|---|
| | | | | | | | female householders | | male householders | |
| | total | total | married couples | female hh, no spouse present | male hh, no spouse present | total | total | living alone | total | living alone |
| **Total households** | **5,860** | **3,352** | **1,450** | **1,342** | **560** | **2,507** | **1,221** | **587** | **1,286** | **556** |
| Under $25,000 | 2,903 | 1,557 | 499 | 901 | 157 | 1,343 | 682 | 469 | 661 | 391 |
| $25,000 to $49,999 | 1,979 | 1,217 | 672 | 307 | 238 | 762 | 354 | 99 | 408 | 127 |
| $50,000 to $74,999 | 640 | 376 | 202 | 85 | 89 | 266 | 124 | 12 | 142 | 33 |
| $75,000 to $99,999 | 183 | 119 | 42 | 31 | 46 | 63 | 27 | – | 36 | 4 |
| $100,000 or more | 154 | 81 | 32 | 19 | 30 | 74 | 34 | 9 | 40 | – |
| Median income | $25,171 | $25,547 | $30,399 | $16,071 | $35,692 | $23,193 | $21,962 | $14,587 | $24,361 | $17,553 |
| **Total households** | **100.0%** | **100.0%** | **100.0%** | **100.0%** | **100.0%** | **100.0%** | **100.0%** | **100.0%** | **100.0%** | **100.0%** |
| Under $25,000 | 49.5 | 46.4 | 34.4 | 67.1 | 28.0 | 53.6 | 55.9 | 79.9 | 51.4 | 70.3 |
| $25,000 to $49,999 | 33.8 | 36.3 | 46.3 | 22.9 | 42.5 | 30.4 | 29.0 | 16.9 | 31.7 | 22.8 |
| $50,000 to $74,999 | 10.9 | 11.2 | 13.9 | 6.3 | 15.9 | 10.6 | 10.2 | 2.0 | 11.0 | 5.9 |
| $75,000 to $99,999 | 3.1 | 3.6 | 2.9 | 2.3 | 8.2 | 2.5 | 2.2 | – | 2.8 | 0.7 |
| $100,000 or more | 2.6 | 2.4 | 2.2 | 1.4 | 5.4 | 3.0 | 2.8 | 1.5 | 3.1 | – |

*Note: (–) means sample is too small to make a reliable estimate.*
*Source: Bureau of the Census, data from the 2000 Current Population Survey, Internet site <http://ferret.bls.census.gov/macro/032000/hhinc/new02_000.htm>; calculations by New Strategist*

## Household Income by Household Type, 1999: Householders Aged 25 to 34

*(number and percent distribution of households headed by householders aged 25 to 34, by household income and type of household, 1999; households in thousands as of 2000)*

| | | family households | | | | nonfamily households | | | | |
|---|---|---|---|---|---|---|---|---|---|---|
| | | | | | | | female householders | | male householders | |
| | total | total | married couples | female hh, no spouse present | male hh, no spouse present | total | total | living alone | total | living alone |
| **Total households** | **18,627** | **13,007** | **9,389** | **2,732** | **886** | **5,620** | **2,172** | **1,569** | **3,448** | **2,279** |
| Under $25,000 | 4,688 | 3,087 | 1,242 | 1,618 | 227 | 1,600 | 644 | 583 | 956 | 807 |
| $25,000 to $49,999 | 6,241 | 4,089 | 2,990 | 779 | 320 | 2,156 | 900 | 723 | 1,256 | 945 |
| $50,000 to $74,999 | 4,158 | 3,136 | 2,779 | 181 | 176 | 1,021 | 338 | 155 | 683 | 330 |
| $75,000 to $99,999 | 1,829 | 1,415 | 1,243 | 98 | 74 | 414 | 116 | 39 | 298 | 101 |
| $100,000 or more | 1,711 | 1,279 | 1,135 | 55 | 89 | 432 | 174 | 67 | 258 | 99 |
| Median income | $42,174 | $45,426 | $53,169 | $20,356 | $40,681 | $35,923 | $33,385 | $29,841 | $37,521 | $31,461 |
| **Total households** | **100.0%** | **100.0%** | **100.0%** | **100.0%** | **100.0%** | **100.0%** | **100.0%** | **100.0%** | **100.0%** | **100.0%** |
| Under $25,000 | 25.2 | 23.7 | 13.2 | 59.2 | 25.6 | 28.5 | 29.7 | 37.2 | 27.7 | 35.4 |
| $25,000 to $49,999 | 33.5 | 31.4 | 31.8 | 28.5 | 36.1 | 38.4 | 41.4 | 46.1 | 36.4 | 41.5 |
| $50,000 to $74,999 | 22.3 | 24.1 | 29.6 | 6.6 | 19.9 | 18.2 | 15.6 | 9.9 | 19.8 | 14.5 |
| $75,000 to $99,999 | 9.8 | 10.9 | 13.2 | 3.6 | 8.4 | 7.4 | 5.3 | 2.5 | 8.6 | 4.4 |
| $100,000 or more | 9.2 | 9.8 | 12.1 | 2.0 | 10.0 | 7.7 | 8.0 | 4.3 | 7.5 | 4.3 |

*Source: Bureau of the Census, data from the 2000 Current Population Survey, Internet site <http://ferret.bls.census.gov/macro/032000/hhinc/new02_000.htm>; calculations by New Strategist*

## Household Income by Household Type, 1999: Householders Aged 35 to 44

*(number and percent distribution of households headed by householders aged 35 to 44, by household income and type of household, 1999; households in thousands as of 2000)*

| | | family households | | | | nonfamily households | | | | |
|---|---|---|---|---|---|---|---|---|---|---|
| | | | | | | | female householders | | male householders | |
| | total | total | married couples | female hh, no spouse present | male hh, no spouse present | total | total | living alone | total | living alone |
| **Total households** | **23,955** | **18,705** | **14,104** | **3,499** | **1,102** | **5,250** | **1,989** | **1,540** | **3,261** | **2,569** |
| Under $25,000 | 4,827 | 3,122 | 1,268 | 1,615 | 239 | 1,706 | 677 | 603 | 1,029 | 911 |
| $25,000 to $49,999 | 6,897 | 4,991 | 3,451 | 1,146 | 394 | 1,907 | 719 | 601 | 1,188 | 990 |
| $50,000 to $74,999 | 5,503 | 4,566 | 3,876 | 452 | 238 | 936 | 357 | 227 | 579 | 418 |
| $75,000 to $99,999 | 3,211 | 2,874 | 2,585 | 168 | 121 | 333 | 117 | 61 | 216 | 109 |
| $100,000 or more | 3,520 | 3,152 | 2,921 | 119 | 112 | 367 | 121 | 48 | 246 | 139 |
| Median income | $50,873 | $56,059 | $64,154 | $27,410 | $43,411 | $34,772 | $34,003 | $30,822 | $35,241 | $31,676 |
| **Total households** | **100.0%** | **100.0%** | **100.0%** | **100.0%** | **100.0%** | **100.0%** | **100.0%** | **100.0%** | **100.0%** | **100.0%** |
| Under $25,000 | 20.2 | 16.7 | 8.0 | 46.2 | 21.7 | 32.5 | 34.0 | 39.2 | 31.6 | 35.5 |
| $25,000 to $49,999 | 28.8 | 26.7 | 24.5 | 32.8 | 35.8 | 36.3 | 36.1 | 39.0 | 36.4 | 38.5 |
| $50,000 to $74,999 | 22.0 | 24.4 | 27.5 | 12.9 | 21.6 | 17.8 | 17.9 | 14.7 | 17.8 | 16.3 |
| $75,000 to $99,999 | 13.4 | 15.4 | 18.3 | 4.8 | 10.0 | 6.3 | 5.9 | 3.0 | 6.6 | 4.2 |
| $100,000 or more | 14.7 | 16.9 | 20.7 | 3.4 | 10.2 | 6.0 | 6.1 | 3.1 | 7.5 | 5.4 |

*Source: Bureau of the Census, data from the 2000 Current Population Survey, Internet site <http://ferret.bls.census.gov/macro/032000/hhinc/new02_000.htm>; calculations by New Strategist*

## Household Income by Household Type, 1999: Householders Aged 45 to 54

*(number and percent distribution of households headed by householders aged 45 to 54, by household income and type of household, 1999; households in thousands as of 2000)*

| | | family households | | | | nonfamily households | | | | |
|---|---|---|---|---|---|---|---|---|---|---|
| | | | | | | | female householders | | male householders | |
| | total | total | married couples | female hh, no spouse present | male hh, no spouse present | total | total | living alone | total | living alone |
| **Total households** | **20,927** | **15,804** | **12,792** | **2,299** | **713** | **5,124** | **2,541** | **2,158** | **2,583** | **2,146** |
| Under $25,000 | 3,853 | 1,958 | 997 | 815 | 146 | 1,894 | 1,017 | 947 | 877 | 820 |
| $25,000 to $49,999 | 5,199 | 3,437 | 2,431 | 781 | 225 | 1,763 | 903 | 800 | 860 | 756 |
| $50,000 to $74,999 | 4,494 | 3,707 | 3,074 | 470 | 163 | 787 | 356 | 263 | 431 | 321 |
| $75,000 to $99,999 | 3,148 | 2,840 | 2,612 | 143 | 85 | 311 | 144 | 83 | 167 | 110 |
| $100,000 or more | 4,233 | 3,861 | 3,677 | 89 | 95 | 371 | 124 | 67 | 247 | 140 |
| Median income | $56,917 | $67,264 | $74,012 | $35,545 | $48,477 | $33,297 | $30,509 | $27,559 | $36,040 | $32,343 |
| **Total households** | **100.0%** | **100.0%** | **100.0%** | **100.0%** | **100.0%** | **100.0%** | **100.0%** | **100.0%** | **100.0%** | **100.0%** |
| Under $25,000 | 18.4 | 12.4 | 7.8 | 35.5 | 20.5 | 37.0 | 40.0 | 43.9 | 34.0 | 38.2 |
| $25,000 to $49,999 | 24.8 | 21.7 | 19.0 | 34.0 | 31.6 | 34.4 | 35.5 | 37.1 | 33.3 | 35.2 |
| $50,000 to $74,999 | 21.5 | 23.5 | 24.0 | 20.4 | 22.9 | 15.4 | 14.0 | 12.2 | 16.7 | 15.0 |
| $75,000 to $99,999 | 15.0 | 18.0 | 20.4 | 6.2 | 11.9 | 6.1 | 5.7 | 3.8 | 6.5 | 5.1 |
| $100,000 or more | 20.2 | 24.4 | 28.7 | 3.9 | 13.3 | 7.2 | 4.9 | 3.1 | 9.6 | 6.5 |

*Source: Bureau of the Census, data from the 2000 Current Population Survey, Internet site <http://ferret.bls.census.gov/macro/032000/hhinc/new02_000.htm>; calculations by New Strategist*

## Household Income by Household Type, 1999: Householders Aged 55 to 64

*(number and percent distribution of households headed by householders aged 55 to 64, by household income and type of household, 1999; households in thousands as of 2000)*

| | | family households | | | | nonfamily households | | | | |
|---|---|---|---|---|---|---|---|---|---|---|
| | | | | | | | female householders | | male householders | |
| | total | total | married couples | female hh, no spouse present | male hh, no spouse present | total | total | living alone | total | living alone |
| **Total households** | **13,592** | **9,569** | **8,138** | **1,080** | **351** | **4,023** | **2,490** | **2,262** | **1,533** | **1,276** |
| Under $25,000 | 3,838 | 1,804 | 1,299 | 408 | 97 | 2,038 | 1,379 | 1,330 | 659 | 597 |
| $25,000 to $49,999 | 3,638 | 2,517 | 2,047 | 352 | 118 | 1,121 | 689 | 618 | 432 | 365 |
| $50,000 to $74,999 | 2,490 | 2,058 | 1,818 | 186 | 54 | 433 | 242 | 186 | 191 | 130 |
| $75,000 to $99,999 | 1,494 | 1,308 | 1,181 | 83 | 44 | 189 | 92 | 67 | 97 | 69 |
| $100,000 or more | 2,130 | 1,884 | 1,793 | 52 | 39 | 246 | 88 | 62 | 158 | 115 |
| Median income | $44,597 | $55,266 | $58,963 | $31,551 | $42,525 | $24,460 | $21,401 | $20,104 | $29,429 | $26,825 |
| **Total households** | **100.0%** | **100.0%** | **100.0%** | **100.0%** | **100.0%** | **100.0%** | **100.0%** | **100.0%** | **100.0%** | **100.0%** |
| Under $25,000 | 28.2 | 18.9 | 16.0 | 37.8 | 27.6 | 50.7 | 55.4 | 58.8 | 43.0 | 46.8 |
| $25,000 to $49,999 | 26.8 | 26.3 | 25.2 | 32.6 | 33.6 | 27.9 | 27.7 | 27.3 | 28.2 | 28.6 |
| $50,000 to $74,999 | 18.3 | 21.5 | 22.3 | 17.2 | 15.4 | 10.8 | 9.7 | 8.2 | 12.5 | 10.2 |
| $75,000 to $99,999 | 11.0 | 13.7 | 14.5 | 7.7 | 12.5 | 4.7 | 3.7 | 3.0 | 6.3 | 5.4 |
| $100,000 or more | 15.7 | 19.7 | 22.0 | 4.8 | 11.1 | 6.1 | 3.5 | 2.7 | 10.3 | 9.0 |

*Source: Bureau of the Census, data from the 2000 Current Population Survey, Internet site <http://ferret.bls.census.gov/macro/032000/hhinc/new02_000.htm>; calculations by New Strategist*

## Household Income by Household Type, 1999: Householders Aged 65 or Older

*(number and percent distribution of households headed by householders aged 65 or older, by household income and type of household, 1999; households in thousands as of 2000)*

| | | family households | | | | nonfamily households | | | | |
|---|---|---|---|---|---|---|---|---|---|---|
| | | | | | | | female householders | | male householders | |
| | total | total | married couples | female hh, no spouse present | male hh, no spouse present | total | total | living alone | total | living alone |
| **Total households** | **21,745** | **11,588** | **9,437** | **1,735** | **416** | **10,156** | **7,626** | **7,427** | **2,530** | **2,356** |
| Under $25,000 | 11,929 | 3,946 | 3,119 | 714 | 113 | 7,981 | 6,281 | 6,195 | 1,700 | 1,630 |
| $25,000 to $49,999 | 5,855 | 4,328 | 3,562 | 632 | 134 | 1,526 | 973 | 898 | 553 | 495 |
| $50,000 to $74,999 | 1,988 | 1,615 | 1,280 | 246 | 89 | 370 | 230 | 211 | 140 | 114 |
| $75,000 to $99,999 | 890 | 765 | 634 | 95 | 36 | 122 | 74 | 63 | 48 | 38 |
| $100,000 or more | 1,084 | 930 | 841 | 46 | 43 | 155 | 66 | 57 | 89 | 77 |
| Median income | $22,812 | $33,274 | $33,719 | $29,182 | $40,257 | $14,579 | $13,271 | $13,045 | $18,521 | $17,848 |
| **Total households** | **100.0%** | **100.0%** | **100.0%** | **100.0%** | **100.0%** | **100.0%** | **100.0%** | **100.0%** | **100.0%** | **100.0%** |
| Under $25,000 | 54.9 | 34.1 | 33.1 | 41.2 | 27.2 | 78.6 | 82.4 | 83.4 | 67.2 | 69.2 |
| $25,000 to $49,999 | 26.9 | 37.3 | 37.7 | 36.4 | 32.2 | 15.0 | 12.8 | 12.1 | 21.9 | 21.0 |
| $50,000 to $74,999 | 9.1 | 13.9 | 13.6 | 14.2 | 21.4 | 3.6 | 3.0 | 2.8 | 5.5 | 4.8 |
| $75,000 to $99,999 | 4.1 | 6.6 | 6.7 | 5.5 | 8.7 | 1.2 | 1.0 | 0.8 | 1.9 | 1.6 |
| $100,000 or more | 5.0 | 8.0 | 8.9 | 2.7 | 10.3 | 1.5 | 0.9 | 0.8 | 3.5 | 3.3 |

*Source: Bureau of the Census, data from the 2000 Current Population Survey, Internet site <http://ferret.bls.census.gov/macro/032000/hhinc/new02_000.htm>; calculations by New Strategist*

# Couples with Children Have Highest Incomes

## Married couples with school-aged children have a median income of $64,311.

The median income of all married couples stood at $56,676 in 1999. Among couples with children under age 18 at home, median income was an even higher $60,168. In 32 percent of the nation's couples, both husband and wife work full-time. Their median income of $76,185 was 34 percent higher than the median for all couples.

Married couples with school-aged children have the highest incomes because they're likely to be in their peak earning years. Couples without children at home have lower incomes because many are older and retired.

Among couples in which both husband and wife work full-time, those without children at home have the highest incomes—a median of $79,788 in 1999. One-third had an income of $100,000 or more. Many are empty-nesters in their peak earning years.

♦ The proportion of married couples in which both husband and wife work full-time will rise as the baby-boom's children leave home and more boomer women take on full-time jobs.

♦ The rising number of dual-earner married couples in their peak earning years will continue to be a powerful boost for the economy. Expect record levels of affluence for another 10 years.

## Household Income of Married Couples by Presence of Children, 1999

*(number and percent distribution of married-couple households by income and presence and age of related children under age 18 at home, 1999; households in thousands as of 2000)*

| | | | with one or more children | | | |
|---|---|---|---|---|---|---|
| | total | no children | total | all under 6 | some under 6 some 6 to 17 | all 6 to 17 |
| **Total couples** | **55,315** | **28,942** | **26,373** | **6,340** | **5,875** | **14,157** |
| Under $25,000 | 8,492 | 5,393 | 3,099 | 856 | 864 | 1,379 |
| $25,000 to $49,999 | 15,177 | 8,061 | 7,115 | 1,808 | 1,863 | 3,443 |
| $50,000 to $74,999 | 13,032 | 6,213 | 6,819 | 1,650 | 1,507 | 3,664 |
| $75,000 to $99,999 | 8,277 | 3,994 | 4,284 | 917 | 761 | 2,606 |
| $100,000 or more | 10,336 | 5,282 | 5,054 | 1,107 | 883 | 3,065 |
| Median income | $56,676 | $53,180 | $60,168 | $56,837 | $52,794 | $64,311 |
| **Total couples** | **100.0%** | **100.0%** | **100.0%** | **100.0%** | **100.0%** | **100.0%** |
| Under $25,000 | 15.4 | 18.6 | 11.8 | 13.5 | 14.7 | 9.7 |
| $25,000 to $49,999 | 27.4 | 27.9 | 26.0 | 28.5 | 31.7 | 24.3 |
| $50,000 to $74,999 | 23.6 | 21.5 | 25.9 | 26.0 | 25.7 | 25.9 |
| $75,000 to $99,999 | 14.0 | 13.8 | 16.2 | 14.5 | 12.0 | 18.4 |
| $100,000 or more | 18.7 | 18.3 | 19.2 | 17.5 | 15.0 | 21.7 |

*Source: Bureau of the Census,* Money Income in the United States: 1999, *Current Population Reports, P60-209, 2000; calculations by New Strategist*

## Household Income of Dual-Earner Married Couples by Presence of Children, 1999

*(number and percent distribution of married couple households in which both husband and wife work full-time, year-round, by income and presence and age of related children under age 18 at home, 1999; households in thousands as of 2000)*

| | | | with one or more children | | | |
|---|---|---|---|---|---|---|
| | total | no children | total | all under 6 | some under 6 some 6 to 17 | all 6 to 17 |
| **Total couples** | **17,450** | **8,332** | **9,118** | **1,884** | **1,656** | **5,579** |
| Under $25,000 | 336 | 166 | 170 | 33 | 48 | 89 |
| $25,000 to $49,999 | 3,062 | 1,217 | 1,844 | 373 | 437 | 1,035 |
| $50,000 to $74,999 | 5,065 | 2,353 | 2,714 | 613 | 488 | 1,612 |
| $75,000 to $99,999 | 3,962 | 1,903 | 2,059 | 403 | 350 | 1,306 |
| $100,000 or more | 5,023 | 2,691 | 2,332 | 462 | 332 | 1,538 |
| Median income | $76,185 | $79,788 | $72,773 | $71,826 | $66,190 | $75,678 |
| **Total couples** | **100.0%** | **100.0%** | **100.0%** | **100.0%** | **100.0%** | **100.0%** |
| Under $25,000 | 1.9 | 1.0 | 1.9 | 1.8 | 2.9 | 1.6 |
| $25,000 to $49,999 | 17.5 | 14.6 | 20.2 | 19.8 | 26.4 | 18.6 |
| $50,000 to $74,999 | 29.0 | 28.2 | 29.8 | 32.5 | 29.5 | 28.9 |
| $75,000 to $99,999 | 22.7 | 22.8 | 22.6 | 21.4 | 21.1 | 23.4 |
| $100,000 or more | 28.8 | 32.3 | 25.6 | 24.5 | 20.1 | 27.6 |

*Source: Bureau of the Census,* Money Income in the United States: 1999, *Current Population Reports, P60-209, 2000; calculations by New Strategist*

# Single Parents Have Low Incomes

## But many male- and female-headed families have incomes close to the average.

Single-parent families, which by definition include children under age 18 in the home, account for the majority of male- and female-headed families. Sixty-nine percent of female-headed families and 54 percent of male-headed families are single parents. The incomes of single-parent families are lower than those of other male- and female-headed families. Female-headed single-parent families had a median income of $19,934 in 1999, while their male counterparts had a median income of $32,427.

Male- and female-headed families without children under age 18 at home have substantially higher incomes. Many of these householders live with other adults such as parents, brothers, or sisters—which adds earners to their households. The median income of male-headed families without children under age 18 stood at $44,234, above the national household median. A substantial 10 percent had incomes of $100,000 or more. Their female counterparts had a median income of $33,935.

♦ Families headed by women are likely to see their incomes grow in the years ahead as women's earnings rise.

## Household Income of Female- and Male-Headed Families by Presence of Children, 1999

*(number and percent distribution of female- and male-headed families with no spouse present, by household income and presence of children under age 18 at home, 1999; households in thousands as of 2000)*

| | female-headed families | | | male-headed families | | |
|---|---|---|---|---|---|---|
| | total | no children | one or more children | total | no children | one or more children |
| **Total households** | **12,687** | **3,951** | **8,736** | **4,028** | **1,860** | **2,169** |
| Under $25,000 | 6,633 | 1,387 | 5,246 | 1,182 | 417 | 765 |
| $25,000 to $49,999 | 3,819 | 1,482 | 2,340 | 1,417 | 636 | 778 |
| $50,000 to $74,999 | 1,427 | 688 | 741 | 776 | 419 | 356 |
| $75,000 to $99,999 | 502 | 258 | 245 | 341 | 196 | 143 |
| $100,000 or more | 306 | 139 | 166 | 314 | 190 | 124 |
| Median income | $23,732 | $33,935 | $19,934 | $37,396 | $44,234 | $32,427 |
| **Total households** | **100.0%** | **100.0%** | **100.0%** | **100.0%** | **100.0%** | **100.0%** |
| Under $25,000 | 52.3 | 35.1 | 60.1 | 29.3 | 22.4 | 35.3 |
| $25,000 to $49,999 | 30.1 | 37.5 | 26.8 | 35.2 | 34.2 | 35.9 |
| $50,000 to $74,999 | 11.2 | 17.4 | 8.5 | 19.3 | 22.5 | 16.4 |
| $75,000 to $99,999 | 4.0 | 6.5 | 2.8 | 8.5 | 10.5 | 6.6 |
| $100,000 or more | 2.4 | 3.5 | 1.9 | 7.8 | 10.2 | 5.7 |

*Source: Bureau of the Census, data from the 2000 Current Population Survey; Internet sites <http://ferret.bls.census.gov/macro/032000/faminc/new03_016.htm> and <http://ferret.bls.census.gov/macro/032000/faminc/new03_011.htm>; calculations by New Strategist*

# Older Women Who Live Alone Have Low Incomes

## Among 25-to-44-year-olds who live alone, however, women's incomes are close to men's.

Women account for 58 percent of the nation's 27 million single-person households. Their median income was just $17,347 in 1999. The median income of men who live alone was a higher $26,852. The gap in median incomes can be explained almost entirely by the age difference between men and women who live alone. Fully 62 percent of women who live alone are aged 55 or older, many of them elderly widows dependent on Social Security. Sixty-eight percent of men who live alone are under age 55, many in their peak earning years.

Within age groups, men and women who live alone have similar incomes. Among 25-to-34-year-olds who live alone, the median income of women is just $1,620 less than that of men. Among 35-to-44-year-olds who live alone, the gap is only $854. The difference in the incomes of men and women who live alone is greatest in the older age groups.

♦ The incomes of older men and women who live alone will converge as career-oriented baby-boom women become widowed.

**Women's incomes are not far behind men's**

*(median income of people who live alone by age and sex, 1999)*

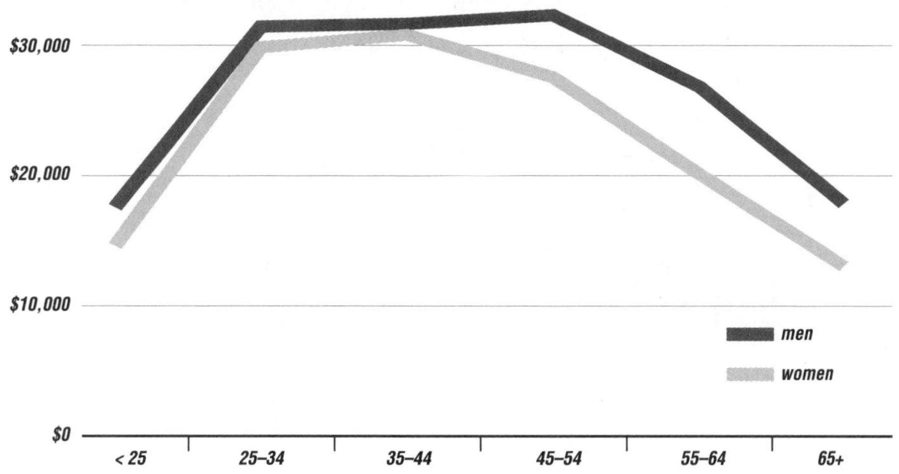

## Household Income of Men Who Live Alone, 1999

*(number and percent distribution of male-headed single-person households by household income and age of householder, 1999; households in thousands as of 2000)*

| | total | 15 to 24 | 25 to 34 | 35 to 44 | 45 to 54 | 55 to 64 | 65 or older |
|---|---|---|---|---|---|---|---|
| **Total households** | **11,181** | **556** | **2,279** | **2,569** | **2,146** | **1,276** | **2,356** |
| Under $25,000 | 5,155 | 391 | 807 | 911 | 820 | 597 | 1,630 |
| $25,000 to $49,999 | 3,677 | 127 | 945 | 990 | 756 | 365 | 495 |
| $50,000 to $74,999 | 1,343 | 33 | 330 | 418 | 321 | 130 | 114 |
| $75,000 to $99,999 | 431 | 4 | 101 | 109 | 110 | 69 | 38 |
| $100,000 or more | 570 | – | 99 | 139 | 140 | 115 | 77 |
| Median income | $26,852 | $17,553 | $31,461 | $31,676 | $32,343 | $26,825 | $17,848 |
| **Total households** | **100.0%** | **100.0%** | **100.0%** | **100.0%** | **100.0%** | **100.0%** | **100.0%** |
| Under $25,000 | 46.1 | 70.3 | 35.4 | 35.5 | 38.2 | 46.8 | 69.2 |
| $25,000 to $49,999 | 32.9 | 22.8 | 41.5 | 38.5 | 35.2 | 28.6 | 21.0 |
| $50,000 to $74,999 | 12.0 | 5.9 | 14.5 | 16.3 | 15.0 | 10.2 | 4.8 |
| $75,000 to $99,999 | 3.9 | 0.7 | 4.4 | 4.2 | 5.1 | 5.4 | 1.6 |
| $100,000 or more | 5.1 | – | 4.3 | 5.4 | 6.5 | 9.0 | 3.3 |

*Note: (–) means sample is too small to make a reliable estimate.*
*Source: Bureau of the Census, data from the 2000 Current Population Survey, Internet site <http://ferret.bls .census.gov/macro/032000/hhinc/new02_000.htm>; calculations by New Strategist*

## Household Income of Women Who Live Alone, 1999

*(number and percent distribution of female-headed single-person households by household income and age of householder, 1999; households in thousands as of 2000)*

| | total | 15 to 24 | 25 to 34 | 35 to 44 | 45 to 54 | 55 to 64 | 65 or older |
|---|---|---|---|---|---|---|---|
| **Total households** | **15,543** | **587** | **1,569** | **1,540** | **2,158** | **2,262** | **7,427** |
| Under $25,000 | 10,122 | 469 | 583 | 603 | 947 | 1,330 | 6,195 |
| $25,000 to $49,999 | 3,737 | 99 | 723 | 601 | 800 | 618 | 898 |
| $50,000 to $74,999 | 1,058 | 12 | 155 | 227 | 263 | 186 | 211 |
| $75,000 to $99,999 | 317 | – | 39 | 61 | 83 | 67 | 63 |
| $100,000 or more | 309 | 9 | 67 | 48 | 67 | 62 | 57 |
| Median income | $17,347 | $14,587 | $29,841 | $30,822 | $27,559 | $20,104 | $13,045 |
| **Total households** | **100.0%** | **100.0%** | **100.0%** | **100.0%** | **100.0%** | **100.0%** | **100.0%** |
| Under $25,000 | 65.1 | 79.9 | 37.2 | 39.2 | 43.9 | 58.8 | 83.4 |
| $25,000 to $49,999 | 24.0 | 16.9 | 46.1 | 39.0 | 37.1 | 27.3 | 12.1 |
| $50,000 to $74,999 | 6.8 | 2.0 | 9.9 | 14.7 | 12.2 | 8.2 | 2.8 |
| $75,000 to $99,999 | 2.0 | – | 2.5 | 4.0 | 3.8 | 3.0 | 0.8 |
| $100,000 or more | 2.0 | 1.5 | 4.3 | 3.1 | 3.1 | 2.7 | 0.8 |

*Note: (–) means sample is too small to make a reliable estimate.*
*Source: Bureau of the Census, data from the 2000 Current Population Survey, Internet site <http://ferret.bls.census.gov/macro/032000/hhinc/new02_000.htm>; calculations by New Strategist*

# College-Educated Householders Earn Top Dollar

## The median income of households headed by college graduates is 66 percent higher than the national average.

The higher the educational degree, the greater the financial reward. At the top are householders with professional degrees, such as doctors and lawyers. Their median household income was an even $100,000 in 1999—meaning fully half had six-digit incomes.

Twenty-seven percent of householders aged 25 or older have at least a bachelor's degree. Their median income stood at $69,804 in 1999. Those with a master's degree had a median income of $74,476. In contrast, householders who went no further than high school had a below-average household income of just $35,744.

♦ As the incomes of college graduates soar, those without a college degree will find themselves at an increasing disadvantage in earning power.

**Incomes rise with education**

*(median income of householders aged 25 or older by education of householder, 1999)*

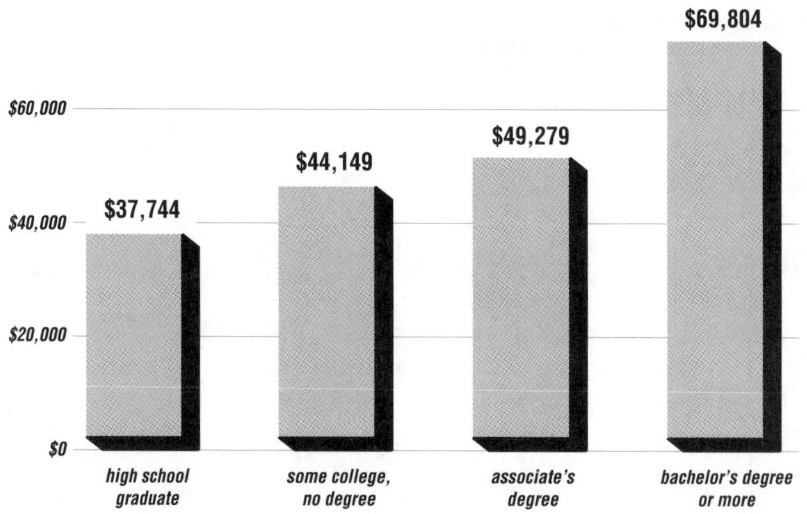

## Household Income by Education of Householder, 1999

*(number and percent distribution of householders aged 25 or older by household income and educational attainment of householder, 1999; households in thousands as of 2000)*

| | | | | | | | bachelor's degree or more | | | | |
|---|---|---|---|---|---|---|---|---|---|---|---|
| | total | less than 9th grade | 9th to 12th grade, no degree | high school graduate, incl. GED | some college, no degree | associate's degree | total | bachelor's degree | master's degree | professional degree | doctoral degree |
| **Total households** | **98,845** | **6,800** | **8,974** | **30,846** | **17,986** | **7,755** | **26,484** | **17,144** | **6,336** | **1,651** | **1,353** |
| Under $25,000 | 29,133 | 4,484 | 5,060 | 10,625 | 4,528 | 1,599 | 2,841 | 2,057 | 567 | 136 | 80 |
| $25,000 to $49,999 | 27,831 | 1,581 | 2,571 | 9,905 | 5,683 | 2,338 | 5,753 | 4,171 | 1,177 | 241 | 166 |
| $50,000 to $74,999 | 18,631 | 502 | 943 | 5,871 | 3,811 | 1,821 | 5,684 | 3,799 | 1,445 | 193 | 246 |
| $75,000 to $99,999 | 10,572 | 134 | 249 | 2,662 | 2,067 | 1,034 | 4,426 | 2,887 | 1,095 | 226 | 220 |
| $100,000 or more | 12,677 | 102 | 150 | 1,784 | 1,898 | 962 | 7,780 | 4,230 | 2,053 | 857 | 640 |
| Median income | $42,038 | $17,261 | $21,737 | $35,744 | $44,149 | $49,279 | $69,804 | $64,406 | $74,476 | $100,000 | $97,325 |
| **Total households** | **100.0%** | **100.0%** | **100.0%** | **100.0%** | **100.0%** | **100.0%** | **100.0%** | **100.0%** | **100.0%** | **100.0%** | **100.0%** |
| Under $25,000 | 29.5 | 65.9 | 56.4 | 34.4 | 25.2 | 20.6 | 10.7 | 11.0 | 8.9 | 8.2 | 5.9 |
| $25,000 to $49,999 | 28.2 | 23.2 | 28.6 | 32.1 | 31.6 | 30.1 | 21.7 | 24.3 | 18.6 | 14.6 | 12.3 |
| $50,000 to $74,999 | 18.8 | 7.4 | 10.5 | 19.0 | 21.2 | 23.5 | 21.5 | 22.2 | 22.8 | 11.7 | 18.2 |
| $75,000 to $99,999 | 10.7 | 1.0 | 2.8 | 8.6 | 11.5 | 13.3 | 16.7 | 16.8 | 17.3 | 13.7 | 16.3 |
| $100,000 or more | 12.8 | 1.5 | 1.7 | 5.8 | 10.6 | 12.4 | 29.4 | 24.7 | 32.4 | 51.9 | 47.3 |

*Source: Bureau of the Census, data from the 2000 Current Population Survey, Internet site <http://ferret.bls.census.gov/macro/032000/hhinc/new01_001.htm>; calculations by New Strategist*

# Women's Incomes Are Growing Faster Than Men's

## Since 1980, women's median income has climbed 54 percent while men's has increased just 8 percent, after adjusting for inflation.

Women's incomes are growing faster than men's as well-educated baby-boom and younger women enter the workforce. Women's median income stood at a record $15,311 in 1999, still well below men's median of $27,275.

Men's median income is far higher than women's because men are more likely to work full-time. Incomes peak among men aged 45 to 54 at $40,939. Women's income peak also occurs in the 45-to-54 age group at $22,588 (including both full- and part-time workers). Women aged 45 to 54 have enjoyed the fastest income growth—a 74 percent increase—between 1980 and 1999, after adjusting for inflation. The median income of men under age 45 fell between 1980 and 1999.

♦ Women will continue to close the income gap with men, but their median income will never equal that of men because many choose to work part-time while their children are young.

**Women's median income grew seven times faster than men's**

*(percent increase in median income of people aged 15 or older, by sex, 1980 to 1999; in 1999 dollars)*

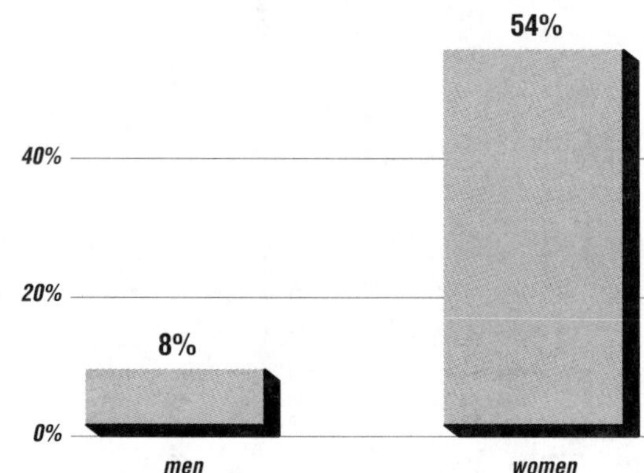

## Median Income of Men by Age, 1980 to 1999

*(median income of men aged 15 or older with income, by age, 1980–99; in 1999 dollars; percent change in income for selected years)*

| | total | under 25 | 25 to 34 | 35 to 44 | 45 to 54 | 55 to 64 | 65 or older |
|---|---|---|---|---|---|---|---|
| 1999 | $27,275 | $8,302 | $29,864 | $36,217 | $40,939 | $33,648 | $19,079 |
| 1998 | 27,077 | 8,371 | 28,738 | 35,954 | 39,782 | 33,500 | 18,567 |
| 1997 | 26,171 | 7,752 | 26,984 | 34,100 | 39,054 | 32,341 | 18,444 |
| 1996 | 25,308 | 7,391 | 26,736 | 34,156 | 38,472 | 31,351 | 17,716 |
| 1995 | 24,664 | 7,557 | 25,809 | 34,347 | 38,902 | 31,681 | 18,020 |
| 1994 | 24,417 | 7,923 | 25,413 | 34,520 | 39,271 | 30,437 | 17,143 |
| 1993 | 24,330 | 7,412 | 25,280 | 34,983 | 38,225 | 28,983 | 17,274 |
| 1992 | 24,290 | 7,478 | 25,527 | 35,020 | 38,214 | 30,416 | 17,334 |
| 1991 | 25,038 | 7,683 | 26,415 | 35,841 | 38,872 | 31,143 | 17,561 |
| 1990 | 25,867 | 8,055 | 27,269 | 37,951 | 39,524 | 31,617 | 18,079 |
| 1989 | 26,728 | 8,482 | 28,707 | 39,550 | 41,599 | 32,819 | 17,610 |
| 1988 | 26,627 | 8,229 | 29,267 | 40,200 | 41,654 | 31,893 | 17,563 |
| 1987 | 26,084 | 8,003 | 29,223 | 39,658 | 41,778 | 32,092 | 17,492 |
| 1986 | 26,014 | 8,031 | 29,127 | 39,784 | 42,191 | 31,973 | 17,548 |
| 1985 | 25,255 | 7,734 | 28,895 | 39,262 | 40,017 | 31,365 | 16,877 |
| 1984 | 25,015 | 7,551 | 29,012 | 39,391 | 39,428 | 31,311 | 16,756 |
| 1983 | 24,473 | 7,166 | 28,109 | 37,535 | 38,664 | 31,270 | 16,295 |
| 1982 | 24,310 | 7,715 | 28,608 | 37,727 | 37,542 | 31,068 | 16,012 |
| 1981 | 24,912 | 5,681 | 29,755 | 39,047 | 38,871 | 32,109 | 15,047 |
| 1980 | 25,364 | 9,306 | 31,539 | 40,560 | 40,434 | 32,215 | 14,856 |
| **Percent change** | | | | | | | |
| 1990–1999 | 5.4% | 3.1% | 9.5% | –4.6% | 3.6% | 6.4% | 5.5% |
| 1980–1999 | 7.5 | –10.8 | –5.3 | –10.7 | 1.2 | 4.4 | 28.4 |

*Source: Bureau of the Census, data from the Current Population Survey, Internet site <www .census.gov/hhes/income/histinc/p08.html>; calculations by New Strategist*

## Median Income of Women by Age, 1980 to 1999

*(median income of women aged 15 or older with income, by age, 1980–99; in 1999 dollars; percent change in income for selected years)*

| | total | under 25 | 25 to 34 | 35 to 44 | 45 to 54 | 55 to 64 | 65 or older |
|---|---|---|---|---|---|---|---|
| 1999 | $15,311 | $6,689 | $19,396 | $20,683 | $22,588 | $15,917 | $10,943 |
| 1998 | 14,749 | 6,678 | 18,660 | 20,733 | 22,065 | 14,999 | 10,736 |
| 1997 | 14,223 | 6,583 | 18,318 | 19,417 | 21,315 | 14,922 | 10,445 |
| 1996 | 13,607 | 6,245 | 17,397 | 19,587 | 20,223 | 14,140 | 10,221 |
| 1995 | 13,261 | 5,804 | 17,006 | 19,018 | 19,375 | 13,534 | 10,227 |
| 1994 | 12,890 | 6,192 | 16,732 | 18,199 | 19,168 | 12,216 | 10,061 |
| 1993 | 12,735 | 6,169 | 16,127 | 18,267 | 18,821 | 12,485 | 9,799 |
| 1992 | 12,722 | 6,139 | 16,186 | 18,307 | 18,824 | 12,032 | 9,717 |
| 1991 | 12,814 | 6,357 | 15,858 | 18,501 | 18,010 | 12,112 | 10,016 |
| 1990 | 12,836 | 6,248 | 16,047 | 18,487 | 18,139 | 11,982 | 10,254 |
| 1989 | 12,930 | 6,367 | 16,433 | 18,548 | 17,659 | 12,311 | 10,285 |
| 1988 | 12,511 | 6,316 | 16,287 | 17,669 | 16,928 | 11,797 | 10,003 |
| 1987 | 12,165 | 6,465 | 16,101 | 17,591 | 16,518 | 11,059 | 10,114 |
| 1986 | 11,568 | 6,147 | 15,672 | 16,818 | 15,778 | 11,213 | 9,766 |
| 1985 | 11,174 | 5,870 | 15,296 | 15,909 | 14,894 | 11,106 | 9,774 |
| 1984 | 11,013 | 5,787 | 15,059 | 15,330 | 14,275 | 10,963 | 9,653 |
| 1983 | 10,569 | 5,783 | 14,223 | 14,820 | 13,725 | 10,252 | 9,365 |
| 1982 | 10,259 | 5,841 | 13,892 | 13,682 | 13,074 | 10,294 | 9,349 |
| 1981 | 10,092 | 3,691 | 14,050 | 13,620 | 12,999 | 9,939 | 8,702 |
| 1980 | 9,959 | 6,324 | 14,115 | 13,087 | 12,962 | 9,971 | 8,555 |
| **Percent change** | | | | | | | |
| 1990–1999 | 19.3% | 7.1% | 20.9% | 11.9% | 24.5% | 32.8% | 6.7% |
| 1980–1999 | 53.7 | 5.8 | 37.4 | 58.0 | 74.3 | 59.6 | 27.9 |

*Source: Bureau of the Census, data from the Current Population Survey, Internet site <www .census.gov/hhes/income/histinc/p08.html>; calculations by New Strategist*

# Among Men, Blacks Post Biggest Income Gains

## Black women also experienced the biggest gains.

The median income of black men grew 25 percent between 1990 and 1999, after adjusting for inflation, to a record high $20,579. In contrast, the median income of all men rose only 5 percent during those years. In 1999, the income of black men was 67 percent as high as that of non-Hispanic white men, up from 59 percent in 1990. Black women, too, saw the greatest income gains during the 1990s. Their median income rose 39 percent compared with a 19 percent gain for all women.

Among both men and women, Hispanics have the lowest median income—just $11,314 for women and $18,234 for men in 1999. Hispanic men are the only racial or ethnic group whose median income failed to reach a record high in 1999.

Among men, non-Hispanic whites have the highest incomes, a median of $30,594 in 1999. Among women, Asians have the highest incomes, a median of $16,840.

♦ The incomes of Hispanics have not grown as rapidly as those of other racial and ethnic groups because millions of immigrants with little earning power are depressing the income statistics for all Hispanics.

## Median Income of Men by Race and Hispanic Origin, 1980 to 1999

*(median income of men aged 15 or older with income, by race and Hispanic origin; percent change, 1980–99; in 1999 dollars)*

| | total | Asian | black | Hispanic | white | non-Hispanic white |
|---|---|---|---|---|---|---|
| 1999 | $27,275 | $27,731 | $20,579 | $18,234 | $28,564 | $30,594 |
| 1998 | 27,077 | 25,679 | 19,748 | 17,638 | 28,257 | 30,522 |
| 1997 | 26,171 | 25,998 | 18,784 | 16,833 | 27,108 | 28,606 |
| 1996 | 25,308 | 24,819 | 17,510 | 16,391 | 26,491 | 27,915 |
| 1995 | 24,664 | 24,228 | 17,497 | 16,223 | 26,121 | 27,855 |
| 1994 | 24,417 | 25,732 | 16,842 | 16,300 | 25,484 | 27,117 |
| 1993 | 24,330 | 24,951 | 16,839 | 15,783 | 25,343 | 26,715 |
| 1992 | 24,290 | 23,618 | 15,513 | 15,921 | 25,418 | 26,598 |
| 1991 | 25,038 | 24,009 | 15,856 | 16,902 | 26,171 | 27,123 |
| 1990 | 25,867 | 24,721 | 16,402 | 17,170 | 26,985 | 27,989 |
| 1989 | 26,728 | 27,690 | 16,941 | 18,004 | 28,031 | 29,101 |
| 1988 | 26,627 | 25,943 | 16,962 | 18,350 | 28,108 | 29,156 |
| 1987 | 26,084 | – | 16,447 | 17,936 | 27,725 | 28,882 |
| 1986 | 26,014 | – | 16,450 | 17,530 | 27,452 | 28,687 |
| 1985 | 25,255 | – | 16,672 | 17,704 | 26,493 | 27,393 |
| 1984 | 25,015 | – | 15,149 | 17,800 | 26,405 | 27,190 |
| 1983 | 24,523 | – | 15,088 | 18,157 | 25,799 | 26,551 |
| 1982 | 24,310 | – | 15,402 | 18,247 | 25,701 | 26,358 |
| 1981 | 24,912 | – | 15,719 | 18,866 | 26,434 | 27,129 |
| 1980 | 25,364 | – | 16,212 | 19,553 | 26,980 | 27,694 |
| **Percent change** | | | | | | |
| 1990–1999 | 5.4% | 12.2% | 25.5% | 6.2% | 5.9% | 9.3% |
| 1980–1999 | 7.5 | – | 26.9 | –6.7 | 5.9 | 10.5 |

*Note: (–) means data not available.*
*Source: Bureau of the Census,* Money Income in the United States:1999 *Current Population Reports, P60-209, 2000; calculations by New Strategist*

## Median Income of Women by Race and Hispanic Origin, 1980 to 1999

*(median income of women aged 15 or older with income, by race and Hispanic origin; percent change, 1980–99; in 1999 dollars)*

| | *total* | *Asian* | *black* | *Hispanic* | *white* | *non-Hispanic white* |
|---|---|---|---|---|---|---|
| 1999 | $15,311 | $16,840 | $14,771 | $11,314 | $15,362 | $15,922 |
| 1998 | 14,749 | 15,564 | 13,427 | 11,102 | 14,940 | 15,553 |
| 1997 | 14,223 | 14,856 | 13,544 | 10,650 | 14,316 | 14,936 |
| 1996 | 13,607 | 15,539 | 12,500 | 10,071 | 13,762 | 14,349 |
| 1995 | 13,261 | 14,061 | 11,982 | 9,760 | 13,464 | 14,001 |
| 1994 | 12,890 | 13,897 | 11,853 | 9,682 | 13,074 | 13,428 |
| 1993 | 12,735 | 14,256 | 10,962 | 9,339 | 12,989 | 13,373 |
| 1992 | 12,722 | 14,097 | 10,553 | 9,865 | 13,018 | 13,362 |
| 1991 | 12,814 | 13,487 | 10,784 | 9,802 | 13,114 | 13,457 |
| 1990 | 12,836 | 14,131 | 10,615 | 9,600 | 13,151 | 13,487 |
| 1989 | 12,930 | 15,059 | 10,581 | 10,274 | 13,183 | 13,453 |
| 1988 | 12,511 | 13,017 | 10,360 | 9,844 | 12,820 | 13,119 |
| 1987 | 12,165 | – | 10,191 | 9,723 | 12,476 | 12,756 |
| 1986 | 11,568 | – | 9,981 | 9,634 | 11,796 | 11,995 |
| 1985 | 11,174 | – | 9,719 | 9,321 | 11,391 | 11,517 |
| 1984 | 11,013 | – | 9,884 | 9,348 | 11,143 | 11,321 |
| 1983 | 10,714 | – | 9,315 | 9,050 | 10,901 | 11,142 |
| 1982 | 10,259 | – | 9,172 | 8,958 | 10,399 | 10,708 |
| 1981 | 10,092 | – | 9,066 | 9,356 | 10,205 | 10,388 |
| 1980 | 9,959 | – | 9,271 | 8,917 | 10,014 | 10,081 |
| **Percent change** | | | | | | |
| 1990–1999 | 19.3% | 19.2% | 39.2% | 17.9% | 16.8% | 18.1% |
| 1980–1999 | 53.7 | – | 59.3 | 26.9 | 53.4 | 57.9 |

*Note: (–) means data not available.*
*Source: Bureau of the Census,* Money Income in the United States:1999*; Current Population Reports, P60-209, 2000; calculations by New Strategist*

# Incomes of Men and Women Peak in the 45-to-54 Age Group

## Men's income peak is almost twice as high as women's.

Men aged 45 to 54 had a median income of $40,939 in 1999. Their female counterparts had a median income of only $22,588. The gap between women's and men's incomes is large because the statistics include both full- and part-time workers, and women are much more likely than men to work part-time.

Nearly one in five men aged 45 to 54 had an income of $75,000 or more in 1999, as did 16 percent of those aged 55 to 64. Incomes are lowest for men under age 25, with a median of just $8,302. Many are college students who work part-time.

Women are much less likely to have high incomes than men. Only 4 percent of women aged 45 to 54 had an income of $75,000 or more. But a significant 14 percent of women in the age group had an income of $50,000 or more. Older women have much lower incomes than their male counterparts because fewer are covered by pensions. Women aged 65 or older had a median income of just $10,943 versus a median of $19,079 for men.

♦ The income gap between older men and women should narrow as working women with pensions of their own replace older women with no work experience.

## Income of Men by Age, 1999: Total Men

*(number and percent distribution of men aged 15 or older by income and age, and median income of those with income, 1999; men in thousands as of 2000)*

| | *total* | *under 25* | *25 to 34* | *35 to 44* | *45 to 54* | *55 to 64* | *65 or older* |
|---|---|---|---|---|---|---|---|
| **Total men** | **103,114** | **19,503** | **18,563** | **22,135** | **17,890** | **11,137** | **13,886** |
| **WITH INCOME** | **96,023** | **14,428** | **17,974** | **21,654** | **17,477** | **10,804** | **13,686** |
| Under $15,000 | 26,416 | 10,055 | 3,099 | 3,203 | 2,578 | 2,378 | 5,102 |
| $15,000 to $24,999 | 17,386 | 2,562 | 4,012 | 3,325 | 2,151 | 1,602 | 3,737 |
| $25,000 to $49,999 | 29,801 | 1,606 | 7,521 | 8,223 | 5,904 | 3,392 | 3,156 |
| $50,000 to $74,999 | 12,559 | 148 | 2,230 | 4,054 | 3,607 | 1,695 | 823 |
| $75,000 or more | 9,866 | 57 | 1,112 | 2,851 | 3,236 | 1,740 | 870 |
| Median income | $27,275 | $8,302 | $29,864 | $36,217 | $40,939 | $33,648 | $19,079 |
| **Total men with income** | **100.0%** | **100.0%** | **100.0%** | **100.0%** | **100.0%** | **100.0%** | **100.0%** |
| Under $15,000 | 27.5 | 69.7 | 17.2 | 14.8 | 14.8 | 22.0 | 37.3 |
| $15,000 to $24,999 | 18.1 | 17.8 | 22.3 | 15.4 | 12.3 | 14.8 | 27.3 |
| $25,000 to $49,999 | 31.0 | 11.1 | 41.8 | 37.0 | 33.8 | 31.4 | 23.1 |
| $50,000 to $74,999 | 13.1 | 1.0 | 12.4 | 18.7 | 20.6 | 15.7 | 6.0 |
| $75,000 or more | 10.3 | 0.4 | 6.2 | 13.2 | 18.5 | 16.1 | 6.4 |

*Source: Bureau of the Census, data from the 2000 Current Population Survey, Internet site <http://ferret.bls .census.gov/macro/032000/perinc/new01_000.htm>calculations by New Strategist*

## Income of Women by Age, 1999: Total Women

*(number and percent distribution of women aged 15 or older by income and age, and median income of those with income, 1999; women in thousands as of 2000)*

| | total | under 25 | 25 to 34 | 35 to 44 | 45 to 54 | 55 to 64 | 65 or older |
|---|---|---|---|---|---|---|---|
| **Total women** | **110,660** | **19,040** | **19,223** | **22,670** | **18,741** | **12,250** | **18,735** |
| **With income** | **99,613** | **13,957** | **17,411** | **21,098** | **17,579** | **11,277** | **18,291** |
| Under $15,000 | 49,023 | 10,739 | 6,761 | 7,877 | 5,959 | 5,399 | 12,285 |
| $15,000 to $24,999 | 19,848 | 2,185 | 4,109 | 4,410 | 3,507 | 2,186 | 3,452 |
| $25,000 to $49,999 | 22,601 | 943 | 5,239 | 6,382 | 5,675 | 2,501 | 1,863 |
| $50,000 to $74,999 | 5,466 | 56 | 844 | 1,671 | 1,667 | 786 | 444 |
| $75,000 or more | 2,676 | 34 | 458 | 758 | 773 | 407 | 246 |
| Median income | $15,311 | $6,689 | $19,396 | $20,683 | $22,588 | $15,917 | $10,943 |
| **Total women with income** | **100.0%** | **100.0%** | **100.0%** | **100.0%** | **100.0%** | **100.0%** | **100.0%** |
| Under $15,000 | 49.2 | 76.9 | 38.8 | 37.3 | 33.9 | 47.9 | 67.2 |
| $15,000 to $24,999 | 19.9 | 15.7 | 23.6 | 20.9 | 19.9 | 19.4 | 18.9 |
| $25,000 to $49,999 | 22.7 | 6.8 | 30.1 | 30.2 | 32.3 | 22.2 | 10.2 |
| $50,000 to $74,999 | 5.5 | 0.4 | 4.8 | 7.9 | 9.5 | 6.0 | 2.4 |
| $75,000 or more | 2.7 | 0.2 | 2.6 | 3.6 | 4.4 | 3.6 | 1.3 |

*Source: Bureau of the Census, data from the 2000 Current Population Survey, Internet site <http://ferret.bls.census.gov/macro/032000/perinc/new01_000.htm>calculations by New Strategist*

# Earnings Gap between Men and Women Is Smallest among Young Adults

## Women have a long way to go before they catch up to men.

Among full-time workers, women earn 73 percent as much as men—$27,370 for women versus $37,574 for men in 1999. The figure varies sharply by age, race, and education, however.

Young women come the closest to matching the earnings of men. Among people under age 25 who work full-time, women earn 91 percent as much as men. The figure drops to 82 percent in the 25-to-34 age group and falls with age to 65 and 66 percent among people aged 55 or older. Some of the decline occurs because older men are much better educated and have more job experience than older women. But the career choices women have made in the past also play a role.

Black and Hispanic women have earnings closer to their male counterparts than non-Hispanic white women do. In part, this is because black and Hispanic men earn much less than non-Hispanic white men.

By education, the gap in earnings between men and women is greatest among those with professional degrees—such as doctors and lawyers. This gap is largely due to demographic differences between male and female professionals since women have only recently entered the professions in significant numbers.

♦ Women will continue to gain on men in earnings, but they are unlikely to completely close the gap because more women than men will make economic sacrifices for their family.

## Median Income of Full-Time Workers by Sex, 1999

*(median income of people aged 15 or older working year-round, full-time by age, race, Hispanic orgin, education, and sex, and women's income as a percent of men's, 1999)*

| | men | women | women's income as a percent of men's |
|---|---|---|---|
| **Total people** | **$37,574** | **$27,370** | **73** |
| **Age** | | | |
| Under age 25 | 19,515 | 17,851 | 91 |
| Aged 25 to 34 | 32,599 | 26,670 | 82 |
| Aged 35 to 44 | 40,916 | 29,155 | 71 |
| Aged 45 to 54 | 46,228 | 30,848 | 67 |
| Aged 55 to 64 | 44,264 | 28,764 | 65 |
| Aged 65 or older | 45,781 | 30,013 | 66 |
| **Race and Hispanic origin** | | | |
| Black | 30,297 | 25,142 | 83 |
| Hispanic | 23,342 | 20,052 | 86 |
| White | 39,331 | 28,023 | 71 |
| Non-Hispanic white | 41,406 | 29,369 | 71 |
| **Education** | | | |
| Total, aged 25 or older | 40,333 | 28,844 | 72 |
| Less than 9th grade | 20,429 | 15,098 | 74 |
| 9th to 12th grade | 25,035 | 17,015 | 68 |
| High school graduate | 33,184 | 23,061 | 69 |
| Some college, no degree | 39,221 | 27,757 | 71 |
| Associate's degree | 41,638 | 30,919 | 74 |
| Bachelor's degree | 52,985 | 37,993 | 72 |
| Master's degree | 66,243 | 48,097 | 73 |
| Professional degree | 100,000 | 59,904 | 60 |
| Doctoral degree | 81,687 | 60,079 | 74 |

*Source: Bureau of the Census,* Money Income in the United States: 1999, *Current Population Reports, P60-209, 2000; calculations by New Strategist*

# Education Boosts Earnings

## Although college costs have soared, the payback is enormous.

Men with at least a bachelor's degree earned a median of $51,815 in 1999. Those who went no further than high school earned just $29,917. Women with at least a bachelor's degree earned a median of $30,730 versus the $17,126 earned by those who went no further than high school. Women's earnings are much lower than men's because these statistics include both full- and part-time workers, and women are much more likely than men to work part-time.

The highest-paid men are those with professional degrees, such as doctors and lawyers. Their median earnings amounted to $86,523 in 1999, and 45 percent earned more than $100,000. The highest-paid women, those with doctorates, earned a median of $46,949 in 1999.

♦ Educational credentials will become more important in the years ahead as the economy continues to reward highly trained workers. A master's degree may become a necessity for a middle-class lifestyle in the 21st century.

♦ Because people tend to marry those with similar educational backgrounds, highly educated couples will continue to dominate the nation's affluent.

## Earnings Distribution of Men Aged 25 or Older by Education, 1999

*(number and percent distribution of men aged 25 or older by earnings and educational attainment, and median earnings of those with earnings, 1999; men in thousands as of 2000)*

| | | | | | | | bachelor's degree or more | | | | |
|---|---|---|---|---|---|---|---|---|---|---|---|
| | total | less than 9th grade | 9th to 12th grade, no degree | high school graduate, incl. GED | some college, no degree | associate's degree | total | bachelor's degree | master's degree | professional degree | doctoral degree |
| **Total men** | **83,611** | **5,918** | **7,298** | **26,651** | **14,540** | **5,952** | **23,251** | **14,909** | **5,166** | **1,752** | **1,425** |
| **With earnings** | **65,412** | **2,833** | **4,608** | **20,656** | **11,908** | **5,175** | **20,232** | **13,057** | **4,462** | **1,480** | **1,233** |
| Under $25,000 | 21,351 | 2,120 | 2,803 | 8,112 | 3,756 | 1,375 | 3,185 | 2,279 | 622 | 149 | 136 |
| $25,000 to $49,999 | 24,772 | 600 | 1,513 | 9,135 | 5,157 | 2,255 | 6,110 | 4,554 | 1,101 | 233 | 226 |
| $50,000 to $74,999 | 11,218 | 79 | 224 | 2,562 | 2,000 | 1,118 | 5,233 | 3,366 | 1,335 | 232 | 298 |
| $75,000 to $99,999 | 3,799 | 16 | 36 | 490 | 565 | 245 | 2,448 | 1,370 | 701 | 200 | 180 |
| $100,000 or more | 4,268 | 15 | 33 | 357 | 427 | 180 | 3,256 | 1,491 | 706 | 663 | 396 |
| Median earnings | $34,850 | $16,704 | $20,604 | $29,917 | $34,270 | $36,885 | $51,815 | $47,419 | $57,841 | $86,523 | $71,531 |
| **Total men with earnings** | **100.0%** | **100.0%** | **100.0%** | **100.0%** | **100.0%** | **100.0%** | **100.0%** | **100.0%** | **100.0%** | **100.0%** | **100.0%** |
| Under $25,000 | 32.6 | 74.8 | 60.8 | 39.3 | 31.5 | 26.6 | 15.7 | 17.5 | 13.9 | 10.1 | 11.0 |
| $25,000 to $49,999 | 37.9 | 21.2 | 32.8 | 44.2 | 43.3 | 43.6 | 30.2 | 34.9 | 24.7 | 15.7 | 18.3 |
| $50,000 to $74,999 | 17.1 | 2.8 | 4.9 | 12.4 | 16.8 | 21.6 | 25.9 | 25.8 | 29.9 | 15.7 | 24.2 |
| $75,000 to $99,999 | 5.8 | 0.6 | 0.8 | 2.4 | 4.7 | 4.7 | 12.1 | 10.5 | 15.7 | 13.5 | 14.6 |
| $100,000 or more | 6.5 | 0.5 | 0.7 | 1.7 | 3.6 | 3.5 | 16.1 | 11.4 | 15.8 | 44.8 | 32.1 |

*Source: Bureau of the Census, data from the 2000 Current Population Survey, Internet site <http://ferret.bls.census.gov/macro/032000/perinc/new03_000.htm>; calculations by New Strategist*

## Earnings Distribution of Women Aged 25 or Older by Education, 1999

*(number and percent distribution of women aged 25 or older by earnings and educational attainment, and median earnings of those with earnings, 1999; women in thousands as of 2000)*

| | | | | | | | bachelor's degree or more | | | | |
|---|---|---|---|---|---|---|---|---|---|---|---|
| | total | less than 9th grade | 9th to 12th grade, no degree | high school graduate, incl. GED | some college, no degree | associate's degree | total | bachelor's degree | master's degree | professional degree | doctoral degree |
| **Total women** | **91,620** | **6,261** | **8,377** | **31,435** | **16,213** | **7,740** | **21,595** | **14,931** | **5,230** | **834** | **599** |
| **WITH EARNINGS** | **58,225** | **1,673** | **3,489** | **18,756** | **11,483** | **5,844** | **16,980** | **11,548** | **4,238** | **687** | **507** |
| Under $25,000 | 33,380 | 1,556 | 3,089 | 13,374 | 6,778 | 3,077 | 5,511 | 4,292 | 962 | 143 | 113 |
| $25,000 to $49,999 | 18,768 | 101 | 364 | 4,838 | 3,846 | 2,319 | 7,300 | 5,027 | 1,890 | 233 | 149 |
| $50,000 to $74,999 | 4,362 | 10 | 24 | 422 | 626 | 345 | 2,935 | 1,632 | 1,041 | 128 | 133 |
| $75,000 to $99,999 | 946 | – | 5 | 56 | 134 | 55 | 696 | 404 | 196 | 65 | 34 |
| $100,000 or more | 768 | 6 | 7 | 66 | 98 | 52 | 539 | 193 | 149 | 118 | 79 |
| Median earnings | $21,417 | $10,754 | $11,432 | $17,126 | $21,426 | $23,760 | $33,370 | $30,730 | $40,553 | $45,926 | $46,949 |
| **Total women with earnings** | **100.0%** | **100.0%** | **100.0%** | **100.0%** | **100.0%** | **100.0%** | **100.0%** | **100.0%** | **100.0%** | **100.0%** | **100.0%** |
| Under $25,000 | 57.3 | 93.0 | 88.5 | 71.3 | 59.0 | 52.7 | 32.5 | 37.2 | 22.7 | 20.8 | 22.3 |
| $25,000 to $49,999 | 32.2 | 6.0 | 10.4 | 25.8 | 33.5 | 39.7 | 43.0 | 43.5 | 44.6 | 33.9 | 29.4 |
| $50,000 to $74,999 | 7.5 | 0.6 | 0.7 | 2.2 | 5.5 | 5.9 | 17.3 | 14.1 | 24.6 | 18.6 | 26.2 |
| $75,000 to $99,999 | 1.6 | – | 0.1 | 0.3 | 1.2 | 0.9 | 4.1 | 3.5 | 4.6 | 9.5 | 6.7 |
| $100,000 or more | 1.3 | 0.4 | 0.2 | 0.4 | 0.9 | 0.9 | 3.2 | 1.7 | 3.5 | 17.2 | 15.6 |

*Note: (–) means sample is too small to make a reliable estimate.*
*Source: Bureau of the Census, data from the 2000 Current Population Survey, Internet site <http://ferret.bls.census.gov/macro/032000/perinc/new03_000.htm>; calculations by New Strategist*

# Women Earn 76 Percent as Much as Men

## The gap is narrower in some occupations than others.

Men who work full-time earned a median of $646 a week in 2000. Women earned a median of $491—or 76 percent of what men earn. But women have been closing the earnings gap, and in many occupations, women now make almost as much as men.

While women in precision production occupations earn only 64 percent as much as their male counterparts, women mechanics and repairers earn 97 percent as much men in the occupation. Women working as computer scientists, registered nurses, pharmacists, therapists, social workers, and computer programmers make at least 85 percent as much as men in those professions.

The earnings gap is wide in many executive, administrative, and managerial jobs. Among administrators in medicine and health, women earn only 65 percent as much as men. Women's earnings are less than 70 percent of men's among financial managers and marketing managers as well.

♦ One reason for the earnings gap is that the average male worker has been on the job longer than the average female worker. As women gain job experience, the earnings gap will continue to shrink.

# Median Weekly Earnings by Sex, 2000

*(median weekly earnings of full-time wage and salary workers aged 16 or older by selected occupation and sex, and women's earnings as a percent of men's, 2000)*

| | men | women | women's earnings as a percent of men's |
|---|---|---|---|
| **Total workers** | **$646** | **$491** | **76.0%** |
| Managerial and professional specialty | 994 | 709 | 71.3 |
| Executive, administrative, and managerial | 1,014 | 686 | 67.7 |
| Officials and administrators, public administration | 980 | 740 | 75.5 |
| Financial managers | 1,201 | 787 | 65.5 |
| Personnel and labor relations managers | 1,153 | 837 | 72.6 |
| Purchasing managers | 1,035 | – | – |
| Managers, marketing, advertising, public relations | 1,250 | 846 | 67.7 |
| Administrators, education and related fields | 1,098 | 827 | 75.3 |
| Managers, medicine and health | 1,039 | 676 | 65.1 |
| Managers, property and real estate | 754 | 565 | 74.9 |
| Professional specialty | 977 | 725 | 74.2 |
| Engineers | 1,126 | 949 | 84.3 |
| Mathematical and computer scientists | 1,055 | 901 | 85.4 |
| Natural scientists | 1,007 | 726 | 72.1 |
| Physicians | 1,553 | 899 | 57.9 |
| Registered nurses | 890 | 782 | 87.9 |
| Pharmacists | 1,312 | 1,152 | 87.8 |
| Therapists | 831 | 727 | 87.5 |
| Teachers, college and university | 1,020 | 805 | 78.9 |
| Teachers, except college and university | 827 | 673 | 81.4 |
| Psychologists | 893 | 698 | 78.2 |
| Social, recreation, and religious workers | 678 | 577 | 85.1 |
| Lawyers and judges | 1,448 | 1,054 | 72.8 |
| Writers, artists, entertainers, and athletes | 789 | 641 | 81.2 |
| Technical, sales, and administrative support | 655 | 452 | 69.0 |
| Health technologists and technicians | 620 | 507 | 81.8 |
| Engineering and related technologists and technicians | 721 | 586 | 81.3 |
| Science technicians | 678 | 460 | 67.8 |
| Technicians, except health, engineering, and science | 957 | 655 | 68.4 |
| Computer programmers | 968 | 868 | 89.7 |
| Legal assistants | 703 | 596 | 84.8 |

*(continued)*

*(continued from previous page)*

| | men | women | women's earnings as a percent of men's |
|---|---|---|---|
| Sales occupations | $684 | $407 | 59.5% |
| Supervisors and proprietors | 695 | 485 | 69.8 |
| Sales representatives, finance and business services | 887 | 591 | 66.6 |
| Sales representatives, commodities, except retail | 832 | 665 | 79.9 |
| Sales workers, retail and personal services | 470 | 301 | 64.0 |
| Administrative support, including clerical | 563 | 449 | 79.8 |
| Supervisors | 703 | 545 | 77.5 |
| Computer equipment operators | 634 | 492 | 77.6 |
| Secretaries, stenographers, and typists | – | 455 | – |
| Information clerks | 486 | 400 | 82.3 |
| Records processing occupations, except financial | 492 | 459 | 93.3 |
| Financial records processing | 544 | 473 | 86.9 |
| Service occupations | 414 | 316 | 76.3 |
| Police and detective | 716 | 559 | 78.1 |
| Food preparation and service occupations | 325 | 294 | 90.5 |
| Health service occupations | 377 | 339 | 89.9 |
| Cleaning and building service occupations | 382 | 307 | 80.4 |
| Personal service occupations | 400 | 321 | 80.3 |
| Precision production, craft, and repair | 628 | 445 | 70.9 |
| Mechanics and repairers | 649 | 627 | 96.6 |
| Construction trades | 599 | 475 | 79.3 |
| Precision production occupations | 645 | 414 | 64.2 |
| Operators, fabricators, and laborers | 487 | 351 | 72.1 |
| Machine operators, assemblers, and inspectors | 496 | 355 | 71.6 |
| Transportation and material moving occupations | 558 | 407 | 72.9 |
| Truck drivers | 573 | 407 | 71.0 |
| Bus drivers | 506 | 401 | 79.2 |
| Handlers, equipment cleaners, helpers, and laborers | 394 | 320 | 81.2 |
| Farming, forestry, and fishing | 347 | 294 | 84.7 |

*Note: (–) means data not available.*
*Source: Bureau of Labor Statistics,* Employment and Earnings, *January 2001; calculations by New Strategist*

# Incomes Are Highest in Suburbia

## Nonmetropolitan households have the lowest incomes.

Householders living in the suburbs of the nation's largest metropolitan areas have the highest incomes. Their median of $51,221 in 1999 was 25 percent higher than the national median. Many suburban householders are middle-aged married couples in their peak earning years. Nonmetropolitan households have the lowest incomes, a median of $33,021 in 1999, or just 81 percent of the national average. The elderly—many of whom have low incomes because they are retired—head a larger share of households in nonmetropolitan areas.

Households in the Northeast, Midwest, and West have above-average incomes, while those in the South are below average. Among the 50 states, Maryland has the highest household income, a median of $51,715 in 1999. Alaska is second, with a median income of $51,660. West Virginia has the lowest median household income, just $28,363 in 1999. The median income gap between Maryland and West Virginia amounted to more than $22,000 in 1999.

♦ The changing structure of the economy may result in smaller income differences by region and metropolitan residence. In the future, because of increased telecommuting, place-of-residence may no longer determine income levels as distinctly as it does today.

## Median Household Income by Metropolitan Status and Region of Residence, 1999

*(number of households, median household income, and index of category median to national median, by metropolitan status and region of residence, 1999; households in thousands as of 2000)*

| | number of households | median income | index |
|---|---|---|---|
| **Total households** | **104,705** | **$40,816** | **100** |
| **Metropolitan status** | | | |
| Inside metropolitan areas | 84,259 | 42,785 | 105 |
| 1 million or more | 56,131 | 45,497 | 111 |
| Inside central cities | 20,214 | 36,485 | 89 |
| Outside central cities | 35,917 | 51,221 | 125 |
| Under 1 million | 28,127 | 38,359 | 94 |
| Inside central cities | 11,611 | 33,756 | 83 |
| Outside central cities | 16,516 | 41,703 | 102 |
| Outside metropolitan areas | 20,447 | 33,021 | 81 |
| **Region** | | | |
| Northeast | 20,087 | 41,984 | 103 |
| Midwest | 24,508 | 42,679 | 105 |
| South | 37,303 | 37,442 | 92 |
| West | 22,808 | 42,720 | 105 |

*Note: The index is calculated by dividing the median for each metropolitan status and region by the national median and multiplying by 100.*

*Source: Bureau of the Census,* Money Income in the United States: 1999, *Current Population Reports, P60-209, 2000; calculations by New Strategist*

## Median Income of Households by State, 1998–99

*(median income of households by state, and index of state to national median, two-year average, 1998–99; ranked by median income)*

| | median income | index |
|---|---|---|
| **United States** | **$40,280** | **100** |
| Maryland | 51,715 | 128 |
| Alaska | 51,660 | 128 |
| New Jersey | 50,428 | 125 |
| Connecticut | 49,167 | 122 |
| Minnesota | 48,112 | 119 |
| Colorado | 47,987 | 119 |
| Washington | 47,054 | 117 |
| New Hampshire | 46,059 | 114 |
| Utah | 45,686 | 113 |
| Illinois | 45,262 | 112 |
| Virginia | 45,031 | 112 |
| Delaware | 44,606 | 111 |
| Michigan | 44,491 | 110 |
| Wisconsin | 44,032 | 109 |
| Massachusetts | 43,736 | 109 |
| Hawaii | 43,051 | 107 |
| California | 42,791 | 106 |
| Rhode Island | 42,260 | 105 |
| Missouri | 41,277 | 102 |
| Nevada | 41,157 | 102 |
| Vermont | 40,936 | 102 |
| Indiana | 40,769 | 101 |
| Oregon | 40,321 | 100 |
| Ohio | 39,701 | 99 |
| Iowa | 39,537 | 98 |
| Georgia | 39,476 | 98 |
| New York | 39,139 | 97 |
| Pennsylvania | 38,936 | 97 |
| Nebraska | 38,002 | 94 |
| Texas | 37,776 | 94 |
| Maine | 37,680 | 94 |
| Arizona | 37,514 | 93 |

*(continued)*

*(continued from previous page)*

| | median income | index |
|---|---|---|
| Kansas | $37,499 | 93 |
| North Carolina | 36,985 | 92 |
| Wyoming | 36,712 | 91 |
| Idaho | 36,698 | 91 |
| Alabama | 36,640 | 91 |
| District of Columbia | 36,429 | 90 |
| Florida | 35,778 | 89 |
| Tennessee | 35,690 | 89 |
| Kentucky | 35,477 | 88 |
| South Carolina | 35,282 | 88 |
| South Dakota | 34,746 | 86 |
| Oklahoma | 33,695 | 84 |
| Louisiana | 32,565 | 81 |
| New Mexico | 32,357 | 80 |
| North Dakota | 31,925 | 79 |
| Montana | 31,759 | 79 |
| Mississippi | 31,152 | 77 |
| Arkansas | 29,019 | 72 |
| West Virginia | 28,363 | 70 |

*Note: The index is calculated by dividing the median income of each state by the national median and multiplying by 100.*
*Source: Bureau of the Census,* Money Income in the United States: 1999, *Current Population Reports, P60-209, 2000; calculations by New Strategist*

# Wages and Salaries Rank Number One

## Wages and salaries are the most important source of income for the largest proportion of Americans.

Among the 196 million Americans aged 15 or older with income in 1999, fully 72 percent earned money from wages or salaries. The average amount they received from wages and salaries was $31,278. Nineteen percent of the population received Social Security payments averaging $8,819 per person in 1999.

Interest is another widely received source of income. More than 104 million people earned interest income in 1999, but the average amount is small. Americans with interest income received an average of $1,958 from this source in 1999. Twenty-one percent of the population aged 15 or older received dividend income (averaging $3,112), while 8 percent received pension income (averaging $13,277).

♦ While most people of working age are dependent primarily on wage and salary income to maintain their lifestyle, older Americans are dependent on a greater variety of income sources—from Social Security to pensions to interest and dividends.

## Sources of Income, 1999

*(number and percent of people aged 15 or older with income and average income for those with income, by selected sources of income, 1999; people in thousands as of 2000)*

| | number | percent | average |
|---|---|---|---|
| **Total people** | **195,636** | **100.0%** | **$29,675** |
| With earnings | 148,847 | 76.1 | 31,521 |
| Wages and salary | 140,107 | 71.6 | 31,278 |
| Nonfarm self-employment | 11,632 | 5.9 | 25,287 |
| Farm self-employment | 1,837 | 0.9 | 8,444 |
| Social Security | 37,794 | 19.3 | 8,819 |
| Public assistance | 2,756 | 1.4 | 3,151 |
| Veterans' benefits | 2,512 | 1.3 | 7,994 |
| Survivors' benefits | 2,687 | 1.4 | 9,833 |
| Disability benefits | 1,616 | 0.8 | 10,306 |
| Pensions | 15,135 | 7.7 | 13,277 |
| Company or union | 9,441 | 4.8 | 10,039 |
| Federal government | 1,298 | 0.7 | 21,863 |
| Military retirement | 933 | 0.5 | 17,148 |
| State or local government | 2,836 | 1.4 | 16,180 |
| Annuities | 255 | 0.1 | 9,675 |
| IRA, KEOGH, or 401K | 398 | 0.2 | 14,466 |
| Interest | 104,493 | 53.4 | 1,958 |
| Dividends | 40,564 | 20.7 | 3,112 |
| Rents, royalties, estates or trusts | 12,437 | 6.4 | 4,564 |
| Education | 7,525 | 3.8 | 4,046 |
| Child support | 5,146 | 2.6 | 4,031 |
| Alimony | 462 | 0.2 | 10,266 |

*Source: Bureau of the Census,* Money Income in the United States: 1999, *Current Population Reports, P60-209, 2000; calculations by New Strategist*

# Majority of Poor Are Black or Hispanic

## Among the nation's 32 million poor, only 46 percent are non-Hispanic white.

The poverty rate has fallen in recent years, but some segments of society continue to be poorer than others. Only 8 percent of non-Hispanic whites are poor versus 24 percent of blacks and 23 percent of Hispanics. Within each racial and ethnic group, children and young adults are more likely to be poor than other age groups. Overall, 17 percent of the nation's children are poor. The figure is 33 percent among black children and 30 percent among Hispanic children.

The poverty rate varies sharply by family type. Regardless of race or Hispanic origin, the incidence of poverty is low among married couples. Overall, only 5 percent of married couples are poor compared with fully 28 percent of female-headed families. Among female-headed families with children, the poverty rate is an even higher 36 percent.

♦ Childhood poverty will remain a chronic problem until single-parent families begin to decline as a share of all families.

**Poverty rates are low for married couples**

*(percent of families in poverty by race, Hispanic origin, and family type, 1999)*

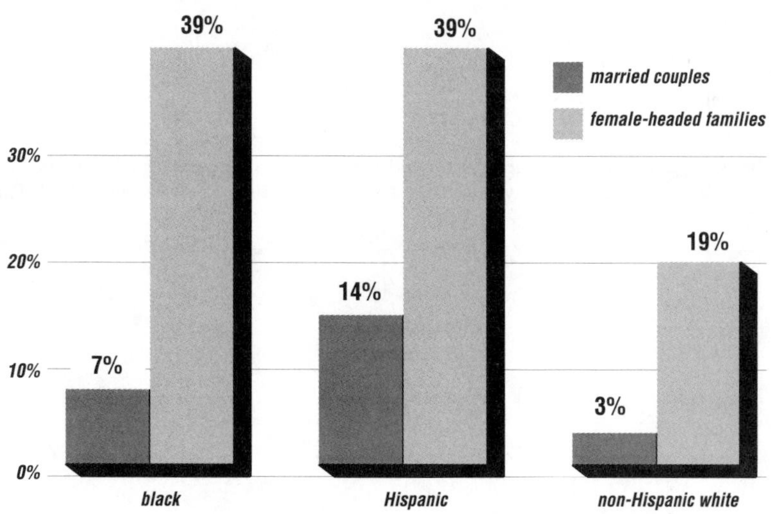

## People in Poverty by Age, Race, and Hispanic Origin, 1999

*(number and percent of people in poverty by age, race, and Hispanic origin, 1999; people in thousands as of 2000)*

| | *total* | *black* | *Hispanic* | *white* | *non-Hispanic white* |
|---|---|---|---|---|---|
| **Number in poverty** | | | | | |
| **Total people** | **32,258** | **8,360** | **7,439** | **21,922** | **14,875** |
| Under age 18 | 12,109 | 3,759 | 3,506 | 7,568 | 4,252 |
| Aged 18 to 24 | 4,603 | 1,165 | 941 | 3,125 | 2,236 |
| Aged 25 to 34 | 3,968 | 893 | 1,121 | 2,792 | 1,732 |
| Aged 35 to 44 | 3,733 | 945 | 811 | 2,614 | 1,845 |
| Aged 45 to 54 | 2,466 | 538 | 422 | 1,749 | 1,361 |
| Aged 55 to 59 | 1,179 | 231 | 141 | 890 | 750 |
| Aged 60 to 64 | 1,033 | 204 | 140 | 776 | 636 |
| Aged 65 or older | 3,167 | 626 | 358 | 2,409 | 2,063 |
| **Percent in poverty** | | | | | |
| **Total people** | **11.8%** | **23.6%** | **22.8%** | **9.8%** | **7.7%** |
| Under age 18 | 16.9 | 33.1 | 30.3 | 13.5 | 9.4 |
| Aged 18 to 24 | 17.3 | 29.3 | 23.8 | 14.8 | 12.9 |
| Aged 25 to 34 | 10.5 | 17.3 | 19.8 | 9.2 | 6.9 |
| Aged 35 to 44 | 8.3 | 16.6 | 16.3 | 7.1 | 5.7 |
| Aged 45 to 54 | 6.7 | 13.1 | 14.0 | 5.7 | 4.9 |
| Aged 55 to 59 | 9.2 | 17.9 | 14.2 | 8.0 | 7.4 |
| Aged 60 to 64 | 9.8 | 19.8 | 18.5 | 8.5 | 7.6 |
| Aged 65 tor older | 9.7 | 22.7 | 20.4 | 8.3 | 7.6 |

*Note: Numbers will not add to total because Hispanics may be of any race and not all races are shown.*
*Source: Bureau of the Census,* Poverty in the United States, *Current Population Reports, P60-210, 2000*

## Families in Poverty by Race, Hispanic Origin, and Presence of Children, 1999

*(number and percent of families in poverty by type of family, presence of related children under age 18 at home, and race and Hispanic origin of householder, 1999; families in thousands as of 2000)*

| | *total* | *black* | *Hispanic* | *white* | *non-Hispanic white* |
|---|---|---|---|---|---|
| TOTAL FAMILIES | | | | | |
| **Number of families in poverty** | **6,676** | **1,898** | **1,525** | **4,377** | **2,942** |
| Married couples | 2,673 | 294 | 728 | 2,161 | 1,448 |
| Female householders, no spouse present | 3,531 | 1,499 | 686 | 1,883 | 1,255 |
| Male householders, no spouse present | 472 | 104 | 111 | 333 | 230 |
| **Percent of families in poverty** | **9.3%** | **21.9%** | **20.2%** | **7.3%** | **5.5%** |
| Married couples | 4.8 | 7.1 | 14.2 | 4.4 | 3.3 |
| Female householders, no spouse present | 27.8 | 39.3 | 38.8 | 22.5 | 18.6 |
| Male householders, no spouse present | 11.7 | 14.7 | 16.8 | 10.8 | 9.3 |
| FAMILIES WITH CHILDREN | | | | | |
| **Number of families in poverty** | **5,129** | **1,615** | **1,330** | **3,236** | **1,984** |
| Married couples | 1,662 | 199 | 607 | 1,333 | 744 |
| Female householders, no spouse present | 3,116 | 1,333 | 630 | 1,656 | 1,079 |
| Male householders, no spouse present | 350 | 83 | 93 | 247 | 161 |
| **Percent of families in poverty** | **13.8%** | **28.9%** | **25.0%** | **10.8%** | **8.0%** |
| Married couples | 6.3 | 8.6 | 16.8 | 5.9 | 3.9 |
| Female householders, no spouse present | 35.7 | 46.1 | 46.6 | 30.1 | 25.4 |
| Male householders, no spouse present | 16.2 | 21.4 | 26.0 | 14.7 | 11.9 |

*Note: Numbers will not add to total because Hispanics may be of any race and not all races are shown.*
*Source: Bureau of the Census,* Poverty in the United States, *Current Population Reports, P60-210, 2000*

CHAPTER

# 5

# Labor Force Trends

♦ **The labor force has never been bigger.**

Never before have so many Americans been in the labor force, both numerically and proportionately. Behind the record levels are working women.

♦ **Working mothers are now the norm, even among women with infants.**

Fifty-eight percent of mothers with children under age 1 are in the labor force. Among those who work, 68 percent have full-time jobs.

♦ **Long-term employment is less common for men.**

In the 55-to-64 age group, the proportion of men who have been with their current employer for at least ten years fell from two-thirds to just over half.

♦ **Most commuters drive to work alone.**

In 1999, 78 percent of commuters drove alone. Only 9 percent carpooled, while just 5 percent used mass transit.

♦ **Big gains for fiftysomething workers.**

The labor force will increase 12 percent between 1998 and 2008, but the number of working men aged 55 to 64 will grow 49 percent. Working women in the age group will expand an even faster 64 percent.

♦ **Asian and Hispanic workers will grow the fastest between 1998 and 2008.**

The number of Asian workers will expand fully 40 percent during those years, while the Hispanic labor force will increase 37 percent. A 20 percent increase is projected for black workers, who will be slightly outnumbered by Hispanics in 2008.

# More Women, Fewer Men at Work

## Women's labor force participation rates have climbed steeply over the past thirty years while men's have declined.

Sixty percent of women aged 16 or older were in the labor force in 2000, up from just 43 percent in 1970. Among men, labor force participation fell from 80 to 75 percent during those years.

Women's labor force participation rate grew in all but the oldest age group. The biggest gain came among women aged 25 to 34. In 1970, just 45 percent of women in the age group were in the labor force. By 2000, the proportion stood at 76 percent as mothers with young children went to work.

Among men, labor force participation has fallen in every age group, the biggest drop (16 percentage points) occurring among men aged 55 to 64. In 1970, 83 percent of men in the age group were in the labor force. By 2000, only 67 percent were working as early retirement grew in popularity.

♦ Declining labor force participation among younger men can be attributed to working women. With most wives earning a pay check, more men can decide to go back to school or stay home for a few years and care for their children.

### Divergent trends for men and women

*(percent of people aged 16 or older in the civilian labor force, by sex, 1970 and 2000)*

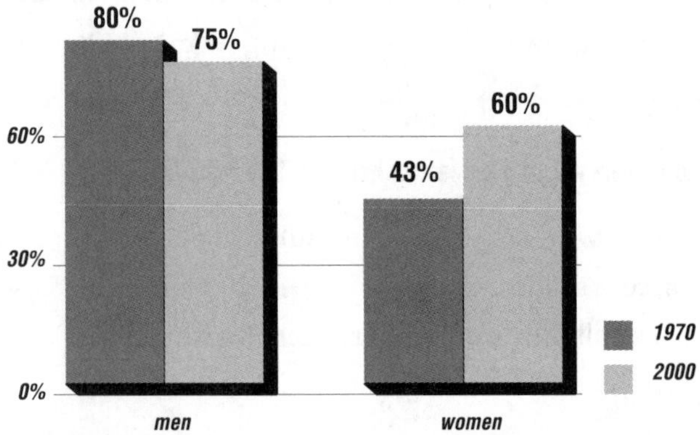

## Labor Force Participation by Sex and Age, 1970 to 2000

*(civilian labor force participation rate of people aged 16 or older by sex and age, 1970–2000; percentage point change, 1970–2000)*

| | *2000* | *1990* | *1980* | *1970* | *percentage point change 1970–2000* |
|---|---|---|---|---|---|
| **Total men** | **74.7%** | **76.1%** | **77.4%** | **79.7%** | **–5.0** |
| Aged 16 to 19 | 53.0 | 55.7 | 60.5 | 56.1 | –3.1 |
| Aged 20 to 24 | 82.6 | 84.3 | 85.9 | 83.3 | –0.7 |
| Aged 25 to 34 | 93.4 | 94.2 | 95.2 | 96.4 | –3.0 |
| Aged 35 to 44 | 92.6 | 94.4 | 95.5 | 96.9 | –4.3 |
| Aged 45 to 54 | 88.6 | 90.7 | 91.2 | 94.3 | –5.7 |
| Aged 55 to 64 | 67.3 | 67.7 | 72.1 | 83.0 | –15.7 |
| Aged 65 or older | 17.5 | 16.4 | 19.0 | 26.8 | –9.3 |
| **Total women** | **60.2** | **57.5** | **51.5** | **43.3** | **16.9** |
| Aged 16 to 19 | 51.3 | 51.8 | 52.9 | 44.0 | 7.3 |
| Aged 20 to 24 | 73.3 | 71.6 | 68.9 | 57.7 | 15.6 |
| Aged 25 to 34 | 76.3 | 73.6 | 65.5 | 45.0 | 31.3 |
| Aged 35 to 44 | 77.3 | 76.5 | 65.5 | 51.1 | 26.2 |
| Aged 45 to 54 | 76.8 | 71.2 | 59.9 | 54.4 | 22.4 |
| Aged 55 to 64 | 51.8 | 45.3 | 41.3 | 43.0 | 8.8 |
| Aged 65 or older | 9.4 | 8.7 | 8.1 | 9.7 | –0.3 |

*Source: Bureau of Labor Statistics,* Employment and Earnings, *January 2001 and January 1991; and* Handbook of Labor Statistics, *Bulletin 2340, 1989; calculations by New Strategist*

# A Record Proportion of Americans Are at Work

## Sixty-seven percent of people aged 16 or older are in the labor force.

Never before have so many Americans been in the labor force, both numerically and proportionately. Of the nation's 210 million people aged 16 or older, 141 million were in the civilian labor force in 2000. The labor force participation rate is at a record high because working women have become the norm. Of the nation's 141 million workers, 47 percent are women.

Men's and women's labor force participation rates are similar for 16-to-19-year-olds, of whom slightly more than half are in the labor force. Men's participation peaks at 93 percent in the 25-to-44 age group. Women's rate peaks at 77 percent in the 35-to-54 age group. Both men's and women's participation fall sharply in the 55-to-64 age group as retirement drains workers from the labor force. Few people aged 65 or older work.

♦ Men's labor force participation rate is likely to stabilize in the years ahead as fewer employers offer generous retirement benefits.

## Employment Status by Sex and Age, 2000

*(number and percent of people aged 16 or older in the civilian labor force by sex, age, and employment status, 2000; numbers in thousands)*

| | civilian noninstitutional population | civilian labor force | | | | |
|---|---|---|---|---|---|---|
| | | | | | unemployed | |
| | | total | percent of population | employed | number | percent of labor force |
| **Total people** | **209,699** | **140,863** | **67.2%** | **135,208** | **5,655** | **4.0%** |
| Aged 16 to 19 | 16,042 | 8,369 | 52.2 | 7,276 | 1,093 | 13.1 |
| Aged 20 to 24 | 18,411 | 14,346 | 77.9 | 13,321 | 1,025 | 7.1 |
| Aged 25 to 34 | 37,417 | 31,669 | 84.6 | 30,501 | 1,168 | 3.7 |
| Aged 35 to 44 | 44,605 | 37,838 | 84.8 | 36,697 | 1,141 | 3.0 |
| Aged 45 to 54 | 36,904 | 30,467 | 82.6 | 29,717 | 749 | 2.5 |
| Aged 55 to 64 | 23,615 | 13,974 | 59.2 | 13,627 | 347 | 2.5 |
| Aged 65 or older | 32,705 | 4,200 | 12.8 | 4,070 | 131 | 3.1 |
| **Total men** | **100,731** | **75,247** | **74.7** | **72,293** | **2,954** | **3.9** |
| Aged 16 to 19 | 8,151 | 4,317 | 53.0 | 3,713 | 604 | 14.0 |
| Aged 20 to 24 | 9,154 | 7,558 | 82.6 | 7,009 | 549 | 7.3 |
| Aged 25 to 34 | 18,289 | 17,073 | 93.4 | 16,494 | 579 | 3.4 |
| Aged 35 to 44 | 21,951 | 20,334 | 92.6 | 19,770 | 564 | 2.8 |
| Aged 45 to 54 | 18,004 | 15,951 | 88.6 | 15,561 | 391 | 2.4 |
| Aged 55 to 64 | 11,257 | 7,574 | 67.3 | 7,389 | 185 | 2.4 |
| Aged 65 or older | 13,925 | 2,439 | 17.5 | 2,357 | 82 | 3.4 |
| **Total women** | **108,968** | **65,616** | **60.2** | **62,915** | **2,701** | **4.1** |
| Aged 16 to 19 | 7,890 | 4,051 | 51.3 | 3,563 | 489 | 12.1 |
| Aged 20 to 24 | 9,257 | 6,788 | 73.3 | 6,312 | 476 | 7.0 |
| Aged 25 to 34 | 19,128 | 14,596 | 76.3 | 14,006 | 590 | 4.0 |
| Aged 35 to 44 | 22,655 | 17,504 | 77.3 | 16,927 | 577 | 3.3 |
| Aged 45 to 54 | 18,901 | 14,515 | 76.8 | 14,156 | 359 | 2.5 |
| Aged 55 to 64 | 12,358 | 6,400 | 51.8 | 6,238 | 162 | 2.5 |
| Aged 65 or older | 18,780 | 1,762 | 9.4 | 1,713 | 49 | 2.8 |

*Note: The civilian labor force equals the number of employed plus the number of unemployed. The civilian population equals the number of people in the labor force plus the number of those not in the labor force.*
*Source: Bureau of Labor Statistics,* Employment and Earnings, *January 2001*

# Labor Force Participation Varies by Race and Hispanic Origin

## Hispanic men and black women are most likely to work.

The gap in the labor force participation rate between men and women is greatest for Hispanics. With 81 percent of Hispanic men and only 57 percent of Hispanic women in the labor force, the 24 percentage point Hispanic gap is far larger than that among whites or blacks. Among blacks, 69 percent of men and 63 percent of women are in the labor force—a gap of just 6 percentage points. Among whites, the gap between men and women in the workforce is 15 percentage points.

Black men are less likely to work than white or Hispanic men. One reason for their lower labor force participation rate is difficulty finding jobs, discouraging many from even looking for work. Despite the booming economy of the late 1990s, many blacks who wanted jobs could not find them. Eight percent of black men were unemployed in 2000 versus 5 percent of Hispanic and 3 percent of white men. Among black men aged 20 to 24, 17 percent were unemployed versus 6 percent of whites and 7 percent of Hispanics.

♦ Many blacks have trouble finding jobs because they live in central cities while most job growth has been in the suburbs.

### Gap is biggest between Hispanic men and women

*(labor force participation rate by race, Hispanic origin, and sex, 2000)*

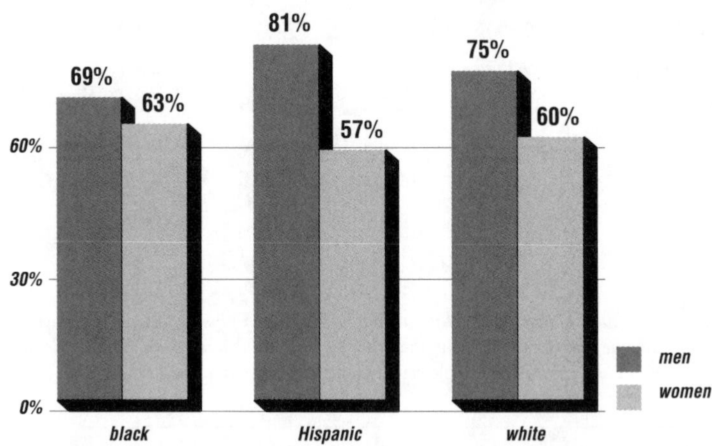

## Employment Status of Blacks by Sex and Age, 2000

*(number and percent of blacks aged 16 or older in the civilian labor force by sex, age, and employment status, 2000; numbers in thousands)*

| | | civilian labor force | | | | |
|---|---|---|---|---|---|---|
| | | | | | unemployed | |
| | civilian noninstitutional population | total | percent of population | employed | number | percent of labor force |
| **Total black men** | **11,320** | **7,816** | **69.0%** | **7,180** | **636** | **8.1%** |
| Aged 16 to 19 | 1,213 | 473 | 39.0 | 438 | 125 | 26.4 |
| Aged 20 to 24 | 1,235 | 906 | 73.4 | 755 | 151 | 16.7 |
| Aged 25 to 34 | 2,300 | 2,019 | 87.7 | 1,882 | 136 | 6.8 |
| Aged 35 to 44 | 2,597 | 2,214 | 85.3 | 2,087 | 127 | 5.7 |
| Aged 45 to 54 | 1,856 | 1,467 | 79.1 | 1,396 | 71 | 4.8 |
| Aged 55 to 64 | 1,015 | 580 | 57.1 | 564 | 16 | 2.7 |
| Aged 65 or older | 1,105 | 157 | 14.2 | 147 | 10 | 6.3 |
| **Total black women** | **13,898** | **8,787** | **63.2** | **8,154** | **633** | **7.2** |
| Aged 16 to 19 | 1,255 | 494 | 39.4 | 380 | 114 | 23.0 |
| Aged 20 to 24 | 1,455 | 1,026 | 70.5 | 887 | 139 | 13.5 |
| Aged 25 to 34 | 2,844 | 2,310 | 81.2 | 2,154 | 156 | 6.8 |
| Aged 35 to 44 | 3,072 | 2,451 | 79.8 | 2,317 | 134 | 5.5 |
| Aged 45 to 54 | 2,262 | 1,694 | 74.9 | 1,635 | 59 | 3.5 |
| Aged 55 to 64 | 1,336 | 647 | 48.4 | 626 | 21 | 3.3 |
| Aged 65 or older | 1,673 | 165 | 9.9 | 155 | 10 | 6.0 |

*Note: The civilian labor force equals the number of employed plus the number of unemployed. The civilian population equals the number of people in the labor force plus the number of those not in the labor force.*
*Source: Bureau of Labor Statistics,* Employment and Earnings, *January 2001*

## Employment Status of Hispanics by Sex and Age, 2000

*(number and percent of Hispanics aged 16 or older in the civilian labor force by sex, age, and employment status, 2000; numbers in thousands)*

| | civilian noninstitutional population | civilian labor force | | | | |
|---|---|---|---|---|---|---|
| | | | | | unemployed | |
| | | total | percent of population | employed | number | percent of labor force |
| **Total Hispanic men** | **11,064** | **8,919** | **80.6%** | **8,478** | **441** | **4.9%** |
| Aged 16 to 19 | 1,205 | 613 | 50.9 | 517 | 96 | 15.7 |
| Aged 20 to 24 | 1,457 | 1,299 | 89.2 | 1,214 | 85 | 6.5 |
| Aged 25 to 34 | 2,820 | 2,652 | 94.0 | 2,554 | 98 | 3.7 |
| Aged 35 to 44 | 2,506 | 2,338 | 93.3 | 2,249 | 89 | 3.8 |
| Aged 45 to 54 | 1,491 | 1,305 | 87.5 | 1,264 | 41 | 3.1 |
| Aged 55 to 64 | 826 | 573 | 69.4 | 550 | 23 | 4.1 |
| Aged 65 or older | 759 | 138 | 18.2 | 130 | 9 | 6.3 |
| **Total Hispanic women** | **11,329** | **6,449** | **56.9** | **6,014** | **435** | **6.7** |
| Aged 16 to 19 | 1,136 | 470 | 41.4 | 385 | 85 | 18.1 |
| Aged 20 to 24 | 1,319 | 856 | 64.9 | 780 | 77 | 8.9 |
| Aged 25 to 34 | 2,806 | 1,833 | 65.3 | 1,716 | 117 | 6.4 |
| Aged 35 to 44 | 2,501 | 1,748 | 69.9 | 1,654 | 94 | 5.4 |
| Aged 45 to 54 | 1,542 | 1,053 | 68.3 | 1,015 | 38 | 3.6 |
| Aged 55 to 64 | 993 | 410 | 41.3 | 389 | 21 | 5.1 |
| Aged 65 or older | 1,032 | 80 | 7.7 | 152 | 4 | 4.8 |

*Note: The civilian labor force equals the number of employed plus the number of unemployed. The civilian population equals the number of people in the labor force plus the number of those not in the labor force.*
*Source: Bureau of Labor Statistics,* Employment and Earnings, *January 2001*

# Employment Status of Whites by Sex and Age, 2000

*(number and percent of whites aged 16 or older in the civilian labor force by sex, age, and employment status, 2000; numbers in thousands)*

| | | civilian labor force | | | | |
|---|---|---|---|---|---|---|
| | | | | | unemployed | |
| | civilian noninstitutional population | total | percent of population | employed | number | percent of labor force |
| **Total white men** | **84,647** | **63,861** | **75.4%** | **61,696** | **2,165** | **3.4%** |
| Aged 16 to 19 | 6,496 | 3,679 | 56.6 | 3,227 | 452 | 12.3 |
| Aged 20 to 24 | 7,420 | 6,308 | 85.0 | 5,939 | 369 | 5.9 |
| Aged 25 to 34 | 14,870 | 14,043 | 94.4 | 13,634 | 409 | 2.9 |
| Aged 35 to 44 | 18,304 | 17,158 | 93.7 | 16,749 | 409 | 2.4 |
| Aged 45 to 54 | 15,356 | 13,783 | 89.8 | 13,484 | 298 | 2.2 |
| Aged 55 to 64 | 9,811 | 6,692 | 68.2 | 6,532 | 159 | 2.4 |
| Aged 65 or older | 12,390 | 2,198 | 17.7 | 2,130 | 68 | 3.1 |
| **Total white women** | **89,781** | **53,714** | **59.8** | **51,780** | **1,934** | **3.6** |
| Aged 16 to 19 | 6,211 | 3,396 | 54.7 | 3,043 | 353 | 10.4 |
| Aged 20 to 24 | 7,300 | 5,455 | 74.7 | 5,140 | 315 | 5.8 |
| Aged 25 to 34 | 15,081 | 11,439 | 75.9 | 11,043 | 396 | 3.5 |
| Aged 35 to 44 | 18,384 | 14,188 | 77.2 | 13,772 | 415 | 2.9 |
| Aged 45 to 54 | 15,736 | 12,186 | 77.4 | 11,899 | 286 | 2.3 |
| Aged 55 to 64 | 10,513 | 5,500 | 52.3 | 5,369 | 131 | 2.4 |
| Aged 65 or older | 16,557 | 1,550 | 9.4 | 1,512 | 38 | 2.4 |

*Note: The civilian labor force equals the number of employed plus the number of unemployed. The civilian population equals the number of people in the labor force plus the number of those not in the labor force.*
*Source: Bureau of Labor Statistics,* Employment and Earnings, *January 2001*

# Working Mothers Are the Norm

## The majority of women with children under age 18 work full-time.

Working mothers are now the norm even among women with infants. Fifty-eight percent of mothers with children under age 1 are in the labor force. Among those who work, 68 percent have full-time jobs.

Labor force participation is higher for mothers with school-aged children than for those with preschoolers. Seventy-eight percent of women with children aged 6 to 17 are in the labor force, and more than three out of four work full-time. Among women with children under age 6, the 65 percent majority are in the labor force and more than 70 percent work full-time.

Sixty-four percent of the nation's married couples with children under age 18 are dual-earners, with both mother and father in the labor force. In just 29 percent of couples, only the father is employed. Even among couples with preschoolers, the 57 percent majority are dual-earners.

♦ The majority of mothers being at work, the nation's schools and workplaces must adapt so that families can thrive.

**Most mothers are in the labor force**

*(percent of women in the labor force by age of children at home, 1999)*

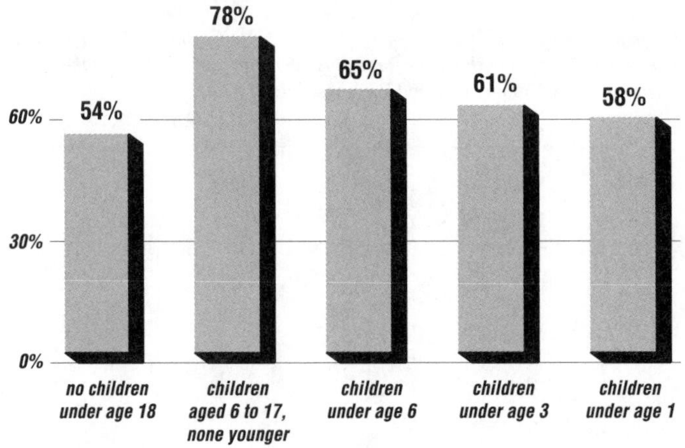

## Labor Force Status of Women by Presence of Children, 1999

*(labor force status of women by presence and age of own children under age 18, 1999; numbers in thousands)*

| | civilian population | | | employed | | | percent of total women who work full-time |
|---|---|---|---|---|---|---|---|
| | | civilian labor force | | | percent of employed who work | | |
| | total | number | percent | total | full-time | part-time | |
| **Total women** | **108,031** | **64,855** | **60.0%** | **62,042** | **74.7%** | **25.3%** | **42.9%** |
| No children under age 18 | 72,446 | 39,169 | 54.1 | 37,504 | 74.8 | 25.2 | 38.7 |
| With children under age 18 | 35,585 | 25,686 | 72.2 | 24,538 | 74.7 | 25.3 | 51.5 |
| Children aged 6 to 17, none younger | 19,572 | 15,311 | 78.2 | 14,747 | 77.5 | 22.5 | 58.4 |
| Children under age 6 | 16,014 | 10,375 | 64.8 | 9,791 | 70.5 | 29.5 | 43.1 |
| Children under age 3 | 9,339 | 5,742 | 61.4 | 5,390 | 68.5 | 31.5 | 39.5 |
| Children under age 1 | 3,166 | 1,792 | 57.9 | 1,668 | 68.2 | 31.8 | 35.9 |

*Source: Bureau of Labor Statistics, Internet sites <www.bls.gov/news.release/famee.t05.htm> and <www.bls.gov/news.release/famee.t06.htm>; calculations by New Strategist*

## Labor Force Status of Parents with Children under Age 18, 1999

*(percent distribution of people aged 16 or older with own children under age 18 by family type, labor force status, and age of own children, 1999; numbers in thousands)*

| | with children under age 18 | | |
|---|---|---|---|
| | *total* | *aged 6 to 17, none younger* | *under age 6* |
| **Married couples** | **100.0%** | **100.0%** | **100.0%** |
| One or both parents employed | 97.3 | 97.1 | 97.6 |
| Mother employed | 68.2 | 74.6 | 60.7 |
| Both parents employed | 64.1 | 69.6 | 57.4 |
| Mother employed, not father | 4.2 | 4.9 | 3.3 |
| Father employed, not mother | 29.1 | 22.6 | 36.9 |
| Neither parent employed | 2.7 | 2.9 | 2.4 |
| **Female-headed families** | **100.0** | **100.0** | **100.0** |
| Mother employed | 74.7 | 79.1 | 67.4 |
| Mother not employed | 25.3 | 20.9 | 32.6 |
| **Male-headed families** | **100.0** | **100.0** | **100.0** |
| Father employed | 86.3 | 84.8 | 88.5 |
| Father not employed | 13.7 | 15.2 | 11.5 |

*Source: Bureau of Labor Statistics, Internet site <www.bls.gov/news.release/famee.t04.htm>*

# More Than Half of Couples Are Dual Earners

## In just one-fifth of married couples is only the husband in the labor force.

Dual incomes are by far the norm among married couples in the U.S. Both husband and wife are in the labor force in 56 percent of married couples. In another 21 percent, the husband is the only worker. Not far behind are the 17 percent of couples in which neither spouse is in the labor force. The wife is the sole worker in 6 percent of couples.

More than 70 percent of couples aged 25 to 54 are dual earners. This lifestyle accounts for a 44 percent minority among couples aged 55 to 64. The wife is the only one employed in a substantial 14 percent of couples aged 55 to 64. In these homes, typically, the older husband is retired while the younger wife is still at work. In 75 percent of couples aged 65 or older, neither husband nor wife is working.

♦ As boomers age into their sixties and begin to retire, the number of couples in which neither spouse is in the labor force will surpass the number in which only the husband is employed.

## Dual-Income Couples by Age, 1998

*(number and percent distribution of married couples by labor force status of husband and wife, 1998; numbers in thousands)*

| | total married couples | husband and wife in labor force | husband only in labor force | wife only in labor force | husband and wife not in labor force |
|---|---|---|---|---|---|
| **Total couples** | **54,317** | **30,591** | **11,582** | **3,087** | **9,057** |
| Under age 25 | 1,373 | 889 | 429 | 24 | 30 |
| Aged 25 to 34 | 9,886 | 6,998 | 2,585 | 204 | 98 |
| Aged 35 to 44 | 14,180 | 10,111 | 3,422 | 416 | 232 |
| Aged 45 to 54 | 11,734 | 8,368 | 2,452 | 555 | 359 |
| Aged 55 to 64 | 7,936 | 3,560 | 1,791 | 1,107 | 1,480 |
| Aged 65 or older | 9,209 | 666 | 902 | 782 | 6,857 |
| **Total couples** | **100.0%** | **56.3%** | **21.3%** | **5.7%** | **16.7%** |
| Under age 25 | 100.0 | 64.7 | 31.2 | 1.7 | 2.2 |
| Aged 25 to 34 | 100.0 | 70.8 | 26.1 | 2.1 | 1.0 |
| Aged 35 to 44 | 100.0 | 71.3 | 24.1 | 2.9 | 1.6 |
| Aged 45 to 54 | 100.0 | 71.3 | 20.9 | 4.7 | 3.1 |
| Aged 55 to 64 | 100.0 | 44.9 | 22.6 | 13.9 | 18.6 |
| Aged 65 or older | 100.0 | 7.2 | 9.8 | 8.5 | 74.5 |

*Source: Bureau of the Census, detailed tables for* Household and Family Characteristics: March 1998, *Current Population Reports, P20-515, 1998; calculations by New Strategist*

# Seventeen Percent of Workers Are Part-Timers

## Among female workers, 25 percent work part-time.

Most of the nation's workers have full-time jobs. Only in the 16-to-19 age group do part-timers outnumber those with full-time jobs. Sixty-five percent of employed people aged 16 to 19 work part-time. Among 20-to-24-year-olds, 25 percent work part-time. The figure drops to just 11 percent among 25-to-54-year-olds, then rises again to 25 percent among those aged 55 or older. The 54 percent majority of the nation's part-time workers are either under age 25 or 55 or older.

Among the 23 million part-time workers, women account for the 68 percent majority. Nevertheless, only among women under age 25 do part-timers outnumber those with full-time jobs. Among employed women aged 25 to 54, 81 percent work full-time.

♦ Many Americans cannot afford part-time work because it offers few benefits such as health insurance or retirement plans.

## Full-Time and Part-Time Workers by Sex and Age, 2000

*(number and percent distribution of employed people aged 16 or older by age, employment status, and sex, 2000; numbers in thousands)*

| | total | | | men | | | women | | |
|---|---|---|---|---|---|---|---|---|---|
| | *total* | *full-time* | *part-time* | *total* | *full-time* | *part-time* | *total* | *full-time* | *part-time* |
| **Total employed** | **135,208** | **112,291** | **22,917** | **72,293** | **64,938** | **7,355** | **62,915** | **47,353** | **15,562** |
| Aged 16 to 19 | 7,275 | 2,521 | 4,754 | 3,713 | 1,480 | 2,233 | 3,562 | 1,041 | 2,521 |
| Aged 20 to 24 | 13,320 | 10,019 | 3,301 | 7,009 | 5,659 | 1,350 | 6,311 | 4,360 | 1,951 |
| Aged 25 to 54 | 96,916 | 86,419 | 10,497 | 51,826 | 49,847 | 1,979 | 45,090 | 36,572 | 8,518 |
| Aged 55 or older | 17,696 | 13,331 | 4,365 | 9,746 | 7,952 | 1,794 | 7,950 | 5,379 | 2,571 |
| **Percent distribution by employment status** | | | | | | | | | |
| **Total employed** | **100.0%** | **83.1%** | **16.9%** | **100.0%** | **89.8%** | **10.2%** | **100.0%** | **75.3%** | **24.7%** |
| Aged 16 to 19 | 100.0 | 34.7 | 65.3 | 100.0 | 39.9 | 60.1 | 100.0 | 29.2 | 70.8 |
| Aged 20 to 24 | 100.0 | 75.2 | 24.8 | 100.0 | 80.7 | 19.3 | 100.0 | 69.1 | 30.9 |
| Aged 25 to 54 | 100.0 | 89.2 | 10.8 | 100.0 | 96.2 | 3.8 | 100.0 | 81.1 | 18.9 |
| Aged 55 or older | 100.0 | 75.3 | 24.7 | 100.0 | 81.6 | 18.4 | 100.0 | 67.7 | 32.3 |
| **Percent distribution by age** | | | | | | | | | |
| **Total employed** | **100.0%** | **100.0%** | **100.0%** | **100.0%** | **100.0%** | **100.0%** | **100.0%** | **100.0%** | **100.0%** |
| Aged 16 to 19 | 5.4 | 2.2 | 20.7 | 5.1 | 2.3 | 30.4 | 5.7 | 2.2 | 16.2 |
| Aged 20 to 24 | 9.9 | 8.9 | 14.4 | 9.7 | 8.7 | 18.4 | 10.0 | 9.2 | 12.5 |
| Aged 25 to 54 | 71.7 | 77.0 | 45.8 | 71.7 | 76.8 | 26.9 | 71.7 | 77.2 | 54.7 |
| Aged 55 or older | 13.1 | 11.9 | 19.0 | 13.5 | 12.2 | 24.4 | 12.6 | 11.4 | 16.5 |

*Source: Bureau of Labor Statistics,* Employment and Earnings*, January 2001; calculations by New Strategist*

# Occupations of Men and Women Differ

## Men are more likely to have blue-collar jobs.

Fully 72 percent of women workers are in white-collar occupations. They are managers, professionals, technicians, sales people, or administrative support workers. A much smaller 48 percent of men are in those occupations, while a substantial 38 percent work in blue-collar jobs such as in precision production, craft, and repair occupations or as operators, fabricators, and laborers. Only 9 percent of women are blue-collar workers.

Women account for the majority of workers in many occupations, including managers of medicine and health, registered nurses, librarians, legal assistants, and secretaries. Between 1983 and 2000, women's share of total workers grew 2.8 percentage points. Women's share of some occupations grew much more than that, making big gains in a number of managerial occupations such as educational administrators (up 26 percentage points to 67 percent) and purchasing managers (up 18 percentage points to 41 percent). Women also made substantial gains as economists (up 15 percentage points to 53 percent) and lawyers and judges (up 14 percentage points to 30 percent).

♦ While women have made inroads on most occupations, they continue to be under-represented in a variety of jobs such as engineer (10 percent are women), computer programmer (27 percent), and police (17 percent).

## Workers by Occupation and Sex, 2000

*(number and percent distribution of employed people aged 16 or older in the civilian labor force, by occupation and sex, 2000; numbers in thousands)*

| | total | men | women |
|---|---|---|---|
| **Total employed** | **135,208** | **72,293** | **62,915** |
| Managerial and professional specialty | 40,887 | 20,543 | 20,345 |
| Executive, administrative, and managerial | 19,774 | 10,814 | 8,960 |
| Professional specialty | 21,113 | 9,728 | 11,385 |
| Technical, sales, and administrative support | 39,442 | 14,288 | 25,154 |
| Technicians and related support | 4,385 | 2,118 | 2,267 |
| Sales occupations | 16,340 | 8,231 | 8,110 |
| Administrative support, including clerical | 18,717 | 3,939 | 14,778 |
| Service occupations | 18,278 | 7,245 | 11,034 |
| Private household | 792 | 35 | 757 |
| Protective service | 2,399 | 1,944 | 455 |
| Service, except private household and protective | 15,087 | 5,265 | 9,822 |
| Precision production, craft, and repair | 14,882 | 13,532 | 1,351 |
| Operators, fabricators, and laborers | 18,319 | 13,988 | 4,331 |
| Machine operators, assemblers, and inspectors | 7,319 | 4,622 | 2,697 |
| Transportation and material moving occupations | 5,557 | 5,003 | 554 |
| Handlers, equipment cleaners, helpers, and laborers | 5,443 | 4,363 | 1,080 |
| Farming, forestry, and fishing | 3,399 | 2,698 | 701 |
| **Total employed** | **100.0%** | **100.0%** | **100.0%** |
| Managerial and professional specialty | 30.2 | 28.4 | 32.3 |
| Executive, administrative, and managerial | 14.6 | 15.0 | 14.2 |
| Professional specialty | 15.6 | 13.5 | 18.1 |
| Technical, sales, and administrative support | 29.2 | 19.8 | 40.0 |
| Technicians and related support | 3.2 | 2.9 | 3.6 |
| Sales occupations | 12.1 | 11.4 | 12.9 |
| Administrative support, including clerical | 13.8 | 5.4 | 23.5 |
| Service occupations | 13.5 | 10.0 | 17.5 |
| Private household | 0.6 | 0.0 | 1.2 |
| Protective service | 1.8 | 2.7 | 0.7 |
| Service, except private household and protective | 11.2 | 7.3 | 15.6 |
| Precision production, craft, and repair | 11.0 | 18.7 | 2.1 |
| Operators, fabricators, and laborers | 13.5 | 19.3 | 6.9 |
| Machine operators, assemblers, and inspectors | 5.4 | 6.4 | 4.3 |
| Transportation and material moving occupations | 4.1 | 6.9 | 0.9 |
| Handlers, equipment cleaners, helpers, and laborers | 4.0 | 6.0 | 1.7 |
| Farming, forestry, and fishing | 2.5 | 3.7 | 1.1 |

*Source: Bureau of Labor Statistics,* Employment and Earnings, *January 2001; calculations by New Strategist*

# Female Workers by Occupation, 1983 and 2000

*(women as a percent of total employed people aged 16 or older in selected occupations, 1983 and 2000, and percentage point change, 1983–2000)*

| | 2000 | 1983 | percentage point change 1983–2000 |
|---|---|---|---|
| **Total, aged 16 or older** | **46.5%** | **43.7%** | **2.8** |
| Managerial and professional specialty | 49.8 | 40.9 | 8.9 |
| Executive, administrative, and managerial | 45.3 | 32.4 | 12.9 |
| Officials and administrators, public administration | 52.7 | 38.5 | 14.2 |
| Financial managers | 50.1 | 38.6 | 11.5 |
| Personnel and labor relations managers | 61.8 | 43.9 | 17.9 |
| Purchasing managers | 41.3 | 23.6 | 17.7 |
| Managers, marketing, advertising, and public relations | 37.6 | 21.8 | 15.8 |
| Administrators, education and related fields | 67.0 | 41.4 | 25.6 |
| Managers, medicine and health | 77.9 | 57.0 | 20.9 |
| Managers, properties and real estate | 50.9 | 42.8 | 8.1 |
| Professional specialty | 53.9 | 48.1 | 5.8 |
| Architects | 23.5 | 12.7 | 10.8 |
| Engineers | 9.9 | 5.8 | 4.1 |
| Mathematical and computer scientists | 31.4 | 29.6 | 1.8 |
| Natural scientists | 33.5 | 20.5 | 13.0 |
| Physicians | 27.9 | 15.8 | 12.1 |
| Dentists | 18.7 | 6.7 | 12.0 |
| Registered nurses | 92.8 | 95.8 | –3.0 |
| Pharmacists | 46.5 | 26.7 | 19.8 |
| Dietitians | 89.9 | 90.8 | –0.9 |
| Therapists | 74.7 | 76.3 | –1.6 |
| Teachers, college and university | 42.4* | 39.3 | 3.1 |
| Teachers, except college and university | 75.4 | 70.9 | 4.5 |
| Librarians, archivists, and curators | 84.4 | 84.4 | 0.0 |
| Economists | 53.3 | 37.9 | 15.4 |
| Psychologists | 64.6 | 57.1 | 7.5 |
| Social, recreation, and religious workers | 56.4 | 43.1 | 13.3 |
| Lawyers and judges | 29.7 | 15.8 | 13.9 |
| Writers, artists, entertainers, and athletes | 50.0 | 42.7 | 7.3 |
| Technical, sales, and administrative support | 63.8 | 64.6 | –0.8 |
| Health technologists and technicians | 80.5 | 84.3 | –3.8 |
| Engineering and related technologists and technicians | 20.4 | 18.4 | 2.0 |
| Science technicians | 41.4 | 29.1 | 12.3 |

*(continued)*

*(continued from previous page)*

| | 2000 | 1983 | percentage point change 1983–2000 |
|---|---|---|---|
| Technicians, except health, engineering, and science | 40.5% | 35.3% | 5.2 |
| Airplane pilots and navigators | 3.7 | 2.1 | 1.6 |
| Computer programmers | 26.5 | 32.5 | –6.0 |
| Legal assistants | 84.4 | 74.0 | 10.4 |
| Sales occupations | 49.6 | 47.5 | 2.1 |
| Supervisors and proprietors | 40.3 | 28.4 | 11.9 |
| Sales representatives, finance and business services | 44.5 | 37.2 | 7.3 |
| Sales representatives, commodities, except retail | 27.5 | 15.1 | 12.4 |
| Sales workers, retail and personal services | 63.5 | 69.7 | –6.2 |
| Administrative support occupations, including clerical | 79.0 | 79.9 | –0.9 |
| Supervisors, administrative support | 60.3 | 53.4 | 6.9 |
| Computer equipment operators | 48.6 | 63.9 | –15.3 |
| Secretaries, stenographers, and typists | 98.0 | 98.2 | –0.2 |
| Information clerks | 88.0 | 88.9 | –0.9 |
| Records processing, except financial | 81.5 | 82.4 | –0.9 |
| Financial records processing | 91.8 | 89.4 | 2.4 |
| Service occupations | 60.4 | 60.1 | 0.3 |
| Private household | 95.5 | 96.1 | –0.6 |
| Firefighting and fire prevention | 3.8 | 1.0 | 2.8 |
| Police and detectives | 16.5 | 9.4 | 7.1 |
| Food preparation and service occupations | 57.7 | 63.3 | –5.6 |
| Health service occupations | 89.5 | 89.2 | 0.3 |
| Cleaning and building service occupations | 45.0 | 38.8 | 6.2 |
| Personal service occupations | 80.5 | 79.2 | 1.3 |
| Precision production, craft, and repair | 9.1 | 8.1 | 1.0 |
| Mechanics and repairers | 5.1 | 3.0 | 2.1 |
| Construction trades | 2.6 | 1.8 | 0.8 |
| Precision production occupations | 25.0 | 21.5 | 3.5 |
| Operators, fabricators, and laborers | 23.6 | 26.6 | –3.0 |
| Machine operators, assemblers, and inspectors | 36.9 | 42.1 | –5.2 |
| Transportation and material moving occupations | 10.0 | 7.8 | 2.2 |
| Truck drivers | 4.7 | 3.1 | 1.6 |
| Bus drivers | 49.6 | 45.5 | 4.1 |
| Taxicab drivers and chauffeurs | 10.8 | 10.4 | 0.4 |
| Handlers, equipment cleaners, helpers, and laborers | 19.8 | 16.8 | 3.0 |
| Farming, forestry, and fishing | 20.6 | 16.0 | 4.6 |

* *Figure is for 1999.*
*Source: Bureau of Labor Statistics,* Employment and Earnings, *January 2001; calculations by New Strategist*

# Whites Are Most Likely to Be Managers or Professionals

## Hispanics are most likely to be blue-collar workers.

Among employed whites, 31 percent are managers or professionals. The proportion is a smaller 22 percent among blacks and just 14 percent among Hispanics. The proportion of workers in technical, sales, and administrative support positions is more similar by race and Hispanic origin, with 29 percent of both white and black workers and 24 percent of Hispanic employees holding those jobs.

Blacks and Hispanics are more likely to be service workers than whites, with 22 percent of black, 20 percent of Hispanic, and only 12 percent of white employees in service work. Blue-collar jobs (precision production, craft, and repair occupations; and operators, fabricators, and laborers) are much more common among Hispanic workers, 36 percent of whom have blue-collar jobs. The proportions are 26 percent among black and 24 percent among white workers.

Blacks and Hispanics each account for 11 percent of employed workers. In many occupations, however, blacks and Hispanics account for a much larger share. Eighteen percent of dietitians are black, as are 17 percent of social, recreation, and religious workers and 18 percent of police. Hispanics account for 32 percent of private household workers, 17 percent of food preparation workers, and 16 percent of construction workers.

♦ Although blacks and Hispanics lag behind whites in upper-level white-collar jobs, they are catching up. Among executive, administrative, and managerial workers in 2000, 8 percent were black and 5 percent were Hispanic.

## Workers by Occupation, Race, and Hispanic Origin, 2000

*(number and percent distribution of employed people aged 16 or older in the civilian labor force, by occupation, race, and Hispanic origin, 2000; numbers in thousands)*

| | *total* | *black* | *Hispanic* | *white* |
|---|---|---|---|---|
| **Total employed** | **135,208** | **15,334** | **14,492** | **113,475** |
| Managerial and professional specialty | 40,833 | 3,343 | 2,036 | 35,291 |
| Executive, administrative, and managerial | 19,740 | 1,518 | 1,072 | 17,362 |
| Professional specialty | 21,092 | 1,840 | 964 | 17,929 |
| Technical, sales, and administrative support | 39,481 | 4,493 | 3,504 | 33,135 |
| Technicians and related support | 4,327 | 491 | 303 | 3,631 |
| Sales occupations | 16,360 | 1,441 | 1,385 | 14,184 |
| Administrative support, including clerical | 18,659 | 2,576 | 1,816 | 15,319 |
| Service occupations | 18,253 | 3,297 | 2,867 | 14,071 |
| Private household | 811 | 123 | 251 | 681 |
| Protective service | 2,434 | 475 | 208 | 1,816 |
| Service, except private household and protective | 15,143 | 2,714 | 2,408 | 11,574 |
| Precision production, craft, and repair | 14,873 | 1,196 | 2,075 | 13,163 |
| Operators, fabricators, and laborers | 18,253 | 2,837 | 3,202 | 14,638 |
| Machine operators, assemblers, and inspectors | 7,301 | 1,073 | 1,416 | 5,787 |
| Transportation and material moving occupations | 5,544 | 920 | 662 | 4,426 |
| Handlers, equipment cleaners, helpers, and laborers | 5,408 | 828 | 1,125 | 4,426 |
| Farming, forestry, and fishing | 3,380 | 169 | 807 | 3,177 |
| **Total employed** | **100.0%** | **100.0%** | **100.0%** | **100.0%** |
| Managerial and professional specialty | 30.2 | 21.8 | 14.0 | 31.1 |
| Executive, administrative, and managerial | 14.6 | 9.9 | 7.4 | 15.3 |
| Professional specialty | 15.6 | 12.0 | 6.7 | 15.8 |
| Technical, sales, and administrative support | 29.2 | 29.3 | 24.2 | 29.2 |
| Technicians and related support | 3.2 | 3.2 | 2.1 | 3.2 |
| Sales occupations | 12.1 | 9.4 | 9.6 | 12.5 |
| Administrative support, including clerical | 13.8 | 16.8 | 12.5 | 13.5 |
| Service occupations | 13.5 | 21.5 | 19.8 | 12.4 |
| Private household | 0.6 | 0.8 | 1.7 | 0.6 |
| Protective service | 1.8 | 3.1 | 1.4 | 1.6 |
| Service, except private household and protective | 11.2 | 17.7 | 16.6 | 10.2 |
| Precision production, craft, and repair | 11.0 | 7.8 | 14.3 | 11.6 |
| Operators, fabricators, and laborers | 13.5 | 18.5 | 22.1 | 12.9 |
| Machine operators, assemblers, and inspectors | 5.4 | 7.0 | 9.8 | 5.1 |
| Transportation and material moving occupations | 4.1 | 6.0 | 4.6 | 3.9 |
| Handlers, equipment cleaners, helpers, and laborers | 4.0 | 5.4 | 7.8 | 3.9 |
| Farming, forestry, and fishing | 2.5 | 1.1 | 5.6 | 2.8 |

*Note: Numbers will not add to total because Hispanics may be of any race and not all races are shown.*
*Source: Bureau of Labor Statistics,* Employment and Earnings, *January 2001; calculations by New Strategist*

## Black and Hispanic Workers by Occupation, 1983 and 2000

*(blacks and Hispanics as a percent of total employed people aged 16 or older in selected occupations, 1983 and 2000; percentage point change, 1983–2000)*

| | black | | | Hispanic | | |
|---|---|---|---|---|---|---|
| | 2000 | 1983 | percentage point change 1983–2000 | 2000 | 1983 | percentage point change 1983–2000 |
| **TOTAL, AGED 16 OR OLDER** | **11.3%** | **9.3%** | **2.0** | **10.7%** | **5.3%** | **5.4** |
| **Managerial/professional specialty** | **8.2** | **5.6** | **2.6** | **5.0** | **2.6** | **2.4** |
| Executive, administrative, managerial | 7.6 | 4.7 | 2.9 | 5.4 | 2.8 | 2.6 |
| Officials and administrators, public administration | 13.1 | 8.3 | 4.8 | 7.0 | 3.8 | 3.2 |
| Financial managers | 6.1 | 3.5 | 2.6 | 4.3 | 3.1 | 1.2 |
| Personnel, labor relations managers | 7.9 | 4.9 | 3.0 | 4.0 | 2.6 | 1.4 |
| Purchasing managers | 7.0 | 5.1 | 1.9 | 3.2 | 1.4 | 1.8 |
| Managers, marketing, advertising, and public relations | 4.2 | 2.7 | 1.5 | 4.2 | 1.7 | 2.5 |
| Administrators, education and related fields | 13.5 | 11.3 | 2.2 | 5.7 | 2.4 | 3.3 |
| Managers, medicine and health | 9.7 | 5.0 | 4.7 | 5.4 | 2.0 | 3.4 |
| Managers, properties and real estate | 8.2 | 5.5 | 2.7 | 7.2 | 5.2 | 2.0 |
| Professional specialty | 8.7 | 6.4 | 2.3 | 4.6 | 2.5 | 2.1 |
| Architects | 1.6 | 1.6 | 0.0 | 5.5 | 1.5 | 4.0 |
| Engineers | 5.7 | 2.7 | 3.0 | 3.7 | 2.2 | 1.5 |
| Mathematical and computer scientists | 8.1 | 5.4 | 2.7 | 3.7 | 2.6 | 1.1 |
| Natural scientists | 5.4 | 2.6 | 2.8 | 3.2 | 2.1 | 1.1 |
| Physicians | 6.3 | 3.2 | 3.1 | 3.7 | 4.5 | –0.8 |
| Dentists | 3.4 | 2.4 | 1.0 | 2.2 | 1.0 | 1.2 |
| Registered nurses | 9.5 | 6.7 | 2.8 | 2.8 | 1.8 | 1.0 |
| Pharmacists | 3.3 | 3.8 | –0.5 | 3.8 | 2.6 | 1.2 |
| Dietitians | 18.4 | 21.0 | –2.6 | 4.8 | 3.7 | 1.1 |
| Therapists | 8.1 | 7.6 | 0.5 | 5.0 | 2.7 | 2.3 |
| Teachers, college and university | 6.5* | 4.4 | 2.1 | 4.2* | 1.8 | 2.4 |
| Teachers, except college, university | 10.4 | 9.1 | 1.3 | 5.2 | 2.7 | 2.5 |
| Librarians, archivists, and curators | 6.0 | 7.8 | –1.8 | 5.8 | 1.6 | 4.2 |
| Economists | 6.3 | 6.3 | 0.0 | 4.4 | 2.7 | 1.7 |
| Psychologists | 8.1 | 8.6 | –0.5 | 4.0 | 1.1 | 2.9 |

*(continued)*

*(continued from previous page)*

| | black | | | Hispanic | | |
|---|---|---|---|---|---|---|
| | 2000 | 1983 | percentage point change 1983–2000 | 2000 | 1983 | percentage point change 1983–2000 |
| Social, recreation, religious workers | 17.4% | 12.1% | 5.3 | 6.4% | 3.8% | 2.6 |
| Lawyers and judges | 5.7 | 2.7 | 3.0 | 4.1 | 1.0 | 3.1 |
| Writers, artists, entertainers, athletes | 6.9 | 4.8 | 2.1 | 5.6 | 2.9 | 2.7 |
| **Technical, sales, admin. support** | **11.4** | **7.6** | **3.8** | **8.9** | **4.3** | **4.6** |
| Health technologists and technicians | 15.0 | 12.7 | 2.3 | 8.2 | 3.1 | 5.1 |
| Engineering and related technologists and technicians | 10.0 | 6.1 | 3.9 | 6.1 | 3.5 | 2.6 |
| Science technicians | 8.7 | 6.6 | 2.1 | 8.4 | 2.8 | 5.6 |
| Technicians, except health, engineering, and science | 7.9 | 5.0 | 2.9 | 5.7 | 2.7 | 3.0 |
| Airplane pilots and navigators | 1.9 | – | – | 4.3 | 1.6 | 2.7 |
| Computer programmers | 8.1 | 4.4 | 3.7 | 3.5 | 2.1 | 1.4 |
| Legal assistants | 8.4 | 4.3 | 4.1 | 9.8 | 3.6 | 6.2 |
| Sales occupations | 8.8 | 4.7 | 4.1 | 8.5 | 3.7 | 4.8 |
| Supervisors and proprietors | 6.6 | 3.6 | 3.0 | 7.3 | 3.4 | 3.9 |
| Sales representatives, finance and business services | 7.6 | 2.7 | 4.9 | 4.9 | 2.2 | 2.7 |
| Sales representatives, commodities, except retail | 2.8 | 2.1 | 0.7 | 6.4 | 2.2 | 4.2 |
| Sales workers, retail and personal services | 12.3 | 6.7 | 5.6 | 11.4 | 4.8 | 6.6 |
| Administrative support occupations, including clerical | 13.7 | 9.6 | 4.1 | 9.7 | 5.0 | 4.7 |
| Supervisors, admin. support | 17.0 | 9.3 | 7.7 | 9.4 | 5.0 | 4.4 |
| Computer equipment operators | 16.6 | 12.5 | 4.1 | 7.4 | 6.0 | 1.4 |
| Secretaries, stenographers, typists | 9.9 | 7.3 | 2.6 | 8.6 | 4.5 | 4.1 |
| Information clerks | 11.3 | 8.5 | 2.8 | 10.4 | 5.5 | 4.9 |
| Records processing, exc. financial | 16.9 | 13.9 | 3.0 | 10.6 | 4.8 | 5.8 |
| Financial records processing | 9.2 | 4.6 | 4.6 | 7.3 | 3.7 | 3.6 |
| **Service occupations** | **18.1** | **16.6** | **1.5** | **15.7** | **6.8** | **8.9** |
| Private household | 14.9 | 27.8 | –12.9 | 31.7 | 8.5 | 23.2 |
| Firefighting and fire prevention | 8.7 | 6.7 | 2.0 | 5.4 | 4.1 | 1.3 |
| Police and detectives | 18.3 | 13.1 | 5.2 | 8.4 | 4.0 | 4.4 |
| Food prep./service occupations | 11.9 | 10.5 | 1.4 | 17.2 | 6.8 | 10.4 |
| Health service occupations | 31.4 | 23.5 | 7.9 | 10.1 | 4.8 | 5.3 |
| Cleaning/bldg. service occupations | 22.2 | 24.4 | –2.2 | 23.4 | 9.2 | 14.2 |
| Personal service occupations | 14.8 | 11.1 | 3.7 | 10.8 | 6.0 | 4.8 |

*(continued)*

*(continued from previous page)*

| | black | | | Hispanic | | |
|---|---|---|---|---|---|---|
| | ***2000*** | ***1983*** | ***percentage point change 1983–2000*** | ***2000*** | ***1983*** | ***percentage point change 1983–2000*** |
| **Precision production, craft, repair** | **8.0%** | **6.8%** | **1.2** | **13.9%** | **6.2%** | **7.7** |
| Mechanics and repairers | 8.2 | 6.8 | 1.4 | 10.7 | 5.3 | 5.4 |
| Construction trades | 7.0 | 6.6 | 0.4 | 16.4 | 6.0 | 10.4 |
| Precision production occupations | 9.5 | 7.3 | 2.2 | 14.4 | 7.4 | 7.0 |
| **Operators, fabricators, and laborers** | **15.4** | **14.0** | **1.4** | **17.5** | **8.3** | **9.2** |
| Machine operators, assemblers, and inspectors | 14.7 | 14.0 | 0.7 | 19.3 | 9.4 | 9.9 |
| Transportation and material moving occupations | 16.5 | 13.0 | 3.5 | 11.9 | 5.9 | 6.0 |
| Truck drivers | 14.4 | 12.3 | 2.1 | 12.5 | 5.7 | 6.8 |
| Bus drivers | 26.1 | 22.2 | 3.9 | 8.0 | 7.0 | 1.0 |
| Taxicab drivers and chauffeurs | 26.0 | 19.6 | 6.4 | 14.0 | 8.6 | 5.4 |
| Handlers, equipment cleaners, helpers, and laborers | 15.3 | 15.1 | 0.2 | 20.7 | 8.6 | 12.1 |
| **Farming, forestry, and fishing** | **4.9** | **7.5** | **–2.6** | **23.7** | **8.2** | **15.5** |

* *Figure is for 1999.*
*Note: (–) means less than 0.5 percent.*
*Source: Bureau of Labor Statistics,* Employment and Earnings, *January 2001; calculations by New Strategist*

# Women's Jobs Are More Concentrated Than Men's

## Men and women are most likely to be managers and professionals in service industries, however.

The largest share of workers by industry and occupation are managers and professionals in service industries, accounting for 14 percent of employed men and 22 percent of employed women. The service industries include subcategories as disparate as hotels and motels, beauty shops, advertising agencies, computer operations, repair shops, amusement parks, health clubs, hospitals, law firms, public and private schools, social service agencies, and accounting firms. Service industry managers and professionals include nurses, teachers, lawyers, and people running Internet start-ups.

No other industry or occupation combination accounts for more than one in ten working men. For men, the second-largest grouping is technical, sales, and administrative support workers in wholesale and retail trade. Among working women, 14 percent are technical, sales, or administrative support workers in the service industries; 12 percent are technical, sales, or administrative support workers in wholesale or retail trade; and 12 percent are service workers in the service industries.

♦ A growing share of men and women are concentrated in the service industries because employment there is growing faster than in any other industry.

## Employment of Men by Industry and Occupation, 2000

*(number and percent distribution of employed men aged 16 or older by industry and occupation, 2000; numbers in thousands)*

| | total | managerial and prof. specialty | technical, sales, admin. support | service | precision prod., craft, repair | operators, fabricators & laborers | farming, forestry, fishing |
|---|---|---|---|---|---|---|---|
| **Total employed men** | **72,294** | **20,544** | **14,287** | **7,244** | **13,532** | **13,987** | **2,698** |
| Agriculture | 2,434 | 125 | 35 | 9 | 51 | 81 | 2,132 |
| Mining | 450 | 103 | 27 | 5 | 191 | 125 | – |
| Construction | 8,520 | 1,191 | 172 | 17 | 5,425 | 1,701 | 15 |
| Manufacturing | 13,458 | 3,456 | 1,548 | 200 | 3,120 | 5,052 | 82 |
| Transportation, public utilities | 6,945 | 1,332 | 1,445 | 157 | 1,241 | 2,753 | 16 |
| Wholesale, retail trade | 14,705 | 1,779 | 6,360 | 2,479 | 1,252 | 2,794 | 40 |
| Finance, insurance, real estate | 3,624 | 1,428 | 1,776 | 202 | 144 | 31 | 42 |
| Services | 18,845 | 9,902 | 2,512 | 2,805 | 1,927 | 1,353 | 345 |
| Public administration | 3,313 | 1,228 | 412 | 1,370 | 181 | 97 | 26 |
| **Percent distribution by industry and occupation** | | | | | | | |
| **Total employed men** | **100.0%** | **28.4%** | **19.8%** | **10.0%** | **18.7%** | **19.3%** | **3.7%** |
| Agriculture | 3.4 | 0.2 | 0.0 | 0.0 | 0.1 | 0.1 | 2.9 |
| Mining | 0.6 | 0.1 | 0.0 | 0.0 | 0.3 | 0.2 | – |
| Construction | 11.8 | 1.6 | 0.2 | 0.0 | 7.5 | 2.4 | 0.0 |
| Manufacturing | 18.6 | 4.8 | 2.1 | 0.3 | 4.3 | 7.0 | 0.1 |
| Transportation, public utilities | 9.6 | 1.8 | 2.0 | 0.2 | 1.7 | 3.8 | 0.0 |
| Wholesale, retail trade | 20.3 | 2.5 | 8.8 | 3.4 | 1.7 | 3.9 | 0.1 |
| Finance, insurance, real estate | 5.0 | 2.0 | 2.5 | 0.3 | 0.2 | 0.0 | 0.1 |
| Services | 26.1 | 13.7 | 3.5 | 3.9 | 2.7 | 1.9 | 0.5 |
| Public administration | 4.6 | 1.7 | 0.6 | 1.9 | 0.3 | 0.1 | 0.0 |

*Note: (–) means sample is too small to make a reliable estimate.*
*Source: Bureau of Labor Statistics,* Employment and Earnings, *January 2001; calculations by New Strategist*

## Employment of Women by Industry and Occupation, 2000

*(number and percent distribution of employed women aged 16 or older by industry and occupation, 2000; numbers in thousands)*

| | total | managerial and prof. specialty | technical, sales, admin. support | service | precision prod., craft, repair | operators, fabricators & laborers | farming, forestry, fishing |
|---|---|---|---|---|---|---|---|
| **Total employed women** | **62,914** | **19,512** | **25,153** | **11,034** | **1,351** | **4,333** | **702** |
| Agriculture | 871 | 85 | 182 | 6 | 3 | 9 | 586 |
| Mining | 71 | 27 | 36 | 2 | 3 | 3 | – |
| Construction | 913 | 293 | 418 | 13 | 130 | 57 | 2 |
| Manufacturing | 6,482 | 1,481 | 1,738 | 71 | 665 | 2,525 | 4 |
| Transportation, public utilities | 2,795 | 638 | 1,624 | 161 | 86 | 285 | – |
| Wholesale, retail trade | 13,127 | 691 | 7,758 | 2,900 | 219 | 756 | 45 |
| Finance, insurance, real estate | 5,103 | 1,450 | 3,456 | 96 | 13 | 11 | 4 |
| Services | 30,850 | 13,689 | 8,769 | 7,446 | 217 | 670 | 60 |
| Public administration | 2,702 | 1,158 | 1,172 | 339 | 15 | 17 | 1 |
| **Percent distribution by industry and occupation** | | | | | | | |
| **Total employed women** | **100.0%** | **31.0%** | **40.0%** | **17.5%** | **2.1%** | **6.9%** | **1.1%** |
| Agriculture | 1.4 | 0.1 | 0.3 | 0.0 | 0.0 | 0.0 | 0.9 |
| Mining | 0.1 | 0.0 | 0.1 | 0.0 | 0.0 | 0.0 | – |
| Construction | 1.5 | 0.5 | 0.7 | 0.0 | 0.2 | 0.1 | 0.0 |
| Manufacturing | 10.3 | 2.4 | 2.8 | 0.1 | 1.1 | 4.0 | 0.0 |
| Transportation, public utilities | 4.4 | 1.0 | 2.6 | 0.3 | 0.1 | 0.5 | – |
| Wholesale, retail trade | 20.9 | 1.1 | 12.3 | 4.6 | 0.3 | 1.2 | 0.1 |
| Finance, insurance, real estate | 8.1 | 2.3 | 5.5 | 0.2 | 0.0 | 0.0 | 0.0 |
| Services | 49.0 | 21.8 | 13.9 | 11.8 | 0.3 | 1.1 | 0.1 |
| Public administration | 4.3 | 1.8 | 1.9 | 0.5 | 0.0 | 0.0 | 0.0 |

*Note: (–) means sample is too small to make a reliable estimate.*
*Source: Bureau of Labor Statistics,* Employment and Earnings, *January 2001; calculations by New Strategist*

# Job Tenure Falls among Men

## The decline was steepest for those aged 55 to 64.

As relationships between employers and employees erode, job tenure—the number of years workers have been with their current employer—is on the decline among men. Since 1983, median job tenure for men aged 25 or older has fallen from 5.9 to 5.0 years. The steepest decline occurred among men aged 55 to 64. In 1983, men in the age group had been with their current employer 15.3 years. By 2000, tenure was down to 10.2 years. Job tenure has remained stable for women over the years as career-oriented women have replaced just-a-job women in the labor force.

Job tenure is down partly because long-term employment has become less common. The proportion of men aged 40 to 64 who have been with their current employer for at least 10 years fell sharply between 1983 and 2000. In the 55-to-64 age group, the figure fell from two-thirds to just over half.

♦ Job tenure declines when workers either voluntarily switch jobs or are laid off. That job tenure has declined most among older men points toward involuntary layoffs as the bigger factor.

### Fewer men have long-term jobs

*(percent of men aged 40 to 64 who have worked for their current employer for at least ten years, 1983 and 2000)*

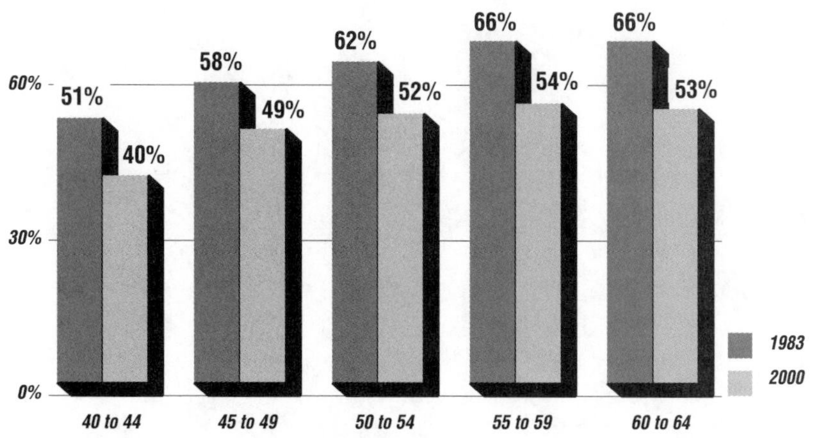

## Job Tenure by Sex and Age, 1983 and 2000

*(median number of years workers aged 25 or older have been with their current employer by sex and age; 1983 and 2000; change in years, 1983–2000)*

| | 2000 | 1983 | change in years 1983–2000 |
|---|---|---|---|
| **Total workers** | **4.7** | **5.0** | **–0.3** |
| **Total male workers** | **5.0** | **5.9** | **–0.9** |
| Aged 25 to 34 | 2.7 | 3.2 | –0.5 |
| Aged 35 to 44 | 5.4 | 7.3 | –1.9 |
| Aged 45 to 54 | 9.5 | 12.8 | –3.3 |
| Aged 55 to 64 | 10.2 | 15.3 | –5.1 |
| Aged 65 or older | 9.1 | 8.3 | 0.8 |
| **Total female workers** | **4.4** | **4.2** | **0.2** |
| Aged 25 to 34 | 2.5 | 2.8 | –0.3 |
| Aged 35 to 44 | 4.3 | 4.1 | 0.2 |
| Aged 45 to 54 | 7.3 | 6.3 | 1.0 |
| Aged 55 to 64 | 9.9 | 9.8 | 0.1 |
| Aged 65 or older | 9.7 | 10.1 | –0.4 |

*Source: Bureau of Labor Statistics, Internet site <www.bls.gov/news.release/tenure.t01.htm>; calculations by New Strategist*

## Long-Term Employment by Sex and Age, 1983 and 2000

*(percent of employed wage or salary workers aged 25 or older who have been with their current employer for ten or more years, by sex and age, 1983 and 2000; percentage point change in share, 1983–2000)*

| | 2000 | 1983 | percentage point change |
|---|---|---|---|
| **Total workers** | **31.7%** | **31.9%** | **–0.2** |
| **Total male workers** | **33.6** | **37.7** | **–4.1** |
| Aged 25 to 29 | 3.0 | 4.0 | –1.0 |
| Aged 30 to 34 | 15.3 | 18.7 | –3.4 |
| Aged 35 to 39 | 29.5 | 36.9 | –7.4 |
| Aged 40 to 44 | 40.4 | 51.1 | –10.7 |
| Aged 45 to 49 | 49.0 | 57.8 | –8.8 |
| Aged 50 to 54 | 51.6 | 62.3 | –10.7 |
| Aged 55 to 59 | 53.7 | 66.2 | –12.5 |
| Aged 60 to 64 | 52.5 | 65.6 | –13.1 |
| Aged 65 or older | 48.9 | 47.6 | 1.3 |
| **Total female workers** | **29.5** | **24.9** | **4.6** |
| Aged 25 to 29 | 1.9 | 2.5 | –0.6 |
| Aged 30 to 34 | 12.6 | 14.8 | –2.2 |
| Aged 35 to 39 | 22.4 | 21.6 | 0.8 |
| Aged 40 to 44 | 31.4 | 23.4 | 8.0 |
| Aged 45 to 49 | 41.5 | 33.0 | 8.5 |
| Aged 50 to 54 | 45.6 | 42.5 | 3.1 |
| Aged 55 to 59 | 52.5 | 51.0 | 1.5 |
| Aged 60 to 64 | 54.0 | 52.6 | 1.4 |
| Aged 65 or older | 51.2 | 54.5 | –3.3 |

*Source: Bureau of Labor Statistics, Internet site <www.bls.gov/news.release/tenure.t02.htm>; calculations by New Strategist*

# Self-Employment Rises with Age

## Older workers are three times as likely to be self-employed as the average worker.

Among the 135 million employed Americans in 2000, only 10 million, or 7 percent, were self-employed. The figure undoubtedly underestimates the number of people who work for themselves because it excludes those who have a business that is not their primary source of income. It also excludes sole proprietorships that are incorporated.

Self-employment rises with age, from just 1 percent of workers aged 16 to 19 to fully 21 percent of workers aged 65 or older. Many older self-employed workers are retired from a primary career and have started a business to supplement their retirement income. Although workers aged 65 or older are most likely to be self-employed, they account for only 9 percent of the self-employed because few people aged 65 or older work.

♦ The number of self-employed will grow as the large baby-boom generation ages and technology allows more people to work on their own.

## Self-Employed Workers by Age, 2000

*(number of employed workers aged 16 or older, number and percent who are self-employed, and percent distribution of self-employed by age, 2000; numbers in thousands)*

| | | self-employed | | percent distribution |
|---|---|---|---|---|
| | total | number | percent | by age |
| **Total aged 16 or older** | **135,208** | **9,907** | **7.3%** | **100.0%** |
| Aged 16 to 19 | 7,277 | 82 | 1.1 | 0.8 |
| Aged 20 to 24 | 13,321 | 262 | 2.0 | 2.6 |
| Aged 25 to 34 | 30,500 | 1,535 | 5.0 | 15.5 |
| Aged 35 to 44 | 36,698 | 2,833 | 7.7 | 28.6 |
| Aged 45 to 54 | 29,717 | 2,711 | 9.1 | 27.4 |
| Aged 55 to 64 | 13,627 | 1,625 | 11.9 | 16.4 |
| Aged 65 or older | 4,069 | 859 | 21.1 | 8.7 |

*Source: Bureau of Labor Statistics,* Employment and Earnings, *January 2001; calculations by New Strategist*

## Twelve Million Workers Have Alternative Jobs

### Among workers aged 65 or older, more than one in five has chosen an alternative work arrangement.

Nontraditional workers include independent contractors, on-call workers (such as substitute teachers), workers for temporary-help agencies, and workers provided by contract firms (such as lawn service companies). These workers are considered alternative because they are not employees of the organization for which they perform their services, nor do they necessarily work standard schedules.

Two out of three alternative workers are independent contractors—freelancers, consultants, and others who obtain customers on their own for whom they provide a product or service. The likelihood of being an independent contractor increases with age to a high of 15 percent among workers aged 65 or older. The likelihood of being an on-call worker, such as a substitute teacher, is also greatest among the oldest workers, at more than 4 percent. Temp work is slightly more prevalent among young adults, while contract work varies little by age.

♦ As the large baby-boom generation ages into its fifties and sixties, the number of independent contractors will surge.

# Workers in Alternative Work Arrangements by Age, 1999

*(number and percent distribution of employed workers by age and work arrangement, 1999; numbers in thousands)*

| | | alternative workers | | | | |
|---|---|---|---|---|---|---|
| | total | total | independent contractors | on-call workers | temporary-help agency workers | workers provided by contract firms |
| **Total employed** | **131,494** | **12,236** | **8,247** | **2,032** | **1,188** | **769** |
| Aged 16 to 19 | 6,662 | 360 | 76 | 179 | 68 | 37 |
| Aged 20 to 24 | 12,462 | 790 | 252 | 202 | 249 | 87 |
| Aged 25 to 34 | 30,968 | 2,532 | 1,479 | 470 | 348 | 235 |
| Aged 35 to 44 | 36,415 | 3,445 | 2,491 | 507 | 231 | 216 |
| Aged 45 to 54 | 28,144 | 2,794 | 2,177 | 303 | 182 | 132 |
| Aged 55 to 64 | 13,062 | 1,541 | 1,212 | 205 | 77 | 47 |
| Aged 65 or older | 3,781 | 775 | 561 | 167 | 33 | 14 |
| **Total employed** | **100.0%** | **9.3%** | **6.3%** | **1.5%** | **0.9%** | **0.6%** |
| Aged 16 to 19 | 100.0 | 5.4 | 1.1 | 2.7 | 1.0 | 0.6 |
| Aged 20 to 24 | 100.0 | 6.3 | 2.0 | 1.6 | 2.0 | 0.7 |
| Aged 25 to 34 | 100.0 | 8.2 | 4.8 | 1.5 | 1.1 | 0.8 |
| Aged 35 to 44 | 100.0 | 9.5 | 6.8 | 1.4 | 0.6 | 0.6 |
| Aged 45 to 54 | 100.0 | 9.9 | 7.7 | 1.1 | 0.6 | 0.5 |
| Aged 55 to 64 | 100.0 | 11.8 | 9.3 | 1.6 | 0.6 | 0.4 |
| Aged 65 or older | 100.0 | 20.5 | 14.8 | 4.4 | 0.9 | 0.4 |

*Note: Independent contractors are workers who obtain customers on their own to provide a product or service, including the self-employed. On-call workers are workers who are called to work only as needed, such as substitute teachers and construction workers supplied by a union hiring hall. Temporary-help agency workers are those who said they are paid by a temporary-help agency. Workers provided by contract firms are those employed by a company that provides employees or their services to others under contract, such as for security, landscaping, and computer programming.*

*Source: Bureau of Labor Statistics,* Contingent and Alternative Employment Arrangements, *February 1999, Internet site <www.bls.gov/news.release/conemp.toc.htm>; calculations by New Strategist*

# More Than 3 Million Americans Get Paid to Work at Home

## Most who work at home are not paid for doing so, however.

Twenty-one million people spent at least a few hours a week working at home in 1997. Most are wage or salary workers not paid for the time they spend working at home—they're the ones finishing up projects on the dining room table after the kids are in bed.

A growing minority of people who work at home are paid for doing so. Seventeen percent of people who work at home are wage or salary workers paid by their employer for the time they log at home. Their number stood at 3.6 million in 1997, up from 1.9 million in 1991, according to the Bureau of Labor Statistics. Another 19 percent of home workers are self-employed.

Most workers paid to work at home are in white-collar jobs, including nearly 2 million in managerial or professional specialty occupations. More than 1 million are sales and administrative support workers. Among the major industry groups, the service industry is the only one with more than 1 million wage or salary workers paid to work at home. Whites are more than twice as likely as blacks or Hispanics to work at home for pay.

♦ The number of workers paid by their employers to work at home will continue to grow as employers realize the savings in overhead costs.

## People Who Work at Home, 1997

*(number and percent of people aged 16 or older employed in nonagricultural industries who work at home on their primary job, by sex, occupation, industry, race, Hispanic origin, and pay status, 1997; numbers in thousands)*

| | total who work at home | | wage or salary workers who work at home for pay | | home-based self-employed | |
|---|---|---|---|---|---|---|
| | number | percent of total workers | number | percent of home workers | number | percent of home workers |
| **Total aged 16 or older** | **21,478** | **17.8%** | **3,644** | **17.0%** | **4,125** | **19.2%** |
| Men | 11,202 | 17.3 | 1,683 | 15.0 | 2,157 | 19.3 |
| Women | 10,275 | 18.3 | 1,960 | 19.1 | 1,968 | 19.2 |
| **Occupation** | | | | | | |
| Managerial & professional specialty | 13,120 | 36.7 | 1,836 | 14.0 | 1,714 | 13.1 |
| Executive, admin., managerial | 5,940 | 34.0 | 867 | 14.6 | 1,014 | 17.1 |
| Professional specialty | 7,180 | 39.2 | 969 | 13.5 | 700 | 9.7 |
| Technical, sales, admin. support | 5,457 | 15.0 | 1,363 | 25.0 | 1,016 | 18.6 |
| Technicians and related support | 417 | 10.6 | 112 | 26.9 | 36 | 8.6 |
| Sales occupations | 3,356 | 22.4 | 640 | 19.1 | 722 | 21.5 |
| Administrative support, inc. clerical | 1,684 | 9.7 | 611 | 36.3 | 259 | 15.4 |
| Service occupations | 1,250 | 7.2 | 256 | 20.5 | 616 | 49.3 |
| Precision production, craft, repair | 1,145 | 8.2 | 116 | 10.1 | 564 | 49.3 |
| Operators, fabricators, and laborers | 506 | 2.9 | 73 | 14.4 | 215 | 42.5 |
| **Industry** | | | | | | |
| Mining | 73 | 12.3 | – | – | – | – |
| Construction | 1,330 | 16.2 | 136 | 10.2 | 726 | 54.6 |
| Manufacturing | 2,318 | 11.5 | 517 | 22.3 | 193 | 8.3 |
| Transportation and public utilities | 963 | 10.9 | 205 | 21.3 | 132 | 13.7 |
| Wholesale trade | 1,202 | 24.4 | 343 | 28.5 | 185 | 15.4 |
| Retail trade | 1,964 | 9.2 | 289 | 14.7 | 532 | 27.1 |
| Finance, insurance, and real estate | 2,008 | 25.7 | 330 | 16.4 | 291 | 14.5 |
| Services | 10,954 | 25.1 | 1,616 | 14.8 | 2,054 | 18.8 |
| Public administration | 666 | 12.3 | 196 | 29.4 | – | – |
| **Race and Hispanic origin** | | | | | | |
| Black | 1,117 | 8.5 | 185 | 16.6 | 135 | 12.1 |
| Hispanic | 830 | 7.2 | 145 | 17.5 | 156 | 18.8 |
| White | 19,646 | 19.2 | 3,345 | 17.0 | 3,868 | 19.7 |

*Note: Numbers will not add to total because wage or salary workers who work at home but are not paid for doing so are not shown.*
*Source: Bureau of Labor Statistics,* Work at Home in 1997, *USDL 98-93, Internet site <www.bls.gov/news.release/homey.nws.htm>; calculations by New Strategist*

# Most Workers Drive to Work Alone

## Few commuters use mass transit to get to work.

Despite the efforts of many to encourage carpooling and the use of public transportation for the commute to work, the great majority of workers drive to work alone. In 1999, 78 percent of workers aged 16 or older drove alone. Only 9 percent carpooled, while just 5 percent used mass transit. Three percent of workers walked to work.

While horror stories about long commutes abound, in fact, the median commuting time to work was just 21 minutes in 1999. Fewer than 5 percent of workers spend an hour or more getting to work. Most commutes are not overly time consuming because half of workers live ten or fewer miles from their workplace. Only 8 percent live thirty or more miles from the job.

The most popular commuting time is 6:00 to 7:00 a.m., when 18 percent of workers leave for work. The 55 percent majority depart for work between 6:00 and 8:30 in the morning.

♦ Cars will continue to dominate the commute to work because of the convenience and control they offer. This is especially true for working parents.

### For most, the commute is short

*(percent distribution of workers by travel time from home to work, 1999)*

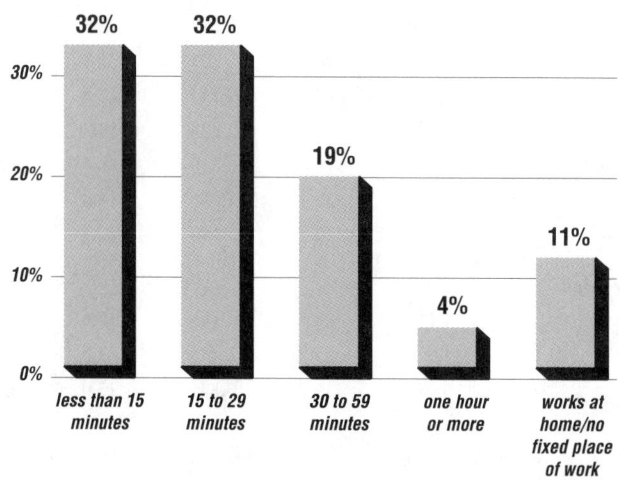

## Journey to Work, 1999

*(number and percent distribution of workers aged 16 or older by principal means of transportation to work last week, travel time and distance from home to work, and departure time to work, 1999; numbers in thousands)*

| | *number* | *percent* |
|---|---|---|
| **Total workers** | **118,041** | **100.0%** |
| **Principal means of transportation to work** | | |
| Drives self | 92,363 | 78.2 |
| Carpool | 11,103 | 9.4 |
| Mass transportation | 5,779 | 4.9 |
| Taxicab | 144 | 0.1 |
| Bicycle or motorcycle | 749 | 0.6 |
| Walks only | 3,627 | 3.1 |
| Other means | 987 | 0.8 |
| Works at home | 3,288 | 2.8 |
| **Travel time from home to work** | | |
| Less than 15 minutes | 38,311 | 32.5 |
| 15 to 29 minutes | 38,138 | 32.3 |
| 30 to 44 minutes | 16,605 | 14.1 |
| 45 to 59 minutes | 6,366 | 5.4 |
| 1 hour or more | 5,356 | 4.5 |
| Works at home | 3,288 | 2.8 |
| No fixed place of work | 9,976 | 8.5 |
| Median travel time (minutes) | 21 | – |
| **Distance from home to work** | | |
| Less than 1 mile | 4,863 | 4.1 |
| 1 to 4 miles | 24,507 | 20.8 |
| 5 to 9 miles | 23,568 | 20.0 |
| 10 to 19 miles | 29,286 | 24.8 |
| 20 to 29 miles | 12,611 | 10.7 |
| 30 miles or more | 9,942 | 8.4 |
| Works at home | 3,288 | 2.8 |
| No fixed place of work | 9,976 | 8.5 |
| Median distance (miles) | 10 | – |

*(continued)*

*(continued from previous page)*

| | *number* | *percent* |
|---|---|---|
| **Departure time to work** | | |
| 12:00 a.m. to 2:59 a.m. | 729 | 0.6% |
| 3:00 a.m. to 5:59 a.m. | 11,355 | 9.6 |
| 6:00 a.m. to 6:59 a.m. | 20,737 | 17.6 |
| 7:00 a.m. to 7:29 a.m. | 16,604 | 14.1 |
| 7:30 a.m. to 7:59 a.m. | 15,328 | 13.0 |
| 8:00 a.m. to 8:29 a.m. | 12,622 | 10.7 |
| 8:30 a.m. to 8:59 a.m. | 5,790 | 4.9 |
| 9:00 a.m. to 9:59 a.m. | 5,646 | 4.8 |
| 10:00 a.m. to 3:59 p.m. | 10,777 | 9.1 |
| 4:00 p.m. to 11:59 p.m. | 7,050 | 6.0 |

*Note: Numbers may not add to total because not reported is not shown; (–) means not applicable.*
*Source: Bureau of the Census,* American Housing Survey for the United States in 1999*; calculations by New Strategist*

# Few Benefits for Part-Time Workers

## A minority of part-time workers receive paid vacations, health insurance, or retirement benefits.

Not surprisingly, large firms offer a broader range of employee benefits than small firms, according to the Bureau of Labor Statistics. But neither large nor small firms offer much to their part-timers. Most large firms offer paid vacations (95 percent), health insurance (76 percent), and retirement plans (79 percent). Among small firms, most offer paid vacations (86 percent) and health insurance (64 percent), while only 46 percent have a retirement plan. Nonproduction bonuses are the only benefit more common at small companies than at large ones—perhaps to make up for the lack of other benefits.

At large firms, a 44 percent minority of part-time employees receive paid vacations, only 21 percent receive health insurance, and just 34 percent have retirement plans. The proportions are even lower for part-time workers at small firms. Nonproduction bonuses are the only benefit more widely available to part-timers at small firms (26 percent) than at large firms (17 percent).

♦ More Americans would choose part-time work if benefits for part-timers were more widely available.

## Employee Benefits for Full- and Part-Time Workers by Size of Firm, 1996–97

*(percent of employees in private, nonfarm industries offered selected employee benefits, by size of firm and full- or part-time employment status, 1996–97)*

| | medium and large firms | | small firms | |
|---|---|---|---|---|
| | full-time | part-time | full-time | part-time |
| **Paid time off** | | | | |
| Holidays | 89% | 40% | 80% | 24% |
| Vacations | 95 | 44 | 86 | 30 |
| Personal leave | 20 | 9 | 14 | 5 |
| Funeral leave | 81 | 34 | 51 | 16 |
| Jury duty leave | 87 | 37 | 59 | 23 |
| Military leave | 47 | 9 | 18 | 5 |
| Family leave | 2 | – | 2 | 1 |
| **Unpaid time off** | | | | |
| Family leave | 93 | 54 | – | – |
| **Disability benefits** | | | | |
| Paid sick leave | 56 | 18 | 50 | 10 |
| Short-term disability coverage | 55 | 18 | 29 | 13 |
| Long-term disability insurance | 43 | 4 | 22 | 2 |
| **Insurance** | | | | |
| Medical care | 76 | 21 | 64 | 6 |
| Dental care | 59 | 16 | 31 | 4 |
| Vision care | 26 | 9 | – | – |
| Life | 87 | 18 | 62 | 7 |
| **Retirement** | | | | |
| Any retirement plan* | 79 | 34 | 46 | 13 |
| Defined benefit plans | 50 | 17 | 15 | 4 |
| Defined contribution plans | 57 | 23 | 38 | 10 |
| Savings and thrift | 39 | 13 | 23 | 4 |
| Deferred profit sharing | 13 | 7 | 12 | 5 |
| Employee stock ownership | 4 | – | 1 | – |
| Money purchase pension | 8 | – | 4 | 2 |

*(continued)*

*(continued from previous page)*

| | medium and large firms | | small firms | |
|---|---|---|---|---|
| | *full-time* | *part-time* | *full-time* | *part-time* |
| **Tax deferred savings arrangements** | | | | |
| With employer contributions | 46% | 15% | 24% | 5% |
| Without employer contributions | 9 | 4 | 4 | 2 |
| **Income continuation plans** | | | | |
| Severance pay | 36 | 10 | 15 | 2 |
| Supplemental unemployment benefits | 5 | – | – | – |
| **Family benefits** | | | | |
| Child care | 10 | 7 | 2 | 2 |
| Adoption assistance | 10 | 3 | 1 | – |
| Long-term care insurance | 7 | 3 | 1 | – |
| Flexible workplace | 2 | – | 1 | 1 |
| **Health promotion programs** | | | | |
| Wellness | 36 | 17 | 8 | 6 |
| Employee assistance | 61 | 36 | 14 | 9 |
| Fitness center | 21 | 11 | 4 | 3 |
| **Miscellaneous benefits** | | | | |
| Job-related travel accident insurance | 42 | 18 | 12 | 4 |
| Nonproduction bonuses | 42 | 17 | 44 | 26 |
| Subsidized commuting | 6 | 2 | 1 | – |
| Educational assistance, total | – | 34 | – | – |
| Job related | 67 | – | 38 | 13 |
| Not job related | 20 | – | 5 | 2 |
| Section 125 cafeteria benefits | 52 | 15 | 23 | 4 |
| Flexible benefit plans | 13 | 3 | 4 | 1 |
| Reimbursement plans | 32 | 11 | 12 | 3 |
| Premium conversion plans | 7 | 1 | 7 | 1 |

* *Includes defined benefit and defined contribution plans. Some employees participate in both types, but are counted just once in the category "any retirement plan."*
*Note: Data for small firms are for 1996 and include those employing fewer than 100 workers; data for medium and large firms are for 1997 and include those employing 100 or more workers. (–) means data not available.*
*Source: Bureau of Labor Statistics,* Employee Benefits in Medium and Large Private Establishments, *1997; and* Employee Benefits in Small Private Establishments, *1996, Internet site <www.bls.gov/ebshome.htm>*

# Fiftysomething Workers Will Expand Rapidly

## The early retirement trend has ended.

As the baby-boom generation enters its late fifties and early sixties, the number of workers aged 55 to 64 will surge. While the labor force as a whole will increase 12 percent between 1998 and 2008, the number of working men aged 55 to 64 will grow 49 percent. The number of working women in the age group will expand an even faster 64 percent. In contrast, the number of workers aged 35 to 44 will decline.

Not only will the number of older workers grow, so will their labor force participation rate. The labor force participation rate of men aged 55 to 64 will climb from 68 to 69 percent—a small, but significant increase because it marks the end of the trend toward ever-earlier retirement. The labor force participation rate of women aged 55 to 64 will rise 6.5 percentage points as career-oriented baby-boom women enter the age group.

♦ While it will become less common for workers to retire in their fifties, most will be out of the labor force by age 65.

### Big gains for workers aged 55 to 64

*(percent change in total number of workers and workers aged 55 to 64, by sex, 1998–2008)*

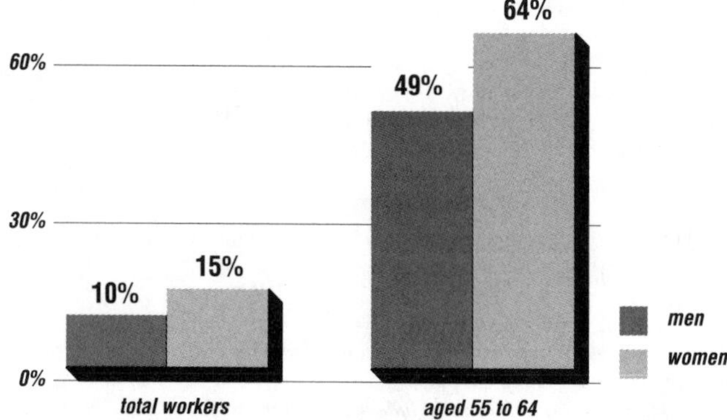

## Labor Force Projections by Sex and Age, 1998 to 2008

*(number and percent of people aged 16 or older in the civilian labor force by sex and age, 1998 and 2008; percent change in number and percentage point change in rate, 1998–2008; numbers in thousands)*

| | number | | | participation rate | | |
|---|---|---|---|---|---|---|
| | 1998 | 2008 | percent change 1998–2008 | 1998 | 2008 | percentage point change 1998–2008 |
| **Total labor force** | **137,673** | **154,576** | **12.3%** | **67.1%** | **67.6%** | **0.5** |
| **Total men in labor force** | **73,959** | **81,132** | **9.7** | **74.9** | **73.7** | **–1.2** |
| Aged 16 to 19 | 4,244 | 4,769 | 12.4 | 53.3 | 52.9 | –0.4 |
| Aged 20 to 24 | 7,221 | 8,279 | 14.7 | 82.0 | 81.4 | –0.6 |
| Aged 25 to 34 | 17,796 | 17,145 | –3.7 | 93.2 | 93.2 | 0.0 |
| Aged 35 to 44 | 20,242 | 18,345 | –9.4 | 92.6 | 92.3 | –0.3 |
| Aged 45 to 54 | 14,963 | 19,006 | 27.0 | 89.2 | 88.8 | –0.4 |
| Aged 55 to 64 | 7,253 | 10,797 | 48.9 | 68.1 | 69.4 | 1.3 |
| Aged 65 or older | 2,240 | 2,790 | 24.6 | 16.5 | 17.8 | 1.3 |
| **Total women in labor force** | **63,714** | **73,444** | **15.3** | **59.8** | **61.9** | **2.1** |
| Aged 16 to 19 | 4,012 | 4,627 | 15.3 | 52.3 | 52.4 | 0.1 |
| Aged 20 to 24 | 6,418 | 7,535 | 17.4 | 73.0 | 74.6 | 1.6 |
| Aged 25 to 34 | 15,017 | 15,253 | 1.6 | 76.3 | 79.0 | 2.7 |
| Aged 35 to 44 | 17,294 | 16,600 | –4.0 | 77.1 | 80.0 | 2.9 |
| Aged 45 to 54 | 13,405 | 17,784 | 32.7 | 76.2 | 80.0 | 3.8 |
| Aged 55 to 64 | 5,962 | 9,791 | 64.2 | 51.2 | 57.7 | 6.5 |
| Aged 65 or older | 1,607 | 1,854 | 15.4 | 8.6 | 9.1 | 0.5 |

*Source: Bureau of Labor Statistics, Internet site <www.bls.gov/emplt983.htm> and <www.bls.gov/emplt985 .htm>*

# Number of Asian and Hispanic Workers Will Grow the Fastest

## Non-Hispanic whites' share of workers will decline.

Between 1998 and 2008, the labor force will grow 12 percent, to 155 million, according to projections by the Bureau of Labor Statistics. The number of minority workers will grow much faster than that of non-Hispanic whites. The number of Asian workers will expand fully 40 percent during those years, while the Hispanic labor force will increase 37 percent. The bureau projects a 20 percent increase for black workers, who will be slightly outnumbered by Hispanics in 2008.

Non-Hispanic white men will account for only 37 percent of the labor force in 2008, down from 40 percent in 1998. As older workers retire and are replaced by more diverse younger workers, non-Hispanic white men will account for 38 percent of those leaving the labor force and for a smaller 30 percent of those joining the labor force.

Non-Hispanic white women will account for 29 percent of workers entering the labor force between 1998 and 2008. Blacks and Hispanics will each account for 16 percent, while Asians will account for 9 percent.

♦ The ability to manage a diverse workforce will become increasingly important as the minority share of American workers grows.

## Labor Force Projections by Race and Hispanic Origin, 1998 to 2008

*(number and percent of people aged 16 or older in the civilian labor force by race and Hispanic origin, 1998 and 2008; percent change in number and percentage point change in participation rate, 1998–2008; numbers in thousands)*

| | number | | | participation rate | | |
|---|---|---|---|---|---|---|
| | 1998 | 2008 | percent change 1998–2008 | 1998 | 2008 | percentage point change 1998–2008 |
| **Total in labor force** | **137,673** | **154,576** | **12.3%** | **67.1%** | **67.6%** | **0.5** |
| **Race** | | | | | | |
| Asian and other | 6,278 | 8,809 | 40.3 | 67.0 | 66.9 | -0.1 |
| Black | 15,982 | 19,101 | 19.5 | 65.6 | 66.3 | 0.7 |
| White | 115,415 | 126,665 | 9.7 | 67.3 | 67.9 | 0.6 |
| **Hispanic origin** | | | | | | |
| Hispanic | 14,317 | 19,585 | 36.8 | 67.9 | 67.7 | -0.2 |
| Non-Hispanic | 123,356 | 134,991 | 9.4 | 67.0 | 67.6 | 0.6 |
| White, non-Hispanic | 101,767 | 109,216 | 7.3 | 67.2 | 67.9 | 0.7 |

*Source: Bureau of Labor Statistics, Internet site <www.bls.gov/emplt983.htm> and <www.bls.gov/emplt985 .htm>*

## Labor Force Entrants and Leavers, 1998 to 2008

*(number and percent distribution of people aged 16 or older in the civilian labor force in 1998 and 2008; number and percent distribution of entrants and leavers, 1998 to 2008, by race, Hispanic origin, and sex; numbers in thousands)*

| | 1998 labor force | entrants 1998–2008 | leavers 1998–2008 | 2008 labor force |
|---|---|---|---|---|
| **Total** | **137,673** | **42,033** | **25,131** | **154,576** |
| Men | 73,959 | 20,963 | 13,790 | 81,132 |
| Women | 63,714 | 21,070 | 11,341 | 73,444 |
| **White non-Hispanic** | **101,767** | **24,619** | **17,170** | **109,216** |
| Men | 54,833 | 12,578 | 9,654 | 57,756 |
| Women | 46,935 | 12,041 | 7,516 | 51,459 |
| **Black non-Hispanic** | **15,589** | **6,928** | **4,789** | **17,728** |
| Men | 7,337 | 3,166 | 2,302 | 8,200 |
| Women | 8,252 | 3,762 | 2,487 | 9,528 |
| **Asian and other, non-Hispanic** | **6,000** | **3,686** | **1,639** | **8,047** |
| Men | 3,219 | 1,788 | 864 | 4,143 |
| Women | 2,782 | 1,898 | 775 | 3,904 |
| **Hispanic** | **14,317** | **6,800** | **1,532** | **19,585** |
| Men | 8,571 | 3,431 | 969 | 11,033 |
| Women | 5,746 | 3,369 | 563 | 8,552 |

*(continued)*

*(continued from previous page)*

| | 1998 labor force | entrants 1998–2008 | leavers 1998–2008 | 2008 labor force |
|---|---|---|---|---|
| **Percent distribution** | | | | |
| **Total** | **100.0%** | **100.0%** | **100.0%** | **100.0%** |
| Men | 53.7 | 49.9 | 54.9 | 52.5 |
| Women | 46.3 | 50.1 | 45.1 | 47.5 |
| **White non-Hispanic** | **73.9** | **58.6** | **68.3** | **70.7** |
| Men | 39.8 | 29.9 | 38.4 | 37.4 |
| Women | 34.1 | 28.6 | 29.9 | 33.3 |
| **Black non-Hispanic** | **11.3** | **16.5** | **19.1** | **11.5** |
| Men | 5.3 | 7.5 | 9.2 | 5.3 |
| Women | 6.0 | 9.0 | 9.9 | 6.2 |
| **Asian and other, non-Hispanic** | **4.4** | **8.8** | **6.5** | **5.2** |
| Men | 2.3 | 4.3 | 3.4 | 2.7 |
| Women | 2.0 | 4.5 | 3.1 | 2.5 |
| **Hispanic** | **10.4** | **16.2** | **6.1** | **12.7** |
| Men | 6.2 | 8.2 | 3.9 | 7.1 |
| Women | 4.2 | 8.0 | 2.2 | 5.5 |

*Source: Bureau of Labor Statistics, Internet site <www.bls.gov/emplt986.htm>*

# White-Collar Jobs Will Grow Fastest

## Computer engineers will be in greatest demand.

Employment in professional specialty and technical jobs will grow the fastest between 1998 and 2008, according to projections by the Bureau of Labor Statistics. It projects professional specialty jobs to gain 27 percent during those years, while technical jobs should grow 22 percent. In contrast, precision production jobs will increase only 8 percent.

A look at the occupations projected to grow the fastest shows computer specialists to be in greatest demand. The agency projects the number of computer engineers and computer support specialists to more than double during the decade, while the number of system analysts will grow 94 percent. Other fast-growing computer occupations include database administrator and desktop publisher.

Some of the occupations expected to see the greatest number of job openings are far from glamorous. While system analyst leads the list, with a gain of 577,000, other big gainers are retail sales clerks, cashiers, truck drivers, and teacher assistants.

♦ One problem for the future economy is how to fill the many low-paying service jobs that are begging for workers. Immigrants are one potential source.

# Employment by Major Occupational Group, 1998 and 2008

*(number and percent distribution of people aged 16 or older employed by major occupational group, 1998 and 2008; percent change, 1998–2008; numbers in thousands)*

| | 1998 | 2008 | percent change 1998–2008 |
|---|---|---|---|
| **Total employed** | **140,514** | **160,795** | **14.4%** |
| Executive, administrative, and managerial | 14,770 | 17,196 | 16.4 |
| Professional specialty | 19,802 | 25,145 | 27.0 |
| Technicians and related support | 4,949 | 6,048 | 22.2 |
| Marketing and sales | 15,341 | 17,627 | 14.9 |
| Administrative support, including clerical | 24,461 | 26,659 | 9.0 |
| Service | 22,548 | 26,401 | 17.1 |
| Agriculture, forestry, fishing | 4,435 | 4,506 | 1.6 |
| Precision production, craft, and repair | 15,619 | 16,871 | 8.0 |
| Operators, fabricators, and laborers | 18,588 | 20,341 | 9.4 |
| | | | percentage point change 1998–2008 |
| **Total employed** | **100.0%** | **100.0%** | – |
| Executive, administrative, and managerial | 10.5 | 10.7 | 0.2 |
| Professional specialty | 14.1 | 15.6 | 1.5 |
| Technicians and related support | 3.5 | 3.8 | 0.3 |
| Marketing and sales | 10.9 | 11.0 | 0.1 |
| Administrative support, including clerical | 17.4 | 16.6 | –0.8 |
| Service | 16.0 | 16.4 | 0.4 |
| Agriculture, forestry, fishing | 3.2 | 2.8 | –0.4 |
| Precision production, craft, and repair | 11.1 | 10.5 | –0.6 |
| Operators, fabricators, and laborers | 13.2 | 12.7 | –0.5 |

*Note: (–) means not applicable.*
*Source: Bureau of Labor Statistics, Internet site <www.bls.gov/news.release/ecopro.t02.htm>; calculations by New Strategist*

## Fastest Growing Occupations, 1998 to 2008

*(number of people aged 16 or older employed in the ten fastest-growing occupations, 1998 to 2008; numerical and percent change, 1998–2008; numbers in thousands)*

| | | | change, 1998–2008 | |
|---|---|---|---|---|
| | 1998 | 2008 | number | percent |
| Computer engineers | 299 | 622 | 323 | 108% |
| Computer support specialists | 429 | 869 | 439 | 102 |
| Systems analysts | 617 | 1,194 | 577 | 94 |
| Database administrators | 87 | 155 | 67 | 77 |
| Desktop publishing specialists | 26 | 44 | 19 | 73 |
| Paralegals and legal assistants | 136 | 220 | 84 | 62 |
| Personal care and home health aides | 746 | 1,179 | 433 | 58 |
| Medical assistants | 252 | 398 | 146 | 58 |
| Social and human service assistants | 268 | 410 | 141 | 53 |
| Physician assistants | 66 | 98 | 32 | 48 |

*Source: Bureau of Labor Statistics, Internet site <www.bls.gov/empoccl.htm>*

## Occupations with the Largest Job Growth, 1998 to 2008

*(number of people aged 16 or older employed in the ten occupations with the largest job growth, 1998 to 2008; numerical and percent change, 1998–2008; numbers in thousands)*

| | | | change, 1998–2008 | |
|---|---|---|---|---|
| | 1998 | 2008 | number | percent |
| Systems analysts | 617 | 1,194 | 577 | 94% |
| Retail salespersons | 4,056 | 4,620 | 563 | 14 |
| Cashiers | 3,198 | 3,754 | 556 | 17 |
| General managers and top executives | 3,362 | 3,913 | 551 | 16 |
| Truck drivers, light and heavy | 2,970 | 3,463 | 493 | 17 |
| Office clerks, general | 3,021 | 3,484 | 463 | 15 |
| Registered nurses | 2,079 | 2,530 | 451 | 22 |
| Computer support specialists | 429 | 869 | 439 | 102 |
| Personal care and home health aides | 746 | 1,179 | 433 | 58 |
| Teacher assistants | 1,192 | 1,567 | 375 | 31 |

*Source: Bureau of Labor Statistics, Internet site <www.bls.gov/empoccl.htm>*

# Service Industry Projected to Grow the Most

## Employment in the service industry will grow twice as fast as total employment between 1998 and 2008.

The number of jobs in the service industry will expand 33 percent between 1998 and 2008. According to the Bureau of Labor Statistics, the five services projected to grow the fastest are computer and data processing, health care, residential care, management and public relations, and personnel supply.

Jobs in goods-producing industries are projected to expand only 1 percent between 1998 and 2008 and will account for only 18 percent of all jobs in 2008. The bureau projects mining and manufacturing employment to decline during those years.

♦ These projections are based on current trends. Unforeseen technological breakthroughs or major new government programs could shift growth from one industry to another during the next decade.

## Employment by Major Industry, 1998 to 2008

*(number and percent distribution of people aged 16 or older employed as wage or salary workers in nonagricultural industries by major industry, 1998 and 2008; percent change in number and percentage point change in distribution, 1998–2008; numbers in thousands)*

| | 1998 | 2008 | percent change 1998–2008 |
|---|---|---|---|
| **Total employed** | **124,887** | **144,526** | **15.7%** |
| Goods producing | 25,347 | 25,694 | 1.4 |
| Mining | 590 | 475 | –19.5 |
| Construction | 5,985 | 6,535 | 9.2 |
| Manufacturing | 18,772 | 18,684 | –0.5 |
| Durable | 11,170 | 11,277 | 1.0 |
| Nondurable | 7,602 | 7,406 | –2.6 |
| Service producing | 99,540 | 118,832 | 19.4 |
| Transportation, communications, and utilities | 6,600 | 7,541 | 14.3 |
| Wholesale trade | 6,831 | 7,330 | 7.3 |
| Retail trade | 22,296 | 25,363 | 13.8 |
| Finance, insurance, and real estate | 7,408 | 8,367 | 12.9 |
| Services | 36,586 | 48,543 | 32.7 |
| Government | 19,819 | 21,688 | 9.4 |
| Federal government | 2,686 | 2,550 | –5.1 |
| State and local government | 17,133 | 19,138 | 11.7 |
| | | | **percentage point change 1998–2008** |
| **Total employed** | **100.0%** | **100.0%** | – |
| Goods producing | 20.3 | 17.8 | –2.5 |
| Mining | 0.5 | 0.3 | –0.1 |
| Construction | 4.8 | 4.5 | –0.3 |
| Manufacturing | 15.0 | 12.9 | –2.1 |
| Durable | 8.9 | 7.8 | –1.1 |
| Nondurable | 6.1 | 5.1 | –1.0 |
| Service producing | 79.7 | 82.2 | 2.5 |
| Transportation, communications, and utilities | 5.3 | 5.2 | –0.1 |
| Wholesale trade | 5.5 | 5.1 | –0.4 |
| Retail trade | 17.9 | 17.5 | –0.3 |
| Finance, insurance, and real estate | 5.9 | 5.8 | –0.1 |
| Services | 29.3 | 33.6 | 4.3 |
| Government | 15.9 | 15.0 | –0.9 |
| Federal government | 2.2 | 1.8 | –0.4 |
| State and local government | 13.7 | 13.2 | –0.5 |

*Source: Bureau of Labor Statistics, Internet site <www.bls.gov/news.release/ecopro.t01.htm>; calculations by New Strategist*

## Industries with Fastest Job Gains, 1998 to 2008

*(number of people aged 16 or older employed in industries with the fastest job gains, 1998–2008; numerical and percent change in employment, 1998–2008; ranked by percent change; numbers in thousands)*

| | 1998 | 2008 | change 1998–2008 number | change 1998–2008 percent |
|---|---|---|---|---|
| Computer and data processing services | 1,599 | 3,472 | 1,873 | 117% |
| Health services, not elsewhere classified | 1,209 | 2,018 | 809 | 67 |
| Residential care | 747 | 1,171 | 424 | 57 |
| Management and public relations | 1,034 | 1,500 | 466 | 45 |
| Personnel supply services | 3,230 | 4,623 | 1,393 | 43 |
| Miscellaneous equipment rental and leasing | 258 | 369 | 111 | 43 |
| Museums, botanical and zoological gardens | 93 | 131 | 38 | 41 |
| Research and testing services | 614 | 861 | 247 | 40 |
| Miscellaneous transportation services | 236 | 329 | 93 | 39 |
| Security and commodity brokers | 645 | 900 | 255 | 40 |

*Source: Bureau of Labor Statistics, Internet site <www.bls.gov/news.release/ecopro.table4.htm>*

# Greatest Demand Will Be for Educated Workers

## Those with associate's degrees will see biggest gain.

Between 1998 and 2008, employment will grow fastest for workers with associate's degrees. Jobs that demand an associate's degree will increase 31 percent during those years compared with a 14 percent gain in all jobs. Workers with bachelor's degrees will also be in great demand, with job growth projected at 24 percent between 1998 and 2008. The Bureau of Labor Statistics projects the slowest growth for jobs requiring moderate- to long-term on-the-job training, which should increase less than 9 percent.

Although the agency projects the fastest growth for jobs requiring an associate's or bachelor's degree, it forecasts the largest job gains for workers with only short-term on-the-job training. Cashiers, truck drivers, and home health aides are among the top ten occupations in projected job gains. Nearly 24 million additional workers with short-term training will be needed by 2008.

♦ As the labor force becomes increasingly educated, the biggest problem for employers will be attracting workers to entry-level jobs. Easing immigration restrictions is one way around this problem.

## Projections of Employment by Education, 1998 and 2008

*(number of people aged 16 or older employed by highest level of educational attainment or job training, 1998 and 2008; percent change in number 1998–2008; net job openings by educational and training category, 1998–2008; numbers in thousands)*

| | 1998 | 2008 | percent change 1998–2008 | net job openings 1998–2008 |
|---|---|---|---|---|
| **Total employed** | **140,514** | **160,795** | **14.4%** | **55,008** |
| First professional degree | 1,908 | 2,215 | 16.1 | 617 |
| Doctoral degree | 996 | 1,228 | 23.3 | 502 |
| Master's degree | 940 | 1,115 | 18.6 | 374 |
| Work experience plus bachelor's or higher degree | 9,595 | 11,276 | 17.5 | 3,372 |
| Bachelor's degree | 17,379 | 21,596 | 24.3 | 7,822 |
| Associate's degree | 4,930 | 6,467 | 31.2 | 2,422 |
| Postsecondary vocational training | 4,508 | 5,151 | 14.3 | 1,680 |
| Work experience in a related occupation | 11,174 | 12,490 | 11.8 | 3,699 |
| Long-term on-the-job training | 13,436 | 14,604 | 8.7 | 4,411 |
| Moderate-term on-the-job training | 20,521 | 21,952 | 7.0 | 6,218 |
| Short-term on-the-job training | 55,125 | 62,701 | 13.7 | 23,890 |

*Note: Net job openings include new positions as well as replacements for retirees, etc.*
*Source: Bureau of Labor Statistics, Internet site <www.bls.gov/empoccl.htm>*

CHAPTER

# 6

## Living Arrangement Trends

♦ **Married couples are slipping as a share of households.**

Married couples accounted for 53 percent of households in 2000, down from 56 percent in 1990.

♦ **Between 1990 and 2000, the number of households headed by 45-to-54-year-olds grew 45 percent.**

In contrast, the number of households headed by 25-to-34-year-olds fell 9 percent.

♦ **Fifty-nine percent of American households are home to only one or two people.**

Overall 2.6 people live in the average U.S. household.

♦ **Fifty-one percent of black children live with only their mother, while just 36 percent live with both parents.**

An increasing proportion of all children—black, white, and Hispanic—live only with their mother, and a shrinking proportion live with two parents.

♦ **Eighty percent of men and 73 percent of women aged 18 or 19 live with their parents.**

Entry-level wages have fallen sharply over the past few decades, forcing young adults to live with their parents until they can afford independence.

♦ **Unmarried couples head nearly 6 million American households.**

Seventy-two percent of cohabiting couples are heterosexual partners, while 28 percent are same-sex couples.

♦ **Men are more likely than women to be married—58 versus 55 percent.**

Men are also more likely than women to have not yet married—31 versus 25 percent.

# Married Couples Still Account for the Majority of Households

## But their dominance is slipping as other household types grow faster.

Between 1990 and 2000, the number of married couples increased only 6 percent, just half the 12 percent gain for all households. Consequently, the married couple share of households slipped to 53 percent from 56 percent in 1990.

Male-headed families grew most rapidly in the 1990s, up 40 percent during the decade. But these households account for a tiny 4 percent of the total. They are greatly outnumbered by the 13 million female-headed families.

Nonfamily households grew 20 percent during the 1990s, and male-headed nonfamily households grew the fastest. Female-headed nonfamily households (most of them headed by women aged 55 or older) are growing relatively slowly as the small Depression-era cohort enters the 55-or-older age group. This household type will grow rapidly when the baby-boom generation ages into its late fifties and sixties.

♦ Single-person households already are one of the most common household types. Their importance will grow as the population ages.

**Little growth for married couples**

*(percent change in number of households by type, 1990–2000)*

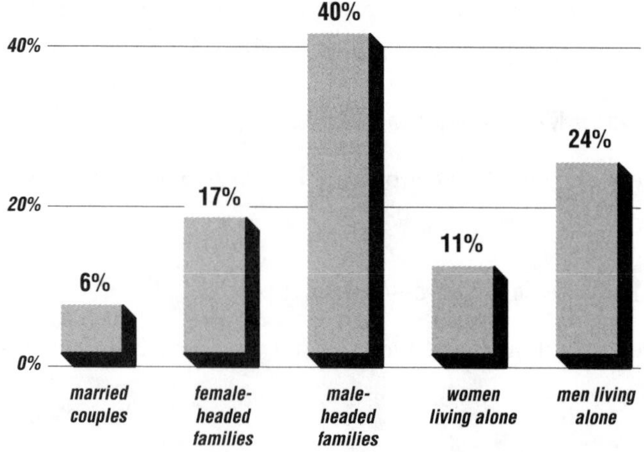

## Households by Type, 1990 and 2000

*(number and percent distribution of households by household type, 1990 and 2000; percent change 1990–2000; numbers in thousands)*

| | 2000 | | 1990 | | percent change |
|---|---|---|---|---|---|
| | number | percent | number | percent | 1990–2000 |
| **Total households** | **104,705** | **100.0%** | **93,347** | **100.0%** | **12.2%** |
| **Family households** | **72,025** | **68.8** | **66,090** | **70.8** | **9.0** |
| Married couples | 55,311 | 52.8 | 52,317 | 56.0 | 5.7 |
| Female householder, no spouse present | 12,687 | 12.1 | 10,890 | 11.7 | 16.5 |
| Male householder, no spouse present | 4,028 | 3.8 | 2,884 | 3.1 | 39.7 |
| **Nonfamily households** | **32,680** | **31.2** | **27,257** | **29.2** | **19.9** |
| Female householder | 18,039 | 17.2 | 15,651 | 16.8 | 15.3 |
| Living alone | 15,543 | 14.8 | 13,950 | 14.9 | 11.4 |
| Male householder | 14,641 | 14.0 | 11,606 | 12.4 | 26.2 |
| Living alone | 11,181 | 10.7 | 9,049 | 9.7 | 23.6 |

*Source: Bureau of the Census, data from the Current Population Survey, Internet site <http:/ferret.bls.census.gov/macro/032000/hhinc/new02_000.htm>; calculations by New Strategist*

# Households Headed by 45-to-54-Year-Olds Have Grown Rapidly

## The number of households headed by 25-to-34-year-olds has declined.

Between 1990 and 2000, the number of households headed by 45-to-54-year-olds grew 45 percent, much faster than the 12 percent gain for all households. Behind the rapid growth is the aging of the baby-boom generation into its late forties and early fifties.

In contrast, the number of households headed by 25-to-34-year-olds fell 9 percent as the small generation X entered the age group. Between 1990 and 2000, the number of householders aged 25 to 34 declined by 1.8 million.

♦ The number of households headed by people aged 65 or older will grow slowly during the next few years as the small generation born during the Depression enters the age group.

### Fewer householders are aged 25 to 34

*(percent change in number of households by age of householder, 1990 to 2000)*

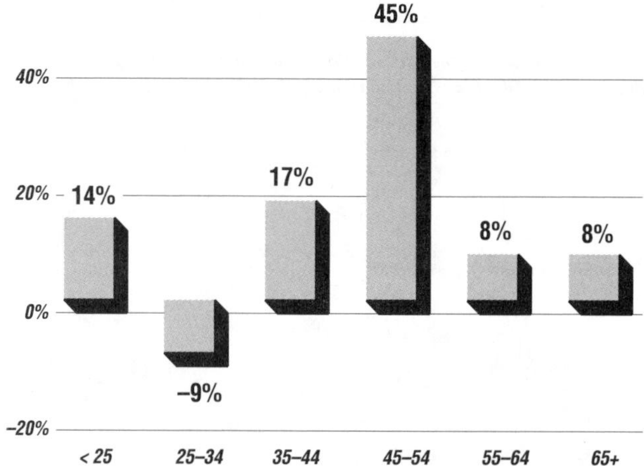

## Households by Age of Householder, 1990 and 2000

*(number of households by age of householder, 1990 and 2000; percent change 1990–2000; numbers in thousands)*

| | *2000* | *1990* | *percent change 1990–2000* |
|---|---|---|---|
| **Total households** | **104,705** | **93,347** | **12.2%** |
| Under age 25 | 5,860 | 5,121 | 14.4 |
| Aged 25 to 34 | 18,627 | 20,472 | –9.0 |
| Aged 35 to 44 | 23,955 | 20,554 | 16.5 |
| Aged 45 to 54 | 20,927 | 14,415 | 45.2 |
| Aged 55 to 64 | 13,592 | 12,529 | 8.5 |
| Aged 65 or older | 21,745 | 20,156 | 7.9 |

*Source: Bureau of the Census, data from the Current Population Survey, Internet site <http://ferret.bls.census.gov/macro/032000/hhinc/new02_000.htm>; calculations by New Strategist*

# Households Vary by Age

## The households of young adults are different from those of middle-aged and older Americans.

Married couples are far less common among the youngest and oldest householders than among the middle-aged. Only 25 percent of households headed by people under age 25 consist of married couples. Among the elderly, married couples head a 43 percent minority of households. In contrast, couples account for the majority of households headed by people aged 25 to 64.

Female-headed families are most common among the youngest householders, at 23 percent. Women living alone are most common among the oldest householders, at 34 percent. Female-headed families account for just 11 percent of households headed by 45-to-54-year-olds and for fewer than 8 percent among 55-to-64-year-olds. Nonfamily households bottom out at 22 percent among 35-to-44-year-olds because women in that age group are least likely to live alone.

♦ With the baby-boom generation now in middle age, household composition has stabilized. More change is in store, however, as boomers age.

**Married couples head most households in the 25-to-64 age groups**

*(percent of households headed by married couples, by age of householder, 2000)*

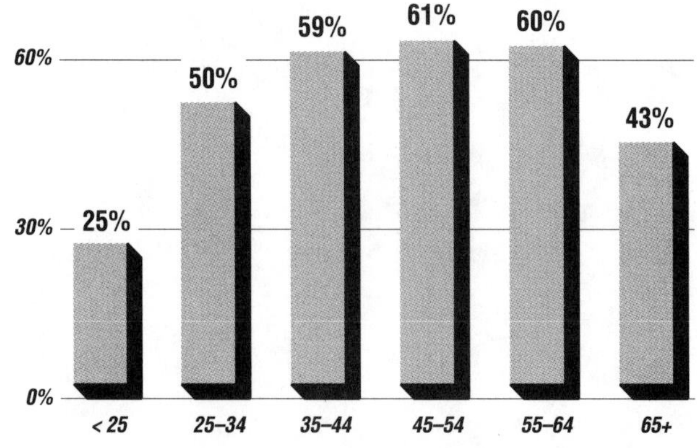

## Households by Household Type and Age of Householder, 2000

*(number and percent distribution of households by household type and age of householder, 2000; numbers in thousands)*

| | total | under 25 | 25 to 34 | 35 to 44 | 45 to 54 | 55 to 64 | 65 or older |
|---|---|---|---|---|---|---|---|
| **Total households** | **104,705** | **5,860** | **18,627** | **23,955** | **20,927** | **13,592** | **21,745** |
| **Family households** | **72,025** | **3,352** | **13,007** | **18,705** | **15,804** | **9,569** | **11,588** |
| Married couples | 55,311 | 1,450 | 9,389 | 14,104 | 12,792 | 8,138 | 9,437 |
| Female householder, no spouse present | 12,687 | 1,342 | 2,732 | 3,499 | 2,299 | 1,080 | 1,735 |
| Male householder, no spouse present | 4,028 | 560 | 886 | 1,102 | 713 | 351 | 416 |
| **Nonfamily households** | **32,680** | **2,507** | **5,620** | **5,250** | **5,124** | **4,023** | **10,156** |
| Female householder | 18,039 | 1,221 | 2,172 | 1,989 | 2,541 | 2,490 | 7,626 |
| Living alone | 15,543 | 587 | 1,569 | 1,540 | 2,158 | 2,262 | 7,427 |
| Male householder | 14,641 | 1,286 | 3,448 | 3,261 | 2,583 | 1,533 | 2,530 |
| Living alone | 11,181 | 556 | 2,279 | 2,569 | 2,146 | 1,276 | 2,356 |
| **Percent distribution by household type** | | | | | | | |
| **Total households** | **100.0%** | **100.0%** | **100.0%** | **100.0%** | **100.0%** | **100.0%** | **100.0%** |
| **Family households** | **68.8** | **57.2** | **69.8** | **78.1** | **75.5** | **70.4** | **53.3** |
| Married couples | 52.8 | 24.7 | 50.4 | 58.9 | 61.1 | 59.9 | 43.4 |
| Female householder, no spouse present | 12.1 | 22.9 | 14.7 | 14.6 | 11.0 | 7.9 | 8.0 |
| Male householder, no spouse present | 3.8 | 9.6 | 4.8 | 4.6 | 3.4 | 2.6 | 1.9 |
| **Nonfamily households** | **31.2** | **42.8** | **30.2** | **21.9** | **24.5** | **29.6** | **46.7** |
| Female householder | 17.2 | 20.8 | 11.7 | 8.3 | 12.1 | 18.3 | 35.1 |
| Living alone | 14.8 | 10.0 | 8.4 | 6.4 | 10.3 | 16.6 | 34.2 |
| Male householder | 14.0 | 21.9 | 18.5 | 13.6 | 12.3 | 11.3 | 11.6 |
| Living alone | 10.7 | 9.5 | 12.2 | 10.7 | 10.3 | 9.4 | 10.8 |

*(continued)*

*(continued from previous page)*

| | *total* | *under 25* | *25 to 34* | *35 to 44* | *45 to 54* | *55 to 64* | *65 or older* |
|---|---|---|---|---|---|---|---|
| **Percent distribution by age** | | | | | | | |
| **Total households** | **100.0%** | **5.6%** | **17.8%** | **22.9%** | **20.0%** | **13.0%** | **20.8%** |
| **Family households** | **100.0** | **4.7** | **18.1** | **26.0** | **21.9** | **13.3** | **16.1** |
| Married couples | 100.0 | 2.6 | 17.0 | 25.5 | 23.1 | 14.7 | 17.1 |
| Female householder, no spouse present | 100.0 | 10.6 | 21.5 | 27.6 | 18.1 | 8.5 | 13.7 |
| Male householder, no spouse present | 100.0 | 13.9 | 22.0 | 27.4 | 17.7 | 8.7 | 10.3 |
| **Nonfamily households** | **100.0** | **7.7** | **17.2** | **16.1** | **15.7** | **12.3** | **31.1** |
| Female householder | 100.0 | 6.8 | 12.0 | 11.0 | 14.1 | 13.8 | 42.3 |
| Living alone | 100.0 | 3.8 | 10.1 | 9.9 | 13.9 | 14.6 | 47.8 |
| Male householder | 100.0 | 8.8 | 23.6 | 22.3 | 17.6 | 10.5 | 17.3 |
| Living alone | 100.0 | 5.0 | 20.4 | 23.0 | 19.2 | 11.4 | 21.1 |

*Source: Bureau of the Census, data from the 2000 Current Population Survey, Internet site <http://ferret.bls.census.gov/macro/032000/hhinc/new02_000.htm>; calculations by New Strategist*

# Big Differences between Black and White Households

## Married couples account for more than half of non-Hispanic white households, but for fewer than one-third of black households.

Female-headed families are almost as common as married couples among black households. Married couples account for 32 percent of black households while female-headed families represent another 30 percent. In contrast, only 9 percent of non-Hispanic white households are female-headed families. The proportion is 19 percent for Hispanics.

Hispanics are less likely to live in nonfamily households than either non-Hispanic whites or blacks. Fewer than 7 percent of Hispanic women live alone compared with 16 percent of black and non-Hispanic white women. Hispanic men also are less likely to live alone than their non-Hispanic white and black counterparts.

♦ Although Hispanics outnumber blacks among married couples, there are many more black than Hispanic households—13 million versus 9 million in 2000.

## Households by Household Type, Race, and Hispanic Origin of Householder, 2000

*(number and percent distribution of households by household type, race, and Hispanic origin of householder, 2000; numbers in thousands)*

| | *total* | *black* | *Hispanic* | *white* | *non-Hispanic white* |
|---|---|---|---|---|---|
| **Total households** | **104,705** | **12,849** | **9,319** | **87,671** | **78,819** |
| **Family households** | **72,025** | **8,664** | **7,561** | **60,251** | **53,066** |
| Married couples | 55,311 | 4,144 | 5,133 | 48,790 | 43,865 |
| Female householder, no spouse present | 12,687 | 3,814 | 1,769 | 8,380 | 6,732 |
| Male householder, no spouse present | 4,028 | 706 | 658 | 3,081 | 2,468 |
| **Nonfamily households** | **32,680** | **4,185** | **1,758** | **27,420** | **25,753** |
| Female householder | 18,039 | 2,309 | 783 | 15,215 | 14,475 |
| Living alone | 15,543 | 2,025 | 630 | 13,109 | 12,508 |
| Male householder | 14,641 | 1,876 | 974 | 12,204 | 11,278 |
| Living alone | 11,181 | 1,580 | 666 | 9,198 | 8,562 |
| **Percent distribution by household type** | | | | | |
| **Total households** | **100.0%** | **100.0%** | **100.0%** | **100.0%** | **100.0%** |
| **Family households** | **68.8** | **67.4** | **81.1** | **68.7** | **67.3** |
| Married couples | 52.8 | 32.3 | 55.1 | 55.7 | 55.7 |
| Female householder, no spouse present | 12.1 | 29.7 | 19.0 | 9.6 | 8.5 |
| Male householder, no spouse present | 3.8 | 5.5 | 7.1 | 3.5 | 3.1 |
| **Nonfamily households** | **31.2** | **32.6** | **18.9** | **31.3** | **32.7** |
| Female householder | 17.2 | 18.0 | 8.4 | 17.4 | 18.4 |
| Living alone | 14.8 | 15.8 | 6.8 | 15.0 | 15.9 |
| Male householder | 14.0 | 14.6 | 10.5 | 13.9 | 14.3 |
| Living alone | 10.7 | 12.3 | 7.1 | 10.5 | 10.9 |

*(continued)*

*(continued from previous page)*

| | total | black | Hispanic | white | non-Hispanic white |
|---|---|---|---|---|---|
| **Percent distribution by race and Hispanic origin** | | | | | |
| **Total households** | **100.0%** | **12.3%** | **8.9%** | **83.7%** | **75.3%** |
| **Family households** | **100.0** | **12.0** | **10.5** | **83.7** | **73.7** |
| Married couples | 100.0 | 7.5 | 9.3 | 88.2 | 79.3 |
| Female householder, no spouse present | 100.0 | 30.1 | 13.9 | 66.1 | 53.1 |
| Male householder, no spouse present | 100.0 | 17.5 | 16.3 | 76.5 | 61.3 |
| **Nonfamily households** | **100.0** | **12.8** | **5.4** | **83.9** | **78.8** |
| Female householder | 100.0 | 12.8 | 4.3 | 84.3 | 80.2 |
| Living alone | 100.0 | 13.0 | 4.1 | 84.3 | 80.5 |
| Male householder | 100.0 | 12.8 | 6.7 | 83.4 | 77.0 |
| Living alone | 100.0 | 14.1 | 6.0 | 82.3 | 76.6 |

*Note: Numbers will not add to total because Hispanics may be of any race and not all races are shown.*
*Source: Bureau of the Census, data from the 2000 Current Population Survey, Internet site <http://ferret.bls.census.gov/macro/032000/hhinc/new02_000.htm>; calculations by New Strategist*

# Hispanic Households Are the Youngest

## Young adults head more than one-third of Hispanic households.

People under age 35 head 36 percent of Hispanic compared with only 21 percent of non-Hispanic white households. The Hispanic population is far more youthful than the non-Hispanic white population, which accounts for the difference in householder ages. People under age 35 head 29 percent of black households.

The differences between non-Hispanic white and Hispanic households are just as extreme at the other end of the age spectrum. While people aged 65 or older head 23 percent of non-Hispanic white households, the elderly head only 11 percent of Hispanic households. Among blacks, people aged 65 or older head 15 percent of households.

♦ In the years ahead, the generation gap between non-Hispanic whites and Hispanics could lead to political conflict over the equitable distribution of the nation's economic resources.

**Non-Hispanic white households are the oldest**

*(percent of households headed by people aged 65 or older, by race and Hispanic origin, 2000)*

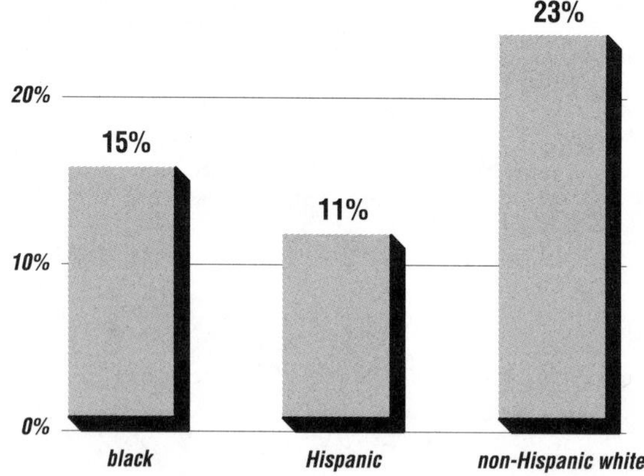

## Households by Age, Race, and Hispanic Origin of Householder, 2000

*(number and percent distribution of households by age, race, and Hispanic origin of householder, 2000; numbers in thousands)*

| | *total* | *black* | *Hispanic* | *white* | *non-Hispanic white* |
|---|---|---|---|---|---|
| **Total households** | **104,705** | **12,849** | **9,319** | **87,671** | **78,819** |
| Under age 25 | 5,860 | 1,002 | 871 | 4,541 | 3,721 |
| Aged 25 to 34 | 18,627 | 2,724 | 2,477 | 14,871 | 12,533 |
| Aged 35 to 44 | 23,955 | 3,149 | 2,494 | 19,808 | 17,440 |
| Aged 45 to 54 | 20,927 | 2,566 | 1,546 | 17,475 | 16,008 |
| Aged 55 to 64 | 13,592 | 1,522 | 929 | 11,599 | 10,704 |
| Aged 65 or older | 21,745 | 1,886 | 1,002 | 19,376 | 18,412 |
| **Percent distribution by age** | | | | | |
| **Total households** | **100.0%** | **100.0%** | **100.0%** | **100.0%** | **100.0%** |
| Under age 25 | 5.6 | 7.8 | 9.3 | 5.2 | 4.7 |
| Aged 25 to 34 | 17.8 | 21.2 | 26.6 | 17.0 | 15.9 |
| Aged 35 to 44 | 22.9 | 24.5 | 26.8 | 22.6 | 22.1 |
| Aged 45 to 54 | 20.0 | 20.0 | 16.6 | 19.9 | 20.3 |
| Aged 55 to 64 | 13.0 | 11.8 | 10.0 | 13.2 | 13.6 |
| Aged 65 or older | 20.8 | 14.7 | 10.8 | 22.1 | 23.4 |
| **Percent distribution by race and Hispanic origin** | | | | | |
| **Total households** | **100.0%** | **12.3%** | **8.9%** | **83.7%** | **75.3%** |
| Under age 25 | 100.0 | 17.1 | 14.9 | 77.5 | 63.5 |
| Aged 25 to 34 | 100.0 | 14.6 | 13.3 | 79.8 | 67.3 |
| Aged 35 to 44 | 100.0 | 13.1 | 10.4 | 82.7 | 72.8 |
| Aged 45 to 54 | 100.0 | 12.3 | 7.4 | 83.5 | 76.5 |
| Aged 55 to 64 | 100.0 | 11.2 | 6.8 | 85.3 | 78.8 |
| Aged 65 or older | 100.0 | 8.7 | 4.6 | 89.1 | 84.7 |

*Note: Numbers will not add to total because Hispanics may be of any race and not all races are shown.*
*Source: Bureau of the Census, data from the 2000 Current Population Survey, Internet site <http://ferret.bls.census.gov/macro/032000/hhinc/new02_003.htm>; calculations by New Strategist*

# Most Households Are Small

## Fifty-nine percent of American households are home to only one or two people.

Two-person households are most common, accounting for 33 percent of the nation's 105 million households. Single-person households represent 26 percent of the total. Three- and four-person households together account for another 31 percent. Only 10 percent of households have five or more people. Overall, the average household in the U.S. was home to 2.6 people in 2000.

♦ Household size, which had been shrinking for decades, has stabilized as the baby-boom generation raises its children. When boomers enter old age, household size will begin to shrink again as the number of single-person households climbs.

### Two-person households are most common

*(percent distribution of households by size, 2000)*

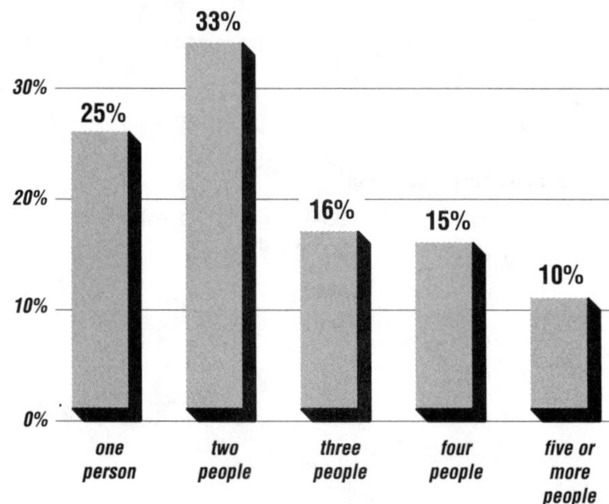

## Households by Size, 2000

*(number and percent distribution of households by size, 2000; numbers in thousands)*

| | *number* | *percent* |
|---|---|---|
| **Total households** | **104,705** | **100.0%** |
| 1 person | 26,724 | 25.5 |
| 2 people | 34,666 | 33.1 |
| 3 people | 17,152 | 16.4 |
| 4 people | 15,309 | 14.6 |
| 5 people | 6,981 | 6.7 |
| 6 people | 2,445 | 2.3 |
| 7 or more people | 1,428 | 1.4 |
| People per household | 2.6 | |

*Source: Bureau of the Census, data from the 2000 Current Population Survey, Internet site <http://ferret.bls.census.gov/macro/032000/hhinc/new01_001.htm>; calculations by New Strategist*

# Seven Million Elderly Women Live Alone

## Nearly half of women aged 65 or older live alone.

There are sharp differences in the ages of men and women who live alone. Most men who live alone are under age 55, while most women who live alone are aged 55 or older. Among men who live alone, the largest share is in the 35-to-44 age group (23 percent). Among women who live alone, the largest share is aged 65 or older (48 percent). Most men live alone before marriage or after divorce. Most women live alone following the death of their spouse.

♦ People who live alone account for 26 percent of all households, making single-person households one of the most common household types.

**Women who live alone are older**

*(percent distribution of women who live alone, by age, 2000)*

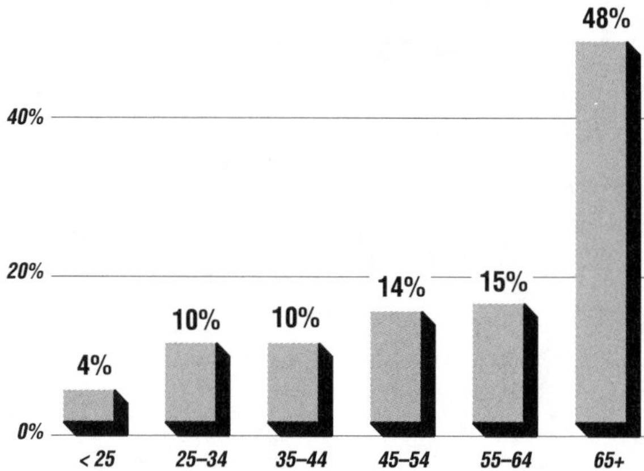

## People Living Alone by Sex and Age, 2000

*(total number of people aged 15 or older, number and percent living alone, and percent distribution of people who live alone, by sex and age, 2000; numbers in thousands)*

| | | living alone | | |
|---|---|---|---|---|
| | total | number | percent | percent distribution |
| **Total men** | **103,114** | **11,181** | **10.8%** | **100.0%** |
| Under age 25 | 19,503 | 556 | 2.9 | 5.0 |
| Aged 25 to 34 | 18,563 | 2,279 | 12.3 | 20.4 |
| Aged 35 to 44 | 22,135 | 2,569 | 11.6 | 23.0 |
| Aged 45 to 54 | 17,890 | 2,146 | 12.0 | 19.2 |
| Aged 55 to 64 | 11,137 | 1,276 | 11.5 | 11.4 |
| Aged 65 or older | 13,886 | 2,356 | 17.0 | 21.1 |
| **Total women** | **110,660** | **15,543** | **14.0** | **100.0** |
| Under age 25 | 19,040 | 587 | 3.1 | 3.8 |
| Aged 25 to 34 | 19,223 | 1,569 | 8.2 | 10.1 |
| Aged 35 to 44 | 22,670 | 1,540 | 6.8 | 9.9 |
| Aged 45 to 54 | 18,741 | 2,158 | 11.5 | 13.9 |
| Aged 55 to 64 | 12,250 | 2,262 | 18.5 | 14.6 |
| Aged 65 or older | 18,735 | 7,427 | 39.6 | 47.8 |

*Source: Bureau of the Census, data from the 2000 Current Population Survey, Internet site <http://ferret.bls .census.gov/macro/032000/hhinc/toc.htm>; calculations by New Strategist*

# More Than One-Third of Households Reside in the South

## The Northeast is home to the smallest number of households.

Thirty-six percent of the nation's households are in the South, making it by far the most populous region. Only 19 percent of households are in the Northeast, a smaller share than the 22 percent in the West. The Midwest is the second most populous region, home to nearly one in four households.

The majority of black households are in the South, while the South and West combined are home to more than three out of four Hispanic households. Blacks head 19 percent of households in the South, while Hispanics head 17 percent of households in the West.

♦ The nation's politics will be shaped increasingly by the concentration of blacks and Hispanics in certain regions and states.

## Households by Region, Race, and Hispanic Origin, 2000

*(number and percent distribution of households by region, race, and Hispanic origin of householder, 2000; numbers in thousands)*

| | *total* | *black* | *Hispanic* | *white* | *non-Hispanic white* |
|---|---|---|---|---|---|
| **Total households** | **104,705** | **12,849** | **9,319** | **87,671** | **78,819** |
| Northeast | 20,087 | 2,316 | 1,469 | 17,110 | 15,843 |
| Midwest | 24,508 | 2,446 | 704 | 21,534 | 20,871 |
| South | 37,303 | 7,001 | 3,286 | 29,494 | 26,336 |
| West | 22,808 | 1,086 | 3,860 | 19,533 | 15,769 |
| **Percent distribution by region** | | | | | |
| **Total households** | **100.0%** | **100.0%** | **100.0%** | **100.0%** | **100.0%** |
| Northeast | 19.2 | 18.0 | 15.8 | 19.5 | 20.1 |
| Midwest | 23.4 | 19.0 | 7.6 | 24.6 | 26.5 |
| South | 35.6 | 54.5 | 35.3 | 33.6 | 33.4 |
| West | 21.8 | 8.5 | 41.4 | 22.3 | 20.0 |
| **Percent distribution by race and Hispanic origin** | | | | | |
| **Total households** | **100.0%** | **12.3%** | **8.9%** | **83.7%** | **75.3%** |
| Northeast | 100.0 | 11.5 | 7.3 | 85.2 | 78.9 |
| Midwest | 100.0 | 10.0 | 2.9 | 87.9 | 85.2 |
| South | 100.0 | 18.8 | 8.8 | 79.1 | 70.6 |
| West | 100.0 | 4.8 | 16.9 | 85.6 | 69.1 |

*Note: Numbers will not add to total because Hispanics may be of any race and not all races are shown.*
*Source: Bureau of the Census, data from the 2000 Current Population Survey, Internet site <http://ferret.bls.census.gov/macro/032000/hhinc/new01_000.htm>; calculations by New Strategist*

# Half the Nation's Households Are in the Suburbs

## Only one in five households is outside a metropolitan area.

Of the nation's 105 million households, 80 percent are in metropolitan areas. The Census Bureau defines metropolitan areas as counties with a city of 50,000 or more population plus any adjacent counties with economic ties to the core county.

The suburbs are home to half of households, and one in three households live in the suburbs of metropolitan areas with populations of 1 million or more. Slightly fewer than one-third of American households are in central cities.

♦ Advances in telecommunications are allowing people to live where they want rather than where they must. This development could slow the growth of the largest metropolitan areas since many Americans prefer smaller towns and cities.

## Households by Metropolitan Status, 2000

*(number and percent distribution of households by metropolitan status and size of metropolitan poulation, 2000; numbers in thousands)*

| | number | percent |
|---|---|---|
| **Total households** | **104,705** | **100.0%** |
| Households in metropolitan areas | 84,259 | 80.5 |
| Central cities | 31,825 | 30.4 |
| Suburbs | 52,433 | 50.1 |
| Households in nonmetropolitan areas | 20,447 | 19.5 |
| **Metropolitan size** | | |
| **Inside metropolitan areas** | **84,259** | **80.5** |
| 1 million or more | 56,131 | 53.6 |
| Inside central cities | 20,214 | 19.3 |
| Outside central cities | 35,917 | 34.3 |
| Under 1 million | 28,127 | 26.9 |
| Inside central cities | 11,611 | 11.1 |
| Outside central cities | 16,516 | 15.8 |

*Source: Bureau of the Census, data from the 2000 Current Population Survey, Internet site <http://ferret.bls.census.gov/macro/032000/hhinc/new01_000.htm>; calculations by New Strategist*

# Most Black Children Live with Mother Only

## Fifty-one percent of black children live with only their mother, up from 44 percent in 1980.

Among whites, 74 percent of children live with both parents. Just 18 percent live with only their mother, up from 14 percent in 1980. Among Hispanic children, 64 percent live with both parents, while 27 percent live with only their mother—up from 20 percent in 1980.

Few children live with only their father: 5 percent of white and 4 percent of Hispanic and black children. Nine percent of black children, 5 percent of Hispanic children, and 3 percent of white children live with someone other than their mother or father, often a grandmother.

♦ While the living arrangements of black children differ from those of white or Hispanic children, the trends are the same for all three groups. An increasing proportion of children live with only their mothers, and a shrinking proportion live with two parents.

**Most white children live with two parents**

*(percent of children under age 18 who live with two parents, by race and Hispanic origin, 1998)*

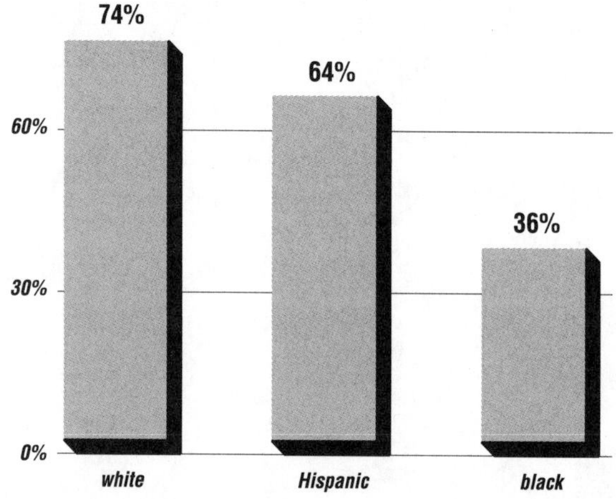

## Living Arrangements of Children by Race and Hispanic Origin, 1980 and 1998

*(number and percent distribution of children under age 18 by living arrangement, race, and Hispanic origin of child, 1980 and 1998; numbers in thousands)*

| | 1998 | | 1980 | |
|---|---|---|---|---|
| | *number* | *percent* | *number* | *percent* |
| **Total children** | **71,377** | **100.0%** | **63,427** | **100.0%** |
| Two parents | 48,642 | 68.1 | 48,624 | 76.7 |
| Mother only | 16,634 | 23.3 | 11,406 | 18.0 |
| Father only | 3,143 | 4.4 | 1,060 | 1.7 |
| Other | 2,959 | 4.1 | 2,337 | 3.7 |
| **Black children** | **11,414** | **100.0** | **9,375** | **100.0** |
| Two parents | 4,137 | 36.2 | 3,956 | 42.2 |
| Mother only | 5,830 | 51.1 | 4,117 | 43.9 |
| Father only | 424 | 3.7 | 180 | 1.9 |
| Other | 1,015 | 8.9 | 1,122 | 12.0 |
| **Hispanic children** | **10,863** | **100.0** | **5,459** | **100.0** |
| Two parents | 6,909 | 63.6 | 4,116 | 75.4 |
| Mother only | 2,915 | 26.8 | 1,069 | 19.6 |
| Father only | 482 | 4.4 | 83 | 1.5 |
| Other | 551 | 5.1 | 191 | 3.5 |
| **White children** | **56,124** | **100.0** | **52,242** | **100.0** |
| Two parents | 41,547 | 74.0 | 43,200 | 82.7 |
| Mother only | 10,210 | 18.2 | 7,059 | 13.5 |
| Father only | 2,562 | 4.6 | 842 | 1.6 |
| Other | 1,799 | 3.2 | 1,141 | 2.2 |

*Note: Numbers will not add to total because Hispanics may be of any race and not all races are shown.*
*Source: Bureau of the Census,* Marital Status and Living Arrangements: March 1998, *Current Population Reports, P20-514, 1998; calculations by New Strategist*

# Most Young Adults Live at Home

## Seventy-seven percent of the nation's 18- and 19-year-olds still live with their parents.

Young men are far more likely to live at home than young women. Eighty percent of men and 73 percent of women aged 18 or 19 live with their parents. Among those aged 20 to 24, 50 percent of men and 37 percent of women still live at home. (These statistics count young adults who live in college dormitories as living at home.) The proportion of young adults who live at home has been rising during the past few years not only because more are going to college, but also because a growing share cannot yet afford the expense of setting up an independent household.

Only 13 percent of men aged 20 to 24 live with their spouse. A larger 26 percent share lives alone or with nonrelatives. Among women in the age group, 24 percent live with their spouse while 23 percent live alone or with nonrelatives. Women are more likely than men to live with their spouse because they marry at a younger age, on average.

Among 25-to-29-year-olds, the majority of women live with their spouse. Among men, the proportion is 41 percent. Twenty percent of men and 12 percent of women in this age group still live at home.

♦ Young adults are more likely to live at home than they once were out of necessity. Entry-level wages have fallen sharply over the past 15 years, forcing young adults to live with their parents until they can afford independence.

## Living Arrangements of Young Adults, 1998

*(number and percent distribution of people aged 18 to 29 by living arrangement and sex, 1998; numbers in thousands)*

| | number | | | percent | | |
|---|---|---|---|---|---|---|
| | *total* | *men* | *women* | *total* | *men* | *women* |
| **Aged 18 to 19** | **7,587** | **3,807** | **3,780** | **100.0%** | **100.0%** | **100.0%** |
| Living with parents | 5,796 | 3,030 | 2,766 | 76.4 | 79.6 | 73.2 |
| Living with spouse | 242 | 62 | 180 | 3.2 | 1.6 | 4.8 |
| Living with other relatives | 698 | 354 | 344 | 9.2 | 9.3 | 9.1 |
| Living alone or with nonrelatives | 851 | 361 | 490 | 11.2 | 9.5 | 13.0 |
| **Aged 20 to 24** | **17,614** | **8,826** | **8,788** | **100.0** | **100.0** | **100.0** |
| Living with parents | 7,575 | 4,368 | 3,207 | 43.0 | 49.5 | 36.5 |
| Living with spouse | 3,314 | 1,179 | 2,135 | 18.8 | 13.4 | 24.3 |
| Living with other relatives | 2,383 | 995 | 1,388 | 13.5 | 11.3 | 15.8 |
| Living alone or with nonrelatives | 4,342 | 2,284 | 2,058 | 24.7 | 25.9 | 23.4 |
| **Aged 25 to 29** | **18,996** | **9,450** | **9,546** | **100.0** | **100.0** | **100.0** |
| Living with parents | 3,013 | 1,848 | 1,165 | 15.9 | 19.6 | 12.2 |
| Living with spouse | 8,816 | 3,914 | 4,902 | 46.4 | 41.4 | 51.4 |
| Living with other relatives | 2,525 | 932 | 1,593 | 13.3 | 9.9 | 16.7 |
| Living alone or with nonrelatives | 4,642 | 2,756 | 1,886 | 24.4 | 29.2 | 19.8 |

*Source: Bureau of the Census,* Marital Status and Living Arrangements: March 1998, *Current Population Reports, P20-514, 1998; calculations by New Strategist*

# Lifestyles of Men and Women Diverge in Old Age

## Older men are much more likely to live with their spouse.

Among men aged 65 or older, 73 percent live with their spouse. Among women in the age group, the proportion is just 41 percent. That women tend to marry slightly older men and men tend to die at a younger age than women accounts for this difference.

Equal shares of women aged 65 or older live alone and live with their spouse, 41 percent in 1998. Among men in the age group, only 17 percent live alone. Elderly women are twice as likely as elderly men to live with other relatives, 17 versus 7 percent. Often, the other relative with whom they live is a son or daughter who helps care for them.

♦ The different living arrangements of older men and women divide the population into two distinct segments: older women who live alone and older couples. The two segments will dominate the elderly population for years to come.

### Older women are more likely than older men to live alone

*(percent of people aged 65 or older who live with their spouse or alone, by sex, 1998)*

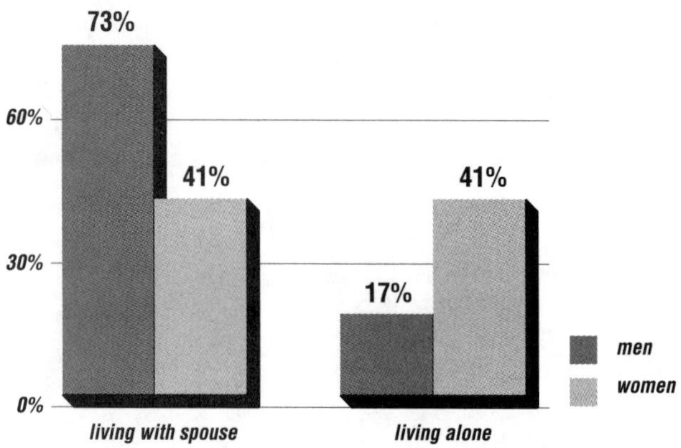

## Living Arrangements of People Aged 65 or Older, 1998

*(number and percent distribution of people aged 65 or older by living arrangement and sex, 1998; numbers in thousands)*

| | *total* | *men* | *women* |
|---|---|---|---|
| **Total people** | **32,084** | **13,525** | **18,559** |
| Living with spouse | 17,382 | 9,821 | 7,561 |
| Living alone | 9,922 | 2,345 | 7,577 |
| Living with other relatives | 4,067 | 952 | 3,115 |
| Living with unrelated people | 713 | 407 | 306 |
| **Total people** | **100.0%** | **100.0%** | **100.0%** |
| Living with spouse | 54.2 | 72.6 | 40.7 |
| Living alone | 30.9 | 17.3 | 40.8 |
| Living with other relatives | 12.7 | 7.0 | 16.8 |
| Living with unrelated people | 2.2 | 3.0 | 1.6 |

*Source: Bureau of the Census,* Marital Status and Living Arrangements: March 1998, *Current Population Reports, P20-514, 1998; and data from the 1998 Current Population Survey, Internet site <www.bls.census.gov/cps>; calculations by New Strategist*

# Most Married Couples Have Children at Home

## The couples most likely to have children at home are aged 35 to 44.

As young adults become increasingly likely to live at home, parenting duties are extending into later life. The majority of married couples under age 55 have children in their home. Even among couples in the 55-to-64 age group, a substantial 29 percent have children living with them.

The majority of married couples under age 45 have children under age 18 at home. In the 45-to-64 age group, the share with children under age 18 at home falls to a minority, but more than one couple in five has grown children living with them.

The couples most likely to have preschoolers at home are under age 35. Those most likely to have teens at home are aged 40 to 44. Half the couples in this age group are living with teens.

♦ The number of married couples with adult children at home will rise as boomers age and their children become young adults.

## Married Couples with Children at Home by Age of Householder and Age of Children, 1998

*(number and percent distribution of total married couples and couples with children at home, by age of householder and age of children, 1998; numbers in thousands)*

| | | with children | | | | | |
|---|---|---|---|---|---|---|---|
| | | | | under age 18 | | | |
| | total | of any age | aged 18 or older | total | 12 to 17 | 6 to 11 | under 6 |
| **Total couples** | **54,317** | **31,288** | **6,019** | **25,269** | **11,406** | **12,285** | **11,773** |
| Under age 20 | 86 | 56 | – | 56 | 1 | – | 55 |
| Aged 20 to 24 | 1,287 | 760 | 5 | 755 | 12 | 99 | 731 |
| Aged 25 to 29 | 3,967 | 2,543 | 8 | 2,535 | 104 | 984 | 2,227 |
| Aged 30 to 34 | 5,919 | 4,712 | 10 | 4,702 | 873 | 2,376 | 3,566 |
| Aged 35 to 39 | 6,941 | 6,047 | 80 | 5,967 | 2,436 | 3,670 | 3,045 |
| Aged 40 to 44 | 7,239 | 6,098 | 473 | 5,625 | 3,636 | 3,093 | 1,477 |
| Aged 45 to 54 | 11,734 | 7,550 | 2,615 | 4,935 | 3,819 | 1,872 | 593 |
| Aged 55 to 64 | 7,936 | 2,332 | 1,741 | 591 | 468 | 153 | 55 |
| Aged 65 or older | 9,209 | 1,191 | 1,087 | 104 | 56 | 38 | 23 |
| **Total couples** | **100.0%** | **57.6%** | **11.1%** | **46.5%** | **21.0%** | **22.6%** | **21.7%** |
| Under age 20 | 100.0 | 65.1 | – | 65.1 | 1.2 | – | 64.0 |
| Aged 20 to 24 | 100.0 | 59.1 | 0.4 | 58.7 | 0.9 | 7.7 | 56.8 |
| Aged 25 to 29 | 100.0 | 64.1 | 0.2 | 63.9 | 2.6 | 24.8 | 56.1 |
| Aged 30 to 34 | 100.0 | 79.6 | 0.2 | 79.4 | 14.7 | 40.1 | 60.2 |
| Aged 35 to 39 | 100.0 | 87.1 | 1.2 | 86.0 | 35.1 | 52.9 | 43.9 |
| Aged 40 to 44 | 100.0 | 84.2 | 6.5 | 77.7 | 50.2 | 42.7 | 20.4 |
| Aged 45 to 54 | 100.0 | 64.3 | 22.3 | 42.1 | 32.5 | 16.0 | 5.1 |
| Aged 55 to 64 | 100.0 | 29.4 | 21.9 | 7.4 | 5.9 | 1.9 | 0.7 |
| Aged 65 or older | 100.0 | 12.9 | 11.8 | 1.1 | 0.6 | 0.4 | 0.2 |

*Note: (–) means sample is too small to make a reliable estimate.*
*Source: Bureau of the Census, detailed tables for* Household and Family Characteristics: March 1998, *Current Population Reports, P20-515, 1998; calculations by New Strategist*

## Married Couples by Age of Householder and Number of Children under Age 18 at Home, 1998

*(number and percent distribution of married couples by age of householder and number of children under age 18 living at home, 1998; numbers in thousands)*

| | | | with children under 18 | | | |
|---|---|---|---|---|---|---|
| | total | no children under 18 | total | one | two | three or more |
| **Total couples** | **54,317** | **29,048** | **25,269** | **9,507** | **10,241** | **5,521** |
| Under age 25 | 1,373 | 562 | 811 | 471 | 240 | 99 |
| Aged 25 to 29 | 3,967 | 1,432 | 2,535 | 1,033 | 1,041 | 461 |
| Aged 30 to 34 | 5,919 | 1,217 | 4,702 | 1,533 | 1,949 | 1,219 |
| Aged 35 to 39 | 6,941 | 974 | 5,967 | 1,495 | 2,758 | 1,714 |
| Aged 40 to 44 | 7,239 | 1,614 | 5,625 | 1,885 | 2,426 | 1,315 |
| Aged 45 to 54 | 11,734 | 6,799 | 4,935 | 2,581 | 1,690 | 663 |
| Aged 55 to 64 | 7,936 | 7,345 | 591 | 444 | 108 | 40 |
| Aged 65 or older | 9,209 | 9,105 | 104 | 66 | 28 | 9 |
| **Total couples** | **100.0%** | **53.5%** | **46.5%** | **17.5%** | **18.9%** | **10.2%** |
| Under age 25 | 100.0 | 40.9 | 59.1 | 34.3 | 17.5 | 7.2 |
| Aged 25 to 29 | 100.0 | 36.1 | 63.9 | 26.0 | 26.2 | 11.6 |
| Aged 30 to 34 | 100.0 | 20.6 | 79.4 | 25.9 | 32.9 | 20.6 |
| Aged 35 to 39 | 100.0 | 14.0 | 86.0 | 21.5 | 39.7 | 24.7 |
| Aged 40 to 44 | 100.0 | 22.3 | 77.7 | 26.0 | 33.5 | 18.2 |
| Aged 45 to 54 | 100.0 | 57.9 | 42.1 | 22.0 | 14.4 | 5.7 |
| Aged 55 to 64 | 100.0 | 92.6 | 7.4 | 5.6 | 1.4 | 0.5 |
| Aged 65 or older | 100.0 | 98.9 | 1.1 | 0.7 | 0.3 | 0.1 |

*Source: Bureau of the Census, detailed tables for* Household and Family Characteristics: March 1998, *Current Population Reports, P20-515, 1998; calculations by New Strategist*

# Most Single Parents Are Women

## Women head 81 percent of the nation's 9 million single-parent families.

Not all male- and female-headed families are single-parent families. Many such householders consist of men or women heading households in which other relatives live, such as an elderly parent, a sister, or a nephew. But the 61 percent majority of the nation's 12.7 million female-headed families include single mothers and children under age 18. In contrast, a 45 percent minority of male-headed families are single-parent families.

Most of the female-headed families with a householder under age 50 include children under age 18. Most of the male-headed families with a householder between the ages of 25 and 49 include children.

♦ As the children of baby boomers grow up and leave home, the number of single-parent families should stabilize or even decline.

## Female- and Male-Headed Families with Children under Age 18 at Home by Age of Householder, 1998

*(total number of female- and male-headed families, and number and percent with children under age 18 at home, by age of householder, 1998; numbers in thousands)*

| | | with children under 18 | |
|---|---|---|---|
| | total | number | percent |
| **Female-headed families** | **12,652** | **7,693** | **60.8%** |
| Aged 15 to 19 | 152 | 76 | 50.0 |
| Aged 20 to 24 | 943 | 790 | 83.8 |
| Aged 25 to 29 | 1,305 | 1,204 | 92.3 |
| Aged 30 to 34 | 1,582 | 1,489 | 94.1 |
| Aged 35 to 39 | 1,818 | 1,684 | 92.6 |
| Aged 40 to 44 | 1,819 | 1,357 | 74.6 |
| Aged 45 to 49 | 1,367 | 740 | 54.1 |
| Aged 50 to 54 | 893 | 226 | 25.3 |
| Aged 55 to 59 | 679 | 95 | 14.0 |
| Aged 60 to 64 | 420 | 10 | 2.4 |
| Aged 65 or older | 1,676 | 22 | 1.3 |
| **Male-headed families** | **3,911** | **1,798** | **46.0** |
| Aged 15 to 19 | 167 | 18 | 10.8 |
| Aged 20 to 24 | 384 | 168 | 43.8 |
| Aged 25 to 29 | 462 | 251 | 54.3 |
| Aged 30 to 34 | 404 | 238 | 58.9 |
| Aged 35 to 39 | 493 | 332 | 67.3 |
| Aged 40 to 44 | 562 | 362 | 64.4 |
| Aged 45 to 49 | 405 | 231 | 57.0 |
| Aged 50 to 54 | 296 | 118 | 39.9 |
| Aged 55 to 59 | 213 | 50 | 23.5 |
| Aged 60 to 64 | 139 | 15 | 10.8 |
| Aged 65 or older | 386 | 14 | 3.6 |

*Source: Bureau of the Census, detailed tables for* Household and Family Characteristics: March 1998*; Current Population Reports, P20-515, 1998; calculations by New Strategist*

# Many Unmarried Couples Are Older

## More than 1 million cohabiting couples are aged 45 or older.

Living together as an unmarried couple is not the sole domain of young Americans. Only 20 percent of cohabiting couples are under age 25. Fifty-seven percent are aged 25 to 44, and 23 percent are aged 45 or older.

More than 70 percent of cohabiting couples are heterosexual partners, while 28 percent are homosexual couples. Among same-sex couples, 52 percent are men.

♦ Baby boomers were the first to make cohabitation common. As boomers age, the number of cohabitors aged 45 and older will soar.

### More than one in four cohabiting couples are same-sex partners

*(percent distribution of cohabiting couples, by sex of partner, 1998)*

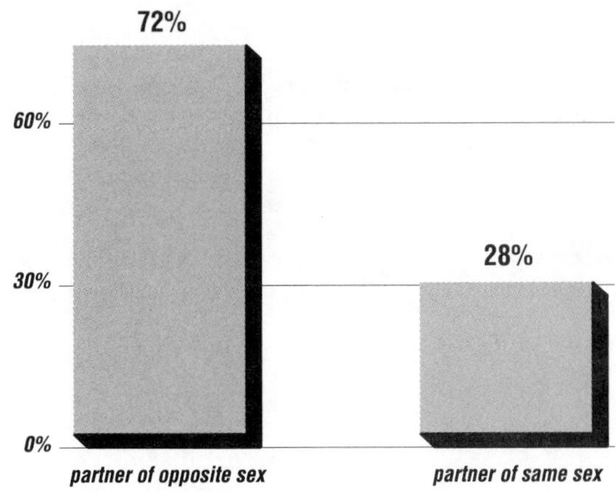

## Characteristics of Cohabiting Couples, 1998

*(number and percent distribution of households with two unrelated adults, by sex of partner and age of householder, 1998; numbers in thousands)*

| | *total* | | *male householder* | | *female householder* | |
|---|---|---|---|---|---|---|
| | *number* | *percent* | *number* | *percent* | *number* | *percent* |
| **Total cohabiting couples** | **5,911** | **100.0%** | **3,217** | **100.0%** | **2,694** | **100.0%** |
| **Partner of opposite sex** | **4,236** | **71.7** | **2,352** | **73.1** | **1,885** | **70.0** |
| Under age 25 | 776 | 13.1 | 408 | 12.7 | 369 | 13.7 |
| Aged 25 to 34 | 1,618 | 27.4 | 891 | 27.7 | 727 | 27.0 |
| Aged 35 to 44 | 857 | 14.5 | 514 | 16.0 | 343 | 12.7 |
| Aged 45 to 64 | 797 | 13.5 | 441 | 13.7 | 356 | 13.2 |
| Aged 65 or older | 188 | 3.2 | 98 | 3.0 | 90 | 3.3 |
| **Partner of same sex** | **1,674** | **28.3** | **865** | **26.9** | **810** | **30.1** |
| Under age 25 | 407 | 6.9 | 204 | 6.3 | 203 | 7.5 |
| Aged 25 to 34 | 571 | 9.7 | 309 | 9.6 | 262 | 9.7 |
| Aged 35 to 44 | 339 | 5.7 | 181 | 5.6 | 158 | 5.9 |
| Aged 45 to 64 | 263 | 4.4 | 140 | 4.4 | 123 | 4.6 |
| Aged 65 or older | 95 | 1.6 | 31 | 1.0 | 64 | 2.4 |

*Source: Bureau of the Census,* Marital Status and Living Arrangements: March 1998, *Current Population Reports, P20-514, 1998; calculations by New Strategist*

# Most Americans Are Married

## Men are more likely to be married than women—58 versus 55 percent in 1998.

Men are also more likely than women to have never married—31 percent of men compared with 25 percent of women. Never-married men outnumber never-married women up to age 65.

The proportion of young adults who have not yet married has been growing for decades as men and women postpone marriage. The median age at first marriage was 26.7 years for men and a record high 25.0 years for women in 1998. By age 30, most men are married, and the proportion peaks at 80 percent among those aged 55 to 64. Among women, the married proportion peaks at 73 percent for those aged 40 to 44.

A substantial 18 percent of women aged 45 to 54 are currently divorced. This figure, while high, greatly understates the incidence of divorce among boomers because it does not include those who have divorced and remarried.

Overall, 10 percent of women are currently widowed compared with 2.5 percent of men. Women are more likely to be widowed than men because they tend to marry men who are older and because men's life expectancy is lower than women's. Most women aged 75 or older are widows, while the proportion of widowers does not top 42 percent in any age group.

♦ With so many young adults going to college, the median age at first marriage is likely to remain high as men and women postpone marriage until they have established a career.

## Median Age at First Marriage by Sex, 1890 to 1998

*(median age at first marriage by sex, 1890 to 1998)*

| | *men* | *women* |
|---|---|---|
| 1998 | 26.7 | 25.0 |
| 1997 | 26.8 | 25.0 |
| 1996 | 27.1 | 24.8 |
| 1995 | 26.9 | 24.5 |
| 1994 | 26.7 | 24.5 |
| 1993 | 26.5 | 24.5 |
| 1992 | 26.5 | 24.4 |
| 1991 | 26.3 | 24.1 |
| 1990 | 26.1 | 23.9 |
| 1980 | 24.7 | 22.0 |
| 1970 | 23.2 | 20.8 |
| 1960 | 22.8 | 20.3 |
| 1950 | 22.8 | 20.3 |
| 1940 | 24.3 | 21.5 |
| 1930 | 24.3 | 21.3 |
| 1920 | 24.6 | 21.2 |
| 1910 | 25.1 | 21.6 |
| 1900 | 25.9 | 21.9 |
| 1890 | 26.1 | 22.0 |
| **Change in age** | | |
| 1950–1998 | 3.9 | 4.7 |
| 1890–1950 | –3.3 | –1.7 |

*Source: Bureau of the Census,* Marital Status and Living Arrangements: March 1998, *Current Population Report P20-514, 1998; calculations by New Strategist*

## Marital Status of Men by Age, 1998

*(number and percent distribution of men aged 15 or older by age and marital status, 1998; numbers in thousands)*

| | total men | never married | married | divorced | widowed |
|---|---|---|---|---|---|
| **Total number** | **101,123** | **31,591** | **58,633** | **8,331** | **2,569** |
| Under age 20 | 9,921 | 9,778 | 121 | 19 | 3 |
| Aged 20 to 24 | 8,826 | 7,360 | 1,332 | 133 | – |
| Aged 25 to 29 | 9,450 | 4,822 | 4,219 | 398 | 10 |
| Aged 30 to 34 | 10,076 | 2,939 | 6,345 | 773 | 20 |
| Aged 35 to 39 | 11,299 | 2,444 | 7,598 | 1,213 | 44 |
| Aged 40 to 44 | 10,756 | 1,676 | 7,633 | 1,397 | 50 |
| Aged 45 to 54 | 16,598 | 1,481 | 12,665 | 2,303 | 150 |
| Aged 55 to 64 | 10,673 | 572 | 8,559 | 1,266 | 275 |
| Aged 65 to 74 | 7,992 | 328 | 6,331 | 626 | 707 |
| Aged 75 to 84 | 4,527 | 145 | 3,327 | 166 | 888 |
| Aged 85 or older | 1,006 | 45 | 502 | 36 | 423 |
| **Total percent** | **100.0%** | **31.2%** | **57.0%** | **8.2%** | **2.5%** |
| Under age 20 | 100.0 | 98.6 | 1.2 | 0.2 | 0.0 |
| Aged 20 to 24 | 100.0 | 83.4 | 15.1 | 1.5 | – |
| Aged 25 to 29 | 100.0 | 51.0 | 44.6 | 4.2 | 0.1 |
| Aged 30 to 34 | 100.0 | 29.2 | 62.0 | 7.7 | 0.2 |
| Aged 35 to 39 | 100.0 | 21.6 | 67.2 | 10.7 | 0.4 |
| Aged 40 to 44 | 100.0 | 15.6 | 70.0 | 12.0 | 0.5 |
| Aged 45 to 54 | 100.0 | 8.9 | 76.3 | 13.9 | 0.9 |
| Aged 55 to 64 | 100.0 | 5.4 | 80.2 | 11.9 | 2.6 |
| Aged 65 to 74 | 100.0 | 4.1 | 79.2 | 7.8 | 8.8 |
| Aged 75 to 84 | 100.0 | 3.2 | 73.5 | 3.7 | 19.6 |
| Aged 85 or older | 100.0 | 4.5 | 49.9 | 3.6 | 42.1 |

*Note: (–) means sample is too small to make a reliable estimate.*
*Source: Bureau of the Census,* Marital Status and Living Arrangements: March 1998, *Current Population Reports, P20-514, 1998; calculations by New Strategist*

## Marital Status of Women by Age, 1998

*(number and percent distribution of women aged 15 or older by age and marital status, 1998; numbers in thousands)*

| | total women | never married | married | divorced | widowed |
|---|---|---|---|---|---|
| **Total number** | **108,168** | **26,713** | **59,333** | **11,093** | **11,029** |
| Under age 20 | 9,545 | 9,235 | 289 | 20 | 2 |
| Aged 20 to 24 | 8,788 | 6,178 | 2,372 | 222 | 17 |
| Aged 25 to 29 | 9,546 | 3,689 | 5,298 | 525 | 35 |
| Aged 30 to 34 | 10,282 | 2,219 | 7,044 | 964 | 55 |
| Aged 35 to 39 | 11,392 | 1,626 | 8,145 | 1,484 | 138 |
| Aged 40 to 44 | 11,015 | 1,095 | 8,016 | 1,738 | 166 |
| Aged 45 to 54 | 17,459 | 1,263 | 12,345 | 3,154 | 697 |
| Aged 55 to 64 | 11,582 | 538 | 7,847 | 1,671 | 1,526 |
| Aged 65 to 74 | 9,882 | 425 | 5,420 | 882 | 3,155 |
| Aged 75 to 84 | 6,754 | 340 | 2,300 | 362 | 3,752 |
| Aged 85 or older | 1,923 | 106 | 258 | 71 | 1,487 |
| **Total percent** | **100.0%** | **24.7%** | **54.9%** | **10.3%** | **10.2%** |
| Under age 20 | 100.0 | 96.8 | 3.0 | 0.2 | 0.0 |
| Aged 20 to 24 | 100.0 | 70.3 | 27.0 | 2.5 | 0.2 |
| Aged 25 to 20 | 100.0 | 38.6 | 55.5 | 5.5 | 0.4 |
| Aged 30 to 34 | 100.0 | 21.6 | 68.5 | 9.4 | 0.5 |
| Aged 35 to 39 | 100.0 | 14.3 | 71.5 | 13.0 | 1.2 |
| Aged 40 to 44 | 100.0 | 9.9 | 72.8 | 15.8 | 1.5 |
| Aged 45 to 54 | 100.0 | 7.2 | 70.7 | 18.1 | 4.0 |
| Aged 55 to 64 | 100.0 | 4.6 | 67.8 | 14.4 | 13.2 |
| Aged 65 to 74 | 100.0 | 4.3 | 54.8 | 8.9 | 31.9 |
| Aged 75 to 84 | 100.0 | 5.0 | 34.1 | 5.4 | 55.6 |
| Aged 85 or older | 100.0 | 5.5 | 13.4 | 3.7 | 77.3 |

*Source: Bureau of the Census,* Marital Status and Living Arrangements: March 1998, *Current Population Reports, P20-514, 1998; calculations by New Strategist*

# Most Blacks Are Not Married

## Only 39 percent of blacks are currently married compared with 59 percent of non-Hispanic whites.

The majority of non-Hispanic whites and Hispanics are married by the time they reach their late twenties. For blacks, marriage does not claim the majority until the 30-to-34 age group. Among non-Hispanic whites aged 25 to 29 in 1998, only 41 percent had never married. But 62 percent of their black counterparts were still single. In the 30-to-34 age group, only 22 percent of whites but 45 percent of blacks had never married.

Blacks are more likely to be divorced than whites or Hispanics, particularly in the 45-to-54 age group. They are also more likely to be widowed in middle age than whites or Hispanics. Fifteen percent of blacks aged 55 to 64 are widowed compared with only 7 percent of non-Hispanic whites and Hispanics in the age group.

♦ Blacks are less likely to marry than whites because many black men have difficulty finding jobs that pay enough to support a family.

## Marital Status by Race, Hispanic Origin, and Age, 1998

*(number of people aged 15 or older and percent distribution by marital status, by race, Hispanic origin, and age, 1998; numbers in thousands)*

| | total | | never | | | |
|---|---|---|---|---|---|---|
| | number | percent | married | married | divorced | widowed |
| **Black** | **24,998** | **100.0%** | **43.5%** | **38.6%** | **10.8%** | **7.0%** |
| Under age 20 | 3,058 | 100.0 | 98.5 | 1.3 | 0.3 | – |
| Aged 20 to 24 | 2,563 | 100.0 | 88.2 | 11.2 | 0.5 | 0.1 |
| Aged 25 to 29 | 2,603 | 100.0 | 61.7 | 34.8 | 3.5 | 0.1 |
| Aged 30 to 34 | 2,697 | 100.0 | 45.4 | 45.4 | 8.6 | 0.5 |
| Aged 35 to 39 | 2,851 | 100.0 | 36.8 | 49.2 | 12.6 | 1.4 |
| Aged 40 to 44 | 2,648 | 100.0 | 28.5 | 52.6 | 16.8 | 2.0 |
| Aged 45 to 54 | 3,663 | 100.0 | 15.3 | 57.3 | 22.0 | 4.4 |
| Aged 55 to 64 | 2,224 | 100.0 | 10.8 | 54.9 | 19.3 | 15.0 |
| Aged 65 to 74 | 1,613 | 100.0 | 6.1 | 47.3 | 13.0 | 33.5 |
| Aged 75 to 84 | 789 | 100.0 | 7.7 | 34.9 | 7.9 | 49.6 |
| Aged 85 or older | 289 | 100.0 | 3.5 | 15.9 | 5.5 | 74.7 |
| **Hispanic** | **21,430** | **100.0** | **34.7** | **54.6** | **7.2** | **3.5** |
| Under age 20 | 2,722 | 100.0 | 95.0 | 4.7 | 0.2 | 0.1 |
| Aged 20 to 24 | 2,663 | 100.0 | 69.3 | 29.4 | 1.1 | 0.2 |
| Aged 25 to 29 | 2,795 | 100.0 | 41.9 | 55.2 | 2.6 | 0.3 |
| Aged 30 to 34 | 2,693 | 100.0 | 23.7 | 69.4 | 6.5 | 0.4 |
| Aged 35 to 39 | 2,505 | 100.0 | 20.4 | 68.5 | 10.1 | 0.9 |
| Aged 40 to 44 | 2,101 | 100.0 | 10.5 | 75.3 | 13.3 | 0.0 |
| Aged 45 to 54 | 2,700 | 100.0 | 10.0 | 73.7 | 13.2 | 3.1 |
| Aged 55 to 64 | 1,633 | 100.0 | 7.3 | 73.2 | 12.9 | 6.7 |
| Aged 65 to 74 | 1,015 | 100.0 | 5.7 | 61.9 | 10.8 | 21.5 |
| Aged 75 to 84 | 480 | 100.0 | 3.1 | 50.0 | 7.5 | 39.6 |
| Aged 85 or older | 123 | 100.0 | 7.3 | 27.6 | 0.8 | 63.4 |

*(continued)*

*(continued from previous page)*

| | total | | never married | married | divorced | widowed |
|---|---|---|---|---|---|---|
| | number | percent | | | | |
| **White** | **174,708** | **100.0%** | **25.4%** | **58.8%** | **9.2%** | **6.6%** |
| Under age 20 | 15,462 | 100.0 | 97.5 | 2.3 | 0.2 | 0.0 |
| Aged 20 to 24 | 14,168 | 100.0 | 74.5 | 23.1 | 2.4 | 0.1 |
| Aged 25 to 29 | 15,298 | 100.0 | 41.1 | 53.4 | 5.2 | 0.3 |
| Aged 30 to 34 | 16,481 | 100.0 | 21.9 | 68.0 | 8.7 | 0.4 |
| Aged 35 to 39 | 18,697 | 100.0 | 15.1 | 72.3 | 11.9 | 0.7 |
| Aged 40 to 44 | 18,039 | 100.0 | 10.6 | 74.1 | 14.4 | 0.8 |
| Aged 45 to 54 | 28,871 | 100.0 | 7.3 | 75.1 | 15.5 | 2.2 |
| Aged 55 to 64 | 19,140 | 100.0 | 4.4 | 75.7 | 12.7 | 7.3 |
| Aged 65 to 74 | 15,760 | 100.0 | 4.0 | 67.6 | 8.0 | 20.4 |
| Aged 75 to 84 | 10,211 | 100.0 | 4.1 | 50.8 | 4.5 | 40.6 |
| Aged 85 or older | 2,582 | 100.0 | 5.3 | 26.4 | 3.5 | 64.8 |
| **Non-Hispanic white** | **154,205** | **100.0** | **24.2** | **59.3** | **9.5** | **6.0** |
| Under age 20 | 12,864 | 100.0 | 97.0 | 1.8 | 0.2 | 0.0 |
| Aged 20 to 24 | 11,631 | 100.0 | 75.7 | 21.5 | 2.6 | 0.1 |
| Aged 25 to 29 | 12,607 | 100.0 | 41.0 | 52.9 | 5.8 | 0.2 |
| Aged 30 to 34 | 13,905 | 100.0 | 21.8 | 68.8 | 9.1 | 0.3 |
| Aged 35 to 39 | 16,318 | 100.0 | 14.3 | 72.7 | 12.2 | 0.7 |
| Aged 40 to 44 | 16,028 | 100.0 | 10.7 | 73.8 | 14.6 | 0.8 |
| Aged 45 to 54 | 26,298 | 100.0 | 6.0 | 75.2 | 15.8 | 2.1 |
| Aged 55 to 64 | 17,560 | 100.0 | 4.1 | 75.9 | 12.7 | 7.3 |
| Aged 65 to 74 | 14,789 | 100.0 | 3.9 | 67.9 | 7.8 | 20.3 |
| Aged 75 to 84 | 9,743 | 100.0 | 4.2 | 50.8 | 4.3 | 40.7 |
| Aged 85 or older | 2,463 | 100.0 | 5.3 | 26.2 | 3.7 | 64.8 |

*Note: (–) means sample is too small to make a reliable estimate.*
*Source: Bureau of the Census,* Marital Status and Living Arrangements: March 1998, *Current Population Reports, P20-514, 1998; calculations by New Strategist*

CHAPTER

# 7

# Population Trends

♦ **The 60-to-64 age group will grow faster than any other between 2001 and 2010.**

In contrast, the number of people aged 30 to 44 will shrink as the small generation X enters middle age.

♦ **By 2010, minorities will account for 33 percent of the U.S. population.**

Hispanics will begin to outnumber non-Hispanic blacks and become the largest minority group in the U.S. in 2002.

♦ **California Has Minority Majority**

Only 48 percent of the state's residents are non-Hispanic white.

♦ **Las Vegas was the fastest-growing metropolitan area during the 1990s.**

Eighty percent of Americans are metropolitan residents, up from only 56 percent in 1950.

♦ **More immigrants came to the U.S. in the 1990s than in the 1980s.**

The last decade of the 20th century may have seen more immigrants enter the U.S. than any other decade in our history.

♦ **More than half of American households owned a computer in 2000.**

Forty-two percent of households had Internet access. The affluent and the educated were most likely to be online.

# More Women Than Men

## American women outnumber men by more than 6 million.

Although there are more women than men in the population, women do not begin to outnumber men until the 25-to-29 age group. By ages 85 and older, there are only 44 men per 100 women. Males slightly outnumber females at younger ages because boys outnumber girls at birth. Women outnumber men at older ages because, throughout life, males have a higher death rate than females. Research has shown that the higher male death rate is primarily due to biological factors rather than lifestyle differences.

In 2001, the largest five-year age group was 40-to-44-year-olds, at 22.9 million. This age group is now filled with the youngest members of the baby-boom generation, born from 1957 to 1961. Boomers, who spanned the ages of 37 to 55 in 2001, are moving up through the age distribution, changing America as they do.

♦ Because the death rate is higher for males than for females, women will continue to greatly outnumber men at older ages.

**Women increasingly outnumber men with age**

*(number of males per 100 females at selected ages, 2001)*

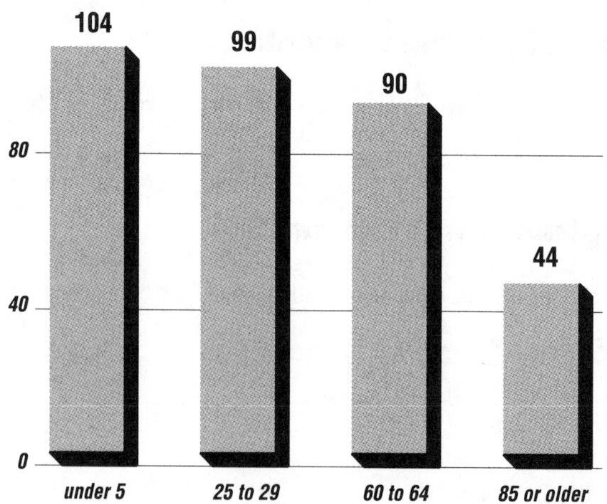

# Population by Age and Sex, 2001

*(number of people by age and sex, and sex ratio by age, 2001; numbers in thousands)*

| | *total* | *male* | *female* | *sex ratio* |
|---|---|---|---|---|
| **Total people** | **277,803** | **135,795** | **142,008** | **96** |
| Under age 5 | 18,899 | 9,654 | 9,245 | 104 |
| Aged 5 to 9 | 19,546 | 10,001 | 9,546 | 105 |
| Aged 10 to 14 | 20,270 | 10,380 | 9,891 | 105 |
| Aged 15 to 19 | 20,065 | 10,313 | 9,751 | 106 |
| Aged 20 to 24 | 19,012 | 9,685 | 9,327 | 104 |
| Aged 25 to 29 | 17,424 | 8,665 | 8,759 | 99 |
| Aged 30 to 34 | 19,639 | 9,694 | 9,944 | 97 |
| Aged 35 to 39 | 21,799 | 10,826 | 10,973 | 99 |
| Aged 40 to 44 | 22,894 | 11,360 | 11,534 | 98 |
| Aged 45 to 49 | 20,457 | 10,055 | 10,401 | 97 |
| Aged 50 to 54 | 18,184 | 8,846 | 9,338 | 95 |
| Aged 55 to 59 | 13,596 | 6,527 | 7,070 | 92 |
| Aged 60 to 64 | 10,953 | 5,178 | 5,774 | 90 |
| Aged 65 to 69 | 9,411 | 4,330 | 5,081 | 85 |
| Aged 70 to 74 | 8,744 | 3,888 | 4,856 | 80 |
| Aged 75 to 79 | 7,401 | 3,100 | 4,301 | 72 |
| Aged 80 to 84 | 5,070 | 1,944 | 3,126 | 62 |
| Aged 85 or older | 4,437 | 1,347 | 3,090 | 44 |
| Aged 18 to 24 | 27,187 | 13,874 | 13,313 | 104 |
| Aged 18 or older | 207,197 | 99,635 | 107,562 | 93 |
| Aged 65 or older | 35,064 | 14,609 | 20,455 | 71 |
| Median age | 36.0 | 34.8 | 37.2 | – |

*Note: The sex ratio is the number of males per 100 females. (–) means not applicable.*
*Source: Bureau of the Census, Internet site <www.census.gov/population/projections/nation/summary/np-t3-b .txt>; calculations by New Strategist*

# Boomers Will Inflate the 55-to-64 Age Group

## The 60-to-64 age group will grow faster than any other between 2001 and 2010.

The United States population is projected to grow 8 percent between 2001 and 2010, according to the Census Bureau. But some age groups will expand rapidly while others will shrink.

The fastest-growing age group will be 60-to-64-year-olds, projected to increase 48 percent between 2001 and 2010 as the baby-boom generation enters its early sixties. In contrast, the number of people aged 30 to 44 will shrink as the small generation X enters middle age.

The millennial generation, many of them the children of boomers, will boost the number of teens and young adults. The 20-to-29 age group will grow more than 12 percent between 2001 and 2010.

♦ Rapid growth in the number of people nearing retirement age will shift the focus of the nation's attention from business goals to leisure pursuits.

## Population by Age and Sex, 2001 to 2010

*(number of people by age, 2001 to 2010; percent change, 2001–10; numbers in thousands)*

| | 2001 | 2005 | 2010 | percent change 2001–10 |
|---|---|---|---|---|
| **Total people** | **277,803** | **287,716** | **299,862** | **7.9%** |
| Under age 5 | 18,899 | 19,212 | 20,099 | 6.3 |
| Aged 5 to 9 | 19,546 | 19,122 | 19,438 | –0.6 |
| Aged 10 to 14 | 20,270 | 20,634 | 19,908 | –1.8 |
| Aged 15 to 19 | 20,065 | 20,990 | 21,668 | 8.0 |
| Aged 20 to 24 | 19,012 | 20,159 | 21,151 | 11.3 |
| Aged 25 to 29 | 17,424 | 18,351 | 19,849 | 13.9 |
| Aged 30 to 34 | 19,639 | 18,582 | 19,002 | –3.2 |
| Aged 35 to 39 | 21,799 | 20,082 | 19,039 | –12.7 |
| Aged 40 to 44 | 22,894 | 22,634 | 20,404 | –10.9 |
| Aged 45 to 49 | 20,457 | 22,230 | 22,227 | 8.7 |
| Aged 50 to 54 | 18,184 | 19,661 | 21,934 | 20.6 |
| Aged 55 to 59 | 13,596 | 16,842 | 19,177 | 41.0 |
| Aged 60 to 64 | 10,953 | 12,848 | 16,252 | 48.4 |
| Aged 65 to 69 | 9,411 | 10,086 | 12,159 | 29.2 |
| Aged 70 to 74 | 8,744 | 8,375 | 8,995 | 2.9 |
| Aged 75 to 79 | 7,401 | 7,429 | 7,175 | –3.1 |
| Aged 80 to 84 | 5,070 | 5,514 | 5,600 | 10.5 |
| Aged 85 or older | 4,437 | 4,968 | 5,786 | 30.4 |
| Aged 18 to 24 | 27,187 | 28,498 | 30,163 | 10.9 |
| Aged 18 or older | 207,197 | 216,098 | 227,761 | 9.9 |
| Aged 65 or older | 35,064 | 36,370 | 39,715 | 13.3 |

*Source: Bureau of the Census, Internet site <www.census.gov/population/projections/nation/summary/np-t3-c .txt>; calculations by New Strategist*

# Asians Are Projected to Grow the Fastest

## Hispanics will outnumber non-Hispanic blacks by more than 2 million in 2005.

The minority share of the U.S. population is growing rapidly. By 2010, 33 percent of Americans will be Asian, black, Hispanic, or Native American, up from 29 percent in 2001. Only 67 percent of the population will be non-Hispanic white.

Asians are the fastest-growing minority, enjoying a 31 percent increase in numbers between 2001 and 2010. Despite this rapid growth, Asians will account for fewer than 5 percent of Americans in 2010.

The number of Hispanics will grow 30 percent between 2001 and 2010, surpassing the number of non-Hispanic blacks and thus becoming the largest minority group in the U.S. in 2002. By 2010, Hispanics will account for 15 percent of the U.S. population.

♦ Because younger generations are much more diverse than older Americans, a multicultural generation gap looms in the years ahead.

**Hispanics overtake non-Hispanic blacks**

*(number of Hispanics and non-Hispanic blacks, 2001 and 2010; numbers in millions)*

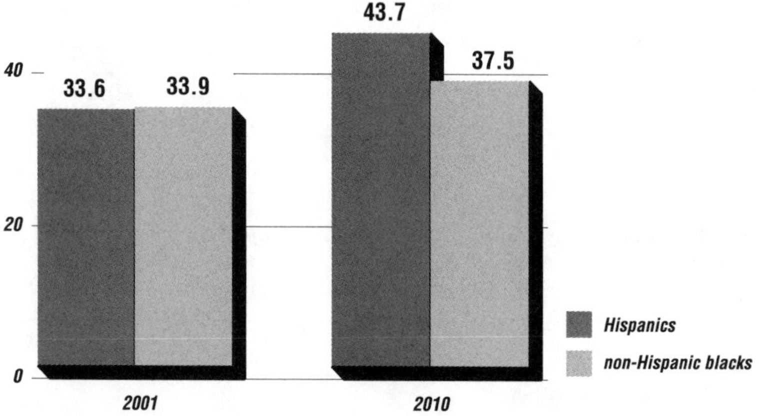

## Population by Race and Hispanic Origin, 2001 to 2010

*(number and percent distribution of people by race and Hispanic origin, 2001 to 2010; percent change in number and percentage point change in share, 2001–10; numbers in thousands)*

| | 2001 | 2005 | 2010 | percent change 2001–10 |
|---|---|---|---|---|
| **Total number** | **277,803** | **287,716** | **299,862** | **7.9%** |
| Asian, non-Hispanic | 10,990 | 12,497 | 14,436 | 31.4 |
| Black, non-Hispanic | 33,876 | 35,446 | 37,483 | 10.6 |
| Hispanic | 33,616 | 38,189 | 43,688 | 30.0 |
| Native American, non-Hispanic | 2,072 | 2,171 | 2,300 | 11.0 |
| White, non-Hispanic | 197,249 | 199,414 | 201,956 | 2.4 |

| | 2001 | 2005 | 2010 | percentage point change, 2001–10 |
|---|---|---|---|---|
| **Total percent** | **100.0%** | **100.0%** | **100.0%** | – |
| Asian, non-Hispanic | 4.0 | 4.3 | 4.8 | 0.9 |
| Black, non-Hispanic | 12.2 | 12.3 | 12.5 | 0.3 |
| Hispanic | 12.1 | 13.3 | 14.6 | 2.5 |
| Native American, non-Hispanic | 0.7 | 0.8 | 0.8 | 0.0 |
| White, non-Hispanic | 71.0 | 69.3 | 67.3 | –3.7 |

*Note: (–) means not applicable.*
*Source: Bureau of the Census, Internet site <www.census.gov/population/projections/nation/summary/np-t4-b.txt>, and <www.census.gov/population/projections/nation/summary/np-t4-c.txt>; calculations by New Strategist*

# Among Hispanics and Asians, Every Age Group Will Grow

## For non-Hispanic whites, many age groups shrink.

Among non-Hispanic whites, population growth will vary dramatically by age between 2001 and 2010, ranging from a hefty 20 percent decline in the number of non-Hispanic whites aged 35 to 39 to a substantial 46 percent gain for those aged 60 to 64. The non-Hispanic black and Native American populations will see losses in some age groups during the coming decade, but the declines are much smaller than those that will occur among non-Hispanic whites.

For Hispanics and non-Hispanic Asians, rapid growth is in store for every age group between 2001 and 2010. Among Hispanics, growth ranges from a low of 11 percent in the 35-to-39 age group to a high of 73 percent for those aged 85 or older. Among Asians, growth ranges from a 10 percent gain in the 30-to-34 age group to a doubling of the 85-or-older population.

♦ The 55-to-64 age group will grow rapidly in every racial and ethnic group thanks to the aging of the baby-boom generation. The concerns of pre-retirees will unite Americans regardless of racial or ethnic background.

## Non-Hispanic Asians by Age, 2001 to 2010

*(number of non-Hispanic Asians by age, 2001 and 2010; percent change 2001–10; numbers in thousands)*

| | 2001 | 2005 | 2010 | percent change 2001–10 |
|---|---|---|---|---|
| **Total people** | **10,990** | **12,497** | **14,436** | **31.4%** |
| Under age 5 | 886 | 970 | 1,067 | 20.4 |
| Aged 5 to 9 | 856 | 937 | 1,050 | 22.7 |
| Aged 10 to 14 | 836 | 996 | 1,108 | 32.5 |
| Aged 15 to 19 | 806 | 887 | 1,096 | 36.0 |
| Aged 20 to 24 | 774 | 894 | 995 | 28.6 |
| Aged 25 to 29 | 848 | 885 | 1,040 | 22.6 |
| Aged 30 to 34 | 966 | 1,026 | 1,065 | 10.2 |
| Aged 35 to 39 | 949 | 1,047 | 1,147 | 20.9 |
| Aged 40 to 44 | 914 | 1,016 | 1,139 | 24.6 |
| Aged 45 to 49 | 797 | 921 | 1,048 | 31.5 |
| Aged 50 to 54 | 663 | 785 | 936 | 41.2 |
| Aged 55 to 59 | 465 | 623 | 778 | 67.3 |
| Aged 60 to 64 | 366 | 453 | 626 | 71.0 |
| Aged 65 to 69 | 290 | 351 | 447 | 54.1 |
| Aged 70 to 74 | 232 | 268 | 333 | 43.5 |
| Aged 75 to 79 | 169 | 202 | 242 | 43.2 |
| Aged 80 to 84 | 97 | 129 | 162 | 67.0 |
| Aged 85 or older | 78 | 107 | 156 | 100.0 |
| Aged 18 to 24 | 1,093 | 1,234 | 1,429 | 30.7 |
| Aged 18 or older | 7,925 | 9,047 | 10,549 | 33.1 |
| Aged 65 or older | 866 | 1,057 | 1,341 | 54.8 |

*Source: Bureau of the Census, Internet sites <www.census.gov/population/projections/nation/summary/np-t4-b .txt> and <www.census.gov/population/projections/nation/summary/np-t4-c.txt>; calculations by New Strategist*

## Non-Hispanic Blacks by Age, 2001 to 2010

*(number of non-Hispanic blacks by age, 2001 and 2010; percent change 2001–10; numbers in thousands)*

| | 2001 | 2005 | 2010 | percent change 2001–10 |
|---|---|---|---|---|
| **Total people** | **33,876** | **35,446** | **37,483** | **10.6%** |
| Under age 5 | 2,607 | 2,686 | 2,854 | 9.5 |
| Aged 5 to 9 | 2,810 | 2,625 | 2,724 | –3.1 |
| Aged 10 to 14 | 3,071 | 3,039 | 2,757 | –10.2 |
| Aged 15 to 19 | 2,926 | 3,176 | 3,215 | 9.9 |
| Aged 20 to 24 | 2,705 | 2,827 | 3,099 | 14.6 |
| Aged 25 to 29 | 2,404 | 2,551 | 2,735 | 13.8 |
| Aged 30 to 34 | 2,519 | 2,504 | 2,601 | 3.3 |
| Aged 35 to 39 | 2,727 | 2,573 | 2,575 | –5.6 |
| Aged 40 to 44 | 2,715 | 2,762 | 2,598 | –4.3 |
| Aged 45 to 49 | 2,302 | 2,600 | 2,687 | 16.7 |
| Aged 50 to 54 | 1,861 | 2,161 | 2,535 | 36.2 |
| Aged 55 to 59 | 1,301 | 1,669 | 2,085 | 60.3 |
| Aged 60 to 64 | 1,065 | 1,216 | 1,595 | 49.8 |
| Aged 65 to 69 | 909 | 995 | 1,170 | 28.7 |
| Aged 70 to 74 | 739 | 746 | 830 | 12.3 |
| Aged 75 to 79 | 553 | 596 | 616 | 11.4 |
| Aged 80 to 84 | 343 | 368 | 409 | 19.2 |
| Aged 85 or older | 319 | 350 | 398 | 24.8 |
| Aged 18 to 24 | 3,892 | 4,060 | 4,453 | 14.4 |
| Aged 18 or older | 23,649 | 25,152 | 27,287 | 15.4 |
| Aged 65 or older | 2,863 | 3,055 | 3,423 | 19.6 |

*Source: Bureau of the Census, Internet sites <www.census.gov/population/projections/nation/summary/np-t4-b .txt> and <www.census.gov/population/projections/nation/summary/np-t4-c.txt>; calculations by New Strategist*

## Hispanics by Age, 2001 to 2010

*(number of Hispanics by age, 2001 and 2010; percent change 2001–10; numbers in thousands)*

| | 2001 | 2005 | 2010 | percent change 2001–10 |
|---|---|---|---|---|
| **Total people** | **33,616** | **38,189** | **43,688** | **30.0%** |
| Under age 5 | 3,651 | 4,027 | 4,476 | 22.6 |
| Aged 5 to 9 | 3,409 | 3,681 | 4,129 | 21.1 |
| Aged 10 to 14 | 3,036 | 3,622 | 3,914 | 28.9 |
| Aged 15 to 19 | 2,916 | 3,307 | 4,011 | 37.6 |
| Aged 20 to 24 | 2,912 | 3,224 | 3,599 | 23.6 |
| Aged 25 to 29 | 2,671 | 3,011 | 3,336 | 24.9 |
| Aged 30 to 34 | 2,733 | 2,888 | 3,212 | 17.5 |
| Aged 35 to 39 | 2,722 | 2,851 | 3,011 | 10.6 |
| Aged 40 to 44 | 2,387 | 2,767 | 2,926 | 22.6 |
| Aged 45 to 49 | 1,862 | 2,278 | 2,738 | 47.0 |
| Aged 50 to 54 | 1,439 | 1,778 | 2,270 | 57.7 |
| Aged 55 to 59 | 1,039 | 1,352 | 1,759 | 69.3 |
| Aged 60 to 64 | 810 | 989 | 1,330 | 64.2 |
| Aged 65 to 69 | 655 | 770 | 963 | 47.0 |
| Aged 70 to 74 | 536 | 599 | 716 | 33.6 |
| Aged 75 to 79 | 390 | 470 | 544 | 39.5 |
| Aged 80 to 84 | 234 | 308 | 387 | 65.4 |
| Aged 85 or older | 213 | 266 | 368 | 72.8 |
| Aged 18 to 24 | 4,114 | 4,536 | 5,235 | 27.2 |
| Aged 18 or older | 21,806 | 24,863 | 28,794 | 32.0 |
| Aged 65 or older | 2,029 | 2,413 | 2,978 | 46.8 |

*Source: Bureau of the Census, Internet sites <www.census.gov/population/projections/nation/summary/np-t4-b.txt> and <www.census.gov/population/projections/nation/summary/np-t4-c.txt>; calculations by New Strategist*

## Non-Hispanic Native Americans by Age, 2001 to 2010

*(number of non-Hispanic Native Americans by age, 2001 and 2010; percent change 2001–10; numbers in thousands)*

| | 2001 | 2005 | 2010 | percent change 2001–10 |
|---|---|---|---|---|
| **Total people** | **2,072** | **2,171** | **2,300** | **11.0%** |
| Under age 5 | 166 | 176 | 188 | 13.3 |
| Aged 5 to 9 | 174 | 171 | 182 | 4.6 |
| Aged 10 to 14 | 211 | 196 | 190 | –10.0 |
| Aged 15 to 19 | 200 | 212 | 197 | –1.5 |
| Aged 20 to 24 | 173 | 192 | 206 | 19.1 |
| Aged 25 to 29 | 156 | 166 | 192 | 23.1 |
| Aged 30 to 34 | 153 | 157 | 166 | 8.5 |
| Aged 35 to 39 | 152 | 147 | 155 | 2.0 |
| Aged 40 to 44 | 152 | 152 | 145 | –4.6 |
| Aged 45 to 49 | 131 | 141 | 144 | 9.9 |
| Aged 50 to 54 | 108 | 120 | 133 | 23.1 |
| Aged 55 to 59 | 80 | 95 | 111 | 38.8 |
| Aged 60 to 64 | 61 | 70 | 88 | 44.3 |
| Aged 65 to 69 | 47 | 52 | 63 | 34.0 |
| Aged 70 to 74 | 38 | 40 | 46 | 21.1 |
| Aged 75 to 79 | 30 | 32 | 35 | 16.7 |
| Aged 80 to 84 | 19 | 23 | 25 | 31.6 |
| Aged 85 or older | 22 | 27 | 34 | 54.5 |
| Aged 18 to 24 | 249 | 271 | 284 | 14.1 |
| Aged 18 or older | 1,398 | 1,495 | 1,622 | 16.0 |
| Aged 65 or older | 156 | 175 | 203 | 30.1 |

*Source: Bureau of the Census, Internet sites <www.census.gov/population/projections/nation/summary/np-t4-b.txt> and <www.census.gov/population/projections/nation/summary/np-t4-c.txt>; calculations by New Strategist*

## Non-Hispanic Whites by Age, 2001 to 2010

*(number of non-Hispanic whites by age, 2001 and 2010; percent change 2001–10; numbers in thousands)*

| | 2001 | 2005 | 2010 | percent change 2001–10 |
|---|---|---|---|---|
| **Total people** | **197,249** | **199,414** | **201,956** | **2.4%** |
| Under age 5 | 11,589 | 11,353 | 11,514 | –0.6 |
| Aged 5 to 9 | 12,298 | 11,707 | 11,352 | –7.7 |
| Aged 10 to 14 | 13,117 | 12,781 | 11,940 | –9.0 |
| Aged 15 to 19 | 13,216 | 13,409 | 13,149 | –0.5 |
| Aged 20 to 24 | 12,449 | 13,022 | 13,253 | 6.5 |
| Aged 25 to 29 | 11,345 | 11,737 | 12,546 | 10.6 |
| Aged 30 to 34 | 13,268 | 12,007 | 11,958 | –9.9 |
| Aged 35 to 39 | 15,250 | 13,464 | 12,151 | –20.3 |
| Aged 40 to 44 | 16,727 | 15,936 | 13,596 | –18.7 |
| Aged 45 to 49 | 15,366 | 16,289 | 15,609 | 1.6 |
| Aged 50 to 54 | 14,113 | 14,816 | 16,060 | 13.8 |
| Aged 55 to 59 | 10,712 | 13,103 | 14,444 | 34.8 |
| Aged 60 to 64 | 8,650 | 10,120 | 12,613 | 45.8 |
| Aged 65 to 69 | 7,511 | 7,918 | 9,516 | 26.7 |
| Aged 70 to 74 | 7,199 | 6,721 | 7,070 | –1.8 |
| Aged 75 to 79 | 6,259 | 6,130 | 5,737 | –8.3 |
| Aged 80 to 84 | 4,377 | 4,685 | 4,617 | 5.5 |
| Aged 85 or older | 3,804 | 4,218 | 4,830 | 27.0 |
| Aged 18 to 24 | 17,839 | 18,398 | 18,762 | 5.2 |
| Aged 18 or older | 152,419 | 155,540 | 159,509 | 4.7 |
| Aged 65 or older | 29,150 | 29,670 | 31,770 | 9.0 |

*Source: Bureau of the Census, Internet sites <www.census.gov/population/projections/nation/summary/np-t4-b.txt> and <www.census.gov/population/projections/nation/summary/np-t4-c.txt>; calculations by New Strategist*

# The South Is the Most Populous Region

## The West is the most diverse.

The South is by far the most populous region, and more than one-third of Americans live there. The Northeast is the least populous region, accounting for 19 percent of the U.S. population.

Only 61 percent of Americans living in the West are non-Hispanic white, while 39 percent are Hispanic, black, Asian, or Native American. In the Pacific division, which includes California and Hawaii, an even smaller 55 percent of the population is non-Hispanic white.

The Midwest is the least diverse region. Eighty-three percent of Midwesterners are non-Hispanic white. Non-Hispanic whites account for fully 89 percent of the population of the West North Central division, which includes Iowa, Kansas, Minnesota, Missouri, Nebraska, North Dakota, and South Dakota.

The South is home to the 56 percent majority of the nation's blacks. Within the region, blacks account for one-fifth of the population.

♦ Even in the Midwest, the diversity of metropolitan areas such as Chicago is growing rapidly.

**The Midwest is the least diverse region**

*(non-Hispanic white share of population, by region, 2001)*

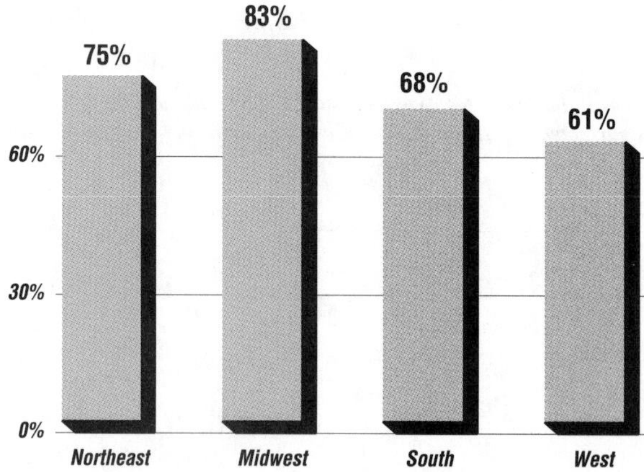

## Population by Region, Race, and Hispanic Origin, 2001

*(number and percent distribution of people by region, division, race, and Hispanic origin, 2001; numbers in thousands)*

| | | non-Hispanic | | | | |
|---|---|---|---|---|---|---|
| | *total* | *Asian* | *black* | *Native American* | *white* | *Hispanic* |
| **UNITED STATES** | **277,803** | **10,990** | **33,876** | **2,072** | **197,249** | **33,616** |
| **Northeast** | **52,282** | **2,176** | **5,626** | **114** | **39,274** | **5,092** |
| New England | 13,642 | 402 | 701 | 31 | 11,663 | 844 |
| Middle Atlantic | 38,641 | 1,774 | 4,926 | 83 | 27,611 | 4,247 |
| **Midwest** | **63,341** | **1,218** | **6,347** | **364** | **52,715** | **2,698** |
| East North Central | 44,414 | 885 | 5,289 | 149 | 35,923 | 2,169 |
| West North Central | 18,927 | 333 | 1,058 | 215 | 16,792 | 529 |
| **South** | **99,226** | **1,978** | **18,900** | **591** | **67,129** | **10,627** |
| South Atlantic | 51,044 | 1,145 | 10,986 | 205 | 35,128 | 3,581 |
| East South Central | 16,839 | 138 | 3,396 | 40 | 13,080 | 185 |
| West South Central | 31,343 | 696 | 4,519 | 346 | 18,921 | 6,861 |
| **West** | **62,953** | **5,618** | **3,002** | **1,003** | **38,131** | **15,200** |
| Mountain | 18,245 | 406 | 523 | 581 | 13,399 | 3,337 |
| Pacific | 44,708 | 5,212 | 2,480 | 421 | 24,732 | 11,863 |
| **Percent distribution by race and Hispanic origin** | | | | | | |
| **UNITED STATES** | **100.0%** | **4.0%** | **12.2%** | **0.7%** | **71.0%** | **12.1%** |
| **Northeast** | **100.0** | **4.2** | **10.8** | **0.2** | **75.1** | **9.7** |
| New England | 100.0 | 2.9 | 5.1 | 0.2 | 85.5 | 6.2 |
| Middle Atlantic | 100.0 | 4.6 | 12.7 | 0.2 | 71.5 | 11.0 |
| **Midwest** | **100.0** | **1.9** | **10.0** | **0.6** | **83.2** | **4.3** |
| East North Central | 100.0 | 2.0 | 11.9 | 0.3 | 80.9 | 4.9 |
| West North Central | 100.0 | 1.8 | 5.6 | 1.1 | 88.7 | 2.8 |
| **South** | **100.0** | **2.0** | **19.0** | **0.6** | **67.7** | **10.7** |
| South Atlantic | 100.0 | 2.2 | 21.5 | 0.4 | 68.8 | 7.0 |
| East South Central | 100.0 | 0.8 | 20.2 | 0.2 | 77.7 | 1.1 |
| West South Central | 100.0 | 2.2 | 14.4 | 1.1 | 60.4 | 21.9 |
| **West** | **100.0** | **8.9** | **4.8** | **1.6** | **60.6** | **24.1** |
| Mountain | 100.0 | 2.2 | 2.9 | 3.2 | 73.4 | 18.3 |
| Pacific | 100.0 | 11.7 | 5.5 | 0.9 | 55.3 | 26.5 |

*(continued)*

*(continued from previous page)*

| | total | non-Hispanic Asian | black | Native American | white | Hispanic |
|---|---|---|---|---|---|---|
| **Percent distribution by region and division** | | | | | | |
| **UNITED STATES** | **100.0%** | **100.0%** | **100.0%** | **100.0%** | **100.0%** | **100.0%** |
| **Northeast** | **18.8** | **19.8** | **16.6** | **5.5** | **19.9** | **15.1** |
| New England | 4.9 | 3.7 | 2.1 | 1.5 | 5.9 | 2.5 |
| Middle Atlantic | 13.9 | 16.1 | 14.5 | 4.0 | 14.0 | 12.6 |
| **Midwest** | **22.8** | **11.1** | **18.7** | **17.6** | **26.7** | **8.0** |
| East North Central | 16.0 | 8.1 | 15.6 | 7.2 | 18.2 | 6.5 |
| West North Central | 6.8 | 3.0 | 3.1 | 10.4 | 8.5 | 1.6 |
| **South** | **35.7** | **18.0** | **55.8** | **28.5** | **34.0** | **31.6** |
| South Atlantic | 18.4 | 10.4 | 32.4 | 9.9 | 17.8 | 10.7 |
| East South Central | 6.1 | 1.3 | 10.0 | 1.9 | 6.6 | 0.6 |
| West South Central | 11.3 | 6.3 | 13.3 | 16.7 | 9.6 | 20.4 |
| **West** | **22.7** | **51.1** | **8.9** | **48.4** | **19.3** | **45.2** |
| Mountain | 6.6 | 3.7 | 1.5 | 28.1 | 6.8 | 9.9 |
| Pacific | 16.1 | 47.4 | 7.3 | 20.3 | 12.5 | 35.3 |

*Source: Projections by New Strategist*

# California Has Minority Majority

## Only 48 percent of the state's residents are non-Hispanic white.

California is not the most diverse state. That honor belongs to Hawaii, where only 28 percent of the population is non-Hispanic white while 60 percent is Asian. In New Mexico, non-Hispanic whites account for just 46 percent of the population, while Hispanics are a close second at 42 percent. In California, the nation's most populous state, 33 percent of residents are Hispanic and 12 percent are Asian. Non-Hispanic whites account for only 54 percent of the population of Texas, the second most-populous state. Thirty-one percent are Hispanic.

At the other extreme, non-Hispanic whites account for more than 95 percent of the populations of Maine, New Hampshire, Vermont, and West Virginia. In many states of the West and Midwest, minorities account for fewer than 15 percent of the population.

♦ As the most populous states become minority-led, the nation's political landscape will change, giving a greater voice to the wants and needs of minorities.

## Population by State, Race, and Hispanic Origin, 2001

*(number of people by state, race, and Hispanic origin, 2001; numbers in thousands)*

| | | non-Hispanic | | | | |
|---|---|---|---|---|---|---|
| | total | Asian | black | Native American | white | Hispanic |
| **United States** | **277,803** | **10,990** | **33,876** | **2,072** | **197,249** | **33,616** |
| Alabama | 4,384 | 30 | 1,139 | 14 | 3,154 | 48 |
| Alaska | 632 | 31 | 23 | 103 | 449 | 27 |
| Arizona | 5,143 | 101 | 157 | 250 | 3,399 | 1,236 |
| Arkansas | 2,640 | 20 | 424 | 13 | 2,123 | 60 |
| California | 33,631 | 3,984 | 2,178 | 180 | 16,199 | 11,089 |
| Colorado | 4,294 | 104 | 166 | 28 | 3,331 | 666 |
| Connecticut | 3,323 | 89 | 292 | 6 | 2,631 | 304 |
| Delaware | 776 | 17 | 152 | 2 | 574 | 31 |
| District of Columbia | 544 | 17 | 323 | 1 | 161 | 43 |
| Florida | 15,532 | 284 | 2,343 | 45 | 10,386 | 2,475 |
| Georgia | 8,230 | 174 | 2,353 | 16 | 5,421 | 266 |
| Hawaii | 1,192 | 721 | 30 | 5 | 337 | 99 |
| Idaho | 1,302 | 14 | 5 | 15 | 1,164 | 104 |
| Illinois | 12,237 | 420 | 1,827 | 18 | 8,603 | 1,369 |
| Indiana | 6,022 | 61 | 497 | 13 | 5,287 | 165 |
| Iowa | 2,852 | 40 | 57 | 8 | 2,681 | 66 |
| Kansas | 2,649 | 49 | 151 | 20 | 2,269 | 160 |
| Kentucky | 3,992 | 29 | 286 | 5 | 3,634 | 38 |
| Louisiana | 4,406 | 56 | 1,427 | 18 | 2,783 | 123 |
| Maine | 1,241 | 10 | 6 | 6 | 1,210 | 10 |
| Maryland | 5,225 | 218 | 1,464 | 13 | 3,319 | 212 |
| Massachusetts | 6,231 | 256 | 351 | 11 | 5,185 | 427 |
| Michigan | 9,755 | 174 | 1,382 | 53 | 7,855 | 290 |
| Minnesota | 4,866 | 145 | 155 | 58 | 4,406 | 103 |
| Mississippi | 2,816 | 21 | 1,031 | 10 | 1,728 | 26 |
| Missouri | 5,508 | 64 | 621 | 18 | 4,706 | 98 |
| Montana | 883 | 6 | 3 | 58 | 799 | 18 |
| Nebraska | 1,685 | 24 | 67 | 14 | 1,497 | 83 |
| Nevada | 2,023 | 94 | 140 | 29 | 1,400 | 360 |
| New Hampshire | 1,228 | 16 | 8 | 2 | 1,180 | 21 |

*(continued)*

*(continued from previous page)*

| | | non-Hispanic | | | | |
|---|---|---|---|---|---|---|
| | **total** | **Asian** | **black** | **Native American** | **white** | **Hispanic** |
| New Jersey | 8,234 | 495 | 1,107 | 14 | 5,539 | 1,080 |
| New Mexico | 1,804 | 22 | 32 | 163 | 835 | 751 |
| New York | 18,506 | 1,066 | 2,686 | 54 | 11,881 | 2,818 |
| North Carolina | 8,006 | 116 | 1,742 | 101 | 5,851 | 197 |
| North Dakota | 625 | 6 | 4 | 32 | 576 | 8 |
| Ohio | 11,133 | 139 | 1,286 | 20 | 9,495 | 194 |
| Oklahoma | 3,394 | 46 | 262 | 255 | 2,681 | 149 |
| Oregon | 3,383 | 116 | 56 | 40 | 2,935 | 235 |
| Pennsylvania | 11,901 | 213 | 1,133 | 14 | 10,191 | 350 |
| Rhode Island | 1,022 | 25 | 42 | 4 | 875 | 77 |
| South Carolina | 3,959 | 37 | 1,169 | 9 | 2,686 | 59 |
| South Dakota | 742 | 5 | 5 | 64 | 657 | 10 |
| Tennessee | 5,647 | 58 | 940 | 11 | 4,565 | 73 |
| Texas | 20,903 | 574 | 2,407 | 59 | 11,335 | 6,529 |
| Utah | 2,308 | 60 | 16 | 28 | 2,033 | 170 |
| Vermont | 597 | 5 | 3 | 1 | 582 | 5 |
| Virginia | 7,019 | 274 | 1,389 | 16 | 5,052 | 288 |
| Washington | 5,869 | 359 | 192 | 93 | 4,812 | 413 |
| West Virginia | 1,752 | 9 | 52 | 2 | 1,678 | 11 |
| Wisconsin | 5,267 | 91 | 298 | 45 | 4,683 | 151 |
| Wyoming | 488 | 4 | 4 | 11 | 439 | 31 |

*Source: Projections by New Strategist*

## Distribution of State Populations by Race and Hispanic Origin, 2001

*(distribution of state populations by race, and Hispanic origin, 2001)*

| | | non-Hispanic | | | | |
|---|---|---|---|---|---|---|
| | *total* | *Asian* | *black* | *Native American* | *white* | *Hispanic* |
| **United States** | **100.0%** | **4.0%** | **12.2%** | **0.7%** | **71.0%** | **12.1%** |
| Alabama | 100.0 | 0.7 | 26.0 | 0.3 | 71.9 | 1.1 |
| Alaska | 100.0 | 4.9 | 3.6 | 16.3 | 71.0 | 4.3 |
| Arizona | 100.0 | 2.0 | 3.0 | 4.9 | 66.1 | 24.0 |
| Arkansas | 100.0 | 0.7 | 16.1 | 0.5 | 80.4 | 2.3 |
| California | 100.0 | 11.8 | 6.5 | 0.5 | 48.2 | 33.0 |
| Colorado | 100.0 | 2.4 | 3.9 | 0.6 | 77.6 | 15.5 |
| Connecticut | 100.0 | 2.7 | 8.8 | 0.2 | 79.2 | 9.2 |
| Delaware | 100.0 | 2.2 | 19.6 | 0.3 | 74.0 | 3.9 |
| District of Columbia | 100.0 | 3.1 | 59.3 | 0.2 | 29.6 | 7.8 |
| Florida | 100.0 | 1.8 | 15.1 | 0.3 | 66.9 | 15.9 |
| Georgia | 100.0 | 2.1 | 28.6 | 0.2 | 65.9 | 3.2 |
| Hawaii | 100.0 | 60.5 | 2.5 | 0.4 | 28.3 | 8.3 |
| Idaho | 100.0 | 1.1 | 0.4 | 1.1 | 89.4 | 8.0 |
| Illinois | 100.0 | 3.4 | 14.9 | 0.1 | 70.3 | 11.2 |
| Indiana | 100.0 | 1.0 | 8.2 | 0.2 | 87.8 | 2.7 |
| Iowa | 100.0 | 1.4 | 2.0 | 0.3 | 94.0 | 2.3 |
| Kansas | 100.0 | 1.8 | 5.7 | 0.8 | 85.7 | 6.0 |
| Kentucky | 100.0 | 0.7 | 7.2 | 0.1 | 91.0 | 1.0 |
| Louisiana | 100.0 | 1.3 | 32.4 | 0.4 | 63.1 | 2.8 |
| Maine | 100.0 | 0.8 | 0.5 | 0.5 | 97.5 | 0.8 |
| Maryland | 100.0 | 4.2 | 28.0 | 0.3 | 63.5 | 4.1 |
| Massachusetts | 100.0 | 4.1 | 5.6 | 0.2 | 83.2 | 6.9 |
| Michigan | 100.0 | 1.8 | 14.2 | 0.5 | 80.5 | 3.0 |
| Minnesota | 100.0 | 3.0 | 3.2 | 1.2 | 90.5 | 2.1 |
| Mississippi | 100.0 | 0.7 | 36.6 | 0.4 | 61.4 | 0.9 |
| Missouri | 100.0 | 1.2 | 11.3 | 0.3 | 85.4 | 1.8 |
| Montana | 100.0 | 0.7 | 0.3 | 6.6 | 90.5 | 2.0 |
| Nebraska | 100.0 | 1.4 | 4.0 | 0.9 | 88.8 | 4.9 |
| Nevada | 100.0 | 4.7 | 6.9 | 1.4 | 69.2 | 17.8 |
| New Hampshire | 100.0 | 1.3 | 0.6 | 0.2 | 96.1 | 1.7 |

*(continued)*

*(continued from previous page)*

| | | non-Hispanic | | | | |
|---|---|---|---|---|---|---|
| | **total** | **Asian** | **black** | **Native American** | **white** | **Hispanic** |
| New Jersey | 100.0% | 6.0% | 13.4% | 0.2% | 67.3% | 13.1% |
| New Mexico | 100.0 | 1.2 | 1.8 | 9.1 | 46.3 | 41.6 |
| New York | 100.0 | 5.8 | 14.5 | 0.3 | 64.2 | 15.2 |
| North Carolina | 100.0 | 1.4 | 21.8 | 1.3 | 73.1 | 2.5 |
| North Dakota | 100.0 | 0.9 | 0.6 | 5.1 | 92.1 | 1.3 |
| Ohio | 100.0 | 1.2 | 11.5 | 0.2 | 85.3 | 1.7 |
| Oklahoma | 100.0 | 1.4 | 7.7 | 7.5 | 79.0 | 4.4 |
| Oregon | 100.0 | 3.4 | 1.7 | 1.2 | 86.8 | 6.9 |
| Pennsylvania | 100.0 | 1.8 | 9.5 | 0.1 | 85.6 | 2.9 |
| Rhode Island | 100.0 | 2.4 | 4.1 | 0.4 | 85.6 | 7.5 |
| South Carolina | 100.0 | 0.9 | 29.5 | 0.2 | 67.8 | 1.5 |
| South Dakota | 100.0 | 0.7 | 0.7 | 8.6 | 88.6 | 1.3 |
| Tennessee | 100.0 | 1.0 | 16.6 | 0.2 | 80.8 | 1.3 |
| Texas | 100.0 | 2.7 | 11.5 | 0.3 | 54.2 | 31.2 |
| Utah | 100.0 | 2.6 | 0.7 | 1.2 | 88.1 | 7.4 |
| Vermont | 100.0 | 0.9 | 0.5 | 0.2 | 97.5 | 0.9 |
| Virginia | 100.0 | 3.9 | 19.8 | 0.2 | 72.0 | 4.1 |
| Washington | 100.0 | 6.1 | 3.3 | 1.6 | 82.0 | 7.0 |
| West Virginia | 100.0 | 0.5 | 3.0 | 0.1 | 95.8 | 0.6 |
| Wisconsin | 100.0 | 1.7 | 5.7 | 0.8 | 88.9 | 2.9 |
| Wyoming | 100.0 | 0.8 | 0.7 | 2.2 | 89.8 | 6.4 |

*Source: Projections by New Strategist*

# Most People Live in Metropolitan Areas

## Las Vegas is the fastest-growing large metropolitan area.

Eighty percent of Americans lived in one of the nation's metropolitan areas in 1999. Nearly 50 years ago, only 56 percent of Americans were metropolitan residents. Within metropolitan areas, the population distribution has changed dramatically as well. The suburbs were home to half of Americans in 1999, up from just 23 percent in 1950. Thirty percent live in the nation's central cities, a figure that has barely changed over the past 50 years. The proportion of people living in the nation's nonmetropolitan areas has fallen sharply, from 44 percent in 1950 to just 19 percent in 1999.

The fastest growing among the nation's 50 largest metropolitan areas is Las Vegas, up an estimated 69 percent between 1990 and 2000. Other rapidly growing metropolitan areas include Phoenix–Mesa, Arizona; Atlanta, Georgia; and Raleigh–Durham–Chapel Hill, North Carolina. Pittsburgh is the only large metropolitan area estimated to have lost population between 1990 and 2000.

♦ Metropolitan areas in the South and West will continue to grow faster than those in the Northeast and Midwest as Americans flock to warmer climates and booming economies.

## Population by Metropolitan Status, 1950 to 1999

*(number and percent distribution of people by metropolitan status, 1950 to 1999; numbers in thousands; metropolitan areas as defined at each time period)*

| | number | | percent distribution by metropolitan status | | | | |
|---|---|---|---|---|---|---|---|
| | | | | metropolitan | | | |
| | total | metropolitan | total | total | central cities | suburbs | nonmetro areas |
| 1999 | 272,691 | 218,607 | 100.0% | 80.2% | 30.2% | 50.0% | 19.8% |
| 1990 | 249,464 | 198,249 | 100.0 | 77.5 | 31.3 | 46.2 | 22.5 |
| 1980 | 227,225 | 177,361 | 100.0 | 74.8 | 30.0 | 44.8 | 25.2 |
| 1970 | 203,212 | 139,480 | 100.0 | 69.0 | 31.4 | 37.6 | 31.0 |
| 1960 | 179,323 | 112,885 | 100.0 | 63.3 | 32.3 | 30.9 | 36.7 |
| 1950 | 150,697 | 84,501 | 100.0 | 56.1 | 32.8 | 23.3 | 43.9 |

*Note: The suburbs are the portion of a metropolitan area that is outside the central city.*
*Source: Bureau of the Census,* Metropolitan Areas and Cities, *1990 Census Profile, No. 3, 1991; and* Historical Statistics of the United States, Colonial Times to 1970, Part 1, *1975; and Internet site <www.census.gov/population/estimates/metro-city/ma99-01.txt>; calculations by New Strategist*

## Populations of the Top 50 Metropolitan Areas, 1990 and 2000

*(number of people in the 50 most populous metropolitan areas, 1990 and 2000; percent change, 1990–2000; ranked by population in 2000; numbers in thousands; metropolitan areas as defined by the Office of Management and Budget as of June 30, 1997)*

| | | 1990 | 2000 | percent change 1990–2000 |
|---|---|---|---|---|
| 1. | Los Angeles–Long Beach, CA PMSA | 8,875,882 | 9,170,556 | 3.3% |
| 2. | New York, NY PMSA | 8,547,307 | 8,806,432 | 3.0 |
| 3. | Chicago, IL PMSA | 7,424,644 | 7,959,512 | 7.2 |
| 4. | Boston–Worcester–Lawrence–Lowell–Brockton, MA–NH NECMA | 5,688,301 | 5,992,945 | 5.4 |
| 5. | Philadelphia, PA–NJ PMSA | 4,925,373 | 4,963,247 | 0.8 |
| 6. | Washington, DC–MD–VA–WV PMSA | 4,237,360 | 4,796,068 | 13.2 |
| 7. | Detroit, MI PMSA | 4,269,297 | 4,363,415 | 2.2 |
| 8. | Houston, TX PMSA | 3,342,687 | 4,052,446 | 21.2 |
| 9. | Atlanta, GA MSA | 2,977,832 | 4,016,548 | 34.9 |
| 10. | Dallas, TX PMSA | 2,690,111 | 3,359,550 | 24.9 |
| 11. | Phoenix–Mesa, AZ MSA | 2,246,023 | 3,205,112 | 42.7 |
| 12. | Riverside–San Bernardino, CA PMSA | 2,631,234 | 3,118,599 | 18.5 |
| 13. | Minneapolis–St. Paul, MN–WI MSA | 2,548,262 | 2,913,004 | 14.3 |
| 14. | Orange County, CA PMSA | 2,418,718 | 2,794,084 | 15.5 |
| 15. | San Diego, CA MSA | 2,513,581 | 2,708,874 | 7.8 |
| 16. | Nassau–Suffolk, NY PMSA | 2,608,488 | 2,680,691 | 2.8 |
| 17. | St. Louis, MO–IL MSA | 2,496,041 | 2,578,501 | 3.3 |
| 18. | Baltimore, MD PMSA | 2,389,232 | 2,500,150 | 4.6 |
| 19. | Seattle–Bellevue–Everett, WA PMSA | 2,047,820 | 2,342,105 | 14.4 |
| 20. | Pittsburgh, PA MSA | 2,395,128 | 2,308,991 | –3.6 |
| 21. | Tampa–St. Petersburg–Clearwater, FL MSA | 2,075,595 | 2,280,318 | 9.9 |
| 22. | Oakland, CA PMSA | 2,087,499 | 2,276,509 | 9.1 |
| 23. | Miami, FL PMSA | 1,942,135 | 2,253,896 | 16.1 |
| 24. | Cleveland–Lorain–Elyria, OH PMSA | 2,203,406 | 2,228,591 | 1.1 |
| 25. | Denver, CO PMSA | 1,628,382 | 2,006,726 | 23.2 |
| 26. | Newark, NJ PMSA | 1,915,923 | 1,968,156 | 2.7 |
| 27. | Portland–Vancouver, OR–WA PMSA | 1,526,705 | 1,908,088 | 25.0 |
| 28. | Kansas City, MO–KS MSA | 1,587,096 | 1,759,672 | 10.9 |
| 29. | San Jose, CA PMSA | 1,497,905 | 1,711,607 | 14.3 |
| 30. | San Francisco, CA PMSA | 1,602,932 | 1,708,573 | 6.6 |
| 31. | Fort Worth–Arlington, TX PMSA | 1,367,839 | 1,653,521 | 20.9 |

*(continued)*

*(continued from previous page)*

| | | 1990 | 2000 | percent change 1990–2000 |
|---|---|---|---|---|
| 32. | New Haven–Bridgeport–Stamford–Waterbury–Danbury, CT NECMA | 1,632,466 | 1,635,506 | 0.2% |
| 33. | Cincinnati, OH–KY–IN PMSA | 1,529,231 | 1,624,595 | 6.2 |
| 34. | San Antonio, TX MSA | 1,327,466 | 1,610,124 | 21.3 |
| 35. | Fort Lauderdale, FL PMSA | 1,262,082 | 1,563,118 | 23.9 |
| 36. | Indianapolis, IN MSA | 1,385,395 | 1,555,173 | 12.3 |
| 37. | Norfolk–Virginia Beach–Newport News, VA–NC MSA | 1,450,863 | 1,554,883 | 7.2 |
| 38. | Sacramento, CA PMSA | 1,353,507 | 1,542,980 | 14.0 |
| 39. | Orlando, FL MSA | 1,239,093 | 1,530,204 | 23.5 |
| 40. | Columbus, OH MSA | 1,350,373 | 1,494,252 | 10.7 |
| 41. | Las Vegas, NV–AZ MSA | 867,853 | 1,464,229 | 68.7 |
| 42. | Milwaukee–Waukesha, WI PMSA | 1,434,366 | 1,458,923 | 1.7 |
| 43. | Charlotte–Gastonia–Rock Hill, NC–SC MSA | 1,168,616 | 1,453,103 | 24.3 |
| 44. | Bergen–Passaic, NJ PMSA | 1,278,847 | 1,344,270 | 5.1 |
| 45. | New Orleans, LA MSA | 1,284,037 | 1,319,172 | 2.7 |
| 46. | Salt Lake City–Ogden, UT MSA | 1,076,650 | 1,298,955 | 20.6 |
| 47. | Nashville, TN MSA | 988,716 | 1,225,002 | 23.9 |
| 48. | Greensboro–Winston-Salem–High Point, NC MSA | 1,053,657 | 1,213,980 | 15.2 |
| 49. | Austin–San Marcos, TX MSA | 850,650 | 1,204,818 | 41.6 |
| 50. | Raleigh–Durham–Chapel Hill, NC MSA | 864,222 | 1,154,456 | 33.6 |

*Note: For definitions of the terms MSA, NECMA, and PMSA, see glossary.*
*Source: TGE Demographics, Inc., Honeoye Falls, New York*

# Americans Are Moving Less

## The mobility rate continues to fall as more people stay put.

Only 15.9 percent of Americans moved between March 1998 and March 1999, far below the 21.2 percent of 1950–51. Most moves are local, owing to housing needs rather than job relocations. Among movers just 6 percent relocated to a different county between 1998 and 1999, while only 3 percent moved to a different state. Many long-distance moves are job related.

Overall, nearly 43 million people moved between 1998 and 1999, an annual figure that has remained about the same throughout the 1990s. Those most likely to move are young adults, many of them seeking jobs. One-third of renters moved between 1998 and 1999 compared with just 8 percent of homeowners. Only 11 percent of those not in the labor force moved versus 28 percent of the unemployed, many of whom move in search of jobs. Fully 40 percent of people in the armed forces moved between 1998 and 1999.

♦ The rise of the two-income couple is one factor behind the decline in mobility rates over the past five decades. When both husband and wife are employed, it is more difficult for families to relocate.

### Mobility is down

*(percent of people aged 1 or older who moved in a 12-month period, selected years, 1950–51 to 1998–99)*

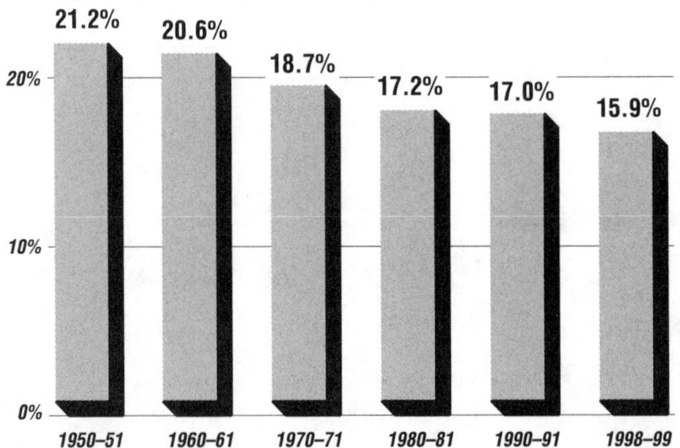

## Geographical Mobility, 1950 to 1999

*(total number of people aged 1 or older, and number and percent distribution by mobility status, 1950–51 to 1998–99; numbers in thousands)*

| | | | | different house in U.S. | | | | | |
|---|---|---|---|---|---|---|---|---|---|
| | total | same house (non-movers) | total movers | total | same county | different county | same state | different state | movers from abroad |
| 1998–99 | 267,933 | 225,297 | 42,636 | 41,207 | 25,268 | 15,939 | 8,423 | 7,516 | 1,429 |
| 1997–98 | 265,209 | 222,702 | 42,507 | 41,304 | 27,082 | 14,222 | 7,867 | 6,355 | 1,203 |
| 1996–97 | 262,976 | 219,585 | 43,391 | 42,088 | 27,740 | 14,348 | 7,960 | 6,389 | 1,303 |
| 1995–96 | 260,406 | 217,868 | 42,537 | 41,176 | 26,696 | 14,480 | 8,009 | 6,471 | 1,361 |
| 1994–95 | 258,248 | 215,931 | 42,317 | 41,539 | 27,908 | 13,631 | 7,888 | 5,743 | 778 |
| 1993–94 | 255,774 | 212,939 | 42,835 | 41,590 | 26,638 | 14,952 | 8,226 | 6,726 | 1,245 |
| 1992–93 | 252,799 | 209,700 | 43,099 | 41,704 | 26,932 | 14,772 | 7,855 | 6,916 | 1,395 |
| 1991–92 | 247,380 | 204,580 | 42,800 | 41,545 | 26,587 | 14,957 | 7,853 | 7,105 | 1,255 |
| 1990–91 | 244,884 | 203,345 | 41,539 | 40,154 | 25,151 | 15,003 | 7,881 | 7,122 | 1,385 |
| 1980–81 | 221,641 | 183,442 | 38,200 | 36,887 | 23,097 | 13,789 | 7,614 | 6,175 | 1,313 |
| 1970–71 | 201,506 | 163,800 | 37,705 | 36,161 | 23,018 | 13,143 | 6,197 | 6,946 | 1,544 |
| 1960–61 | 177,354 | 140,821 | 36,533 | 35,535 | 24,289 | 11,246 | 5,493 | 5,753 | 998 |
| 1950–51 | 148,400 | 116,936 | 31,464 | 31,158 | 20,694 | 10,464 | 5,276 | 5,188 | 306 |
| **Percent distribution by mobility status** | | | | | | | | | |
| 1998–99 | 100.0% | 84.1% | 15.9% | 15.4% | 9.4% | 5.9% | 3.1% | 2.8% | 0.5% |
| 1997–98 | 100.0 | 84.0 | 16.0 | 15.6 | 10.2 | 5.4 | 3.0 | 2.4 | 0.5 |
| 1996–97 | 100.0 | 83.5 | 16.5 | 16.0 | 10.5 | 5.5 | 3.0 | 2.4 | 0.5 |
| 1995–96 | 100.0 | 83.7 | 16.3 | 15.8 | 10.3 | 5.6 | 3.1 | 2.5 | 0.5 |
| 1994–95 | 100.0 | 83.6 | 16.4 | 16.1 | 10.8 | 5.3 | 3.1 | 2.2 | 0.3 |
| 1993–94 | 100.0 | 83.3 | 16.7 | 16.3 | 10.4 | 5.8 | 3.2 | 2.6 | 0.5 |
| 1992–93 | 100.0 | 83.0 | 17.0 | 16.5 | 10.7 | 5.8 | 3.1 | 2.7 | 0.6 |
| 1991–92 | 100.0 | 82.7 | 17.3 | 16.8 | 10.7 | 6.0 | 3.2 | 2.9 | 0.5 |
| 1990–91 | 100.0 | 83.0 | 17.0 | 16.4 | 10.3 | 6.1 | 3.2 | 2.9 | 0.6 |
| 1980–81 | 100.0 | 82.8 | 17.2 | 16.6 | 10.4 | 6.2 | 3.4 | 2.8 | 0.6 |
| 1970–71 | 100.0 | 81.3 | 18.7 | 17.9 | 11.4 | 6.5 | 3.1 | 3.4 | 0.8 |
| 1960–61 | 100.0 | 79.4 | 20.6 | 20.0 | 13.7 | 6.3 | 3.1 | 3.2 | 0.6 |
| 1950–51 | 100.0 | 78.8 | 21.2 | 21.0 | 13.9 | 7.1 | 3.6 | 3.5 | 0.2 |

*Source: Bureau of the Census, Internet site <www.census.gov/population/socdemo/migration/tab-a-1.txt>*

## Geographic Mobility by Selected Characteristics, 1998–99

*(total number of people aged 1 or older, and percent distribution by mobility status between March 1998 and March 1999, by age, housing tenure, and employment status; numbers in thousands)*

| | total | | | movers | | | | | | |
|---|---|---|---|---|---|---|---|---|---|---|
| | number | percent | same house (nonmovers) | total | same county | different county same state | different state same division | different division same region | different region | movers from abroad |
| **Total, aged 1 or older** | **267,933** | **100.0%** | **84.1%** | **15.9%** | **9.4%** | **3.1%** | **1.2%** | **0.4%** | **1.2%** | **0.5%** |
| Aged 1 to 4 | 15,792 | 100.0 | 76.2 | 23.8 | 15.5 | 3.9 | 1.4 | 0.5 | 1.9 | 0.6 |
| Aged 5 to 9 | 20,557 | 100.0 | 81.1 | 18.9 | 12.5 | 2.8 | 1.4 | 0.3 | 1.2 | 0.5 |
| Aged 10 to 14 | 19,909 | 100.0 | 86.3 | 13.7 | 8.5 | 2.5 | 1.0 | 0.2 | 1.2 | 0.3 |
| Aged 15 to 17 | 11,955 | 100.0 | 86.8 | 13.2 | 8.2 | 2.3 | 0.8 | 0.2 | 0.9 | 0.7 |
| Aged 18 to 19 | 7,909 | 100.0 | 79.7 | 20.3 | 11.3 | 4.4 | 1.6 | 0.6 | 1.6 | 0.9 |
| Aged 20 to 24 | 18,058 | 100.0 | 66.8 | 33.2 | 19.2 | 7.1 | 2.5 | 0.9 | 2.4 | 1.2 |
| Aged 25 to 29 | 18,639 | 100.0 | 68.3 | 31.7 | 18.0 | 6.7 | 2.3 | 0.9 | 2.6 | 1.2 |
| Aged 30 to 34 | 19,835 | 100.0 | 77.2 | 22.8 | 13.6 | 4.7 | 1.7 | 0.6 | 1.5 | 0.9 |
| Aged 35 to 39 | 22,529 | 100.0 | 84.6 | 15.4 | 8.8 | 3.2 | 1.2 | 0.4 | 1.2 | 0.6 |
| Aged 40 to 44 | 22,215 | 100.0 | 87.2 | 12.8 | 7.6 | 2.4 | 1.1 | 0.3 | 1.1 | 0.3 |
| Aged 45 to 49 | 19,166 | 100.0 | 89.8 | 10.2 | 5.7 | 2.5 | 0.9 | 0.2 | 0.8 | 0.2 |
| Aged 50 to 54 | 16,066 | 100.0 | 91.3 | 8.7 | 4.9 | 1.8 | 0.7 | 0.2 | 0.8 | 0.2 |
| Aged 55 to 59 | 12,601 | 100.0 | 92.8 | 7.2 | 3.6 | 1.6 | 1.0 | 0.2 | 0.5 | 0.3 |
| Aged 60 to 61 | 4,322 | 100.0 | 94.0 | 6.0 | 3.1 | 1.0 | 0.7 | 0.3 | 0.6 | 0.3 |
| Aged 62 to 64 | 5,986 | 100.0 | 93.9 | 6.1 | 3.0 | 1.5 | 0.5 | 0.3 | 0.7 | 0.1 |

*(continued)*

(continued from previous page)

| | total | | | movers | | | | | | |
|---|---|---|---|---|---|---|---|---|---|---|
| | number | percent | same house (nonmovers) | total | same county | different county same state | different state same division | different division same region | different region | movers from abroad |
| Aged 65 to 69 | 9,320 | 100.0% | 94.8% | 5.2% | 3.1% | 1.2% | 0.3% | 0.1% | 0.4% | 0.1% |
| Aged 70 to 74 | 8,524 | 100.0 | 95.5 | 4.4 | 2.4 | 1.1 | 0.3 | 0.1 | 0.4 | 0.1 |
| Aged 75 to 79 | 6,952 | 100.0 | 95.8 | 4.2 | 2.6 | 0.7 | 0.3 | 0.2 | 0.4 | 0.0 |
| Aged 80 to 84 | 4,545 | 100.0 | 96.2 | 3.8 | 2.3 | 0.5 | 0.3 | 0.1 | 0.5 | 0.1 |
| Aged 85 or older | 3,054 | 100.0 | 96.1 | 3.9 | 2.0 | 0.6 | 0.7 | 0.1 | 0.6 | – |
| **Housing tenure** | | | | | | | | | | |
| Owner | 186,416 | 100.0 | 91.7 | 8.3 | 4.9 | 1.8 | 0.6 | 0.2 | 0.6 | 0.2 |
| Renter | 81,517 | 100.0 | 66.8 | 33.2 | 19.7 | 6.1 | 2.6 | 0.8 | 2.7 | 1.3 |
| **Employment status** | | | | | | | | | | |
| **Total, aged 16 or older** | **207,777** | **100.0** | **84.7** | **15.3** | **8.8** | **3.2** | **1.2** | **0.4** | **1.2** | **0.5** |
| Employed | 131,806 | 100.0 | 83.2 | 16.8 | 9.8 | 3.6 | 1.3 | 0.4 | 1.2 | 0.5 |
| Unemployed | 6,314 | 100.0 | 72.4 | 27.5 | 15.4 | 5.7 | 1.6 | 0.8 | 2.8 | 1.3 |
| Armed forces | 739 | 100.0 | 60.4 | 39.5 | 12.0 | 3.5 | 6.4 | 2.6 | 10.8 | 4.2 |
| Not in labor force | 68,918 | 100.0 | 88.9 | 11.1 | 6.1 | 2.2 | 0.9 | 0.3 | 1.0 | 0.6 |

*Note: (–) means sample is too small to make a reliable estimate.*
*Source: Bureau of the Census, Internet sites <www.census.gov/population/socdemo/migration/p20-531/tab01.txt>, <www.census.gov/population/socdemo/migration/p20-531/tab03.txt>, and <www.census.gov/population/socdemo/migration/p20-531/tab07.txt>; calculations by New Strategist*

# Immigration Adds Millions to Population

## More immigrants came to the U.S. in the 1990s than in the 1980s.

Fully 7.6 million immigrants were granted permanent legal residence during the eight years between 1991 and 1998, already surpassing the 7.3 million who came here during the decade of the 1980s. Once the numbers are in for the entire 1990s, they are likely to show that the last decade of the 20th century saw more immigrants enter the U.S. than any other decade in our history.

The impact of immigration varies dramatically by state. Fully 61 percent of the 660,477 immigrants who arrived in the U.S. in 1998 planned to live in one of just five states: California, New York, Florida, Texas, and New Jersey.

The largest number of immigrants are from Mexico, accounting for 22 percent of the total. Fully 47 percent of Mexican immigrants plan to live in California. California is also popular among other immigrant groups. It is the state of intended residence for 34 percent of Chinese immigrants, 48 percent of immigrants from the Philippines, and 37 percent of those from Vietnam. More than 80 percent of Cuban immigrants plan to live in Florida.

♦ The arrival of tens of thousands of immigrants who need jobs, schools, and health care creates severe problems for some states. There are no easy political solutions, since a few states are strongly affected while others are untouched.

**California is the top state for immigrants**

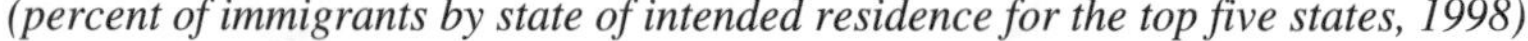

*(percent of immigrants by state of intended residence for the top five states, 1998)*

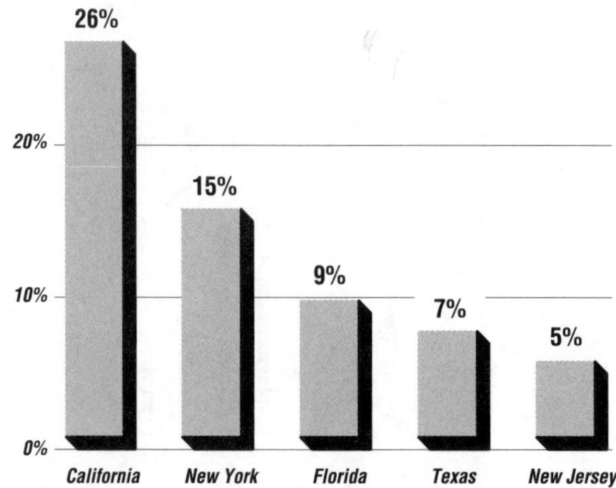

## Immigration to the U.S., 1901 to 1998

*(number of immigrants granted permanent residence in the U.S. by decade, 1901–98; and by single year, 1981–98)*

| | *number of immigrants* |
|---|---|
| 1998 | 660,477 |
| 1997 | 798,378 |
| 1996 | 915,900 |
| 1995 | 720,461 |
| 1994 | 804,416 |
| 1993 | 904,292 |
| 1992 | 973,977 |
| 1991 | 1,827,167 |
| 1990 | 1,536,483 |
| 1989 | 1,090,924 |
| 1988 | 643,025 |
| 1987 | 601,516 |
| 1986 | 601,708 |
| 1985 | 570,009 |
| 1984 | 543,903 |
| 1983 | 559,763 |
| 1982 | 594,131 |
| 1981 | 596,600 |
| 1991–98 | 7,605,068 |
| 1981–90 | 7,338,062 |
| 1971–80 | 4,493,314 |
| 1961–70 | 3,321,677 |
| 1951–60 | 2,515,479 |
| 1941–50 | 1,035,039 |
| 1931–40 | 528,431 |
| 1921–30 | 4,107,209 |
| 1911–20 | 5,735,811 |
| 1901–10 | 8,795,386 |

*Note: Immigrants are people granted legal permanent residence in the United States. They either arrive in the U.S. with immigrant visas issued abroad or adjust their status in the United States from temporary to permanent residence.*
*Source: Immigration and Naturalization Service,* 1998 Statistical Yearbook of the Immigration and Naturalization Service, *2000*

## Immigrants by Country of Birth and State of Intended Residence, 1998

*(number and percent distribution of immigrants admitted to the U.S. from the 10 leading countries of birth and percent distribution by intended state of residence, 1998; for the five states receiving the largest total number of immigrants)*

| | total | total for top five states | California | New York | Florida | Texas | New Jersey |
|---|---|---|---|---|---|---|---|
| **Total immigrants** | **660,477** | **405,169** | **170,126** | **96,559** | **59,965** | **44,428** | **34,091** |
| Mexico | 131,575 | 90,245 | 62,113 | 1,616 | 2,788 | 22,956 | 772 |
| China | 36,884 | 24,537 | 12,582 | 8,850 | 628 | 1,159 | 1,318 |
| India | 36,482 | 19,220 | 7,177 | 4,017 | 1,079 | 2,663 | 4,284 |
| Philippines | 34,466 | 21,028 | 16,202 | 1,490 | 837 | 851 | 1,648 |
| Dominican Republic | 20,387 | 14,849 | 72 | 10,719 | 1,483 | 97 | 2,478 |
| Vietnam | 17,649 | 9,449 | 6,519 | 646 | 437 | 1,576 | 271 |
| Cuba | 17,375 | 15,531 | 289 | 322 | 14,265 | 218 | 437 |
| Jamaica | 15,146 | 12,000 | 186 | 5,874 | 4,795 | 108 | 1,037 |
| El Salvador | 14,590 | 10,071 | 6,348 | 1,088 | 400 | 1,694 | 541 |
| Korea | 14,268 | 7,445 | 4,466 | 1,449 | 202 | 392 | 936 |
| **Percent distribution by country of origin** | | | | | | | |
| **Total immigrants** | **100.0%** | **100.0%** | **100.0%** | **100.0%** | **100.0%** | **100.0%** | **100.0%** |
| Mexico | 19.9 | 22.3 | 36.5 | 1.7 | 4.6 | 51.7 | 2.3 |
| China | 5.6 | 6.1 | 7.4 | 9.2 | 1.0 | 2.6 | 3.9 |
| India | 5.5 | 4.7 | 4.2 | 4.2 | 1.8 | 6.0 | 12.6 |
| Philippines | 5.2 | 5.2 | 9.5 | 1.5 | 1.4 | 1.9 | 4.8 |
| Dominican Republic | 3.1 | 3.7 | 0.0 | 11.1 | 2.5 | 0.2 | 7.3 |
| Vietnam | 2.7 | 2.3 | 3.8 | 0.7 | 0.7 | 3.5 | 0.8 |
| Cuba | 2.6 | 3.8 | 0.2 | 0.3 | 23.8 | 0.5 | 1.3 |
| Jamaica | 2.3 | 3.0 | 0.1 | 6.1 | 8.0 | 0.2 | 3.0 |
| El Salvador | 2.2 | 2.5 | 3.7 | 1.1 | 0.7 | 3.8 | 1.6 |
| Korea | 2.2 | 1.8 | 2.6 | 1.5 | 0.3 | 0.9 | 2.7 |

*(continued)*

*(continued from previous page)*

| | *total* | *total for top five states* | *California* | *New York* | *Florida* | *Texas* | *New Jersey* |
|---|---|---|---|---|---|---|---|
| **Percent distribution by state of intended residence** | | | | | | | |
| **Total immigrants** | **100.0%** | **61.3%** | **25.8%** | **14.6%** | **9.1%** | **6.7%** | **5.2%** |
| Mexico | 100.0 | 68.6 | 47.2 | 1.2 | 2.1 | 17.4 | 0.6 |
| China | 100.0 | 66.5 | 34.1 | 24.0 | 1.7 | 3.1 | 3.6 |
| India | 100.0 | 52.7 | 19.7 | 11.0 | 3.0 | 7.3 | 11.7 |
| Philippines | 100.0 | 61.0 | 47.0 | 4.3 | 2.4 | 2.5 | 4.8 |
| Dominican Republic | 100.0 | 72.8 | 0.4 | 52.6 | 7.3 | 0.5 | 12.2 |
| Vietnam | 100.0 | 53.5 | 36.9 | 3.7 | 2.5 | 8.9 | 1.5 |
| Cuba | 100.0 | 89.4 | 1.7 | 1.9 | 82.1 | 1.3 | 2.5 |
| Jamaica | 100.0 | 79.2 | 1.2 | 38.8 | 31.7 | 0.7 | 6.8 |
| El Salvador | 100.0 | 69.0 | 43.5 | 7.5 | 2.7 | 11.6 | 3.7 |
| Korea | 100.0 | 52.2 | 31.3 | 10.2 | 1.4 | 2.7 | 6.6 |

*Note: Total includes immigrants from other countries not shown separately. Immigrants are people granted legal permanent residence in the United States. They either arrive in the U.S. with immigrant visas issued abroad or adjust their status in the United States from temporary to permanent residence.*
*Source: Immigration and Naturalization Service,* 1998 Statistical Yearbook of the Immigration and Naturalization Service, *2000; calculations by New Strategist*

# The Foreign-Born Are Diverse

## One in 10 Americans was born in a foreign country.

More than 28 million U.S. residents were born in a foreign country, most of them having arrived in the U.S. since 1980. The largest share (34 percent) were born in Central America, primarily Mexico. Another 26 percent were born in Asia, while 15 percent are from Europe.

Many of the foreign-born are high school drop-outs, but some are highly educated. Many have low incomes, but some are top earners. While only 13 percent of native-born Americans did not graduate from high school, the figure is a much higher 27 percent among the foreign-born. In fact, the foreign-born account for more than one-fourth of the nation's high school drop-outs. But the foreign-born are also more likely than the native-born to have a graduate-level degree, 10 versus 8 percent.

Among full-time workers, the earnings of the foreign-born are below those of the native-born. Still, many foreign-born workers earn relatively high incomes. Twenty-three percent of foreign-born men who work full-time have earnings of $50,000 or more compared with 33 percent of their native-born counterparts.

♦ The number of foreign-born in the U.S. will continue to expand as long as immigration remains high, creating a dynamic multicultural market.

## Foreign-Born Population by Region of Birth and Year of Entry, 2000

*(number and percent distribution of foreign-born people by region of birth and year of entry in the U.S., 2000; numbers in thousands)*

| | *number* | *percent* |
|---|---|---|
| **Region of birth** | | |
| **Total foreign-born** | **28,379** | **100.0%** |
| Europe | 4,355 | 15.3 |
| Asia | 7,246 | 25.5 |
| Central America | 9,789 | 34.5 |
| Caribbean | 2,813 | 9.9 |
| South America | 1,876 | 6.6 |
| Other | 2,301 | 8.1 |
| **Year of entry** | | |
| **Total foreign-born** | **28,379** | **100.0** |
| Since 1990 | 11,206 | 39.5 |
| 1980 to 1989 | 8,022 | 28.3 |
| 1970 to 1979 | 4,605 | 16.2 |
| Before 1970 | 4,547 | 16.0 |

*Note: The majority of those born in Central America are from Mexico. "Others" are from Africa, Bermuda, Canada, and Oceania.*
*Source: Bureau of the Census, Internet site <www.census.gov/population/www/socdemo/foreign.html>; calculations by New Strategist*

## Characteristics of the Foreign-Born Population, 2000

*(number and percent distribution of native- and foreign-born people by selected characteristics, and the foreign born as a percent of the total population, 2000; numbers in thousands)*

| | | native born | | foreign-born | | |
|---|---|---|---|---|---|---|
| | total population | number | percent distribution | number | percent distribution | percent of total |
| **Total people** | **274,087** | **245,708** | **100.0%** | **28,379** | **100.0%** | **10.4%** |
| **Age** | | | | | | |
| Aged 0 to 4 | 19,607 | 19,319 | 7.9 | 289 | 1.0 | 1.5 |
| Aged 5 to 9 | 20,379 | 19,719 | 8.0 | 659 | 2.3 | 3.2 |
| Aged 10 to 14 | 20,328 | 19,269 | 7.8 | 1,059 | 3.7 | 5.2 |
| Aged 15 to 19 | 20,102 | 18,490 | 7.5 | 1,612 | 5.7 | 8.0 |
| Aged 20 to 24 | 18,441 | 16,075 | 6.5 | 2,366 | 8.3 | 12.8 |
| Aged 25 to 29 | 18,268 | 15,366 | 6.3 | 2,902 | 10.2 | 15.9 |
| Aged 30 to 34 | 19,518 | 16,284 | 6.6 | 3,233 | 11.4 | 16.6 |
| Aged 35 to 44 | 44,805 | 38,571 | 15.7 | 6,235 | 22.0 | 13.9 |
| Aged 45 to 54 | 36,631 | 32,342 | 13.2 | 4,289 | 15.1 | 11.7 |
| Aged 55 to 64 | 23,387 | 20,766 | 8.5 | 2,621 | 9.2 | 11.2 |
| Aged 65 to 74 | 17,796 | 16,019 | 6.5 | 1,778 | 6.3 | 10.0 |
| Aged 75 to 84 | 11,685 | 10,721 | 4.4 | 965 | 3.4 | 8.3 |
| Aged 85 or older | 3,140 | 2,767 | 1.1 | 373 | 1.3 | 11.9 |
| **Sex** | | | | | | |
| Female | 140,154 | 125,975 | 51.3 | 14,179 | 50.0 | 10.1 |
| Male | 133,933 | 119,733 | 48.7 | 14,200 | 50.0 | 10.6 |
| **Educational attainment** | | | | | | |
| **People aged 25 or older** | **175,230** | **152,836** | **100.0** | **22,394** | **100.0** | **12.8** |
| Not a high school graduate | 27,854 | 20,456 | 13.4 | 7,397 | 33.0 | 26.6 |
| High school graduate | 58,086 | 52,492 | 34.3 | 5,593 | 25.0 | 9.6 |
| Some college or associate's degree | 44,445 | 40,820 | 26.7 | 3,625 | 16.2 | 8.2 |
| Bachelor's degree | 29,840 | 26,225 | 17.2 | 3,615 | 16.1 | 12.1 |
| Advanced degree | 15,006 | 12,843 | 8.4 | 2,162 | 9.7 | 14.4 |

*(continued)*

*(continued from previous page)*

| | total population | native born number | native born percent distribution | foreign-born number | foreign-born percent distribution | percent of total |
|---|---|---|---|---|---|---|
| **Labor force status** | | | | | | |
| **People aged 16 or older** | **209,067** | **182,969** | **100.0%** | **26,099** | **100.0%** | **12.5%** |
| In civilian labor force | 140,454 | 123,070 | 67.3 | 17,385 | 66.6 | 12.4 |
| Employed | 134,338 | 117,806 | 64.4 | 16,532 | 63.3 | 12.3 |
| Unemployed | 6,116 | 5,264 | 2.9 | 852 | 3.3 | 13.9 |
| Not in labor force | 68,613 | 59,899 | 32.7 | 8,714 | 33.4 | 12.7 |
| **Earnings of full-time, year-round workers in 1999** | | | | | | |
| **Men with earnings** | **57,511** | **49,659** | **100.0** | **7,852** | **100.0** | **13.7** |
| Under $10,000 | 1,981 | 1,600 | 3.2 | 382 | 4.9 | 19.3 |
| $10,000 to $19,999 | 8,234 | 6,051 | 12.2 | 2,183 | 27.8 | 26.5 |
| $20,000 to $24,999 | 5,511 | 4,531 | 9.1 | 980 | 12.5 | 17.8 |
| $25,000 to $34,999 | 10,993 | 9,639 | 19.4 | 1,354 | 17.2 | 12.3 |
| $35,000 to $49,999 | 12,631 | 11,488 | 23.1 | 1,143 | 14.6 | 9.0 |
| $50,000 to $74,999 | 10,667 | 9,642 | 19.4 | 1,024 | 13.0 | 9.6 |
| $75,000 or more | 7,494 | 6,708 | 13.5 | 786 | 10.0 | 10.5 |
| **Women with earnings** | **40,404** | **36,018** | **100.0** | **4,385** | **100.0** | **10.9** |
| Under $10,000 | 2,298 | 1,978 | 5.5 | 320 | 7.3 | 13.9 |
| $10,000 to $19,999 | 10,176 | 8,610 | 23.9 | 1,566 | 35.7 | 15.4 |
| $20,000 to $24,999 | 5,898 | 5,346 | 14.8 | 551 | 12.6 | 9.3 |
| $25,000 to $34,999 | 9,410 | 8,625 | 23.9 | 785 | 17.9 | 8.3 |
| $35,000 to $49,999 | 7,353 | 6,715 | 18.6 | 638 | 14.5 | 8.7 |
| $50,000 to $74,999 | 3,757 | 3,392 | 9.4 | 365 | 8.3 | 9.7 |
| $75,000 or more | 1,512 | 1,353 | 3.8 | 159 | 3.6 | 10.5 |

*Source: Bureau of the Census, Internet site <www.census.gov/population/www/socdemo/foreign.html>;*

# The Majority of Americans Are Protestant

## Only 14 percent have no religious preference.

The 54 percent majority of Americans aged 18 or older are Protestant, while 25 percent are Catholic. People of other religions, such as Muslims, Hindus, and Buddhists, account for 4 percent of the population, while 2 percent are Jewish.

The religious makeup of America is changing. The Protestant share fell 10 percentage points between 1978 and 1998. The proportion of those who have no religious preference rose from 8 to 14 percent during those years.

The religious makeup of the population will change even more as younger generations replace older ones. Among people aged 50 or older, more than 6 out of 10 are Protestant, but among people under age 40, fewer than half are Protestant. Twenty-four percent of the youngest adults say they have no religious preference. Some will choose a particular faith as they age, but many will continue to seek spiritual fulfillment apart from organized religion.

♦ As younger generations with diverse religious preferences replace older, more Protestant generations, tolerance for religious diversity will grow in the nation's communities.

## Religious Preference, 1978 and 1998

"What is your religious preference? Is it Protestant, Catholic, Jewish, some other religion, or no religion?"

*(percent of people aged 18 or older responding by sex, race, age, and education, 1978 and 1998)*

| | Protestant | | Catholic | | Jewish | | other | | none | |
|---|---|---|---|---|---|---|---|---|---|---|
| | 1998 | 1978 | 1998 | 1978 | 1998 | 1978 | 1998 | 1978 | 1998 | 1978 |
| **Total people** | **54%** | **64%** | **25%** | **25%** | **2%** | **2%** | **4%** | **1%** | **14%** | **8%** |
| Men | 50 | 62 | 25 | 23 | 2 | 3 | 5 | 2 | 18 | 11 |
| Women | 58 | 66 | 26 | 26 | 2 | 1 | 4 | 1 | 11 | 6 |
| Black | 76 | 89 | 7 | 5 | 0 | 0 | 6 | 1 | 11 | 4 |
| White | 53 | 61 | 26 | 27 | 2 | 2 | 4 | 1 | 14 | 8 |
| Aged 18 to 29 | 44 | 58 | 25 | 26 | 1 | 1 | 6 | 2 | 24 | 12 |
| Aged 30 to 39 | 49 | 61 | 29 | 27 | 0 | 2 | 7 | 1 | 15 | 9 |
| Aged 40 to 49 | 57 | 63 | 22 | 26 | 2 | 2 | 4 | 1 | 14 | 8 |
| Aged 50 to 59 | 58 | 66 | 26 | 27 | 3 | 1 | 4 | 1 | 10 | 4 |
| Aged 60 to 69 | 61 | 70 | 27 | 23 | 2 | 3 | 2 | 0 | 9 | 3 |
| Aged 70 or older | 69 | 76 | 22 | 17 | 3 | 3 | 0 | 0 | 6 | 4 |
| Not a high school graduate | 57 | 72 | 28 | 22 | 0 | 1 | 2 | 0 | 13 | 5 |
| High school graduate | 57 | 62 | 24 | 28 | 1 | 1 | 4 | 1 | 14 | 7 |
| Bachelor's degree | 49 | 56 | 25 | 24 | 3 | 5 | 7 | 1 | 16 | 15 |
| Graduate degree | 52 | 56 | 22 | 21 | 7 | 6 | 5 | 3 | 13 | 13 |

*Note: Numbers may not add to 100 because "don't know" is not shown.*
*Source: General Social Surveys, National Opinion Research Center, University of Chicago; calculations by New Strategist*

# More Than 40 Percent of Households Have Internet Access

## Affluent, educated householders are most likely to tap into the Internet.

More than half of American households—51 percent—owned a computer in 2000, according to a survey by the National Telecommunications and Information Administration. Forty-two percent had Internet access.

The proportion with computers and online access varies sharply by demographic characteristic. Fully 86 percent of households with incomes of $75,000 or more owned a computer, and 78 percent had Internet access. Among householders with a postgraduate degree, 79 percent were computer owners and 70 percent had Internet access. Asians are most likely to be wired while non-Hispanic blacks are least likely.

There is little difference in Internet use among people ranging in age from school children to the middle-aged. The majority of people aged 9 to 49 were Internet users in 2000. E-mailing is the most common online activity, 80 percent doing so. Searching for information is second, while checking the news ranks third. Thirty percent of Internet users shop and pay bills online.

**Many children are online**

*(percent of people using the Internet by age, 2000)*

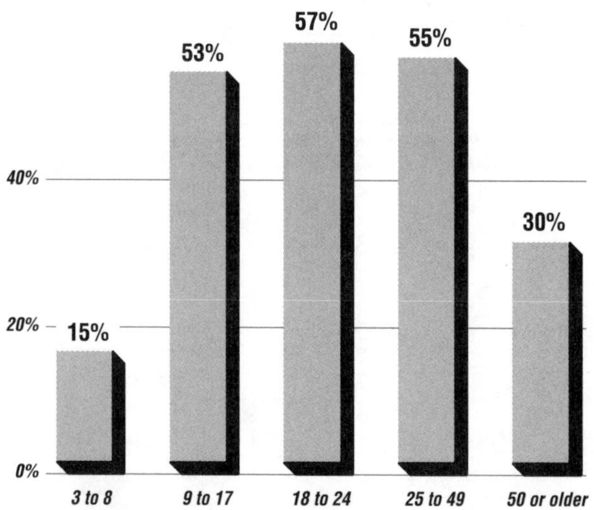

## Households with Computers and Internet Access, 2000

*(percent of households with computers and percent of households with Internet access, by selected characteristics, 2000)*

| | *computer* | *Internet access* |
|---|---|---|
| **Total households** | **51.0%** | **41.5%** |
| **Race and Hispanic origin** | | |
| White, non-Hispanic | 55.7 | 46.1 |
| Black, non-Hispanic | 32.6 | 23.5 |
| Asian | 65.6 | 56.8 |
| Hispanic | 33.7 | 23.6 |
| **Household income** | | |
| Under $15,000 | 19.2 | 12.7 |
| $15,000 to $24,999 | 30.1 | 21.3 |
| $25,000 to $34,999 | 44.6 | 34.0 |
| $35,000 to $49,999 | 58.6 | 46.1 |
| $50,000 to $74,999 | 73.2 | 60.9 |
| $75,000 or more | 86.3 | 77.7 |
| **Education** | | |
| Not a high school graduate | 18.2 | 11.7 |
| High school graduate | 39.6 | 29.9 |
| Some college | 60.3 | 49.0 |
| College graduate | 74.0 | 64.0 |
| Postgraduate | 79.0 | 69.9 |

*Source: National Telecommunications and Information Administration,* Falling through the Net: Toward Digital Inclusion—A Report on Americans' Access to Technology Tools, *October 2000*

## Internet Users by Age, 1998 and 2000

*(percent of people aged 3 or older who use the Internet by age, 1998 and 2000; percentage point change, 1998–2000)*

| | 2000 | 1998 | percentage point change |
|---|---|---|---|
| **Total, aged 3 or older** | **44.4%** | **32.7%** | **11.7** |
| Aged 3 to 8 | 15.3 | 11.0 | 4.3 |
| Aged 9 to 17 | 53.4 | 43.0 | 10.4 |
| Aged 18 to 24 | 56.8 | 44.3 | 12.5 |
| Aged 25 to 49 | 55.4 | 40.9 | 14.5 |
| Aged 50 or older | 29.6 | 19.3 | 10.3 |

*Source: National Telecommunications and Information Administration,* Falling through the Net: Toward Digital Inclusion—A Report on Americans' Access to Technology Tools, *October 2000*

## Online Activities of Internet Users, 2000

*(percent of Internet users who regularly participate in selected online activities, 2000)*

| | |
|---|---|
| E-mail | 79.9% |
| Search for information | 58.8 |
| Check news | 43.2 |
| Take course | 35.4 |
| Do job-related tasks | 35.3 |
| Shop and pay bills | 30.0 |
| Search for job | 16.1 |
| Make phone calls | 5.7 |
| Other | 9.1 |

*Source: National Telecommunications and Information Administration,* Falling through the Net: Toward Digital Inclusion—A Report on Americans' Access to Technology Tools, *October 2000*

# Attendance at Art Events Soars with Education

## Participation in the arts is less affected by educational attainment.

Attendance at art events rises sharply with education. People with no more than a high school diploma are less likely than the average person to attend any type of art program. Those with at least some college education have above-average attendance rates. College graduates—especially those who have been to graduate school—are much more likely than average to attend art events. Fully 70 percent of those with graduate-level experience visited an art museum in the past 12 months, for example, compared with just 35 percent of all adults.

Education is not as influential in determining participation in art activities. The best educated people, in fact, are less likely than average to participate in weaving and pottery. Those who went no further than high school have above-average participation rates in those activities.

♦ As the educational level of the population increases, attendance at art events will rise, crowding museums and concert halls.

## Attendance at Art Events, 1997

*(percent of people aged 18 or older attending art event or reading literature at least once in the past 12 months, by educational attainment, 1997)*

| | total | high school graduate | some college | college graduate | graduate school |
|---|---|---|---|---|---|
| Read literature* | 63.1% | 57.6% | 72.1% | 79.5% | 86.3% |
| Visited art/craft fair | 47.5 | 42.9 | 57.8 | 65.2 | 69.3 |
| Visited historic park | 46.9 | 40.5 | 56.3 | 66.6 | 72.7 |
| Visited art museum | 34.9 | 24.6 | 43.2 | 57.7 | 69.8 |
| Attended musical play | 24.5 | 15.7 | 28.4 | 43.6 | 50.3 |
| Attended non-musical play | 15.8 | 9.1 | 18.9 | 27.7 | 37.2 |
| Attended classical music | 15.6 | 8.3 | 18.1 | 28.0 | 44.5 |
| Attended dance, except ballet | 12.4 | 9.2 | 13.7 | 17.8 | 24.7 |
| Attended jazz performance | 11.9 | 6.8 | 15.4 | 21.3 | 27.7 |
| Attended ballet | 5.8 | 3.6 | 6.5 | 10.8 | 14.4 |
| Attended opera | 4.7 | 1.7 | 5.2 | 10.2 | 14.3 |

** Literature is defined as plays, poetry, novels, or short stories.*
*Source: National Endowment for the Arts,* 1997 Survey of Public Participation in the Arts, Summary Report, *Internet site <http://arts.endow.gov/pub/Survey/SurveyPDF.html>*

## Participation in the Arts, 1997

*(percent of people aged 18 or older participating in art activity at least once in the past 12 months, by educational attainment, 1997)*

| | total | high school graduate | some college | college graduate | graduate school |
|---|---|---|---|---|---|
| Buying art | 35.1% | 30.9% | 34.6% | 40.6% | 40.5% |
| Weaving | 27.6 | 28.2 | 31.9 | 32.0 | 25.8 |
| Photography | 16.9 | 13.1 | 21.5 | 23.1 | 21.8 |
| Drawing | 15.9 | 15.0 | 20.3 | 18.0 | 18.2 |
| Pottery | 15.1 | 16.0 | 18.1 | 13.3 | 13.0 |
| Dance, except ballet | 12.6 | 12.3 | 15.7 | 10.3 | 15.2 |
| Writing | 12.1 | 9.2 | 17.0 | 13.9 | 19.4 |
| Classical music | 11.0 | 8.0 | 14.2 | 18.2 | 19.8 |
| Singing in groups | 10.4 | 8.7 | 12.6 | 9.0 | 11.8 |
| Musical play | 7.7 | 5.0 | 10.9 | 11.8 | 15.1 |
| Nonmusical play | 2.7 | 1.8 | 3.9 | 3.7 | 2.7 |
| Jazz | 2.2 | 1.5 | 2.6 | 3.3 | 4.3 |
| Opera | 1.8 | 1.2 | 2.6 | 2.4 | 5.1 |
| Ballet | 0.5 | 0.1 | 1.1 | 0.2 | 0.5 |

*Source: National Endowment for the Arts,* 1997 Survey of Public Participation in the Arts, Summary Report, *Internet site <http://arts.endow.gov/pub/Survey/SurveyPDF.html>*

# Violent Crime Is Most Likely among the Young

## Violent crime rates among people under age 25 are more than twice the average.

While crime rates fell during the 1990s, there was no change in the pattern of crime—teens and young adults are crime's most likely victims. The rate among 16-to-19 year olds stood at more than 77 violent crimes per 1,000 people in 1999. Among people aged 65 or older, the rate is just 4 per 1,000.

Overall, the violent crime rate fell 34 percent between 1993 and 1999. But males are still more likely than females to be victims of violent crime, and blacks more likely than whites. People living in low-income households are more likely to be victims of violent crime than those who live in higher-income households.

In contrast to violent crime, household property crime does not vary much by household income. Blacks, however, are more likely to be victims of property crime than whites, and renters more than homeowners.

These numbers are based on the Bureau of Justice Statistics National Criminal Victimization Survey, which asks people whether they have been a crime victim in the past year. The level of crime found by the survey is much greater than that reported to police because many crimes go unreported. A comparison of survey results with police reports shows that only 36 percent of crimes are reported to police, ranging from 28 percent of rapes and sexual assaults to 84 percent of motor vehicle thefts.

## Violent Crime, 1999

*(number of violent crimes and personal thefts per 1,000 people aged 12 or older by selected characteristics, 1999)*

| | violent crimes | | | | | | |
|---|---|---|---|---|---|---|---|
| | | | | assault | | | |
| | total | rape, sexual assault | robbery | total | aggravated | simple | personal theft |
| **Total people** | **32.8** | **1.7** | **3.6** | **27.4** | **6.7** | **20.8** | **0.9** |
| **Sex** | | | | | | | |
| Female | 28.8 | 3.0 | 2.3 | 23.6 | 4.8 | 18.8 | 0.9 |
| Male | 37.0 | 0.4 | 5.0 | 31.6 | 8.7 | 22.9 | 0.9 |
| **Age** | | | | | | | |
| Aged 12 to 15 | 74.4 | 4.0 | 6.7 | 63.7 | 13.1 | 50.6 | 3.1 |
| Aged 16 to 19 | 77.4 | 6.9 | 8.2 | 62.3 | 16.8 | 45.5 | 1.5 |
| Aged 20 to 24 | 68.5 | 4.3 | 7.7 | 56.4 | 16.7 | 39.7 | 1.0 |
| Aged 25 to 34 | 36.3 | 1.7 | 4.1 | 30.5 | 8.3 | 22.2 | 1.2 |
| Aged 35 to 49 | 25.2 | 0.8 | 2.8 | 21.6 | 4.7 | 16.9 | 0.4 |
| Aged 50 to 64 | 14.4 | 0.2 | 1.9 | 12.3 | 1.8 | 10.5 | 0.6 |
| Aged 65 or older | 3.8 | 0.1 | 0.7 | 3.0 | 1.1 | 1.9 | 0.6 |
| **Race** | | | | | | | |
| Black | 41.6 | 2.6 | 7.7 | 31.3 | 10.6 | 20.8 | 1.3 |
| White | 31.9 | 1.6 | 3.1 | 27.2 | 6.2 | 21.1 | 0.8 |
| Other | 24.5 | 1.7 | 2.5 | 20.3 | 5.7 | 14.6 | 1.5 |
| **Hispanic origin** | | | | | | | |
| Hispanic | 33.8 | 1.9 | 5.6 | 26.3 | 8.9 | 17.4 | 1.5 |
| Non-Hispanic | 32.4 | 1.7 | 3.4 | 27.3 | 6.4 | 20.9 | 0.9 |
| **Household income** | | | | | | | |
| Less than $7,500 | 57.5 | 4.3 | 8.1 | 45.1 | 14.5 | 30.6 | 1.9 |
| $7,500 to $14,999 | 44.5 | 1.6 | 6.9 | 35.9 | 10.0 | 26.0 | 1.1 |
| $15,000 to $24,999 | 35.3 | 3.2 | 4.8 | 27.2 | 7.2 | 20.1 | 0.8 |
| $25,000 to $34,999 | 37.9 | 1.2 | 3.1 | 33.7 | 6.9 | 26.7 | 1.2 |
| $35,000 to $49,999 | 30.3 | 1.6 | 3.5 | 25.3 | 5.5 | 19.7 | 0.5 |
| $50,000 to $74,999 | 33.3 | 1.5 | 2.2 | 29.7 | 7.1 | 22.6 | 0.4 |
| $75,000 or more | 22.9 | 0.8 | 1.8 | 20.3 | 4.0 | 16.3 | 1.2 |

*(continued)*

*(continued from previous page)*

| | violent crimes | | | | | | |
|---|---|---|---|---|---|---|---|
| | | | | assault | | | |
| | total | rape, sexual assault | robbery | total | aggravated | simple | personal theft |
| **Marital status** | | | | | | | |
| Never married | 60.6 | 3.9 | 7.2 | 49.5 | 12.6 | 36.9 | 1.6 |
| Married | 14.4 | 0.3 | 1.1 | 12.9 | 2.7 | 10.3 | 0.4 |
| Divorced/separated | 53.6 | 2.9 | 5.8 | 45.0 | 11.6 | 33.3 | 1.2 |
| Widowed | 6.0 | 0.0 | 1.9 | 4.1 | 1.3 | 2.8 | 1.0 |
| **Region** | | | | | | | |
| Northeast | 29.6 | 1.5 | 3.6 | 24.5 | 5.1 | 19.4 | 1.0 |
| Midwest | 35.5 | 1.6 | 3.2 | 30.8 | 7.7 | 23.0 | 1.0 |
| South | 30.2 | 1.8 | 3.3 | 25.1 | 6.6 | 18.4 | 0.7 |
| West | 36.9 | 1.9 | 4.6 | 30.4 | 7.0 | 23.4 | 1.2 |
| **Residence** | | | | | | | |
| Urban | 39.8 | 2.3 | 6.7 | 30.9 | 8.5 | 22.4 | 1.6 |
| Suburban | 32.8 | 1.6 | 2.8 | 28.4 | 6.6 | 21.7 | 0.9 |
| Rural | 24.9 | 1.3 | 1.7 | 22.0 | 4.8 | 17.1 | 0.2 |

*Note: Violent crime as defined in the National Crime Victimization Survey includes rape/sexual assault, robbery, and assault. It does not include murder or manslaughter because it is based on interviews with victims. Personal theft includes pocket picking, purse snatching, and attempted purse snatching.*
*Source: Bureau of Justice Statistics,* Criminal Victimization 1999: Changes 1998-99 with Trends 1993–99, *NCJ 182734, 2000*

## Household Property Crime, 1999

*(number of household property crimes per 1,000 households by selected characteristics, 1999)*

| | *total* | *burglary* | *motor vehicle theft* | *theft* |
|---|---|---|---|---|
| **Total households** | **198.0** | **34.1** | **10.0** | **153.9** |
| **Race of householder** | | | | |
| Black | 249.9 | 52.6 | 16.0 | 181.2 |
| White | 190.0 | 31.5 | 9.0 | 149.5 |
| Other | 206.3 | 31.2 | 11.6 | 163.6 |
| **Hispanic origin** | | | | |
| Hispanic | 232.5 | 37.2 | 17.3 | 178.0 |
| Non-Hispanic | 194.6 | 33.7 | 9.3 | 151.5 |
| **Household income** | | | | |
| Less than $7,500 | 220.8 | 67.0 | 6.2 | 147.6 |
| $7,500 to $14,999 | 200.1 | 44.2 | 10.1 | 145.9 |
| $15,000 to $24,999 | 214.9 | 38.9 | 11.2 | 164.9 |
| $25,000 to $34,999 | 199.1 | 37.1 | 10.4 | 151.7 |
| $35,000 to $49,999 | 207.6 | 30.9 | 11.7 | 165.0 |
| $50,000 to $74,999 | 213.6 | 24.1 | 10.3 | 179.1 |
| $75,000 or more | 220.4 | 23.1 | 9.7 | 187.7 |
| **Region** | | | | |
| Northeast | 159.5 | 26.2 | 9.2 | 124.1 |
| Midwest | 199.9 | 36.6 | 7.8 | 155.4 |
| South | 191.4 | 34.6 | 10.5 | 146.3 |
| West | 243.1 | 37.5 | 12.3 | 193.3 |
| **Residence** | | | | |
| Urban | 256.3 | 46.2 | 15.9 | 194.2 |
| Suburban | 181.4 | 27.1 | 8.5 | 145.8 |
| Rural | 159.8 | 32.6 | 5.7 | 121.5 |
| **Homeownership** | | | | |
| Owned | 170.4 | 26.5 | 8.4 | 135.5 |
| Rented | 251.9 | 48.9 | 13.0 | 190.0 |

*Source: Bureau of Justice Statistics,* Criminal Victimization 1999: Changes 1998-99 With Trends 1993–99, *NCJ 182734, 2000*

CHAPTER

# 8

# Spending Trends

♦ **Spending by the average household rose a modest 2 percent during the 1990s.**

The average household spent only $851 more in 1999 than in 1990, after adjusting for inflation.

♦ **Households headed by people aged 45 to 54 spend the most.**

Those headed by people under age 25 spend the least—only $21,725 in 1999.

♦ **Households with incomes of $70,000 or more spend twice the average.**

While the affluent are only 19 percent of households, they account for 36 percent of spending.

♦ **Married couples with children spend much more than average.**

In 1999, couples with kids spent an average of $51,186 versus the $37,027 spent by the average household.

♦ **Non-Hispanic whites spend more than non-Hispanic blacks or Hispanics.**

But non-Hispanic blacks spend much more than average on poultry, fish, and seafood. Hispanics spend more than average on children's clothes.

♦ **Incomes are highest in the Northeast, but spending is highest in the West.**

Households in the West spent $42,364 in 1999, 14 percent more than the average household.

♦ **College graduates earn more and spend more than the average household.**

In 1999, households headed by college graduates spent $53,658, 45 percent more than the average.

# Spending Rose 2 Percent during 1990s

## The average household spent less in 1999 than in 1990 on many discretionary items.

Between 1990 and 1999, spending by the average household rose a modest 2 percent, after adjusting for inflation, despite the booming economy. In 1999, the average household spent $37,027, only $851 more than the $36,176 of 1990, according to the Bureau of Labor Statistics' Consumer Expenditure Survey. Each year the Consumer Expenditure Survey collects household spending data on nearly 1,000 product and service categories.

The average household spent less in 1999 on many categories of products and services than in 1990. Food spending fell 8 percent during the decade, after adjusting for inflation. Both food-at-home (groceries) and food-away-from-home (restaurants) spending was down. Spending on alcoholic beverages fell 15 percent, as did spending on apparel. The average household cut its gift spending by 7 percent.

Spending on many nondiscretionary items rose during the 1990s. Spending on property taxes was up 48 percent between 1990 and 1999, for example, while spending on household services (mostly daycare) rose 17 percent. Spending on health insurance climbed 25 percent during the decade, after adjusting for inflation. While spending on entertainment rose 4 percent, spending on fees and admissions to entertainment events fell 3 percent during the 1990s. Education spending rose 23 percent as college tuition soared.

♦ It is more myth than reality that a consumer spending spree caused the booming economy of the 1990s. The average household has been cautious with its money, a fact that may help soften any recession that lies ahead.

## Spending Trends, 1990 and 1999

*(average annual spending of consumer units by product and service category, 1990 and 1999; percent change 1990–99; in 1999 dollars)*

| | *1999* | *1990* | *percent change 1990–99* |
|---|---|---|---|
| **Number of consumer units (in 000s)** | **108,465** | **96,968** | **11.9%** |
| **Average before-tax income** | **$43,951** | **$40,648** | **8.1** |
| **Average annual spending** | **37,027** | **36,176** | **2.4** |
| **FOOD** | **$5,031** | **$5,476** | **–8.1%** |
| **Food at home** | **2,915** | **3,168** | **–8.0** |
| Cereals and bakery products | 448 | 469 | –4.5 |
| Cereals and cereal products | 160 | 164 | –2.4 |
| Bakery products | 288 | 306 | –5.9 |
| Meats, poultry, fish, and eggs | 749 | 851 | –12.0 |
| Beef | 220 | 278 | –20.9 |
| Pork | 157 | 168 | –6.5 |
| Other meats | 97 | 126 | –23.0 |
| Poultry | 136 | 138 | –1.4 |
| Fish and seafood | 106 | 105 | 1.0 |
| Eggs | 32 | 38 | –15.8 |
| Dairy products | 322 | 376 | –14.4 |
| Fresh milk and cream | 122 | 178 | –31.5 |
| Other dairy products | 200 | 198 | 1.0 |
| Fruits and vegetables | 500 | 520 | –3.8 |
| Fresh fruits | 152 | 162 | –6.2 |
| Fresh vegetables | 149 | 150 | –0.7 |
| Processed fruits | 113 | 119 | –5.0 |
| Processed vegetables | 86 | 89 | –3.4 |
| Other food at home | 896 | 951 | –5.8 |
| Sugar and other sweets | 112 | 120 | –6.7 |
| Fats and oils | 84 | 87 | –3.4 |
| Miscellaneous foods | 420 | 428 | –1.9 |
| Nonalcoholic beverages | 242 | 272 | –11.0 |
| Food prepared by household on trips | 39 | 45 | –13.3 |

*(continued)*

*(continued from previous page)*

| | 1999 | 1990 | percent change 1990–99 |
|---|---|---|---|
| **Food away from home** | **$2,116** | **$2,308** | **–8.3%** |
| **ALCOHOLIC BEVERAGES** | **318** | **373** | **–14.7** |
| **HOUSING** | **12,057** | **11,093** | **8.7** |
| **Shelter** | **7,016** | **6,164** | **13.8** |
| Owned dwellings | 4,525 | 3,764 | 20.2 |
| Mortgage interest and charges | 2,547 | 2,316 | 10.0 |
| Property taxes | 1,123 | 761 | 47.6 |
| Maintenance, repairs, insurance, other expenses | 855 | 688 | 24.3 |
| Rented dwellings | 2,027 | 1,954 | 3.7 |
| Other lodging | 464 | 445 | 4.3 |
| **Utilities, fuels, public services** | **2,377** | **2,409** | **–1.3** |
| Natural gas | 270 | 314 | –14.0 |
| Electricity | 899 | 966 | –6.9 |
| Fuel oil and other fuels | 74 | 127 | –41.7 |
| Telephone services | 849 | 755 | 12.5 |
| Water and other public services | 285 | 246 | 15.9 |
| **Household services** | **666** | **569** | **17.0** |
| Personal services | 323 | 279 | 15.8 |
| Other household services | 343 | 289 | 18.7 |
| **Housekeeping supplies** | **498** | **518** | **–3.9** |
| Laundry and cleaning supplies | 121 | 144 | –16.0 |
| Other household products | 250 | 218 | 14.7 |
| Postage and stationery | 127 | 156 | –18.6 |
| **Household furnishings and equipment** | **1,499** | **1,434** | **4.5** |
| Household textiles | 114 | 126 | –9.5 |
| Furniture | 365 | 395 | –7.6 |
| Floor coverings | 44 | 117 | –62.4 |
| Major appliances | 183 | 187 | –2.1 |
| Small appliances, miscellaneous housewares | 102 | 96 | 6.3 |
| Miscellaneous household equipment | 692 | 512 | 35.2 |

*(continued)*

*(continued from previous page)*

| | *1999* | *1990* | *percent change 1990–99* |
|---|---|---|---|
| **APPAREL AND SERVICES** | **$1,743** | **$2,062** | **–15.5%** |
| **Men and boys** | **421** | **501** | **–16.0** |
| Men, aged 16 or older | 328 | 413 | –20.6 |
| Boys, aged 2 to 15 | 93 | 89 | 4.5 |
| **Women and girls** | **655** | **858** | **–23.7** |
| Women, aged 16 or older | 548 | 747 | –26.6 |
| Girls, aged 2 to 15 | 107 | 111 | –3.6 |
| **Children under age 2** | **67** | **89** | **–24.7** |
| **Footwear** | **303** | **287** | **5.6** |
| **Other apparel products and services** | **297** | **329** | **–9.7** |
| **TRANSPORTATION** | **7,011** | **6,526** | **7.4** |
| **Vehicle purchases** | **3,305** | **2,714** | **21.8** |
| Cars and trucks, new | 1,628 | 1,477 | 10.2 |
| Cars and trucks, used | 1,641 | 1,208 | 35.8 |
| Other vehicles | 36 | 28 | 28.6 |
| **Gasoline and motor oil** | **1,055** | **1,335** | **–21.0** |
| **Other vehicle expenses** | **2,254** | **2,093** | **7.7** |
| Vehicle finance charges | 320 | 382 | –16.2 |
| Maintenance and repairs | 664 | 751 | –11.6 |
| Vehicle insurance | 756 | 718 | 5.3 |
| Vehicle rental, leases, licenses, other charges | 513 | 242 | 112.0 |
| **Public transportation** | **397** | **385** | **3.1** |
| **HEALTH CARE** | **1,959** | **1,887** | **3.8** |
| Health insurance | 923 | 741 | 24.6 |
| Medical services | 558 | 716 | –22.1 |
| Drugs | 370 | 321 | 15.3 |
| Medical supplies | 109 | 108 | 0.9 |
| **ENTERTAINMENT** | **1,891** | **1,813** | **4.3** |
| Fees and admissions | 459 | 473 | –3.0 |
| Television, radio, sound equipment | 608 | 579 | 5.0 |
| Pets, toys, and playground equipment | 346 | 352 | –1.7 |
| Other entertainment supplies, services | 478 | 409 | 16.9 |

*(continued)*

*(continued from previous page)*

| | 1999 | 1990 | percent change 1990–99 |
|---|---|---|---|
| **PERSONAL CARE PRODUCTS AND SERVICES** | **$408** | **$464** | **–12.1%** |
| **READING** | **159** | **195** | **–18.5** |
| **EDUCATION** | **635** | **518** | **22.6** |
| **TOBACCO PRODUCTS AND SMOKING SUPPLIES** | **300** | **349** | **–14.0** |
| **MISCELLANEOUS** | **889** | **1,073** | **–17.1** |
| **CASH CONTRIBUTIONS** | **1,190** | **1,040** | **14.4** |
| **PERSONAL INSURANCE AND PENSIONS** | **3,436** | **3,304** | **4.0** |
| Life and other personal insurance | 394 | 440 | –10.5 |
| Pensions and Social Security | 3,042 | 2,865 | 6.2 |
| **PERSONAL TAXES** | **3,588** | **3,763** | **–4.7** |
| Federal income taxes | 2,802 | 2,956 | –5.2 |
| State and local income taxes | 616 | 711 | –13.4 |
| Other taxes | 170 | 96 | 77.1 |
| **GIFTS** | **1,083** | **1,161** | **–6.7** |
| **Food** | **83** | **121** | **–31.4** |
| **Housing** | **292** | **296** | **–1.4** |
| Housekeeping supplies | 41 | 45 | –8.9 |
| Household textiles | 17 | 18 | –5.6 |
| Appliances and misc. housewares | 32 | 34 | –5.9 |
| Major appliances | 9 | 9 | 0.0 |
| Small appliances and misc. housewares | 24 | 25 | –4.0 |
| Miscellaneous household equipment | 66 | 64 | 3.1 |
| Other housing | 136 | 136 | 0.0 |
| **Apparel and services** | **210** | **301** | **–30.2** |
| Males, aged 2 or older | 54 | 78 | –30.8 |
| Females, aged 2 or older | 71 | 121 | –41.3 |
| Children under age 2 | 33 | 40 | –17.5 |
| Other apparel products and services | 52 | 61 | –14.8 |
| Jewelry and watches | 27 | 32 | –15.6 |
| All other apparel products and services | 25 | 29 | –13.8 |

*(continued)*

*(continued from previous page)*

| | 1999 | 1990 | percent change 1990–99 |
|---|---|---|---|
| **Transportation** | **$63** | **$68** | **–7.4%** |
| **Health care** | **40** | **57** | **–29.8** |
| **Entertainment** | **98** | **84** | **16.7** |
| Toys, games, hobbies, and tricycles | 32 | 32 | 0.0 |
| Other entertainment | 66 | 52 | 26.9 |
| **Education** | **166** | **122** | **36.1** |
| **All other gifts** | **131** | **112** | **17.0** |

*Note: The Bureau of Labor Statistics uses consumer unit rather than household as the sampling unit in the Consumer Expenditure Survey. For the definition of consumer unit, see Glossary. Spending on gifts is also included in the preceding product and service categories.*
*Source: Bureau of Labor Statistics, 1990 and 1999 Consumer Expenditure Surveys, Internet site <www.bls.gov/csxhome.htm>; calculations by New Strategist*

# Householders Aged 45 to 54 Spend the Most

## Young adults spend the least.

Households headed by people aged 45 to 54 spent an average of $46,538 in 1999, 26 percent more than the average household. In second place are householders aged 35 to 44, who spent an average of $42,836, according to the Bureau of Labor Statistics' Consumer Expenditure Survey. Householders aged 35 to 54 spend more than younger and older householders not only because they have higher incomes, but also because their households are more likely to include children.

Households headed by people under age 25 spend less than any other age group, just $21,725 in 1999. This figure is below the spending of even the oldest householders, those aged 75 or older, who spent $22,900 in 1999. Similarly, the spending of householders aged 55 to 64 surpasses that of 25-to-34-year-olds on most items, including new cars and trucks, entertainment, women's clothes, and personal care products and services.

The indexed spending table in this section shows spending by age of householder in comparison to what the average household spends. An index of 100 means a household spends an average amount on an item. An index above 100 means households in the age group spend more than average on an item, while an index below 100 reveals below-average spending. A look at the table shows that spending by households headed by people under age 25 is below average on most items. Spending is close to the average on most items for households headed by 25-to-34-year-olds, and above average in most categories for householders aged 35 to 64. Spending then falls below average again in most categories for householders aged 65 or older.

There are some exceptions, however. Householders under age 25 spend 63 percent more than average on rent. They spend 48 percent more than average on baby clothes, and twice the average on education because many are in college. The oldest householders spend 16 percent more than the average household on fuel oil and 56 percent more on health care. Householders aged 45 to 54 spend 24 percent less than average on rent since most are homeowners. They spend 54 percent less than average on household personal services, a category that includes day care expenses, which most no longer have. Householders aged 45 to 54 spend 28 percent more than average on new cars and trucks and more than twice as much as the average household on gifts of education (their children's college bills).

The market share table in this section shows how much of total spending by category is accounted for by three broad age groups of householders. Middle-aged householders (aged 35 to 54) accounted for 50 percent of all household spending in 1999. Middle-aged householders dominate spending on many items, ranging from food-away-from-home to entertainment. Householders under age 35 account for only 22 percent of spending, while householders aged 55 or older account for a larger 28 percent. In no category do young adults account for more than half of all household spending, although they come close with a 48 percent share of spending on infants' clothes. Older Americans dominate spending on drugs as well as gifts of health care.

♦ The spending of older householders will grow in importance as the large baby-boom generation enters the 55-or-older age group.

**Spending peaks in middle age**

*(average annual spending of consumer units by age of consumer unit reference person, 1999)*

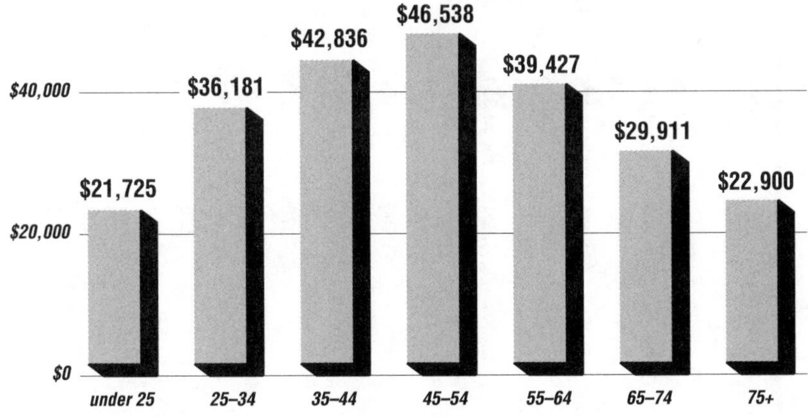

## Spending by Age of Householder, 1999

*(average annual spending of consumer units (CU's) by product and service category and age of consumer unit reference person, 1999)*

| | | | | | | | aged 65 or older | | |
|---|---|---|---|---|---|---|---|---|---|
| | *total* | *under 25* | *25 to 34* | *35 to 44* | *45 to 54* | *55 to 64* | *total* | *65 to 74* | *75 or older* |
| **Number of consumer units (in 000s)** | **108,465** | **8,164** | **19,332** | **24,405** | **20,903** | **13,647** | **22,015** | **11,578** | **10,437** |
| **Average number of persons per CU** | **2.5** | **1.8** | **2.9** | **3.2** | **2.7** | **2.2** | **1.7** | **1.9** | **1.5** |
| **Average before-tax income** | **$43,951** | **$18,276** | **$42,470** | **$53,579** | **$59,822** | **$49,436** | **$26,581** | **$28,928** | **$23,937** |
| **Average annual spending** | **37,027** | **21,725** | **36,181** | **42,836** | **46,538** | **39,427** | **26,553** | **29,911** | **22,900** |
| **FOOD** | **$5,031** | **$3,354** | **$5,140** | **$6,109** | **$5,945** | **$5,056** | **$3,511** | **$4,146** | **$2,841** |
| **Food at home** | **2,915** | **1,828** | **2,890** | **3,537** | **3,340** | **2,920** | **2,266** | **2,575** | **1,943** |
| Cereals and bakery products | 448 | 271 | 432 | 561 | 509 | 433 | 357 | 399 | 314 |
| Cereals and cereal products | 160 | 102 | 170 | 211 | 175 | 140 | 116 | 130 | 101 |
| Bakery products | 288 | 169 | 262 | 350 | 335 | 294 | 242 | 269 | 213 |
| Meats, poultry, fish, and eggs | 749 | 469 | 751 | 897 | 878 | 761 | 563 | 664 | 457 |
| Beef | 220 | 155 | 221 | 266 | 257 | 230 | 154 | 187 | 119 |
| Pork | 157 | 93 | 154 | 185 | 185 | 165 | 121 | 146 | 95 |
| Other meats | 97 | 61 | 95 | 119 | 111 | 94 | 77 | 94 | 60 |
| Poultry | 136 | 82 | 148 | 162 | 160 | 136 | 96 | 109 | 82 |
| Fish and seafood | 106 | 59 | 103 | 125 | 130 | 102 | 87 | 98 | 77 |
| Eggs | 32 | 19 | 31 | 40 | 34 | 35 | 27 | 30 | 24 |
| Dairy products | 322 | 195 | 322 | 410 | 354 | 305 | 255 | 289 | 220 |
| Fresh milk and cream | 122 | 78 | 124 | 158 | 130 | 107 | 99 | 108 | 89 |
| Other dairy products | 200 | 117 | 198 | 252 | 224 | 198 | 156 | 181 | 131 |

*(continued)*

*(continued from previous page)*

| | total | under 25 | 25 to 34 | 35 to 44 | 45 to 54 | 55 to 64 | aged 65 or older | | |
|---|---|---|---|---|---|---|---|---|---|
| | | | | | | | total | 65 to 74 | 75 or older |
| Fruits and vegetables | $500 | $283 | $475 | $572 | $563 | $525 | $450 | $497 | $401 |
| Fresh fruits | 152 | 77 | 136 | 173 | 173 | 161 | 149 | 165 | 131 |
| Fresh vegetables | 149 | 79 | 146 | 161 | 168 | 171 | 131 | 148 | 114 |
| Processed fruits | 113 | 77 | 105 | 133 | 129 | 108 | 100 | 106 | 93 |
| Processed vegetables | 86 | 49 | 87 | 104 | 93 | 86 | 71 | 78 | 63 |
| Other food at home | 896 | 610 | 910 | 1,097 | 1,037 | 895 | 641 | 726 | 551 |
| Sugar and other sweets | 112 | 71 | 99 | 134 | 128 | 118 | 93 | 106 | 80 |
| Fats and oils | 84 | 54 | 80 | 96 | 96 | 86 | 70 | 81 | 59 |
| Miscellaneous foods | 420 | 300 | 463 | 517 | 464 | 401 | 290 | 322 | 258 |
| Nonalcoholic beverages | 242 | 167 | 236 | 301 | 301 | 241 | 158 | 176 | 139 |
| Food prepared by household on trips | 39 | 19 | 32 | 49 | 47 | 50 | 29 | 42 | 15 |
| **Food away from home** | **2,116** | **1,526** | **2,250** | **2,572** | **2,605** | **2,136** | **1,245** | **1,571** | **898** |
| **ALCOHOLIC BEVERAGES** | **318** | **369** | **365** | **384** | **320** | **330** | **172** | **219** | **122** |
| **HOUSING** | **12,057** | **6,585** | **12,520** | **14,215** | **14,513** | **12,093** | **8,946** | **9,605** | **8,230** |
| **Shelter** | **7,016** | **4,140** | **7,613** | **8,605** | **8,534** | **6,660** | **4,578** | **4,929** | **4,188** |
| Owned dwellings | 4,525 | 596 | 3,936 | 6,110 | 6,203 | 4,813 | 2,973 | 3,424 | 2,472 |
| Mortgage interest and charges | 2,547 | 311 | 2,694 | 3,990 | 3,642 | 2,328 | 745 | 1,038 | 420 |
| Property taxes | 1,123 | 168 | 751 | 1,297 | 1,444 | 1,380 | 1,149 | 1,222 | 1,069 |
| Maintenance, repairs, insurance, other | 855 | 117 | 490 | 823 | 1,117 | 1,105 | 1,078 | 1,164 | 983 |
| Rented dwellings | 2,027 | 3,296 | 3,447 | 2,121 | 1,532 | 1,206 | 1,182 | 968 | 1,420 |
| Other lodging | 464 | 248 | 230 | 374 | 799 | 641 | 423 | 537 | 296 |

*(continued)*

*(continued from previous page)*

| | | | | | | | aged 65 or older | | |
|---|---|---|---|---|---|---|---|---|---|
| | *total* | *under 25* | *25 to 34* | *35 to 44* | *45 to 54* | *55 to 64* | *total* | *65 to 74* | *75 or older* |
| **Utilities, fuels, public services** | **$2,377** | **$1,166** | **$2,249** | **$2,587** | **$2,819** | **$2,608** | **$2,145** | **$2,369** | **$1,897** |
| Natural gas | 270 | 92 | 238 | 283 | 304 | 327 | 284 | 290 | 276 |
| Electricity | 899 | 426 | 811 | 969 | 1,074 | 997 | 848 | 933 | 753 |
| Fuel oil and other fuels | 74 | 14 | 47 | 72 | 94 | 80 | 102 | 117 | 86 |
| Telephone services | 849 | 562 | 924 | 950 | 1,008 | 869 | 614 | 711 | 506 |
| Water and other public services | 285 | 72 | 229 | 313 | 339 | 335 | 298 | 319 | 276 |
| **Household services** | **666** | **181** | **772** | **830** | **606** | **476** | **746** | **458** | **1,064** |
| Personal services | 323 | 121 | 573 | 500 | 148 | 60 | 311 | 87 | 559 |
| Other household services | 343 | 60 | 199 | 330 | 459 | 416 | 435 | 372 | 505 |
| **Housekeeping supplies** | **498** | **221** | **441** | **604** | **574** | **570** | **423** | **493** | **349** |
| Laundry and cleaning supplies | 121 | 64 | 117 | 149 | 135 | 124 | 102 | 118 | 85 |
| Other household products | 250 | 86 | 211 | 315 | 298 | 296 | 199 | 231 | 166 |
| Postage and stationery | 127 | 71 | 113 | 139 | 141 | 149 | 122 | 144 | 98 |
| **Household furnishings and equipment** | **1,499** | **877** | **1,445** | **1,590** | **1,980** | **1,779** | **1,054** | **1,356** | **730** |
| Household textiles | 114 | 41 | 101 | 114 | 169 | 111 | 106 | 143 | 67 |
| Furniture | 365 | 283 | 435 | 403 | 446 | 382 | 205 | 265 | 138 |
| Floor coverings | 44 | 11 | 37 | 37 | 52 | 94 | 31 | 32 | 30 |
| Major appliances | 183 | 91 | 176 | 192 | 215 | 196 | 175 | 190 | 158 |
| Small appliances, misc. housewares | 102 | 47 | 82 | 90 | 131 | 144 | 99 | 147 | 49 |
| Miscellaneous household equipment | 692 | 405 | 615 | 754 | 968 | 853 | 438 | 578 | 288 |
| **APPAREL AND SERVICES** | **1,743** | **1,192** | **2,047** | **2,053** | **2,048** | **1,722** | **1,070** | **1,235** | **901** |
| **Men and boys** | **421** | **238** | **519** | **517** | **517** | **406** | **219** | **300** | **134** |

*(continued)*

*(continued from previous page)*

| | total | under 25 | 25 to 34 | 35 to 44 | 45 to 54 | 55 to 64 | aged 65 or older total | 65 to 74 | 75 or older |
|---|---|---|---|---|---|---|---|---|---|
| Men, aged 16 or older | $328 | $209 | $387 | $331 | $438 | $364 | $195 | $266 | $120 |
| Boys, aged 2 to 15 | 93 | 29 | 133 | 186 | 79 | 41 | 24 | 34 | 13 |
| **Women and girls** | **655** | **422** | **709** | **764** | **817** | **671** | **416** | **525** | **301** |
| Women, aged 16 or older | 548 | 377 | 579 | 561 | 687 | 625 | 394 | 491 | 292 |
| Girls, aged 2 to 15 | 107 | 45 | 130 | 203 | 130 | 46 | 22 | 34 | 9 |
| **Children under age 2** | **67** | **99** | **139** | **80** | **40** | **41** | **17** | **22** | **11** |
| **Footwear** | **303** | **234** | **374** | **373** | **327** | **308** | **165** | **219** | **108** |
| **Other apparel products and services** | **297** | **199** | **306** | **319** | **347** | **296** | **253** | **169** | **347** |
| **TRANSPORTATION** | **7,011** | **5,037** | **7,150** | **8,041** | **9,010** | **7,330** | **4,385** | **5,457** | **3,196** |
| **Vehicle purchases** | **3,305** | **2,859** | **3,500** | **3,807** | **4,117** | **3,406** | **1,911** | **2,422** | **1,344** |
| Cars and trucks, new | 1,628 | 857 | 1,377 | 1,722 | 2,079 | 2,109 | 1,304 | 1,661 | 907 |
| Cars and trucks, used | 1,641 | 1,974 | 2,034 | 2,058 | 1,988 | 1,283 | 606 | 758 | 437 |
| Other vehicles | 36 | 28 | 89 | 27 | 51 | 14 | 2 | 3 | – |
| **Gasoline and motor oil** | **1,055** | **708** | **1,066** | **1,259** | **1,349** | **1,093** | **644** | **807** | **463** |
| **Other vehicle expenses** | **2,254** | **1,253** | **2,249** | **2,565** | **3,085** | **2,339** | **1,443** | **1,724** | **1,131** |
| Vehicle finance charges | 320 | 209 | 402 | 394 | 431 | 320 | 104 | 146 | 57 |
| Maintenance and repairs | 664 | 402 | 554 | 743 | 890 | 724 | 519 | 596 | 434 |
| Vehicle insurance | 756 | 408 | 705 | 806 | 1,052 | 803 | 566 | 638 | 485 |
| Vehicle rental, leases, licenses, other | 513 | 234 | 588 | 620 | 712 | 493 | 255 | 344 | 155 |
| **Public transportation** | **397** | **217** | **335** | **411** | **459** | **492** | **387** | **504** | **258** |

*(continued)*

(continued from previous page)

| | | | | | | | aged 65 or older | | |
|---|---|---|---|---|---|---|---|---|---|
| | *total* | *under 25* | *25 to 34* | *35 to 44* | *45 to 54* | *55 to 64* | *total* | *65 to 74* | *75 or older* |
| **HEALTH CARE** | **$1,959** | **$551** | **$1,170** | **$1,631** | **$2,183** | **$2,450** | **$3,019** | **$2,991** | **$3,052** |
| Health insurance | 923 | 233 | 597 | 746 | 942 | 1,063 | 1,554 | 1,572 | 1,534 |
| Medical services | 558 | 184 | 351 | 531 | 754 | 751 | 601 | 574 | 632 |
| Drugs | 370 | 97 | 162 | 254 | 368 | 497 | 706 | 696 | 719 |
| Medical supplies | 109 | 36 | 60 | 101 | 118 | 139 | 158 | 149 | 168 |
| **ENTERTAINMENT** | **1,891** | **1,149** | **1,776** | **2,254** | **2,368** | **2,176** | **1,239** | **1,567** | **875** |
| Fees and admissions | 459 | 262 | 395 | 528 | 578 | 560 | 336 | 438 | 223 |
| Television, radios, sound equipment | 608 | 485 | 636 | 707 | 741 | 578 | 412 | 477 | 341 |
| Pets, toys, playground equipment | 346 | 185 | 375 | 454 | 418 | 354 | 186 | 250 | 117 |
| Other entertainment supplies, services | 478 | 217 | 369 | 565 | 631 | 684 | 305 | 403 | 194 |
| **PERSONAL CARE PRODUCTS AND SERVICES** | **408** | **254** | **381** | **471** | **475** | **449** | **333** | **370** | **295** |
| **READING** | **159** | **70** | **116** | **157** | **210** | **195** | **163** | **184** | **141** |
| **EDUCATION** | **635** | **1,277** | **453** | **637** | **1,125** | **552** | **139** | **165** | **111** |
| **TOBACCO PRODUCTS AND SMOKING SUPPLIES** | **300** | **220** | **295** | **370** | **395** | **329** | **148** | **204** | **86** |
| **MISCELLANEOUS** | **889** | **370** | **745** | **984** | **1,104** | **1,041** | **807** | **803** | **812** |
| **CASH CONTRIBUTIONS** | **1,190** | **186** | **589** | **1,074** | **1,426** | **1,762** | **1,640** | **1,684** | **1,593** |
| **PERSONAL INSURANCE AND PENSIONS** | **3,436** | **1,110** | **3,433** | **4,455** | **5,415** | **3,941** | **980** | **1,280** | **647** |
| Life and other personal insurance | 394 | 61 | 238 | 418 | 616 | 533 | 333 | 429 | 226 |
| Pensions and Social Security | 3,042 | 1,049 | 3,195 | 4,037 | 4,799 | 3,408 | 647 | 851 | 421 |

(continued)

(continued from previous page)

| | | | | | | | aged 65 or older | | |
|---|---|---|---|---|---|---|---|---|---|
| | *total* | *under 25* | *25 to 34* | *35 to 44* | *45 to 54* | *55 to 64* | *total* | *65 to 74* | *75 or older* |
| **PERSONAL TAXES** | **$3,588** | **$845** | **$3,065** | **$3,963** | **$5,363** | **$6,628** | **$1,256** | **$1,361** | **$1,137** |
| Federal income taxes | 2,802 | 630 | 2,316 | 3,037 | 4,178 | 5,696 | 827 | 905 | 739 |
| State and local income taxes | 616 | 208 | 671 | 797 | 955 | 691 | 169 | 178 | 159 |
| Other taxes | 170 | 7 | 78 | 128 | 230 | 241 | 260 | 278 | 240 |
| **GIFTS** | **1,083** | **515** | **739** | **956** | **1,690** | **1,537** | **884** | **948** | **814** |
| **Food** | **83** | **19** | **40** | **48** | **194** | **138** | **43** | **63** | **22** |
| **Housing** | **292** | **139** | **238** | **275** | **425** | **375** | **238** | **278** | **196** |
| Housekeeping supplies | 41 | 14 | 39 | 52 | 44 | 48 | 32 | 37 | 27 |
| Household textiles | 17 | 3 | 11 | 11 | 27 | 21 | 22 | 33 | 11 |
| Appliances and misc. housewares | 32 | 5 | 19 | 23 | 46 | 58 | 36 | 38 | 33 |
| Major appliances | 9 | 2 | 4 | 6 | 13 | 14 | 10 | 4 | 17 |
| Small appliances and misc. housewares | 24 | 2 | 15 | 17 | 34 | 44 | 25 | 34 | 16 |
| Miscellaneous household equipment | 66 | 42 | 48 | 61 | 83 | 102 | 58 | 79 | 37 |
| Other housing | 136 | 75 | 120 | 128 | 225 | 146 | 90 | 92 | 89 |
| **Apparel and services** | **210** | **118** | **206** | **190** | **269** | **298** | **160** | **176** | **143** |
| Males, aged 2 or older | 54 | 24 | 49 | 39 | 70 | 88 | 51 | 65 | 36 |
| Females, aged 2 or older | 71 | 35 | 46 | 58 | 110 | 99 | 67 | 55 | 79 |
| Children under age 2 | 33 | 23 | 43 | 45 | 30 | 38 | 14 | 17 | 11 |
| All other apparel products and services | 52 | 36 | 67 | 47 | 59 | 74 | 29 | 40 | 18 |
| Jewelry and watches | 27 | 22 | 53 | 25 | 23 | 26 | 11 | 18 | 3 |
| All other apparel products and services | 25 | 14 | 14 | 22 | 36 | 48 | 18 | 22 | 14 |

(continued)

*(continued from previous page)*

| | total | under 25 | 25 to 34 | 35 to 44 | 45 to 54 | 55 to 64 | aged 65 or older | | |
|---|---|---|---|---|---|---|---|---|---|
| | | | | | | | total | 65 to 74 | 75 or older |
| **Transportation** | **$63** | **$65** | **$30** | **$56** | **$90** | **$93** | **$57** | **$64** | **$49** |
| **Health care** | **40** | **5** | **9** | **24** | **46** | **43** | **90** | **57** | **128** |
| **Entertainment** | **98** | **63** | **74** | **89** | **106** | **142** | **107** | **99** | **115** |
| Toys, games, hobbies, and tricycles | 32 | 10 | 23 | 28 | 41 | 52 | 30 | 42 | 16 |
| Other entertainment | 66 | 53 | 51 | 61 | 65 | 90 | 77 | 57 | 99 |
| **Education** | **166** | **42** | **31** | **126** | **422** | **254** | **78** | **92** | **63** |
| **All other gifts** | **131** | **65** | **111** | **148** | **138** | **193** | **110** | **120** | **99** |

*Note: The Bureau of Labor Statistics uses consumer unit rather than household as the sampling unit in the Consumer Expenditure Survey. For the definition of consumer unit, see Glossary. Gift spending is also included in the preceding product and service categories.*
*Source: Bureau of Labor Statistics, 1999 Consumer Expenditure Survey; Internet site <www.bls.gov/csxstnd.htm>*

## Indexed Spending by Age of Householder, 1999

*(indexed average annual spending of consumer units by product and service category and age of consumer unit reference person, 1999)*

| | total | under 25 | 25 to 34 | 35 to 44 | 45 to 54 | 55 to 64 | aged 65 or older: total | aged 65 or older: 65 to 74 | aged 65 or older: 75 or older |
|---|---|---|---|---|---|---|---|---|---|
| **Number of consumer units (in 000s)** | **108,465** | **8,164** | **19,332** | **24,405** | **20,903** | **13,647** | **22,015** | **11,578** | **10,437** |
| **Indexed average before-tax income** | **100** | **42** | **97** | **122** | **136** | **112** | **60** | **66** | **54** |
| **Indexed average annual spending** | **100** | **59** | **98** | **116** | **126** | **106** | **72** | **81** | **62** |
| **FOOD** | **100** | **67** | **102** | **121** | **118** | **100** | **70** | **82** | **56** |
| **Food at home** | **100** | **63** | **99** | **121** | **115** | **100** | **78** | **88** | **67** |
| Cereals and bakery products | 100 | 60 | 96 | 125 | 114 | 97 | 80 | 89 | 70 |
| Cereals and cereal products | 100 | 64 | 106 | 132 | 109 | 88 | 73 | 81 | 63 |
| Bakery products | 100 | 59 | 91 | 122 | 116 | 102 | 84 | 93 | 74 |
| Meats, poultry, fish, and eggs | 100 | 63 | 100 | 120 | 117 | 102 | 75 | 89 | 61 |
| Beef | 100 | 70 | 100 | 121 | 117 | 105 | 70 | 85 | 54 |
| Pork | 100 | 59 | 98 | 118 | 118 | 105 | 77 | 93 | 61 |
| Other meats | 100 | 63 | 98 | 123 | 114 | 97 | 79 | 97 | 62 |
| Poultry | 100 | 60 | 109 | 119 | 118 | 100 | 71 | 80 | 60 |
| Fish and seafood | 100 | 56 | 97 | 118 | 123 | 96 | 82 | 92 | 73 |
| Eggs | 100 | 59 | 97 | 125 | 106 | 109 | 84 | 94 | 75 |
| Dairy products | 100 | 61 | 100 | 127 | 110 | 95 | 79 | 90 | 68 |
| Fresh milk and cream | 100 | 64 | 102 | 130 | 107 | 88 | 81 | 89 | 73 |
| Other dairy products | 100 | 59 | 99 | 126 | 112 | 99 | 78 | 91 | 66 |

*(continued)*

(continued from previous page)

| | | | | | | | aged 65 or older | | |
|---|---|---|---|---|---|---|---|---|---|
| | total | under 25 | 25 to 34 | 35 to 44 | 45 to 54 | 55 to 64 | total | 65 to 74 | 75 or older |
| Fruits and vegetables | 100 | 57 | 95 | 114 | 113 | 105 | 90 | 99 | 80 |
| Fresh fruits | 100 | 51 | 89 | 114 | 114 | 106 | 98 | 109 | 86 |
| Fresh vegetables | 100 | 53 | 98 | 108 | 113 | 115 | 88 | 99 | 77 |
| Processed fruits | 100 | 68 | 93 | 118 | 114 | 96 | 88 | 94 | 82 |
| Processed vegetables | 100 | 57 | 101 | 121 | 108 | 100 | 83 | 91 | 73 |
| Other food at home | 100 | 68 | 102 | 122 | 116 | 100 | 72 | 81 | 61 |
| Sugar and other sweets | 100 | 63 | 88 | 120 | 114 | 105 | 83 | 95 | 71 |
| Fats and oils | 100 | 64 | 95 | 114 | 114 | 102 | 83 | 96 | 70 |
| Miscellaneous foods | 100 | 71 | 110 | 123 | 110 | 95 | 69 | 77 | 61 |
| Nonalcoholic beverages | 100 | 69 | 98 | 124 | 124 | 100 | 65 | 73 | 57 |
| Food prepared by household on trips | 100 | 49 | 82 | 126 | 121 | 128 | 74 | 108 | 38 |
| **Food away from home** | **100** | **72** | **106** | **122** | **123** | **101** | **59** | **74** | **42** |
| **ALCOHOLIC BEVERAGES** | **100** | **116** | **115** | **121** | **101** | **104** | **54** | **69** | **38** |
| **HOUSING** | **100** | **55** | **104** | **118** | **120** | **100** | **74** | **80** | **68** |
| **Shelter** | **100** | **59** | **109** | **123** | **122** | **95** | **65** | **70** | **60** |
| Owned dwellings | 100 | 13 | 87 | 135 | 137 | 106 | 66 | 76 | 55 |
| Mortgage interest and charges | 100 | 12 | 106 | 157 | 143 | 91 | 29 | 41 | 16 |
| Property taxes | 100 | 15 | 67 | 115 | 129 | 123 | 102 | 109 | 95 |
| Maintenance, repairs, insurance, other | 100 | 14 | 57 | 96 | 131 | 129 | 126 | 136 | 115 |
| Rented dwellings | 100 | 163 | 170 | 105 | 76 | 59 | 58 | 48 | 70 |
| Other lodging | 100 | 53 | 50 | 81 | 172 | 138 | 91 | 116 | 64 |

(continued)

(continued from previous page)

| | | | | | | | aged 65 or older | | |
|---|---|---|---|---|---|---|---|---|---|
| | *total* | *under 25* | *25 to 34* | *35 to 44* | *45 to 54* | *55 to 64* | *total* | *65 to 74* | *75 or older* |
| **Utilities, fuels, public services** | **100** | **49** | **95** | **109** | **119** | **110** | **90** | **100** | **80** |
| Natural gas | 100 | 34 | 88 | 105 | 113 | 121 | 105 | 107 | 102 |
| Electricity | 100 | 47 | 90 | 108 | 119 | 111 | 94 | 104 | 84 |
| Fuel oil and other fuels | 100 | 19 | 64 | 97 | 127 | 108 | 138 | 158 | 116 |
| Telephone services | 100 | 66 | 109 | 112 | 119 | 102 | 72 | 84 | 60 |
| Water and other public services | 100 | 25 | 80 | 110 | 119 | 118 | 105 | 112 | 97 |
| **Household services** | **100** | **27** | **116** | **125** | **91** | **71** | **112** | **69** | **160** |
| Personal services | 100 | 37 | 177 | 155 | 46 | 19 | 96 | 27 | 173 |
| Other household services | 100 | 17 | 58 | 96 | 134 | 121 | 127 | 108 | 147 |
| **Housekeeping supplies** | **100** | **44** | **89** | **121** | **115** | **114** | **85** | **99** | **70** |
| Laundry and cleaning supplies | 100 | 53 | 97 | 123 | 112 | 102 | 84 | 98 | 70 |
| Other household products | 100 | 34 | 84 | 126 | 119 | 118 | 80 | 92 | 66 |
| Postage and stationery | 100 | 56 | 89 | 109 | 111 | 117 | 96 | 113 | 77 |
| **Household furnishings and equipment** | **100** | **59** | **96** | **106** | **132** | **119** | **70** | **90** | **49** |
| Household textiles | 100 | 36 | 89 | 100 | 148 | 97 | 93 | 125 | 59 |
| Furniture | 100 | 78 | 119 | 110 | 122 | 105 | 56 | 73 | 38 |
| Floor coverings | 100 | 25 | 84 | 84 | 118 | 214 | 70 | 73 | 68 |
| Major appliances | 100 | 50 | 96 | 105 | 117 | 107 | 96 | 104 | 86 |
| Small appliances, misc. housewares | 100 | 46 | 80 | 88 | 128 | 141 | 97 | 144 | 48 |
| Miscellaneous household equipment | 100 | 59 | 89 | 109 | 140 | 123 | 63 | 84 | 42 |
| **APPAREL AND SERVICES** | **100** | **68** | **117** | **118** | **117** | **99** | **61** | **71** | **52** |
| **Men and boys** | **100** | **57** | **123** | **123** | **123** | **96** | **52** | **71** | **32** |

*(continued)*

*(continued from previous page)*

| | | | | | | | aged 65 or older | | |
|---|---|---|---|---|---|---|---|---|---|
| | *total* | *under 25* | *25 to 34* | *35 to 44* | *45 to 54* | *55 to 64* | *total* | *65 to 74* | *75 or older* |
| Men, aged 16 or older | 100 | 64 | 118 | 101 | 134 | 111 | 59 | 81 | 37 |
| Boys, aged 2 to 15 | 100 | 31 | 143 | 200 | 85 | 44 | 26 | 37 | 14 |
| **Women and girls** | **100** | **64** | **108** | **117** | **125** | **102** | **64** | **80** | **46** |
| Women, aged 16 or older | 100 | 69 | 106 | 102 | 125 | 114 | 72 | 90 | 53 |
| Girls, aged 2 to 15 | 100 | 42 | 121 | 190 | 121 | 43 | 21 | 32 | 8 |
| **Children under age 2** | **100** | **148** | **207** | **119** | **60** | **61** | **25** | **33** | **16** |
| **Footwear** | **100** | **77** | **123** | **123** | **108** | **102** | **54** | **72** | **36** |
| **Other apparel products and services** | **100** | **67** | **103** | **107** | **117** | **100** | **85** | **57** | **117** |
| **TRANSPORTATION** | **100** | **72** | **102** | **115** | **129** | **105** | **63** | **78** | **46** |
| **Vehicle purchases** | **100** | **87** | **106** | **115** | **125** | **103** | **58** | **73** | **41** |
| Cars and trucks, new | 100 | 53 | 85 | 106 | 128 | 130 | 80 | 102 | 56 |
| Cars and trucks, used | 100 | 120 | 124 | 125 | 121 | 78 | 37 | 46 | 27 |
| Other vehicles | 100 | 78 | 247 | 75 | 142 | 39 | 6 | 8 | – |
| **Gasoline and motor oil** | **100** | **67** | **101** | **119** | **128** | **104** | **61** | **76** | **44** |
| **Other vehicle expenses** | **100** | **56** | **100** | **114** | **137** | **104** | **64** | **76** | **50** |
| Vehicle finance charges | 100 | 65 | 126 | 123 | 135 | 100 | 33 | 46 | 18 |
| Maintenance and repairs | 100 | 61 | 83 | 112 | 134 | 109 | 78 | 90 | 65 |
| Vehicle insurance | 100 | 54 | 93 | 107 | 139 | 106 | 75 | 84 | 64 |
| Vehicle rental, leases, licenses, other | 100 | 46 | 115 | 121 | 139 | 96 | 50 | 67 | 30 |
| **Public transportation** | **100** | **55** | **84** | **104** | **116** | **124** | **97** | **127** | **65** |

*(continued)*

*(continued from previous page)*

| | total | under 25 | 25 to 34 | 35 to 44 | 45 to 54 | 55 to 64 | aged 65 or older total | 65 to 74 | 75 or older |
|---|---|---|---|---|---|---|---|---|---|
| **HEALTH CARE** | **100** | **28** | **60** | **83** | **111** | **125** | **154** | **153** | **156** |
| Health insurance | 100 | 25 | 65 | 81 | 102 | 115 | 168 | 170 | 166 |
| Medical services | 100 | 33 | 63 | 95 | 135 | 135 | 108 | 103 | 113 |
| Drugs | 100 | 26 | 44 | 69 | 99 | 134 | 191 | 188 | 194 |
| Medical supplies | 100 | 33 | 55 | 93 | 108 | 128 | 145 | 137 | 154 |
| **ENTERTAINMENT** | **100** | **61** | **94** | **119** | **125** | **115** | **66** | **83** | **46** |
| Fees and admissions | 100 | 57 | 86 | 115 | 126 | 122 | 73 | 95 | 49 |
| Television, radio, sound equipment | 100 | 80 | 105 | 116 | 122 | 95 | 68 | 78 | 56 |
| Pets, toys, playground equipment | 100 | 53 | 108 | 131 | 121 | 102 | 54 | 72 | 34 |
| Other entertainment supplies, services | 100 | 45 | 77 | 118 | 132 | 143 | 64 | 84 | 41 |
| **PERSONAL CARE PRODUCTS AND SERVICES** | **100** | **62** | **93** | **115** | **116** | **110** | **82** | **91** | **72** |
| **READING** | **100** | **44** | **73** | **99** | **132** | **123** | **103** | **116** | **89** |
| **EDUCATION** | **100** | **201** | **71** | **100** | **177** | **87** | **22** | **26** | **17** |
| **TOBACCO PRODUCTS AND SMOKING SUPPLIES** | **100** | **73** | **98** | **123** | **132** | **110** | **49** | **68** | **29** |
| **MISCELLANEOUS** | **100** | **42** | **84** | **111** | **124** | **117** | **91** | **90** | **91** |
| **CASH CONTRIBUTIONS** | **100** | **16** | **49** | **90** | **120** | **148** | **138** | **142** | **134** |
| **PERSONAL INSURANCE AND PENSIONS** | **100** | **32** | **100** | **130** | **158** | **115** | **29** | **37** | **19** |
| Life and other personal insurance | 100 | 15 | 60 | 106 | 156 | 135 | 85 | 109 | 57 |
| Pensions and Social Security | 100 | 34 | 105 | 133 | 158 | 112 | 21 | 28 | 14 |

*(continued)*

(continued from previous page)

| | | | | | | | aged 65 or older | | |
|---|---|---|---|---|---|---|---|---|---|
| | *total* | *under 25* | *25 to 34* | *35 to 44* | *45 to 54* | *55 to 64* | *total* | *65 to 74* | *75 or older* |
| **PERSONAL TAXES** | **100** | **24** | **85** | **110** | **149** | **185** | **35** | **38** | **32** |
| Federal income taxes | 100 | 22 | 83 | 108 | 149 | 203 | 30 | 32 | 26 |
| State and local income taxes | 100 | 34 | 109 | 129 | 155 | 112 | 27 | 29 | 26 |
| Other taxes | 100 | 4 | 46 | 75 | 135 | 142 | 153 | 164 | 141 |
| **GIFTS** | **100** | **48** | **68** | **88** | **156** | **142** | **82** | **88** | **75** |
| **Food** | **100** | **23** | **48** | **58** | **234** | **166** | **52** | **76** | **27** |
| **Housing** | **100** | **48** | **82** | **94** | **146** | **128** | **82** | **95** | **67** |
| Housekeeping supplies | 100 | 34 | 95 | 127 | 107 | 117 | 78 | 90 | 66 |
| Household textiles | 100 | 18 | 65 | 65 | 159 | 124 | 129 | 194 | 65 |
| Appliances and misc. housewares | 100 | 16 | 59 | 72 | 144 | 181 | 113 | 119 | 103 |
| Major appliances | 100 | 22 | 44 | 67 | 144 | 156 | 111 | 44 | 189 |
| Small appliances and misc. housewares | 100 | 8 | 63 | 71 | 142 | 183 | 104 | 142 | 67 |
| Miscellaneous household equipment | 100 | 64 | 73 | 92 | 126 | 155 | 88 | 120 | 56 |
| Other housing | 100 | 55 | 88 | 94 | 165 | 107 | 66 | 68 | 65 |
| **Apparel and services** | **100** | **56** | **98** | **90** | **128** | **142** | **76** | **84** | **68** |
| Males, aged 2 or older | 100 | 44 | 91 | 72 | 130 | 163 | 94 | 120 | 67 |
| Females, aged 2 or older | 100 | 49 | 65 | 82 | 155 | 139 | 94 | 77 | 111 |
| Children under age 2 | 100 | 70 | 130 | 136 | 91 | 115 | 42 | 52 | 33 |
| All other apparel products and services | 100 | 69 | 129 | 90 | 113 | 142 | 56 | 77 | 35 |
| Jewelry and watches | 100 | 81 | 196 | 93 | 85 | 96 | 41 | 67 | 11 |
| All other apparel products and services | 100 | 56 | 56 | 88 | 144 | 192 | 72 | 88 | 56 |

(continued)

(continued from previous page)

| | total | under 25 | 25 to 34 | 35 to 44 | 45 to 54 | 55 to 64 | aged 65 or older | | |
|---|---|---|---|---|---|---|---|---|---|
| | | | | | | | total | 65 to 74 | 75 or older |
| **Transportation** | **100** | **103** | **48** | **89** | **143** | **148** | **90** | **102** | **78** |
| **Health care** | **100** | **13** | **23** | **60** | **115** | **108** | **225** | **143** | **320** |
| **Entertainment** | **100** | **64** | **76** | **91** | **108** | **145** | **109** | **101** | **117** |
| Toys, games, hobbies, and tricycles | 100 | 31 | 72 | 88 | 128 | 163 | 94 | 131 | 50 |
| Other entertainment | 100 | 80 | 77 | 92 | 98 | 136 | 117 | 86 | 150 |
| **Education** | **100** | **25** | **19** | **76** | **254** | **153** | **47** | **55** | **38** |
| **All other gifts** | **100** | **50** | **85** | **113** | **105** | **147** | **84** | **92** | **76** |

*Note: The Bureau of Labor Statistics uses consumer unit rather than household as the sampling unit in the Consumer Expenditure Survey. For the definition of consumer unit, see Glossary. An index of 100 is the average for all households. An index of 132 means households in the group spend 32 percent more than the average household. An index of 75 means households in the group spend 25 percent less than the average household. (–) means sample is too small to make a reliable estimate.*
*Source: Bureau of Labor Statistics, 1999 Consumer Expenditure Survey; calculations by New Strategist*

## Market Shares by Age of Householder, 1999

*(share of total annual spending accounted for by consumer unit age group, 1999)*

| | *total* | *under 35* | *35 to 54* | *55 or older* |
|---|---|---|---|---|
| **Share of total consumer units** | **100.0%** | **25.4%** | **41.8%** | **32.9%** |
| **Share of total annual spending** | **100.0** | **21.8** | **50.3** | **27.0** |
| **FOOD** | **100.0%** | **23.2%** | **50.1%** | **26.8%** |
| **Food at home** | **100.0** | **22.4** | **49.4** | **28.4** |
| Cereals and bakery products | 100.0 | 21.7 | 50.1 | 28.3 |
| Cereals and cereal products | 100.0 | 23.7 | 50.8 | 25.7 |
| Bakery products | 100.0 | 20.6 | 49.8 | 29.9 |
| Meats, poultry, fish, and eggs | 100.0 | 22.6 | 49.5 | 28.0 |
| Beef | 100.0 | 23.2 | 49.7 | 27.4 |
| Pork | 100.0 | 21.9 | 49.2 | 28.9 |
| Other meats | 100.0 | 22.2 | 49.7 | 28.3 |
| Poultry | 100.0 | 23.9 | 49.5 | 26.9 |
| Fish and seafood | 100.0 | 21.5 | 50.2 | 28.8 |
| Eggs | 100.0 | 21.7 | 48.6 | 30.9 |
| Dairy products | 100.0 | 22.4 | 49.8 | 27.0 |
| Fresh milk and cream | 100.0 | 22.9 | 49.7 | 27.5 |
| Other dairy products | 100.0 | 22.1 | 49.9 | 28.3 |
| Fruits and vegetables | 100.0 | 21.2 | 47.4 | 31.5 |
| Fresh fruits | 100.0 | 19.8 | 47.5 | 33.2 |
| Fresh vegetables | 100.0 | 21.5 | 46.0 | 32.3 |
| Processed fruits | 100.0 | 21.7 | 48.5 | 29.0 |
| Processed vegetables | 100.0 | 22.3 | 48.1 | 29.3 |
| Other food at home | 100.0 | 23.2 | 49.9 | 27.1 |
| Sugar and other sweets | 100.0 | 20.5 | 48.9 | 30.1 |
| Fats and oils | 100.0 | 21.8 | 47.7 | 29.8 |
| Miscellaneous foods | 100.0 | 25.0 | 48.0 | 26.0 |
| Nonalcoholic beverages | 100.0 | 22.6 | 51.0 | 25.8 |
| Food prepared by household on trips | 100.0 | 18.3 | 51.5 | 31.2 |
| **Food away from home** | **100.0** | **24.4** | **51.1** | **24.6** |
| **ALCOHOLIC BEVERAGES** | **100.0** | **29.2** | **46.6** | **24.0** |
| **HOUSING** | **100.0** | **22.6** | **49.7** | **27.7** |
| **Shelter** | **100.0** | **23.8** | **51.0** | **25.2** |

*(continued)*

*(continued from previous page)*

| | *total* | *under 35* | *35 to 54* | *55 or older* |
|---|---|---|---|---|
| Owned dwellings | 100.0% | 16.5% | 56.8% | 26.7% |
| Mortgage interest and charges | 100.0 | 19.8 | 62.8 | 17.4 |
| Property taxes | 100.0 | 13.1 | 50.8 | 36.2 |
| Maintenance, repairs, insurance, other | 100.0 | 11.2 | 46.8 | 41.9 |
| Rented dwellings | 100.0 | 42.5 | 38.1 | 19.3 |
| Other lodging | 100.0 | 12.9 | 51.3 | 35.9 |
| **Utilities, fuels, public services** | **100.0** | **20.6** | **47.3** | **32.1** |
| Natural gas | 100.0 | 18.3 | 45.3 | 36.6 |
| Electricity | 100.0 | 19.6 | 47.3 | 33.1 |
| Fuel oil and other fuels | 100.0 | 12.7 | 46.4 | 41.6 |
| Telephone services | 100.0 | 24.4 | 48.1 | 27.6 |
| Water and other public services | 100.0 | 16.2 | 47.6 | 36.0 |
| **Household services** | **100.0** | **22.7** | **45.6** | **31.7** |
| Personal services | 100.0 | 34.4 | 43.7 | 21.9 |
| Other household services | 100.0 | 11.7 | 47.4 | 41.0 |
| **Housekeeping supplies** | **100.0** | **19.1** | **49.5** | **31.6** |
| Laundry and cleaning supplies | 100.0 | 21.2 | 49.2 | 30.0 |
| Other household products | 100.0 | 17.6 | 51.3 | 31.1 |
| Postage and stationery | 100.0 | 20.1 | 46.0 | 34.3 |
| **Household furnishings and equipment** | **100.0** | **21.6** | **49.3** | **29.2** |
| Household textiles | 100.0 | 18.5 | 51.1 | 31.1 |
| Furniture | 100.0 | 27.1 | 48.4 | 24.6 |
| Floor coverings | 100.0 | 16.9 | 41.7 | 41.2 |
| Major appliances | 100.0 | 20.9 | 46.2 | 32.9 |
| Small appliances, miscellaneous housewares | 100.0 | 17.8 | 44.6 | 37.5 |
| Miscellaneous household equipment | 100.0 | 20.2 | 51.5 | 28.4 |
| **APPAREL AND SERVICES** | **100.0** | **26.1** | **49.1** | **24.9** |
| **Men and boys** | **100.0** | **26.2** | **51.3** | **22.7** |
| Men, aged 16 or older | 100.0 | 25.8 | 48.4 | 26.0 |
| Boys, aged 2 to 15 | 100.0 | 27.8 | 61.4 | 10.8 |
| **Women and girls** | **100.0** | **24.1** | **50.3** | **25.8** |
| Women, aged 16 or older | 100.0 | 24.0 | 47.2 | 28.9 |
| Girls, aged 2 to 15 | 100.0 | 24.8 | 66.1 | 9.6 |
| **Children under age 2** | **100.0** | **48.1** | **38.4** | **12.8** |
| **Footwear** | **100.0** | **27.8** | **48.5** | **23.8** |
| **Other apparel products and services** | **100.0** | **23.4** | **46.7** | **29.8** |

*(continued)*

*(continued from previous page)*

| | total | under 35 | 35 to 54 | 55 or older |
|---|---|---|---|---|
| **TRANSPORTATION** | **100.0%** | **23.6%** | **50.6%** | **25.8%** |
| **Vehicle purchases** | **100.0** | **25.4** | **49.9** | **24.7** |
| Cars and trucks, new | 100.0 | 19.0 | 48.4 | 32.6 |
| Cars and trucks, used | 100.0 | 31.1 | 51.6 | 17.3 |
| Other vehicles | 100.0 | 49.9 | 44.2 | 6.0 |
| **Gasoline and motor oil** | **100.0** | **23.1** | **51.5** | **25.4** |
| **Other vehicle expenses** | **100.0** | **21.0** | **51.0** | **26.1** |
| Vehicle finance charges | 100.0 | 27.3 | 53.7 | 19.2 |
| Maintenance and repairs | 100.0 | 19.4 | 51.0 | 29.6 |
| Vehicle insurance | 100.0 | 20.7 | 50.8 | 28.6 |
| Vehicle rental, leases, licenses, other | 100.0 | 23.9 | 53.9 | 22.2 |
| **Public transportation** | **100.0** | **19.2** | **45.6** | **35.4** |
| **HEALTH CARE** | **100.0** | **12.8** | **40.2** | **47.0** |
| Health insurance | 100.0 | 13.4 | 37.9 | 48.7 |
| Medical services | 100.0 | 13.7 | 47.5 | 38.8 |
| Drugs | 100.0 | 9.8 | 34.6 | 55.6 |
| Medical supplies | 100.0 | 12.3 | 41.7 | 45.5 |
| **ENTERTAINMENT** | **100.0** | **21.3** | **50.0** | **27.8** |
| Fees and admissions | 100.0 | 19.6 | 50.2 | 30.2 |
| Television, radio, sound equipment | 100.0 | 24.6 | 49.7 | 25.7 |
| Pets, toys, playground equipment | 100.0 | 23.3 | 52.8 | 23.8 |
| Other entertainment supplies, services | 100.0 | 17.2 | 52.0 | 30.0 |
| **PERSONAL CARE PRODUCTS AND SERVICES** | **100.0** | **21.3** | **48.4** | **30.4** |
| **READING** | **100.0** | **16.3** | **47.7** | **36.2** |
| **EDUCATION** | **100.0** | **27.9** | **56.7** | **15.4** |
| **TOBACCO PRODUCTS AND SMOKING SUPPLIES** | **100.0** | **23.1** | **53.1** | **23.8** |
| **MISCELLANEOUS** | **100.0** | **18.1** | **48.8** | **33.2** |
| **CASH CONTRIBUTIONS** | **100.0** | **9.0** | **43.4** | **46.6** |
| **PERSONAL INSURANCE AND PENSIONS** | **100.0** | **20.2** | **59.5** | **20.2** |
| Life and other personal insurance | 100.0 | 11.9 | 54.0 | 34.2 |
| Pensions and Social Security | 100.0 | 21.3 | 60.3 | 18.4 |

*(continued)*

*(continued from previous page)*

| | total | under 35 | 35 to 54 | 55 or older |
|---|---|---|---|---|
| **PERSONAL TAXES** | **100.0%** | **16.0%** | **53.7%** | **30.3%** |
| Federal income taxes | 100.0 | 16.4 | 53.1 | 31.6 |
| State and local income taxes | 100.0 | 21.0 | 58.0 | 19.7 |
| Other taxes | 100.0 | 8.5 | 43.0 | 48.9 |
| **GIFTS** | **100.0** | **15.7** | **49.9** | **34.4** |
| **Food** | **100.0** | **10.3** | **58.1** | **31.4** |
| **Housing** | **100.0** | **18.1** | **49.2** | **32.7** |
| Housekeeping supplies | 100.0 | 19.5 | 49.2 | 30.6 |
| Household textiles | 100.0 | 12.9 | 45.2 | 41.8 |
| Appliances and misc. housewares | 100.0 | 11.8 | 43.9 | 45.6 |
| Major appliances | 100.0 | 9.6 | 42.8 | 42.1 |
| Small appliances and misc. houseware | 100.0 | 11.8 | 43.2 | 44.2 |
| Miscellaneous household equipment | 100.0 | 17.8 | 45.0 | 37.3 |
| Other housing | 100.0 | 19.9 | 53.1 | 26.9 |
| **Apparel and services** | **100.0** | **21.7** | **45.0** | **33.3** |
| Males, aged 2 or older | 100.0 | 19.5 | 41.2 | 39.7 |
| Females, aged 2 or older | 100.0 | 15.3 | 48.2 | 36.7 |
| Children under age 2 | 100.0 | 28.5 | 48.2 | 23.1 |
| All other apparel products and services | 100.0 | 28.2 | 42.2 | 29.2 |
| Jewelry and watches | 100.0 | 41.1 | 37.3 | 20.4 |
| All other apparel products and services | 100.0 | 14.2 | 47.6 | 38.8 |
| **Transportation** | **100.0** | **16.3** | **47.5** | **36.9** |
| **Health care** | **100.0** | **4.0** | **35.7** | **59.2** |
| **Entertainment** | **100.0** | **18.3** | **41.3** | **40.4** |
| Toys, games, hobbies, and tricycles | 100.0 | 15.2 | 44.4 | 39.5 |
| Other entertainment | 100.0 | 19.8 | 39.8 | 40.8 |
| **Education** | **100.0** | **5.2** | **66.1** | **28.8** |
| **All other gifts** | **100.0** | **18.8** | **45.7** | **35.6** |

*Note: The Bureau of Labor Statistics uses consumer unit rather than household as the sampling unit in the Consumer Expenditure Survey. For the definition of consumer unit, see Glossary. Numbers may not add to total because of rounding.*
*Source: Bureau of Labor Statistics, 1999 Consumer Expenditure Survey; calculations by New Strategist*

# Spending Rises with Income

## Households with incomes of $70,000 or more spend nearly twice as much as the average household.

Households with incomes of $70,000 or more spent an average of $76,812 in 1999, 96 percent more than the average household. The most affluent households are also the largest, housing an average of 3.1 people, according to the Bureau of Labor Statistics' Consumer Expenditure Survey. High-income households spend more than average on nearly every category of goods and services.

The indexed spending table in this section shows spending by household income in comparison to what the average household spends. An index of 100 means a household spends an average amount on an item. An index above 100 means households in the income group spend more than average on the item, while an index below 100 reveals below-average spending. A look at the table shows that spending is below average on most items for households with incomes below $30,000, close to the average on most items for households with incomes between $30,000 and $50,000, and above average in most categories for households with incomes of $50,000 or more.

There are some exceptions, however. Households with incomes below $30,000 spend close to or more than average on rent, drugs, and tobacco. Households with incomes of $70,000 or more spend 36 percent less than average on rent and only an average amount on tobacco. The most affluent households spend at least twice the average on a variety of items such as alcoholic beverages, "other" lodging (college dorm rooms as well as hotels and motels), new cars and trucks, entertainment, and education.

The market share table in this section shows how much of total spending by category is accounted for by four broad income groups: households with annual incomes below $20,000, between $20,000 and $40,000, between $40,000 and $70,000, and $70,000 or more. While 33 percent of all households have annual incomes below $20,000, these households account for only 16 percent of spending. In contrast, while households with incomes of $70,000 or more are just 19 percent of households, they account for a much larger 36 percent of spending. The share of spending accounted for by the most affluent households is above

40 percent on a variety of items including mortgage interest, "other" lodging, household services, fees and admissions to entertainment events, education, and personal insurance and pensions.

♦ Spending patterns by income group will remain unchanged because of stability in demographic characteristics of those with low or high incomes. Young adults and the elderly will continue to dominate low-income households, and middle-aged two-earner couples will continue to dominate high-income households.

**High-income households account for a disproportionately large share of spending**

*(share of spending accounted for by consumer unit income group, 1999)*

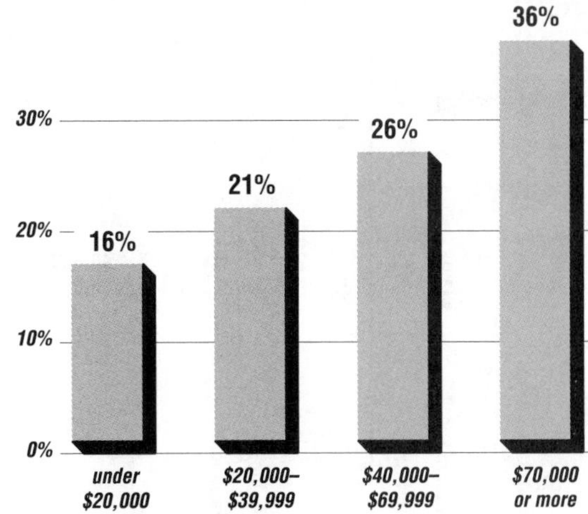

## Spending by Household Income, 1999

*(average annual spending of consumer units (CU's) by product and service category and household income, 1999; data shown for complete income reporters only)*

| | *total complete reporters* | *Under $10,000* | *$10,000 – $19,999* | *$20,000 – $29,999* | *$30,000 – $39,999* | *$40,000 – $49,999* | *$50,000 – $69,999* | *$70,000 or more* |
|---|---|---|---|---|---|---|---|---|
| **Number of consumer units in (000s)** | **81,692** | **11,497** | **15,634** | **11,560** | **9,453** | **7,381** | **10,999** | **15,168** |
| **Average number of persons per CU** | **2.5** | **1.8** | **2.1** | **2.5** | **2.5** | **2.6** | **2.9** | **3.1** |
| **Average before-tax income** | **$43,951** | **$5,592** | **$14,563** | **$24,467** | **$34,353** | **$44,321** | **$58,473** | **$113,441** |
| **Average annual spending** | **39,174** | **15,976** | **21,800** | **28,963** | **35,077** | **40,868** | **49,615** | **76,812** |
| **FOOD** | **$5,216** | **$2,677** | **$3,321** | **$4,322** | **$5,060** | **$5,823** | **$6,527** | **$8,725** |
| **Food at home** | **3,010** | **1,813** | **2,229** | **2,697** | **2,918** | **3,457** | **3,724** | **4,328** |
| Cereals and bakery products | 461 | 291 | 341 | 395 | 440 | 518 | 581 | 667 |
| Cereals and cereal products | 163 | 111 | 126 | 140 | 170 | 193 | 195 | 217 |
| Bakery products | 298 | 180 | 216 | 255 | 271 | 325 | 387 | 450 |
| Meats, poultry, fish, and eggs | 758 | 502 | 591 | 709 | 742 | 854 | 913 | 1,023 |
| Beef | 219 | 138 | 162 | 192 | 212 | 261 | 274 | 308 |
| Pork | 157 | 103 | 127 | 169 | 156 | 187 | 186 | 187 |
| Other meats | 99 | 63 | 85 | 101 | 94 | 104 | 124 | 125 |
| Poultry | 140 | 96 | 102 | 128 | 133 | 158 | 167 | 199 |
| Fish and seafood | 109 | 74 | 85 | 86 | 112 | 112 | 125 | 165 |
| Eggs | 33 | 26 | 30 | 32 | 36 | 33 | 36 | 39 |

*(continued)*

*(continued from previous page)*

| | *total complete reporters* | *Under $10,000* | *$10,000 – $19,999* | *$20,000 – $29,999* | *$30,000 – $39,999* | *$40,000 – $49,999* | *$50,000 – $69,999* | *$70,000 or more* |
|---|---|---|---|---|---|---|---|---|
| Dairy products | $338 | $195 | $241 | $296 | $334 | $383 | $428 | $499 |
| Fresh milk and cream | 128 | 84 | 99 | 113 | 140 | 137 | 162 | 170 |
| Other dairy products | 210 | 111 | 142 | 184 | 194 | 245 | 266 | 329 |
| Fruits and vegetables | 515 | 312 | 396 | 471 | 486 | 591 | 598 | 753 |
| Fresh fruits | 158 | 97 | 120 | 144 | 144 | 182 | 177 | 239 |
| Fresh vegetables | 153 | 92 | 118 | 141 | 149 | 172 | 176 | 224 |
| Processed fruits | 116 | 67 | 89 | 106 | 108 | 129 | 141 | 172 |
| Processed vegetables | 88 | 56 | 69 | 80 | 85 | 109 | 104 | 119 |
| Other food at home | 938 | 511 | 660 | 825 | 916 | 1,112 | 1,204 | 1,386 |
| Sugar and other sweets | 119 | 72 | 89 | 109 | 112 | 129 | 159 | 165 |
| Fats and oils | 85 | 53 | 69 | 82 | 88 | 107 | 95 | 107 |
| Miscellaneous foods | 438 | 221 | 296 | 378 | 431 | 532 | 567 | 668 |
| Nonalcoholic beverages | 254 | 148 | 187 | 226 | 250 | 289 | 333 | 354 |
| Food prepared by household on trips | 43 | 18 | 19 | 30 | 36 | 56 | 50 | 91 |
| **Food away from home** | **2,206** | **864** | **1,092** | **1,625** | **2,142** | **2,365** | **2,803** | **4,398** |
| **ALCOHOLIC BEVERAGES** | **348** | **158** | **191** | **267** | **292** | **345** | **443** | **696** |
| **HOUSING** | **12,315** | **5,962** | **7,652** | **9,423** | **10,862** | **12,644** | **14,873** | **23,066** |
| **Shelter** | **7,062** | **3,476** | **4,277** | **5,309** | **6,323** | **7,405** | **8,306** | **13,380** |

*(continued)*

(continued from previous page)

| | total complete reporters | Under $10,000 | $10,000 – $19,999 | $20,000 – $29,999 | $30,000 – $39,999 | $40,000 – $49,999 | $50,000 – $69,999 | $70,000 or more |
|---|---|---|---|---|---|---|---|---|
| Owned dwellings | $4,507 | $1,207 | $1,811 | $2,749 | $3,556 | $4,376 | $5,945 | $10,739 |
| Mortgage interest and charges | 2,517 | 436 | 585 | 1,207 | 1,958 | 2,680 | 3,631 | 6,546 |
| Property taxes | 1,080 | 414 | 641 | 770 | 851 | 930 | 1,311 | 2,324 |
| Maintenance, repairs, insurance, other | 909 | 358 | 585 | 772 | 747 | 767 | 1,002 | 1,869 |
| Rented dwellings | 2,081 | 2,098 | 2,285 | 2,300 | 2,469 | 2,674 | 1,850 | 1,325 |
| Other lodging | 475 | 171 | 179 | 260 | 297 | 355 | 511 | 1,315 |
| **Utilities, fuels, public services** | **2,368** | **1,439** | **1,878** | **2,159** | **2,297** | **2,491** | **2,795** | **3,411** |
| Natural gas | 262 | 151 | 214 | 232 | 241 | 270 | 302 | 398 |
| Electricity | 888 | 570 | 744 | 840 | 860 | 922 | 1,043 | 1,202 |
| Fuel oil and other fuels | 77 | 46 | 67 | 76 | 85 | 76 | 76 | 106 |
| Telephone services | 851 | 528 | 639 | 752 | 850 | 914 | 1,018 | 1,241 |
| Water and other public services | 290 | 144 | 214 | 258 | 261 | 309 | 356 | 463 |
| **Household services** | **717** | **237** | **364** | **377** | **385** | **624** | **801** | **1,898** |
| Personal services | 357 | 106 | 174 | 164 | 178 | 353 | 441 | 933 |
| Other household services | 361 | 130 | 190 | 213 | 207 | 271 | 359 | 965 |
| **Housekeeping supplies** | **549** | **251** | **313** | **451** | **515** | **575** | **784** | **945** |
| Laundry and cleaning supplies | 131 | 78 | 100 | 131 | 119 | 143 | 168 | 180 |
| Other household products | 278 | 115 | 134 | 213 | 255 | 292 | 424 | 509 |
| Postage and stationery | 140 | 58 | 78 | 107 | 141 | 141 | 191 | 256 |

(continued)

(continued from previous page)

| | total complete reporters | Under $10,000 | $10,000 – $19,999 | $20,000 – $29,999 | $30,000 – $39,999 | $40,000 – $49,999 | $50,000 – $69,999 | $70,000 or more |
|---|---|---|---|---|---|---|---|---|
| **Household furnishings and equipment** | **$1,619** | **$560** | **$821** | **$1,127** | **$1,343** | **$1,549** | **$2,188** | **$3,431** |
| Household textiles | 125 | 45 | 69 | 115 | 106 | 116 | 169 | 236 |
| Furniture | 391 | 143 | 198 | 266 | 364 | 304 | 515 | 840 |
| Floor coverings | 46 | – | 24 | 20 | 34 | 53 | 50 | 106 |
| Major appliances | 190 | 75 | 127 | 174 | 158 | 209 | 228 | 340 |
| Small appliances, misc. housewares | 114 | 38 | 48 | 78 | 93 | 96 | 183 | 246 |
| Miscellaneous household equipment | 752 | 234 | 354 | 474 | 587 | 771 | 1,043 | 1,664 |
| **APPAREL AND SERVICES** | **1,871** | **799** | **1,100** | **1,553** | **1,904** | **1,677** | **2,139** | **3,625** |
| **Men and boys** | **451** | **157** | **182** | **353** | **513** | **413** | **554** | **943** |
| Men, aged 16 or older | 352 | 105 | 121 | 270 | 407 | 323 | 411 | 786 |
| Boys, aged 2 to 15 | 99 | 51 | 61 | 84 | 105 | 90 | 143 | 158 |
| **Women and girls** | **707** | **342** | **519** | **566** | **680** | **603** | **808** | **1,289** |
| Women, aged 16 or older | 594 | 305 | 448 | 451 | 584 | 511 | 662 | 1,080 |
| Girls, aged 2 to 15 | 113 | 37 | 70 | 115 | 97 | 92 | 146 | 208 |
| **Children under age 2** | **74** | **42** | **35** | **64** | **74** | **107** | **87** | **125** |
| **Footwear** | **327** | **140** | **222** | **354** | **425** | **299** | **375** | **475** |
| **Other apparel products and services** | **311** | **119** | **142** | **214** | **212** | **255** | **315** | **793** |
| **TRANSPORTATION** | **7,222** | **2,538** | **4,090** | **5,485** | **6,973** | **8,352** | **9,380** | **13,363** |
| **Vehicle purchases** | **3,407** | **1,119** | **1,937** | **2,500** | **3,239** | **4,138** | **4,317** | **6,437** |

(continued)

*(continued from previous page)*

| | total complete reporters | Under $10,000 | $10,000 – $19,999 | $20,000 – $29,999 | $30,000 – $39,999 | $40,000 – $49,999 | $50,000 – $69,999 | $70,000 or more |
|---|---|---|---|---|---|---|---|---|
| Cars and trucks, new | $1,616 | $459 | $871 | $996 | $1,237 | $1,769 | $1,781 | $3,773 |
| Cars and trucks, used | 1,756 | 659 | 1,060 | 1,490 | 1,916 | 2,326 | 2,503 | 2,589 |
| Other vehicles | 35 | – | 6 | 14 | 86 | 43 | 33 | 75 |
| **Gasoline and motor oil** | **1,071** | **468** | **663** | **928** | **1,124** | **1,246** | **1,451** | **1,666** |
| **Other vehicle expenses** | **2,335** | **790** | **1,280** | **1,781** | **2,296** | **2,610** | **3,145** | **4,322** |
| Vehicle finance charges | 329 | 84 | 128 | 237 | 360 | 414 | 533 | 585 |
| Maintenance and repairs | 711 | 285 | 494 | 576 | 705 | 811 | 870 | 1,200 |
| Vehicle insurance | 781 | 279 | 473 | 677 | 798 | 870 | 1,050 | 1,308 |
| Vehicle rental, leases, licenses, other | 514 | 142 | 184 | 291 | 433 | 514 | 692 | 1,229 |
| **Public transportation** | **408** | **162** | **211** | **276** | **314** | **358** | **468** | **939** |
| **HEALTH CARE** | **2,042** | **1,085** | **1,766** | **2,019** | **1,970** | **2,023** | **2,391** | **2,870** |
| Health insurance | 945 | 515 | 840 | 969 | 965 | 1,032 | 1,065 | 1,220 |
| Medical services | 579 | 258 | 362 | 517 | 552 | 522 | 748 | 1,016 |
| Drugs | 398 | 259 | 464 | 430 | 351 | 331 | 419 | 459 |
| Medical supplies | 119 | 53 | 101 | 102 | 102 | 138 | 159 | 174 |
| **ENTERTAINMENT** | **1,978** | **733** | **990** | **1,323** | **1,682** | **1,882** | **2,754** | **4,121** |
| Fees and admissions | 482 | 148 | 185 | 262 | 335 | 489 | 634 | 1,189 |
| Television, radios, sound equipment | 632 | 317 | 428 | 511 | 607 | 629 | 862 | 1,023 |
| Pets, toys, playground equipment | 368 | 137 | 206 | 263 | 284 | 431 | 513 | 710 |
| Other entertainment supplies, services | 496 | 131 | 171 | 288 | 456 | 333 | 746 | 1,199 |

*(continued)*

*(continued from previous page)*

| | total complete reporters | Under $10,000 | $10,000 – $19,999 | $20,000 – $29,999 | $30,000 – $39,999 | $40,000 – $49,999 | $50,000 – $69,999 | $70,000 or more |
|---|---|---|---|---|---|---|---|---|
| **PERSONAL CARE PRODUCTS AND SERVICES** | **$447** | **$224** | **$247** | **$385** | **$452** | **$500** | **$525** | **$794** |
| **READING** | **169** | **68** | **104** | **132** | **147** | **166** | **209** | **330** |
| **EDUCATION** | **593** | **527** | **262** | **309** | **347** | **425** | **602** | **1,430** |
| **TOBACCO PRODUCTS AND SMOKING SUPPLIES** | **315** | **235** | **274** | **305** | **336** | **376** | **391** | **328** |
| **MISCELLANEOUS** | **959** | **367** | **470** | **742** | **890** | **986** | **1,107** | **2,004** |
| **CASH CONTRIBUTIONS** | **1,348** | **264** | **553** | **850** | **1,070** | **1,121** | **1,852** | **3,288** |
| **PERSONAL INSURANCE AND PENSIONS** | **4,352** | **338** | **780** | **1,849** | **3,092** | **4,548** | **6,421** | **12,172** |
| Life and other personal insurance | 408 | 126 | 168 | 264 | 342 | 349 | 517 | 970 |
| Pensions and Social Security | 3,944 | 213 | 611 | 1,585 | 2,750 | 4,199 | 5,904 | 11,202 |
| **PERSONAL TAXES** | **3,588** | **172** | **268** | **980** | **1,895** | **2,916** | **4,401** | **12,380** |
| Federal income taxes | 2,802 | 102 | 115 | 637 | 1,392 | 2,157 | 3,303 | 10,096 |
| State and local income taxes | 616 | 17 | 60 | 198 | 366 | 603 | 906 | 1,912 |
| Other taxes | 170 | 53 | 94 | 144 | 137 | 156 | 192 | 372 |
| **GIFTS** | **1,143** | **481** | **605** | **824** | **935** | **850** | **1,289** | **2,619** |
| **Food** | **86** | **23** | **18** | **32** | **65** | **50** | **78** | **282** |
| **Housing** | **306** | **130** | **180** | **220** | **243** | **227** | **358** | **678** |
| Housekeeping supplies | 47 | 14 | 23 | 41 | 46 | 31 | 77 | 88 |

*(continued)*

*(continued from previous page)*

| | total complete reporters | Under $10,000 | $10,000 – $19,999 | $20,000 – $29,999 | $30,000 – $39,999 | $40,000 – $49,999 | $50,000 – $69,999 | $70,000 or more |
|---|---|---|---|---|---|---|---|---|
| Household textiles | $18 | $8 | $13 | $10 | $17 | $20 | $17 | $39 |
| Appliances and misc. housewares | 36 | 3 | 20 | 26 | 33 | 38 | 42 | 80 |
| Major appliances | 9 | 1 | 14 | 6 | 4 | 22 | 8 | 9 |
| Small appliances and misc. housewares | 27 | 2 | 6 | 20 | 29 | 16 | 33 | 71 |
| Miscellaneous household equipment | 72 | 22 | 37 | 66 | 55 | 56 | 79 | 167 |
| Other housing | 133 | 81 | 88 | 77 | 92 | 82 | 144 | 304 |
| **Apparel and services** | **230** | **117** | **152** | **202** | **220** | **202** | **259** | **419** |
| Males, aged 2 or older | 59 | 29 | 33 | 48 | 59 | 60 | 61 | 118 |
| Females, aged 2 or older | 81 | 34 | 63 | 72 | 70 | 46 | 91 | 158 |
| Children under age 2 | 36 | 21 | 16 | 34 | 33 | 35 | 41 | 69 |
| All other apparel products and services | 54 | 33 | 39 | 49 | 59 | 62 | 66 | 74 |
| Jewelry and watches | 28 | 14 | 14 | 35 | 25 | 38 | 39 | 35 |
| All other apparel products and services | 26 | 18 | 25 | 14 | 33 | 25 | 28 | 40 |
| **Transportation** | **68** | **41** | **31** | **83** | **34** | **43** | **87** | **134** |
| **Health care** | **46** | **31** | **46** | **45** | **37** | **17** | **35** | **85** |
| **Entertainment** | **107** | **32** | **64** | **75** | **79** | **102** | **144** | **225** |
| Toys, games, hobbies, and tricycles | 34 | 12 | 18 | 32 | 28 | 41 | 52 | 55 |
| Other entertainment | 73 | 19 | 46 | 43 | 51 | 61 | 92 | 170 |
| **Education** | **153** | **43** | **32** | **55** | **72** | **63** | **182** | **509** |
| **All other gifts** | **148** | **65** | **81** | **111** | **185** | **146** | **146** | **286** |

*Note: The Bureau of Labor Statistics uses consumer unit rather than household as the sampling unit in the Consumer Expenditure Survey. For the definition of consumer unit, see Glossary. Gift spending is also included in the preceding product and service categories.*
*Source: Bureau of Labor Statistics, 1999 Consumer Expenditure Survey; Internet site <www.bls.gov/csxstnd.htm>; calculations by New Strategist*

## Indexed Spending by Household Income, 1999

*(indexed average annual spending of consumer units by product and service category and household income of consumer unit reference person, 1999)*

| | *total complete reporters* | *Under $10,000* | *$10,000 – $19,999* | *$20,000 – $29,999* | *$30,000 – $39,999* | *$40,000 – $49,999* | *$50,000 – $69,999* | *$70,000 or more* |
|---|---|---|---|---|---|---|---|---|
| **Number of consumer units (in 000s)** | **81,692** | **11,497** | **15,634** | **11,560** | **9,453** | **7,381** | **10,999** | **15,168** |
| **Indexed average before-tax income** | **100** | **13** | **33** | **56** | **78** | **101** | **133** | **258** |
| **Indexed average annual spending** | **100** | **41** | **56** | **74** | **90** | **104** | **127** | **196** |
| **FOOD** | **100** | **51** | **64** | **83** | **97** | **112** | **125** | **167** |
| **Food at home** | **100** | **60** | **74** | **90** | **97** | **115** | **124** | **144** |
| Cereals and bakery products | 100 | 63 | 74 | 86 | 95 | 112 | 126 | 145 |
| Cereals and cereal products | 100 | 68 | 77 | 86 | 104 | 118 | 120 | 133 |
| Bakery products | 100 | 60 | 72 | 86 | 91 | 109 | 130 | 151 |
| Meats, poultry, fish, and eggs | 100 | 66 | 78 | 94 | 98 | 113 | 120 | 135 |
| Beef | 100 | 63 | 74 | 88 | 97 | 119 | 125 | 141 |
| Pork | 100 | 66 | 81 | 108 | 99 | 119 | 118 | 119 |
| Other meats | 100 | 64 | 86 | 102 | 95 | 105 | 125 | 126 |
| Poultry | 100 | 69 | 73 | 91 | 95 | 113 | 119 | 142 |
| Fish and seafood | 100 | 68 | 78 | 79 | 103 | 103 | 115 | 151 |
| Eggs | 100 | 79 | 92 | 97 | 109 | 100 | 109 | 118 |

*(continued)*

*(continued from previous page)*

| | total complete reporters | Under $10,000 | $10,000 – $19,999 | $20,000 – $29,999 | $30,000 – $39,999 | $40,000 – $49,999 | $50,000 – $69,999 | $70,000 or more |
|---|---|---|---|---|---|---|---|---|
| Dairy products | 100 | 58 | 71 | 88 | 99 | 113 | 127 | 148 |
| Fresh milk and cream | 100 | 65 | 77 | 88 | 109 | 107 | 127 | 133 |
| Other dairy products | 100 | 53 | 68 | 88 | 92 | 117 | 127 | 157 |
| Fruits and vegetables | 100 | 61 | 77 | 91 | 94 | 115 | 116 | 146 |
| Fresh fruits | 100 | 61 | 76 | 91 | 91 | 115 | 112 | 151 |
| Fresh vegetables | 100 | 60 | 77 | 92 | 97 | 112 | 115 | 146 |
| Processed fruits | 100 | 58 | 77 | 91 | 93 | 111 | 122 | 148 |
| Processed vegetables | 100 | 64 | 78 | 91 | 97 | 124 | 118 | 135 |
| Other food at home | 100 | 55 | 70 | 88 | 98 | 119 | 128 | 148 |
| Sugar and other sweets | 100 | 61 | 75 | 92 | 94 | 108 | 134 | 139 |
| Fats and oils | 100 | 63 | 81 | 96 | 104 | 126 | 112 | 126 |
| Miscellaneous foods | 100 | 50 | 68 | 86 | 98 | 121 | 129 | 153 |
| Nonalcoholic beverages | 100 | 58 | 74 | 89 | 98 | 114 | 131 | 139 |
| Food prepared by household on trips | 100 | 42 | 43 | 70 | 84 | 130 | 116 | 212 |
| **Food away from home** | **100** | **39** | **50** | **74** | **97** | **107** | **127** | **199** |
| **ALCOHOLIC BEVERAGES** | **100** | **45** | **55** | **77** | **84** | **99** | **127** | **200** |
| **HOUSING** | **100** | **48** | **62** | **77** | **88** | **103** | **121** | **187** |
| **Shelter** | **100** | **49** | **61** | **75** | **90** | **105** | **118** | **189** |

*(continued)*

*(continued from previous page)*

| | total complete reporters | Under $10,000 | $10,000 – $19,999 | $20,000 – $29,999 | $30,000 – $39,999 | $40,000 – $49,999 | $50,000 – $69,999 | $70,000 or more |
|---|---|---|---|---|---|---|---|---|
| Owned dwellings | 100 | 27 | 40 | 61 | 79 | 97 | 132 | 238 |
| Mortgage interest and charges | 100 | 17 | 23 | 48 | 78 | 106 | 144 | 260 |
| Property taxes | 100 | 38 | 59 | 71 | 79 | 86 | 121 | 215 |
| Maintenance, repairs, insurance, other | 100 | 39 | 64 | 85 | 82 | 84 | 110 | 206 |
| Rented dwellings | 100 | 101 | 110 | 111 | 119 | 128 | 89 | 64 |
| Other lodging | 100 | 36 | 38 | 55 | 63 | 75 | 108 | 277 |
| **Utilities, fuels, public services** | **100** | **61** | **79** | **91** | **97** | **105** | **118** | **144** |
| Natural gas | 100 | 58 | 82 | 89 | 92 | 103 | 115 | 152 |
| Electricity | 100 | 64 | 84 | 95 | 97 | 104 | 117 | 135 |
| Fuel oil and other fuels | 100 | 60 | 87 | 99 | 110 | 99 | 99 | 138 |
| Telephone services | 100 | 62 | 75 | 88 | 100 | 107 | 120 | 146 |
| Water and other public services | 100 | 50 | 74 | 89 | 90 | 107 | 123 | 160 |
| **Household services** | **100** | **33** | **51** | **53** | **54** | **87** | **112** | **265** |
| Personal services | 100 | 30 | 49 | 46 | 50 | 99 | 124 | 261 |
| Other household services | 100 | 36 | 53 | 59 | 57 | 75 | 99 | 267 |
| **Housekeeping supplies** | **100** | **46** | **57** | **82** | **94** | **105** | **143** | **172** |
| Laundry and cleaning supplies | 100 | 60 | 76 | 100 | 91 | 109 | 128 | 137 |
| Other household products | 100 | 41 | 48 | 77 | 92 | 105 | 153 | 183 |
| Postage and stationery | 100 | 42 | 56 | 76 | 101 | 101 | 136 | 183 |

*(continued)*

(continued from previous page)

| | total complete reporters | Under $10,000 | $10,000 – $19,999 | $20,000 – $29,999 | $30,000 – $39,999 | $40,000 – $49,999 | $50,000 – $69,999 | $70,000 or more |
|---|---|---|---|---|---|---|---|---|
| **Household furnishings and equipment** | **100** | **35** | **51** | **70** | **83** | **96** | **135** | **212** |
| Household textiles | 100 | 36 | 55 | 92 | 85 | 93 | 135 | 189 |
| Furniture | 100 | 36 | 51 | 68 | 93 | 78 | 132 | 215 |
| Floor coverings | 100 | – | 53 | 43 | 74 | 115 | 109 | 230 |
| Major appliances | 100 | 39 | 67 | 92 | 83 | 110 | 120 | 179 |
| Small appliances, misc. housewares | 100 | 33 | 42 | 68 | 82 | 84 | 161 | 216 |
| Miscellaneous household equipment | 100 | 31 | 47 | 63 | 78 | 103 | 139 | 221 |
| **APPAREL AND SERVICES** | **100** | **43** | **59** | **83** | **102** | **90** | **114** | **194** |
| **Men and boys** | **100** | **35** | **40** | **78** | **114** | **92** | **123** | **209** |
| Men, aged 16 or older | 100 | 30 | 34 | 77 | 116 | 92 | 117 | 223 |
| Boys, aged 2 to 15 | 100 | 51 | 62 | 85 | 106 | 91 | 144 | 160 |
| **Women and girls** | **100** | **48** | **73** | **80** | **96** | **85** | **114** | **182** |
| Women, aged 16 or older | 100 | 51 | 75 | 76 | 98 | 86 | 111 | 182 |
| Girls, aged 2 to 15 | 100 | 33 | 62 | 102 | 86 | 81 | 129 | 184 |
| **Children under age 2** | **100** | **57** | **48** | **86** | **100** | **145** | **118** | **169** |
| **Footwear** | **100** | **43** | **68** | **108** | **130** | **91** | **115** | **145** |
| **Other apparel products and services** | **100** | **38** | **46** | **69** | **68** | **82** | **101** | **255** |
| **TRANSPORTATION** | **100** | **35** | **57** | **76** | **97** | **116** | **130** | **185** |
| **Vehicle purchases** | **100** | **33** | **57** | **73** | **95** | **121** | **127** | **189** |

(continued)

(continued from previous page)

| | total complete reporters | Under $10,000 | $10,000 – $19,999 | $20,000 – $29,999 | $30,000 – $39,999 | $40,000 – $49,999 | $50,000 – $69,999 | $70,000 or more |
|---|---|---|---|---|---|---|---|---|
| Cars and trucks, new | 100 | 28 | 54 | 62 | 77 | 109 | 110 | 233 |
| Cars and trucks, used | 100 | 38 | 60 | 85 | 109 | 132 | 143 | 147 |
| Other vehicles | 100 | – | 18 | 40 | 246 | 123 | 94 | 214 |
| **Gasoline and motor oil** | **100** | **44** | **62** | **87** | **105** | **116** | **135** | **156** |
| **Other vehicle expenses** | **100** | **34** | **55** | **76** | **98** | **112** | **135** | **185** |
| Vehicle finance charges | 100 | 25 | 39 | 72 | 109 | 126 | 162 | 178 |
| Maintenance and repairs | 100 | 40 | 69 | 81 | 99 | 114 | 122 | 169 |
| Vehicle insurance | 100 | 36 | 61 | 87 | 102 | 111 | 134 | 167 |
| Vehicle rental, leases, licenses, other | 100 | 28 | 36 | 57 | 84 | 100 | 135 | 239 |
| **Public transportation** | **100** | **40** | **52** | **68** | **77** | **88** | **115** | **230** |
| **HEALTH CARE** | **100** | **53** | **86** | **99** | **96** | **99** | **117** | **141** |
| Health insurance | 100 | 55 | 89 | 103 | 102 | 109 | 113 | 129 |
| Medical services | 100 | 45 | 63 | 89 | 95 | 90 | 129 | 175 |
| Drugs | 100 | 65 | 117 | 108 | 88 | 83 | 105 | 115 |
| Medical supplies | 100 | 45 | 85 | 86 | 86 | 116 | 134 | 146 |
| **ENTERTAINMENT** | **100** | **37** | **50** | **67** | **85** | **95** | **139** | **208** |
| Fees and admissions | 100 | 31 | 38 | 54 | 70 | 101 | 132 | 247 |
| Television, radio, sound equipment | 100 | 50 | 68 | 81 | 96 | 100 | 136 | 162 |
| Pets, toys, playground equipment | 100 | 37 | 56 | 71 | 77 | 117 | 139 | 193 |
| Other entertainment supplies, services | 100 | 26 | 34 | 58 | 92 | 67 | 150 | 242 |

(continued)

(continued from previous page)

| | total complete reporters | Under $10,000 | $10,000 – $19,999 | $20,000 – $29,999 | $30,000 – $39,999 | $40,000 – $49,999 | $50,000 – $69,999 | $70,000 or more |
|---|---|---|---|---|---|---|---|---|
| **PERSONAL CARE PRODUCTS AND SERVICES** | **100** | **50** | **55** | **86** | **101** | **112** | **117** | **178** |
| **READING** | **100** | **40** | **61** | **78** | **87** | **98** | **124** | **195** |
| **EDUCATION** | **100** | **89** | **44** | **52** | **59** | **72** | **102** | **241** |
| **TOBACCO PRODUCTS AND SMOKING SUPPLIES** | **100** | **75** | **87** | **97** | **107** | **119** | **124** | **104** |
| **MISCELLANEOUS** | **100** | **38** | **49** | **77** | **93** | **103** | **115** | **209** |
| **CASH CONTRIBUTIONS** | **100** | **20** | **41** | **63** | **79** | **83** | **137** | **244** |
| **PERSONAL INSURANCE AND PENSIONS** | **100** | **8** | **18** | **42** | **71** | **105** | **148** | **280** |
| Life and other personal insurance | 100 | 31 | 41 | 65 | 84 | 86 | 127 | 238 |
| Pensions and Social Security | 100 | 5 | 16 | 40 | 70 | 106 | 150 | 284 |
| **PERSONAL TAXES** | **100** | **5** | **7** | **27** | **53** | **81** | **123** | **345** |
| Federal income taxes | 100 | 4 | 4 | 23 | 50 | 77 | 118 | 360 |
| State and local income taxes | 100 | 3 | 10 | 32 | 59 | 98 | 147 | 310 |
| Other taxes | 100 | 31 | 55 | 85 | 81 | 92 | 113 | 219 |
| **GIFTS** | **100** | **42** | **53** | **72** | **82** | **74** | **113** | **229** |
| **Food** | **100** | **27** | **21** | **37** | **76** | **58** | **91** | **328** |
| **Housing** | **100** | **42** | **59** | **72** | **79** | **74** | **117** | **222** |
| Housekeeping supplies | 100 | 31 | 48 | 87 | 98 | 66 | 164 | 187 |

(continued)

*(continued from previous page)*

| | total complete reporters | Under $10,000 | $10,000 – $19,999 | $20,000 – $29,999 | $30,000 – $39,999 | $40,000 – $49,999 | $50,000 – $69,999 | $70,000 or more |
|---|---|---|---|---|---|---|---|---|
| Household textiles | 100 | 44 | 71 | 56 | 94 | 111 | 94 | 217 |
| Appliances and misc. housewares | 100 | 7 | 57 | 72 | 92 | 106 | 117 | 222 |
| Major appliances | 100 | 11 | 152 | 67 | 44 | 244 | 89 | 100 |
| Small appliances and misc. housewares | 100 | 6 | 23 | 74 | 107 | 59 | 122 | 263 |
| Miscellaneous household equipment | 100 | 31 | 51 | 92 | 76 | 78 | 110 | 232 |
| Other housing | 100 | 61 | 66 | 58 | 69 | 62 | 108 | 229 |
| **Apparel and services** | **100** | **51** | **66** | **88** | **96** | **88** | **113** | **182** |
| Males, aged 2 or older | 100 | 49 | 56 | 81 | 100 | 102 | 103 | 200 |
| Females, aged 2 or older | 100 | 42 | 77 | 89 | 86 | 57 | 112 | 195 |
| Children under age 2 | 100 | 59 | 45 | 94 | 92 | 97 | 114 | 192 |
| All other apparel products and services | 100 | 61 | 73 | 91 | 109 | 115 | 122 | 137 |
| Jewelry and watches | 100 | 50 | 52 | 125 | 89 | 136 | 139 | 125 |
| All other apparel products and services | 100 | 71 | 95 | 54 | 127 | 96 | 108 | 154 |
| **Transportation** | **100** | **60** | **46** | **122** | **50** | **63** | **128** | **197** |
| **Health care** | **100** | **68** | **100** | **98** | **80** | **37** | **76** | **185** |
| **Entertainment** | **100** | **30** | **60** | **70** | **74** | **95** | **135** | **210** |
| Toys, games, hobbies, and tricycles | 100 | 36 | 54 | 94 | 82 | 121 | 153 | 162 |
| Other entertainment | 100 | 26 | 63 | 59 | 70 | 84 | 126 | 233 |
| **Education** | **100** | **28** | **21** | **36** | **47** | **41** | **119** | **333** |
| **All other gifts** | **100** | **44** | **55** | **75** | **125** | **99** | **99** | **193** |

*Note: The Bureau of Labor Statistics uses consumer unit rather than household as the sampling unit in the Consumer Expenditure Survey. For the definition of consumer unit, see Glossary. An index of 100 is the average for all households. An index of 132 means households in the group spend 32 percent more than the average household. An index of 75 means households in the group spend 25 percent less than the average household.*
*Source: Bureau of Labor Statistics, 1999 Consumer Expenditure Survey; calculations by New Strategist*

## Market Shares by Household Income, 1999

*(share of total household spending accounted for by income group, 1999)*

| | total complete reporters | under $20,000 | $20,000–$39,999 | $40,000–$69,999 | $70,000 or more |
|---|---|---|---|---|---|
| **Total consumer units** | **100.0%** | **33.2%** | **25.7%** | **22.5%** | **18.6%** |
| **Share of total spending** | **100.0** | **16.4** | **20.8** | **26.5** | **36.4** |
| **FOOD** | **100.0%** | **19.4%** | **22.0%** | **26.9%** | **31.1%** |
| **Food at home** | **100.0** | **22.6** | **23.9** | **27.0** | **26.7** |
| Cereals and bakery products | 100.0 | 23.1 | 23.2 | 27.1 | 26.9 |
| Cereals and cereal products | 100.0 | 24.4 | 24.2 | 26.8 | 24.7 |
| Bakery products | 100.0 | 22.4 | 22.6 | 27.3 | 28.0 |
| Meats, poultry, fish, and eggs | 100.0 | 24.2 | 24.6 | 26.4 | 25.1 |
| Beef | 100.0 | 23.0 | 23.6 | 27.6 | 26.1 |
| Pork | 100.0 | 24.7 | 26.7 | 26.7 | 22.1 |
| Other meats | 100.0 | 25.4 | 25.4 | 26.4 | 23.4 |
| Poultry | 100.0 | 23.7 | 23.9 | 26.3 | 26.4 |
| Fish and seafood | 100.0 | 24.4 | 23.1 | 24.7 | 28.1 |
| Eggs | 100.0 | 28.7 | 26.3 | 23.7 | 21.9 |
| Dairy products | 100.0 | 21.7 | 23.8 | 27.3 | 27.4 |
| Fresh milk and cream | 100.0 | 23.9 | 25.1 | 26.7 | 24.7 |
| Other dairy products | 100.0 | 20.4 | 23.1 | 27.6 | 29.1 |
| Fruits and vegetables | 100.0 | 23.3 | 23.9 | 26.0 | 27.1 |
| Fresh fruits | 100.0 | 23.1 | 23.4 | 25.5 | 28.1 |
| Fresh vegetables | 100.0 | 23.2 | 24.3 | 25.6 | 27.2 |
| Processed fruits | 100.0 | 22.9 | 23.7 | 26.4 | 27.5 |
| Processed vegetables | 100.0 | 23.0 | 24.0 | 27.1 | 25.1 |
| Other food at home | 100.0 | 21.1 | 23.7 | 27.0 | 27.4 |
| Sugar and other sweets | 100.0 | 22.8 | 23.9 | 27.8 | 25.7 |
| Fats and oils | 100.0 | 24.3 | 25.6 | 26.4 | 23.4 |
| Miscellaneous foods | 100.0 | 20.0 | 23.6 | 28.4 | 28.3 |
| Nonalcoholic beverages | 100.0 | 22.3 | 23.0 | 27.9 | 25.9 |
| Food prepared by household on trips | 100.0 | 14.2 | 19.6 | 27.4 | 39.3 |
| **Food away from home** | **100.0** | **14.0** | **21.7** | **26.8** | **37.0** |
| **ALCOHOLIC BEVERAGES** | **100.0** | **16.9** | **20.6** | **26.1** | **37.1** |
| **HOUSING** | **100.0** | **18.7** | **21.0** | **25.5** | **34.8** |
| **Shelter** | **100.0** | **18.5** | **20.0** | **25.3** | **35.2** |

*(continued)*

*(continued from previous page)*

| | total complete reporters | under $20,000 | $20,000–$39,999 | $40,000–$69,999 | $70,000 or more |
|---|---|---|---|---|---|
| Owned dwellings | 100.0% | 11.5% | 17.8% | 26.5% | 44.2% |
| Mortgage interest and charges | 100.0 | 6.9 | 15.8 | 29.0 | 48.3 |
| Property taxes | 100.0 | 16.8 | 19.2 | 24.1 | 39.0 |
| Maintenance, repairs, insurance, other | 100.0 | 17.9 | 21.5 | 22.5 | 38.2 |
| Rented dwellings | 100.0 | 35.2 | 29.4 | 23.6 | 11.8 |
| Other lodging | 100.0 | 12.3 | 14.0 | 21.2 | 51.4 |
| **Utilities, fuels, public services** | **100.0** | **23.7** | **24.1** | **25.4** | **26.7** |
| Natural gas | 100.0 | 23.7 | 23.2 | 24.8 | 28.2 |
| Electricity | 100.0 | 25.1 | 24.6 | 25.2 | 25.1 |
| Fuel oil and other fuels | 100.0 | 24.0 | 26.7 | 22.2 | 25.6 |
| Telephone services | 100.0 | 23.1 | 24.1 | 25.8 | 27.1 |
| Water and other public services | 100.0 | 21.1 | 23.0 | 26.2 | 29.6 |
| **Household services** | **100.0** | **14.3** | **13.7** | **22.9** | **49.2** |
| Personal services | 100.0 | 13.5 | 12.3 | 25.6 | 48.5 |
| Other household services | 100.0 | 15.2 | 14.0 | 20.2 | 49.6 |
| **Housekeeping supplies** | **100.0** | **17.3** | **22.5** | **28.7** | **31.0** |
| Laundry and cleaning supplies | 100.0 | 22.0 | 24.7 | 27.1 | 25.5 |
| Other household products | 100.0 | 15.1 | 21.5 | 30.0 | 33.0 |
| Postage and stationery | 100.0 | 16.5 | 22.5 | 27.5 | 33.0 |
| **Household furnishings, equipment** | **100.0** | **14.6** | **19.4** | **26.8** | **39.3** |
| Household textiles | 100.0 | 15.6 | 22.8 | 26.6 | 35.1 |
| Furniture | 100.0 | 14.8 | 20.4 | 24.8 | 39.9 |
| Floor coverings | 100.0 | 17.5 | 14.7 | 25.0 | 42.8 |
| Major appliances | 100.0 | 18.4 | 22.6 | 26.1 | 33.2 |
| Small appliances, misc. housewares | 100.0 | 12.7 | 19.1 | 29.2 | 40.1 |
| Misc. household equipment | 100.0 | 13.4 | 17.0 | 27.9 | 41.1 |
| **APPAREL AND SERVICES** | **100.0** | **17.3** | **23.5** | **23.5** | **35.0** |
| **Men and boys** | **100.0** | **12.6** | **24.2** | **24.8** | **38.8** |
| Men, aged 16 or older | 100.0 | 10.8 | 24.2 | 24.0 | 41.5 |
| Boys, aged 2 to 15 | 100.0 | 19.1 | 24.3 | 27.7 | 29.6 |
| **Women and girls** | **100.0** | **20.9** | **22.5** | **23.1** | **33.9** |
| Women, aged 16 or older | 100.0 | 21.7 | 22.1 | 22.8 | 33.8 |
| Girls, aged 2 to 15 | 100.0 | 16.5 | 24.3 | 24.8 | 34.2 |
| **Children under age 2** | **100.0** | **17.2** | **23.8** | **28.9** | **31.4** |
| **Footwear** | **100.0** | **18.0** | **30.4** | **23.7** | **26.0** |
| **Other apparel products and services** | **100.0** | **14.1** | **17.6** | **21.1** | **47.3** |

*(continued)*

*(continued from previous page)*

| | total complete reporters | under $20,000 | $20,000–$39,999 | $40,000–$69,999 | $70,000 or more |
|---|---|---|---|---|---|
| **TRANSPORTATION** | **100.0%** | **15.8%** | **21.9%** | **27.9%** | **34.4%** |
| **Vehicle purchases** | **100.0** | **15.5** | **21.4** | **28.0** | **35.1** |
| Cars and trucks, new | 100.0 | 14.3 | 17.6 | 24.7 | 43.4 |
| Cars and trucks, used | 100.0 | 16.8 | 24.6 | 31.2 | 27.4 |
| Other vehicles | 100.0 | – | 34.1 | 23.8 | 39.8 |
| **Gasoline and motor oil** | **100.0** | **17.0** | **24.4** | **28.8** | **28.9** |
| **Other vehicle expenses** | **100.0** | **15.2** | **22.2** | **28.2** | **34.4** |
| Vehicle finance charges | 100.0 | 11.0 | 22.9 | 33.2 | 33.0 |
| Maintenance and repairs | 100.0 | 18.9 | 22.9 | 26.8 | 31.3 |
| Vehicle insurance | 100.0 | 16.6 | 24.1 | 28.2 | 31.1 |
| Vehicle rental, leases, licenses, other | 100.0 | 10.7 | 17.8 | 27.2 | 44.4 |
| **Public transportation** | **100.0** | **15.5** | **18.5** | **23.4** | **42.7** |
| **HEALTH CARE** | **100.0** | **24.0** | **25.2** | **24.7** | **26.1** |
| Health insurance | 100.0 | 24.7 | 26.3 | 25.0 | 23.0 |
| Medical services | 100.0 | 18.3 | 23.7 | 25.5 | 32.6 |
| Drugs | 100.0 | 31.4 | 25.5 | 21.7 | 21.4 |
| Medical supplies | 100.0 | 22.6 | 22.1 | 28.5 | 27.1 |
| **ENTERTAINMENT** | **100.0** | **14.8** | **19.3** | **27.3** | **38.7** |
| Fees and admissions | 100.0 | 11.6 | 15.7 | 26.9 | 45.8 |
| Television, radio, sound equipment | 100.0 | 20.0 | 22.6 | 27.4 | 30.1 |
| Pets, toys, playground equipment | 100.0 | 15.9 | 19.0 | 29.4 | 35.8 |
| Other entertainment supplies, services | 100.0 | 10.3 | 18.9 | 26.3 | 44.9 |
| **PERSONAL CARE PRODUCTS AND SERVICE** | **100.0** | **17.6** | **23.9** | **25.9** | **32.0** |
| **READING** | **100.0** | **17.4** | **21.1** | **25.5** | **36.3** |
| **EDUCATION** | **100.0** | **20.0** | **14.1** | **20.1** | **44.8** |
| **TOBACCO PRODUCTS AND SMOKING SUPPLIES** | **100.0** | **27.2** | **26.0** | **27.5** | **19.3** |
| **MISCELLANEOUS** | **100.0** | **14.8** | **21.7** | **24.8** | **38.8** |
| **CASH CONTRIBUTIONS** | **100.0** | **10.6** | **18.1** | **26.0** | **45.3** |
| **PERSONAL INSURANCE AND PENSIONS** | **100.0** | **4.5** | **14.2** | **29.3** | **51.9** |
| Life and other personal insurance | 100.0 | 12.2 | 18.9 | 24.8 | 44.1 |
| Pensions and Social Security | 100.0 | 3.7 | 13.8 | 29.8 | 52.7 |

*(continued)*

*(continued from previous page)*

| | total complete reporters | under $20,000 | $20,000–$39,999 | $40,000–$69,999 | $70,000 or more |
|---|---|---|---|---|---|
| **PERSONAL TAXES** | **100.0%** | **2.1%** | **9.0%** | **23.9%** | **64.1%** |
| Federal income taxes | 100.0 | 1.3 | 8.0 | 22.8 | 66.9 |
| State and local income taxes | 100.0 | 2.3 | 11.4 | 28.6 | 57.6 |
| Other taxes | 100.0 | 14.9 | 21.3 | 23.5 | 40.6 |
| **GIFTS** | **100.0** | **16.1** | **19.7** | **21.9** | **42.5** |
| **Food** | **100.0** | **7.7** | **14.0** | **17.5** | **60.9** |
| **Housing** | **100.0** | **17.2** | **19.4** | **22.5** | **41.1** |
| Housekeeping supplies | 100.0 | 13.5 | 23.7 | 28.0 | 34.8 |
| Household textiles | 100.0 | 19.8 | 18.8 | 22.8 | 40.2 |
| Appliances and misc. housewares | 100.0 | 11.9 | 20.8 | 25.2 | 41.3 |
| Major appliances | 100.0 | 30.7 | 14.6 | 34.1 | 18.6 |
| Small appliances and misc. housewares | 100.0 | 5.2 | 22.9 | 21.8 | 48.8 |
| Misc. household equipment | 100.0 | 14.1 | 21.8 | 21.8 | 43.1 |
| Other housing | 100.0 | 21.3 | 16.2 | 20.1 | 42.4 |
| **Apparel and services** | **100.0** | **19.8** | **23.5** | **23.1** | **33.8** |
| Males, aged 2 or older | 100.0 | 17.6 | 23.1 | 23.1 | 37.1 |
| Females, aged 2 or older | 100.0 | 20.7 | 22.6 | 20.3 | 36.2 |
| Children under age 2 | 100.0 | 16.0 | 23.0 | 24.1 | 35.6 |
| All other apparel products and services | 100.0 | 22.5 | 25.5 | 26.8 | 25.4 |
| Jewelry and watches | 100.0 | 16.9 | 28.0 | 31.0 | 23.2 |
| All other apparel products and services | 100.0 | 28.2 | 22.3 | 23.2 | 28.6 |
| **Transportation** | **100.0** | **17.1** | **23.1** | **22.9** | **36.6** |
| **Health care** | **100.0** | **28.7** | **23.2** | **13.6** | **34.3** |
| **Entertainment** | **100.0** | **15.7** | **18.5** | **26.7** | **39.0** |
| Toys, games, hobbies, and tricycles | 100.0 | 15.4 | 22.8 | 31.5 | 30.0 |
| Other entertainment | 100.0 | 15.8 | 16.4 | 24.5 | 43.2 |
| **Education** | **100.0** | **7.0** | **10.5** | **19.7** | **61.8** |
| **All other gifts** | **100.0** | **16.7** | **25.1** | **22.2** | **35.9** |

*Note: The Bureau of Labor Statistics uses consumer unit rather than household as the sampling unit in the Consumer Expenditure Survey. For the definition of consumer unit, see Glossary. Numbers may not add to total because of rounding.*
*Source: Bureau of Labor Statistics, 1999 Consumer Expenditure Survey; calculations by New Strategist*

# Couples with Children Spend the Most

## Married couples with children spend 38 percent more than the average household.

Married couples with children spend much more than average because they have the highest incomes and the largest households. In 1999, couples with kids spent an average of $51,186, compared with $37,027 spent by the average household, according to the Bureau of Labor Statistics' Consumer Expenditure Survey.

Married couples without children at home spend 14 percent more than average. Most are empty-nesters with grown children living elsewhere or young couples who have not yet had children. Single-parent households spent $27,918 in 1999, while single-person households spent the least, just $22,404.

The indexed spending table in this section shows spending by household type in comparison to what the average household spends. An index of 100 means a household spends an average amount on the item. An index above 100 means the household type spends more than average on an item, while an index below 100 reveals below-average spending. A look at the table shows that spending is well below average for single-parent and single-person households, although single-parent households spend close to the average on most foods. Single-parent households spend 64 percent more than average on household personal services, much of which is day care expenses.

Married couples without children at home spend more than average on many items. But they spend less than average on products and services for children such as household personal services (with an index of just 24), children's clothing, and education.

The market share table in this section shows how much of total spending by category is accounted for by each household type. Spending by household type closely matches each type's share of total households. Married couples with children account for 38 percent of households and 36 percent of household spending, for example. Within categories, however, market shares vary sharply by household type. Married couples with children account for more than half of all spending on some items such as household personal services (day care) and children's clothing. Married couples without children at home account for more than one-third of spending on "other" lodging (hotels and motels), floor coverings, drugs, and gifts. Single-parents account for less than 10 percent of spending on all but children's clothing. Single-person households account for a disproportionately large share of spending on alcoholic beverages, rent, fees and admissions to entertainment events, cash contributions, and many types of gifts.

♦ The spending of married couples without children may grow faster than average in the years ahead as two-income baby-boom couples enter the empty-nest years.

**Spending is below average for single parents**

*(average annual spending of consumer units, by type, 1999)*

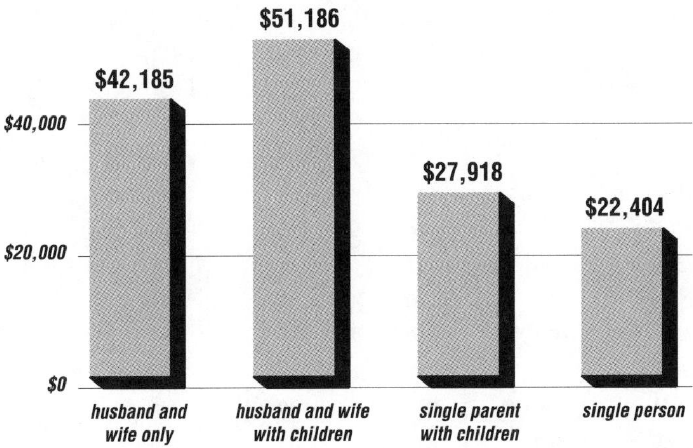

## Spending by Household Type, 1999

*(average annual spending of consumer units (CU's) by product and service category and type of consumer unit, 1999)*

| | total | married couples: total | married couples: husband and wife only | married couples: husband and wife with children | single parent with children under age 18 | single person |
|---|---|---|---|---|---|---|
| **Number of consumer units (in 000s)** | **108,465** | **56,427** | **23,404** | **28,535** | **6,571** | **31,550** |
| **Average number of persons per CU** | **2.5** | **3.2** | **2** | **3.9** | **2.9** | **1.0** |
| **Avg. before-tax income** | **$43,951** | **$59,128** | **$54,067** | **$63,666** | **$25,685** | **$25,247** |
| **Avg. annual spending** | **37,027** | **47,188** | **42,185** | **51,186** | **27,918** | **22,404** |
| **FOOD** | **$5,031** | **$6,372** | **$5,380** | **$7,034** | **$4,526** | **$2,685** |
| **Food at home** | **2,915** | **3,695** | **3,000** | **4,146** | **2,942** | **1,449** |
| Cereals and bakery products | 448 | 567 | 446 | 653 | 509 | 222 |
| Cereals and cereal products | 160 | 200 | 144 | 239 | 204 | 73 |
| Bakery products | 288 | 367 | 302 | 413 | 305 | 149 |
| Meats, poultry, fish, and eggs | 749 | 939 | 771 | 1,031 | 770 | 340 |
| Beef | 220 | 287 | 233 | 322 | 207 | 91 |
| Pork | 157 | 195 | 167 | 206 | 167 | 67 |
| Other meats | 97 | 120 | 97 | 136 | 109 | 48 |
| Poultry | 136 | 166 | 123 | 190 | 143 | 63 |
| Fish and seafood | 106 | 132 | 118 | 135 | 110 | 55 |
| Eggs | 32 | 40 | 32 | 43 | 34 | 16 |
| Dairy products | 322 | 419 | 329 | 484 | 301 | 155 |
| Fresh milk and cream | 122 | 157 | 110 | 189 | 123 | 58 |
| Other dairy products | 200 | 262 | 220 | 295 | 178 | 98 |
| Fruits and vegetables | 500 | 633 | 548 | 680 | 457 | 264 |
| Fresh fruits | 152 | 193 | 170 | 204 | 134 | 85 |
| Fresh vegetables | 149 | 190 | 174 | 196 | 128 | 76 |
| Processed fruits | 113 | 141 | 115 | 160 | 111 | 60 |
| Processed vegetables | 86 | 109 | 89 | 120 | 84 | 42 |
| Other food at home | 896 | 1,136 | 906 | 1,297 | 904 | 468 |
| Sugar and other sweets | 112 | 144 | 124 | 156 | 115 | 57 |
| Fats and oils | 84 | 104 | 92 | 110 | 90 | 42 |
| Miscellaneous foods | 420 | 530 | 398 | 632 | 439 | 221 |
| Nonalcoholic beverages | 242 | 302 | 241 | 340 | 243 | 128 |
| Food prepared by hh on trips | 39 | 56 | 51 | 59 | 18 | 20 |
| **Food away from home** | **2,116** | **2,677** | **2,380** | **2,888** | **1,584** | **1,236** |

*(continued)*

*(continued from previous page)*

| | | married couples | | | | |
|---|---|---|---|---|---|---|
| | total | total | husband and wife only | husband and wife with children | single parent with children under age 18 | single person |
| **ALCOHOLIC BEVERAGES** | **$318** | **$337** | **$388** | **$299** | **$144** | **$286** |
| **HOUSING** | **12,057** | **14,790** | **12,965** | **16,348** | **10,103** | **8,207** |
| **Shelter** | **7,016** | **8,412** | **7,271** | **9,415** | **5,873** | **5,143** |
| Owned dwellings | 4,525 | 6,406 | 5,336 | 7,380 | 2,646 | 2,309 |
| Mortgage interest/charges | 2,547 | 3,768 | 2,571 | 4,775 | 1,590 | 1,004 |
| Property taxes | 1,123 | 1,517 | 1,458 | 1,587 | 539 | 731 |
| Maintenance, repairs, insurance, other | 855 | 1,120 | 1,307 | 1,018 | 516 | 573 |
| Rented dwellings | 2,027 | 1,370 | 1,195 | 1,460 | 3,088 | 2,517 |
| Other lodging | 464 | 637 | 740 | 575 | 139 | 317 |
| **Utilities, fuels, public services** | **2,377** | **2,860** | **2,585** | **3,015** | **2,194** | **1,551** |
| Natural gas | 270 | 322 | 290 | 337 | 248 | 184 |
| Electricity | 899 | 1,094 | 1,009 | 1,142 | 852 | 566 |
| Fuel oil and other fuels | 74 | 96 | 101 | 92 | 40 | 45 |
| Telephone services | 849 | 979 | 855 | 1,047 | 833 | 592 |
| Water, other public services | 285 | 370 | 331 | 395 | 221 | 165 |
| **Household services** | **666** | **848** | **534** | **1,126** | **696** | **469** |
| Personal services | 323 | 411 | 77 | 687 | 529 | 193 |
| Other household services | 343 | 437 | 457 | 440 | 167 | 276 |
| **Housekeeping supplies** | **498** | **676** | **622** | **727** | **356** | **238** |
| Laundry and cleaning supplies | 121 | 156 | 134 | 168 | 136 | 55 |
| Other household products | 250 | 356 | 317 | 392 | 139 | 106 |
| Postage and stationery | 127 | 164 | 171 | 166 | 81 | 77 |
| **Household furnishings and equipment** | **1,499** | **1,994** | **1,953** | **2,066** | **984** | **807** |
| Household textiles | 114 | 146 | 139 | 153 | 101 | 69 |
| Furniture | 365 | 483 | 428 | 526 | 255 | 198 |
| Floor coverings | 44 | 62 | 72 | 59 | 29 | 21 |
| Major appliances | 183 | 230 | 229 | 237 | 111 | 109 |
| Small appliances, misc. housewares | 102 | 129 | 156 | 113 | 38 | 69 |
| Misc. household equipment | 692 | 944 | 929 | 978 | 452 | 340 |
| **APPAREL, SERVICES** | **1,743** | **2,169** | **1,680** | **2,520** | **1,946** | **933** |
| **Men and boys** | **421** | **573** | **443** | **664** | **369** | **175** |
| Men, aged 16 or older | 328 | 446 | 420 | 457 | 145 | 165 |
| Boys, aged 2 to 15 | 93 | 127 | 22 | 207 | 224 | 10 |

*(continued)*

*(continued from previous page)*

| | | married couples | | | | |
|---|---|---|---|---|---|---|
| | total | total | husband and wife only | husband and wife with children | single parent with children under age 18 | single person |
| **Women and girls** | **$655** | **$799** | **$667** | **$903** | **$913** | **$337** |
| Women, aged 16 or older | 548 | 653 | 641 | 659 | 649 | 328 |
| Girls, aged 2 to 15 | 107 | 146 | 26 | 244 | 265 | 9 |
| **Children under age 2** | **67** | **100** | **31** | **150** | **75** | **10** |
| **Footwear** | **303** | **367** | **246** | **445** | **396** | **135** |
| **Other apparel products and services** | **297** | **329** | **292** | **358** | **193** | **276** |
| **TRANSPORTATION** | **7,011** | **9,289** | **8,067** | **10,214** | **4,694** | **3,536** |
| **Vehicle purchases** | **3,305** | **4,421** | **3,791** | **4,946** | **2,260** | **1,507** |
| Cars and trucks, new | 1,628 | 2,304 | 2,354 | 2,303 | 556 | 753 |
| Cars and trucks, used | 1,641 | 2,076 | 1,419 | 2,582 | 1,678 | 728 |
| Other vehicles | 36 | 41 | 18 | 61 | 25 | 25 |
| **Gasoline and motor oil** | **1,055** | **1,376** | **1,146** | **1,522** | **720** | **565** |
| **Other vehicle expenses** | **2,254** | **2,977** | **2,549** | **3,289** | **1,484** | **1,215** |
| Vehicle finance charges | 320 | 438 | 319 | 530 | 236 | 120 |
| Maintenance and repairs | 664 | 874 | 766 | 934 | 422 | 382 |
| Vehicle insurance | 756 | 968 | 836 | 1,063 | 510 | 429 |
| Vehicle rental, leases, licenses, other | 513 | 698 | 628 | 761 | 316 | 283 |
| **Public transportation** | **397** | **515** | **580** | **457** | **230** | **250** |
| **HEALTH CARE** | **1,959** | **2,522** | **2,908** | **2,200** | **1,003** | **1,336** |
| Health insurance | 923 | 1,201 | 1,390 | 1,049 | 481 | 614 |
| Medical services | 558 | 736 | 747 | 718 | 306 | 346 |
| Drugs | 370 | 443 | 612 | 303 | 165 | 304 |
| Medical supplies | 109 | 141 | 159 | 130 | 51 | 72 |
| **ENTERTAINMENT** | **1,891** | **616** | **596** | **659** | **284** | **277** |
| Fees and admissions | 459 | 717 | 579 | 815 | 537 | 415 |
| Television, radio, sound equipment | 608 | 449 | 377 | 516 | 297 | 185 |
| Pets, toys, playground equip. | 346 | 449 | 377 | 516 | 297 | 185 |
| Other entertainment supplies, services | 478 | 737 | 723 | 793 | 249 | 163 |
| **PERSONAL CARE PRODUCTS, SERVICES** | **408** | **506** | **471** | **541** | **362** | **254** |
| **READING** | **159** | **201** | **215** | **197** | **71** | **122** |

*(continued)*

*(continued from previous page)*

| | | married couples | | | | |
|---|---|---|---|---|---|---|
| | **total** | **total** | **husband and wife only** | **husband and wife with children** | **single parent with children under age 18** | **single person** |
| **EDUCATION** | **$635** | **$829** | **$528** | **$1,115** | **$426** | **$421** |
| **TOBACCO PRODUCTS, SMOKING SUPPLIES** | **300** | **324** | **269** | **342** | **239** | **189** |
| **MISCELLANEOUS** | **889** | **1,042** | **931** | **1,091** | **843** | **688** |
| **CASH CONTRIBUTIONS** | **1,190** | **1,477** | **1,816** | **1,201** | **368** | **1,018** |
| **PERSONAL INSURANCE AND PENSIONS** | **3,436** | **4,812** | **4,291** | **5,301** | **1,827** | **1,689** |
| Life, other personal insurance | 394 | 602 | 548 | 644 | 170 | 133 |
| Pensions, Social Security | 3,042 | 4,210 | 3,743 | 4,658 | 1,657 | 1,556 |
| **PERSONAL TAXES** | **3,588** | **5,029** | **4,207** | **6,013** | **909** | **2,218** |
| Federal income taxes | 2,802 | 4,005 | 3,222 | 4,915 | 592 | 1,679 |
| State and local income taxes | 616 | 794 | 723 | 890 | 258 | 419 |
| Other taxes | 170 | 230 | 262 | 208 | 59 | 121 |
| **GIFTS** | **1,083** | **1,378** | **1,707** | **1,160** | **589** | **801** |
| **Food** | **83** | **126** | **175** | **82** | **28** | **40** |
| **Housing** | **292** | **377** | **441** | **347** | **187** | **200** |
| Housekeeping supplies | 41 | 54 | 57 | 53 | 22 | 25 |
| Household textiles | 17 | 17 | 20 | 16 | 6 | 20 |
| Appliances and miscellaneous housewares | 32 | 45 | 70 | 29 | 12 | 19 |
| Major appliances | 9 | 9 | 15 | 5 | 2 | 10 |
| Small appliances and misc. housewares | 24 | 36 | 55 | 23 | 10 | 9 |
| Misc. household equipment | 66 | 87 | 116 | 66 | 46 | 47 |
| Other housing | 136 | 175 | 178 | 184 | 101 | 90 |
| **Apparel and services** | **210** | **249** | **286** | **221** | **163** | **156** |
| Males, aged 2 or older | 54 | 74 | 97 | 58 | 28 | 26 |
| Females, aged 2 or older | 71 | 85 | 113 | 66 | 63 | 51 |
| Children under age 2 | 33 | 47 | 31 | 61 | 30 | 10 |
| All other apparel products and services | 52 | 43 | 45 | 36 | 41 | 69 |
| Jewelry and watches | 27 | 15 | 17 | 13 | 14 | 53 |
| All other apparel products and services | 25 | 28 | 29 | 23 | 27 | 16 |
| **Transportation** | **63** | **72** | **82** | **66** | **13** | **46** |
| **Health care** | **40** | **34** | **48** | **22** | **13** | **61** |

*(continued)*

*(continued from previous page)*

| | | married couples | | | | |
|---|---|---|---|---|---|---|
| | total | total | husband and wife only | husband and wife with children | single parent with children under age 18 | single person |
| **Entertainment** | **$98** | **$120** | **$155** | **$95** | **$39** | **$80** |
| Toys, games, hobbies, tricycles | 32 | 40 | 52 | 29 | 12 | 22 |
| Other entertainment | 66 | 80 | 102 | 66 | 28 | 58 |
| **Education** | **166** | **259** | **337** | **219** | **50** | **84** |
| **All other gifts** | **131** | **142** | **182** | **107** | **95** | **133** |

*Note: The Bureau of Labor Statistics uses consumer unit rather than household as the sampling unit in the Consumer Expenditure Survey. For the definition of consumer unit, see Glossary. Gift spending is also included in the preceding product and service categories.*
*Source: Bureau of Labor Statistics, 1999 Consumer Expenditure Survey; Internet site <www.bls.gov/csxstnd.htm>*

## Indexed Spending by Household Type, 1999

*(indexed average annual spending of consumer units by product and service category and type of consumer unit, 1999)*

| | | married couples | | | | |
|---|---|---|---|---|---|---|
| | *total* | *total* | *husband and wife only* | *husband and wife with children* | *single parent with children under age 18* | *single person* |
| **Number of consumer units (in 000s)** | **108,465** | **56,427** | **23,404** | **28,535** | **6,571** | **31,550** |
| **Indexed average before-tax income** | **100** | **135** | **123** | **145** | **58** | **57** |
| **Indexed average annual spending** | **100** | **127** | **114** | **138** | **75** | **61** |
| **FOOD** | **100** | **127** | **107** | **140** | **90** | **53** |
| **Food at home** | **100** | **127** | **103** | **142** | **101** | **50** |
| Cereals and bakery products | 100 | 127 | 100 | 146 | 114 | 50 |
| Cereals and cereal products | 100 | 125 | 90 | 149 | 128 | 46 |
| Bakery products | 100 | 127 | 105 | 143 | 106 | 52 |
| Meats, poultry, fish, and eggs | 100 | 125 | 103 | 138 | 103 | 45 |
| Beef | 100 | 130 | 106 | 146 | 94 | 41 |
| Pork | 100 | 124 | 106 | 131 | 106 | 43 |
| Other meats | 100 | 124 | 100 | 140 | 112 | 49 |
| Poultry | 100 | 122 | 90 | 140 | 105 | 46 |
| Fish and seafood | 100 | 125 | 111 | 127 | 104 | 52 |
| Eggs | 100 | 125 | 100 | 134 | 106 | 50 |
| Dairy products | 100 | 130 | 102 | 150 | 93 | 48 |
| Fresh milk and cream | 100 | 129 | 90 | 155 | 101 | 48 |
| Other dairy products | 100 | 131 | 110 | 148 | 89 | 49 |
| Fruits and vegetables | 100 | 127 | 110 | 136 | 91 | 53 |
| Fresh fruits | 100 | 127 | 112 | 134 | 88 | 56 |
| Fresh vegetables | 100 | 128 | 117 | 132 | 86 | 51 |
| Processed fruits | 100 | 125 | 102 | 142 | 98 | 53 |
| Processed vegetables | 100 | 127 | 103 | 140 | 98 | 49 |
| Other food at home | 100 | 127 | 101 | 145 | 101 | 52 |
| Sugar and other sweets | 100 | 129 | 111 | 139 | 103 | 51 |
| Fats and oils | 100 | 124 | 110 | 131 | 107 | 50 |
| Miscellaneous foods | 100 | 126 | 95 | 150 | 105 | 53 |
| Nonalcoholic beverages | 100 | 125 | 100 | 140 | 100 | 53 |
| Food prepared by hh on trips | 100 | 144 | 131 | 151 | 46 | 51 |
| **Food away from home** | **100** | **127** | **112** | **136** | **75** | **58** |

*(continued)*

*(continued from previous page)*

| | | married couples | | | | |
|---|---|---|---|---|---|---|
| | total | total | husband and wife only | husband and wife with children | single parent with children under age 18 | single person |
| **ALCOHOLIC BEVERAGES** | **100** | **106** | **122** | **94** | **45** | **90** |
| **HOUSING** | **100** | **123** | **108** | **136** | **84** | **68** |
| **Shelter** | **100** | **120** | **104** | **134** | **84** | **73** |
| Owned dwellings | 100 | 142 | 118 | 163 | 58 | 51 |
| Mortgage interest/charges | 100 | 148 | 101 | 187 | 62 | 39 |
| Property taxes | 100 | 135 | 130 | 141 | 48 | 65 |
| Maintenance, repairs, insurance, other | 100 | 131 | 153 | 119 | 60 | 67 |
| Rented dwellings | 100 | 68 | 59 | 72 | 152 | 124 |
| Other lodging | 100 | 137 | 159 | 124 | 30 | 68 |
| **Utilities, fuels, public services** | **100** | **120** | **109** | **127** | **92** | **65** |
| Natural gas | 100 | 119 | 107 | 125 | 92 | 68 |
| Electricity | 100 | 122 | 112 | 127 | 95 | 63 |
| Fuel oil and other fuels | 100 | 130 | 136 | 124 | 54 | 61 |
| Telephone services | 100 | 115 | 101 | 123 | 98 | 70 |
| Water, other public services | 100 | 130 | 116 | 139 | 78 | 58 |
| **Household services** | **100** | **127** | **80** | **169** | **105** | **70** |
| Personal services | 100 | 127 | 24 | 213 | 164 | 60 |
| Other household services | 100 | 127 | 133 | 128 | 49 | 80 |
| **Housekeeping supplies** | **100** | **136** | **125** | **146** | **71** | **48** |
| Laundry and cleaning supplies | 100 | 129 | 111 | 139 | 112 | 45 |
| Other household products | 100 | 142 | 127 | 157 | 56 | 42 |
| Postage and stationery | 100 | 129 | 135 | 131 | 64 | 61 |
| **Household furnishings and equipment** | **100** | **133** | **130** | **138** | **66** | **54** |
| Household textiles | 100 | 128 | 122 | 134 | 89 | 61 |
| Furniture | 100 | 132 | 117 | 144 | 70 | 54 |
| Floor coverings | 100 | 141 | 164 | 134 | 66 | 48 |
| Major appliances | 100 | 126 | 125 | 130 | 61 | 60 |
| Small appliances, misc. housewares | 100 | 126 | 153 | 111 | 37 | 68 |
| Misc. household equipment | 100 | 136 | 134 | 141 | 65 | 49 |
| **APPAREL, SERVICES** | **100** | **124** | **96** | **145** | **112** | **54** |
| **Men and boys** | **100** | **136** | **105** | **158** | **88** | **42** |
| Men, aged 16 or older | 100 | 136 | 128 | 139 | 44 | 50 |
| Boys, aged 2 to 15 | 100 | 137 | 24 | 223 | 241 | 11 |

*(continued)*

*(continued from previous page)*

| | | married couples | | | | |
|---|---|---|---|---|---|---|
| | *total* | *total* | *husband and wife only* | *husband and wife with children* | *single parent with children under age 18* | *single person* |
| **Women and girls** | **100** | **122** | **102** | **138** | **139** | **51** |
| Women, aged 16 or older | 100 | 119 | 117 | 120 | 118 | 60 |
| Girls, aged 2 to 15 | 100 | 136 | 24 | 228 | 248 | 8 |
| **Children under age 2** | **100** | **149** | **46** | **224** | **112** | **15** |
| **Footwear** | **100** | **121** | **81** | **147** | **131** | **45** |
| **Other apparel products and services** | **100** | **111** | **98** | **121** | **65** | **93** |
| **TRANSPORTATION** | **100** | **132** | **115** | **146** | **67** | **50** |
| **Vehicle purchases** | **100** | **134** | **115** | **150** | **68** | **46** |
| Cars and trucks, new | 100 | 142 | 145 | 141 | 34 | 46 |
| Cars and trucks, used | 100 | 127 | 86 | 157 | 102 | 44 |
| Other vehicles | 100 | 114 | 50 | 169 | 69 | 69 |
| **Gasoline and motor oil** | **100** | **130** | **109** | **144** | **68** | **54** |
| **Other vehicle expenses** | **100** | **132** | **113** | **146** | **66** | **54** |
| Vehicle finance charges | 100 | 137 | 100 | 166 | 74 | 38 |
| Maintenance and repairs | 100 | 132 | 115 | 141 | 64 | 58 |
| Vehicle insurance | 100 | 128 | 111 | 141 | 67 | 57 |
| Vehicle rental, leases, licenses, other | 100 | 136 | 122 | 148 | 62 | 55 |
| **Public transportation** | **100** | **130** | **146** | **115** | **58** | **63** |
| **HEALTH CARE** | **100** | **129** | **148** | **112** | **51** | **68** |
| Health insurance | 100 | 130 | 151 | 114 | 52 | 67 |
| Medical services | 100 | 132 | 134 | 129 | 55 | 62 |
| Drugs | 100 | 120 | 165 | 82 | 45 | 82 |
| Medical supplies | 100 | 129 | 146 | 119 | 47 | 66 |
| **ENTERTAINMENT** | **100** | **33** | **32** | **35** | **15** | **15** |
| Fees and admissions | 100 | 156 | 126 | 178 | 117 | 90 |
| Television, radios, sound equipment | 100 | 74 | 62 | 85 | 49 | 30 |
| Pets, toys, playground equip. | 100 | 130 | 109 | 149 | 86 | 53 |
| Other entertainment supplies, services | 100 | 154 | 151 | 166 | 52 | 34 |
| **PERSONAL CARE PRODUCTS, SERVICES** | **100** | **124** | **115** | **133** | **89** | **62** |
| **READING** | **100** | **126** | **135** | **124** | **45** | **77** |

*(continued)*

*(continued from previous page)*

| | | married couples | | | | |
|---|---|---|---|---|---|---|
| | ***total*** | ***total*** | ***husband and wife only*** | ***husband and wife with children*** | ***single parent with children under age 18*** | ***single person*** |
| **EDUCATION** | **100** | **131** | **83** | **176** | **67** | **66** |
| **TOBACCO PRODUCTS, SMOKING SUPPLIES** | **100** | **108** | **90** | **114** | **80** | **63** |
| **MISCELLANEOUS** | **100** | **117** | **105** | **123** | **95** | **77** |
| **CASH CONTRIBUTIONS** | **100** | **124** | **153** | **101** | **31** | **86** |
| **PERSONAL INSURANCE AND PENSIONS** | **100** | **140** | **125** | **154** | **53** | **49** |
| Life, other personal insurance | 100 | 153 | 139 | 163 | 43 | 34 |
| Pensions and Social Security | 100 | 138 | 123 | 153 | 54 | 51 |
| **PERSONAL TAXES** | **100** | **140** | **117** | **168** | **25** | **62** |
| Federal income taxes | 100 | 143 | 115 | 175 | 21 | 60 |
| State and local income taxes | 100 | 129 | 117 | 144 | 42 | 68 |
| Other taxes | 100 | 135 | 154 | 122 | 35 | 71 |
| **GIFTS** | **100** | **127** | **158** | **107** | **54** | **74** |
| **Food** | **100** | **152** | **211** | **99** | **34** | **48** |
| **Housing** | **100** | **129** | **151** | **119** | **64** | **68** |
| Housekeeping supplies | 100 | 132 | 139 | 129 | 54 | 61 |
| Household textiles | 100 | 100 | 118 | 94 | 35 | 118 |
| Appliances and miscellaneous housewares | 100 | 141 | 219 | 91 | 38 | 59 |
| Major appliances | 100 | 100 | 167 | 56 | 22 | 111 |
| Small appliances and misc. housewares | 100 | 150 | 229 | 96 | 42 | 38 |
| Misc. household equipment | 100 | 132 | 176 | 100 | 70 | 71 |
| Other housing | 100 | 129 | 131 | 135 | 74 | 66 |
| **Apparel and services** | **100** | **119** | **136** | **105** | **78** | **74** |
| Males, aged 2 or older | 100 | 137 | 180 | 107 | 52 | 48 |
| Females, aged 2 or older | 100 | 120 | 159 | 93 | 89 | 72 |
| Children under age 2 | 100 | 142 | 94 | 185 | 91 | 30 |
| All other apparel products and services | 100 | 83 | 87 | 69 | 79 | 133 |
| Jewelry and watches | 100 | 56 | 63 | 48 | 52 | 196 |
| All other apparel products and services | 100 | 112 | 116 | 92 | 108 | 64 |
| **Transportation** | **100** | **114** | **130** | **105** | **21** | **73** |
| **Health care** | **100** | **85** | **120** | **55** | **33** | **153** |

*(continued)*

*(continued from previous page)*

| | total | married couples total | husband and wife only | husband and wife with children | single parent with children under age 18 | single person |
|---|---|---|---|---|---|---|
| **Entertainment** | **100** | **122** | **158** | **97** | **40** | **82** |
| Toys, games, hobbies, and tricycles | 100 | 125 | 163 | 91 | 38 | 69 |
| Other entertainment | 100 | 121 | 155 | 100 | 42 | 88 |
| **Education** | **100** | **156** | **203** | **132** | **30** | **51** |
| **All other gifts** | **100** | **108** | **139** | **82** | **73** | **102** |

*Note: The Bureau of Labor Statistics uses consumer unit rather than household as the sampling unit in the Consumer Expenditure Survey. For the definition of consumer unit, see Glossary. An index of 100 is the average for all households. An index of 132 means households of that type spend 32 percent more than the average household. An index of 75 means households of that type spend 25 percent less than the average household. (–) means sample is too small to make a reliable estimate.*

*Source: Bureau of Labor Statistics, 1999 Consumer Expenditure Survey; calculations by New Strategist*

## Market Shares by Household Type, 1999

*(share of total annual spending accounted for by type of consumer unit, 1999)*

| | | married couples | | | | |
|---|---|---|---|---|---|---|
| | *total* | *total* | *husband and wife only* | *husband and wife with children* | *single parent with children under age 18* | *single person* |
| **Share of total consumer units** | **100.0%** | **70.0%** | **26.5%** | **38.1%** | **3.5%** | **16.7%** |
| **Share of total annual spending** | **100.0** | **66.3** | **24.6** | **36.4** | **4.6** | **17.6** |
| **FOOD** | **100.0%** | **65.9%** | **23.1%** | **36.8%** | **5.5%** | **15.5%** |
| **Food at home** | **100.0** | **65.9** | **22.2** | **37.4** | **6.1** | **14.5** |
| Cereals and bakery products | 100.0 | 65.8 | 21.5 | 38.3 | 6.9 | 14.4 |
| Cereals, cereal products | 100.0 | 65.0 | 19.4 | 39.3 | 7.7 | 13.3 |
| Bakery products | 100.0 | 66.3 | 22.6 | 37.7 | 6.4 | 15.0 |
| Meats, poultry, fish, eggs | 100.0 | 65.2 | 22.2 | 36.2 | 6.2 | 13.2 |
| Beef | 100.0 | 67.9 | 22.9 | 38.5 | 5.7 | 12.0 |
| Pork | 100.0 | 64.6 | 23.0 | 34.5 | 6.4 | 12.4 |
| Other meats | 100.0 | 64.4 | 21.6 | 36.9 | 6.8 | 14.4 |
| Poultry | 100.0 | 63.5 | 19.5 | 36.8 | 6.4 | 13.5 |
| Fish and seafood | 100.0 | 64.8 | 24.0 | 33.5 | 6.3 | 15.1 |
| Eggs | 100.0 | 65.0 | 21.6 | 35.4 | 6.4 | 14.5 |
| Dairy products | 100.0 | 67.7 | 22.0 | 39.5 | 5.7 | 14.0 |
| Fresh milk and cream | 100.0 | 66.9 | 19.5 | 40.8 | 6.1 | 13.8 |
| Other dairy products | 100.0 | 68.2 | 23.7 | 38.8 | 5.4 | 14.3 |
| Fruits and vegetables | 100.0 | 65.9 | 23.6 | 35.8 | 5.5 | 15.4 |
| Fresh fruits | 100.0 | 66.1 | 24.1 | 35.3 | 5.3 | 16.3 |
| Fresh vegetables | 100.0 | 66.3 | 25.2 | 34.6 | 5.2 | 14.8 |
| Processed fruits | 100.0 | 64.9 | 22.0 | 37.3 | 6.0 | 15.4 |
| Processed vegetables | 100.0 | 65.9 | 22.3 | 36.7 | 5.9 | 14.2 |
| Other food at home | 100.0 | 66.0 | 21.8 | 38.1 | 6.1 | 15.2 |
| Sugar and other sweets | 100.0 | 66.9 | 23.9 | 36.6 | 6.2 | 14.8 |
| Fats and oils | 100.0 | 64.4 | 23.6 | 34.5 | 6.5 | 14.5 |
| Miscellaneous foods | 100.0 | 65.6 | 20.4 | 39.6 | 6.3 | 15.3 |
| Nonalcoholic beverages | 100.0 | 64.9 | 21.5 | 37.0 | 6.1 | 15.4 |
| Food prepared by hh on trips | 100.0 | 74.7 | 28.2 | 39.8 | 2.8 | 14.9 |
| **Food away from home** | **100.0** | **65.8** | **24.3** | **35.9** | **4.5** | **17.0** |

*(continued)*

*(continued from previous page)*

| | | married couples | | | | |
|---|---|---|---|---|---|---|
| | *total* | *total* | *husband and wife only* | *husband and wife with children* | *single parent with children under age 18* | *single person* |
| **ALCOHOLIC BEVERAGES** | **100.0%** | **55.1%** | **26.3%** | **24.7%** | **2.7%** | **26.2%** |
| **HOUSING** | **100.0** | **63.8** | **23.2** | **35.7** | **5.1** | **19.8** |
| **Shelter** | **100.0** | **62.4** | **22.4** | **35.3** | **5.1** | **21.3** |
| Owned dwellings | 100.0 | 73.6 | 25.4 | 42.9 | 3.5 | 14.8 |
| Mortgage interest/charges | 100.0 | 77.0 | 21.8 | 49.3 | 3.8 | 11.5 |
| Property taxes | 100.0 | 70.3 | 28.0 | 37.2 | 2.9 | 18.9 |
| Maintenance, repairs, insurance, other | 100.0 | 68.1 | 33.0 | 31.3 | 3.7 | 19.5 |
| Rented dwellings | 100.0 | 35.2 | 12.7 | 18.9 | 9.2 | 36.1 |
| Other lodging | 100.0 | 71.4 | 34.4 | 32.6 | 1.8 | 19.9 |
| **Utilities, fuels, public services** | **100.0** | **62.6** | **23.5** | **33.4** | **5.6** | **19.0** |
| Natural gas | 100.0 | 62.0 | 23.2 | 32.8 | 5.6 | 19.8 |
| Electricity | 100.0 | 63.3 | 24.2 | 33.4 | 5.7 | 18.3 |
| Fuel oil and other fuels | 100.0 | 67.5 | 29.5 | 32.7 | 3.3 | 17.7 |
| Telephone services | 100.0 | 60.0 | 21.7 | 32.4 | 5.9 | 20.3 |
| Water, other public services | 100.0 | 67.5 | 25.1 | 36.5 | 4.7 | 16.8 |
| **Household services** | **100.0** | **66.2** | **17.3** | **44.5** | **6.3** | **20.5** |
| Personal services | 100.0 | 66.2 | 5.1 | 56.0 | 9.9 | 17.4 |
| Other household services | 100.0 | 66.3 | 28.7 | 33.7 | 2.9 | 23.4 |
| **Housekeeping supplies** | **100.0** | **70.6** | **27.0** | **38.4** | **4.3** | **13.9** |
| Laundry, cleaning supplies | 100.0 | 67.1 | 23.9 | 36.5 | 6.8 | 13.2 |
| Other household products | 100.0 | 74.1 | 27.4 | 41.3 | 3.4 | 12.3 |
| Postage and stationery | 100.0 | 67.2 | 29.1 | 34.4 | 3.9 | 17.6 |
| **Household furnishings and equipment** | **100.0** | **69.2** | **28.1** | **36.3** | **4.0** | **15.7** |
| Household textiles | 100.0 | 66.6 | 26.3 | 35.3 | 5.4 | 17.6 |
| Furniture | 100.0 | 68.8 | 25.3 | 37.9 | 4.2 | 15.8 |
| Floor coverings | 100.0 | 73.3 | 35.3 | 35.3 | 4.0 | 13.9 |
| Major appliances | 100.0 | 65.4 | 27.0 | 34.1 | 3.7 | 17.3 |
| Small appliances, misc. housewares | 100.0 | 65.8 | 33.0 | 29.1 | 2.3 | 19.7 |
| Misc. household equipment | 100.0 | 71.0 | 29.0 | 37.2 | 4.0 | 14.3 |
| **APPAREL, SERVICES** | **100.0** | **64.7** | **20.8** | **38.0** | **6.8** | **15.6** |
| **Men and boys** | **100.0** | **70.8** | **22.7** | **41.5** | **5.3** | **12.1** |
| Men, aged 16 or older | 100.0 | 70.7 | 27.6 | 36.7 | 2.7 | 14.6 |
| Boys, aged 2 to 15 | 100.0 | 71.0 | 5.1 | 58.6 | 14.6 | 3.1 |

*(continued)*

*(continued from previous page)*

| | total | married couples: total | married couples: husband and wife only | married couples: husband and wife with children | single parent with children under age 18 | single person |
|---|---|---|---|---|---|---|
| **Women and girls** | **100.0%** | **63.5%** | **22.0%** | **36.3%** | **8.4%** | **15.0%** |
| Women, aged 16 or older | 100.0 | 62.0 | 25.2 | 31.6 | 7.2 | 17.4 |
| Girls, aged 2 to 15 | 100.0 | 71.0 | 5.2 | 60.0 | 15.0 | 2.4 |
| **Children under age 2** | **100.0** | **77.6** | **10.0** | **58.9** | **6.8** | **4.3** |
| **Footwear** | **100.0** | **63.0** | **17.5** | **38.6** | **7.9** | **13.0** |
| **Other apparel products and services** | **100.0** | **57.6** | **21.2** | **31.7** | **3.9** | **27.0** |
| **TRANSPORTATION** | **100.0** | **68.9** | **24.8** | **38.3** | **4.1** | **14.7** |
| **Vehicle purchases** | **100.0** | **69.6** | **24.8** | **39.4** | **4.1** | **13.3** |
| Cars and trucks, new | 100.0 | 73.6 | 31.2 | 37.2 | 2.1 | 13.5 |
| Cars and trucks, used | 100.0 | 65.8 | 18.7 | 41.4 | 6.2 | 12.9 |
| Other vehicles | 100.0 | 59.2 | 10.8 | 44.6 | 4.2 | 20.2 |
| **Gasoline and motor oil** | **100.0** | **67.9** | **23.4** | **38.0** | **4.1** | **15.6** |
| **Other vehicle expenses** | **100.0** | **68.7** | **24.4** | **38.4** | **4.0** | **15.7** |
| Vehicle finance charges | 100.0 | 71.2 | 21.5 | 43.6 | 4.5 | 10.9 |
| Maintenance and repairs | 100.0 | 68.5 | 24.9 | 37.0 | 3.9 | 16.7 |
| Vehicle insurance | 100.0 | 66.6 | 23.9 | 37.0 | 4.1 | 16.5 |
| Vehicle rental, leases, licenses, other | 100.0 | 70.8 | 26.4 | 39.0 | 3.7 | 16.0 |
| **Public transportation** | **100.0** | **67.5** | **31.5** | **30.3** | **3.5** | **18.3** |
| **HEALTH CARE** | **100.0** | **67.0** | **32.0** | **29.5** | **3.1** | **19.8** |
| Health insurance | 100.0 | 67.7 | 32.5 | 29.9 | 3.2 | 19.3 |
| Medical services | 100.0 | 68.6 | 28.9 | 33.9 | 3.3 | 18.0 |
| Drugs | 100.0 | 62.3 | 35.7 | 21.5 | 2.7 | 23.9 |
| Medical supplies | 100.0 | 67.3 | 31.5 | 31.4 | 2.8 | 19.2 |
| **ENTERTAINMENT** | **100.0** | **16.9** | **6.8** | **9.2** | **0.9** | **4.3** |
| Fees and admissions | 100.0 | 81.3 | 27.2 | 46.7 | 7.1 | 26.3 |
| Television, radio, sound equipment | 100.0 | 38.4 | 13.4 | 22.3 | 3.0 | 8.9 |
| Pets, toys, playground equipment | 100.0 | 67.5 | 23.5 | 39.2 | 5.2 | 15.6 |
| Other entertainment supplies, services | 100.0 | 80.2 | 32.6 | 43.6 | 3.2 | 9.9 |
| **PERSONAL CARE PRODUCTS, SERVICES** | **100.0** | **64.5** | **24.9** | **34.9** | **5.4** | **18.1** |
| **READING** | **100.0** | **65.8** | **29.2** | **32.6** | **2.7** | **22.3** |

*(continued)*

*(continued from previous page)*

| | | married couples | | | | |
|---|---|---|---|---|---|---|
| | *total* | *total* | *husband and wife only* | *husband and wife with children* | *single parent with children under age 18* | *single person* |
| **EDUCATION** | **100.0%** | **67.9%** | **17.9%** | **46.2%** | **4.1%** | **19.3%** |
| **TOBACCO PRODUCTS, SMOKING SUPPLIES** | **100.0** | **56.2** | **19.3** | **30.0** | **4.8** | **18.3** |
| **MISCELLANEOUS** | **100.0** | **61.0** | **22.6** | **32.3** | **5.7** | **22.5** |
| **CASH CONTRIBUTIONS** | **100.0** | **64.6** | **32.9** | **26.6** | **1.9** | **24.9** |
| **PERSONAL INSURANCE AND PENSIONS** | **100.0** | **72.9** | **26.9** | **40.6** | **3.2** | **14.3** |
| Life, other pers. insurance | 100.0 | 79.5 | 30.0 | 43.0 | 2.6 | 9.8 |
| Pensions, Social Security | 100.0 | 72.0 | 26.5 | 40.3 | 3.3 | 14.9 |
| **PERSONAL TAXES** | **100.0** | **72.9** | **25.3** | **44.1** | **1.5** | **18.0** |
| Federal income taxes | 100.0 | 74.4 | 24.8 | 46.1 | 1.3 | 17.4 |
| State and local income taxes | 100.0 | 67.1 | 25.3 | 38.0 | 2.5 | 19.8 |
| Other taxes | 100.0 | 70.4 | 33.3 | 32.2 | 2.1 | 20.7 |
| **GIFTS** | **100.0** | **66.2** | **34.0** | **28.2** | **3.3** | **21.5** |
| **Food** | **100.0** | **79.0** | **45.5** | **26.0** | **2.0** | **14.0** |
| **Housing** | **100.0** | **67.2** | **32.6** | **31.3** | **3.9** | **19.9** |
| Housekeeping supplies | 100.0 | 68.5 | 30.0 | 34.0 | 3.3 | 17.7 |
| Household textiles | 100.0 | 52.0 | 25.4 | 24.8 | 2.1 | 34.2 |
| Appliances and misc. housewares | 100.0 | 73.2 | 47.2 | 23.8 | 2.3 | 17.3 |
| Major appliances | 100.0 | 52.0 | 36.0 | 14.6 | 1.3 | 32.3 |
| Small appliances and misc. housewares | 100.0 | 78.0 | 49.4 | 25.2 | 2.5 | 10.9 |
| Misc. household equipment | 100.0 | 68.6 | 37.9 | 26.3 | 4.2 | 20.7 |
| Other housing | 100.0 | 66.9 | 28.2 | 35.6 | 4.5 | 19.2 |
| **Apparel and services** | **100.0** | **61.7** | **29.4** | **27.7** | **4.7** | **21.6** |
| Males, aged 2 or older | 100.0 | 71.3 | 38.8 | 28.3 | 3.1 | 14.0 |
| Females, aged 2 or older | 100.0 | 62.3 | 34.3 | 24.5 | 5.4 | 20.9 |
| Children under age 2 | 100.0 | 74.1 | 20.3 | 48.6 | 5.5 | 8.8 |
| All other apparel products and services | 100.0 | 43.0 | 18.7 | 18.2 | 4.8 | 38.6 |
| Jewelry and watches | 100.0 | 28.9 | 13.6 | 12.7 | 3.1 | 57.1 |
| All other apparel products and services | 100.0 | 58.3 | 25.0 | 24.2 | 6.5 | 18.6 |
| **Transportation** | **100.0** | **59.5** | **28.1** | **27.6** | **1.3** | **21.2** |
| **Health care** | **100.0** | **44.2** | **25.9** | **14.5** | **2.0** | **44.4** |

*(continued)*

*(continued from previous page)*

| | total | married couples: total | married couples: husband and wife only | married couples: husband and wife with children | single parent with children under age 18 | single person |
|---|---|---|---|---|---|---|
| **Entertainment** | **100.0%** | **63.7%** | **34.1%** | **25.5%** | **2.4%** | **23.7%** |
| Toys, games, hobbies, and tricycles | 100.0 | 65.0 | 35.1 | 23.8 | 2.3 | 20.0 |
| Other entertainment | 100.0 | 63.1 | 33.3 | 26.3 | 2.6 | 25.6 |
| **Education** | **100.0** | **81.2** | **43.8** | **34.7** | **1.8** | **14.7** |
| **All other gifts** | **100.0** | **56.4** | **30.0** | **21.5** | **4.4** | **29.5** |

*Note: The Bureau of Labor Statistics uses consumer unit rather than household as the sampling unit in the Consumer Expenditure Survey. For the definition of consumer unit, see Glossary. Numbers may not add to total due to rounding.*

*Source: Bureau of Labor Statistics, 1999 Consumer Expenditure Survey; calculations by New Strategist*

# Spending of Blacks, Hispanics Is above Average on Many Items

## Hispanics spend more than average on most foods, while blacks are big spenders on children's clothes.

Spending patterns by race and Hispanic origin are more complex than total spending figures would suggest. Overall, non-Hispanic white and "other" households spent an average of $38,687 in 1999 compared with $27,314 spent by non-Hispanic blacks and $33,105 spent by Hispanics. But an examination of the indexed spending table in this section shows that both non-Hispanic blacks and Hispanics spend more than the average household on a number of items.

The indexed spending table shows household spending for each racial and Hispanic origin group relative to what the average household spends. An index of 100 means a household spends an average amount on an item. An index above 100 means households in the group spend more than average on the item, while an index below 100 reveals below-average spending.

A look at the table shows below-average spending on most items by non-Hispanic black and Hispanic households, and average spending by non-Hispanic white households. There are some important exceptions, however. Non-Hispanic black households spend much more than average on poultry, pork, fish, and seafood. They spend 8 percent more on telephone services, 61 percent more on boys' clothes, 47 percent more on girls' clothes, and 65 percent more on footwear.

Hispanic households spend much more than average on most foods, probably because their households are larger than average—3.5 people compared with 2.5 in the average household. Hispanics households spend 31 percent more than average on laundry and cleaning products, 44 percent more on boys' clothes, 61 percent more on girls' clothes, 70 percent more on infants' clothes, and 62 percent more on footwear. They spend 19 percent more than the average household on used cars and trucks.

Because non-Hispanic black and Hispanic households account for a small share of total households, and because their spending is below average as well, they account for a small share of the overall household market in most product and service categories.

♦ The spending of non-Hispanic black households is likely to remain below average because few are headed by married couples, the most affluent household type. The spending of Hispanics will remain below average because many are recent immigrants with low incomes.

## Non-Hispanic black and Hispanic households spend more than average on children's clothing

*(indexed average annual spending of consumer units on boys' and girls' clothes, by race and Hispanic origin of consumer unit reference person, 1999)*

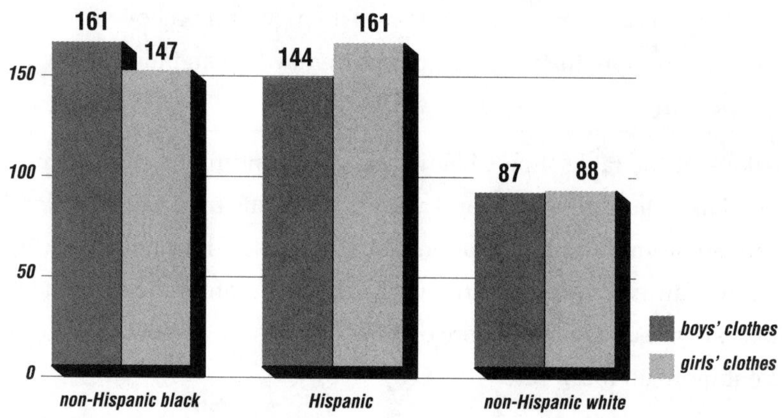

# Spending by Race and Hispanic Origin, 1999

*(average annual spending of consumer units (CU's) by product and service category and race and Hispanic origin of consumer unit reference person, 1999)*

| | | non-Hispanic | | | |
|---|---|---|---|---|---|
| | *total* | *total* | *white/other* | *black* | *Hispanic* |
| **Number of consumer units (in 000s)** | **108,465** | **99,354** | **87,924** | **11,431** | **9,111** |
| **Average number of persons per CU** | **2.5** | **2.4** | **2.4** | **2.7** | **3.5** |
| **Average before-tax income** | **$43,951** | **$44,955** | **$46,746** | **$30,325** | **$33,803** |
| **Average annual spending** | **37,027** | **37,385** | **38,687** | **27,314** | **33,105** |
| **FOOD** | **$5,031** | **$4,986** | **$5,100** | **$4,089** | **$5,493** |
| **Food at home** | **2,915** | **2,854** | **2,883** | **2,625** | **3,556** |
| Cereals and bakery products | 448 | 444 | 450 | 396 | 495 |
| Cereals and cereal products | 160 | 156 | 155 | 161 | 204 |
| Bakery products | 288 | 288 | 295 | 235 | 291 |
| Meats, poultry, fish, and eggs | 749 | 716 | 697 | 864 | 1,097 |
| Beef | 220 | 210 | 209 | 216 | 331 |
| Pork | 157 | 150 | 142 | 210 | 230 |
| Other meats | 97 | 94 | 94 | 93 | 128 |
| Poultry | 136 | 129 | 124 | 170 | 206 |
| Fish and seafood | 106 | 103 | 98 | 140 | 142 |
| Eggs | 32 | 30 | 29 | 35 | 60 |
| Dairy products | 322 | 317 | 328 | 232 | 377 |
| Fresh milk and cream | 122 | 118 | 122 | 84 | 165 |
| Other dairy products | 200 | 199 | 206 | 147 | 211 |
| Fruits and vegetables | 500 | 484 | 492 | 420 | 663 |
| Fresh fruits | 152 | 147 | 150 | 121 | 216 |
| Fresh vegetables | 149 | 141 | 145 | 108 | 224 |
| Processed fruits | 113 | 111 | 112 | 106 | 134 |
| Processed vegetables | 86 | 85 | 85 | 85 | 89 |
| Other food at home | 896 | 894 | 916 | 714 | 924 |
| Sugar and other sweets | 112 | 112 | 113 | 100 | 111 |
| Fats and oils | 84 | 82 | 81 | 87 | 104 |
| Miscellaneous foods | 420 | 422 | 436 | 311 | 393 |
| Nonalcoholic beverages | 242 | 239 | 243 | 203 | 279 |
| Food prepared by household on trips | 39 | 40 | 43 | 13 | 38 |
| **Food away from home** | **2,116** | **2,132** | **2,217** | **1,464** | **1,937** |
| **ALCOHOLIC BEVERAGES** | **318** | **322** | **345** | **144** | **269** |

*(continued)*

*(continued from previous page)*

| | total | non-Hispanic total | non-Hispanic white/other | non-Hispanic black | Hispanic |
|---|---|---|---|---|---|
| **HOUSING** | **$12,057** | **$12,155** | **$12,484** | **$9,609** | **$11,001** |
| **Shelter** | **7,016** | **7,038** | **7,250** | **5,409** | **6,778** |
| Owned dwellings | 4,525 | 4,648 | 4,901 | 2,705 | 3,186 |
| Mortgage interest and charges | 2,547 | 2,605 | 2,727 | 1,664 | 1,919 |
| Property taxes | 1,123 | 1,168 | 1,239 | 623 | 634 |
| Maintenance, repairs, insurance, other | 855 | 875 | 934 | 418 | 633 |
| Rented dwellings | 2,027 | 1,899 | 1,811 | 2,571 | 3,420 |
| Other lodging | 464 | 491 | 538 | 133 | 171 |
| **Utilities, fuels, public services** | **2,377** | **2,401** | **2,397** | **2,431** | **2,124** |
| Natural gas | 270 | 274 | 270 | 305 | 228 |
| Electricity | 899 | 913 | 912 | 923 | 743 |
| Fuel oil and other fuels | 74 | 78 | 83 | 40 | 30 |
| Telephone services | 849 | 847 | 838 | 918 | 872 |
| Water and other public services | 285 | 288 | 293 | 245 | 251 |
| **Household services** | **666** | **684** | **715** | **441** | **470** |
| Personal services | 323 | 328 | 336 | 265 | 269 |
| Other household services | 343 | 356 | 380 | 175 | 201 |
| **Housekeeping supplies** | **498** | **503** | **521** | **359** | **445** |
| Laundry and cleaning supplies | 121 | 118 | 116 | 130 | 158 |
| Other household products | 250 | 253 | 266 | 154 | 211 |
| Postage and stationery | 127 | 132 | 139 | 75 | 77 |
| **Household furnishings and equipment** | **1,499** | **1,529** | **1,600** | **969** | **1,184** |
| Household textiles | 114 | 114 | 118 | 89 | 110 |
| Furniture | 365 | 366 | 375 | 301 | 352 |
| Floor coverings | 44 | 45 | 48 | 22 | 27 |
| Major appliances | 183 | 185 | 189 | 156 | 158 |
| Small appliances, miscellaneous housewares | 102 | 103 | 111 | 41 | 85 |
| Miscellaneous household equipment | 692 | 714 | 759 | 359 | 453 |
| **APPAREL AND SERVICES** | **1,743** | **1,712** | **1,691** | **1,880** | **2,071** |
| **Men and boys** | **421** | **411** | **419** | **349** | **525** |
| Men, aged 16 or older | 328 | 322 | 337 | 199 | 391 |
| Boys, aged 2 to 15 | 93 | 89 | 81 | 150 | 134 |
| **Women and girls** | **655** | **655** | **647** | **723** | **651** |
| Women, aged 16 or older | 548 | 554 | 552 | 566 | 479 |
| Girls, aged 2 to 15 | 107 | 101 | 94 | 157 | 172 |
| **Children under age 2** | **67** | **62** | **62** | **66** | **114** |
| **Footwear** | **303** | **285** | **259** | **499** | **490** |
| **Other apparel products and services** | **297** | **297** | **304** | **242** | **291** |

*(continued)*

*(continued from previous page)*

| | | non-Hispanic | | | |
|---|---|---|---|---|---|
| | *total* | *total* | *white/other* | *black* | *Hispanic* |
| **TRANSPORTATION** | **$7,011** | **$7,031** | **$7,273** | **$5,163** | **$6,801** |
| **Vehicle purchases** | **3,305** | **3,300** | **3,414** | **2,428** | **3,362** |
| Cars and trucks, new | 1,628 | 1,653 | 1,740 | 982 | 1,352 |
| Cars and trucks, used | 1,641 | 1,612 | 1,634 | 1,446 | 1,959 |
| Other vehicles | 36 | 35 | 39 | – | 50 |
| **Gasoline and motor oil** | **1,055** | **1,049** | **1,086** | **765** | **1,116** |
| **Other vehicle expenses** | **2,254** | **2,279** | **2,353** | **1,706** | **1,979** |
| Vehicle finance charges | 320 | 325 | 331 | 275 | 276 |
| Maintenance and repairs | 664 | 671 | 698 | 463 | 586 |
| Vehicle insurance | 756 | 764 | 785 | 605 | 672 |
| Vehicle rental, leases, licenses, other | 513 | 519 | 539 | 363 | 445 |
| **Public transportation** | **397** | **402** | **420** | **264** | **344** |
| **HEALTH CARE** | **1,959** | **2,036** | **2,155** | **1,115** | **1,119** |
| Health insurance | 923 | 958 | 1,009 | 566 | 534 |
| Medical services | 558 | 580 | 623 | 248 | 313 |
| Drugs | 370 | 385 | 402 | 248 | 211 |
| Medical supplies | 109 | 113 | 121 | 53 | 62 |
| **ENTERTAINMENT** | **1,891** | **1,951** | **2,082** | **933** | **1,245** |
| Fees and admissions | 459 | 478 | 518 | 167 | 253 |
| Television, radios, sound equipment | 608 | 613 | 620 | 556 | 554 |
| Pets, toys, playground equipment | 346 | 358 | 386 | 138 | 211 |
| Other entertainment supplies, services | 478 | 502 | 557 | 73 | 226 |
| **PERSONAL CARE PRODUCTS AND SERVICES** | **408** | **409** | **410** | **401** | **404** |
| **READING** | **159** | **168** | **179** | **81** | **71** |
| **EDUCATION** | **635** | **659** | **695** | **387** | **366** |
| **TOBACCO PRODUCTS AND SMOKING SUPPLIES** | **300** | **312** | **324** | **216** | **172** |
| **MISCELLANEOUS** | **889** | **906** | **944** | **613** | **697** |
| **CASH CONTRIBUTIONS** | **1,190** | **1,237** | **1,324** | **567** | **679** |
| **PERSONAL INSURANCE AND PENSIONS** | **3,436** | **3,502** | **3,682** | **2,116** | **2,718** |
| Life and other personal insurance | 394 | 413 | 425 | 322 | 191 |
| Pensions and Social Security | 3,042 | 3,089 | 3,257 | 1,794 | 2,528 |

*(continued)*

*(continued from previous page)*

| | total | non-Hispanic total | non-Hispanic white/other | non-Hispanic black | Hispanic |
|---|---|---|---|---|---|
| **PERSONAL TAXES** | **$3,588** | **$3,712** | **$3,986** | **$1,477** | **$2,334** |
| Federal income taxes | 2,802 | 2,893 | 3,117 | 1,065 | 1,880 |
| State and local income taxes | 616 | 638 | 675 | 343 | 387 |
| Other taxes | 170 | 181 | 194 | 69 | 68 |
| **GIFTS** | **1,083** | **1,114** | **1,172** | **663** | **749** |
| **Food** | **83** | **87** | **95** | **29** | **35** |
| **Housing** | **292** | **303** | **319** | **181** | **172** |
| Housekeeping supplies | 41 | 42 | 44 | 24 | 25 |
| Household textiles | 17 | 17 | 18 | 10 | 11 |
| Appliances and miscellaneous housewares | 32 | 34 | 37 | 10 | 16 |
| Major appliances | 9 | 9 | 10 | 2 | 2 |
| Small appliances and misc. housewares | 24 | 25 | 27 | 8 | 14 |
| Miscellaneous household equipment | 66 | 70 | 74 | 41 | 26 |
| Other housing | 136 | 140 | 146 | 95 | 95 |
| **Apparel and services** | **210** | **205** | **204** | **215** | **256** |
| Males, aged 2 or older | 54 | 54 | 56 | 42 | 54 |
| Females, aged 2 or older | 71 | 71 | 70 | 75 | 73 |
| Children under age 2 | 33 | 32 | 32 | 33 | 40 |
| All other apparel products and services | 52 | 48 | 46 | 65 | 90 |
| Jewelry and watches | 27 | 25 | 26 | 14 | 44 |
| All other apparel products and services | 25 | 23 | 20 | 51 | 46 |
| **Transportation** | **63** | **64** | **65** | **55** | **60** |
| **Health care** | **40** | **43** | **48** | **6** | **7** |
| **Entertainment** | **98** | **103** | **111** | **34** | **50** |
| Toys, games, hobbies, and tricycles | 32 | 32 | 35 | 14 | 26 |
| Other entertainment | 66 | 70 | 77 | 20 | 24 |
| **Education** | **166** | **176** | **189** | **74** | **62** |
| **All other gifts** | **131** | **133** | **142** | **68** | **108** |

*Note: The Bureau of Labor Statistics uses consumer unit rather than household as the sampling unit in the Consumer Expenditure Survey. For the definition of consumer unit, see the Glossary. Gift spending is also included in the preceding product and service categories.*
*Source: Bureau of Labor Statistics, 1999 Consumer Expenditure Survey; Internet site <www.bls.gov/csxstnd.htm>*

## Indexed Spending by Race and Hispanic Origin, 1999

*(indexed average annual spending of consumer units by product and service category and race and Hispanic origin of consumer unit reference person, 1999)*

| | | non-Hispanic | | | |
|---|---|---|---|---|---|
| | *total* | *total* | *white/other* | *black* | *Hispanic* |
| **Number of consumer units (in 000s)** | **108,465** | **99,354** | **87,924** | **11,431** | **9,111** |
| **Indexed average before-tax income** | **100** | **102** | **106** | **69** | **77** |
| **Indexed average annual spending** | **100** | **101** | **104** | **74** | **89** |
| **FOOD** | **100** | **99** | **101** | **81** | **109** |
| **Food at home** | **100** | **98** | **99** | **90** | **122** |
| Cereals and bakery products | 100 | 99 | 100 | 88 | 110 |
| Cereals and cereal products | 100 | 98 | 97 | 101 | 128 |
| Bakery products | 100 | 100 | 102 | 82 | 101 |
| Meats, poultry, fish, and eggs | 100 | 96 | 93 | 115 | 146 |
| Beef | 100 | 95 | 95 | 98 | 150 |
| Pork | 100 | 96 | 90 | 134 | 146 |
| Other meats | 100 | 97 | 97 | 96 | 132 |
| Poultry | 100 | 95 | 91 | 125 | 151 |
| Fish and seafood | 100 | 97 | 92 | 132 | 134 |
| Eggs | 100 | 94 | 91 | 109 | 188 |
| Dairy products | 100 | 98 | 102 | 72 | 117 |
| Fresh milk and cream | 100 | 97 | 100 | 69 | 135 |
| Other dairy products | 100 | 100 | 103 | 74 | 106 |
| Fruits and vegetables | 100 | 97 | 98 | 84 | 133 |
| Fresh fruits | 100 | 97 | 99 | 80 | 142 |
| Fresh vegetables | 100 | 95 | 97 | 72 | 150 |
| Processed fruits | 100 | 98 | 99 | 94 | 119 |
| Processed vegetables | 100 | 99 | 99 | 99 | 103 |
| Other food at home | 100 | 100 | 102 | 80 | 103 |
| Sugar and other sweets | 100 | 100 | 101 | 89 | 99 |
| Fats and oils | 100 | 98 | 96 | 104 | 124 |
| Miscellaneous foods | 100 | 100 | 104 | 74 | 94 |
| Nonalcoholic beverages | 100 | 99 | 100 | 84 | 115 |
| Food prepared by household on trips | 100 | 103 | 110 | 33 | 97 |
| **Food away from home** | **100** | **101** | **105** | **69** | **92** |
| **ALCOHOLIC BEVERAGES** | **100** | **101** | **108** | **45** | **85** |

*(continued)*

*(continued from previous page)*

| | | non-Hispanic | | | |
|---|---|---|---|---|---|
| | *total* | *total* | *white/other* | *black* | *Hispanic* |
| **HOUSING** | **100** | **101** | **104** | **80** | **91** |
| **Shelter** | **100** | **100** | **103** | **77** | **97** |
| Owned dwellings | 100 | 103 | 108 | 60 | 70 |
| Mortgage interest and charges | 100 | 102 | 107 | 65 | 75 |
| Property taxes | 100 | 104 | 110 | 55 | 56 |
| Maintenance, repairs, insurance, other | 100 | 102 | 109 | 49 | 74 |
| Rented dwellings | 100 | 94 | 89 | 127 | 169 |
| Other lodging | 100 | 106 | 116 | 29 | 37 |
| **Utilities, fuels, public services** | **100** | **101** | **101** | **102** | **89** |
| Natural gas | 100 | 101 | 100 | 113 | 84 |
| Electricity | 100 | 102 | 101 | 103 | 83 |
| Fuel oil and other fuels | 100 | 105 | 112 | 54 | 41 |
| Telephone services | 100 | 100 | 99 | 108 | 103 |
| Water and other public services | 100 | 101 | 103 | 86 | 88 |
| **Household services** | **100** | **103** | **107** | **66** | **71** |
| Personal services | 100 | 102 | 104 | 82 | 83 |
| Other household services | 100 | 104 | 111 | 51 | 59 |
| **Housekeeping supplies** | **100** | **101** | **105** | **72** | **89** |
| Laundry and cleaning supplies | 100 | 98 | 96 | 107 | 131 |
| Other household products | 100 | 101 | 106 | 62 | 84 |
| Postage and stationery | 100 | 104 | 109 | 59 | 61 |
| **Household furnishings and equipment** | **100** | **102** | **107** | **65** | **79** |
| Household textiles | 100 | 100 | 104 | 78 | 96 |
| Furniture | 100 | 100 | 103 | 82 | 96 |
| Floor coverings | 100 | 102 | 109 | 50 | 61 |
| Major appliances | 100 | 101 | 103 | 85 | 86 |
| Small appliances, miscellaneous housewares | 100 | 101 | 109 | 40 | 83 |
| Miscellaneous household equipment | 100 | 103 | 110 | 52 | 65 |
| **APPAREL AND SERVICES** | **100** | **98** | **97** | **108** | **119** |
| **Men and boys** | **100** | **98** | **100** | **83** | **125** |
| Men, aged 16 or older | 100 | 98 | 103 | 61 | 119 |
| Boys, aged 2 to 15 | 100 | 96 | 87 | 161 | 144 |
| **Women and girls** | **100** | **100** | **99** | **110** | **99** |
| Women, aged 16 or older | 100 | 101 | 101 | 103 | 87 |
| Girls, aged 2 to 15 | 100 | 94 | 88 | 147 | 161 |
| **Children under age 2** | **100** | **93** | **93** | **99** | **170** |
| **Footwear** | **100** | **94** | **85** | **165** | **162** |
| **Other apparel products and services** | **100** | **100** | **102** | **81** | **98** |

*(continued)*

*(continued from previous page)*

| | | non-Hispanic | | | |
|---|---|---|---|---|---|
| | **total** | **total** | **white/other** | **black** | **Hispanic** |
| **TRANSPORTATION** | **100** | **100** | **104** | **74** | **97** |
| **Vehicle purchases** | **100** | **100** | **103** | **73** | **102** |
| Cars and trucks, new | 100 | 102 | 107 | 60 | 83 |
| Cars and trucks, used | 100 | 98 | 100 | 88 | 119 |
| Other vehicles | 100 | 97 | 108 | – | 139 |
| **Gasoline and motor oil** | **100** | **99** | **103** | **73** | **106** |
| **Other vehicle expenses** | **100** | **101** | **104** | **76** | **88** |
| Vehicle finance charges | 100 | 102 | 103 | 86 | 86 |
| Maintenance and repairs | 100 | 101 | 105 | 70 | 88 |
| Vehicle insurance | 100 | 101 | 104 | 80 | 89 |
| Vehicle rental, leases, licenses, other | 100 | 101 | 105 | 71 | 87 |
| **Public transportation** | **100** | **101** | **106** | **66** | **87** |
| **HEALTH CARE** | **100** | **104** | **110** | **57** | **57** |
| Health insurance | 100 | 104 | 109 | 61 | 58 |
| Medical services | 100 | 104 | 112 | 44 | 56 |
| Drugs | 100 | 104 | 109 | 67 | 57 |
| Medical supplies | 100 | 104 | 111 | 49 | 57 |
| **ENTERTAINMENT** | **100** | **103** | **110** | **49** | **66** |
| Fees and admissions | 100 | 104 | 113 | 36 | 55 |
| Television, radio, sound equipment | 100 | 101 | 102 | 91 | 91 |
| Pets, toys, playground equipment | 100 | 103 | 112 | 40 | 61 |
| Other entertainment supplies, services | 100 | 105 | 117 | 15 | 47 |
| **PERSONAL CARE PRODUCTS AND SERVICES** | **100** | **100** | **100** | **98** | **99** |
| **READING** | **100** | **106** | **113** | **51** | **45** |
| **EDUCATION** | **100** | **104** | **109** | **61** | **58** |
| **TOBACCO PRODUCTS AND SMOKING SUPPLIES** | **100** | **104** | **108** | **72** | **57** |
| **MISCELLANEOUS** | **100** | **102** | **106** | **69** | **78** |
| **CASH CONTRIBUTIONS** | **100** | **104** | **111** | **48** | **57** |
| **PERSONAL INSURANCE AND PENSIONS** | **100** | **102** | **107** | **62** | **79** |
| Life and other personal insurance | 100 | 105 | 108 | 82 | 48 |
| Pensions and Social Security | 100 | 102 | 107 | 59 | 83 |

*(continued)*

*(continued from previous page)*

| | total | non-Hispanic total | non-Hispanic white/other | black | Hispanic |
|---|---|---|---|---|---|
| **PERSONAL TAXES** | **100** | **103** | **111** | **41** | **65** |
| Federal income taxes | 100 | 103 | 111 | 38 | 67 |
| State and local income taxes | 100 | 104 | 110 | 56 | 63 |
| Other taxes | 100 | 106 | 114 | 41 | 40 |
| **GIFTS** | **100** | **103** | **108** | **61** | **69** |
| **Food** | **100** | **105** | **114** | **35** | **42** |
| **Housing** | **100** | **104** | **109** | **62** | **59** |
| Housekeeping supplies | 100 | 102 | 107 | 59 | 61 |
| Household textiles | 100 | 100 | 106 | 59 | 65 |
| Appliances and miscellaneous housewares | 100 | 106 | 116 | 31 | 50 |
| Major appliances | 100 | 100 | 111 | 22 | 22 |
| Small appliances and misc. housewares | 100 | 104 | 113 | 33 | 58 |
| Miscellaneous household equipment | 100 | 106 | 112 | 62 | 39 |
| Other housing | 100 | 103 | 107 | 70 | 70 |
| **Apparel and services** | **100** | **98** | **97** | **102** | **122** |
| Males, aged 2 or older | 100 | 100 | 104 | 78 | 100 |
| Females, aged 2 or older | 100 | 100 | 99 | 106 | 103 |
| Children under age 2 | 100 | 97 | 97 | 100 | 121 |
| All other apparel products and services | 100 | 92 | 88 | 125 | 173 |
| Jewelry and watches | 100 | 93 | 96 | 52 | 163 |
| All other apparel products and services | 100 | 92 | 80 | 204 | 184 |
| **Transportation** | **100** | **102** | **103** | **87** | **95** |
| **Health care** | **100** | **108** | **120** | **15** | **18** |
| **Entertainment** | **100** | **105** | **113** | **35** | **51** |
| Toys, games, hobbies, and tricycles | 100 | 100 | 109 | 44 | 81 |
| Other entertainment | 100 | 106 | 117 | 30 | 36 |
| **Education** | **100** | **106** | **114** | **45** | **37** |
| **All other gifts** | **100** | **102** | **108** | **52** | **82** |

*Note: The Bureau of Labor Statistics uses consumer unit rather than household as the sampling unit in the Consumer Expenditure Survey. For the definition of consumer unit, see Glossary. An index of 100 is the average for all households. An index of 132 means households in the group spend 32 percent more than the average household. An index of 75 means households in the group spend 25 percent less than the average household. (–) means sample is too small to make a reliable estimate.*
*Source: Bureau of Labor Statistics, 1999 Consumer Expenditure Survey; calculations by New Stratetgist*

## Market Shares by Race and Hispanic Origin, 1999

*(share of total annual spending accounted for by race and Hispanic origin group, 1999)*

| | | non-Hispanic | | | |
|---|---|---|---|---|---|
| | *total* | *total* | *white/other* | *black* | *Hispanic* |
| **Share of total consumer units** | **100.0%** | **91.6%** | **81.1%** | **10.5%** | **8.4%** |
| **Share of total annual spending** | **100.0** | **92.5** | **84.7** | **7.8** | **7.5** |
| **FOOD** | **100.0%** | **90.8%** | **82.2%** | **8.6%** | **9.2%** |
| **Food at home** | **100.0** | **89.7** | **80.2** | **9.5** | **10.2** |
| Cereals and bakery products | 100.0 | 90.8 | 81.4 | 9.3 | 9.3 |
| Cereals and cereal products | 100.0 | 89.3 | 78.5 | 10.6 | 10.7 |
| Bakery products | 100.0 | 91.6 | 83.0 | 8.6 | 8.5 |
| Meats, poultry, fish, and eggs | 100.0 | 87.6 | 75.4 | 12.2 | 12.3 |
| Beef | 100.0 | 87.4 | 77.0 | 10.3 | 12.6 |
| Pork | 100.0 | 87.5 | 73.3 | 14.1 | 12.3 |
| Other meats | 100.0 | 88.8 | 78.6 | 10.1 | 11.1 |
| Poultry | 100.0 | 86.9 | 73.9 | 13.2 | 12.7 |
| Fish and seafood | 100.0 | 89.0 | 74.9 | 13.9 | 11.3 |
| Eggs | 100.0 | 85.9 | 73.5 | 11.5 | 15.7 |
| Dairy products | 100.0 | 90.2 | 82.6 | 7.6 | 9.8 |
| Fresh milk and cream | 100.0 | 88.6 | 81.1 | 7.3 | 11.4 |
| Other dairy products | 100.0 | 91.1 | 83.5 | 7.7 | 8.9 |
| Fruits and vegetables | 100.0 | 88.7 | 79.8 | 8.9 | 11.1 |
| Fresh fruits | 100.0 | 88.6 | 80.0 | 8.4 | 11.9 |
| Fresh vegetables | 100.0 | 86.7 | 78.9 | 7.6 | 12.6 |
| Processed fruits | 100.0 | 90.0 | 80.3 | 9.9 | 10.0 |
| Processed vegetables | 100.0 | 90.5 | 80.1 | 10.4 | 8.7 |
| Other food at home | 100.0 | 91.4 | 82.9 | 8.4 | 8.7 |
| Sugar and other sweets | 100.0 | 91.6 | 81.8 | 9.4 | 8.3 |
| Fats and oils | 100.0 | 89.4 | 78.2 | 10.9 | 10.4 |
| Miscellaneous foods | 100.0 | 92.0 | 84.2 | 7.8 | 7.9 |
| Nonalcoholic beverages | 100.0 | 90.5 | 81.4 | 8.8 | 9.7 |
| **Food prepared by household on trips** | **100.0** | **93.9** | **89.4** | **3.5** | **8.2** |
| **Food away from home** | **100.0** | **92.3** | **84.9** | **7.3** | **7.7** |
| **ALCOHOLIC BEVERAGES** | **100.0** | **92.8** | **87.9** | **4.8** | **7.1** |

*(continued)*

*(continued from previous page)*

| | total | non-Hispanic total | non-Hispanic white/other | non-Hispanic black | Hispanic |
|---|---|---|---|---|---|
| **HOUSING** | **100.0%** | **92.3%** | **83.9%** | **8.4%** | **7.7%** |
| **Shelter** | **100.0** | **91.9** | **83.8** | **8.1** | **8.1** |
| Owned dwellings | 100.0 | 94.1 | 87.8 | 6.3 | 5.9 |
| Mortgage interest and charges | 100.0 | 93.7 | 86.8 | 6.9 | 6.3 |
| Property taxes | 100.0 | 95.3 | 89.4 | 5.8 | 4.7 |
| Maintenance, repairs, insurance, other | 100.0 | 93.7 | 88.6 | 5.2 | 6.2 |
| Rented dwellings | 100.0 | 85.8 | 72.4 | 13.4 | 14.2 |
| Other lodging | 100.0 | 96.9 | 94.0 | 3.0 | 3.1 |
| **Utilities, fuels, public services** | **100.0** | **92.5** | **81.7** | **10.8** | **7.5** |
| Natural gas | 100.0 | 93.0 | 81.1 | 11.9 | 7.1 |
| Electricity | 100.0 | 93.0 | 82.2 | 10.8 | 6.9 |
| Fuel oil and other fuels | 100.0 | 96.6 | 90.9 | 5.7 | 3.4 |
| Telephone services | 100.0 | 91.4 | 80.0 | 11.4 | 8.6 |
| Water and other public services | 100.0 | 92.6 | 83.3 | 9.1 | 7.4 |
| **Household services** | **100.0** | **94.1** | **87.0** | **7.0** | **5.9** |
| Personal services | 100.0 | 93.0 | 84.3 | 8.6 | 7.0 |
| Other household services | 100.0 | 95.1 | 89.8 | 5.4 | 4.9 |
| **Housekeeping supplies** | **100.0** | **92.5** | **84.8** | **7.6** | **7.5** |
| Laundry and cleaning supplies | 100.0 | 89.3 | 77.7 | 11.3 | 11.0 |
| Other household products | 100.0 | 92.7 | 86.3 | 6.5 | 7.1 |
| Postage and stationery | 100.0 | 95.2 | 88.7 | 6.2 | 5.1 |
| **Household furnishings and equipment** | **100.0** | **93.4** | **86.5** | **6.8** | **6.6** |
| Household textiles | 100.0 | 91.6 | 83.9 | 8.2 | 8.1 |
| Furniture | 100.0 | 91.9 | 83.3 | 8.7 | 8.1 |
| Floor coverings | 100.0 | 93.7 | 88.4 | 5.3 | 5.2 |
| Major appliances | 100.0 | 92.6 | 83.7 | 9.0 | 7.3 |
| Small appliances, misc. housewares | 100.0 | 92.5 | 88.2 | 4.2 | 7.0 |
| Miscellaneous household equipment | 100.0 | 94.5 | 88.9 | 5.5 | 5.5 |
| **APPAREL AND SERVICES** | **100.0** | **90.0** | **78.6** | **11.4** | **10.0** |
| **Men and boys** | **100.0** | **89.4** | **80.7** | **8.7** | **10.5** |
| Men, aged 16 or older | 100.0 | 89.9 | 83.3 | 6.4 | 10.0 |
| Boys, aged 2 to 15 | 100.0 | 87.7 | 70.6 | 17.0 | 12.1 |
| **Women and girls** | **100.0** | **91.6** | **80.1** | **11.6** | **8.3** |
| Women, aged 16 or older | 100.0 | 92.6 | 81.7 | 10.9 | 7.3 |
| Girls, aged 2 to 15 | 100.0 | 86.5 | 71.2 | 15.5 | 13.5 |
| **Children under age 2** | **100.0** | **84.8** | **75.0** | **10.4** | **14.3** |
| **Footwear** | **100.0** | **86.2** | **69.3** | **17.4** | **13.6** |
| **Other apparel products and services** | **100.0** | **91.6** | **83.0** | **8.6** | **8.2** |

*(continued)*

*(continued from previous page)*

| | total | non-Hispanic total | non-Hispanic white/other | non-Hispanic black | Hispanic |
|---|---|---|---|---|---|
| **TRANSPORTATION** | **100.0%** | **91.9%** | **84.1%** | **7.8%** | **8.1%** |
| **Vehicle purchases** | **100.0** | **91.5** | **83.7** | **7.7** | **8.5** |
| Cars and trucks, new | 100.0 | 93.0 | 86.6 | 6.4 | 7.0 |
| Cars and trucks, used | 100.0 | 90.0 | 80.7 | 9.3 | 10.0 |
| Other vehicles | 100.0 | 89.1 | 87.8 | – | 11.7 |
| **Gasoline and motor oil** | **100.0** | **91.1** | **83.4** | **7.6** | **8.9** |
| **Other vehicle expenses** | **100.0** | **92.6** | **84.6** | **8.0** | **7.4** |
| Vehicle finance charges | 100.0 | 93.0 | 83.8 | 9.1 | 7.2 |
| Maintenance and repairs | 100.0 | 92.6 | 85.2 | 7.3 | 7.4 |
| Vehicle insurance | 100.0 | 92.6 | 84.2 | 8.4 | 7.5 |
| Vehicle rental, leases, licenses, other | 100.0 | 92.7 | 85.2 | 7.5 | 7.3 |
| **Public transportation** | **100.0** | **92.8** | **85.8** | **7.0** | **7.3** |
| **HEALTH CARE** | **100.0** | **95.2** | **89.2** | **6.0** | **4.8** |
| Health insurance | 100.0 | 95.1 | 88.6 | 6.5 | 4.9 |
| Medical services | 100.0 | 95.2 | 90.5 | 4.7 | 4.7 |
| Drugs | 100.0 | 95.3 | 88.1 | 7.1 | 4.8 |
| Medical supplies | 100.0 | 95.0 | 90.0 | 5.1 | 4.8 |
| **ENTERTAINMENT** | **100.0** | **94.5** | **89.2** | **5.2** | **5.5** |
| Fees and admissions | 100.0 | 95.4 | 91.5 | 3.8 | 4.6 |
| Television, radio, sound equipment | 100.0 | 92.4 | 82.7 | 9.6 | 7.7 |
| Pets, toys, playground equipment | 100.0 | 94.8 | 90.4 | 4.2 | 5.1 |
| Other entertainment supplies, services | 100.0 | 96.2 | 94.5 | 1.6 | 4.0 |
| **PERSONAL CARE PRODUCTS AND SERVICES** | **100.0** | **91.8** | **81.5** | **10.4** | **8.3** |
| **READING** | **100.0** | **96.8** | **91.3** | **5.4** | **3.8** |
| **EDUCATION** | **100.0** | **95.1** | **88.7** | **6.4** | **4.8** |
| **TOBACCO PRODUCTS AND SMOKING SUPPLIES** | **100.0** | **95.3** | **87.5** | **7.6** | **4.8** |
| **MISCELLANEOUS** | **100.0** | **93.4** | **86.1** | **7.3** | **6.6** |
| **CASH CONTRIBUTIONS** | **100.0** | **95.2** | **90.2** | **5.0** | **4.8** |
| **PERSONAL INSURANCE AND PENSIONS** | **100.0** | **93.4** | **86.9** | **6.5** | **6.6** |
| Life and other personal insurance | 100.0 | 96.0 | 87.4 | 8.6 | 4.1 |
| Pensions and Social Security | 100.0 | 93.0 | 86.8 | 6.2 | 7.0 |

*(continued)*

*(continued from previous page)*

| | | non-Hispanic | | | |
|---|---|---|---|---|---|
| | total | total | white/other | black | Hispanic |
| **PERSONAL TAXES** | **100.0%** | **94.8%** | **90.1%** | **4.3%** | **5.5%** |
| Federal income taxes | 100.0 | 94.6 | 90.2 | 4.0 | 5.6 |
| State and local income taxes | 100.0 | 94.9 | 88.8 | 5.9 | 5.3 |
| Other taxes | 100.0 | 97.5 | 92.5 | 4.3 | 3.4 |
| **GIFTS** | **100.0** | **94.2** | **87.7** | **6.5** | **5.8** |
| **Food** | **100.0** | **96.0** | **92.8** | **3.7** | **3.5** |
| **Housing** | **100.0** | **95.1** | **88.6** | **6.5** | **4.9** |
| Housekeeping supplies | 100.0 | 93.8 | 87.0 | 6.2 | 5.1 |
| Household textiles | 100.0 | 91.6 | 85.8 | 6.2 | 5.4 |
| Appliances and miscellaneous housewares | 100.0 | 97.3 | 93.7 | 3.3 | 4.2 |
| Major appliances | 100.0 | 91.6 | 90.1 | 2.3 | 1.9 |
| Small appliances and misc. housewares | 100.0 | 95.4 | 91.2 | 3.5 | 4.9 |
| Miscellaneous household equipment | 100.0 | 97.2 | 90.9 | 6.5 | 3.3 |
| Other housing | 100.0 | 94.3 | 87.0 | 7.4 | 5.9 |
| **Apparel and services** | **100.0** | **89.4** | **78.7** | **10.8** | **10.2** |
| Males, aged 2 or older | 100.0 | 91.6 | 84.1 | 8.2 | 8.4 |
| Females, aged 2 or older | 100.0 | 91.6 | 79.9 | 11.1 | 8.6 |
| Children under age 2 | 100.0 | 88.8 | 78.6 | 10.5 | 10.2 |
| All other apparel products and services | 100.0 | 84.6 | 71.7 | 13.2 | 14.5 |
| Jewelry and watches | 100.0 | 84.8 | 78.1 | 5.5 | 13.7 |
| All other apparel products and services | 100.0 | 84.3 | 64.8 | 21.5 | 15.5 |
| **Transportation** | **100.0** | **93.1** | **83.6** | **9.2** | **8.0** |
| **Health care** | **100.0** | **98.5** | **97.3** | **1.6** | **1.5** |
| **Entertainment** | **100.0** | **96.3** | **91.8** | **3.7** | **4.3** |
| Toys, games, hobbies, and tricycles | 100.0 | 91.6 | 88.7 | 4.6 | 6.8 |
| Other entertainment | 100.0 | 97.2 | 94.6 | 3.2 | 3.1 |
| **Education** | **100.0** | **97.1** | **92.3** | **4.7** | **3.1** |
| **All other gifts** | **100.0** | **93.0** | **87.9** | **5.5** | **6.9** |

*Note: The Bureau of Labor Statistics uses consumer unit rather than household as the sampling unit in the Consumer Expenditure Survey. For the definition of consumer unit, see Glossary. Numbers may not add to total because of rounding.*
*Source: Bureau of Labor Statistics, 1999 Consumer Expenditure Survey; calculations by New Strategist*

# Spending Is Highest in the West

## Households in the South spend the least.

While incomes are highest in the Northeast, spending is highest in the West. The average household in the West spent $42,364 in 1999, 14 percent more than the national average. In the Northeast, despite having the highest incomes, households spent only 4 percent more than average, or $38,446 in 1999. In the Midwest, the average household spent 2 percent less than average. In the South, the average household spent fully 10 percent less than average, or $33,328 in 1999. By product and service category, however, spending varies by region.

The indexed spending table in this section shows spending by the average household in each region relative to the national average. An index of 100 means a household spends an average amount on an item. An index above 100 means households in the region spend more than average on the item, while an index below 100 reveals below-average spending.

Households in the West and Northeast spend more than average on most foods, in part because food prices may be higher in those regions than in the South or Midwest. Spending on housing is also above average in the West and Northeast. Households in the Northeast spend 64 percent more than average on property taxes. Households in the Midwest spend 17 percent more than average on laundry and cleaning supplies, 10 to 14 percent more on boys' and girls' clothes, and 16 percent more than average on used cars and trucks. Households in the South spend less than average on most items with some exceptions, such as electricity and drugs.

The market share table in this section shows how much of total spending by category is accounted for by households in each region. In most categories, spending closely matches each region's share of total households. The South, which is home to 35 percent of households, accounts for 31 percent of all household spending. With 22 percent of households, the West accounts for 25 percent of household spending. There are some exceptions, however. Households in the South, for example, account for a disproportionately large share of spending on electricity (42 percent), while those in the West account for only 18 percent of spending on this item.

♦ Because regional spending patterns are partly determined by climate, spending by region is not likely to change much in the years ahead.

## Spending varies by region

*(average annual spending of consumer units, by region, 1999)*

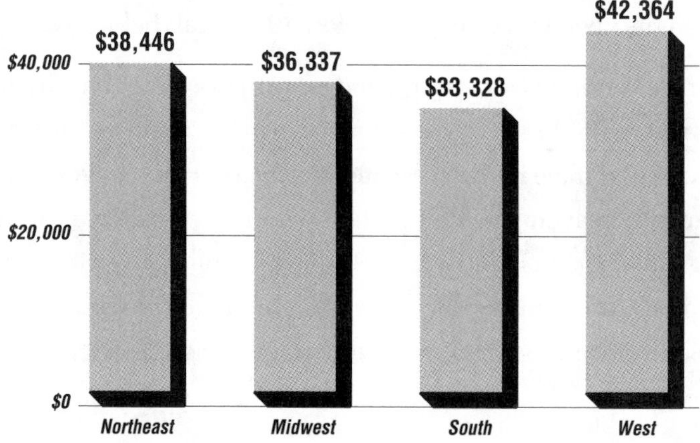

## Spending by Region, 1999

*(average annual spending of consumer units (CU's) by product and service category and region of residence, 1999)*

| | *total* | *Northeast* | *Midwest* | *South* | *West* |
|---|---|---|---|---|---|
| **Number of consumer units (in 000s)** | **108,465** | **20,979** | **25,765** | **37,816** | **23,906** |
| **Average number of persons per CU** | **2.5** | **2.5** | **2.5** | **2.5** | **2.6** |
| **Average before-tax income** | **$43,951** | **$48,307** | **$41,983** | **$40,387** | **$47,494** |
| **Average annual spending** | **37,027** | **38,446** | **36,337** | **33,328** | **42,364** |
| **FOOD** | **$5,031** | **$5,480** | **$4,865** | **$4,615** | **$5,462** |
| **Food at home** | **2,915** | **3,084** | **2,740** | **2,729** | **3,245** |
| Cereals and bakery products | 448 | 487 | 428 | 416 | 485 |
| Cereals and cereal products | 160 | 170 | 149 | 153 | 174 |
| Bakery products | 288 | 317 | 280 | 263 | 311 |
| Meats, poultry, fish, and eggs | 749 | 830 | 655 | 739 | 793 |
| Beef | 220 | 238 | 209 | 212 | 229 |
| Pork | 157 | 147 | 151 | 170 | 151 |
| Other meats | 97 | 115 | 96 | 89 | 95 |
| Poultry | 136 | 162 | 105 | 136 | 147 |
| Fish and seafood | 106 | 133 | 71 | 100 | 130 |
| Eggs | 32 | 36 | 24 | 31 | 41 |
| Dairy products | 322 | 361 | 307 | 290 | 355 |
| Fresh milk and cream | 122 | 135 | 120 | 112 | 129 |
| Other dairy products | 200 | 226 | 187 | 178 | 226 |
| Fruits and vegetables | 500 | 564 | 438 | 451 | 584 |
| Fresh fruits | 152 | 177 | 131 | 129 | 192 |
| Fresh vegetables | 149 | 168 | 123 | 132 | 184 |
| Processed fruits | 113 | 136 | 100 | 101 | 125 |
| Processed vegetables | 86 | 84 | 84 | 89 | 84 |
| Other food at home | 896 | 843 | 912 | 832 | 1,029 |
| Sugar and other sweets | 112 | 111 | 113 | 104 | 122 |
| Fats and oils | 84 | 84 | 75 | 83 | 94 |
| Miscellaneous foods | 420 | 386 | 443 | 382 | 485 |
| Nonalcoholic beverages | 242 | 224 | 243 | 233 | 270 |
| Food prepared by household on trips | 39 | 38 | 37 | 30 | 57 |
| **Food away from home** | **2,116** | **2,396** | **2,126** | **1,887** | **2,216** |
| **ALCOHOLIC BEVERAGES** | **318** | **367** | **324** | **256** | **365** |

*(continued)*

*(continued from previous page)*

| | *total* | *Northeast* | *Midwest* | *South* | *West* |
|---|---|---|---|---|---|
| **HOUSING** | **$12,057** | **$13,365** | **$11,526** | **$10,338** | **$14,201** |
| **Shelter** | **7,016** | **8,255** | **6,492** | **5,541** | **8,829** |
| Owned dwellings | 4,525 | 5,312 | 4,452 | 3,542 | 5,470 |
| Mortgage interest and charges | 2,547 | 2,628 | 2,385 | 2,027 | 3,474 |
| Property taxes | 1,123 | 1,843 | 1,213 | 765 | 962 |
| Maintenance, repairs, insurance, other | 855 | 841 | 854 | 749 | 1,033 |
| Rented dwellings | 2,027 | 2,423 | 1,599 | 1,645 | 2,743 |
| Other lodging | 464 | 520 | 441 | 354 | 616 |
| **Utilities, fuels, public services** | **2,377** | **2,455** | **2,401** | **2,445** | **2,177** |
| Natural gas | 270 | 363 | 378 | 157 | 253 |
| Electricity | 899 | 844 | 829 | 1,087 | 726 |
| Fuel oil and other fuels | 74 | 189 | 65 | 42 | 35 |
| Telephone services | 849 | 846 | 858 | 862 | 822 |
| Water and other public services | 285 | 213 | 272 | 296 | 342 |
| **Household services** | **666** | **658** | **587** | **555** | **933** |
| Personal services | 323 | 288 | 327 | 264 | 441 |
| Other household services | 343 | 370 | 260 | 291 | 492 |
| **Housekeeping supplies** | **498** | **502** | **541** | **458** | **512** |
| Laundry and cleaning supplies | 121 | 102 | 141 | 116 | 126 |
| Other household products | 250 | 267 | 262 | 239 | 238 |
| Postage and stationery | 127 | 134 | 137 | 103 | 149 |
| **Household furnishings and equipment** | **1,499** | **1,496** | **1,506** | **1,339** | **1,749** |
| Household textiles | 114 | 118 | 122 | 94 | 134 |
| Furniture | 365 | 364 | 336 | 352 | 418 |
| Floor coverings | 44 | 44 | 47 | 40 | 46 |
| Major appliances | 183 | 200 | 181 | 171 | 189 |
| Small appliances, miscellaneous housewares | 102 | 104 | 108 | 85 | 118 |
| Miscellaneous household equipment | 692 | 666 | 711 | 597 | 844 |
| **APPAREL AND SERVICES** | **1,743** | **1,817** | **1,591** | **1,598** | **2,070** |
| **Men and boys** | **421** | **434** | **452** | **351** | **487** |
| Men, aged 16 or older | 328 | 341 | 350 | 259 | 402 |
| Boys, aged 2 to 15 | 93 | 93 | 102 | 92 | 85 |
| **Women and girls** | **655** | **684** | **574** | **628** | **760** |
| Women, aged 16 or older | 548 | 589 | 452 | 517 | 663 |
| Girls, aged 2 to 15 | 107 | 95 | 122 | 111 | 97 |
| **Children under age 2** | **67** | **69** | **60** | **69** | **69** |
| **Footwear** | **303** | **301** | **272** | **298** | **347** |
| **Other apparel products and services** | **297** | **329** | **233** | **253** | **407** |

*(continued)*

*(continued from previous page)*

| | *total* | *Northeast* | *Midwest* | *South* | *West* |
|---|---|---|---|---|---|
| **TRANSPORTATION** | **$7,011** | **$6,466** | **$6,939** | **$6,863** | **$7,802** |
| **Vehicle purchases** | **3,305** | **2,706** | **3,382** | **3,466** | **3,495** |
| Cars and trucks, new | 1,628 | 1,516 | 1,451 | 1,777 | 1,681 |
| Cars and trucks, used | 1,641 | 1,179 | 1,905 | 1,647 | 1,755 |
| Other vehicles | 36 | 12 | 27 | 41 | 59 |
| **Gasoline and motor oil** | **1,055** | **907** | **1,038** | **1,069** | **1,180** |
| **Other vehicle expenses** | **2,254** | **2,315** | **2,169** | **2,043** | **2,625** |
| Vehicle finance charges | 320 | 232 | 337 | 362 | 314 |
| Maintenance and repairs | 664 | 661 | 572 | 613 | 847 |
| Vehicle insurance | 756 | 825 | 722 | 709 | 807 |
| Vehicle rental, leases, licenses, other | 513 | 596 | 537 | 359 | 657 |
| **Public transportation** | **397** | **538** | **349** | **286** | **503** |
| **HEALTH CARE** | **1,959** | **1,804** | **2,087** | **1,956** | **1,962** |
| Health insurance | 923 | 840 | 1,009 | 926 | 896 |
| Medical services | 558 | 568 | 559 | 524 | 600 |
| Drugs | 370 | 292 | 405 | 412 | 334 |
| Medical supplies | 109 | 103 | 114 | 93 | 132 |
| **ENTERTAINMENT** | **1,891** | **1,828** | **2,067** | **1,567** | **2,268** |
| Fees and admissions | 459 | 505 | 462 | 377 | 544 |
| Television, radio, sound equipment | 608 | 656 | 596 | 570 | 640 |
| Pets, toys, playground equipment | 346 | 321 | 373 | 318 | 381 |
| Other entertainment supplies, services | 478 | 345 | 636 | 303 | 704 |
| **PERSONAL CARE PRODUCTS AND SERVICES** | **408** | **404** | **401** | **385** | **457** |
| **READING** | **159** | **195** | **166** | **117** | **189** |
| **EDUCATION** | **635** | **939** | **568** | **452** | **728** |
| **TOBACCO PRODUCTS AND SMOKING SUPPLIES** | **300** | **318** | **346** | **302** | **232** |
| **MISCELLANEOUS** | **889** | **858** | **875** | **793** | **1,081** |
| **CASH CONTRIBUTIONS** | **1,190** | **1,113** | **1,163** | **1,141** | **1,365** |
| **PERSONAL INSURANCE AND PENSIONS** | **3,436** | **3,494** | **3,418** | **2,946** | **4,181** |
| Life and other personal insurance | 394 | 403 | 378 | 411 | 379 |
| Pensions and Social Security | 3,042 | 3,092 | 3,041 | 2,535 | 3,801 |

*(continued)*

*(continued from previous page)*

| | *total* | *Northeast* | *Midwest* | *South* | *West* |
|---|---|---|---|---|---|
| **PERSONAL TAXES** | **$3,588** | **$3,819** | **$4,388** | **$2,483** | **$4,193** |
| Federal income taxes | 2,802 | 2,864 | 3,531 | 1,964 | 3,230 |
| State and local income taxes | 616 | 699 | 715 | 361 | 815 |
| Other taxes | 170 | 256 | 141 | 158 | 148 |
| **GIFTS** | **1,083** | **1,229** | **1,064** | **922** | **1,231** |
| **Food** | **83** | **110** | **84** | **61** | **93** |
| **Housing** | **292** | **315** | **302** | **253** | **321** |
| Housekeeping supplies | 41 | 40 | 44 | 31 | 52 |
| Household textiles | 17 | 13 | 16 | 15 | 25 |
| Appliances and miscellaneous housewares | 32 | 47 | 42 | 20 | 29 |
| Major appliances | 9 | 17 | 10 | 5 | 6 |
| Small appliances and misc. housewares | 24 | 30 | 31 | 16 | 23 |
| Miscellaneous household equipment | 66 | 66 | 78 | 52 | 75 |
| Other housing | 136 | 150 | 122 | 135 | 140 |
| **Apparel and services** | **210** | **223** | **192** | **206** | **223** |
| Males, aged 2 or older | 54 | 53 | 67 | 42 | 61 |
| Females, aged 2 or older | 71 | 79 | 52 | 80 | 70 |
| Children under age 2 | 33 | 34 | 29 | 36 | 31 |
| All other apparel products and services | 52 | 56 | 44 | 49 | 60 |
| Jewelry and watches | 27 | 35 | 22 | 23 | 31 |
| All other apparel products and services | 25 | 21 | 22 | 26 | 30 |
| **Transportation** | **63** | **51** | **50** | **58** | **98** |
| **Health care** | **40** | **22** | **46** | **41** | **48** |
| **Entertainment** | **98** | **105** | **92** | **74** | **137** |
| Toys, games, hobbies, and tricycles | 32 | 39 | 32 | 29 | 31 |
| Other entertainment | 66 | 66 | 60 | 46 | 106 |
| **Education** | **166** | **295** | **166** | **107** | **147** |
| **All other gifts** | **131** | **108** | **133** | **122** | **165** |

*Note: The Bureau of Labor Statistics uses consumer unit rather than household as the sampling unit in the Consumer Expenditure Survey. For the definition of consumer unit, see Glossary. Gift spending is also included in the preceding product and service categories.*
*Source: Bureau of Labor Statistics, 1999 Consumer Expenditure Survey; Internet site <www.bls.gov/csxstnd.htm>*

# Indexed Spending by Region, 1999

*(indexed average annual spending of consumer units by product and service category and region of residence, 1999)*

| | *total* | *Northeast* | *Midwest* | *South* | *West* |
|---|---|---|---|---|---|
| **Number of consumer units (in 000s)** | **108,465** | **20,979** | **25,765** | **37,816** | **23,906** |
| **Indexed average before-tax income** | **100** | **110** | **96** | **92** | **108** |
| **Indexed average annual spending** | **100** | **104** | **98** | **90** | **114** |
| **FOOD** | **100** | **109** | **97** | **92** | **109** |
| **Food at home** | **100** | **106** | **94** | **94** | **111** |
| Cereals and bakery products | 100 | 109 | 96 | 93 | 108 |
| Cereals and cereal products | 100 | 106 | 93 | 96 | 109 |
| Bakery products | 100 | 110 | 97 | 91 | 108 |
| Meats, poultry, fish, and eggs | 100 | 111 | 87 | 99 | 106 |
| Beef | 100 | 108 | 95 | 96 | 104 |
| Pork | 100 | 94 | 96 | 108 | 96 |
| Other meats | 100 | 119 | 99 | 92 | 98 |
| Poultry | 100 | 119 | 77 | 100 | 108 |
| Fish and seafood | 100 | 125 | 67 | 94 | 123 |
| Eggs | 100 | 113 | 75 | 97 | 128 |
| Dairy products | 100 | 112 | 95 | 90 | 110 |
| Fresh milk and cream | 100 | 111 | 98 | 92 | 106 |
| Other dairy products | 100 | 113 | 94 | 89 | 113 |
| Fruits and vegetables | 100 | 113 | 88 | 90 | 117 |
| Fresh fruits | 100 | 116 | 86 | 85 | 126 |
| Fresh vegetables | 100 | 113 | 83 | 89 | 123 |
| Processed fruits | 100 | 120 | 88 | 89 | 111 |
| Processed vegetables | 100 | 98 | 98 | 103 | 98 |
| Other food at home | 100 | 94 | 102 | 93 | 115 |
| Sugar and other sweets | 100 | 99 | 101 | 93 | 109 |
| Fats and oils | 100 | 100 | 89 | 99 | 112 |
| Miscellaneous foods | 100 | 92 | 105 | 91 | 115 |
| Nonalcoholic beverages | 100 | 93 | 100 | 96 | 112 |
| Food prepared by household on trips | 100 | 97 | 95 | 77 | 146 |
| **Food away from home** | **100** | **113** | **100** | **89** | **105** |
| **ALCOHOLIC BEVERAGES** | **100** | **115** | **102** | **81** | **115** |

*(continued)*

*(continued from previous page)*

| | *total* | *Northeast* | *Midwest* | *South* | *West* |
|---|---|---|---|---|---|
| **HOUSING** | **100** | **111** | **96** | **86** | **118** |
| **Shelter** | **100** | **118** | **93** | **79** | **126** |
| Owned dwellings | 100 | 117 | 98 | 78 | 121 |
| Mortgage interest and charges | 100 | 103 | 94 | 80 | 136 |
| Property taxes | 100 | 164 | 108 | 68 | 86 |
| Maintenance, repairs, insurance, other | 100 | 98 | 100 | 88 | 121 |
| Rented dwellings | 100 | 120 | 79 | 81 | 135 |
| Other lodging | 100 | 112 | 95 | 76 | 133 |
| **Utilities, fuels, public services** | **100** | **103** | **101** | **103** | **92** |
| Natural gas | 100 | 134 | 140 | 58 | 94 |
| Electricity | 100 | 94 | 92 | 121 | 81 |
| Fuel oil and other fuels | 100 | 255 | 88 | 57 | 47 |
| Telephone services | 100 | 100 | 101 | 102 | 97 |
| Water and other public services | 100 | 75 | 95 | 104 | 120 |
| **Household services** | **100** | **99** | **88** | **83** | **140** |
| Personal services | 100 | 89 | 101 | 82 | 137 |
| Other household services | 100 | 108 | 76 | 85 | 143 |
| **Housekeeping supplies** | **100** | **101** | **109** | **92** | **103** |
| Laundry and cleaning supplies | 100 | 84 | 117 | 96 | 104 |
| Other household products | 100 | 107 | 105 | 96 | 95 |
| Postage and stationery | 100 | 106 | 108 | 81 | 117 |
| **Household furnishings and equipment** | **100** | **100** | **100** | **89** | **117** |
| Household textiles | 100 | 104 | 107 | 82 | 118 |
| Furniture | 100 | 100 | 92 | 96 | 115 |
| Floor coverings | 100 | 100 | 107 | 91 | 105 |
| Major appliances | 100 | 109 | 99 | 93 | 103 |
| Small appliances, miscellaneous housewares | 100 | 102 | 106 | 83 | 116 |
| Miscellaneous household equipment | 100 | 96 | 103 | 86 | 122 |
| **APPAREL AND SERVICES** | **100** | **104** | **91** | **92** | **119** |
| **Men and boys** | **100** | **103** | **107** | **83** | **116** |
| Men, aged 16 or older | 100 | 104 | 107 | 79 | 123 |
| Boys, aged 2 to 15 | 100 | 100 | 110 | 99 | 91 |
| **Women and girls** | **100** | **104** | **88** | **96** | **116** |
| Women, aged 16 or older | 100 | 107 | 82 | 94 | 121 |
| Girls, aged 2 to 15 | 100 | 89 | 114 | 104 | 91 |
| **Children under age 2** | **100** | **103** | **90** | **103** | **103** |
| **Footwear** | **100** | **99** | **90** | **98** | **115** |
| **Other apparel products and services** | **100** | **111** | **78** | **85** | **137** |

*(continued)*

*(continued from previous page)*

| | *total* | *Northeast* | *Midwest* | *South* | *West* |
|---|---|---|---|---|---|
| **TRANSPORTATION** | **100** | **92** | **99** | **98** | **111** |
| **Vehicle purchases** | **100** | **82** | **102** | **105** | **106** |
| Cars and trucks, new | 100 | 93 | 89 | 109 | 103 |
| Cars and trucks, used | 100 | 72 | 116 | 100 | 107 |
| Other vehicles | 100 | 33 | 75 | 114 | 164 |
| **Gasoline and motor oil** | **100** | **86** | **98** | **101** | **112** |
| **Other vehicle expenses** | **100** | **103** | **96** | **91** | **116** |
| Vehicle finance charges | 100 | 73 | 105 | 113 | 98 |
| Maintenance and repairs | 100 | 100 | 86 | 92 | 128 |
| Vehicle insurance | 100 | 109 | 96 | 94 | 107 |
| Vehicle rental, leases, licenses, other | 100 | 116 | 105 | 70 | 128 |
| **Public transportation** | **100** | **136** | **88** | **72** | **127** |
| **HEALTH CARE** | **100** | **92** | **107** | **100** | **100** |
| Health insurance | 100 | 91 | 109 | 100 | 97 |
| Medical services | 100 | 102 | 100 | 94 | 108 |
| Drugs | 100 | 79 | 109 | 111 | 90 |
| Medical supplies | 100 | 94 | 105 | 85 | 121 |
| **ENTERTAINMENT** | **100** | **97** | **109** | **83** | **120** |
| Fees and admissions | 100 | 110 | 101 | 82 | 119 |
| Television, radio, sound equipment | 100 | 108 | 98 | 94 | 105 |
| Pets, toys, playground equipment | 100 | 93 | 108 | 92 | 110 |
| Other entertainment supplies, services | 100 | 72 | 133 | 63 | 147 |
| **PERSONAL CARE PRODUCTS AND SERVICES** | **100** | **99** | **98** | **94** | **112** |
| **READING** | **100** | **123** | **104** | **74** | **119** |
| **EDUCATION** | **100** | **148** | **89** | **71** | **115** |
| **TOBACCO PRODUCTS AND SMOKING SUPPLIES** | **100** | **106** | **115** | **101** | **77** |
| **MISCELLANEOUS** | **100** | **97** | **98** | **89** | **122** |
| **CASH CONTRIBUTIONS** | **100** | **94** | **98** | **96** | **115** |
| **PERSONAL INSURANCE AND PENSIONS** | **100** | **102** | **99** | **86** | **122** |
| Life and other personal insurance | 100 | 102 | 96 | 104 | 96 |
| Pensions and Social Security | 100 | 102 | 100 | 83 | 125 |

*(continued)*

*(continued from previous page)*

| | total | Northeast | Midwest | South | West |
|---|---|---|---|---|---|
| **PERSONAL TAXES** | **100** | **106** | **122** | **69** | **117** |
| Federal income taxes | 100 | 102 | 126 | 70 | 115 |
| State and local income taxes | 100 | 113 | 116 | 59 | 132 |
| Other taxes | 100 | 151 | 83 | 93 | 87 |
| **GIFTS** | **100** | **113** | **98** | **85** | **114** |
| **Food** | **100** | **133** | **101** | **73** | **112** |
| **Housing** | **100** | **108** | **103** | **87** | **110** |
| Housekeeping supplies | 100 | 98 | 107 | 76 | 127 |
| Household textiles | 100 | 76 | 94 | 88 | 147 |
| Appliances and miscellaneous housewares | 100 | 147 | 131 | 63 | 91 |
| Major appliances | 100 | 189 | 111 | 56 | 67 |
| Small appliances and misc. housewares | 100 | 125 | 129 | 67 | 96 |
| Miscellaneous household equipment | 100 | 100 | 118 | 79 | 114 |
| Other housing | 100 | 110 | 90 | 99 | 103 |
| **Apparel and services** | **100** | **106** | **91** | **98** | **106** |
| Males, aged 2 or older | 100 | 98 | 124 | 78 | 113 |
| Females, aged 2 or older | 100 | 111 | 73 | 113 | 99 |
| Children under age 2 | 100 | 103 | 88 | 109 | 94 |
| All other apparel products and services | 100 | 108 | 85 | 94 | 115 |
| Jewelry and watches | 100 | 130 | 81 | 85 | 115 |
| All other apparel products and services | 100 | 84 | 88 | 104 | 120 |
| **Transportation** | **100** | **81** | **79** | **92** | **156** |
| **Health care** | **100** | **55** | **115** | **103** | **120** |
| **Entertainment** | **100** | **107** | **94** | **76** | **140** |
| Toys, games, hobbies, and tricycles | 100 | 122 | 100 | 91 | 97 |
| Other entertainment | 100 | 100 | 91 | 70 | 161 |
| **Education** | **100** | **178** | **100** | **64** | **89** |
| **All other gifts** | **100** | **82** | **102** | **93** | **126** |

*Note: The Bureau of Labor Statistics uses consumer unit rather than household as the sampling unit in the Consumer Expenditure Survey. For the definition of consumer unit, see Glossary. An index of 100 is the average for all households. An index of 132 means households in the region spend 32 percent more than the average household. An index of 75 means households in the region spend 25 percent less than the average household. (–) means sample is too small to make a reliable estimate.*
*Source: Bureau of Labor Statistics 1999, Consumer Expenditure Survey; calculations by New Strategist*

## Market Shares by Region, 1999

*(share of total annual spending accounted for by consumer units in region, 1999)*

| | *total* | *Northeast* | *Midwest* | *South* | *West* |
|---|---|---|---|---|---|
| **Share of total consumer units** | **100.0%** | **19.3%** | **23.8%** | **34.9%** | **22.0%** |
| **Share of total annual spending** | **100.0** | **20.1** | **23.3** | **31.4** | **25.2** |
| **FOOD** | **100.0%** | **21.1%** | **23.0%** | **32.0%** | **23.9%** |
| **Food at home** | **100.0** | **20.5** | **22.3** | **32.6** | **24.5** |
| Cereals and bakery products | 100.0 | 21.0 | 22.7 | 32.4 | 23.9 |
| Cereals and cereal products | 100.0 | 20.6 | 22.1 | 33.3 | 24.0 |
| Bakery products | 100.0 | 21.3 | 23.1 | 31.8 | 23.8 |
| Meats, poultry, fish, and eggs | 100.0 | 21.4 | 20.8 | 34.4 | 23.3 |
| Beef | 100.0 | 20.9 | 22.6 | 33.6 | 22.9 |
| Pork | 100.0 | 18.1 | 22.8 | 37.8 | 21.2 |
| Other meats | 100.0 | 22.9 | 23.5 | 32.0 | 21.6 |
| Poultry | 100.0 | 23.0 | 18.3 | 34.9 | 23.8 |
| Fish and seafood | 100.0 | 24.3 | 15.9 | 32.9 | 27.0 |
| Eggs | 100.0 | 21.8 | 17.8 | 33.8 | 28.2 |
| Dairy products | 100.0 | 21.7 | 22.6 | 31.4 | 24.3 |
| Fresh milk and cream | 100.0 | 21.4 | 23.4 | 32.0 | 23.3 |
| Other dairy products | 100.0 | 21.9 | 22.2 | 31.0 | 24.9 |
| Fruits and vegetables | 100.0 | 21.8 | 20.8 | 31.4 | 25.7 |
| Fresh fruits | 100.0 | 22.5 | 20.5 | 29.6 | 27.8 |
| Fresh vegetables | 100.0 | 21.8 | 19.6 | 30.9 | 27.2 |
| Processed fruits | 100.0 | 23.3 | 21.0 | 31.2 | 24.4 |
| Processed vegetables | 100.0 | 18.9 | 23.2 | 36.1 | 21.5 |
| Other food at home | 100.0 | 18.2 | 24.2 | 32.4 | 25.3 |
| Sugar and other sweets | 100.0 | 19.2 | 24.0 | 32.4 | 24.0 |
| Fats and oils | 100.0 | 19.3 | 21.2 | 34.4 | 24.7 |
| Miscellaneous foods | 100.0 | 17.8 | 25.1 | 31.7 | 25.5 |
| Nonalcoholic beverages | 100.0 | 17.9 | 23.9 | 33.6 | 24.6 |
| Food prepared by household on trips | 100.0 | 18.8 | 22.5 | 26.8 | 32.2 |
| **Food away from home** | **100.0** | **21.9** | **23.9** | **31.1** | **23.1** |
| **ALCOHOLIC BEVERAGES** | **100.0** | **22.3** | **24.2** | **28.1** | **25.3** |

*(continued)*

*(continued from previous page)*

| | *total* | *Northeast* | *Midwest* | *South* | *West* |
|---|---|---|---|---|---|
| **HOUSING** | **100.0%** | **21.4%** | **22.7%** | **29.9%** | **26.0%** |
| **Shelter** | **100.0** | **22.8** | **22.0** | **27.5** | **27.7** |
| Owned dwellings | 100.0 | 22.7 | 23.4 | 27.3 | 26.6 |
| Mortgage interest and charges | 100.0 | 20.0 | 22.2 | 27.7 | 30.1 |
| Property taxes | 100.0 | 31.7 | 25.7 | 23.8 | 18.9 |
| Maintenance, repairs, insurance, other | 100.0 | 19.0 | 23.7 | 30.5 | 26.6 |
| Rented dwellings | 100.0 | 23.1 | 18.7 | 28.3 | 29.8 |
| Other lodging | 100.0 | 21.7 | 22.6 | 26.6 | 29.3 |
| **Utilities, fuels, public services** | **100.0** | **20.0** | **24.0** | **35.9** | **20.2** |
| Natural gas | 100.0 | 26.0 | 33.3 | 20.3 | 20.7 |
| Electricity | 100.0 | 18.2 | 21.9 | 42.2 | 17.8 |
| Fuel oil and other fuels | 100.0 | 49.4 | 20.9 | 19.8 | 10.4 |
| Telephone services | 100.0 | 19.3 | 24.0 | 35.4 | 21.3 |
| Water and other public services | 100.0 | 14.5 | 22.7 | 36.2 | 26.4 |
| **Household services** | **100.0** | **19.1** | **20.9** | **29.1** | **30.9** |
| Personal services | 100.0 | 17.2 | 24.0 | 28.5 | 30.1 |
| Other household services | 100.0 | 20.9 | 18.0 | 29.6 | 31.6 |
| **Housekeeping supplies** | **100.0** | **19.5** | **25.8** | **32.1** | **22.7** |
| Laundry and cleaning supplies | 100.0 | 16.3 | 27.7 | 33.4 | 23.0 |
| Other household products | 100.0 | 20.7 | 24.9 | 33.3 | 21.0 |
| Postage and stationery | 100.0 | 20.4 | 25.6 | 28.3 | 25.9 |
| **Household furnishings and equipment** | **100.0** | **19.3** | **23.9** | **31.1** | **25.7** |
| Household textiles | 100.0 | 20.0 | 25.4 | 28.7 | 25.9 |
| Furniture | 100.0 | 19.3 | 21.9 | 33.6 | 25.2 |
| Floor coverings | 100.0 | 19.3 | 25.4 | 31.7 | 23.0 |
| Major appliances | 100.0 | 21.1 | 23.5 | 32.6 | 22.8 |
| Small appliances, misc. housewares | 100.0 | 19.7 | 25.2 | 29.1 | 25.5 |
| Miscellaneous household equipment | 100.0 | 18.6 | 24.4 | 30.1 | 26.9 |
| **APPAREL AND SERVICES** | **100.0** | **20.2** | **21.7** | **32.0** | **26.2** |
| **Men and boys** | **100.0** | **19.9** | **25.5** | **29.1** | **25.5** |
| Men, aged 16 or older | 100.0 | 20.1 | 25.3 | 27.5 | 27.0 |
| Boys, aged 2 to 15 | 100.0 | 19.3 | 26.1 | 34.5 | 20.1 |
| **Women and girls** | **100.0** | **20.2** | **20.8** | **33.4** | **25.6** |
| Women, aged 16 or older | 100.0 | 20.8 | 19.6 | 32.9 | 26.7 |
| Girls, aged 2 to 15 | 100.0 | 17.2 | 27.1 | 36.2 | 20.0 |
| **Children under age 2** | **100.0** | **19.9** | **21.3** | **35.9** | **22.7** |
| **Footwear** | **100.0** | **19.2** | **21.3** | **34.3** | **25.2** |
| **Other apparel products and services** | **100.0** | **21.4** | **18.6** | **29.7** | **30.2** |

*(continued)*

*(continued from previous page)*

| | *total* | *Northeast* | *Midwest* | *South* | *West* |
|---|---|---|---|---|---|
| **TRANSPORTATION** | **100.0%** | **17.8%** | **23.5%** | **34.1%** | **24.5%** |
| **Vehicle purchases** | **100.0** | **15.8** | **24.3** | **36.6** | **23.3** |
| Cars and trucks, new | 100.0 | 18.0 | 21.2 | 38.1 | 22.8 |
| Cars and trucks, used | 100.0 | 13.9 | 27.6 | 35.0 | 23.6 |
| Other vehicles | 100.0 | 6.4 | 17.8 | 39.7 | 36.1 |
| **Gasoline and motor oil** | **100.0** | **16.6** | **23.4** | **35.3** | **24.7** |
| **Other vehicle expenses** | **100.0** | **19.9** | **22.9** | **31.6** | **25.7** |
| Vehicle finance charges | 100.0 | 14.0 | 25.0 | 39.4 | 21.6 |
| Maintenance and repairs | 100.0 | 19.3 | 20.5 | 32.2 | 28.1 |
| Vehicle insurance | 100.0 | 21.1 | 22.7 | 32.7 | 23.5 |
| Vehicle rental, leases, licenses, other | 100.0 | 22.5 | 24.9 | 24.4 | 28.2 |
| **Public transportation** | **100.0** | **26.2** | **20.9** | **25.1** | **27.9** |
| **HEALTH CARE** | **100.0** | **17.8** | **25.3** | **34.8** | **22.1** |
| Health insurance | 100.0 | 17.6 | 26.0 | 35.0 | 21.4 |
| Medical services | 100.0 | 19.7 | 23.8 | 32.7 | 23.7 |
| Drugs | 100.0 | 15.3 | 26.0 | 38.8 | 19.9 |
| Medical supplies | 100.0 | 18.3 | 24.8 | 29.7 | 26.7 |
| **ENTERTAINMENT** | **100.0** | **18.7** | **26.0** | **28.9** | **26.4** |
| Fees and admissions | 100.0 | 21.3 | 23.9 | 28.6 | 26.1 |
| Television, radio, sound equipment | 100.0 | 20.9 | 23.3 | 32.7 | 23.2 |
| Pets, toys, playground equipment | 100.0 | 17.9 | 25.6 | 32.0 | 24.3 |
| Other entertainment supplies, services | 100.0 | 14.0 | 31.6 | 22.1 | 32.5 |
| **PERSONAL CARE PRODUCTS AND SERVICES** | **100.0** | **19.2** | **23.3** | **32.9** | **24.7** |
| **READING** | **100.0** | **23.7** | **24.8** | **25.7** | **26.2** |
| **EDUCATION** | **100.0** | **28.6** | **21.2** | **24.8** | **25.3** |
| **TOBACCO PRODUCTS AND SMOKING SUPPLIES** | **100.0** | **20.5** | **27.4** | **35.1** | **17.0** |
| **MISCELLANEOUS** | **100.0** | **18.7** | **23.4** | **31.1** | **26.8** |
| **CASH CONTRIBUTIONS** | **100.0** | **18.1** | **23.2** | **33.4** | **25.3** |
| **PERSONAL INSURANCE AND PENSIONS** | **100.0** | **19.7** | **23.6** | **29.9** | **26.8** |
| Life and other personal insurance | 100.0 | 19.8 | 22.8 | 36.4 | 21.2 |
| Pensions and Social Security | 100.0 | 19.7 | 23.7 | 29.1 | 27.5 |

*(continued)*

*(continued from previous page)*

| | *total* | *Northeast* | *Midwest* | *South* | *West* |
|---|---|---|---|---|---|
| **PERSONAL TAXES** | **100.0%** | **20.6%** | **29.1%** | **24.1%** | **25.8%** |
| Federal income taxes | 100.0 | 19.8 | 29.9 | 24.4 | 25.4 |
| State and local income taxes | 100.0 | 21.9 | 27.6 | 20.4 | 29.2 |
| Other taxes | 100.0 | 29.1 | 19.7 | 32.4 | 19.2 |
| **GIFTS** | **100.0** | **21.9** | **23.3** | **29.7** | **25.1** |
| **Food** | **100.0** | **25.6** | **24.0** | **25.6** | **24.7** |
| **Housing** | **100.0** | **20.9** | **24.6** | **30.2** | **24.2** |
| Housekeeping supplies | 100.0 | 18.9 | 25.5 | 26.4 | 28.0 |
| Household textiles | 100.0 | 14.8 | 22.4 | 30.8 | 32.4 |
| Appliances and miscellaneous housewares | 100.0 | 28.4 | 31.2 | 21.8 | 20.0 |
| Major appliances | 100.0 | 36.5 | 26.4 | 19.4 | 14.7 |
| Small appliances and misc. housewares | 100.0 | 24.2 | 30.7 | 23.2 | 21.1 |
| Miscellaneous household equipment | 100.0 | 19.3 | 28.1 | 27.5 | 25.0 |
| Other housing | 100.0 | 21.3 | 21.3 | 34.6 | 22.7 |
| **Apparel and services** | **100.0** | **20.5** | **21.7** | **34.2** | **23.4** |
| Males, aged 2 or older | 100.0 | 19.0 | 29.5 | 27.1 | 24.9 |
| Females, aged 2 or older | 100.0 | 21.5 | 17.4 | 39.3 | 21.7 |
| Children under age 2 | 100.0 | 19.9 | 20.9 | 38.0 | 20.7 |
| All other apparel products and services | 100.0 | 20.8 | 20.1 | 32.9 | 25.4 |
| Jewelry and watches | 100.0 | 25.1 | 19.4 | 29.7 | 25.3 |
| All other apparel products and services | 100.0 | 16.2 | 20.9 | 36.3 | 26.4 |
| **Transportation** | **100.0** | **15.7** | **18.9** | **32.1** | **34.3** |
| **Health care** | **100.0** | **10.6** | **27.3** | **35.7** | **26.4** |
| **Entertainment** | **100.0** | **20.7** | **22.3** | **26.3** | **30.8** |
| Toys, games, hobbies, and tricycles | 100.0 | 23.6 | 23.8 | 31.6 | 21.4 |
| Other entertainment | 100.0 | 19.3 | 21.6 | 24.3 | 35.4 |
| **Education** | **100.0** | **34.4** | **23.8** | **22.5** | **19.5** |
| **All other gifts** | **100.0** | **15.9** | **24.1** | **32.5** | **27.8** |

*Note: The Bureau of Labor Statistics uses consumer unit rather than household as the sampling unit in the Consumer Expenditure Survey. For the definition of consumer unit, see Glossary. Numbers may not add to total because of rounding.*
*Source: Bureau of Labor Statistics 1999, Consumer Expenditure Survey; calculations by New Strategist*

# College Graduates Spend More

## The incomes of college graduates are much higher than average, and they spend more on most items.

College graduates have much higher incomes than those who did not graduate from college. Consequently, they spend more. In 1999, households headed by college graduates spent $53,658, 45 percent more than the $37,027 spent by the average household.

The indexed spending table in this section compares the spending of households by education with average household spending. An index of 100 means a household in the educational group spends an average amount on an item. An index above 100 means households in the group spend more than average on the item, while an index below 100 signifies below-average spending.

Households headed by college graduates spend like the sophisticated consumers they are. Their spending on beef, pork, and eggs is below average, but they spend well above average on fish and seafood, fresh fruits and vegetables, restaurant meals, and alcoholic beverages. They spend only an average amount on laundry and cleaning supplies, but much more than average on household textiles (bedroom and bathroom linens, for example). They spend nearly twice the average on fees and admissions to entertainment events, but only about half the average on tobacco.

The market share table shows how much of total household spending by category is accounted for by households in each educational group. College graduates spend disproportionately more than their share of households, while those who did not graduate from college spend less.

College graduates head 26 percent of households, but account for 37 percent of household spending. On some items their spending is even higher. They account for 52 percent of spending on "other" lodging, which includes dorm rooms, hotels, and motels.

They account for 43 percent of spending on leased vehicles and 51 percent of spending on public transportation (including airline fares). They account for 51 percent of spending on fees and admission to entertainment events and for 52 percent of all education spending. They account for more than half of all spending on cash contributions.

♦ As the educational level of the population rises, college graduates will dominate spending on a growing number of products and services.

**College graduates spend big on many items**

*(indexed average annual spending of consumer units headed by college graduates on selected items, 1999)*

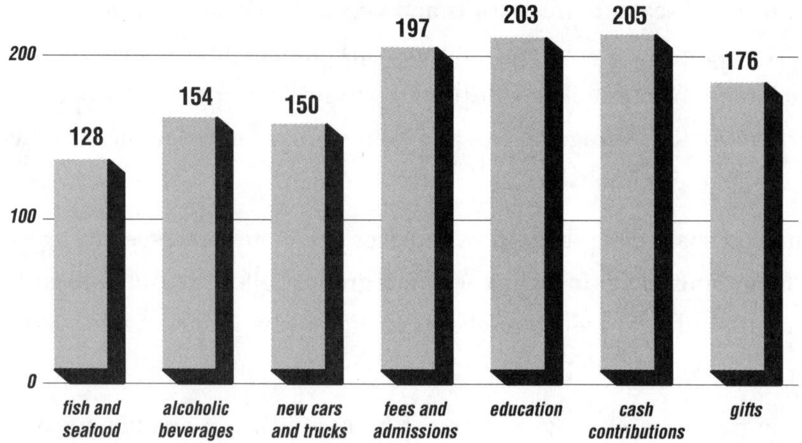

## Spending by Education of Householder, 1999

*(average annual spending of consumer units (CU's) by product and service category and educational attainment of consumer unit reference person, 1999)*

| | total | not a high school graduate | high school graduate | some college or associate's degree | college degree or more |
|---|---|---|---|---|---|
| **Number of consumer units (in 000s)** | **108,465** | **17,154** | **32,049** | **31,327** | **27,936** |
| **Average number of persons per CU** | **2.5** | **2.7** | **2.6** | **2.5** | **2.4** |
| **Average before-tax income** | **$43,951** | **$22,396** | **$36,900** | **$39,353** | **$70,324** |
| **Average annual spending** | **37,027** | **22,597** | **31,112** | **36,274** | **53,658** |
| **FOOD** | **$5,031** | **$3,790** | **$4,598** | **$4,952** | **$6,433** |
| **Food at home** | **2,915** | **2,641** | **2,836** | **2,821** | **3,295** |
| Cereals and bakery products | 448 | 407 | 436 | 430 | 511 |
| Cereals and cereal products | 160 | 161 | 151 | 149 | 182 |
| Bakery products | 288 | 247 | 285 | 279 | 329 |
| Meats, poultry, fish, and eggs | 749 | 778 | 768 | 709 | 751 |
| Beef | 220 | 234 | 227 | 217 | 207 |
| Pork | 157 | 167 | 178 | 145 | 137 |
| Other meats | 97 | 95 | 101 | 93 | 99 |
| Poultry | 136 | 136 | 139 | 127 | 143 |
| Fish and seafood | 106 | 106 | 89 | 98 | 136 |
| Eggs | 32 | 39 | 35 | 29 | 29 |
| Dairy products | 322 | 276 | 310 | 313 | 378 |
| Fresh milk and cream | 122 | 122 | 124 | 114 | 130 |
| Other dairy products | 200 | 155 | 186 | 199 | 248 |
| Fruits and vegetables | 500 | 462 | 462 | 463 | 610 |
| Fresh fruits | 152 | 142 | 135 | 141 | 194 |
| Fresh vegetables | 149 | 143 | 138 | 135 | 179 |
| Processed fruits | 113 | 92 | 103 | 106 | 147 |
| Processed vegetables | 86 | 85 | 86 | 81 | 91 |
| Other food at home | 896 | 718 | 860 | 907 | 1,044 |
| Sugar and other sweets | 112 | 96 | 110 | 106 | 129 |
| Fats and oils | 84 | 80 | 85 | 81 | 86 |
| Miscellaneous foods | 420 | 310 | 397 | 431 | 507 |
| Nonalcoholic beverages | 242 | 213 | 239 | 248 | 259 |
| Food prepared by household on trips | 39 | 20 | 29 | 40 | 63 |
| **Food away from home** | **2,116** | **1,149** | **1,761** | **2,130** | **3,138** |
| **ALCOHOLIC BEVERAGES** | **318** | **169** | **236** | **338** | **489** |

*(continued)*

*(continued from previous page)*

| | total | not a high school graduate | high school graduate | some college or associate's degree | college degree or more |
|---|---|---|---|---|---|
| **HOUSING** | **$12,057** | **$7,513** | **$9,972** | **$11,610** | **$17,766** |
| **Shelter** | **7,016** | **4,197** | **5,526** | **6,709** | **10,803** |
| Owned dwellings | 4,525 | 2,027 | 3,466 | 4,213 | 7,626 |
| Mortgage interest and charges | 2,547 | 969 | 1,809 | 2,420 | 4,506 |
| Property taxes | 1,123 | 617 | 972 | 953 | 1,799 |
| Maintenance, repairs, insurance, other | 855 | 442 | 684 | 840 | 1,321 |
| Rented dwellings | 2,027 | 2,052 | 1,800 | 2,060 | 2,234 |
| Other lodging | 464 | 117 | 260 | 436 | 943 |
| **Utilities, fuels, public services** | **2,377** | **2,007** | **2,291** | **2,306** | **2,784** |
| Natural gas | 270 | 233 | 257 | 251 | 330 |
| Electricity | 899 | 796 | 921 | 871 | 970 |
| Fuel oil and other fuels | 74 | 72 | 86 | 60 | 78 |
| Telephone services | 849 | 686 | 761 | 841 | 1,058 |
| Water and other public services | 285 | 221 | 266 | 283 | 347 |
| **Household services** | **666** | **255** | **492** | **618** | **1,173** |
| Personal services | 323 | 146 | 266 | 319 | 500 |
| Other household services | 343 | 108 | 226 | 298 | 673 |
| **Housekeeping services** | **498** | **319** | **443** | **508** | **672** |
| Laundry and cleaning supplies | 121 | 109 | 122 | 123 | 126 |
| Other household products | 250 | 152 | 217 | 248 | 356 |
| Postage and stationery | 127 | 59 | 103 | 137 | 190 |
| **Household furnishings and equipment** | **1,499** | **735** | **1,222** | **1,469** | **2,335** |
| Household textiles | 114 | 53 | 108 | 113 | 163 |
| Furniture | 365 | 216 | 287 | 340 | 576 |
| Floor coverings | 44 | 21 | 34 | 44 | 68 |
| Major appliances | 183 | 122 | 164 | 163 | 266 |
| Small appliances, miscellaneous housewares | 102 | 46 | 85 | 88 | 172 |
| Miscellaneous household equipment | 692 | 279 | 544 | 722 | 1,089 |
| **APPAREL AND SERVICES** | **1,743** | **1,073** | **1,525** | **1,726** | **2,451** |
| **Men and boys** | **421** | **237** | **370** | **402** | **622** |
| Men, aged 16 or older | 328 | 166 | 282 | 299 | 520 |
| Boys, aged 2 to 15 | 93 | 71 | 88 | 102 | 102 |
| **Women and girls** | **655** | **395** | **528** | **689** | **938** |
| Women, aged 16 or older | 548 | 328 | 427 | 572 | 807 |
| Girls, aged 2 to 15 | 107 | 67 | 101 | 117 | 130 |
| **Children under age 2** | **67** | **57** | **55** | **65** | **90** |
| **Footwear** | **303** | **245** | **298** | **297** | **354** |
| **Other apparel products and services** | **297** | **139** | **274** | **272** | **447** |

*(continued)*

*(continued from previous page)*

| | total | not a high school graduate | high school graduate | some college or associate's degree | college degree or more |
|---|---|---|---|---|---|
| **TRANSPORTATION** | **$7,011** | **$4,553** | **$6,220** | **$7,212** | **$9,205** |
| **Vehicle purchases** | **3,305** | **2,356** | **2,930** | **3,414** | **4,198** |
| Cars and trucks, new | 1,628 | 868 | 1,317 | 1,631 | 2,449 |
| Cars and trucks, used | 1,641 | 1,442 | 1,589 | 1,749 | 1,704 |
| Other vehicles | 36 | 45 | 24 | – | 45 |
| **Gasoline and motor oil** | **1,055** | **792** | **1,028** | **1,100** | **1,195** |
| **Other vehicle expenses** | **2,254** | **1,261** | **2,018** | **2,352** | **3,026** |
| Vehicle finance charges | 320 | 193 | 325 | 360 | 350 |
| Maintenance and repairs | 664 | 402 | 561 | 712 | 891 |
| Vehicle insurance | 756 | 487 | 731 | 772 | 934 |
| Vehicle rental, leases, licenses, other | 513 | 179 | 401 | 510 | 850 |
| **Public transportation** | **397** | **144** | **245** | **346** | **786** |
| **HEALTH CARE** | **1,959** | **1,551** | **1,858** | **1,813** | **2,490** |
| Health insurance | 923 | 775 | 914 | 858 | 1,096 |
| Medical services | 558 | 331 | 489 | 500 | 840 |
| Drugs | 370 | 381 | 362 | 336 | 412 |
| Medical supplies | 109 | 63 | 93 | 118 | 143 |
| **ENTERTAINMENT** | **1,891** | **881** | **1,567** | **2,001** | **2,766** |
| Fees and admissions | 459 | 110 | 275 | 443 | 904 |
| Television, radio, sound equipment | 608 | 432 | 553 | 611 | 776 |
| Pets, toys, playground equipment | 346 | 198 | 293 | 348 | 495 |
| Other entertainment supplies, services | 478 | 140 | 445 | 599 | 591 |
| **PERSONAL CARE PRODUCTS AND SERVICES** | **408** | **253** | **370** | **417** | **545** |
| **READING** | **159** | **62** | **113** | **151** | **281** |
| **EDUCATION** | **635** | **111** | **292** | **691** | **1,288** |
| **TOBACCO PRODUCTS AND SMOKING SUPPLIES** | **300** | **376** | **379** | **295** | **169** |
| **MISCELLANEOUS** | **889** | **518** | **768** | **867** | **1,283** |
| **CASH CONTRIBUTIONS** | **1,190** | **461** | **666** | **1,016** | **2,435** |
| **PERSONAL INSURANCE AND PENSIONS** | **3,436** | **1,286** | **2,549** | **3,185** | **6,056** |
| Life and other personal insurance | 394 | 228 | 305 | 327 | 675 |
| Pensions and Social Security | 3,042 | 1,058 | 2,245 | 2,858 | 5,380 |

*(continued)*

*(continued from previous page)*

| | total | not a high school graduate | high school graduate | some college or associate's degree | college degree or more |
|---|---|---|---|---|---|
| **PERSONAL TAXES** | **$3,588** | **$785** | **$2,082** | **$2,746** | **$7,952** |
| Federal income taxes | 2,802 | 561 | 1,501 | 2,076 | 6,457 |
| State and local income taxes | 616 | 167 | 416 | 531 | 1,212 |
| Other taxes | 170 | 57 | 165 | 138 | 283 |
| **GIFTS** | **1,083** | **548** | **817** | **929** | **1,901** |
| **Food** | **83** | **34** | **45** | **63** | **180** |
| **Housing** | **292** | **150** | **233** | **230** | **519** |
| Housekeeping supplies | 41 | 17 | 32 | 42 | 63 |
| Household textiles | 17 | 4 | 17 | 16 | 26 |
| Appliances and miscellaneous housewares | 32 | 11 | 36 | 20 | 55 |
| Major appliances | 9 | 3 | 14 | 5 | 11 |
| Small appliances and misc. housewares | 24 | 9 | 22 | 15 | 45 |
| Miscellaneous household equipment | 66 | 32 | 50 | 61 | 112 |
| Other housing | 136 | 86 | 98 | 90 | 262 |
| **Apparel and services** | **210** | **142** | **183** | **202** | **293** |
| Males, aged 2 or older | 54 | 39 | 54 | 45 | 74 |
| Females, aged 2 or older | 71 | 37 | 66 | 77 | 93 |
| Children under age 2 | 33 | 25 | 28 | 31 | 47 |
| All other apparel products and services | 52 | 42 | 35 | 50 | 79 |
| Jewelry and watches | 27 | 12 | 16 | 29 | 46 |
| All other apparel products and services | 25 | 30 | 20 | 21 | 33 |
| **Transportation** | **63** | **24** | **64** | **55** | **96** |
| **Health care** | **40** | **29** | **35** | **30** | **64** |
| **Entertainment** | **98** | **44** | **79** | **124** | **126** |
| Toys, games, hobbies, and tricycles | 32 | 24 | 27 | 37 | 37 |
| Other entertainment | 66 | 20 | 53 | 87 | 89 |
| **Education** | **166** | **17** | **89** | **101** | **419** |
| **All other gifts** | **131** | **109** | **88** | **124** | **203** |

*Note: The Bureau of Labor Statistics uses consumer unit rather than household as the sampling unit in the Consumer Expenditure Survey. For the definition of consumer unit, see Glossary. Gift spending is also included in the preceding product and service categories.*
*Source: Bureau of Labor Statistics, 1999 Consumer Expenditure Survey; Internet site <www.bls.gov/csxstnd.htm>*

## Indexed Spending by Education, 1999

*(indexed average annual spending of consumer units by product and service category and educational attainment of consumer unit reference person, 1999)*

| | *total* | *not a high school graduate* | *high school graduate* | *some college or associate's degree* | *college degree or more* |
|---|---|---|---|---|---|
| **Number of consumer units (in 000s)** | **108,465** | **17,154** | **32,049** | **31,327** | **27,936** |
| **Indexed average before-tax income** | **100** | **51** | **84** | **90** | **160** |
| **Indexed average annual spending** | **100** | **61** | **84** | **98** | **145** |
| **FOOD** | **100** | **75** | **91** | **98** | **128** |
| **Food at home** | **100** | **91** | **97** | **97** | **113** |
| Cereals and bakery products | 100 | 91 | 97 | 96 | 114 |
| Cereals and cereal products | 100 | 101 | 94 | 93 | 114 |
| Bakery products | 100 | 86 | 99 | 97 | 114 |
| Meats, poultry, fish, and eggs | 100 | 104 | 103 | 95 | 100 |
| Beef | 100 | 106 | 103 | 99 | 94 |
| Pork | 100 | 106 | 113 | 93 | 87 |
| Other meats | 100 | 98 | 104 | 96 | 102 |
| Poultry | 100 | 100 | 102 | 93 | 105 |
| Fish and seafood | 100 | 100 | 84 | 92 | 128 |
| Eggs | 100 | 122 | 109 | 89 | 91 |
| Dairy products | 100 | 86 | 96 | 97 | 117 |
| Fresh milk and cream | 100 | 100 | 102 | 93 | 107 |
| Other dairy products | 100 | 78 | 93 | 100 | 124 |
| Fruits and vegetables | 100 | 92 | 92 | 93 | 122 |
| Fresh fruits | 100 | 93 | 89 | 93 | 128 |
| Fresh vegetables | 100 | 96 | 93 | 91 | 120 |
| Processed fruits | 100 | 81 | 91 | 94 | 130 |
| Processed vegetables | 100 | 99 | 100 | 94 | 106 |
| Other food at home | 100 | 80 | 96 | 101 | 117 |
| Sugar and other sweets | 100 | 86 | 98 | 95 | 115 |
| Fats and oils | 100 | 95 | 101 | 97 | 102 |
| Miscellaneous foods | 100 | 74 | 95 | 103 | 121 |
| Nonalcoholic beverages | 100 | 88 | 99 | 102 | 107 |
| Food prepared by household on trips | 100 | 51 | 74 | 102 | 162 |
| **Food away from home** | **100** | **54** | **83** | **101** | **148** |
| **ALCOHOLIC BEVERAGES** | **100** | **53** | **74** | **106** | **154** |

*(continued)*

*(continued from previous page)*

| | total | not a high school graduate | high school graduate | some college or associate's degree | college degree or more |
|---|---|---|---|---|---|
| **HOUSING** | **100** | **62** | **83** | **96** | **147** |
| **Shelter** | **100** | **60** | **79** | **96** | **154** |
| Owned dwellings | 100 | 45 | 77 | 93 | 169 |
| Mortgage interest and charges | 100 | 38 | 71 | 95 | 177 |
| Property taxes | 100 | 55 | 87 | 85 | 160 |
| Maintenance, repairs, insurance, other | 100 | 52 | 80 | 98 | 155 |
| Rented dwellings | 100 | 101 | 89 | 102 | 110 |
| Other lodging | 100 | 25 | 56 | 94 | 203 |
| **Utilities, fuels, public services** | **100** | **84** | **96** | **97** | **117** |
| Natural gas | 100 | 86 | 95 | 93 | 122 |
| Electricity | 100 | 89 | 102 | 97 | 108 |
| Fuel oil and other fuels | 100 | 97 | 116 | 81 | 105 |
| Telephone services | 100 | 81 | 90 | 99 | 125 |
| Water and other public services | 100 | 78 | 93 | 99 | 122 |
| **Household services** | **100** | **38** | **74** | **93** | **176** |
| Personal services | 100 | 45 | 82 | 99 | 155 |
| Other household services | 100 | 31 | 66 | 87 | 196 |
| **Housekeeping supplies** | **100** | **64** | **89** | **102** | **135** |
| Laundry and cleaning supplies | 100 | 90 | 101 | 102 | 104 |
| Other household products | 100 | 61 | 87 | 99 | 142 |
| Postage and stationery | 100 | 46 | 81 | 108 | 150 |
| **Household furnishings and equipment** | **100** | **49** | **82** | **98** | **156** |
| Household textiles | 100 | 46 | 95 | 99 | 143 |
| Furniture | 100 | 59 | 79 | 93 | 158 |
| Floor coverings | 100 | 48 | 77 | 100 | 155 |
| Major appliances | 100 | 67 | 90 | 89 | 145 |
| Small appliances, miscellaneous housewares | 100 | 45 | 83 | 86 | 169 |
| Miscellaneous household equipment | 100 | 40 | 79 | 104 | 157 |
| **APPAREL AND SERVICES** | **100** | **62** | **87** | **99** | **141** |
| **Men and boys** | **100** | **56** | **88** | **95** | **148** |
| Men, aged 16 or older | 100 | 51 | 86 | 91 | 159 |
| Boys, aged 2 to 15 | 100 | 76 | 95 | 110 | 110 |
| **Women and girls** | **100** | **60** | **81** | **105** | **143** |
| Women, aged 16 or older | 100 | 60 | 78 | 104 | 147 |
| Girls, aged 2 to 15 | 100 | 63 | 94 | 110 | 121 |
| **Children under age 2** | **100** | **85** | **82** | **97** | **134** |
| **Footwear** | **100** | **81** | **98** | **98** | **117** |
| **Other apparel products and services** | **100** | **47** | **92** | **92** | **151** |

*(continued)*

*(continued from previous page)*

| | *total* | *not a high school graduate* | *high school graduate* | *some college or associate's degree* | *college degree or more* |
|---|---|---|---|---|---|
| **TRANSPORTATION** | **100** | **65** | **89** | **103** | **131** |
| **Vehicle purchases** | **100** | **71** | **89** | **103** | **127** |
| Cars and trucks, new | 100 | 53 | 81 | 100 | 150 |
| Cars and trucks, used | 100 | 88 | 97 | 107 | 104 |
| Other vehicles | 100 | 125 | 67 | – | 125 |
| **Gasoline and motor oil** | **100** | **75** | **97** | **104** | **113** |
| **Other vehicle expenses** | **100** | **56** | **90** | **104** | **134** |
| Vehicle finance charges | 100 | 60 | 102 | 112 | 109 |
| Maintenance and repairs | 100 | 61 | 84 | 107 | 134 |
| Vehicle insurance | 100 | 64 | 97 | 102 | 124 |
| Vehicle rental, leases, licenses, other | 100 | 35 | 78 | 99 | 166 |
| **Public transportation** | **100** | **36** | **62** | **87** | **198** |
| **HEALTH CARE** | **100** | **79** | **95** | **93** | **127** |
| Health insurance | 100 | 84 | 99 | 93 | 119 |
| Medical services | 100 | 59 | 88 | 90 | 151 |
| Drugs | 100 | 103 | 98 | 91 | 111 |
| Medical supplies | 100 | 58 | 85 | 109 | 131 |
| **ENTERTAINMENT** | **100** | **47** | **83** | **106** | **146** |
| Fees and admissions | 100 | 24 | 60 | 96 | 197 |
| Television, radio, sound equipment | 100 | 71 | 91 | 101 | 128 |
| Pets, toys, playground equipment | 100 | 57 | 85 | 101 | 143 |
| Other entertainment supplies, services | 100 | 29 | 93 | 125 | 124 |
| **PERSONAL CARE PRODUCTS AND SERVICES** | **100** | **62** | **91** | **102** | **134** |
| **READING** | **100** | **39** | **71** | **95** | **177** |
| **EDUCATION** | **100** | **17** | **46** | **109** | **203** |
| **TOBACCO PRODUCTS AND SMOKING SUPPLIES** | **100** | **125** | **126** | **98** | **56** |
| **MISCELLANEOUS** | **100** | **58** | **86** | **97** | **144** |
| **CASH CONTRIBUTIONS** | **100** | **39** | **56** | **85** | **205** |
| **PERSONAL INSURANCE AND PENSIONS** | **100** | **37** | **74** | **93** | **176** |
| Life and other personal insurance | 100 | 58 | 77 | 83 | 171 |
| Pensions and Social Security | 100 | 35 | 74 | 94 | 177 |

*(continued)*

*(continued from previous page)*

| | total | not a high school graduate | high school graduate | some college or associate's degree | college degree or more |
|---|---|---|---|---|---|
| **PERSONAL TAXES** | **100** | **22** | **58** | **77** | **222** |
| Federal income taxes | 100 | 20 | 54 | 74 | 230 |
| State and local income taxes | 100 | 27 | 68 | 86 | 197 |
| Other taxes | 100 | 34 | 97 | 81 | 166 |
| **GIFTS** | **100** | **51** | **75** | **86** | **176** |
| **Food** | **100** | **41** | **54** | **76** | **217** |
| **Housing** | **100** | **51** | **80** | **79** | **178** |
| Housekeeping supplies | 100 | 41 | 78 | 103 | 154 |
| Household textiles | 100 | 24 | 100 | 92 | 153 |
| Appliances and miscellaneous housewares | 100 | 34 | 113 | 63 | 172 |
| Major appliances | 100 | 33 | 156 | 56 | 122 |
| Small appliances and misc. housewares | 100 | 38 | 92 | 63 | 188 |
| Miscellaneous household equipment | 100 | 48 | 76 | 92 | 170 |
| Other housing | 100 | 63 | 72 | 66 | 193 |
| **Apparel and services** | **100** | **68** | **87** | **96** | **140** |
| Males, aged 2 or older | 100 | 72 | 100 | 84 | 137 |
| Females, aged 2 or older | 100 | 52 | 93 | 108 | 131 |
| Children under age 2 | 100 | 76 | 85 | 94 | 142 |
| All other apparel products and services | 100 | 81 | 67 | 96 | 152 |
| Jewelry and watches | 100 | 44 | 59 | 107 | 170 |
| All other apparel products and services | 100 | 120 | 80 | 84 | 132 |
| **Transportation** | **100** | **38** | **102** | **87** | **152** |
| **Health care** | **100** | **73** | **88** | **75** | **160** |
| **Entertainment** | **100** | **45** | **81** | **127** | **129** |
| Toys, games, hobbies, and tricycles | 100 | 75 | 84 | 115 | 116 |
| Other entertainment | 100 | 30 | 80 | 132 | 135 |
| **Education** | **100** | **10** | **54** | **61** | **252** |
| **All other gifts** | **100** | **83** | **67** | **94** | **155** |

*Note: The Bureau of Labor Statistics uses consumer unit rather than household as the sampling unit in the Consumer Expenditure Survey. For the definition of consumer unit, see Glossary. An index of 100 is the average for all households. An index of 132 means households in the group spend 32 percent more than the average household. An index of 75 means households in the group spend 25 percent less than the average household. (–) means sample is too small to make a reliable estimate.*
*Source: Bureau of Labor Statistics 1999, Consumer Expenditure Survey; calculations by New Strategist*

## Market Shares by Education, 1999

*(share of total annual spending accounted for by educational group, 1999)*

| | total | not a high school graduate | high school graduate | some college or associate's degree | college degree or more |
|---|---|---|---|---|---|
| **Share of total consumer units** | **100.0%** | **15.8%** | **29.5%** | **28.9%** | **25.8%** |
| **Share of total annual spending** | **100.0** | **9.7** | **24.8** | **28.3** | **37.3** |
| **FOOD** | **100.0%** | **11.9%** | **27.0%** | **28.4%** | **32.9%** |
| **Food at home** | **100.0** | **14.3** | **28.7** | **27.9** | **29.1** |
| Cereals and bakery products | 100.0 | 14.4 | 28.8 | 27.7 | 29.4 |
| Cereals and cereal products | 100.0 | 15.9 | 27.9 | 26.9 | 29.3 |
| Bakery products | 100.0 | 13.6 | 29.2 | 28.0 | 29.4 |
| Meats, poultry, fish, and eggs | 100.0 | 16.4 | 30.3 | 27.4 | 25.8 |
| Beef | 100.0 | 16.8 | 30.5 | 28.5 | 24.2 |
| Pork | 100.0 | 16.8 | 33.5 | 26.8 | 22.5 |
| Other meats | 100.0 | 15.5 | 30.8 | 27.7 | 26.3 |
| Poultry | 100.0 | 15.8 | 30.2 | 27.0 | 27.1 |
| Fish and seafood | 100.0 | 15.8 | 24.8 | 26.7 | 33.0 |
| Eggs | 100.0 | 19.3 | 32.3 | 25.8 | 23.3 |
| Dairy products | 100.0 | 13.6 | 28.4 | 28.1 | 30.2 |
| Fresh milk and cream | 100.0 | 15.8 | 30.0 | 26.9 | 27.4 |
| Other dairy products | 100.0 | 12.3 | 27.5 | 28.8 | 31.9 |
| Fruits and vegetables | 100.0 | 14.6 | 27.3 | 26.7 | 31.4 |
| Fresh fruits | 100.0 | 14.8 | 26.2 | 26.8 | 32.9 |
| Fresh vegetables | 100.0 | 15.2 | 27.4 | 26.3 | 30.9 |
| Processed fruits | 100.0 | 12.9 | 26.9 | 27.2 | 33.5 |
| Processed vegetables | 100.0 | 15.6 | 29.5 | 27.1 | 27.3 |
| Other food at home | 100.0 | 12.7 | 28.4 | 29.2 | 30.0 |
| Sugar and other sweets | 100.0 | 13.6 | 29.0 | 27.4 | 29.7 |
| Fats and oils | 100.0 | 15.1 | 29.9 | 28.0 | 26.4 |
| Miscellaneous foods | 100.0 | 11.7 | 27.9 | 29.6 | 31.1 |
| Nonalcoholic beverages | 100.0 | 13.9 | 29.2 | 29.6 | 27.6 |
| Food prepared by household on trips | 100.0 | 8.1 | 22.0 | 29.4 | 41.6 |
| **Food away from home** | **100.0** | **8.6** | **24.6** | **29.1** | **38.2** |
| **ALCOHOLIC BEVERAGES** | **100.0** | **8.4** | **21.9** | **30.7** | **39.6** |

*(continued)*

*(continued from previous page)*

| | total | not a high school graduate | high school graduate | some college or associate's degree | college degree or more |
|---|---|---|---|---|---|
| **HOUSING** | **100.0%** | **9.9%** | **24.4%** | **27.8%** | **38.0%** |
| **Shelter** | | | | | |
| Owned dwellings | 100.0 | 7.1 | 22.6 | 26.9 | 43.4 |
| Mortgage interest and charges | 100.0 | 6.0 | 21.0 | 27.4 | 45.6 |
| Property taxes | 100.0 | 8.7 | 25.6 | 24.5 | 41.3 |
| Maintenance, repairs, insurance, other | 100.0 | 8.2 | 23.6 | 28.4 | 39.8 |
| Rented dwellings | 100.0 | 16.0 | 26.2 | 29.3 | 28.4 |
| Other lodging | 100.0 | 4.0 | 16.6 | 27.2 | 52.3 |
| **Utilities, fuels, public services** | **100.0** | **13.4** | **28.5** | **28.0** | **30.2** |
| Natural gas | 100.0 | 13.6 | 28.1 | 26.9 | 31.5 |
| Electricity | 100.0 | 14.0 | 30.3 | 28.0 | 27.8 |
| Fuel oil and other fuels | 100.0 | 15.4 | 34.3 | 23.3 | 27.1 |
| Telephone services | 100.0 | 12.8 | 26.5 | 28.6 | 32.1 |
| Water and other public services | 100.0 | 12.3 | 27.6 | 28.6 | 31.4 |
| **Household services** | **100.0** | **6.1** | **21.8** | **26.8** | **45.4** |
| Personal services | 100.0 | 7.1 | 24.3 | 28.5 | 39.9 |
| Other household services | 100.0 | 5.0 | 19.5 | 25.1 | 50.5 |
| **Housekeeping supplies** | **100.0** | **10.1** | **26.3** | **29.5** | **34.8** |
| Laundry and cleaning supplies | 100.0 | 14.2 | 29.8 | 29.4 | 26.8 |
| Other household products | 100.0 | 9.6 | 25.6 | 28.7 | 36.7 |
| Postage and stationery | 100.0 | 7.3 | 24.0 | 31.2 | 38.5 |
| **Household furnishings and equipment** | **100.0** | **7.8** | **24.1** | **28.3** | **40.1** |
| Household textiles | 100.0 | 7.4 | 28.0 | 28.5 | 36.8 |
| Furniture | 100.0 | 9.4 | 23.2 | 26.9 | 40.6 |
| Floor coverings | 100.0 | 7.5 | 22.8 | 28.9 | 39.8 |
| Major appliances | 100.0 | 10.5 | 26.5 | 25.8 | 37.4 |
| Small appliances, misc. housewares | 100.0 | 7.1 | 24.6 | 24.9 | 43.4 |
| Miscellaneous household equipment | 100.0 | 6.4 | 23.2 | 30.1 | 40.5 |
| **APPAREL AND SERVICES** | **100.0** | **9.7** | **25.9** | **28.6** | **36.2** |
| **Men and boys** | **100.0** | **8.9** | **26.0** | **27.5** | **38.1** |
| Men, aged 16 or older | 100.0 | 8.0 | 25.4 | 26.3 | 40.8 |
| Boys, aged 2 to 15 | 100.0 | 12.1 | 28.0 | 31.8 | 28.2 |
| **Women and girls** | **100.0** | **9.5** | **23.8** | **30.4** | **36.9** |
| Women, aged 16 or older | 100.0 | 9.5 | 23.0 | 30.2 | 37.9 |
| Girls, aged 2 to 15 | 100.0 | 9.9 | 27.9 | 31.6 | 31.3 |
| **Children under age 2** | **100.0** | **13.5** | **24.3** | **28.1** | **34.6** |
| **Footwear** | **100.0** | **12.8** | **29.1** | **28.3** | **30.1** |
| **Other apparel products and services** | **100.0** | **7.4** | **27.3** | **26.5** | **38.8** |

*(continued)*

*(continued from previous page)*

| | total | not a high school graduate | high school graduate | some college or associate's degree | college degree or more |
|---|---|---|---|---|---|
| **TRANSPORTATION** | **100.0%** | **10.3%** | **26.2%** | **29.7%** | **33.8%** |
| Vehicle purchases | 100.0 | 11.3 | 26.2 | 29.8 | 32.7 |
| Cars and trucks, new | 100.0 | 8.4 | 23.9 | 28.9 | 38.7 |
| Cars and trucks, used | 100.0 | 13.9 | 28.6 | 30.8 | 26.7 |
| Other vehicles | 100.0 | 19.8 | 19.7 | – | 32.2 |
| **Gasoline and motor oil** | **100.0** | **11.9** | **28.8** | **30.1** | **29.2** |
| **Other vehicle expenses** | **100.0** | **8.8** | **26.5** | **30.1** | **34.6** |
| Vehicle finance charges | 100.0 | 9.5 | 30.0 | 32.5 | 28.2 |
| Maintenance and repairs | 100.0 | 9.6 | 25.0 | 31.0 | 34.6 |
| Vehicle insurance | 100.0 | 10.2 | 28.6 | 29.5 | 31.8 |
| Vehicle rental, leases, licenses, other | 100.0 | 5.5 | 23.1 | 28.7 | 42.7 |
| **Public transportation** | **100.0** | **5.7** | **18.2** | **25.1** | **51.0** |
| **HEALTH CARE** | **100.0** | **12.5** | **28.0** | **26.7** | **32.7** |
| Health insurance | 100.0 | 13.3 | 29.3 | 26.9 | 30.6 |
| Medical services | 100.0 | 9.4 | 25.9 | 25.9 | 38.8 |
| Drugs | 100.0 | 16.3 | 28.9 | 26.2 | 28.7 |
| Medical supplies | 100.0 | 9.1 | 25.2 | 31.4 | 33.8 |
| **ENTERTAINMENT** | **100.0** | **7.4** | **24.5** | **30.6** | **37.7** |
| Fees and admissions | 100.0 | 3.8 | 17.7 | 27.9 | 50.7 |
| Television, radio, sound equipment | 100.0 | 11.2 | 26.9 | 29.0 | 32.9 |
| Pets, toys, playground equipment | 100.0 | 9.1 | 25.0 | 29.1 | 36.8 |
| Other entertainment supplies, services | 100.0 | 4.6 | 27.5 | 36.2 | 31.8 |
| **PERSONAL CARE PRODUCTS AND SERVICES** | **100.0** | **9.8** | **26.8** | **29.6** | **34.4** |
| **READING** | **100.0** | **6.2** | **21.0** | **27.5** | **45.5** |
| **EDUCATION** | **100.0** | **2.8** | **13.6** | **31.4** | **52.2** |
| **TOBACCO PRODUCTS AND SMOKING SUPPLIES** | **100.0** | **19.8** | **37.3** | **28.4** | **14.5** |
| **MISCELLANEOUS** | **100.0** | **9.2** | **25.5** | **28.2** | **37.2** |
| **CASH CONTRIBUTIONS** | **100.0** | **6.1** | **16.5** | **24.7** | **52.7** |
| **PERSONAL INSURANCE AND PENSIONS** | **100.0** | **5.9** | **21.9** | **26.8** | **45.4** |
| Life and other personal insurance | 100.0 | 9.2 | 22.9 | 24.0 | 44.1 |
| Pensions and Social Security | 100.0 | 5.5 | 21.8 | 27.1 | 45.6 |

*(continued)*

*(continued from previous page)*

| | total | not a high school graduate | high school graduate | some college or associate's degree | college degree or more |
|---|---|---|---|---|---|
| **PERSONAL TAXES** | **100.0%** | **3.5%** | **17.1%** | **22.1%** | **57.1%** |
| Federal income taxes | 100.0 | 3.2 | 15.8 | 21.4 | 59.4 |
| State and local income taxes | 100.0 | 4.3 | 20.0 | 24.9 | 50.7 |
| Other taxes | 100.0 | 5.3 | 28.7 | 23.5 | 42.9 |
| **GIFTS** | **100.0** | **8.0** | **22.3** | **24.8** | **45.2** |
| **Food** | **100.0** | **6.5** | **16.0** | **21.8** | **55.9** |
| **Housing** | **100.0** | **8.1** | **23.6** | **22.7** | **45.8** |
| Housekeeping supplies | 100.0 | 6.6 | 23.1 | 29.9 | 39.6 |
| Household textiles | 100.0 | 3.7 | 29.5 | 26.6 | 39.4 |
| Appliances and misc. housewares | 100.0 | 5.4 | 33.2 | 18.2 | 44.3 |
| Major appliances | 100.0 | 5.3 | 46.0 | 16.2 | 31.5 |
| Small appliances and misc. housewares | 100.0 | 5.9 | 27.1 | 18.2 | 48.3 |
| Miscellaneous household equipment | 100.0 | 7.7 | 22.4 | 26.7 | 43.7 |
| Other housing | 100.0 | 10.0 | 21.3 | 19.2 | 49.6 |
| **Apparel and services** | **100.0** | **10.7** | **25.7** | **27.8** | **35.9** |
| Males, aged 2 or older | 100.0 | 11.4 | 29.5 | 24.2 | 35.3 |
| Females, aged 2 or older | 100.0 | 8.2 | 27.5 | 31.2 | 33.7 |
| Children under age 2 | 100.0 | 12.0 | 25.1 | 27.2 | 36.7 |
| All other apparel products and services | 100.0 | 12.8 | 19.9 | 27.7 | 39.1 |
| Jewelry and watches | 100.0 | 7.0 | 17.5 | 31.0 | 43.9 |
| All other apparel products and services | 100.0 | 19.0 | 23.6 | 24.3 | 34.0 |
| **Transportation** | **100.0** | **6.0** | **30.0** | **25.0** | **39.2** |
| **Health care** | **100.0** | **11.5** | **25.9** | **21.8** | **41.2** |
| **Entertainment** | **100.0** | **7.1** | **23.8** | **36.6** | **33.1** |
| Toys, games, hobbies, and tricycles | 100.0 | 11.9 | 24.9 | 33.3 | 29.8 |
| Other entertainment | 100.0 | 4.8 | 23.7 | 38.0 | 34.7 |
| **Education** | **100.0** | **1.6** | **15.8** | **17.7** | **65.0** |
| **All other gifts** | **100.0** | **13.2** | **19.8** | **27.2** | **39.9** |

*Note: The Bureau of Labor Statistics uses consumer unit rather than household as the sampling unit in the Consumer Expenditure Survey. For the definition of consumer unit, see Glossary. Numbers may not add to total because of rounding.*
*Source: Bureau of Labor Statistics, 1999 Consumer Expenditure Survey; calculations by New Strategist*

CHAPTER

# 9

# Wealth Trends

♦ **Net worth peaks in the 65-to-74 age group.**

The median net worth of American households stood at $71,600 in 1998, up 20 percent from the $59,700 of 1989 after adjusting for inflation.

♦ **Most households own financial assets.**

The median value of financial assets owned by the average household stood at a modest $22,400 in 1998—despite the rapid rise in the stock market during the 1990s.

♦ **Half of households are invested in the stock market.**

The percentage of households owning stocks either directly or indirectly rose from 32 percent in 1989 to 49 percent in 1998.

♦ **Americans' nonfinancial assets are much more valuable than their financial assets.**

The median value of nonfinancial assets owned by the average household stood at $97,800 in 1998, much greater than its $22,400 median in financial assets.

♦ **Most households have debt.**

Seventy-four percent of households are in debt, owing a median of $33,300 in 1998.

# Net Worth Rises for Most

## Net worth peaks in the 65-to-74 age group.

The median net worth of American households stood at $71,600 in 1998, up 20 percent from the $59,700 of 1989 after adjusting for inflation. Net worth, which is one of the most important measures of wealth, is what remains after a household's debts are subtracted from its assets. The booming stock market of the 1990s explains much of the rise in net worth.

Not surprisingly, net worth is greatest for those with the highest incomes. Households with incomes of $100,000 or more had a median net worth of more than $500,000 in 1998. Since 1989, median net worth rose for all but the top income group.

Net worth rises with age because people tend to pay off their debts. Householders under age 35 had a median net worth of just $9,000 in 1998. Net worth peaks in the 65-to-74 age group at $146,500. Householders aged 55 or older saw their net worth grow between 1989 and 1998, while the net worth of younger householders declined. Behind the decline in median net worth was the rise in homeownership, as middle-aged and younger householders took on more mortgage debt.

Net worth rose sharply for nonwhites and Hispanics between 1989 and 1998—up 93 percent. Despite the increase, the net worth of nonwhites and Hispanics lags far behind that of non-Hispanic whites, $16,400 versus $94,900 in 1998.

♦ For most households, homeownership is the largest component of net worth. As people pay off their mortgages over the years, net worth grows.

### Median net worth rises with age

*(median net worth of households by age of householder, 1998)*

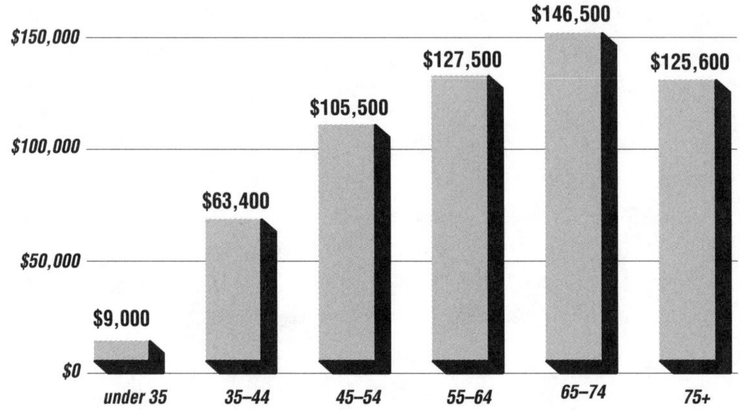

## Net Worth of Households, 1989 and 1998

*(median net worth of households by selected characteristics of householders, 1989 and 1998; percent change, 1989–98)*

| | 1998 | 1989 | percent change 1989–98 |
|---|---|---|---|
| **Total households** | **$71,600** | **$59,700** | **19.9%** |
| **Income** | | | |
| Under $10,000 | 3,600 | 1,900 | 89.5 |
| $10,000 to $24,999 | 24,800 | 22,800 | 8.8 |
| $25,000 to $49,999 | 60,300 | 58,100 | 3.8 |
| $50,000 to $99,999 | 152,000 | 131,400 | 15.7 |
| $100,000 or more | 510,800 | 542,100 | –5.8 |
| **Age of householder** | | | |
| Under age 35 | 9,000 | 9,900 | –9.1 |
| Aged 35 to 44 | 63,400 | 71,800 | –11.7 |
| Aged 45 to 54 | 105,500 | 125,700 | –16.1 |
| Aged 55 to 64 | 127,500 | 124,600 | 2.3 |
| Aged 65 to 74 | 146,500 | 97,100 | 50.9 |
| Aged 75 or older | 125,600 | 92,200 | 36.2 |
| **Education of householder** | | | |
| No high school diploma | 20,900 | 30,700 | –31.9 |
| High school diploma | 53,800 | 46,900 | 14.7 |
| Some college | 73,900 | 58,500 | 26.3 |
| College degree | 146,400 | 141,400 | 3.5 |
| **Race or ethnicity of householder** | | | |
| Non-Hispanic white | 94,900 | 90,500 | 4.9 |
| Nonwhite or Hispanic | 16,400 | 8,500 | 92.9 |

*Source: Federal Reserve Board,* Recent Changes in U.S. Family Finances: Results from the 1998 Survey of Consumer Finances, *Federal Reserve Bulletin, January 2000; calculations by New Strategist*

# The Majority of Households Own Financial Assets

## Nearly half own retirement accounts.

Ninety-three percent of households own financial assets, which range from transaction accounts (checking and saving) to stocks, retirement accounts, and life insurance. The median value of financial assets owned by the average household stood at a modest $22,400 in 1998—despite the rapid rise in the stock market during the 1990s.

Transaction accounts are the most commonly owned financial asset, held by 91 percent of households. Their median value was just $3,100. The second most common financial asset is a retirement account, owned by 49 percent of households. More than half of householders aged 35 to 64 have retirement accounts. Most do not have much in the accounts, however. By age, householders aged 55 to 64 have the most—a median of only $46,800.

Nineteen percent of households own stock directly. The median value of stock owners' holdings was just $17,500 in 1998. Seventeen percent of households own mutual funds, with a median value of $25,000.

♦ The financial assets of Americans grew rapidly during the 1990s because of the booming stock market. A slowdown in the stock market could end the gains in financial assets.

## Ownership of Financial Assets, 1998

*(percent of households owning financial assets, and median value of asset for owners, by selected characteristics of households and type of asset, 1998)*

| | any financial asset | transaction accounts | CDs | savings bonds | bonds | stocks | mutual funds | retirement accounts | life insurance | other managed | other financial |
|---|---|---|---|---|---|---|---|---|---|---|---|
| PERCENT OWNING ASSET | | | | | | | | | | | |
| **Total households** | **92.9%** | **90.5%** | **15.3%** | **19.3%** | **3.0%** | **19.2%** | **16.5%** | **48.8%** | **29.6%** | **5.9%** | **9.4%** |
| **Income** | | | | | | | | | | | |
| Under $10,000 | 70.6 | 61.9 | 7.7 | 3.5 | – | 3.8 | 1.9 | 6.4 | 15.7 | – | 8.0 |
| $10,000 to $24,999 | 89.9 | 86.5 | 16.8 | 10.2 | 1.3 | 7.2 | 7.6 | 25.4 | 20.9 | 4.9 | 8.2 |
| $25,000 to $49,999 | 97.3 | 95.8 | 15.9 | 20.4 | 2.4 | 17.7 | 14.0 | 54.2 | 28.1 | 3.9 | 10.2 |
| $50,000 to $99,999 | 99.8 | 99.3 | 16.4 | 30.6 | 3.3 | 27.7 | 25.8 | 73.5 | 39.8 | 8.0 | 9.1 |
| $100,000 or more | 100.0 | 100.0 | 16.8 | 32.3 | 12.2 | 56.6 | 44.8 | 88.6 | 50.1 | 15.8 | 12.7 |
| **Age of householder** | | | | | | | | | | | |
| Under age 35 | 88.6 | 84.6 | 6.2 | 17.2 | 1.0 | 13.1 | 12.2 | 39.8 | 18.0 | 1.9 | 10.1 |
| Aged 35 to 44 | 93.3 | 90.5 | 9.4 | 24.9 | 1.5 | 18.9 | 16.0 | 59.5 | 29.0 | 3.9 | 11.8 |
| Aged 45 to 54 | 94.9 | 93.5 | 11.8 | 21.8 | 2.8 | 22.6 | 23.0 | 59.2 | 32.9 | 6.5 | 9.1 |
| Aged 55 to 64 | 95.6 | 93.9 | 18.6 | 18.1 | 3.5 | 25.0 | 15.2 | 58.3 | 35.8 | 6.5 | 8.4 |
| Aged 65 to 74 | 95.6 | 94.1 | 29.9 | 16.1 | 7.2 | 21.0 | 18.0 | 46.1 | 39.1 | 11.8 | 7.3 |
| Aged 75 or older | 92.1 | 89.7 | 35.9 | 12.0 | 5.9 | 18.0 | 15.1 | 16.7 | 32.6 | 11.6 | 6.4 |
| **Race and ethnicity of householder** | | | | | | | | | | | |
| Non-Hispanic white | 96.3 | 94.7 | 17.9 | 22.2 | 3.7 | 22.1 | 18.8 | 53.7 | 32.1 | 7.1 | 9.7 |
| Nonwhite or Hispanic | 81.2 | 75.8 | 6.4 | 9.2 | 0.4 | 9.1 | 8.4 | 32.0 | 20.8 | 1.7 | 8.3 |

*(continued)*

*(continued from previous page)*

| | *any financial asset* | *transaction accounts* | *CDs* | *savings bonds* | *bonds* | *stocks* | *mutual funds* | *retirement accounts* | *life insurance* | *other managed* | *other financial* |
|---|---|---|---|---|---|---|---|---|---|---|---|
| **MEDIAN VALUE OF ASSET FOR OWNERS** | | | | | | | | | | | |
| **Total households** | **$22,400** | **$3,100** | **$15,000** | **$1,000** | **$44,800** | **$17,500** | **$25,000** | **$24,000** | **$7,300** | **$31,500** | **$3,000** |
| **Income** | | | | | | | | | | | |
| Under $10,000 | 1,100 | 500 | 7,000 | 1,800 | – | 14,000 | 6,000 | 7,500 | 3,000 | – | 500 |
| $10,000 to $24,999 | 4,800 | 1,300 | 20,000 | 1,000 | 8,400 | 10,000 | 26,000 | 8,000 | 5,000 | 30,000 | 1,100 |
| $25,000 to $49,999 | 17,600 | 2,500 | 14,500 | 600 | 25,000 | 8,000 | 11,000 | 13,000 | 5,000 | 15,000 | 2,000 |
| $50,000 to $99,999 | 57,200 | 6,000 | 13,300 | 1,000 | 18,000 | 15,000 | 25,000 | 31,000 | 9,500 | 32,000 | 5,000 |
| $100,000 or more | 244,300 | 19,000 | 22,000 | 1,500 | 108,000 | 55,000 | 65,000 | 93,000 | 18,000 | 100,000 | 25,000 |
| **Age of householder** | | | | | | | | | | | |
| Under age 35 | 4,500 | 1,500 | 2,500 | 500 | 3,000 | 5,000 | 7,000 | 7,000 | 2,700 | 19,400 | 1,000 |
| Aged 35 to 44 | 22,900 | 2,800 | 8,000 | 700 | 55,300 | 12,000 | 14,000 | 21,000 | 8,500 | 25,000 | 2,500 |
| Aged 45 to 54 | 37,800 | 4,500 | 11,500 | 1,000 | 31,700 | 24,000 | 30,000 | 34,000 | 10,000 | 39,300 | 6,000 |
| Aged 55 to 64 | 45,600 | 4,100 | 17,000 | 1,500 | 100,000 | 21,000 | 58,000 | 46,800 | 9,500 | 65,000 | 10,000 |
| Aged 65 to 74 | 45,800 | 5,600 | 20,000 | 2,000 | 52,000 | 50,000 | 60,000 | 38,000 | 8,500 | 41,300 | 6,000 |
| Aged 75 or older | 36,600 | 6,100 | 30,000 | 5,000 | 18,800 | 50,000 | 59,000 | 30,000 | 5,000 | 30,000 | 8,200 |
| **Race and ethnicity of householder** | | | | | | | | | | | |
| Non-Hispanic white | 29,900 | 3,700 | 17,000 | 1,000 | 46,000 | 20,000 | 29,000 | 26,000 | 7,500 | 32,000 | 4,000 |
| Nonwhite or Hispanic | 6,400 | 1,500 | 6,300 | 700 | 14,200 | 9,000 | 10,000 | 13,000 | 5,000 | 23,000 | 1,000 |

*Note: (–) means sample is too small to make a reliable estimate.*
*Source: Federal Reserve Board,* Recent Changes in U.S. Family Finances: Results from the 1998 Survey of Consumer Finances, *Federal Reserve Bulletin, January 2000*

# Big Gains in Stock Ownership

## Nearly half of American households are invested in stocks.

Between 1989 and 1998, as the stock market roared into record territory, American households bought into the action. The percentage of households owning stocks either directly or indirectly (through mutual funds and retirement accounts) rose from 32 percent in 1989 to 49 percent in 1998. The value of stocks more than doubled, rising from just $10,800 in 1989 to $25,000 (in 1998 dollars). By 1998, stocks accounted for the 54 percent majority of household financial assets, up from just 28 percent in 1989.

The increase in stock ownership occurred in every age and income group. By 1998, the majority of householders aged 35 to 64 owned stock, as did most households with incomes of $25,000 or more. Most own only a modest amount of stock, however, the value exceeding $100,000 only among households with incomes of $100,000 or more. Among the most affluent households, stocks accounted for 63 percent of household financial assets in 1998, up from just 35 percent in 1989.

♦ Millions of Americans invested in the stock market during the 1990s. This investment boosted their net worth, but it also makes them vulnerable to a downturn in the market.

### Stock ownership peaks in the 45-to-54 age group

*(percent of households owning stock directly or indirectly, by age, 1998)*

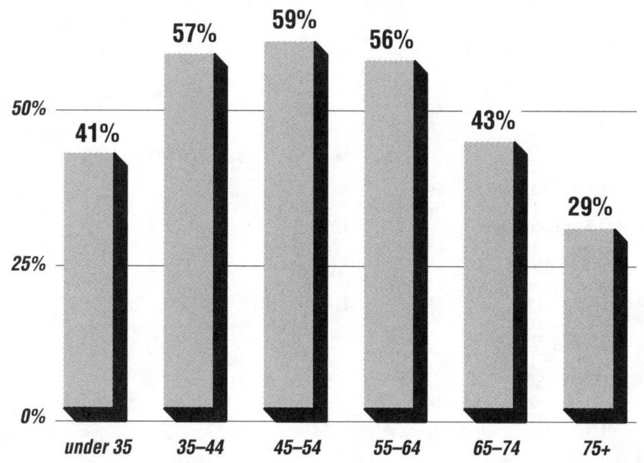

## Stock Ownership by Age of Householder, 1989 and 1998

*(percentage of households owning stocks directly or indirectly, median value of stocks for owners, and share of total household financial assets accounted for by stock holdings, by age of householder, 1989 and 1998; percentage point change in ownership and share of finanacial assets and percent change in value, 1989–98; in 1998 dollars)*

| | *1998* | *1989* | *percentage point change 1989–98* |
|---|---|---|---|
| **Percent owning stock** | | | |
| **Total households** | **48.8%** | **31.6%** | **17.2** |
| Under age 35 | 40.7 | 22.4 | 18.3 |
| Aged 35 to 44 | 56.5 | 38.9 | 17.6 |
| Aged 45 to 54 | 58.6 | 41.8 | 16.8 |
| Aged 55 to 64 | 55.9 | 36.2 | 19.7 |
| Aged 65 to 74 | 42.6 | 26.7 | 15.9 |
| Aged 75 or older | 29.4 | 25.9 | 3.5 |

| | *1998* | *1989* | *percent change 1989–98* |
|---|---|---|---|
| **Median value of stock** | | | |
| **Total households** | **$25,000** | **$10,800** | **131.5%** |
| Under age 35 | 7,000 | 3,800 | 84.2 |
| Aged 35 to 44 | 20,000 | 6,600 | 203.0 |
| Aged 45 to 54 | 38,000 | 16,700 | 127.5 |
| Aged 55 to 64 | 47,000 | 23,400 | 100.9 |
| Aged 65 to 74 | 56,000 | 25,800 | 117.1 |
| Aged 75 or older | 60,000 | 31,800 | 88.7 |

| | *1998* | *1989* | *percentage point change 1989–98* |
|---|---|---|---|
| **Share of financial assets** | | | |
| **Total households** | **53.9%** | **27.8%** | **26.1** |
| Under age 35 | 44.8 | 20.2 | 24.6 |
| Aged 35 to 44 | 54.7 | 29.2 | 25.5 |
| Aged 45 to 54 | 55.7 | 33.5 | 22.2 |
| Aged 55 to 64 | 58.3 | 27.6 | 30.7 |
| Aged 65 to 74 | 51.3 | 26.0 | 25.3 |
| Aged 75 or older | 48.7 | 25.0 | 23.7 |

*Source: Federal Reserve Board,* Recent Changes in U.S. Family Finances: Results from the 1998 Survey of Consumer Finances, *Federal Reserve Bulletin, January 2000*

## Stock Ownership by Household Income, 1989 and 1998

*(percentage of households owning stocks directly or indirectly, median value of stocks for owners, and share of total household financial assets accounted for by stock holdings, by household income, 1989 and 1998; percentage point change in ownership and share of finanacial assets and percent change in value, 1989–98; in 1998 dollars)*

| | 1998 | 1989 | percentage point change 1989–98 |
|---|---|---|---|
| **Percent owning stock** | | | |
| **Total households** | **48.8%** | **31.6%** | **17.2** |
| Under $10,000 | 7.7 | – | – |
| $10,000 to $24,999 | 24.7 | 12.7 | 12 |
| $25,000 to $49,999 | 52.7 | 31.5 | 21.2 |
| $50,000 to $99,999 | 74.3 | 51.5 | 22.8 |
| $100,000 or more | 91.0 | 81.8 | 9.2 |

| | 1998 | 1989 | percent change 1989–98 |
|---|---|---|---|
| **Median value of stock** | | | |
| **Total households** | **$25,000** | **$10,800** | **131.5%** |
| Under $10,000 | 4,000 | – | – |
| $10,000 to $24,999 | 9,000 | 6,400 | 40.6 |
| $25,000 to $49,999 | 11,500 | 6,000 | 91.7 |
| $50,000 to $99,999 | 35,700 | 10,200 | 250.0 |
| $100,000 or more | 150,000 | 53,500 | 180.4 |

| | 1998 | 1989 | percentage point change 1989–98 |
|---|---|---|---|
| **Share of financial assets** | | | |
| **Total households** | **53.9%** | **27.8%** | **26.1** |
| Under $10,000 | 24.8 | – | – |
| $10,000 to $24,999 | 27.5 | 11.7 | 15.8 |
| $25,000 to $49,999 | 39.1 | 16.9 | 22.2 |
| $50,000 to $99,999 | 48.8 | 23.2 | 25.6 |
| $100,000 or more | 63.0 | 35.3 | 27.7 |

*Note: (–) means sample is too small to make a reliable estimate.*
*Source: Federal Reserve Board,* Recent Changes in U.S. Family Finances: Results from the 1998 Survey of Consumer Finances, *Federal Reserve Bulletin, January 2000*

# Nonfinancial Assets Are Most Important

## For the average household, nonfinancial assets are more than four times as valuable as financial assets.

The median value of nonfinancial assets owned by the average American household stood at $97,800 in 1998, much greater than its $22,400 in median financial assets. Vehicles are the most common nonfinancial asset, owned by 83 percent of households. The second most commonly held nonfinancial asset is a home, owned by 66 percent. Homes are by far the most valuable asset owned by Americans, accounting for the largest share of net worth. In 1998, the median value of owned homes stood at $100,000.

Because homeownership is such an important nonfinancial asset, the value of nonfinancial assets owned by households varies greatly by income and age—as does homeownership. The richest households are most likely to own a home, and they have the most in nonfinancial assets, a median of $380,000 including $240,000 in their primary residence in 1998. By age, the value of nonfinancial assets peaks in the 45-to-64 age group as do home values.

♦ The homeownership rate has reached record levels. This should boost net worth in the years ahead as people pay off their mortgages.

## Ownership of Nonfinancial Assets, 1998

*(percent of households owning nonfinancial assets, and median value of asset for owners, by selected characteristics of households and type of asset, 1998)*

| | any nonfinancial asset | vehicles | primary residence | other residential property | equity in non-residential property | business equity | other non-financial |
|---|---|---|---|---|---|---|---|
| **PERCENT OWNING ASSET** | | | | | | | |
| **Total households** | **89.9%** | **82.8%** | **66.2%** | **12.8%** | **8.6%** | **11.5%** | **8.5%** |
| **Income** | | | | | | | |
| Under $10,000 | 62.7 | 51.3 | 34.5 | – | – | 3.8 | 2.6 |
| $10,000 to $24,999 | 85.9 | 78.0 | 51.7 | 5.8 | 5.0 | 5.0 | 5.6 |
| $25,000 to $49,999 | 95.6 | 89.6 | 68.2 | 11.4 | 7.6 | 10.3 | 9.4 |
| $50,000 to $99,999 | 98.0 | 93.6 | 85.0 | 19.0 | 12.0 | 15.0 | 10.2 |
| $100,000 or more | 98.9 | 88.7 | 93.3 | 37.3 | 22.6 | 34.7 | 17.1 |
| **Age of householder** | | | | | | | |
| Under age 35 | 83.3 | 78.3 | 38.9 | 3.5 | 2.7 | 7.2 | 7.3 |
| Aged 35 to 44 | 92.0 | 85.5 | 67.1 | 12.2 | 7.5 | 14.7 | 8.8 |
| Aged 45 to 54 | 92.9 | 87.5 | 74.4 | 16.2 | 12.2 | 16.2 | 9.2 |
| Aged 55 to 64 | 93.8 | 88.7 | 80.3 | 20.4 | 10.4 | 14.3 | 8.5 |
| Aged 65 to 74 | 92.0 | 83.4 | 81.5 | 18.4 | 15.3 | 10.1 | 10.3 |
| Aged 75 or older | 87.2 | 69.8 | 77.0 | 13.6 | 8.1 | 2.7 | 7.0 |
| **Race and ethnicity of householder** | | | | | | | |
| Non-Hispanic white | 93.8 | 87.3 | 71.8 | 14.1 | 9.4 | 13.2 | 10.0 |
| Nonwhite or Hispanic | 76.4 | 67.2 | 46.8 | 8.4 | 5.8 | 5.4 | 3.1 |

*(continued)*

(continued from previous page)

| | any nonfinancial asset | vehicles | primary residence | other residential property | equity in non-residential property | business equity | other non-financial |
|---|---|---|---|---|---|---|---|
| **MEDIAN VALUE OF ASSET FOR OWNERS** | | | | | | | |
| **Total households** | **$97,800** | **$10,800** | **$100,000** | **$65,000** | **$38,000** | **$60,000** | **$10,000** |
| **Income** | | | | | | | |
| Under $10,000 | 16,300 | 4,000 | 51,000 | – | – | 37,500 | 5,000 |
| $10,000 to $24,999 | 43,700 | 5,700 | 71,900 | 70,000 | 25,000 | 31,100 | 5,000 |
| $25,000 to $49,999 | 83,500 | 10,200 | 85,000 | 50,000 | 28,000 | 37,500 | 6,000 |
| $50,000 to $99,999 | 156,300 | 16,600 | 130,000 | 60,000 | 30,000 | 26,000 | 12,000 |
| $100,000 or more | 380,000 | 26,800 | 240,000 | 132,000 | 114,100 | 230,000 | 36,000 |
| **Age of householder** | | | | | | | |
| Under age 35 | 22,700 | 8,900 | 84,000 | 42,500 | 25,000 | 34,000 | 5,000 |
| Aged 35 to 44 | 103,500 | 11,400 | 101,000 | 45,000 | 20,000 | 62,500 | 8,000 |
| Aged 45 to 54 | 126,800 | 12,800 | 120,000 | 74,000 | 45,000 | 100,000 | 14,000 |
| Aged 55 to 64 | 126,900 | 13,500 | 110,000 | 70,000 | 54,000 | 62,500 | 28,000 |
| Aged 65 to 74 | 109,900 | 10,800 | 95,000 | 75,000 | 45,000 | 61,100 | 10,000 |
| Aged 75 or older | 96,100 | 7,000 | 85,000 | 103,000 | 54,000 | 40,000 | 10,000 |
| **Race and ethnicity of householder** | | | | | | | |
| Non-Hispanic white | 107,600 | 11,800 | 100,000 | 67,000 | 42,500 | 67,600 | 10,000 |
| Nonwhite or Hispanic | 52,000 | 8,000 | 85,000 | 59,000 | 24,000 | 30,000 | 5,000 |

*Source: Federal Reserve Board,* Recent Changes in U.S. Family Finances: Results from the 1998 Survey of Consumer Finances, *Federal Reserve Bulletin, January 2000*

# Most Households Have Debt

## Three out of four owe money on mortgages, credit cards, installment loans, or other lines of credit.

Seventy-four percent of households have debt, owing a median of $33,300 in 1998. Those most likely to be in debt are middle-income and younger householders. Debt peaks at 89 percent among households with incomes of $50,000 to $99,999, then drops slightly to 88 percent among those with incomes of $100,000 or more. Householders aged 35 to 54 are most likely to have debt, with 87 percent owing money.

Three types of debt are common—mortgage and home equity loans (43 percent), installment loans such as for vehicles (44 percent), and credit card debt (44 percent). For every age and income group, the largest debts are mortgages. The median amount owed on mortgage and home equity loans stood at $62,000 in 1998. Younger householders have the largest mortgage debt because their loans are relatively new. After age 45, the median amount owed for mortgages and home equity loans drops sharply.

More than half the householders under age 55 and in the $50,000 to $99,999 income group carry credit card debt. Although horror stories about credit card debt are many, the median amount owed by the average household is a relatively modest $1,700.

♦ Most households are cautious about taking on debt, and mortgages account for the largest share of debt by far. As people pay off their mortgages, net worth rises.

## Households with Debt, 1998

*(percent of households with debt, and median value of debt for those with debt, by selected characteristics of households and type of debt, 1998)*

| | any debt | mortgage and home equity | installment | other lines of credit | credit card | other residential property | other debt |
|---|---|---|---|---|---|---|---|
| **PERCENT WITH DEBT** | | | | | | | |
| **Total households** | **74.1%** | **43.1%** | **43.7%** | **2.3%** | **44.1%** | **5.1%** | **8.8%** |
| **Income** | | | | | | | |
| Under $10,000 | 41.7 | 8.3 | 25.7 | – | 20.6 | – | 3.6 |
| $10,000 to $24,999 | 63.7 | 21.3 | 34.4 | 1.2 | 37.9 | 1.8 | 7.0 |
| $25,000 to $49,999 | 79.6 | 43.7 | 50.0 | 2.9 | 49.9 | 4.1 | 7.7 |
| $50,000 to $99,999 | 89.4 | 71.0 | 55.0 | 3.3 | 56.7 | 7.7 | 12.2 |
| $100,000 or more | 87.8 | 73.4 | 43.2 | 2.6 | 40.4 | 16.4 | 14.8 |
| **Age of householder** | | | | | | | |
| Under age 35 | 81.2 | 33.2 | 60.0 | 2.4 | 50.7 | 2.0 | 9.6 |
| Aged 35 to 44 | 87.6 | 58.7 | 53.3 | 3.6 | 51.3 | 6.7 | 11.4 |
| Aged 45 to 54 | 87.0 | 58.8 | 51.2 | 3.6 | 52.5 | 6.7 | 11.1 |
| Aged 55 to 64 | 76.4 | 49.4 | 37.9 | 1.6 | 45.7 | 7.8 | 8.3 |
| Aged 65 to 74 | 51.4 | 26.0 | 20.2 | – | 29.2 | 5.1 | 4.1 |
| Aged 75 or older | 24.6 | 11.5 | 4.2 | – | 11.2 | 1.8 | 2.0 |
| **Race and ethnicity of householder** | | | | | | | |
| Non-Hispanic white | 74.9 | 46.7 | 44.3 | 2.4 | 44.4 | 5.4 | 8.8 |
| Nonwhite or Hispanic | 71.1 | 30.7 | 41.6 | 1.9 | 43.3 | 4.0 | 8.8 |

*(continued)*

*(continued from previous page)*

| | any debt | mortgage and home equity | installment | other lines of credit | credit card | other residential property | other debt |
|---|---|---|---|---|---|---|---|
| **MEDIAN VALUE OF DEBT FOR DEBTOR HOUSEHOLDS** | | | | | | | |
| **Total households** | **$33,300** | **$62,000** | **$8,700** | **$2,500** | **$1,700** | **$40,000** | **$3,000** |
| **Income** | | | | | | | |
| Under $10,000 | 4,100 | 16,000 | 4,000 | – | 1,100 | – | 600 |
| $10,000 to $24,999 | 8,000 | 34,200 | 6,000 | 1,100 | 1,000 | 34,000 | 1,300 |
| $25,000 to $49,999 | 27,100 | 47,000 | 8,000 | 3,000 | 1,900 | 20,000 | 2,200 |
| $50,000 to $99,999 | 75,000 | 75,000 | 11,300 | 2,800 | 2,400 | 42,000 | 3,800 |
| $100,000 or more | 135,400 | 123,800 | 15,400 | 5,000 | 3,200 | 60,000 | 10,000 |
| **Age of householder** | | | | | | | |
| Under age 35 | 19,200 | 71,000 | 9,100 | 1,000 | 1,500 | 55,000 | 1,700 |
| Aged 35 to 44 | 55,700 | 70,000 | 7,700 | 1,400 | 2,000 | 40,000 | 3,000 |
| Aged 45 to 54 | 48,400 | 68,800 | 10,000 | 3,000 | 1,800 | 40,000 | 5,000 |
| Aged 55 to 64 | 34,600 | 49,400 | 8,300 | 4,900 | 2,000 | 41,000 | 5,000 |
| Aged 65 to 74 | 11,900 | 29,000 | 6,500 | – | 1,100 | 56,000 | 4,500 |
| Aged 75 or older | 8,000 | 21,200 | 8,900 | – | 700 | 29,800 | 1,700 |
| **Race and ethnicity of householder** | | | | | | | |
| Non-Hispanic white | 40,000 | 62,000 | 9,000 | 2,800 | 2,000 | 42,600 | 3,000 |
| Nonwhite or Hispanic | 15,300 | 62,000 | 7,200 | 700 | 1,100 | 30,000 | 1,700 |

*Note: (–) means sample is too small to make a reliable estimate.*
*Source: Federal Reserve Board,* Recent Changes in U.S. Family Finances: Results from the 1998 Survey of Consumer Finances, *Federal Reserve Bulletin, January 2000*

# Pension Plans Cover 44 Percent of Workers

## Women are almost as likely to have pension coverage as men.

Among workers with earnings in 1998, 46 percent of men and 42 percent of women were covered by pensions. Pension coverage peaks among workers aged 45 to 64, at 58 percent for men and 53 percent for women.

Pension coverage is almost as high among black workers as among whites. Forty-one percent of black workers had pension coverage in 1998 compared with 44 percent of whites. Fifty-five percent of black women aged 45 to 64 had pension coverage, a higher share than the 53 percent of white women.

Hispanic workers are much less likely to have pension coverage than either white or black workers. In 1998, only 28 percent of Hispanic workers were covered by pensions.

♦ A large share of baby-boom women will have pension coverage in old age because of their propensity to work. Consequently, many of today's dual-income couples will be dual-pension couples in retirement.

## Pension Coverage, 1998

*(number and percent of workers covered by pensions, by sex, age, race, and Hispanic origin, 1998; numbers in thousands)*

| | total | | white | | black | | Hispanic | |
|---|---|---|---|---|---|---|---|---|
| | number | percent | number | percent | number | percent | number | percent |
| **Total workers with coverage** | **64,009** | **43.8%** | **54,474** | **44.4%** | **6,763** | **40.7%** | **4,176** | **28.4%** |
| **Men with coverage** | **35,428** | **45.8** | **30,727** | **46.6** | **3,204** | **41.6** | **2,326** | **27.5** |
| Aged 15 to 24 | 1,783 | 14.1 | 1,548 | 14.4 | 150 | 10.9 | 172 | 9.6 |
| Aged 25 to 44 | 19,188 | 50.2 | 16,393 | 51.2 | 1,906 | 45.4 | 1,411 | 29.6 |
| Aged 45 to 64 | 13,718 | 58.3 | 12,123 | 58.9 | 1,107 | 56.5 | 712 | 40.7 |
| Aged 65 or older | 739 | 25.4 | 663 | 24.9 | 41 | 25.2 | 31 | 20.9 |
| **Women with coverage** | **28,581** | **41.5** | **23,748** | **41.8** | **3,559** | **39.9** | **1,850** | **29.6** |
| Aged 15 to 24 | 1,380 | 11.6 | 1,108 | 11.4 | 181 | 11.3 | 134 | 10.0 |
| Aged 25 to 44 | 15,461 | 45.8 | 12,651 | 46.6 | 2,089 | 43.0 | 1,146 | 33.6 |
| Aged 45 to 64 | 11,190 | 53.2 | 9,493 | 53.1 | 1,252 | 55.2 | 553 | 38.8 |
| Aged 65 or older | 550 | 24.4 | 496 | 24.6 | 37 | 19.9 | 16 | 22.6 |

*Note: Numbers will not add to total because not all races are shown and Hispanics may be of any race.*
*Source: Bureau of the Census,* Statistical Abstract of the United States: 2000

**Appendix 1.**

## A Note on 2000 Census Data

*The American Marketplace: Demographics and Spending Patterns* does not include 2000 census data, which have only begun to be released—a process that will take at least three years to complete. Consequently, most of the population and household data in *The American Marketplace: Demographics and Spending Patterns* originate from the Census Bureau's Current Population Survey, which is benchmarked each decade to census numbers. The benchmarking of the CPS follows the census by two or three years.

Because the 2000 census found more people in the U.S. than the Census Bureau had estimated, the CPS estimates and projections of populations and households are too low. The Census Bureau estimated there were 275 million people in the U.S. in 2000, for example, while the 2000 census counted 281 million. Rather than growing a projected 10 percent during the 1990s, the U.S. population grew a considerably larger 13 percent.

Such a gap between estimates and reality has occurred before. The 1980 census found millions more people than had been estimated by the bureau. It took the agency until 1983 to benchmark the CPS to match census figures. This is the situation again today, and researchers will have to wait a few years before CPS and census are once more in alignment.

Users of demographic statistics should keep in mind that the figures in this and other demographic reference books now being published are somewhat below the actual numbers. The trends described in *The American Marketplace: Demographics and Spending Patterns*, however, are not affected by the census count. And it is the trends—not the exact numbers—that are most important in demographic research. Trends reveal opportunities, numbers tell you their size. Just bear in mind that the many opportunities described in *The American Marketplace: Demographics and Spending Patterns* are even bigger than the numbers suggest.

For more information about 2000 census data, including the release schedule, see Internet site <www.census.gov/dmd/www/2khome.htm>.

Appendix 2.

# For More Information

The federal government is a rich source of data on almost every aspect of American life. Below are the Internet addresses of agencies collecting the data analyzed in this book. Also shown are the phone numbers of subject specialists, organized alphabetically by topic. A list of State Data Centers and Small Business Development Centers is also below to help you track down demographic and economic information for your state or local area. E-mail addresses are shown when available.

## Internet addresses

| | |
|---|---|
| Bureau of the Census | <www.census.gov> |
| Bureau of Justice Statistics | <www.ojp.usdoj.gov/bjs> |
| Bureau of Labor Statistics | <www.bls.gov> |
| Consumer Expenditure Survey | <www.bls.gov/csxhome> |
| Current Population Survey | <www.bls.census.gov/cps> |
| Department of Agriculture Economic Research Service | <www.ers.usda.gov> |
| Department of Agriculture, Food Surveys Research Group | <www.barc.usda.gov/bhnrc/foodsurvey/home.htm> |
| Immigration and Naturalization Service | <www.ins.usdoj.gov/graphics/aboutins/statistics/index.htm> |
| National Center For Education Statistics | <http://nces.ed.gov/> |
| National Center For Health Statistics | <www.cdc.gov/nchs> |
| National Endowment for the Arts | <www.ntia.doc.gov> |
| National Opinion Research Center | <www.norc.uchicago.edu> |
| National Telecommunications and Information Administration | <www.ntia.doc.gov> |
| Survey of Consumer Finances | <www.federalreserve.gov/pubs/OSS/oss2/scfindex.html> |
| U.S. Substance Abuse and Mental Health Services Administration | <www.samhsa.gov> |

## Subject Specialists

| | |
|---|---|
| Absences from work, Staff | 202-691-6378 |
| Aging population, Staff | 301-457-2422 |
| Ancestry, Staff | 301-457-2403 |
| Apportionment, Ed Byerly | 301-457-2381 |
| Bureau of Justice Statistics, | 202-307-0765; askbjs@ojp.usdoj.gov |
| Business expenditures, Sheldon Ziman | 301-457-3315 |
| Business investment, Charles Funk | 301-457-3324 |
| Census Bureau customer service, Staff | 301-457-4100 |
| Census 2000: | |
| • Address list, Joel Sobel | 301-457-1106 |
| • Aging population, Staff | 301-457-2378 |
| • American Community Survey, Larry McGinn | 301-457-8050 |
| • Am. Indian and Alaska Native Program, Sydnee Chattin-Reynolds | 301-457-2032 |

- Annexations/boundary changes, Joe Marinucci ........ 301-457-1099
- Apportionment/redistricting, Edwin Byerly ........ 301-457-2381
- Armed forces, Staff ........ 301-457-2422
- Census history, Dave Pemberton ........ 301-457-1167
- Census in schools, Kim Crews ........ 301-457-3626
- Census operations, Mike Stump ........ 301-457-3577
- Citizenship, Diane Schmidley ........ 301-457-2403
- Commuting and place of work, Gloria Swieczkowski ........ 301-457-2454
- Confidentiality and privacy, Jerry Gates ........ 301-457-2515
- Count review, Paul Campbell ........ 301-457-2390
- Data dissemination, Customer Services ........ 301-457-4100
- Disability, Jack McNeil ........ 301-457-8520
- Education, Staff ........ 301-457-2464
- Emigration, Staff ........ 301-457-2438
- Employment projections, demographic, Howard Fullerton ........ 202-691-5711
- Employment/unemployment, Staff ........ 301-457-3242
- Foreign born, Dianne Schmidley ........ 301-457-2403
- Geographic entities, Staff ........ 301-457-1099
- Group quarters population, Denise Smith ........ 301-457-2378
- Hispanic origin, ethnicity, ancestry, Kevin Deardorff/Roberto Ramirez ........ 301-457-2403
- Homeless, Edison Gore ........ 301-457-3998
- Housing, Staff ........ 301-457-3242
- Immigration, Dianne Schmidley ........ 301-457-2403
- Income, Kirby Posey ........ 301-457-3243
- Labor force status/work experience, Thomas Palumbo ........ 301-457-3220
- Language spoken in home, Wendy Bruno ........ 301-457-2464
- Living arrangements, Staff ........ 301-457-2465
- Metropolitan areas, concepts and standards, Michael Ratcliffe ........ 301-457-2419
- Microdata files, Amanda Shields ........ 301-457-1326
- Migration, Kris Hansen/Carol Faber ........ 301-457-2454
- Occupation/industry, Staff ........ 301-457-3210
- Outlying areas, Idabelle Hovland ........ 301-457-8443
- Persons without conventional housing, Edison Gore ........ 301-457-3998
- Population (general information), Staff ........ 301-457-2422
- Questionnaire content, Louisa Miller ........ 301-457-2073
- Race, Staff ........ 301-457-2402
- Residence rules, Karen Mills ........ 301-457-2390
- Response rates, Staff ........ 301-457-3691
- Sampling, Rajendra Singh ........ 301-457-4199
- Service based enumeration, Annetta Clark Smith ........ 301-457-2378
- Special places/group quarters, Denise Smith ........ 301-457-2378
- Special populations, Staff ........ 301-457-2378
- Special tabulations, Marie Pees ........ 301-457-2447
- Undercount, Rajendra Singh ........ 301-457-4199
  - Demographic, Greg Robinson ........ 301-457-2103
- Urban/rural, Ryan Short ........ 301-457-1099
- U.S. citizens abroad, Staff ........ 301-457-2422

- User maps, Staff ........ 301-457-1101
- Veteran status, Thomas Palumbo ........ 301-457-3220
- Voting districts, John Byle ........ 301-457-1099
- Welfare-to-work, Gail Reid ........ 301-457-4600
- Women, Staff ........ 301-457-2378
- ZIP codes, Staff ........ 301-457-2422

Characteristics of business owners, Valerie Strang ........ 301-457-3316
Child care, Martin O'Connell/Kristin Smith ........ 301-457-2465
Children, Staff ........ 301-457-2465
Citizenship, Staff ........ 301-457-2403
Communications and Utilities:

- Current programs, Ruth Bramblett ........ 301-457-2766
- Economic census, Jim Barron ........ 301-457-2824

Commuting and place of work, Phil Salopek/Celia Boertlein ........ 301-457-2454
Construction:

- Building permits, Staff ........ 301-457-1321
- Census, Pat Horning ........ 301-457-4680
- Housing starts and completions, Staff ........ 301-457-1321
- Residential characteristics, price index and sales, Staff ........ 301-457-1321
- Residential improvements and repairs, Joe Huesman ........ 301-457-4822
- Value of new construction, Mike Davis ........ 301-457-1605

Consumer Expenditure Survey, Staff ........ 202-691-6900
Contingent workers, Sharon Cohany ........ 202-691-6378
County Business Patterns, Paul Hanczaryk ........ 301-457-2580
County populations, Staff ........ 301-457-2422
Crime, Marilyn Monahan ........ 301-457-3925
Current Population Survey, general information, Staff ........ 301-457-3806
Demographic surveys, general information, Staff ........ 301-457-2422
Dept. of Agriculture, Economic Research Service ........ 202-694-5050; service@ers.usda.gov
Dept. of Agriculture, Food Surveys Research Grp. ........ 301-504-0170; fsrg@rbhnrc.usda.gov
Disability, Jack McNeil ........ 301-457-8520
Discouraged workers, Staff ........ 202-691-6378
Displaced workers, Steve Hipple ........ 202-691-6378
Economic census, Paul Zeisset/Robert Marske ........ 301-457-4151/2547

- Accommodations and food services, Fay Dorsett ........ 301-457-2687
- Construction, Pat Horning ........ 301-457-4680
- Finance and insurance, Faye Jacobs ........ 301-457-2824
- General information, Robert Marske ........ 301-457-2547
- Internet dissemination, Paul Zeisset ........ 301-457-4151
- Manufacturing:
  - Consumer goods industries, Robert Reinard ........ 301-457-4810
  - Investment goods industries, Kenneth Hansen ........ 301-457-4755
  - Primary goods industries, Nat Shelton ........ 301-457-4643
- Mining, Pat Horning ........ 301-457-4680
- Minority/women-owned businesses, Valerie Strang ........ 301-457-3316
- North American Industry Class. System, Wanda Dougherty ........ 301-457-2795
- Puerto Rico and the Insular Areas, Irma Harahush ........ 301-457-3314

- Real estate and rental/leasing, Pam Palmer ........ 301-457-2824
- Retail trade, Fay Dorsett ........ 301-457-2687
- Services, Jack Moody ........ 301-457-2689
- Transportation and Utilities:
  - Commodity Flow Survey, John Fowler ........ 301-457-2108
  - Economic census, Jim Barron ........ 301-457-2824
  - Vehicle Inventory and Use Survey, Kim Moore ........ 301-457-2797
- Wholesale Trade, Donna Hambric ........ 301-457-2725

Economic studies, Arnold Reznek ........ 301-457-1856
Education surveys, Steve Tourkin ........ 301-457-3791
Educational attainment, Staff ........ 301-457-2464
Emigration, Staff ........ 301-457-2438
Employee Benefits Survey, Staff ........ 202-691-6199
Employment and Earnings Periodical, John Stinson ........ 202-691-6373
Employment and unemployment trends, Staff ........ 202-691-6378
Enterprise statistics, Eddie Salyers ........ 301-457-3318
Equal employment opportunity data, Staff ........ 301-457-3242
Fertility, Amara Bachu ........ 301-457-2449
Finance, insurance and real estate, Economic Census, Faye Jacobs ........ 301-457-2824
Flexitime and shift work, Thomas Beers ........ 202-691-6378
Foreign Born:

- Current Population Survey, Staff ........ 301-457-2403
- Decennial census, Kevin Deardorff ........ 301-457-2403

Geographic Concepts:

- American Indian areas, Vince Osler ........ 301-457-1099
- Census blocks, Valerie Murdock ........ 301-457-1099
- Census county divisions, Pat Ream ........ 301-457-1099
- Census designated places, Pat Ream ........ 301-457-1099
- Census tracts, Dan Flynn ........ 301-457-1099
- Centers of population, Staff ........ 301-457-1128
- Congressional districts, boundaries, Donna Zorn ........ 301-457-1128
- Metropolitan areas, Rodger Johnson ........ 301-457-2419
- Postal geography, Dan Sweeney ........ 301-457-1106
- School districts, Laura Muller ........ 301-457-1099
- Traffic analysis zones, Carrie Saunders ........ 301-457-1099
- Urban/rural concepts, Ryan Short ........ 301-457-1099
- Urbanized areas, Ryan Short ........ 301-457-1099
- Voting districts, John Byle ........ 301-457-1099
- Zip codes, agriculture and demographic data, Staff ........ 301-457-4100
- Zip codes, economic data, Fay Dorsett ........ 301457-2687

Governments:

- Criminal justice, Charlene Sebold ........ 301-457-1591
- Education and library statistics, Johnny Monaco ........ 301-457-2584
- Education, elementary-secondary, Larry MacDonald ........ 301-457-1563
- Employment, Ellen Thompson ........ 301-457-1531
- Federal expenditure data, Gerard Keffer ........ 301-457-1522
- Finance, Donna Hirsch ........ 301-457-1486

• Government information, Staff ........................................ 301-457-1580
• Governmental organization, Robert McArthur ........................................ 301-457-1582
Group quarters population, Denise Smith ........................................ 301-457-2378
Health insurance statistics, Staff ........................................ 301-457-3242
Health surveys, Adrienne Oneto ........................................ 301-457-3879
Hispanic statistics, Staff ........................................ 301-457-2403
Home-based work, Staff ........................................ 202-691-6378
Homeless, Edison Gore ........................................ 301-457-3998
Households and families, Staff ........................................ 301-457-2465
Household wealth, Staff ........................................ 301-457-3242
Housing:
• American Housing Survey, Jane Kneessi/Barbara Williams ........................................ 301-457-3235
• Census, Staff ........................................ 301-457-3237
• Homeownership, vacancy data, Linda Cavanaugh/Robert Callis ........................................ 301-457-3199
• Housing affordability, Peter Fronczek/Howard Savage ........................................ 301-457-3199
• Market absorption, Alan Friedman ........................................ 301-457-3199
• New York City Housing and Vacancy Survey, Peter Fronczek ........................................ 301-457-3199
• Residential finance, Howard Savage ........................................ 301-457-3199
Illegal immigration, Staff ........................................ 301-457-3428
Immigration, general information, Staff ........................................ 301-457-2422
Income statistics, Staff ........................................ 301-457-3242
Industry and commodity classification, James Kristoff ........................................ 301-457-4631
Industry Employment Projections:
• Aggregate economy, GDP, Betty Su ........................................ 202-691-5729
• Demographics, Howard Fullerton ........................................ 202-691-5711
• Employment impact studies, Norman Saunders ........................................ 202-691-5701
• Employment requirements table, Art Andreassen ........................................ 202-691-5689
• Personal consumption expenditures, Mitra Toossi ........................................ 202-691-5721
• Foreign trade, Mirko Novakovic ........................................ 202-691-5008
• Investment, government, Jay Berman ........................................ 202-691-5692
• Industry classification issues (NAICS), Norman Saunders ........................................ 202-691-5701
• Industry output and employment, Jay Berman ........................................ 202-691-5733
• Industry projections coordination, James Franklin ........................................ 202-691-5709
• Input-output tables, Art Andreassen ........................................ 202-691-5689
• Input-output theory and practice, Charles Bowman ........................................ 202-691-5702
• Labor force, Howard Fullerton ........................................ 202-691-5711
• National income and product accounts, Norman Saunders ........................................ 202-691-5701
• Population, Howard Fullerton ........................................ 202-691-5711
• Productivity, James Franklin ........................................ 202-691-5709
• Value added, Charles Bowman ........................................ 202-691-5702
International Statistics:
• Africa, Asia, Latin Am., North Am., and Oceania, Patricia Rowe ........................................ 301-457-1358
• Aging population, Victoria Velkoff ........................................ 301-457-1371
• China, People's Republic, Loraine West ........................................ 301-457-1363
• Europe, former Soviet Union, Marc Rubin ........................................ 301-457-1362
• Health, Karen Stanecki ........................................ 301-457-1406
• International data base, Pat Dickerson/Peter Johnson ........................................ 301-457-1403

- Technical assistance and training, Diana Lopez-Meisel ............ 301-457-1444
- Women in development, Victoria Velkoff ............ 301-457-1371

Job tenure, Jennifer Martel ............ 202-691-6378
Journey to work, Phil Salopek/Gloria Swieczkowski ............ 301-457-2454
Labor force concepts, Staff ............ 202-691-6378
Language, Staff ............ 301-457-2464
Longitudinal data/gross flows, Staff ............ 202-691-6345
Longitudinal surveys, Ron Dopkowski ............ 301-457-3801
Manufacturing and Mining:

- Concentration, Patrick Duck ............ 301-457-4699
- Exports from manufacturing establishments, John Gates ............ 301-457-4589
- Financial statistics (Quarterly Financial Report), Ronald Horton ............ 301-457-3343
- Foreign direct investment, Ron Taylor ............ 301-457-1313
- Fuels, electric energy consumed and prod. index, Pat Horning ............ 301-457-4680
- General information and data request, Nishea Quash ............ 301-457-4673
- Industries:
  - Electrical and trans. equip., instruments, and misc., Milbren Thomas ............ 301-457-4821
  - Food, textiles, and apparel, Robert Reinard ............ 301-457-4637
  - Metals and industrial machinery, Kenneth Hansen ............ 301-457-4757
  - Wood, furniture, paper, printing, chemicals, petroleum products, rubber, plastics, Robert Reinard ............ 301-457-4810
- Mining, Pat Horning ............ 301-457-4680
- Monthly shipments, inventories, and orders, Lee Wentela ............ 301-457-4832
- Technology, research and development, and capacity use, Ron Taylor ............ 301-457-4683

Marital and family characteristics of workers, Staff ............ 202-691-6378
Metropolitan areas, Staff ............ 301-457-2422
Metropolitan standards, Rodger Johnson ............ 301-457-2419
Migration, Kristin Hansen/Carol Faber ............ 301-457-2454
Mineral industries, Pat Horning ............ 301-457-4680
Minimum wage data, Steven Haugen ............ 202-691-6378
Minority/women-owned businesses, Valerie Strang ............ 301-457-3316
Minority workers, Staff ............ 202-691-6378
Multiple jobholders, Staff ............ 202-691-6373
National Center for Education Statistics, Staff ............ 202-502-7300
National Center for Health Statistics, Staff ............ 301-458-4636
National Endowment for the Arts ............ 202-682-5400
National estimates and projections, Staff ............ 301-457-2422
National Opinion Research Center, Staff ............ 773-753-7500; norcinfo@norcmail.uchicago.edu
National Sporting Goods Association ............ 847-296-6742; info@nsga.org
National Telecommunications and Information Administration ............ 202-482-7002
North Am. Industry Class. System (NAICS), Wanda Dougherty ............ 301-457-2795
Occupational and industrial statistics, Staff ............ 301-457-3242
Occupational data, Staff ............ 202-691-6378
Occupational Employment Statistics Survey, Staff ............ 202-691-6569
Occupational Outlook:

- College graduate job outlook, Tina Shelley ............ 202-691-5726
- Education and training categories, Doug Braddock ............ 202-691-5695

• Industry-occupation matrix , Alan Eck ........ 202-691-5705
• Mobility and tenure, Alan Eck ........ 202-691-5705
• Occupation information, general, Chet Levine ........ 202-691-5715
• Occupational Outlook Quarterly, Kathleen Green ........ 202-691-5717
• Replacement and separation rates, Alan Eck ........ 202-691-5705
• Training statistics, Alan Eck ........ 202-691-5705
• Wage data (BLS sources), Sean Kirby ........ 202-691-5719

Occupational Projections:

• Computer, Carolyn Veneri ........ 202-691-5714
• Construction, Doug Braddock ........ 202-691-5695
• Education, Arlene Dohm ........ 202-691-5727
• Engineering, Doug Braddock ........ 202-691-5695
• Food and lodging, Carolyn Veneri ........ 202-691-5714
• Health, Theresa Cosca ........ 202-691-5712
• Legal, Tina Shelley ........ 202-691-5726
• Mechanics and repairers, Theresa Cosca ........ 202-691-5712
• Sales, Doug Braddock ........ 202-691-5695
• Scientific, Tina Shelley ........ 202-691-5726

Older workers, Staff ........ 202-691-6378
Outlying areas, population, Michael Levin ........ 301-457-1444
Part-time workers, Staff ........ 202-691-6378
Place of birth, Kristin Hansen/Carol Faber ........ 301-457-2454
Population information, Staff ........ 301-457-2422
Poverty statistics, Staff ........ 301-457-3242
Prisoner surveys, Marilyn Monahan ........ 301-457-3925
Puerto Rico, Idabelle Hovland ........ 301-457-8443
Quarterly Financial Report, Ronald Horton ........ 301-457-3343
Race, concepts and interpretation, Staff ........ 301-457-2402
Race statistics, Staff ........ 301-457-2422
Reapportionment and redistricting, Marshall Turner, Jr. ........ 301-457-4015

Retail Trade:

• Advance monthly, Scott Scheleur ........ 301-457-2713
• Economic census, Fay Dorsett ........ 301-457-2687
• Monthly sales and inventory, Nancy Piesto ........ 301-457-2706
• Quarterly Financial Report, Ronald Horton ........ 301-457-3343

Sampling methods, census, Rajendra Singh ........ 301-457-4199
School enrollment, Staff ........ 301-457-2464
Seasonal adjustment methodology, labor, Robert McIntire ........ 202-691-6345

Services:

• Current Reports, Ruth Bramblett ........ 301-457-2766
• Economic census, Jack Moody ........ 301-457-2689
• Services information, Staff ........ 800-541-8345

Small area population estimates, Staff ........ 301-457-3242
Special censuses, Josephine Ruffin ........ 301-457-1429
Special surveys, Ron Dopkowski ........ 301-457-3801
Special tabulations, Marie Pees ........ 301-457-2447

State populations and projections, Staff .......... 301-457-2422
Statistics of U.S. businesses, Melvin Cole .......... 301-457-3320
Survey of Income and Program Participation (SIPP), Staff .......... 301-457-3242
Transportation:
- Commodity Flow Survey, John Fowler .......... 301-457-2108
- Economic census, Pam Palmer .......... 301-457-2811
- Vehicle inventory and use, Kim Moore .......... 301-457-2797
- Warehousing and trucking, Ruth Bramblett .......... 301-457-2766

Undercount, demographic analysis, Gregg Robinson .......... 301-457-2103
Union membership, Staff .......... 202-691-6378
Urban/rural population, Michael Ratcliff/Rodger Johnson .......... 301-457-2419

## Census Regional Offices

Information specialists in the Census Bureau's 12 regional offices answer thousands of questions each year. If you have questions about the Census Bureau's products and services, you can contact the regional office that serves your state. The states served by each regional office are listed in parentheses.

- **Atlanta** (AL, FL, GA) .......... 404-730-3833; atlanta.regional.office@census.gov
- **Boston** (CT, MA, ME, NH, NY, RI, VT) .......... 617-424-0510; boston.regional.office@census.gov
- **Charlotte** (KY, NC, SC, TN, VA) .......... 704-344-6144; charlotte.regional.office@census.gov
- **Chicago** (IL, IN, WI) .......... 312-353-9747; chicago.regional.office@census.gov
- **Dallas** (LA, MS, TX) .......... 214-655-3050; dallas.regional.office@census.gov
- **Denver** (AZ, CO, MT, NE, ND, NM, NV, SD, UT, WY) .......... 303-969-7750; denver_regional_office@census.gov
- **Detroit** (MI, OH, WV) .......... 313-259-1875; detroit.regional.office@census.gov
- **Kansas City** (AR, IA, KS, MN, MO, OK) .......... 913-551-6711; kansas.regional.office@census.gov
- **Los Angeles** (CA southern, HI) .......... 818-904-6339; la.regional.office@census.gov
- **New York** (NY, NJ selected counties) .......... 212-264-4730; ny.regional.office@census.gov
- **Philadelphia** (DE, DC, MD, NJ selected counties, PA) .......... 215-656-7578; philly.regional.office@census.gov
- **Seattle** (CA northern, AK, ID, OR, WA) .......... 206-553-5835; seattle.regional.office@census.gov
- **Puerto Rico** and the **U.S. Virgin Islands** are serviced by the Boston regional office. All other outlying areas are serviced by the Los Angeles regional office.

## State Data Centers and Business and Industry Data Centers

For demographic and economic information about states and local areas, contact your State Data Center (SDC) or Business and Industry Data Center (BIDC). Every state has a State Data Center. Below are listed the leading centers for each state-usually a state government agency, university, or library that heads a network of affiliate centers. Asterisks (*) identify states that also have BIDCs. In some states, one agency serves as the lead for both the SDC and the BIDC. The BIDC is listed separately if a separate agency serves as the lead.

**Alabama**, Annette Watters, University of Alabama .......... 205-348-619; awatters@cba.ua.edu
**Alaska**, Kathryn Lizik, Department of Labor .......... 907-465-2437; kathryn_lizik@labor.state.ak.us
**American Samoa**, Vaitoelav Filiga, Dept. of Commerce .......... 684-633-5155; vfiliga@samotelco.com
* **Arizona**, Betty Jeffries, Dept. of Economic Security .......... 602-542-5984; popstats@de.state.az.us
**Arkansas**, Sarah Breshears, Univ. of Arkansas/Little Rock .......... 501-569-8530; sgbreshears@ualr.edu

**California**, Linda Gage, Department of Finance ............................ 916-323-4086; filgage@dof.ca.gov
**Colorado**, Rebecca Picaso, Dept. of Local Affairs .................. 303-866-2156; rebecca.picaso@state.co
**Connecticut**, Bill Kraynak, Office of Policy and Management ..................................................... ............................................................................ 860-418-6230; william.kraynak@po.state.ct.us
* **Delaware**, O'Shell Howell, Economic Development Office ....... 302-739-427; oshowell@state.de.us
**District of Columbia**, Herb Bixhorn, Mayor's Office of Planning .................................................. ..................................................................................... 202-442-7603; hbixhorn@dcgov.com
* **Florida**, Pam Schenker, Dept. of Labor and Employment Security ................................................ ........................................................................... 850-488-1048; pamela_schenker@awi.state.fl.us
**Georgia**, Robert Giacomini, Office of Planning and Budget ........................................................ ......................................................................... 404-463-1115; robert.giacomini@sdrc.gadata.org
**Guam**, Eugene Yungi Li, Department of Commerce . 671-475-0205; e-mail unavailable at this time
**Hawaii**, Jan Nakamoto, Dept. of Business, Ec. Dev., and Tourism .................................................. .............................................................................. 808-586-2493; jnakamot@dbedt.hawaii.gov
**Idaho**, Alan Porter, Department of Commerce ...................... 208-334-2470; aporter@idoc.state.id.us
**Illinois**, Suzanne Ebetsch, Bureau of the Budget ....... 217-782-1381; sebetsch@commerce.state.il.us
* **Indiana**, Roberta Brooker, State Library ............................. 317-232-3733; rbooker@statelib.lib.in.us
Indiana BIDC, Carol Rogers, Business Research Center ............... 317-274-2205; rogersc@iupui.edu
**Iowa**, Beth Henning, State Library ......................................... 515-281-4350; b.henning@lib.state.ia.us
**Kansas**, Marc Galbraith, State Library ................................................. 785-296-3296; ksstl3lb@ink.org
* **Kentucky**, Ron Crouch, University of Louisville ........ 502-852-7990; rtcrou01gwise@louisville.edu
**Louisiana**, Karen Paterson, Office of Planning and Budget ......................................................... ................................................................................ 225-219-4025; webmaster@doa.state.la.us
* **Maine**, Eric VonMagnus, State Planning Office ........... 207-287-2989; eric.vonmagnus@state.me.us
* **Maryland**, Jane Traynham, Office of Planning ............ 410-767-4450; jtraynham@mdp.state.md.us
* **Massachusetts**, John Gaviglio, Institute for Social and Ec. Research ........................................... ................................................................................... 413-545-3460; miser@miser.umass.edu
**Michigan**, Carolyn Lauer, Dept. of Management and Budget .... 517-373-7910; Lauerc@state.mi.us
* **Minnesota**, David Birkholz, State Demographer's Office ......................................................... ..................................................................... 651-297-2360; david.birkholz@mnplan.state.mm.us
Minnesota BIDC, Barbara Ronningen, State Demographer's Office ................................................. ................................................................ 651-296-4886; barbara.ronningen@mnplan.state.mm.us
* **Mississippi**, Rachel McNeely, University of Mississippi ....... 662-915-7288; rmcneely@olemiss.edu
Mississippi BIDC, Deloise Tate, Dept. of Ec. and Comm. Dev. .................................................... ...................................................................................... 601-359-3593; dtate@mississippi.org
* **Missouri**, Debra Pitts, State Library ............................... 573-526-7648; pittsd@mail.sos.state.mo.us
Missouri BIDC, Fred Goss, Small Business Devel. Center ............ 573-341-4559; fredgoss@umr.edu
* **Montana**, Allan B. Cox, Department of Commerce ....................... 406-444-4393; jclack@state.mt.us
**Nebraska**, Jerome Deichert, University of Nebraska at Omaha ..................................................... ........................................................................... 402-554-2134; jerome_deichert@unomaha.edu
**Nevada**, Joyce M. Cox, State Library and Archives .................... 775-684-3303; jmcox@clan.lib.nv.us
**New Hampshire**, Thomas Duffy, Office of State Planning .. 603-271-2155; t_duffy@osp.state.nh.us
* **New Jersey**, David Joye, Department of Labor .......................... 609-984-2595; djoye@dol.state.nj.us
* **New Mexico**, Kevin Kargacin, University of New Mexico .......... 505-277-6626; kargacin@unm.edu
New Mexico BIDC, Karma Shore, Econ. Development Dept. ......... 505-827-0264; kshore@unm.edu
* **New York**, Staff, Department of Economic Development .............................................................. ........................................................................... 518-292-5300; rscardamalia@empire.state.ny.us

* **North Carolina**, Staff, State Library ........................................ 919-733-3270; francine@ospl.state.nc.us
**North Dakota**, Richard Rathge, State Univ. ........... 701-231-8621; richard_rathge@ndsu.nodak.edu
**Northern Mariana Islands**, Diego Sasamoto, Dept. of Commerce ........................................................ 670-664-3034; cad@itecnmi.com
* **Ohio**, Barry Bennett, Department of Development ......... 614-466-2115; bbennett@odod.state.oh.us
* **Oklahoma**, Jeff Wallace, Department of Commerce ... 405-815-5184; jeff_wallace@odoc.state.ok.us
**Oregon**, George Hough, Portland State University ................ 503-725-5159; houghg@mail.pdx.edu
* **Pennsylvania**, Diane Shoop, Pennsylvania State Univ. / Harrisburg ........................................................ 717-948-6096; des102@psu.edu
**Puerto Rico**, Lillian Torres Aguirre, Planning Bd. .................... 787-728-4430; torres_l@jp.prstar.net
**Rhode Island**, Mark Brown, Dept. of Admin. ............... 401-222-6183 mbrown@planning.state.ri.us
**South Carolina**, Mike MacFarlane, Budget and Control Board ........................................................ 803-734-3780; mmacfarl@drss.state.sc.us
**South Dakota**, Nancy Nelson, Univ. of South Dakota .................... 605-677-5287; nnelson@usd.edu
**Tennessee**, Betty Vickers, University of Tennessee ......................... 423-974-6080; bvickers@utk.edu
* **Texas**, Steve Murdock, Texas A&M Univ. ......... 409-845-5115 / 5332; smurdock@rsocsun.tamu.edu
Texas BIDC, Donna Osborne, Dept. of Economic Dev. ........... 512-936-0223; donna@ded.state.tx.us
* **Utah**, Lisa Hillman, Office of Planning and Budget ............. 801-537-9013; lhillman@gov.state.ut.us
**Vermont**, Sharon Whitaker, Univ. of Vermont ................ 802-656-3021; sharon.whitaker@uvm.edu
**Virgin Islands**, Frank Mills, Univ. of the Virgin Islands ..................... 340-693-1027; fmills@uvi.edu
* **Virginia**, Don Lillywhite, Virginia Employment Commission ........................................................ 804-786-8026; dlillywhite@vec.state.va.us
* **Washington**, Yi Zhao, Office of Financial Management ........... 360-902-0599; yi.zhao@ofm.wa.gov
* **West Virginia**, Delphine Coffey, Office of Comm. and Ind. Dev. 304-558-4010; dcoffey@wvdo.org
West Virginia BIDC, Randy Childs, Center for Economic Research ........................................................ 304-293-6524; childs@be.wvu.edu
* **Wisconsin**, Robert Naylor, Dept of Administration ....... 608-266-1927; bob.naylor@doa.state.wi.us
Wisconsin BIDC, Dan Veroff, Univ. of Wisconsin ............ 608-265-9545; dlveroff@facstaff.wisc.edu
**Wyoming**, Wenlin Liu, Dept. of Admin. and Information .............. 307-766-2925; wliu@state.wy.us

# Glossary

**adjusted for inflation** Income or a change in income that has been adjusted for the rise in the cost of living, or the consumer price index (CPI-U-XI).

**American Housing Survey** The AHS collects national and metropolitan-level data on the nation's housing, including apartments, single-family homes, and mobile homes. The national survey, with a sample of 55,000 homes, is conducted by the Census Bureau for the Department of Housing and Urban Development every other year.

**Asian** In this book, the term "Asian" includes both Asians and Pacific Islanders.

**baby boom** Americans born between 1946 and 1964. Baby boomers were aged 37 to 55 in 2001.

**baby bust** Americans born between 1965 and 1976, also known as Generation X. In 2001, baby busters were aged 25 to 36.

**central cities** The largest city in a metropolitan area is called the central city. The balance of the metropolitan area outside the central city is regarded as the "suburbs."

**complete income reporters** (on spending tables only) Survey respondents who told government interviewers how much money they received from major sources of income, such as wages and salaries, self-employment income, and Social Security income.

**Consolidated metropolitan statistical area or CMSA** An area that meets the requirements for recognition as an MSA (metropolitan statistical area) and also has a population of 1 million or more may be recognized as a consolidated metropolitan statistical area (or CMSA) if it includes separate component areas that meet the statistical criteria specified in the standards for metropolitan areas, and if local opinion indicates there is support for the component areas. The components of CMSAs are called primary metropolitan statistical areas (or PMSAs).

**Consumer Expenditure Survey** The Consumer Expenditure Survey (CEX) is an ongoing study of the day-to-day spending of American households administered by the Bureau of Labor Statistics. The survey is used to update prices for the Consumer Price Index. The CEX includes an interview survey and a diary survey. The average spending figures shown in this book are the integrated data from both the diary and interview components of the survey. Two separate, nationally representative samples are used for the interview and diary surveys. For the interview survey, about 5,000 consumer units are interviewed on a rotating panel basis each quarter for five consecutive quarters. For the diary survey, 5,000 consumer units keep weekly diaries of spending for two consecutive weeks.

**consumer unit** (on Spending tables only) For convenience, the terms consumer unit and household are used interchangeably in the spending tables of this book, although consumer units are somewhat different from the Census Bureau's households. Consumer units are all related members of a household, or financially independent members of a household. A household may include more than one consumer unit.

**1994–96 Continuing Survey of Food** Intakes by Individuals This survey was conducted by the Agricultural Research Service of the U.S. Department of Agriculture to measure the food consumption of individuals. In taking the survey, a nationally representative sample of 21,700 people of all ages and 11,800 children aged 0 to 19 were asked to provide information on their food intakes for two nonconsecutive days.

**Current Population Survey** A nationally representative survey of the civilian noninstitutional population aged 15 or older. It is taken monthly by the Census Bureau for the Bureau of Labor Statistics, collecting information from 50,000 households on employment and unemployment. In March of each year, the survey includes a demographic supplement which is the source of most national data on the characteristics of Americans, such as their educational attainment, living arrangements, and incomes.

**crime** The crime statistics in this book are based on the Bureau of Justice Statistics National Crime Victimization Survey.

**1994–96 Diet and Health Knowledge Survey** This survey was conducted by the Agricultural Research Service of the U.S. Department of Agriculture to measure the public's knowledge about healthy eating. It was designed as a follow-up to the 1994-96 Continuing Survey of Food Intakes by Individuals, with telephone interviews placed to 5,800 individuals who had taken part in the Continuing Survey of Food Intakes about two weeks earlier.

**disability** People aged 15 or older were identified as having a disability if they met any of the following criteria: 1) used a wheelchair, cane, crutches, or walker; 2) had difficulty performing one or more functional activities (seeing, hearing, speaking, lifting/carrying, climbing stairs, walking, or grasping small objects); 3) had difficulty with one or more activities of daily living (or ADLs, which include getting around inside the home, getting in or out of bed or a chair, bathing, dressing, eating, and toileting); 4) had difficulty with one or more instrumental activities of daily living (or IADLs, which include going outside the home, keeping track of money and bills, preparing meals, doing light housework, taking prescription medicines, and using the telephone); 5) had one or more specified conditions such as a learning disability, mental retardation, or another developmental disability, Alzheimer's disease, or some other type of mental or emotional condition; 6) had any other mental or emotional condition that seriously interfered with everyday activities (frequently depressed or anxious, trouble getting along with others, trouble concentrating, or trouble coping with day-to-day stress); 7) had a condition that limited the ability to work around the house; 8) if aged 16 to 67, had a condition that made it difficult to work at a job or business; or 9) received federal benefits based on an inability to work. People were considered to have a severe disability if they met criteria 1, 6, or 9, or had Alzheimer's disease, mental retardation, or another developmental disability, or were unable to perform or needed help to perform one or more activities in criteria 2, 3, 4, 7, or 8. Children under age 5 were identified as disabled if they had a developmental delay or a condition that limited the ability to use arms or legs or a condition that limited walking, running, or playing. Children aged 6 to 14 were identified as severely disabled if they met any of the following criteria: 1) had a mental retardation or some other developmental disability; 2) they had a developmental condition for which they had received therapy or diagnostic services; 3) they used an ambulatory aid; 4) they had a severe limitation in the ability to see, hear, or speak; or 5) they needed personal assistance for an activity of daily living.

**dual-earner couple** A married couple in which both husband and wife are in the labor force.

**earnings** A type of income, earnings is the amount of money a person receives from his or her job. See also Income.

**employed** All civilians who did any work as a paid employee or farmer/self-employed worker, or who worked 15 hours or more as an unpaid farm worker or in a family-owned business, during the reference period. All those who have jobs but who are temporarily absent from their jobs due to illness, bad weather, vacation, labor management dispute, or personal reasons are considered employed.

**expenditure** The transaction cost including excise and sales taxes of goods and services acquired during the survey period. The full cost of each purchase is recorded even though full payment may not have been made at the date of purchase.

Average expenditure figures may be artificially low for infrequently purchased items such as cars because figures are calculated using all consumer units within a demographic segment rather than just purchasers. Expenditure estimates include money spent on gifts for others.

**family** A group of two or more people (one of whom is the householder) related by birth, marriage, or adoption and living in the same household.

**family household** A household maintained by a householder who lives with one or more people related to him or her by blood, marriage, or adoption.

**female/male householder** A woman or man who maintains a household without a spouse present. May head family or nonfamily households.

**full-time employment** Full-time is 35 or more hours of work per week during a majority of the weeks worked during the preceding calendar year.

**full-time, year-round** Indicates 50 or more weeks of full-time employment during the previous calendar year.

**General Social Survey** The General Social Survey (GSS) is a biennial survey of the attitudes of Americans taken by the University of Chicago's National Opinion Research Center (NORC). NORC conducts the GSS through face-to-face interviews with an independently drawn, representative sample of 1,500 to 3,000 noninstitutionalized English-speaking people aged 18 or older who live in the United States.

**Generation X** Americans born between 1965 and 1976, also known as the baby-bust generation. Generation Xers were aged 25 to 36 in 2001.

**Hispanic** People or householders who identify their origin as Mexican, Puerto Rican, Central or South American, or some other Hispanic origin. People of Hispanic origin may be of any race. In other words, there are Asian Hispanics, black Hispanics, Native American Hispanics, and white Hispanics.

**household** All the persons who occupy a housing unit. A household includes the related family members and all the unrelated persons, if any, such as lodgers, foster children, wards, or employees who share the housing unit. A person living alone is counted as a household. A group of unrelated people who share a housing unit as roommates or unmarried partners is also counted as a household. Households do not include group quarters such as college dormitories, prisons, or nursing homes.

**household, race/Hispanic origin of** Households are categorized according to the race or Hispanic origin of the householder only.

**householder** The householder is the person (or one of the persons) in whose name the housing unit is owned or rented or, if there is no such person, any adult member. With married couples, the householder may be either the husband or wife. The householder is the reference person for the household.

**householder, age of** The age of the householder is used to categorize households into age groups such as those used in this book. Married couples, for example, are classified according to the age of either the husband or wife, depending on which one identified him or herself as the householder.

**housing unit** A housing unit is a house, an apartment, a group of rooms, or a single room occupied or intended for occupancy as separate living quarters. Separate living quarters are those in which the occupants do not live and eat with any other persons in the structure and that have direct access from the outside of the building or through a common hall that is used or intended for use by the occupants of another unit or by the general public. The occupants may be a single family, one person living alone, two or more families living together, or any other group of related or unrelated persons who share living arrangements.

**immigration** The relatively permanent movement (change of residence) of persons into the country of reference.

**income** Money received in the preceding calendar year by each person aged 15 or older from each of the following sources: (1) earnings from longest job (or self-employment); (2) earnings from jobs other than longest job; (3) unemployment compensation; (4) workers' compensation; (5) Social Security; (6) Supplemental Security income; (7) public assistance; (8) veterans' payments; (9) survivor benefits; (10) disability benefits; (11) retirement pensions; (12) interest; (13) dividends; (14) rents and royalties or estates and trusts; (15) educational assistance; (16) alimony; (17) child support; (18) financial assistance from outside the household, and other periodic income. Income is reported in several ways in this book. Household income is the combined income of all household members. Income of persons is all income accruing to a person from all sources. Earnings is the amount of money a person receives from his or her job.

**income fifths or quintiles** Where the total number of households are divided into fifths based on household income. One-fifth of households fall into the lowest income quintile, one-fifth into the second income quintile, and so on. This is a useful way to compare the characteristics of low-, middle, and high-income households.

**industry** Refers to the industry in which a person worked longest in the preceding calendar year.

**job tenure** The length of time a person has been employed continuously by the same employer.

**labor force** The labor force tables in this book show the civilian labor force only. The labor force includes both the employed and the unemployed (people who are looking for work). People are counted as in the labor force if they were working or looking for work during the reference week in which the Census Bureau fields the Current Population Survey.

**labor force participation rate** The percent of a population that is in the labor force, which includes both the employed and unemployed. Labor force participation rates may be shown for sex-age groups or other special populations such as mothers of children of a given age.

**married couples with or without children under age 18** Refers to married couples with or without children under age 18 living in the same household. Couples without children under age 18 may be parents of grown children who live elsewhere, or they could be childless couples.

**median** The median is the amount that divides the population or households into two equal portions: one below and one above the median. Medians can be calculated for income, age, and many other characteristics.

**median income** The amount that divides the income distribution into two equal groups, half having incomes above the median, half having incomes below the median. The medians for households or families are based on all households or families. The median for persons are based on all persons aged 15 or older with income.

**metropolitan statistical area (MSA)** To be defined as a metropolitan statistical area (or MSA), an area must include a city with 50,000 or more inhabitants, or a Census Bureau-defined urbanized area of at least 50,000 inhabitants and a total metropolitan population of at least 100,000 (75,000 in New England). The county (or counties) that contains the largest city becomes the "central county" (counties), along with any adjacent counties that have at least 50 percent of their population in the urbanized area surrounding the largest city. Additional "outlying counties" are included in the MSA if they meet specified requirements of commuting to the central counties and other selected requirements of metropolitan character (such as population density and percent urban). In New England, MSAs are defined in terms of cities and towns rather than counties. For this reason, the concept of NECMA is used to define metropolitan areas in the New England division.

**millennial generation** Americans born between 1977 and 1994. Millennials were aged 7 to 24 in 2001.

**National Ambulatory Medical Care Survey** The NAMCS is an annual survey of visits to nonfederally employed office-based physicians who are primarily engaged in direct patient care. Data are collected from physicians rather than patients, with each physician assigned a one-week reporting period. During that week, a systematic random sample of visit characteristics are recorded by the physician or office staff.

**National Crime Victimization Survey** The NCVS is the nation's primary source of information on criminal victimization. Each year since 1973, data have been collected by the Census Bureau for the Bureau of Justice Statistics from a nationally representative sample of about 43,000 households comprising more than 80,000 people aged 12 or older on the frequency, characteristics, and consequences of criminal victimization in the United States. The survey measures rape, sexual assault, robbery, simple and aggravated assault, personal larceny, property theft, household burglary, and motor vehicle theft.

**National Health Interview Survey** The NHIS is a continuing nationwide sample survey of the civilian noninstitutional population of the U.S. conducted by the Census Bureau for the National Center for Health Statistics. Each year, data are collected from more than 100,000 people about their illnesses, injuries, impairments, chronic and acute conditions, activity limitations, and the use of health services.

**net worth** The amount of money left over after a household's debts are subtracted from its assets.

**New England county metropolitan area or NECMAs** NECMAs are the county-based alternative to the city- and town-based New England MSAs and CMSAs. NECMAs are defined as the county containing the first-named city in the MSA/CMSA title (this county may include the first-named cities of other MSAs/CMSAs as well), and each additional county having at least half its population in the MSAs/CMSAs whose first-named cities are in the previously identified county. There are twelve NECMAs, including one for the Boston-Worcester-Lawrence, MA-NH-ME-CT CMSA and one for the Connecticut portion of the New York-Northern New Jersey-Long Island, NY-NJ-CT-PA CMSA. Central cities of NECMAs are those cities in the NECMA that qualify as central cities of an MSA or a CMSA.

**nonfamily household** A household maintained by a householder who lives alone or who lives with people to whom he or she is not related.

**nonfamily householder** A householder who lives alone or with nonrelatives.

**nonmetropolitan area** Counties that are not classified as metropolitan areas.

**occupation** Occupational classification is based on the kind of work a person did at his or her job during the previous calendar year. If a person changed jobs during the year, the data refer to the occupation of the job held the longest during that year.

**occupied housing units** A housing unit is classified as occupied if a person or group of people is living in it or if the occupants are only temporarily absent-on vacation, example. By definition, the count of occupied housing units is the same as the count of households.

**outside central city** The portion of a metropolitan county or counties that falls outside of the central city or cities; generally regarded as the suburbs.

**own children** Own children are sons and daughters, including stepchildren and adopted children, of the householder. The totals include never-married children living away from home in college dormitories.

**owner occupied** A housing unit is "owner occupied" if the owner lives in the unit, even if it is mortgaged or not fully paid for. A cooperative or condominium unit is "owner occupied" only if the owner lives in it. All other occupied units are classified as "renter occupied."

**part-time employment** Part-time employment is less than 35 hours of work per week in a majority of the weeks worked during the year.

**percent change** The change (either positive or negative) in a measure that is expressed as a proportion of the starting measure. When median income changes from $20,000 to $25,000, for example, this is a 25 percent increase.

**percentage point change** The change (either positive or negative) in a value which is already expressed as a percentage. When a labor force participation rate changes from 70 percent of 75 percent, for example, this is a 5 percentage point increase.

**poverty level** The official income threshold below which families and persons are classified as living in poverty. The threshold rises each year with inflation and varies depending on family size and age of householder.

**Primary metropolitan statistical area or PMSA** PMSAs are metropolitan statistical areas that are components of consolidated metropolitan statistical areas (CMSAs).

**proportion or share** The value of a part expressed as a percentage of the whole. If there are 4 million people aged 25 and 3 million of them are white, then the white proportion is 75 percent.

**race** Race is self-reported and appears in four categories in this book: Asian, black, Native American, and white. A household is assigned the race of the householder.

**regions** The four major regions and nine census divisions of the United States are the state groupings as shown below:

**Northeast:**
–New England: Connecticut, Maine, Massachusetts, New Hampshire, Rhode Island, and Vermont
–Middle Atlantic: New Jersey, New York, and Pennsylvania

*Midwest:*
–East North Central: Illinois, Indiana, Michigan, Ohio, and Wisconsin
–West North Central: Iowa, Kansas, Minnesota, Missouri, Nebraska, North Dakota, and South Dakota

*South:*
–South Atlantic: Delaware, District of Columbia, Florida, Georgia, Maryland, North Carolina, South Carolina, Virginia, and West Virginia
–East South Central: Alabama, Kentucky, Mississippi, and Tennessee
–West South Central: Arkansas, Louisiana, Oklahoma, and Texas

*West:*
–Mountain: Arizona, Colorado, Idaho, Montana, Nevada, New Mexico, Utah, and Wyoming
–Pacific: Alaska, California, Hawaii, Oregon, and Washington

**renter occupied** *See* Owner occupied.

**rounding** Percentages are rounded to the nearest tenth of a percent; therefore, the percentages in a distribution do not always add exactly to 100.0 percent. The totals, however, are always shown as 100.0. Moreover, individual figures are rounded to the nearest thousand without being adjusted to group totals, which are independently rounded; percentages are based on the unrounded numbers.

**self-employment** A person is categorized as self-employed if he or she was self-employed in the job held longest during the reference period. Persons who report self-employment from a second job are excluded, but those who report wage-and-salary income from a second job are included. Unpaid workers in family businesses are excluded. Self-employment statistics exclude people who work for themselves in an incorporated business.

**sex ratio** The number of men per 100 women.

**suburbs** The portion of a metropolitan area that is outside the central city.

**Survey of Consumer Finances** The Survey of Consumer Finances is a triennial survey taken by the Federal Reserve Board. It collects data on the assets, debts, and net worth of American households. For the 1998 survey, the Federal Reserve Board interviewed a random sample of 2,813 households and a supplemental sample of 1,496 wealthy households based on tax-return data.

**unemployed** Unemployed people are those who, during the survey period, had no employment but were available and looking for work. Those who were laid off from their jobs and were waiting to be recalled are also classified as unemployed.

# Bibliography


Bureau of Justice Statistics

Internet site <www.ojp.usdoj.gov/bjs>

—*Criminal Victimization 1999: Changes 1998–99 with Trends 1993–99*, NCJ 182734, 2000

Bureau of the Census

Internet site <www.census.gov>

—2000 Current Population Survey, unpublished data

—*Americans with Disabilities: 1997*, detailed tables from Current Population Reports, P70-73, 2001

—American Housing Survey for the United States in 1999

—*Educational Attainment in the United States: March 2000*, detailed tables from Current Population Reports, P20-536, 2000

—*Geographic Mobility: March 1998 to March 1999*, Current Population Reports, P20-531, 2000

—*Household and Family Characteristics: March 1998*, detailed tables from Current Population Reports, P20-515, 1998

—Housing Vacancy Surveys, unpublished data

—*Marital Status and Living Arrangements: March 1998*, Current Population Reports, P20-514, 1998

—*Metropolitan Areas and Cities*, 1990 Census Profile, No. 3, 1991

—*Money Income in the United States: 1999*, Current Population Reports, P60-209, 2000

—*Population Projections of the United States by Age, Sex, Race, and Hispanic Origin: 1995 to 2050*, Current Population Reports, P25-1130, 1996

—*Poverty in the United States: 1999*, Current Population Reports, P60-210, 2000

—*School Enrollment: Social and Economic Characteristics of Students: October 1999*, detailed tables from Current Population Reports, P20-533, 2001

—*Statistical Abstract of the United States: 1999* (119th edition) Washington, DC 1999

—*Statistical Abstract of the United States: 2000* (120th edition) Washington, DC 2001

Bureau of Labor Statistics

Internet site <www.bls.gov>

—1990 and 1999 Consumer Expenditure Surveys, unpublished data

—2000 Current Population Survey, unpublished data

—*Contingent and Alternative Employment Arrangements*, February 1999

—*Employee Benefits in Medium and Large Private Establishments*, 1997

—*Employee Benefits in Small Private Establishments*, 1996

—*Employment and Earnings*, January 1991

—*Employment and Earnings*, January 2001

—*Handbook of Labor Statistics*, Bulletin 2340, 1989

—*Monthly Labor Review*, November 1999

—*Work at Home in 1997*, USDL 98-93

Federal Reserve Board

Internet site <www.federalreserve.gov/pubs/OSS/oss2/scfindex.html>

—*Recent Change in U.S. Family Finance: Results from the 1998 Survey of Consumer Finances*, Federal Reserve Bulletin, January 2000

Immigration and Naturalization Service

Internet site <www.ins.usdoj.gov/graphics/aboutins/statistics/index.htm>

—*1998 Statistical Yearbook of the Immigration and Naturalization Service*, 2000

National Center for Education Statistics

Internet site <http://nces.ed.gov>

—*Digest of Education Statistics: 2001*, NCES 2001034, 2001

—National Household Education Survey 1999, unpublished data

—*Projections of Education Statistics to 2010*, NCES 2000071, 2000

National Center for Health Statistics

Internet site <www.cdc.gov/nchs>

—An Overview of Home Health and Hospice Care Patients: 1996 National Home and Hospice Care Survey, Advance Data, No. 297, 1998

—*Births: Final Data for 1998*, National Vital Statistics Report, Vol. 48, No. 3, 2000

—*Births: Preliminary Data for 1999*, National Vital Statistics Report, Vol. 48, No. 14, 2000

—Current Estimates from the National Health Interview Survey, 1996, Series 10, No. 200, 1999

—*Deaths: Final Data for 1998*, National Vital Statistics Report, Vol. 48, No. 11, 2000

—*Health, United States*, 2000

—National Ambulatory Medical Care Survey: 1998 Summary, Advance Data No. 315, 2000

National Endowment for the Arts

Internet site <http://arts.endow.gov>

—1997 Survey of Public Participation in the Arts, Summary Report, 1998

National Opinion Research Center

Internet site <www.norc.uchicago.edu>

—General Social Surveys, unpublished data

National Sporting Goods Association

Internet site <www.nsga.org>

National Telecommunications and Information Administration

Internet site <www.ntia.doc.gov>

—*Falling through the Net: Toward Digital Inclusion—A Report on Americans' Access to Technology Tools*, October 2000

U.S. Department of Agriculture, Economic Research Service

Internet site <www.ers.usda.gov>

—*Economic Research Service, Food Consumption, Prices, and Expenditures*, 1970–1997

U.S. Department of Agriculture, Food Surveys Research Group

Internet site <www.barc.usda.gov/bhnrc/foodsurvey/home.htm>

—ARS Food Surveys Research Group, 1994–96 Continuing Survey of Food Intakes by Individuals

—ARS Food Surveys Research Group, 1994–96 Diet and Health Knowledge Survey

U.S. Substance Abuse and Mental Health Services Administration

Internet site <www.samhsa.gov>

—National Household Survey on Drug Abuse, 1999

# Index


accidents, among leading causes of death, 107
activities of daily living (ADLs), 94
administrative support occupations:
  employment in, by industry and sex, 236–38;
  employment in, by race and Hispanic origin, 231–35;
  employment in, by sex, 227–230;
  employment, projected, 261;
  weekly earnings, by sex, 200;
  women, employment in, 230
adoption assistance, as an employee benefit, 253
adult education, participation in, 56–57
advanced degree holders:
  arts events, attendance, 355;
  computer use, 350–51;
  foreign-born population, 346;
  health status, self-reported, 60–61;
  Internet access, 350–51;
  religious preference, 348–49
affluence, effect on college attendance, 28–29
agriculture:
  employment in, by occupation and sex, 236–38;
  employment, projected, 264–66
AIDS victims, by sex and race and Hispanic origin, 103
air conditioning, central, 130
Akron, OH:
  homeownership rates, 123
Alabama:
  college graduates, 11;
  high school graduates, 11;
  homeownership rates, 121;
  income, median household, 204;
  population, by race and Hispanic origin, 328;
  population distribution by race and Hispanic origin, 330
Alaska:
  college graduates, 11;
  high school graduates, 11;
  homeownership rates, 121;
  income, median household, 203;
  population, by race and Hispanic origin, 328;
  population distribution by race and Hispanic origin, 330
Albany–Schenectady–Troy, NY:
  homeownership rates, 123
alcohol use, by age and level of drinking, 80
alcoholic beverages, consumption of, 64
alcoholic beverages, spending on:
  by age of householder, 371, indexed, 378, market share, 384;
  by educational attainment, 455, indexed, 459, market share, 463;
  by household income, 391, indexed, 398, market share, 404;
  by household type, 411, indexed, 416, market share, 421;
  by race and Hispanic origin, 427, indexed, 431, market share 435;
  by region, 441, indexed, 445, market share, 449;
  household average, 364
aliens, non-resident, degrees conferred, 37–38
alimony, as source of income, 205–06
American Indians. *See* Native Americans.
apparel and services, spending on by product or service:
  by age of householder, 372–73, indexed, 379–80, market share, 385;
  by educational attainment, 456, indexed, 460, market share, 464;
  by household income, 393, indexed, 400, market share, 405;
  by household type, 411–12, indexed, 416–17, market share, 421–22;
  by race and Hispanic origin, 428, indexed, 432, market share, 436;
  by region, 442, indexed, 446, market share, 450;
  household average, 365
Arizona:
  college graduates, 11;
  high school graduates, 11;
  homeownership rates, 121;
  income, median household, 203;
  population, by race and Hispanic origin, 328;
  population distribution by race and Hispanic origin, 330
Arkansas:
  college graduates, 11;
  high school graduates, 11;
  homeownership rates, 121;
  income, median household, 204;
  population, by race and Hispanic origin, 328;
  population distribution by race and Hispanic origin, 330
art buying, participation in, by educational attainment, 356
art/craft fairs, attendance, by educational attainment, 355
art museums, attendance, by educational attainment, 355
arthritis, 87

arts events, attendance, by educational attainment, 355
arts, participation in, 355–56
Asian Americans:
AIDS victims, 105;
births by age of mother, 71;
college enrollments, 36;
college graduates, 9;
computer use, 350–51;
degrees conferred, 37–38;
high school graduates, 8;
homeownership, by status, 116–117;
income, median, 154–55;
income, median, by type of household, 156–57;
Internet access, 350–51;
labor force, projected, 256–57;
population, by age, projected, 318–19;
population, by region and census division, 324–26;
population, projected, 317–18;
Scholastic Assessment Test (SAT) scores, 26–27
assault, 358–59
associate degree earners:
by field of study and sex, 40–41;
by race and Hispanic origin, 37;
by sex and age, 4–6;
earnings by sex, 196 ;
employment, projected, 267–68;
foreign-born population, 346;
income, household, 182–83;
projected, 53
asthma, 90
Atlanta, GA MSA:
college graduates, 10;
high school graduates, 10;
homeownership rates, 123;
population, 334
Austin–San Marcos, TX MSA:
homeownership rates, 123;
population, 1950–1999, 333;
automobiles, as means of travel to work, 248–49. *See also* Vehicles.

baby-boom generation. *See* Middle-aged adults.
bachelor's degree earners. *See* College graduates.
ballet:
attendance at, by educational attainment, 355;
participation in, by educational attainment, 356
Baltimore, MD PMSA:
college graduates, 11;
high school graduates, 11;
homeownership rates, 123;
population, 1950–1999, 332
basketball for recreation, 77
bathrooms, 126,128
Bergen–Passaic, NJ PMSA:
college graduates, 11;
high school graduates, 11;
homeownership rates, 123;
population, 1950–1999, 333
beverage consumption, by type of beverage, 62–64
bicycle or motorcycle, as means of travel to work, 248–49
bicycle riding for recreation, 77
billiards or pool for recreation, 77
Birmingham, AL:
homeownership rates, 123
births, 68–74:
by age and birth order, 74;
by age, race and Hispanic origin of mother, 70–71;
projected, 68–69;
to unmarried women, by age and race, 72–73
Black Americans:
assets held, financial, by type of asset, 470–72;
assets held non-financial by type of asset, 476–78;
births by age of mother, 71;
births to unmarried women, 72;
children, living arrangements, 290–91;
college enrollments, 30–31;
college graduates, 9;
crime victims, 357–60;
debt, household, by type of debt, 479–81;
employment status by sex and age, 217;
health status, self-reported, 60–61;
high school graduates, 8;
homeownership, by status, 116–117;
households by age, 280–81;
households by region, 286–87;
households by type, 277–79;
income, median 154–55;
income, median, by age of householder, 160–61;
income, median, by type of household, 156–57;
labor force, projected, 256–57;
marital status by age, 307–09;
net worth of households, 468–69;
occupations, employment in, by occupation, 231–35;
pension coverage, 482–83;
physician's visits, 95–96;
population, by age, projected, 318,320;
population, by region and census division, 324–26;
population, projected, 317–18;
poverty status, by age, 207–08;
religious preference, 348–49;
Scholastic Assessment Test (SAT) scores, 26–27
Black Americans, non-Hispanic:
AIDS victims, 105;
college enrollments, 36;
college graduates, 9;
computer use, 350–51;
degrees conferred, 37–38;
high school attenders, non-graduates, 23;

high school graduates, 8;
Internet access, 350–51;
labor force, entrants and leavers, projected, 257–59;
population, by age, projected, 318,320;
population, by region and census division, 324–26;
population, projected, 317–18;
spending, by product or service, 425–30, indexed, 431–34, market share, 435–38
Boston, MA–NH PMSA:
college graduates, 10;
high school graduates, 10;
homeownership rates, 123
Boston–Worcester–Lawrence–Lowell–Brockton, MA–NH NECMA:
college graduates, 10;
high school graduates, 10;
population, 1950–1999, 332
bottled gas, for heating, 130
bowling for recreation, 77
Buffalo–Niagara Falls, NY MSA:
college graduates, 10;
high school graduates, 10;
homeownership rates, 123

California:
college graduates, 11;
high school graduates, 11;
homeownership rates, 121;
immigration to, 342–43;
income, median household, 203;
population, by race and Hispanic origin, 328;
population distribution by race and Hispanic origin, 330
camping for recreation, 77
cancer, among leading causes of death, 107
candy, consumption of, 64
carpool, as means of travel to work, 248–49
cash contributions, spending on:
by age of householder, 374, indexed, 381, market share, 386;
by educational attainment, 457, indexed, 461, market share, 465;
by household income, 395, indexed, 402, market share, 406;
by household type, 413, indexed, 418, market share, 423;
by race and Hispanic origin, 429, indexed, 433, market share, 437;
by region, 443, indexed, 447, market share, 451;
household average, 366
cashiers, 263
Catholic religion, preference for, 349
central cities:
crime victims 357–60;
educational attainment, 12–14;
homeownership status, 120;
households, 201–02, 288–89;
income, median household, 201–02;
population, 1950–1999, 332–33
cerebrovascular diseases, among leading causes of death, 107
certificates of deposit (CDs), 471–72
Charlotte–Gastonia–Rock Hill, NC–SC MSA:
college graduates, 10;
high school graduates, 10;
homeownership rates, 123;
population, 1950–1999, 333
cheese, consumption of, 63
Chicago, IL PMSA:
college graduates, 10;
high school graduates, 10;
homeownership rates, 123
Chicago–Gary–Kenosha, IL–IN–WI CMSA:
college graduates, 10;
high school graduates, 10;
population, 1950–1999, 332
child care, as an employee benefit, 253
child support, as source of income, 205–06
children:
effect on household incomes, 174–78, 209;
foreign-born, 346;
geographic mobility, 338–39;
Internet users, 352;
living arrangements, by race and Hispanic origin, 290–91;
living at home, by age of child and age of householder, 297–98;
living in single-parent households, 299–300;
population, by race and Hispanic origin, projected, 318–23;
population, by sex, 312–13;
population, by sex, projected, 314–15;
presence in families of workers, by type of family, 222;
presence in families of working women, 220–21;
school enrollments, 17;
spending by product or service, 368–87, indexed, 377–83, market share, 384–87
China, immigration from, 342–43
cigarette smoking, 79
Cincinnati, OH–KY–IN PMSA:
college graduates, 10;
high school graduates, 10;
homeownership rates, 123
Cincinnati–Hamilton, OH–KY–IN CMSA:
college graduates, 10;
high school graduates, 10;
population, 1950–1999, 332
circulatory disorders, 89–90, 107
cities. *See* Central cities.

classical music:
attendance, by educational attainment, 355;
participation in, by educational attainment, 356
Cleveland–Lorain–Elyria, OH PMSA:
college graduates, 10;
high school graduates, 10;
homeownership rates, 123;
population, 1950–1999, 332
Cleveland–Akron, OH CMSA:
college graduates, 10;
high school graduates, 10
clothes dryers, 130
clothing, children's, spending on:
household average, 365;
by age of householder, 373, indexed, 380, market share, 385;
by educational attainment, 456, indexed, 460, market share, 464;
by household income, 393, indexed, 400, market share, 405;
by household type, 412, indexed, 417, market share, 422;
by race and Hispanic origin, 428, indexed, 432, market share, 436;
by region, 442, indexed, 446, market share, 450
clothing, men and boys, spending on by product:
by age of householder, 372–73, indexed, 379–80, market share, 385;
by educational attainment, 456, indexed, 460, market share, 464;
by household income, 393, indexed, 400, market share, 405;
by household type, 411–12, indexed, 416–17, market share, 421–22;
by race and Hispanic origin, 428, indexed, 432, market share, 436;
by region, 442, indexed, 446, market share, 450;
household average, 365;
clothing, women and girls, spending on:
by age of householder, 373, indexed, 380, market share, 385;
by educational attainment, 456, indexed, 460, market share, 464;
by household income, 393, indexed, 400, market share, 405;
by household type, 412, indexed, 417, market share, 422;
by race and Hispanic origin, 428, indexed, 432, market share, 436;
by region, 442, indexed, 446, market share, 450;
household average, 365;
coal or coke, for heating, 130
coffee, consumption of, 64
college, attended, non-graduates:
arts events, attendance, 355;
net worth of households, 469;
spending by product or service, 453–58, indexed, 459–62, market share, 463–66
college enrollments:
by age, 33–34;
by age, projected, 46–47;
by attendance status, 34–35;
by level of degree, projected, 49–50;
by race and Hispanic origin, 32,35–36;
by sex, 30–31;
by type of institution, projected, 51–52;
families with children in college, 28–29
college graduates:
arts events, attendance, 355;
by field of study and sex, 42;
by race and Hispanic origin, 7,9;
by sex and age, 4–6;
by state, 10–11;
computer use, 350–51;
earnings by sex, 196;
foreign-born population, 346;
health status, self-reported, 60–61;
household income, 182–83;
Internet access, 350–51;
net worth of households, 468–69;
projected, 53;
religious preference, 348–49;
spending by product or service, 453–58, indexed, 459–62, market share, 463–66
colleges:
four-year, projected enrollments, 52;
two-year, projected enrollments, 51
Colorado:
college graduates, 11;
high school graduates, 11;
homeownership rates, 121;
income, median household, 203;
population, by race and Hispanic origin, 328;
population distribution by race and Hispanic origin, 330
Columbus, OH MSA:
college graduates, 10;
high school graduates, 10;
homeownership rates, 123;
population, 1950–1999, 333
commuting. *See* Journey to work.
computer engineers, 262
computer ownership, 350–51:
by educational attainment, 351
by household income, 351
by race and Hispanic origin, 351
computer support specialists, 262–63
Connecticut:
college graduates, 11;
high school graduates, 11;

homeownership rates, 121;
income, median household, 203;
population, by race and Hispanic origin, 328;
population distribution by race and Hispanic origin, 330
construction industries:
employment in, by occupation and sex, 236–38;
employment, projected, 264–66
consumer units:
by age of householder, 370, market share, 384;
by educational attainment, 455, market share, 459;
by household income, 390, market share, 404;
by household type, 410, market share, 420;
by race and Hispanic origin, 427, market share, 435;
by region, 441, market share, 445;
total, 363
Consumer Expenditure Survey, 362
contract workers, 244–45
contractors, independent, 244–45
couples, cohabiting, by age and sex, 301–02
credit card debt, 479–81
crime, perceived as neighborhood problem, 140
crime victims:
of property crimes, 360;
of violent crimes, 357–58
Cuba, immigration from, 342–43

dairy products, frozen, consumption of, 63
Dallas, TX PMSA:
homeownership rates, 123
Dallas–Ft. Worth, TX CMSA:
college graduates, 10;
high school graduates, 10;
population, 1950–1999, 332
dance performances:
attendance at, by educational attainment, 355;
participation in, by educational attainment, 356
database administrators, 262
Dayton–Springfield, OH:
homeownership rates, 123
debt, by type of debt, 479–81
Delaware:
college graduates, 11;
high school graduates, 11;
homeownership rates, 121;
income, median household, 203;
population, by race and Hispanic origin, 328;
population distribution by race and Hispanic origin, 330
dental care insurance, as an employee benefit, 252
Denver, CO PMSA:
college graduates, 10;
high school graduates, 10;
homeownership rates, 123
Denver–Boulder–Greeley, CO CMSA:
college graduates, 10;
high school graduates, 10;
population, 1950–1999, 332
desktop publishing specialists, 262
Detroit, MI PMSA:
college graduates, 10;
high school graduates, 10;
homeownership rates, 123
Detroit–Ann Arbor–Flint, MI CMSA:
college graduates, 10;
high school graduates, 10;
population, 1950–1999, 332
diabetes:
among leading causes of death, 107;
chronic condition, 89
diet, attitudes toward, by sex, 65
digestive conditions:
acute, 85;
chronic, 88
disabilities:
disabled people by sex and age, 91–92;
disabled people by type of disability and age, 93–94
disability benefits:
as source of income, 205–06;
coverage, by employment status, 252
dishwasher, 130
disposal in kitchen sink, 130
distance from home to work, 249
District of Columbia:
college graduates, 11;
high school graduates, 11;
homeownership rates, 121;
income, median household, 204;
population, by race and Hispanic origin, 328;
population distribution by race and Hispanic origin, 330
dividends, as source of income, 205–06
doctor's visits. *See* Physician's visits.
doctoral degree earners:
by field of study and sex, 44;
by race and Hispanic origin, 37;
by sex and age, 4–6;
earnings by sex, 196;
employment, projected, 267–68;
income, household, 182–83;
projected, 53
Dominican Republic, immigration from, 342–43
dramatic performances:
attendance at, by educational attainment, 355;
participation in, by educational attainment, 356
drawing, participation in, by educational attainment, 356
drug use, illicit, by age, 81
dual-earners. *See* Households, married-couple.

e-mail use, 350
ear conditions:
acute, 86;
hearing impairments, 88
earnings. *See also* Income:
as source of income, 205–06;
by educational attainment, 195–97;
foreign-born workers, 347;
median weekly, by sex, 198–200
East North Central census division:
population by race and Hispanic origin, 324–26
East South Central census division:
population by race and Hispanic origin, 324–26
education, as source of income, 205–06
education, spending on:
by age of householder, 374, indexed, 381, market share, 386;
by educational attainment, 457, indexed, 461, market share, 465;
by household income, 395 , indexed, 402, market share, 406;
by household type, 413, indexed, 418, market share, 423;
by race and Hispanic origin, 429, indexed, 433, market share, 437;
by region, 443, indexed, 447, market share, 451;
household average, 366
education trends, 3–57:
adult education, 56–57;
attainment, 4–14,24–25;
attitudes toward, 18–19;
degrees conferred, 37–45;
degrees conferred, projected, 53;
enrollments, 15–17, 20–23,30–36;
enrollments, projected, 46–53
educational assistance, as an employee benefit, 253
educational attainment:
art activities, participation in, 356;
art events, attendance at, 354–55;
computer use, 351;
employment by, projected, 267–68;
foreign-born, 346;
Internet access, 351;
religious preference, 349;
spending, 453–66
eggs, consumption of, 63
El Salvador, immigration from, 342–43
elderly:
AIDS cases. 104;
alcohol use, 80;
alternative work arrangements, 245;
assets, financial, 471–72;
assets held, financial, by type of asset, 470–72;
assets held, non-financial, by type of asset, 476–78;
assets, non-financial, 476–78;
cohabiting couples, 301–02;
college graduates, by race and Hispanic origin, 9;
college students, 33–34;
crime, victims of violent, 358;
debt, by type of debt, 479–81;
debt, household, by type of debt, 479–81;
disabilities, by type of disability, 91–94;
drug use, illicit, 81;
dual-income couples, 224;
educational attainment, 5–6;
employment, long-term, 241;
employment status, 215,226;
exercise, 76;
foreign-born, 346;
geographic mobility, 338–39;
health conditions, 84–90;
health insurance coverage, 82–83;
health status, self-reported, 61;
high school graduates, by race and Hispanic origin, 8;
home health services, 100–01;
homeownership, 112–14;
hospice care, 102;
hospital care, 97–99;
householders, 272–81;
householders by household type, 275–76;
householders by race and Hispanic origin, 280–81;
income, median, 150–51,158–59;
income, median, by household type, 173;
income, median, by race and Hispanic origin, 160–64;
income, median, of people living alone, by sex, 179–81;
Internet users, 352;
job tenure, 240;
labor force, participation in, 1970–2000, 213;
labor force, participation in, by race and Hispanic origin, 216–219;
labor force, participation in, projected, 255;
living alone, 284–85;
living arrangements, by sex, 294–95;
marital status, 304–09;
net worth of households, 468–69;
pension coverage, 482–83;
physician visits, 95–96;
population, by race and Hispanic origin, projected, 318–23;
population, by sex, 312–13;
population, by sex, projected, 314–15;
school enrollment, 17;
self-employment, 243;
single parents with child at home, 299–300;
smoking, 79;

spending by product or service, 368–87, indexed, 377–83, market share, 384–87;
stock ownership, 473–74;
vitamin and supplement use, 67
electricity:
costs, monthly, by homeownership status, 142;
for heating, 130
elementary schools:
enrollments, 15–17;
parent satisfaction with, 18–19
employee benefits, by size of firm and employment status, 251–53
employment. *See* Labor force.
employment status:
by race and Hispanic origin, 216–19;
by sex and age, 214–15,225–26;
movers, 339;
parents with children, 222;
women by presence of children, 220–21
endocrine disorders, chronic, 89
entertainment, spending on by product:
by product and age of householder, 374, indexed, 381, market share, 386;
by product and educational attainment, 457, indexed, 461, market share, 465;
by product and household income, 394, indexed, 401, market share, 406;
by product and household type, 412, indexed, 417, market share, 422;
by product and race and Hispanic origin, 429, indexed, 433, market share, 437;
by product and region, 443, indexed, 447, market share, 451;
household average, 365
executive administrative and managerial occupations:
earnings, weekly, by sex, 199;
employment in, by industry and sex, 236–38;
employment in, by sex, 227–230;
employment, projected, 1998–2008, 261;
women, employment in, 229
exercise:
by recreational activity, 77;
by sex, age and frequency, 75–76;
with equipment, 77
eye conditions:
acute, 86;
visual impairments, 88

families. *See* Households, family.
family benefits, as an employee benefit, 253
family leave, as an employee benefit, 252
farm self-employment, as source of income, 205–06
farming, forestry and fishing occupations:
earnings, weekly, by sex, 200;
employment in, by industry and sex, 236–38;
employment in, by race and Hispanic origin, 231–35;
employment in by sex, 227–230;
women, employment in, 230
fats and oils, consumption of, 63
finance, insurance and real estate industries:
employment in by occupation and sex, 236–38;
employment, projected, 264–66
fireplaces, 130
fish, consumption of, 63
fishing for recreation, 77
Florida:
college graduates, 11;
high school graduates, 11;
homeownership rates, 121;
immigration to, 342–43;
income, median household, 204;
population, by race and Hispanic origin, 328;
population distribution by race and Hispanic origin, 330
flour and cereal products, consumption of, 64
food consumption, by type of food, 62–64
food, spending on by product:
by age of householder, 370, indexed, 377, market share, 384;
by educational attainment, 455, indexed, 459, market share, 463;
by household income, 390–91, indexed, 397–98, market share, 404;
by household type, 410, indexed, 415, market share, 420;
by race and Hispanic origin, 427, indexed, 431, market share, 435 ;
by region, 441, indexed, 445, market share, 449;
household average, 363
footwear, spending on:
by age of householder, 373, indexed, 380, market share, 385;
by educational attainment, 456, indexed, 460, market share, 464;
by household income, 393, indexed, 400, market share, 405;
by household type, 412, indexed, 417, market share, 422;
by race and Hispanic origin, 428, indexed, 432, market share, 436;
by region, 442, indexed, 446, market share, 450
household average, 365;
foreign-born population, 344–47:
by age, 346;
by educational attainment, 346;
by region of birth, 345;
by year of entry, 345;
earnings by sex, 347;
labor force status, 347

Fort Lauderdale, FL PMSA:
college graduates, 10;
high school graduates, 10;
homeownership rates, 123;
population, 1950–1999, 333
Fort Worth–Arlington, TX PMSA:
college graduates, 10;
high school graduates, 10;
homeownership rates, 123;
population, 1950–1999, 332
Fresno, CA:
homeownership rates, 123
fruit juices, consumption of, 64
fruits:
canned, consumption of, 64;
fresh, consumption of, 63–64;
frozen, consumption of, 64
fuel oil:
cost, monthly, by homeownership status, 142;
for heating, 130
full-time workers:
by sex and age, 225–26;
employment benefits by type of benefit and size of firm, 251–53;
women, by presence of children, 220–21
funeral leave, as an employee benefit, 252

garage or carport, 130
gas, piped:
costs, monthly, by homeownership status, 142;
for heating, 130
general managers and top executives, 263
genitourinary disorders, chronic, 89
geographic mobility, 1950–1999, 336–37
Georgia:
college graduates, 11;
high school graduates, 11;
homeownership rates, 121;
income, median household, 203;
population, by race and Hispanic origin, 328;
population distribution by race and Hispanic origin, 330
gifts, spending on, by type of gift:
by age of householder, 375–76, indexed, 382–83, market share, 386;
by educational attainment, 458, indexed, 462, market share 466;
by household income, 395–96, indexed, 402–03, market share, 407;
by household type, 413–14, indexed, 418–19, market share, 423–24;
by race and Hispanic origin, 430, indexed, 434, market share, 438;
by region, 444, indexed, 448, market share, 452;
household average, 366–67
golf for recreation, 77
graduate schools:
enrollments, 36;
enrollments, projected, 49
Grand Rapids–Muskegon–Holland, MI:
homeownership rates, 123
Greensboro–Winston-Salem–High Point, NC MSA:
homeownership rates, 123;
population, 1950–1999, 333
Greenville–Spartanburg–Anderson, SC:
homeownership rates, 123

Hartford, CT MSA:
college graduates, 10;
high school graduates, 10;
homeownership rates, 123
Hawaii:
college graduates, 11;
high school graduates, 11;
homeownership rates, 121;
income, median household, 203;
population, by race and Hispanic origin, 328;
population distribution by race and Hispanic origin, 330
headaches, 89
health care, spending, on by product:
by age of householder, 374, indexed, 381, market share, 386;
by educational attainment, 457, indexed, 461, market share, 465;
by household income, 394, indexed, 401, market share, 406;
by household type, 412, indexed, 417, market share, 422;
by race and Hispanic origin, 429, indexed, 433, market share, 437;
by region, 443, indexed, 447, market share, 451;
household average, 365
health conditions:
acute, by age and type of condition, 85–86;
chronic, by age and type of condition, 87–90
health insurance, coverage by age, 82–83
health promotion programs, as an employee benefit, 253
health, 59–109:
acute conditions, 85–86;
AIDS victims, 104;
alcohol use, 78,80;
beverage consumption, 62–64;
births, 68–74;
chronic conditions, 87–90;
death, leading causes of, 106–07;
diet, attitudes toward, 65;
disabilities, 91–94;

drug use, illicit, 81;
exercise, 75–77;
food consumption, 62–64;
health status, self-reported, 60–61;
home health services, 100–01;
hospice care, 102;
hospital stays, 97–99;
life expectancy, 108–09;
physician's visits, 95–96;
smoking, 78–79;
vitamin and supplement use, 66–67
hearing impairments, 88
heart disease:
among leading causes of death, 107;
chronic condition, 89
heating fuels, 129–30
high blood pressure (hypertension), 90
high school, attended, non-graduates:
by race and Hispanic origin, 22–23;
earnings by sex, 196;
health status, self-reported, 60–61;
household income, 182–83;
net worth of households, 469;
religious preference, 348–49;
spending by product or service, 453–58, indexed, 459–62, market share, 463–66
high school graduates:
arts events, attendance, 355;
by race and Hispanic origin, 7–8;
by sex and age, 4–6;
by state, 10–11;
computer use, 350–51;
earnings by sex, 196 ;
foreign-born population, 346;
health status, self-reported, 60–61;
household income, 182–83;
Internet access, 350–51;
net worth of households, 469;
projected, 24–25;
spending by product or service, 453–58, indexed,459–62, market share, 463–66
hiking for recreation, 77
Hispanic Americans:
AIDS victims, 105;
assets held, financial by type of asset, 470–72;
assets held, non-financial, type of asset, 476–78;
births by age of mother, 71;
births to unmarried women, 72;
children, living arrangements, 290–91;
college enrollments, 32, 36;
college graduates, 9;
computer use, 350–51;
crime victims, 357–60;
debt, household, by type of debt, 479–81;
degrees conferred, 37–38;
employment status by sex and age, 218;
high school attenders, non-graduates, 23;
high school graduates, 8;
homeownership, by status, 116–117;
households by age, 280–81;
households by region, 286–87;
households by type, 277–79;
income, median, 154–55;
income, median, by age of householder, 160,162;
income, median, by type of household, 156–57;
Internet access, 350–51;
labor force entrants and leavers, projected, 257–59;
labor force, projected, 256–57;
marital status by age, 307–09;
net worth of households, 468–69;
occupations, employment in, by occupation, 231–35;
pension coverage, 482–83;
population, by age, projected, 318,321;
population, by region and census division, 324–26;
population, projected, 317–18;
poverty status, by age, 207–08;
Scholastic Assessment Test (SAT) scores, 26–27;
spending, by product or service, 425–30, indexed, 431–34, market share, 435–38
historic parks, attendance at, by educational attainment, 355
holidays, paid, as an employee benefit, 252
home health services, 100–01
homeowners:
by household type, 114–15;
by housing type and size, 127–28;
by metropolitan area, 123–25;
by metropolitan status, 120;
by race and Hispanic origin, 116–17;
by region, 118–19;
by state, 121–22;
crime victims, 360;
housing costs, 141–42;
housing unit, opinion of, 133–35;
movers, 339;
neighborhood, characteristics of, 138–140;
neighborhood, opinion of, 136–37;
schools, opinions of, 18–19

homeownership:
by age and household type, 112–113,115;
by homeownership status, 112,114–15;
by metropolitan area, 123–25;
by metropolitan status, 120;
by race and Hispanic origin, 116–17;
by region, 118–19;
by state, 121–22

Honolulu:
homeownership rates, 123
hospice care, 102
hospital stays, 97–99
household services and products, spending on:
by age of householder, 372, indexed, 379, market share, 385;
by educational attainment, 456, indexed, 460, market share, 464;
by household income, 392, indexed, 399, market share, 405;
by household type, 411, indexed, 416, market share, 421;
by race and Hispanic origin, 428, indexed, 432, market share, 436;
by region, 442, indexed, 446, market share, 450;
household average, 364
households:
assets held, financial, by type of asset, 470–72;
assets held, non-financial, by type of asset, 476–78;
by age and race and Hispanic origin, 280–81;
by age of householder, 272–73;
by metropolitan status, 288–89;
by region and race and Hispanic origin, 286–87;
by size, 282–83;
by type and age of householder, 274–76;
by type and race and Hispanic origin, 277–79;
by type, as percent of all households, 270–71;
debt, by type of debt, 479–81;
marital status by sex, 305–06;
net worth, of households, 468–69;
pension coverage, 482–83;
people living alone, 284–85;
same-sex partners, 301–02;
single parents with children at home, 299–300;
stock ownership, 473–75;
unrelated adults, by age and sex, 301–02
households, family, female-headed:
as percent of all households, 270–71;
by age and type of household, 167–73;
by age of householder, 274–76;
by presence of children, 299–300;
by race and Hispanic origin, 277–79;
homeownership, 112–114;
income, median, 152–53, 165–66;
income, median by presence of children, 177–78;
income, median by race, 156–57;
labor force participation by presence of children, 222;
poverty status, by presence of children, 209;
poverty status, by race and Hispanic origin, 209
households, family, male-headed:
as percent of all households, 270–71;
by age and type of household, 167–73;
by age of householder, 274–76
by presence of children, 299–300;
by race and Hispanic origin, 277–79;
homeownership, 112–114;
income, median, 152–53, 165–66;
income, median by presence of children, 177–78;
income, median by race, 156–57;
labor force participation by presence of children, 222;
poverty status, by presence of children, 209;
poverty status, by race and Hispanic origin, 209
households, family, married-couple. *See also* Couples, cohabiting:
as percent of all households, 270–7;
by age of householder, 274–76;
by race and Hispanic origin, 277–79;
child present, spending, by product or service, 408–14, indexed, 415–19, market share, 420–24;
dual earners, 223–24;
dual-earner couple incomes, by presence of children, 176;
educational attainment, 54–55;
homeownership, 112–115;
households by age and type of household, 167–73;
households by median income, 165–66;
income by presence of children, 174–76;
income, median, 152–53;
income, median by race, 156–57;
labor force participation by presence of children, 222;
poverty status, by presence of children, 209;
poverty status, by race and Hispanic origin, 209;
spending, by product or service, 408–14, indexed, 415–19, market share, 420–24;
with children at home, 296–98
households, non-family. *See* Men or women living alone.

housing, spending on by product or service:
by age of householder, 371, indexed, 378, market share, 384–85;
by educational attainment, 456, indexed, 460, market share, 464;
by household income, 391–92, indexed, 398–400, market share,404–05;
by household type, 411, indexed, 416, market share, 421;
by race and Hispanic origin, 428, indexed, 432, market share, 436;
by region, 442, indexed, 446, market share, 450;
household average, 364
housing stock, 126–28:
amenities, 131–32;
size of units, 128;
units in structure, 127

housing, 111–44:
costs, by homeownership status, 141–42;
homeownership, 112–115;
housing stock, 126–28;
value, purchase price, and source of down payment, 143–44
Houston, TX PMSA:
college graduates, 10;
high school graduates, 10;
homeownership rates, 123
Houston–Galveston–Brazoria, TX CMSA:
college graduates, 10;
high school graduates, 10;
population, 1950–1999, 332
husbands, educational attainment compared to wives', 54–55

Idaho:
college graduates, 11;
high school graduates, 11;
homeownership rates, 121;
income, median household, 204;
population, by race and Hispanic origin, 328;
population distribution by race and Hispanic origin, 330
Illinois:
college graduates, 11;
high school graduates, 11;
homeownership rates, 121;
income, median household, 203;
population, by race and Hispanic origin, 328;
population distribution by race and Hispanic origin, 330
immigrants, by country of birth and state of intended residence, 342–43
immigration, 340–343
income, aggregate household, 148–49
income, before-tax:
by age of householder, 370, indexed, 377;
by educational attainment, 455, indexed, 459;
by household income, 390, indexed, 397;
by household type, 410, indexed, 415;
by race and Hispanic origin, 427, indexed, 431;
by region, 441, indexed, 445;
household average, 363
income continuation plans, as an employee benefit, 253
income, median household:
by age and type of household, 167–73;
by age of householder, 150–51,158–59;
by educational attainment, 182–83;
by metropolitan status, 201–02;
by race and age of householder, 160–64;
by race and Hispanic origin of householder, 154–55;
by race and type of household, 156–57;
by region, 201–02;
by state, ranked, 203–04;
by type of household, 152–53,165–66,174–76;
sources of, 205–06
income trends, 145–209:
affluence, 146–47;
households, distribution by aggregate household income, 148–49;
households, distribution by income, 146–47;
poverty, 207–09
India, immigration from, 342–43
Indiana:
college graduates, 11;
high school graduates, 11;
homeownership rates, 121;
income, median household, 203;
population, by race and Hispanic origin, 328;
population distribution by race and Hispanic origin, 330
Indianapolis, IN MSA:
college graduates, 10;
high school graduates, 10;
homeownership rates, 123;
population, 1950–1999, 333
industries:
employment in, by occupation and sex, 236–38;
employment projected, 264–66
injuries, 86
installment debt, 480
instrumental activities of daily living (IADLs), 94
insurance, as an employee benefit, 252. *See also* Personal insurance and pensions.
interest income, as source of income, 205–06
Internet use, by type of activity, 353
Internet access, 350–51:
by educational attainment, 350–51;
by household income, 350–51;
by race and Hispanic origin, 351;
users by age, 350,352
Iowa:
college graduates, 11;
high school graduates, 11;
homeownership rates, 121;
income, median household, 203;
population, by race and Hispanic origin, 328;
population distribution by race and Hispanic origin, 330
Jacksonville, FL:
homeownership rates, 123
Jamaica, immigration from, 342–43
jazz performances, participation in, by educational attainment, 356
Jewish religion, preference for, 349

job tenure by age and sex, 239–41
journey to work:
distance to work, 249;
time and means of transportation, 248–50;
time of departure, 250
jury duty leave, as an employee benefit, 252

Kansas:
college graduates, 11;
high school graduates, 11;
homeownership rates, 121;
income, median household, 203;
population, by race and Hispanic origin, 328;
population distribution by race and Hispanic origin, 330
Kansas City, MO–KS MSA:
college graduates, 10;
high school graduates, 10;
homeownership rates, 123;
population, 1950–1999, 332
Kentucky:
college graduates, 11;
high school graduates, 11;
homeownership rates, 121;
income, median household, 204;
population, by race and Hispanic origin, 328;
population distribution by race and Hispanic origin, 330
kerosene, for heating, 130
Korea, immigration from, 342–43

labor force:
alternative work arrangements, 244–47;
dual earner couples, 223–24;
employee benefits, 251–53;
employment status by age and sex, 214–15;
entrants and leavers, by sex and race and Hispanic origin, 257–53;
families by type of family and presence of children, 220–22;
foreign born workers, 347;
full-time workers, 225–26;
industries, employment in, 236–38;
job tenure by age and sex, 239–41;
journey to work, 248–50;
occupations, employment in, by race and Hispanic origin, 231–35;
occupations, employment in, by sex, 227–30;
occupations, employment of women in, 228–30;
part-time workers, 225–26;
participation in, by sex, race and Hispanic origin, 216– 19;
self-employment, 242–47,249;
women, participation of, by presence of children in family, 220–22;
work at home, by occupation, 246–47
labor force trends, 211–268:
employment by educational attainment, projected, 267–68;
employment by industry, projected, 264–66;
employment by occupation, projected, 260–61;
employment, long-term, by age and sex, 241;
entrants and leavers, projected, by sex and race and Hispanic origin, 257–58;
job tenure by age and sex, 239–41;
labor force projected, by age and sex, 254–55;
labor force, projected, by race and Hispanic origin, 256–57
occupations, projected growth, 262–63;
participation by age and sex, 1970–2000, 212–13
Las Vegas, NV–AZ MSA:
homeownership rates, 123;
population, 1950–1999, 333
leave, paid, as an employee benefit, 252
life expectancy, 108–09
life insurance:
as a financial asset, 471–72;
as an employee benefit, 252
litter, perceived as neighborhood problem, 140
liver disease, among leading causes of death, 107
living arrangements, 269–309. *See also* Household types:
cohabiting couples, 301–02;
households by age of householder, 272–73;
households by type of households, 270–71;
median age at first marriage, 1890–1998, 303–04
Los Angeles–Long Beach, CA PMSA:
college graduates, 10;
high school graduates, 10;
homeownership rates, 124;
population, 1950–1999, 332
Los Angeles–Riverside–Orange, CA CMSA:
college graduates, 10;
high school graduates, 10
Louisiana:
college graduates, 11;
high school graduates, 11;
homeownership rates, 121;
income, median household, 204;
population, by race and Hispanic origin, 328;
population distribution by race and Hispanic origin, 330
Louisville, KY:
homeownership rates, 124

Maine:
college graduates, 11;
high school graduates, 11;
homeownership rates, 121;

income, median household, 203;
population, by race and Hispanic origin, 328;
population distribution by race and Hispanic origin, 330
manufacturing industries:
employment in, by occupation and sex, 236–38;
employment, projected, 264–66
marital status. *See also* Households, family, married couple:
by race and Hispanic origin, 307–09;
by sex, 303–06;
cohabiting couples, 301–02;
elderly, 294–95;
home health patients, 100–01;
hospice care patients, 102;
median age at first marriage by sex, 304;
young adults, 292–93
Maryland:
college graduates, 11;
high school graduates, 11;
homeownership rates, 121;
income, median household, 203;
population, by race and Hispanic origin, 328;
population distribution by race and Hispanic origin, 330
mass transportation, as means of travel to work, 248–49
Massachusetts:
college graduates, 11;
high school graduates, 11;
homeownership rates, 121;
income, median household, 203;
population, by race and Hispanic origin, 328;
population distribution by race and Hispanic origin, 330
master's degree earners:
by field of study and sex, 43;
by race and Hispanic origin, 37;
earnings by sex, 196;
employment, projected, 267–68;
household income, 182–83;
projected, 53
meat, consumption of, 63
medical assistants, 262
medical care insurance, as an employee benefit, 252
Memphis, TN–AR–MS:
homeownership rates, 124
men:
AIDS victims, 103–04;
college enrollments, 30–31;
crime victims, 357–60;
degrees conferred, projected, 53;
diet, attitudes toward, 65;
disabled, by age and severity, 91–92;
distribution by age and income, 190–91;
earnings by educational attainment, 195–96;
earnings, median weekly, 198–200;
earnings of foreign-born workers, 347;
educational attainment. by age, 4–5;
employment status by age, 214–15;
employment status by age and race and Hispanic origin, 216–19;
full-time workers, 194, 225–26;
health status, self-reported, 60–61;
home health services, 100–01;
hospice care, 102;
hospital stays, 97–99;
income, median, by age, 184–85;
income, median by race and Hispanic origin, 187–88;
income, median, of full-time workers, 193–94;
industries, employment in, by occupation, 236–37;
job tenure by age, 239–41;
labor force entrants and leavers, projected, 257–59;
labor force participation by age, 212–13;
labor force participation, projected, by age, 254–55;
life expectancy, 108–09;
living arrangements, 292–95;
marital status, 305;
median age at first marriage, 303–04;
occupations, employment in, by occupation, 227–30;
part-time workers, 225–26;
physician's visits, 95–96;
population by age, 312–13;
population by age, projected, 314–15;
religious preference, 348–49;
Scholastic Assessment Test (SAT) scores, 26–27;
smoking, by age, 79;
vitamin and supplement use, 66–67;
with income, distribution by age and income, 190–91
men living alone:
as percent of all households, 270–71;
by age, 274–76, 284–85;
by median income, 165–66;
by race and Hispanic origin, 277–79;
by type of household, 167–73;
homeownership, 112–114;
income, median, 152–53, 179–80;
income, median by race, 156–57
menstrual and female genital disorders:
acute, 86;
chronic disease, 89
mental disability, 93
metropolitan areas. *See also* Individual MSAs:
crime victims 357–60;
educational attainment, 12–14;
homeownership status, 120;
households, 201–02, 288–89;

income, median household, 201–02;
population, 1950–1999, 332–33
Mexican Americans, Scholastic Assessment Test (SAT) scores, 26–27
Mexico, immigration from, 342–43
Miami, FL PMSA:
college graduates, 10;
high school graduates, 10;
homeownership rates, 124;
population, 1950–1999, 332
Miami–Fort Lauderdale, FL CMSA:
college graduates, 10;
high school graduates, 10
Michigan:
college graduates, 11;
high school graduates, 11;
homeownership rates, 121;
income, median household, 203;
population, by race and Hispanic origin, 328;
population distribution by race and Hispanic origin, 330
Middle Atlantic census division:
population by race and Hispanic origin, 324–26
middle-aged adults:
AIDS cases. 104;
alcohol use, 80;
alternative work arrangements, 245;
assets held, financial, by type of asset, 470–72;
assets held, non-financial, by type of asset, 476–78;
cohabiting couples, 301–02;
college graduates, by race and Hispanic origin, 9;
college students, 33–34;
crime victims, 357–60;
debt, by type of debt, 479–81;
disabilities, by type of disability, 91–94;
drug use, illicit, 81;
dual-income couples, 224;
educational attainment, 5–6;
employment, long-term, 241;
employment status, 215, 226;
exercise, 76;
foreign-born, 346;
geographic mobility, 338–39;
health conditions, 84–90;
health insurance coverage, 82–83;
health status, self-reported, 61;
high school graduates, by race and Hispanic origin, 8;
home health services, 100–01;
homeownership, 112–14;
hospice care, 102;
hospital care, 97–99;
householders, 272–74;
householders by household type, 275–76;
householders by race and Hispanic origin, 280–81;
income, median, 150–51,158–59;
income, median, by household type, 169–72;
income, median, by race and Hispanic origin, 160–64;
income, median of people living alone, by sex, 179–81;
Internet users, 352;
job tenure, 240;
labor force, participation in, 213, 216–219;
labor force, participation in, projected, 255;
living alone, 284–85;
marital status, 304–09;
net worth of household, 468–69;
pension coverage, 482–83;
physician visits, 95–96;
population, by race and Hispanic origin, projected, 318–23;
population, by sex, 312–13;
population, by sex, projected, 314–15;
school enrollment, 17;
self-employment, 243;
single parents with child at home, 299–300;
smokers, 79;
spending by product or service, 368–87, indexed, 377–83, market share, 384–87;
stock ownership, 473–74;
vitamin and supplement use, 67
Middlesex–Somerset–Huntington, NJ:
homeownership rates, 124
Midwest region:
crime, victims of property, 360;
crime, victims of violent, 358–59;
homeownership, by status, 118–19;
hospital stays, 97–99;
households, 201–02;
households, by race and Hispanic origin, 286–87;
income, median household, 201–02;
population by race and Hispanic origin, 324–26;
spending by product or service, 439–44, indexed, 445–48, market share, 449–52
migraine headaches, 89
military leave, as an employee benefit, 252
milk, consumption of, 63
Milwaukee–Waukesha, WI PMSA:
college graduates, 11;
high school graduates, 11;
homeownership rates, 124;
population, 1950–1999, 33
Milwaukee–Racine, WI:
college graduates, 11;
high school graduates, 11
mining industries:
employment in, by occupation and sex, 236–38;
employment, projected, 264–66

Minneapolis–St. Paul, MN–WI MSA:
college graduates, 11;
high school graduates, 11;
homeownership rates, 124;
population, 1950–1999, 332
Minnesota:
college graduates, 11;
high school graduates, 11;
homeownership rates, 121;
income, median household, 203;
population, by race and Hispanic origin, 328;
population distribution by race and Hispanic origin, 330
Mississippi:
college graduates, 11;
high school graduates, 11;
homeownership rates, 121;
income, median household, 204;
population, by race and Hispanic origin, 328;
population distribution by race and Hispanic origin, 330
Missouri:
college graduates, 11;
high school graduates, 11;
homeownership rates, 121;
income, median household, 203;
population, by race and Hispanic origin, 328;
population distribution by race and Hispanic origin, 330
mobile homes, 127
Monmouth–Ocean, NJ:
homeownership rates, 124
Montana:
college graduates, 11;
high school graduates, 11;
homeownership rates, 121;
income, median household, 204;
population, by race and Hispanic origin, 328;
population distribution by race and Hispanic origin, 330
mortgage:
as debt, 479–81;
median monthly payment, 142
Mountain census division:
population by race and Hispanic origin, 324–26
movers, 338–39
musculoskeletal conditions, 87–88
musical plays:
attendance at, by educational attainment, 355;
participation in, by educational attainment, 356
mutual funds, 471–72

Nashville, TN MSA:
homeownership rates, 124;
population, 1950–1999, 333
Nassau–Suffolk, NY PMSA:
college graduates, 11;
high school graduates, 11;
homeownership rates, 124;
population, 1950–1999, 332
Native Americans:
AIDS victims, 105;
births by age of mother, 71;
college enrollments, 36;
degrees conferred, 37–38;
homeownership, by status, 116–117;
population, by age, projected, 318,322;
population, by region and census division, 324–26;
population, projected, 317–18;
Scholastic Assessment Test (SAT) scores, 26–27
Nebraska:
college graduates, 11;
high school graduates, 11;
homeownership rates, 121;
income, median household, 203;
population, by race and Hispanic origin, 328;
population distribution by race and Hispanic origin, 330
neighborhoods:
characteristics of, 138–40;
opinions of, by homeownership status, 136–37
nephritis, among leading causes of death, 107
nervous disorders, chronic, 89
Nevada:
college graduates, 11;
high school graduates, 11;
homeownership rates, 121;
income, median household, 203;
population, by race and Hispanic origin, 328;
population distribution by race and Hispanic origin, 330
New England census division:
population by race and Hispanic origin, 324–26
New Hampshire:
college graduates, 11;
high school graduates, 11;
homeownership rates, 121;
income, median household, 203;
population, by race and Hispanic origin, 328;
population distribution by race and Hispanic origin, 330
New Haven–Bridgeport–Stamford–Waterbury–Danbury, CT NECMA:
population, 1950–1999, 333
New Jersey:
college graduates, 11;
high school graduates, 11;
homeownership rates, 121;
immigration to, 342–43
income, median household, 203;

population, by race and Hispanic origin, 329;
population distribution by race and Hispanic origin, 331
New Mexico:
homeownership rates, 122
college graduates, 11;
high school graduates, 11;
homeownership rates, 122;
income, median household, 204;
population, by race and Hispanic origin, 329;
population distribution by race and Hispanic origin, 331
New Orleans, LA MSA:
college graduates, 11;
high school graduates, 11;
homeownership rates, 124;
population, 1950–1999, 333
New York:
college graduates, 11;
high school graduates, 11;
homeownership rates, 122;
immigration to, 342–43
income, median household, 203;
population, by race and Hispanic origin, 329;
population distribution by race and Hispanic origin, 331
New York, NY PMSA:
college graduates, 11;
high school graduates, 11;
homeownership rates, 124;
population, 1950–1999, 332
New York–Northern NJ–Long Island, NY–NJ–PA–CT:
college graduates, 11;
high school graduates, 11;
Newark, NJ PMSA:
college graduates, 11;
high school graduates, 11;
homeownership rates, 124;
population, 1950–1999, 332
non-metropolitan areas:
crime, victims of property, 360;
crime, victims of violent, 358;
educational attainment, 12–14;
homeownership status, 120;
households, 201–02, 288–89;
income, median household, 201–02
population, 1950–1999, 332–33
Norfolk–Virginia Beach, VA–NC MSA:
college graduates, 11;
high school graduates, 11;
homeownership rates, 124;
population, 1950–1999, 333
North Carolina:
college graduates, 11;
high school graduates, 11;
homeownership rates, 122;
income, median household, 204;
population, by race and Hispanic origin, 329;
population distribution by race and Hispanic origin, 331
North Dakota:
college graduates, 11;
high school graduates, 11;
homeownership rates, 122;
income, median household, 204;
population, by race and Hispanic origin, 329;
population distribution by race and Hispanic origin, 331
Northeast region of the US:
crime, victims of property, 360;
crime, victims of violent, 358–59;
homeownership, by status, 118–19;
hospital stays, 97–99;
households, 201–02;
households, by race and Hispanic origin, 286–87;
income, median household, 201–02
population by race and Hispanic origin, 324–26;
spending by product or service, 439–44, indexed, 445–48, market share, 449–52
nurses, registered, 263

Oakland, CA PMSA:
college graduates, 11
high school graduates, 11
homeownership rates, 124
population, 1950–1999, 332
occupations. *See also* Particular occupational groups:
employment in, by industry and sex, 236–38;
employment in, by race and Hispanic origin, 231–35;
employment in, by sex, 227–230;
fastest-growing, 262;
with largest job growth, 263
odors, perceived as neighborhood problem, 140
office clerks, 26
Ohio:
college graduates, 11;
high school graduates, 11;
homeownership rates, 122;
income, median household, 203;
population, by race and Hispanic origin, 329;
population distribution by race and Hispanic origin, 331
Oklahoma:
college graduates, 11;
high school graduates, 11;

homeownership rates, 122;
income, median household, 204;
population, by race and Hispanic origin, 329;
population distribution by race and Hispanic origin, 331
Oklahoma City, OK:
homeownership rates, 124
Omaha, NE–IA:
homeownership rates, 124
on-the-job training, total employed with, projected, 267–68
opera performances:
attendance at, by educational attainment, 355;
participation in, by educational attainment, 356
operators, fabricators and laborers:
earnings, weekly, by sex, 200
employment in, by industry and sex, 236–38;
employment in, by race and Hispanic origin, 231–35;
employment in by sex, 227–230;
employment, projected, 1998–2008, 261;
women, employment in, 230
Orange County, CA PMSA:
college graduates, 10;
high school graduates, 10;;
homeownership rates, 124
population, 1950–1999, 332
Oregon:
college graduates, 11;
high school graduates, 11;
homeownership rates, 122;
income, median household, 203;
population, by race and Hispanic origin, 329;
population distribution by race and Hispanic origin, 331
Orlando, FL MSA:
homeownership rates, 124;
population, 1950–1999, 333

Pacific census division:
population by race and Hispanic origin, 324–26
paralegals and legal assistants, 262
part-time workers:
by sex and age, 225–26;
employment benefits by type of benefit and size of firm, 251–53;
women, by presence of children, 220–21
peanuts, consumption of, 64
Pennsylvania:
college graduates, 11;
high school graduates, 11;
homeownership rates, 122;
income, median household, 203;
population, by race and Hispanic origin, 329;
population distribution by race and Hispanic origin, 331
pensions. *See also* Personal insurance and pensions:
as source of income, 205–06
coverage of households, 482–83
personal care and home health aides, 262–63
personal care products and services, spending on:
by age of householder, 374, indexed, 381, market share, 386;
by educational attainment, 457, indexed, 461, market share, 465;
by household income, 395, indexed, 402, market share, 406;
by household type, 412, indexed, 417, market share, 422;
by race and Hispanic origin, 429, indexed, 433, market share, 437;
by region, 443, indexed, 447, market share, 451;
household average, 366
personal insurance and pensions, spending on, by type of insurance:
by age of householder, 374, indexed, 381, market share, 386–87;
by educational attainment, 457, indexed, 461, market share, 465;
by household income, 395, indexed, 402, market share, 406;
by household type, 413, indexed, 418, market share, 423;
by race and Hispanic origin, 429, indexed, 433, market share, 437;
by region, 443, indexed, 447, market share, 451;
household average, 366
personal leave, as an employee benefit, 252
personal taxes, spending on by type of tax:
by age of householder, 375, indexed, 382, market share, 387;
by educational attainment, 458, indexed, 462, market share, 466;
by household income, 395, indexed, 402, market share, 407;
by household type, 413, indexed, 418, market share, 423;
by race and Hispanic origin, 430, indexed, 434, market share, 438;
by region, 444, indexed, 448, market share, 452;
household average, 366
Ph.D. *See* Doctoral degree earners.
Philadelphia, PA–NJ MSA:
college graduates, 11;
high school graduates, 11;
homeownership rates, 124
Philadelphia–Atlantic City, PA–NJ–DE–MD CMSA:
college graduates, 11;
high school graduates, 11;
population, 1950–1999, 332

Philippines, immigration from, 342–43
Phoenix–Mesa, AZ MSA:
college graduates, 11;
high school graduates, 11;
homeownership rates, 124;
population, 1950–1999, 332
photography, participation in, by educational attainment, 356
physician assistants, 262
physician's visits, 95–96
Pittsburgh, PA MSA:
college graduates, 11;
high school graduates, 11;
homeownership rates, 124;
population, 1950–1999, 332
pneumonia and influenza, among leading causes of death, 107
population, 311–60:
art events, attendance at, 354–55;
arts, participation in, 354,356;
by age and race and Hispanic origin, projected, 318–33;
by age and sex, 312–13;
by age and sex, projected, 314–15;
by metropolitan area, 334–35;
by metropolitan status, 332–33;
by race and Hispanic origin, projected, 316–17;
by region, census division and race and Hispanic origin, 324–26;
by state, 329–331;
computer owners, 350–51;
crime victims, 357–60;
foreign born population, 344–47;
geographic mobility, 336–39;
immigration to the US, 1901–98, 341–43;
Internet users, 350–52;
religious preference, 349
porch, deck or patio, 130
Portland–Vancouver, OR–WA PMSA:
college graduates, 11;
high school graduates, 11;
homeownership rates, 124;
population, 1950–1999, 332
Portland–Salem, OR–WA CMSA:
college graduates, 11;
high school graduates, 11
pottery-making, participation in, by educational attainment, 356
poverty status, by age, race and Hispanic origin, 207–08
precision production, craft and repair occupations:
earnings, weekly, by sex, 200
employment in, by industry and sex, 236–38
employment in, by race and Hispanic origin, 231–35
employment in by sex, 227–230
employment, projected, 1998–2008, 261
women, employment in, 230
professional degree earners:
by field of study and sex, 44;
by race and Hispanic origin, 38;
by sex and age, 4–6;
earnings by sex, 196;
employment, projected, 267–68;
household income, 182–83;
projected, 53
professional schools:
enrollments, 36;
enrollments, projected, 50
professional specialty occupations:
earnings, weekly, by sex, 199
employment in, by industry and sex, 236–38;
employment in, by race and Hispanic origin, 231–35;
employment in, by sex, 227–230;
employment, projected, 1998–2008, 261;
women, employment in, 229
property, as nonfinancial asset, 476–78
Protestant religions, preference for, 349
Providence–Fall River, RI–MA MSA:
college graduates, 11;
high school graduates, 11;
homeownership rates, 124
public administration and government:
employment in, by occupation and sex, 236–38
employment, projected, 264–66
public assistance, as source of income, 205–06
public transportation, spending on:
by age of householder, 373, indexed, 380, market share, 386;
by educational attainment, 457, indexed:, 461, market share, 465;
by household income, 394, indexed, 401, market share, 406;
by household type, 412, indexed, 417, market share, 422;
by race and Hispanic origin, 429, indexed, 433, market share, 437;
by region, 443, indexed, 447, market share, 451;
household average, 365
Puerto Ricans, Scholastic Assessment Test (SAT) scores, 26–27

Raleigh–Durham–Chapel Hill, NC MSA:
homeownership rates, 124;
population, 1950–1999, 333
rape, 358–59
reading, spending on:
by age of householder, 374, indexed, 381, market share, 386;
by educational attainment, 457, indexed, 461, market share, 465;

by household income, 395, indexed 402, market share, 406;
by household type, 412, indexed, 417, market share, 422;
by race and Hispanic origin, 429, indexed, 433, market share, 437;
by region, 443, indexed, 447, market share, 451;
household average, 366
recreational activity, 77
religious preference, by age, sex, race, and educational attainment, 349
renters:
by household type, 114–15;
by housing type and size, 127–28;
by metropolitan area, 123–25;
by metropolitan status, 120;
by race and Hispanic origin, 116–17;
by region. 118–19;
by state, 121–22;
crime victims, 360;
housing costs, 141–42;
housing unit, opinion of, 133–35;
movers, 339;
neighborhood, characteristics of, 138–140;
neighborhood, opinions of, 136–37;
schools, opinions of, 18–19
rents, royalties, estates or trusts, as source of income, 205–06
residence, primary, as nonfinancial asset, 476–78
respiratory conditions:
acute, 85;
chronic, 90;
leading cause of death, 107
retail salespersons, 263
retirement accounts, 471–72
retirement plans, by type of firm and employment status, 252
Rhode Island:
college graduates, 11;
high school graduates, 11;
homeownership rates, 122;
income, median household, 203;
population, by race and Hispanic origin, 329;
population distribution by race and Hispanic origin, 331
Richmond–Petersburg, VA:
homeownership rates, 124
Riverside–San Bernardino, CA PMSA:
college graduates, 10;
high school graduates, 10;
homeownership rates, 124;
population, 1950–1999, 332
robbery, 358–59
Rochester, NY:
homeownership rates, 124
rural areas. *See* Non-metropolitan areas.

Sacramento, CA:
homeownership rates, 124
Sacramento–Yolo, CA CMSA:
college graduates, 11;
high school graduates, 11;
population, 1950–1999, 333
Saint Louis, MO–IL MSA:
college graduates, 11;
high school graduates, 11;
homeownership rates, 124;
population, 1950–1999, 332
sales occupations:
earnings, weekly, by sex, 200;
employment in, by industry and sex, 236–38;
employment in, by race and Hispanic origin, 231–35;
employment in by sex, 227–230;
employment, projected, 1998–2008, 261;
women, employment in, 230
Salt Lake City–Ogden, UT MSA:
college graduates, 11;
high school graduates, 11;
homeownership rates, 124;
population, 1950–1999, 333
San Antonio, TX MSA:
college graduates, 11;
high school graduates, 11;
homeownership rates, 124;
population, 1950–1999, 332
San Diego, CA MSA:
college graduates, 11;
high school graduates, 11;
homeownership rates, 124;
population, 1950–1999, 332
San Francisco, CA PMSA:
college graduates, 11;
high school graduates, 11;
homeownership rates, 124;
population, 1950–1999, 332
San Francisco–Oakland–San Jose, CA CMSA:
college graduates, 11;
high school graduates, 11
San Jose, CA PMSA:
college graduates, 11;
high school graduates, 11;
homeownership rates, 124;
population, 1950–1999, 332
savings bonds, 471–72
Scholastic Assessment Test (SAT), 26–27
schools, K–12:
enrollments, 15–17;
enrollments, projected, 20–21,24–25;

leavers, 22–23;
leavers, foreign-born, 346
Scranton–Wilkes-Barre–Hazelton, PA:
homeownership rates, 124
Seattle–Bellevue–Everett, WA PMSA:
college graduates, 11;
high school graduates, 11;
homeownership rates, 125;
population, 1950–1999, 332
Seattle–Tacoma–Bremerton, WA CMSA:
college graduates, 11;
high school graduates, 11
self-employment, 247. *See also* Labor force and farm self-employment.
service occupations:
earnings, weekly, by sex, 200
employment in, by industry and sex, 236–38;
employment in, by race and Hispanic origin, 231–35;
employment in by sex, 227–230;
employment, projected, 1998–2008, 261;
women, employment in, 230
services industries:
employment in by occupation and sex, 236–38;
employment, projected, 264–66
services, perceived as neighborhood problem, 140
shelter, spending on by type of shelter:
by age of householder, 371, indexed, 378, market share, 384–85;
by educational attainment, 456, indexed, 460, market share, 464;
by household income, 392, indexed, 398–99, market share, 404–05;
by household type, 411, indexed, 416, market share, 421;
by race and Hispanic origin, 428, indexed, 432, market share, 436
by region, 442, indexed, 446, market share, 450;
household average, 364
sick leave, paid, as an employee benefit, 252
singing groups, participation in, by educational attainment, 356
single parents. *See* Households, family, female-headed or male-headed.
skin conditions:
acute, 86;
chronic, 87
smoking by age and sex, 79. *See also* tobacco products.
social and human service assistants, 262
Social Security, as source of income, 205–06
soft drinks, consumption of, 64
solar energy, for heating, 130
South Atlantic census division:
population by race and Hispanic origin, 324–26
South Carolina:
college graduates, 11;
high school graduates, 11;
homeownership rates, 122;
income, median household, 203;
population, by race and Hispanic origin, 329;
population distribution by race and Hispanic origin, 331
South Dakota:
college graduates, 11;
high school graduates, 11;
homeownership rates, 122;
income, median household, 204;
population, by race and Hispanic origin, 329;
population distribution by race and Hispanic origin, 331
South region of the US:
crime victims 357–60;
homeownership, by status, 118–19;
hospital stays, 97–99;
households, 201–02;
households, by race and Hispanic origin, 286–87;
income, median household, 201–02;
population by race and Hispanic origin, 324–26;
spending by product or service, 439–44, indexed, 445–48, market share, 449–52
spending, 361–466:
annual, 362–67;
annual, by product and age of householder, 366–76, indexed, 377–83, market share, 384–87;
by product and educational attainment, 453–58, indexed, 459–62, market share, 463–66;
by product and household income, 388–396, indexed, 397–403, market share, 404–07;
by product and household type, 408–14, indexed, 415–19, market share, 420–24;
by product and race and Hispanic origin, 425–30, indexed, 431–34, market share, 435–38;
by product or service and region, 439–44, indexed, 445–48, market share, 449–52
states of the United States. *See also* the individual states
educational attainment, 11;
homeownership rates, 121–22;
income, median household, 203–04;
population, by race and Hispanic origin, 328–29;
population distribution by race and Hispanic origin, 330–31
stock ownership:
by age of householder, 473–75;
by income of household, 473, 475
stocks, as financial assets, 471–72
street noise, perceived as neighborhood problem, 140

suburbs:
crime victims 357–60;
educational attainment, 12–14;
homeownership status, 120;
households, 201–02, 288–89;
income, median household, 201–02;
population, 1950–1999, 332–33
suicide, among leading causes of death, 107
survivors' benefits, as source of income, 205–06
sweeteners, consumption of, 64
swimming for recreation, 77
Syracuse, NY:
homeownership rates, 125
systems analysts, 262–263

Tampa–St. Petersburg–Clearwater, FL MSA:
college graduates, 11;
high school graduates, 11;
homeownership rates, 125;
population, 1950–1999, 332
tax-deferred savings arrangements, as an employee benefit, 253
taxes, real estate, median monthly payment, 142
taxes, personal. *See* Personal taxes.
taxicab, as means of travel to work, 248–49
tea, consumption of, 64
teacher assistants, 263
technical occupations:
earnings, weekly, by sex, 199;
employment in, by industry and sex, 236–38;
employment in, by race and Hispanic origin, 231–35;
employment in by sex, 227–230;
employment, projected, 1998–2008, 261;
women, employment in, 229–30
telephones, 132
temporary workers, 244–45
Tennessee:
college graduates, 11;
high school graduates, 11;
homeownership rates, 122;
income, median household, 204;
population, by race and Hispanic origin, 329;
population distribution by race and Hispanic origin, 331
Texas:
college graduates, 11;
high school graduates, 11;
homeownership rates, 122;
immigration to, 342–43
income, median household, 203;
population, by race and Hispanic origin, 329;
population distribution by race and Hispanic origin, 331
theft, by type, 357–60
tobacco products and smoking supplies, spending on:
by age of householder, 374, indexed, 381, market share, 386;
by educational attainment, 457, indexed, 461, market share, 465;
by household income, 395, indexed, 402, market share, 406;
by household type, 413, indexed, 418, market share, 423;
by race and Hispanic origin, 429, indexed, 433, market share, 437;
by region, 443, indexed, 447, market share, 451;
household average, 366
transaction accounts, 471–72
transportation and public utilities:
employment in, by occupation and sex, 236–38;
employment, projected, 264–66
transportation, spending on by product or service:
by age of householder, 373, indexed, 380, market share, 386;
by and race and Hispanic origin, 429, indexed, 433, market share, 437;
by educational attainment, 457, indexed, 461, market share, 465;
by household income, 393–94, indexed, 400–01, market, 406;
by household type, 412, indexed, 417, market share, 422;
by region, 443, indexed, 447, market share, 451;
household average, 365
trash disposal, monthly cost of, by homeownership status, 142
travel to work. *See* Journey to work.
truck drivers, 263
Tucson, AZ:
homeownership rates, 125
Tulsa, OK:
homeownership rates, 125

urinary conditions, acute, 86
Utah:
college graduates, 11;
high school graduates, 11;
homeownership rates, 122;
income, median household, 203;
population, by race and Hispanic origin, 329;
population distribution by race and Hispanic origin, 331
utilities, fuels, public services, spending on by product or service:
by age of householder, 372, indexed, 379, market, 385;
by educational attainment, 456, indexed, 460, market share, 464;

by household income, 390–91, indexed, 399, market share, 405;
by household type, 411, indexed, 416, market share, 421;
by race and Hispanic origin, 428, indexed, 432,
market share, 436
by region, 442, indexed, 446, market share, 450;
household 364

vacation as an employee benefit, 252
vegetables, consumption of, 64
vehicle products and services, spending on by product or service:
by age of householder, 373, indexed, 380, market share, 386;
by educational attainment, 457, indexed, 461, market share, 465;
by household income, 394, indexed, 401, market share, 406;
by household type, 412, indexed, 417, market share, 422;
by race and Hispanic origin, 429, indexed, 433,
market share, 437;
by region, 443, indexed, 447, market share, 451;
household average, 365;
vehicle purchases, spending on, by vehicle type:
by age of householder, 373, indexed, 380, market share, 386;
by educational attainment, 457, indexed, 461, market share, 465
by household income, 393–94, indexed, 400–01, market share, 406;
by household type, 412, indexed, 417, market share, 422;
by race and Hispanic origin, 429, indexed, 433,
market share, 437;
by region, 443, indexed, 447, market share, 451;
household average, 365;
vehicles, as non-financial assets, 476–78
Ventura, CA:
homeownership rates, 125
Vermont:
college graduates, 11;
high school graduates, 11;
homeownership rates, 122;
income, median household, 203;
population, by race and Hispanic origin, 329;
population distribution by race and Hispanic origin, 331
veterans benefits, as source of income, 205–06
Vietnam, immigration from, 342–43
Virginia:
college graduates, 11;
high school graduates, 11;
homeownership rates, 122;
income, median household, 203;
population, by race and Hispanic origin, 329;
population distribution by race and Hispanic origin, 331
vision insurance, as an employee benefit, 252
visual impairments, 88
vitamins and mineral supplements, use of, 66–67
vocational training, total employed with, projected,
267–68

walking:
assisted, 93;
means of travel to work, 248–49;
recreational, 77
washing machine, 130
Washington:
college graduates, 11;
high school graduates, 11;
homeownership rates, 122;
income, median household, 203;
population, by race and Hispanic origin, 329;
population distribution by race and Hispanic origin, 331
Washington, DC–MD–VA–WV CMSA:
college graduates, 11;
high school graduates, 11;
homeownership rates, 125;
population, 1950–1999, 332
water, bottled, consumption of, 64
water, monthly cost of, by homeownership status, 142
wealth 467–83:
assets, financial, by type of asset, 470–71;
assets, median value of, by type of asset, 470,472;
assets, non-financial, by type of asset, 476–78;
debt, by type of debt, 479–81;
net worth of households, 469;
stock ownership, 473–75
weaving, participation in, by educational attainment, 356
West North Central census division
population by race and Hispanic origin, 324–26
West Palm Beach–Boca Raton, FL:
homeownership rates, 125
West, region of the US:
crime victims 357–60;
homeownership, by status, 118–19;
hospital stays, 97–99;
households, 201–02;
households, by race and Hispanic origin, 286–87;
income, median household, 201–02;
population by race and Hispanic origin, 324–26;
spending by product or service, 439–44, indexed, 445–48, market share, 449–52

West South Central census division:
population by race and Hispanic origin, 324–26
West Virginia:
college graduates, 11;
high school graduates, 11;
homeownership rates, 122;
income, median household, 204;
population, by race and Hispanic origin, 329;
population distribution by race and Hispanic origin, 331
wheelchair use, 93
White Americans:
births by age of mother, 71;
births to unmarried women, 72;
children, living arrangements, 290–91;
college graduates, 9;
crime victims, 357–60;
employment status by sex and age, 219;
health status, self-reported, 60–61;
high school graduates, 8;
homeownership, by status, 116–117;
households by age, 280–81;
households by region, 286–87;
households by type, 277–79;
income, median, 154–55;
income, median, by age of householder, 160,163;
income, median, by type of household, 156–57;
labor force, projected, 256–57;
marital status by age, 307–09;
occupations, employment in, by occupation, 231–35;
physician's visits, 95–96;
poverty status, by age, 207–08;
religious preference, 348–49;
Scholastic Assessment Test (SAT) scores, 26–27

White Americans, non-Hispanic:
AIDS victims, 105;
assets held, financial, by type of asset, 470–72;
assets held, non-financial, by type of asset, 476–78;
births by age of mother, 71;
college enrollments, 30–31;
college graduates, 9;
computer use, 350–51;
debt, household, by type of debt, 479–81;
degrees conferred, 37–38;
high school attenders, non-graduates, 23;
high school graduates, 8;
homeownership, by status, 116–117;
households by age, 280–81;
households by region, 286–87;
households by type, 277–79;
income, median, 154–55;
income, median, by age of householder, 160,164;
income, median, by type of household, 156–57;
Internet access, 350–51;
labor force, entrants and leavers, projected, 257–59;
labor force, projected, 256–57;
marital status by age, 307–09;
net worth of households, 468–69;
pension coverage, 482–83;
population, by age, projected, 318,323;
population, by region and census division, 324–26;
population, projected, 317–18;
poverty status, by age, 207–08;
spending, by product or service, 425–30, indexed, 431–34, market share, 435–38
wholesale / retail trade:
employment in, by occupation and sex, 236–38;
employment, projected, 264–66
Wisconsin:
college graduates, 11;
high school graduates, 11;
homeownership rates, 122;
income, median household, 203;
population, by race and Hispanic origin, 329;
population distribution by race and Hispanic origin, 331
wives, educational attainment compared to husbands', 54–55
women. *See also* Household, family, female-headed:
AIDS victims, 103–04;
college enrollments, 30–31;
crime victims, 358;
degrees conferred, projected, 53;
diet, attitudes toward, 65;
disabled, by age and severity, 91–92;
distribution by age and income, 190,192;
earnings as a percent of men's earnings, 198–200;
earnings by educational attainment, 195,197;
earnings, median weekly, 198–200;
earnings of foreign-born workers, 347;
educational attainment, by age, 4,6;
employment benefits, by size of firm and employment status, 251–53;
employment status by age, 214–15;
employment status by age and race and Hispanic origin, 216–19;
full-time workers, 195, 225–26;
health status, self-reported, 60–61;
home health services, 100–01;
hospice care, 102;
hospital stays, 97–99;
income, median, by age, 184,186;
income, median by race and Hispanic origin, 187,189;
income, median, of full-time workers, by age, 193,195;

industries, employment in, by occupation, 236,238;
job tenure by age, 239–41;
labor force entrants and leavers, projected, 257–59;
labor force participation by age, 212–13;
labor force participation by presence of children, 220–21;
labor force participation, projected, by age, 254–55;
life expectancy, 108–09;
living arrangements by age, 292–95;
marital status by age, 306;
median age at first marriage, 303–04;
menstrual and genital tract disorders, 86,88;
occupations, employment in, by occupation, 227–30;
part-time workers by age and sex, 225–26;
physician's visits, 95–96;
population by age, 312–13;
population by age, projected, 314–15;
religious preference, 348–49;
Scholastic Assessment Test (SAT) scores, 26–27;
smokers, by age, 79;
vitamin and supplement use, 66–67;
with income, distribution by age and income, 190,192
women living alone:
as percent of all households, 270–71;
by age, 274–76,284–85;
by race and Hispanic origin, 277–79;
homeownership, 112–114;
households by age and type of household, 167–73;
households by median income, 165–66;
income, median, 152–53,179,181;
income, median by race, 156–57
wood, for heating, 130
work arrangements, alternative, 244–45
work at home, 246–47
working mothers, 220–21
writing, participation in, by educational attainment, 356
Wyoming:
college graduates, 11;
high school graduates, 11;
homeownership rates, 122;
income, median household, 204;
population, by race and Hispanic origin, 329;
population distribution by race and Hispanic origin, 331

yoghurt, consumption of, 63
young adults:
AIDS cases. 104;
alcohol use, 80;
alternative work arrangements, 245;
cohabiting couples, 301–02;
college graduates, by race and Hispanic origin, 9;
college students, 33–34;
crime victims, 358;
disabilities, by type of disability, 91–94;
drug use, illicit, 81;
dual-income couples, 224;
educational attainment, 5–6;
employment, long-term, 241;
employment status, 215, 226;
exercise, 76;
foreign-born, 346;
geographic mobility, 338–39;
health conditions, 84–90;
health insurance coverage, 82–83;
health status, self-reported, 61;
high school graduates, by race and Hispanic origin, 8;
home health services, 100–01;
homeownership, 112–14;
hospice care, 102;
hospital care, 97–99;
householders, 272–74;
householders by household type, 275–76;
householders by race and Hispanic origin, 280–81;
income, median, 150–51,158–59;
income, median, by household type, 168
income, median, by race and Hispanic origin, 160–64;
income, median of full-time workers, 193–94;
income, median of people living alone, by sex, 179–81;
Internet users, 352;
job tenure, 240;
labor force, participation in, 1970–2000, 213;
labor force, participation in, by race and Hispanic origin, 216–219;
labor force, participation in, projected, 255;
living alone, 284–85;
living arrangements, by sex, 292–93;
marital status, 304–09;
physician visits, 95–96;
population, by race and Hispanic origin, projected, 318–23;
population, by sex, 312–13;
population, by sex, projected, 314–15;
school enrollment, 17;
self-employment, 243;
single parents with child at home, 299–300;
smokers, 79;
spending by product or service, 368–87, indexed, 377–83, market share, 384–87;
vitamin and supplement use, 67